20·00

DEATH AND THE FUTURE LIFE IN VICTORIAN LITERATURE AND THEOLOGY

Death, judgment, heaven and hell – the four last things of Christian eschatology – have long been the subject of anxious speculation and fierce controversy, and never more so in the modern era than in Victorian Britain. Michael Wheeler looks at the literary implications of Victorian views of death and the life beyond, and the fear and hope embodied in the theological positions of some of the major novelists and poets of the age. Victorian writings on the mysteries of death and the future life are shown to reopen key questions about the nature of religious experience, belief and language in the nineteenth century.

The analyses of each of the four last things and their part in nineteenth-century thought draw on a wide range of sermons, tracts, biographical writings, anthologies of sacred poetry and popular 'guides to heaven' from 1830 to 1890, in addition to the more established canon of Victorian literary and theological writings. There follow readings of four central texts, contrasting the broadly liberal theology of Tennyson's *In Memoriam* and Dickens's *Our Mutual Friend* with the Catholic authority invoked in Newman's *The Dream of Gerontius* and Hopkins's *The Wreck of the Deutschland*.

DEATH AND THE FUTURE LIFE IN VICTORIAN LITERATURE AND THEOLOGY

Michael Wheeler

Professor of English Literature
Lancaster University

The right of the University of Cambridge to print and sell all manner of books was granted by Henry VIII in 1534. The University has printed and published continuously since 1584.

CAMBRIDGE UNIVERSITY PRESS

CAMBRIDGE

NEW YORK   PORT CHESTER

MELBOURNE   SYDNEY

Published by the Press Syndicate of the University of Cambridge
The Pitt Building, Trumpington Street, Cambridge CB2 1RP
40 West 20th Street, New York, NY 10011, USA
10 Stamford Road, Oakleigh, Melbourne 3166, Australia

First published 1990

Printed in Great Britain at
the University Press, Cambridge

British Library cataloguing in publication data
Wheeler, Michael, 1947–
Death and the future life in Victorian
literature and theology.
1. English literature, 1837–1900 – Critical studies
I. Title
820'.9'008

Library of Congress cataloguing in publication data
Wheeler, Michael, 1947–
Death and the future life in Victorian literature
and theology/ Michael Wheeler.
p.   ca.
Includes bibliographical references.
ISBN 0 521 30617 5
1. English literature – 19th century – History and criticism.
2. Death – Religious aspects – Christianity – History – 19th century.
3. Theology, Doctrinal – Great Britain – History – 19th century.
4. Future life – Christianity – History – 19th century.   5. Future life
in literature.   6. Death in literature.   I. Title.
PR468.D42W4   1990
820.9'354'09034 – dc20   89-77366   CIP

ISBN 0 521 30617 5 hardback

For Joshua, Charlotte, and Emily

Contents

Illustrations

Preface

When writing about the symbolic function of eschatological allusions in Dickens, more years ago than I care to remember, I found that although nineteenth-century theological controversies concerning eternal punishment and the future life had been thoroughly investigated by Geoffrey Rowell in his book *Hell and the Victorians* (1974), no large-scale work on the literary implications of this crucial, but now somewhat inaccessible, area of Victorian thought and belief had been carried out. A long period of research followed, during which many sermons and tracts, biographies and reminiscences, anthologies of sacred poems for mourners and popular guides to heaven were examined, as well as the relevant canonical works of the period, both theological and literary.

As the work went on it became clear that a number of different books could have been written, each reflecting a particular aspect of, or approach to, this large area of interest. First, there was the possibility of foregrounding the social history of death, as John Morley does, for example, and relating this to both the theology and the literature of the period. Secondly, a more 'thanatological' study would have focused upon death and bereavement as rites of passage, taking the work of Victor Turner, Elisabeth Kübler-Ross, and Philippe Ariès as points of departure, and considering certain ideas and images of a future life as projections of the experience of those rites. Thirdly, it would have been feasible to carry out a comprehensive survey of all those ideas and images in the Victorian period, of the kind that Colleen McDannell and Bernhard Lang have since done more selectively in their history of heaven in the West.

Would-be readers of all three unwritten books will, I hope, find some material of particular interest to them in the chapters that follow. I have concentrated, however, on re-examining the theological questions associated with death, judgment, heaven, and hell in the nineteenth century, and showing how these questions are reflected in the work of the creative writers. But the word 'reflected' suggests some kind of gap or separation between theology and literature, whereas in fact the writing project examined in this book is one that is *shared* by Victorian creative writers and theologians in their engagement with the great mysteries of the four last things, and with the challenges associated with those mysteries in the nineteenth century, including problems of evidence and authority, of interpretation, and of language.

Eschatology was a highly controversial subject in the Victorian Age, as a glance through any collection of religious tracts or indeed serious general periodicals of the period will reveal. In the absence of definite and coherent teaching on judgment, heaven, and hell in the New Testament, a wide range of doctrinal positions, each based upon a few individual texts, were defended on sectarian lines. Four conflicting views on eternal damnation were current in the 1870s, for example, and ideas of heaven as community and heaven as a place of worship proved difficult to reconcile. Some of the radical truth claims in the New Testament concerning the future life, which had always seemed either enigmatic or contradictory, now became questionable in the light of the Higher Criticism. In grappling with these particular themes and debates, theologians and creative writers reopened some of the key questions concerning the nature of religious belief and language. Both preachers and poets, for example, confronted the problem of finding a discourse which could convey an idea of the transcendent in an increasingly scientific-materialist world. The sense of the miraculous captured in the biblical account of a girl being raised from the dead in a house in first-century Palestine is difficult to transfer to a suburban villa where the doctor is expected, in Victorian fiction. Hans Frei, in his study of the relationship between realist narrative and the 'Eclipse of Biblical Narrative', shows how in the second half of the eighteenth century (in England the period of the rise of the novel) a great reversal had taken place in German biblical criticism: interpretation had become a matter of 'fitting the biblical story into another world with another story rather than incorporating that world into the biblical story'. The Victorian novelist or poet who attempted to write of the 'invisible world' in a secular form and from a this-worldly perspective faced a similar challenge. In the attempt to speak of that which is 'beyond words' or to narrate the unnarratable, such as death and the future life, language comes under great pressure, and communication – in deathbed scenes, for example – can break down. Such a breakdown also occurs in the gospel story of the raising of Lazarus, and it is in these critical moments of stress or fracture in the discourse of consolation that both the provisional nature of the writing project *and* the grounds of Christian faith are laid bare.

At the centre of these concerns lies a tension between what can broadly be defined as 'horizontal' ontological and epistemological models, which tend to be anthropocentric, historical, experiential, and gradualist in orientation, and 'vertical' models, which are often theocentric, eschatological, scriptural, and catastrophist. I discuss the processes of death and bereavement in Victorian deathbed and graveyard scenes, for example, and show how in the horizontal dimension, the dying person passes from life to death (or the 'next world', depending on one's perspective), via an ambiguous phase that is marked off by two disruptive (and 'vertical') moments: that in which death is anticipated, and the moment of death itself. In the Victorian Age, highly conventionalized social customs and funerary rituals eased the transition from the deathbed to the bed that is the grave, and consolatory Christian literature emphasized the continuities between this life and the next, and particularly the idea of heaven as community. The burial service in the Book of Common Prayer, however, far from reinforcing these manageable stages of separation, consoled Victorian mourners (as it had their ancestors) through affirmations of faith which are based upon some of the most challenging paradoxes and contraries in the New Testament, including passages from John 11 and 1 Corinthians 15 which speak of life in death, of incorruption in corruption, of rising in descending. Such paradoxes and contraries are finally resolved only through faith.

The horizontal dimension of temporal process and deferral comes to the fore in the Victorian novel, and 'the sense of an ending'; in millenarian epic poems on 'the course of time'; and in doctrines of purgatory and the 'intermediate state' between death and the last judgment, whereby final divine dispensations are deferred. In moments of spiritual crisis, however, whether in fiction, poetry, or spiritual autobiography, the horizontality of everyday existence is disrupted as a person experiences some kind of vision of judgment, as in Browning's *Easter-Day*, for example. But whereas death and judgment are problematic subjects for the writer because of their contradictory or ambiguous nature as process in and through time, heaven and hell present the quite opposite problem of being fixed states. In each case, however, it is often in the poet's or the hymnist's use of tense and mode that conflicting ideas of time and eternity are most effectively reconciled. What I call the 'eternal present', for example, collapses earthly time in a way that is inscribed in the theology of the kingdom, and in the doctrine of the communion of saints. Thus the mourner's or elegist's experience of separation – I / you, life / death, earth / heaven – is subsumed in a larger scheme of Christian faith, the 'double consciousness' of which holds the this-worldly and the other-worldly in creative tension, and which speaks of a kingdom that is here *and* elsewhere, of a paradise that is now *and* not yet.

In order to combine breadth of interdisciplinary discussion with depth of textual analysis, the book is arranged in two parts. Following an introduction on the grounds of hope of a future life in the Bible, and associated problems of evidence and authority, language, and interpretation, I examine in Part I each of the four last things in separate chapters, drawing upon a wide range of material from the period 1830–90, some of which is familiar – novels by the Brontës and George Eliot, poems by Browning and Arnold, autobiographical works by Newman and Carlyle, and paintings by Martin and Millais – some unfamiliar – tracts by Father Furniss of Dublin, the literary and devotional works of Revd Edward Henry Bickersteth, Vicar of Hampstead and later Bishop of Exeter, and the memoirs of Catharine Tait, wife of a future Archbishop of Canterbury. In Part II, rereadings of four literary texts of major critical interest are informed by the concepts, models, and methodologies identified in Part I. Tennyson and Dickens, both of whom sympathized with Anglican Broad Church opinion on most of the major doctrinal issues of the day, grounded their writing on the subject of death and the future life in *In Memoriam* and *Our Mutual Friend* on the authority of the heart and a liberal interpretation of scripture. In contrast, Newman and Hopkins, both Roman Catholic priests writing for English Catholics, based their treatments of purgatory and martyrdom in *The Dream of Gerontius* and *The Wreck of the Deutschland* on the authority and theology of the church to which they had converted.

It is perhaps a sign of our times that three leading literary critics have in recent years turned their attention to the relationship between literature and theology: Northrop Frye in *The Great Code*, Frank Kermode in *The Genesis of Secrecy*, and George Steiner in *After Babel*. The work of these three critics reflects something of the range of pressing and challenging topics which are of concern to both disciplines, including the study of language, narrative, and myth, and which are the subject of the journal *Literature & Theology*. I wish first to acknowledge my debt to the increasing number of scholars now working in the field of literature and theology, and particularly to my former colleagues on the journal – David Jasper, Terry Wright, Nicholas Sagovsky, Alison Milbank, John Milbank, and Mark Ledbetter.

Versions of sections in Chapters 1, 5, and 7 have appeared in the form of conference papers published by the Macmillan Press Ltd, and edited by David Jasper and T. R. Wright: 'Tennyson, Newman and the Question of Authority', in *The Interpretation of Belief: Coleridge, Schleiermacher and Romanticism* (1986), and '"Can These Dry Bones Live?": Questions of Belief in a Future Life', in *The Critical Spirit and the Will to Believe: Essays in Nineteenth-Century Literature and Religion* (1989).

I am indebted to the following institutions: Lancaster University and its Humanities Research Committee, for granting funds for special research leave, 1986–7, and for a term's study leave in 1989; the Institute for Advanced Studies in the Humanities, University of Edinburgh, for awarding a Visiting Fellowship, Michaelmas 1986; and The British Academy, for awarding a research grant for that term. Also to the librarians and staffs of the British Library, London; the Bodleian Library, Oxford; Cambridge University Library; Edinburgh University Library; the Harry Ransom Humanities Research Center, University of Texas at Austin; Lancaster University Library; Lincolnshire Central Reference Library, Lincoln; the National Library of Scotland, Edinburgh; New College Library, Edinburgh; St Deiniol's Library, Hawarden; and Stonyhurst College Library.

I would like to thank a number of individuals who have helped me with patience and kindness: A. S. Byatt; Arthur Sale; at Lancaster, John Andrews, Pat Armitage, Chip Coakley, Davina Chaplin, Keith Hanley, Vimala Herman, Carole Lord, Denis McCaldin (without whose help I could not have written on Elgar), Alan Robinson, Patrick Sherry, and David Webb; at Edinburgh and St Andrews Universities, Michael Alexander, Ian Campbell, Evelyn Carruthers, Peter Jones, and Karl Guthke; and particularly Andrew Brown, David Carroll, Alison Milbank, and Christopher Walsh, whose continued support and enthusiasm have sustained me. The dedicatees, and their mother, know how profoundly grateful I am to them, in so many ways.

MDW

Introduction

> Blessed be the God and Father of our Lord Jesus Christ, which according to his abundant mercy hath begotten us again unto a lively hope by the resurrection of Jesus Christ from the dead,
>
> To an inheritance incorruptible, and undefiled, and that fadeth not away, reserved in heaven for you,
>
> Who are kept by the power of God through faith unto salvation ready to be revealed in the last time.   (1 Peter 1.3–5)

Many modern scholars reject Petrine authority for the 'First Epistle General of Peter'. Others argue that the epistle was probably written by Silvanus (5.12), but that it embodies the apostle's testimony. With the question of authority still in the balance, however, Peter's traditional title of 'apostle of hope' survives. The epistle itself, addressed to young Christian communities which can expect to suffer persecution, conveys a radiant message of hope for those who are committed to a difficult pilgrimage. The future is to be anticipated in joyful expectation, and embraced in certainty.

The passage quoted above is the opening of a doxology for the risen Christ, and its tone is necessarily direct and authoritative. This was not the place in which to introduce commentary upon the nature of the 'last time', or of Christ's promise of eternal life. Each of the key terms in the passage, however, would have had a very specific resonance for its first readers, and was to be the subject of much detailed exegesis in the nineteenth century, as we will see in later chapters. 'Lively' or 'living', for example, suggests a divinely inspired hope, since life is God's prerogative.[1] 'Hope' was a recognized technical term of the Pharisees, used by Paul in his testimony to the Sanhedrin in Jerusalem: 'I am a Pharisee, a son of a Pharisee: of the hope and resurrection of the dead I am called in question' (Acts 23.6). These words caused a dispute between the Pharisees, who believed in the resurrection of the body, and the Sadducees, who denied it. The concept of the resurrection of the body was an apocalyptic hope current in traditional Palestinian Judaism at the time of Christ, and often came into conflict with that of the immortality of the soul and a future life immediately after death, in Hellenistic Judaism.[2] Although the matter is still contested, most theologians today consider resurrection to be the basis of sound doctrine, as the whole person is thereby raised to new life, and no final separation between the body and the soul is implied.[3] At a time when persecution was an imminent threat, as in 1 Peter, teaching on the resurrection of the body would have been sharply relevant.

The closing words of verse 5, 'in the last time' (en kairō eschatō; NEB 'at the end of time') introduce the concept of the eschaton. The nineteenth-century term 'eschatology' has been used in several different but related senses.[4] Here I will apply it in the traditional sense of 'death, judgment, heaven, and hell' (OED), and the science or study of these four last things. In 1 Peter the end of all things is said to be 'at hand' (4.7). The apostles lived in the end-time, as Christ had already died and been raised from the dead. Thus, paradoxically, the 'lively hope' of the doxology is already an 'eschatological blessing'.[5] (Similarly, New Testament metaphors of 'first fruits' and an 'earnest' of blessings to come, associated with the gift of the Holy Spirit, emphasize a continuity between eternal life as a present possession and as a future promise.)[6]

For the first Christians, the end-time was to be completed in the parousia ('coming' or 'presence'), usually identified with the return or second coming of Christ.[7] Jesus's own teaching on the parousia had been received as a definitive prophecy of the imminent end of the present world order, and of the coming of the kingdom. As the decades passed, however, without the hoped for parousia being fulfilled, the question of the state of the dead between their 'falling asleep' and the general resurrection became increasingly pressing, and Christian writers encountered difficulties in harmonizing the idea of a post-mortem existence with God, in heaven, and Jewish eschatology which looked to the final judgment. (In the Middle Ages, Roman Catholic teaching on purgatory was to draw upon patristic writings which grappled with the same problem.) The writer of the Second Epistle of Peter (which has no connection with the first) anticipates 'that there shall come in the last days scoffers, walking after their own lusts, And saying, Where is the promise of his coming? for since the fathers fell asleep, all things continue as they were from the beginning of the creation' (2 Peter 3.3–4).

Paul tackled these and other difficulties in the finest chapter on the subject of death and the future life in the Bible, 1 Corinthians 15, where he wrote to members of the church in Corinth who shared the hostility of Hellenistic Judaism towards the resurrection of the body:

> But if there be no resurrection of the dead, then is Christ not risen.
>
> . . .
>
> For if the dead arise not, then is not Christ raised:
> And if Christ be not raised, your faith is vain; ye are yet in your sins.
> Then they also which are fallen asleep in Christ are perished.
> If in this life only we have hope in Christ, we are of all men most miserable.
>
> (1 Corinthians 15.13, 16–19)

Paul, a Pharisee before his conversion, would have believed in a *general* resurrection. His analogy, however, of the sowing of the 'bare grain' (15.37) denotes a quality of relationship, not of substance, in the Christian scheme, and he avoids description of the *modus operandi* of resurrection: 'It is sown a natural body; it is raised a spiritual body' (15.44).[8] Similarly, the last judgment is a mystery: 'Behold, I shew you a mystery; We shall not all sleep, but we shall all be changed, in a moment, in the twinkling of an eye, at the last trump' (15.51–2). It is thus implied that not all who read the epistle will have died when the trumpet sounds. Like the writer of 1 Peter, Paul addresses those who are 'waiting for the coming of our Lord Jesus Christ' (1 Corinthians 1.7).

In the interim, however, the early church had to wait and to endure, 'knowing that tribulation worketh patience; And patience, experience; and experience hope: And hope maketh not ashamed' (Romans 5.3–5).[9] This hope is 'for that we seek not' (Romans 8.24–5), and Paul writes to the Colossians of 'the hope which is laid up for you in heaven, whereof ye heard before in the word of the truth of the gospel' (Colossians 1.5). For Paul, the four last things are mysteries hidden with God, and his teaching on the Christian hope speaks to the pilgrim church of the new covenant, going forward in confidence into 'that we see not'. 'Paradise' was for him 'now and not yet'.[10]

In the New Testament the object of the Christian hope remains indefinite: outside the Book of Revelation there are no detailed descriptions of the future life. One explanation for the infrequency and generality of Jesus's teaching on the subject in the gospels is that he took life after death for granted.[11] His reported sayings on the four last things, his raising of Lazarus from the dead, and his teaching on the kingdom are in various ways difficult to interpret. The description of the last judgment in Matthew 25, for example, modifies Jewish apocalyptic by suggesting that groups of individuals rather than nations will be judged, and judged according to their works. But no reference is made to Christ's redemptive act in dying upon the cross.[12] The final verse of the chapter ('And these shall go away into everlasting punishment: but the righteous into eternal life'), the subject of much heated debate in the nineteenth century, may have been a Matthean addition, recalling Daniel 12.2. The story of the raising of Lazarus from the dead poses more problems than it solves, as Tennyson knew:

> Behold a man raised up by Christ!
> The rest remaineth unrevealed;
> He told it not; or something seal'd
> The lips of that Evangelist.[13]

Most of Jesus's teaching on the kingdom is conveyed through parables, a form which at once reveals and conceals.[14] Even the most direct teaching is suggestive rather than explanatory. In the farewell discourses in the fourth gospel, for example, words which have encouraged not only ecumenists but also those who look to the unification of all world faiths ('In my Father's house are many mansions', 14.2) are followed by the unequivocal saying, 'no man cometh unto the Father, but by me' (14.6).

The Book of Revelation, on the other hand, presents difficulties of interpretation of a different order, for what James Hastings called 'the "Divina Commedia" of Scripture' can be read as all too literal a description of the events of the *eschaton*.[15] In the nineteenth century many believed that the seven seals and the four horsemen, the dragon, and the lake of brimstone were more than chiliastic symbols. At the end of the century, one theologian acknowledged the fact that the Revelation had 'suffered many things from the strained ingenuity of the dogmatic interpreter'. He himself focused upon the *parousia*, the 'objective, visible return' of Christ, as the 'decisive event of the future' in his analysis of the book.[16] Northrop Frye, however, who prefers to interpret the Revelation as a 'progression of antitypes', drawing upon the Old Testament in a 'mosaic of allusions', reminds us of the problems associated with an 'objective' reading: 'The author speaks of setting down what he has seen in a vision, but the Book of Revelation is not a visualized book in the ordinary sense of the word, as any illustrator who has struggled with its seven-headed and ten-horned monsters will testify.'[17] Inspired by the

Book of Revelation, many Victorian illustrators and painters, poets, novelists, and preachers attempted to combine sublimity with realism, the visionary with the matter-of-fact, in their portrayals of the last days.

In contrast to those who searched the New Testament for evidence of the location and dimensions of heaven, Friedrich Schleiermacher, the great Protestant theologian of the early nineteenth century, wrote on the subject of the future life:

all the indications [the Redeemer] gives are either purely figurative, or otherwise so indefinite in tenor that nothing can be gathered from them more than what for every Christian is so much the essential thing in every conception he may form of existence after death, that without it such existence would be mere perdition – namely, the persistent union of believers with the Redeemer.[18]

The one statement of Jesus which may be said to summarize the gospel message also underlines the grounds of the Christian hope, but without offering Martha, the sister of Lazarus, a mental picture of the future life: 'I am the resurrection, and the life: he that believeth in me, though he were dead, yet shall he live: And whosoever liveth and believeth in me shall never die' (John 11.25–6).

The lively hope of resurrection in Jesus Christ was reflected in the new tone of early Christian funerary inscriptions in the Roman catacombs.[19] Meditating on these, Walter Pater's Marius became 'as by some gleam of foresight, aware of the whole force of evidence for a certain strange, new hope, defining in its turn some new and weighty motive of action, which lay in deaths so tragic for the "Christian superstition"' (*Marius the Epicurean*, 1885; 21). Expressions of Christian hope often spring from suffering or persecution, and are eloquent testimony of faith among the bereaved. For Victorian Anglicans, and for many nonconformists,[20] it was in the order for the Burial of the Dead in the Book of Common Prayer (1662) that New Testament teaching on the Christian hope was encountered most dramatically and memorably. The words from the fourth gospel quoted above – 'I am the resurrection and the life' – affirmed in the opening sentence the doctrine on which the funeral service was based. From 1549 onwards, the lesson which followed had been taken from 1 Corinthians 15, beginning at verse 20.[21] The final collect refers to Christ's teaching, by his 'holy Apostle Saint Paul', that we should 'not be sorry, as men without hope, for them that sleep in him'. 'Our hope' is that our brother or sister 'rests' in Christ. E. H. Bickersteth, a leading Evangelical who was Vicar of Hampstead and later Bishop of Exeter, wrote on the burial service: 'It is throughout the language of holy hope.'[22] This is the theme of Bickersteth's meditations on the Order for the Burial of the Dead, entitled *The Shadowed Home, and the Light Beyond* (1875), which was written to console the bereaved between a death and a burial. Anthologies of verse fulfilled a similar function in the nineteenth century. A collection of *Sacred Poems for Mourners* (1846), for example, edited by Priscilla Maurice, followed the sequence of the burial service, offering simple reflections on the words of the prayer book and the New Testament teaching and symbolism which they embody. Richard Chenevix Trench's 'Life through Death' begins: 'The seed must die, before the corn appears / Out of the ground, in blade and fruitful ears.'[23] L. C. Briggs's 'The Linden Trees' in the *Illustrated Book of Sacred Poems* (1867) is also typical of the sentimental graveyard tradition of the period:

> While that blest word,
> 'The Resurrection and the life,' is heard,
> And they repeat
> The hopes of those who trust in heaven to meet,
> And rest for aye at the Redeemer's feet.[24]

The indefinite nature of New Testament teaching on the future life, which is reflected in the Book of Common Prayer, allowed Victorian preachers and poets considerable latitude of interpretation, and the idea of heaven as a blessed home or country in which friends and loved ones meet is the most characteristic of the age.

Far more contentious was the question of judgment and God's elect. The words spoken over the dead in the Book of Common Prayer – 'in sure and certain hope of the Resurrection to eternal life' – were the subject of much debate in the 1860s during a prolonged series of ecclesiastical exchanges on the subject of liturgical reform, to which Dickens refers in *Our Mutual Friend* (1864–5).[25] C. J. Vaughan, for example, Vicar of Doncaster and later Dean of Llandaff, drew attention to the dilemma of the minister who 'must give thanks to God for the sure and certain hope of another world by the grave of the drunkard or the adulterer'.[26] The effect, however, of removing the words 'sure and certain', either compulsorily or at the discretion of the priest, would in Vaughan's view be worse than keeping the time-honoured phrase, even though it was considered by some to be complacent, and to hint at the possibility of universal salvation. The nature and scope of the Christian hope in the New Testament were matters of general interest and concern in the nineteenth century, but it was often in the familiar words from the burial service, spoken over the body of a dear brother or sister departed, that a subject of universal significance was brought home to individual mourners.

Heaven, that long home or blessed country, represented for many Victorian writers and thinkers the fulfilment of their Christian hope. Ruskin, for example, claimed a special place for hope in the Christian scheme, and specifically in relation to heaven. In his commentary on the sculptures on the capitals of the Ducal Palace in Venice, which portray the three virtues, he writes:

> Of all the virtues, this is the most distinctively Christian (it could not, of course, enter definitely into any Pagan scheme); and above all others, it seems to me the *testing* virtue, – that by the possession of which we may most certainly determine whether we are Christians or not; for many men have charity, that is to say, general kindness of heart, or even a kind of faith, who have not any habitual *hope* of, or longing for, heaven.[27]

J. M. Neale's hymn 'The world is very evil' encourages belief in heaven, a 'sweet and blessed country, / The home of God's elect':

> Strive, man, to win that glory;
> Toil, man, to gain that light;
> Send hope before to grasp it,
> Till hope be lost in sight . . .[28]

And one of H. W. Baker's hymns in *Hymns Ancient and Modern* begins:

> There is a blessed home
> Beyond this land of woe,
> Where trials never come,
> Nor tears of sorrow flow;
> Where faith is lost in sight,
> And patient hope is crown'd,
> And everlasting light
> Its glory throws around.[29]

This kind of affirmation – 'There *is* a blessed home' – is typical of Victorian hymnody. As we have already seen, however, New Testament teaching on the future life presents numerous problems of interpretation. Nineteenth-century eschatological controversies focused upon the conflict between the certainty of the hope affirmed in the Bible and the prayer book, and the uncertainties of biblical evidence. Before examining that conflict in detail in Part One of this study, in relation to the treatment of death, judgment, heaven, and hell in Victorian literature and theology, I must first consider two broad issues that are central to a discussion of the great themes of eschatology: the questions of biblical authority and the limits of religious language. For in the years from around 1830 to around 1890 these issues were both urgent and challenging.

THE QUESTION OF BIBLICAL AUTHORITY

The debate in the 1860s over the words 'sure and certain hope' in the burial service raised the familiar problem of religious authority. As the forms of service printed in the Book of Common Prayer do not have the same authority as the creeds and the thirty-nine articles of the Church of England, what authority do these words have? Is this sure and certain hope grounded in the New Testament, and does the New Testament itself have divine authority? To what extent can individual biblical texts on the subject be received as authoritative? Article VI states that 'Holy Scripture containeth all things necessary to salvation', and article XX that although the church has 'authority in Controversies of Faith . . . yet it is not lawful for the Church to ordain any thing that is contrary to God's Word written, neither may it so expound one place of Scripture, that it be repugnant to another'. The substance of both these articles figured prominently in discussion on the question of the authority of scripture in the nineteenth century, a large and complex subject which was often closely linked to the specific issue of the future state. As the question of authority will be central to my later discussion, its salient points should be briefly outlined here.

For Bernard Ramm, 'revelation is the key to religious authority'. Whereas the Roman Catholic Church bases its authority upon God's revelation (contained in oral tradition and the scriptures) and his 'one true Church', the Protestant principle of authority is defined by Ramm as 'the Holy Spirit speaking in the Scriptures': 'there is an *external* principle (the *inspired* Scripture) and an *internal* principle (the witness of the Holy Spirit). It is the principle of an objective *divine* revelation, with an anterior *divine* witness.'[30] In the early nineteenth century the Tractarians agreed with the Roman Catholics that authority lay in the Bible *and* in tradition, and in his *Lectures on the Prophetical Office of the*

Church (1837) Newman argued that freedom of private judgment in the interpretation of scripture without reference to tradition would lead to latitudinarianism.[31] Newman was writing at a time when many practising Christians in Britain believed in the inerrancy of the Bible as the inspired word of God.[32] The whole question of authority, however, was to be thrown into the melting-pot over the subsequent twenty-five years.

It has been suggested that if Coleridge's *Confessions of an Inquiring Spirit*, published posthumously in 1840, had been more widely read, much of the misunderstanding over the interpretation of the Bible in the later nineteenth century might have been avoided.[33] Coleridge affirms the Protestant principle of authority (based upon the reading, in faith, of the inspired scriptures), while attacking what he calls 'Bibliolatry'. He encourages his Friend to read the contents of the Bible 'with only the same piety which you freely accord on other occasions to the writings of men, considered the best and wisest of their several ages!'[34] Those who believe in the literal truth of every word of the Bible fall into error through the practice of 'bringing together into logical dependency detached sentences from books composed at the distance of centuries, nay, sometimes a *millennium*, from each other, under different dispensations, and for different objects'.[35]

Coleridge, however, was ahead of his time, having been one of the first Englishmen to recognize the significance of German biblical criticism. It was not until the 1860s, during the controversy following the publication of *Essays and Reviews* (1860), that this kind of approach to biblical interpretation made a considerable impact upon the public mind. In his brilliant article on the interpretation of scripture, Benjamin Jowett argued, like Coleridge, that the Bible should be read like any other book, and that passages from one part of the Bible should not be applied uncritically to other passages.[36] Now the orthodox position on 'life everlasting' and 'everlasting fire' had traditionally been based upon a number of scattered biblical texts (including Isaiah 33.14, Daniel 12.2, and Matthew 25.46), and the Athanasian Creed. The application of historical critical methods to the Bible therefore strengthened a liberal challenge to the doctrine of everlasting punishment, and it is no coincidence that the two contributors taken to law were Rowland Williams (on 'Bunsen's Biblical Researches') and H. B. Wilson (on the question of eternal punishment). The connection was stated explicitly in the declaration of nearly eleven thousand clergy, both Tractarian and Evangelical, that the Church of England believed in the inspired scripture and taught, 'in the words of our Blessed Lord, that the "punish-ment" of the "cursed" equally with the "life" of the "righteous" is "everlasting"' (Matthew 25).[37]

The new questions concerning the authority of the Bible which arose in the 1860s threw many thinking people into a state of near panic. They had to choose between the excesses of the radical Tübingen school and the blinkered conservatism of English scholarship.[38] The English scene was dominated by Pusey, who countered the late dating of Daniel with the observation that Christians, unlike 'the critics', believed that miracu-lous prophecies could happen, and H. P. Liddon, whose Bampton lec-tures of 1866, entitled *The Divinity of Our Lord*, attempted to refute Renan, Baur, and Strauss.[39] The middle ground, however, was soon taken by three scholars – Lightfoot, Hort, and Westcott – who came to be known as the 'Cambridge Three', and whose biblical criticism was as rigorous as that of the Germans. Lightfoot, moreover, managed to explode the more exaggerated claims of the Tübingen school.[40]

The contributors to *Essays and Reviews* had known that there was a gap between doctrine preached by the Church of England and the actual beliefs of educated people. In *Literature and Dogma* (1873), Matthew Arnold took the argument further, stating that '*the masses* are losing the Bible and its religion', largely as a result of Protestantism's having made the Bible 'its fixed authority'.[41] Interestingly, the issues of biblical auth-ority and the nature of the future state are again drawn together in Arnold's preface to the popular edition.[42] His attack on the 'mechanical and materialising theology' of his day was extended in *God and the Bible* (1875), a sequel to *Literature and Dogma*, where he claimed that Jesus's words to Martha were intended to 'transform' the materialist Jewish concept of the resurrection of the body, but that his words provided the basis for the evolution of a miracle story 'exactly effacing the truth which [he] wished to convey'.[43] Our 'hope of immortality', our 'common materialistic notions about the resurrection of the body and the world to come', are 'in direct conflict with the new and loftier conceptions of life and death which Jesus himself strove to establish'.[44] As a moralist and an idealist, Arnold rejects the view, based upon a literal reading of the Bible, that Christianity is nothing but a promise of paradise to the saint and a threat of hell-fire to the worldly man, based on the authority of Christ who rose from the dead and ascended into heaven.[45] 'Of Biblical learning', he writes, 'we have not enough.'[46]

Critics of *Lux Mundi* (1889), edited by Charles Gore, a leading High

Churchman, believed that the opposite was now true, and that of biblical learning we had too much. In his own essay on 'The Holy Spirit and Inspiration', quoted earlier, Gore adopted Plato's idea of authority as a 'necessary schooling of the individual temperament' which 'leaves much for the individual to do'.[47] He uses the word 'myth' in relation to the Bible's earlier narratives, before the call of Abraham, and welcomes the results of historical criticism where it is fairly used.[48] The controversy which ensued has been fully documented and need not be rehearsed here.[49] By the end of the century Dean Farrar of Canterbury could assert in *The Bible, Its Meaning and Supremacy* (1897) that no scholar of note questioned the main conclusions of the 'Higher Criticism', and that it was better for Christianity not to base the Bible's authority on an idea of biblical infallibility. Rather, the doctrine of the Church of England is that 'Scripture *contains* the word of God'.[50]

F. W. Farrar, author of *Eric; or, Little by Little* (1858) and the famous *Life of Christ* (1874), was himself one of the major contributors to nineteenth-century debates on the future life. In his famous sermons on *Eternal Hope* (1878) he had argued that the 'common view' of everlasting punishment, which he abhorred, was based partly upon mistranslations in the Authorized Version, and that the common view was the product of what he later described in *The Bible, Its Meaning and Supremacy* as 'the wresting of texts'. In this later work he quoted Coleridge's *Confessions of an Inquiring Spirit*, and predicted that the printing of the Revised Version (1881–5) in paragraphs instead of verses would gradually help to dissipate the 'delusion' that the Bible 'was originally written in that atomistic form' enshrined in the Authorized Version.[51] The doctrine of 'eternal torment' had often been 'proved' by Isaiah 23.14, yet 'even a moderate study of the context might have sufficed to show that the verse has not the most remote connexion with that terrific dogma'.[52]

In *The Bible, Its Meaning and Supremacy*, Farrar quoted Newman: '"The *translated Bible*," Cardinal Newman says with reluctant admiration, "is *the stronghold of heresy*."'[53] In Farrar's view, the Bible's influence on literature, and specifically on Wordsworth, Tennyson, Browning, George Eliot, Carlyle, Newman, and Ruskin, had been 'invaluable and supreme'.[54] For some Victorian writers who addressed themselves to the subject of the future life, however, the question of the authority of the translated Bible was pressing.

ANALOGY AND THE LIMITS OF LANGUAGE

Behind these arguments concerning translation and proof texts lay a series of fundamental problems associated with the nature of religious language itself. Nineteenth-century literalists based their conceptions of heaven and hell on the narrow ground of one or two isolated biblical texts, and thus on a limited range of analogues and symbols. The same was often true of those who attempted to portray heaven and hell imaginatively, in verse or prose. Indeed, the realist novelist or painter was in certain respects in a more difficult position than the theologian. Chris Brooks examines religious symbolism in the novels of Dickens, the paintings of the Pre-Raphaelites, and the architecture of Butterfield, and finds in all these artists' work a 'mode of the Victorian imagination' which he describes as 'symbolic realism'. This mode, he argues, is grounded in typology, 'the technique of biblical exegesis, Patristic in origin, whereby events and persons in the Old Testament are interpreted both as historically real and as divinely ordained prefigurations of events in the New Testament, most centrally, of the life of Christ'.[55] Thus typology is a particular version of symbolic realism which allows 'events to be read as simultaneously real and symbolic'. Brooks's study focuses upon aesthetics, and does not explore the closely related subject of analogy, and the inheritance of Joseph Butler's *Analogy of Religion* (1736) in the Victorian period.[56] Butler's seminal work profoundly influenced thinkers as varied as Coleridge, Newman, Keble, and Maurice. The book opens with a chapter entitled 'Of a Future Life', in which Butler examines the 'presumption or probability' of a future existence for man in the light of the 'analogy of nature, and the several changes which we have undergone', and other examples of transformation such as that of the worm turning into the fly.[57] James Buchanan, Professor of Systematic Theology at the Free Church New College, Edinburgh, wrote a treatise entitled *Analogy* in the 1860s which was based upon Butler, but which applied the word more widely. Following Butler, Buchanan commented that some analogous facts are 'applicable to such truths as are common to Natural and Revealed religion', and argued that the 'doctrine of a future state of existence after death belongs to this class'.[58] He defined analogies as

a sort of rational imagery, by which the nature and relations of things 'seen and temporal' are made to symbolize those which are 'unseen and eternal'. 'Earthly things' become the exponents and types of 'heavenly things'.[59]

Perhaps the most influential statement on analogy in the nineteenth century, however, was Coleridge's in *Aids to Reflection* (1825), where he compares it with metaphor:

Analogies are used in aid of *Conviction*: Metaphors, as means of Illustration. The language is analogous, wherever a thing, power, or principle in a higher dignity is expressed by the same thing, power, or principle in a lower but more known form. Such, for instance, is the language of John iii.6. *That which is born of the Flesh, is Flesh; that which is born of the Spirit, is Spirit.* The latter half of the verse contains the fact *asserted*; the former half the *analogous* fact, by which it is rendered intelligible. If any man choose to call this *metaphorical* or figurative, I ask him whether . . . he regards the divine Justice, for instance, as a *metaphorical* term, a mere figure of speech? If he disclaims this, then I answer, neither do I regard the words *born again*, or *spiritual life*, as figures or metaphors. I have only to add, that these analogies are the material, or (to speak chemically) the *base*, of Symbols and symbolical expressions; the nature of which is always *tau*tegorical (*i.e.*, expressing the *same* subject but with a *difference* in contra-distinction from metaphors and similitudes), that are always *allegorical* (*i.e.*, expressing a *different* subject but with a resemblance) . . .[60]

Coleridge's description of analogy as a means of expressing some 'higher dignity' which is the object of conviction via a 'lower but more known form' can be applied to the analogue, or parallel relationship between, sleep:waking (the analogous fact) and death:resurrection (the fact asserted), which was to be the 'base' of much of the religious symbolism in the apologetics and the consolatory writings of the Victorian Age. Central to Coleridge's argument, and to the claims of Victorian eschatology, is the belief that the analogical language of the New Testament renders intelligible a higher reality than that which is susceptible to scientific-materialist analysis.

Typology and analogy, then, were both seen in the nineteenth century as means by which language could transcend its human limits, and point towards 'heavenly things'. Whereas typology, however, could easily be adapted to nineteenth-century progressive or developmental models of creation, analogy, traditionally understood by less imaginative thinkers than Coleridge as reflecting a static, divinely ordered cosmos, adapted less well to a world in which language, including biblical language, came to be understood as a human construction. The question of the function and limits of religious language has, of course, continued to exercise twentieth-century theologians and literary critics. In his Bampton Lectures entitled *The Glass of Vision* (1948), Austin Farrer distinguishes between the 'great images' and 'subordinate images' of the Judaeo-Christian tradition, and argues that Christ himself expressed thought in certain dominant images, such as the 'Kingdom of God' and the 'Son of Man', and, in historical time, 'clothed himself in the archetypal images, and then began to do and to suffer'.[61] In his fourth lecture, Farrer considers how it is that these images are able to signify divine realities, and argues that 'analogy is the proper form of metaphysical thought, in the realm of *thought* there is no getting behind it'.[62] In a later lecture he states that 'faith discerns not the images, but what the images signify: and yet we cannot discern it except *through* the images'.[63] Farrer's ideas have aroused considerable interest. H. D. Lewis, for example, devoted a chapter of his study on *Our Experience of God* (1959) to 'Experience and Images', and more recently Farrer has figured in the debate between Helen Gardner and Frank Kermode over the interpretation of Mark's gospel, Farrer's central text in *A Glass of Vision*.[64]

In *God-Talk* (1967), John MacQuarrie was particularly interested in analogy applied to God himself:

analogical language – and all symbolic language – has a paradoxical character. Simply to affirm an analogue or symbol is to fall into that over-literalness which, if we are applying the image to God, leads into an attitude of idolatry. Whatever symbol or analogue is affirmed must be at the same time denied; or, better still, whenever one symbol is affirmed, others that will modify or correct it must be affirmed at the same time.[65]

As an illustration of the need for modifying symbols in theology, MacQuarrie cited what was at the time a recent and controversial argument, in John Robinson's *Honest to God* (1963), that symbols of depth are more helpful than symbols of height in relation to God and his nature. For MacQuarrie, Robinson had simply replaced one set of limiting ideas with another, and a 'big advance' toward a 'more adequate thought of God' would be made if these two symbols were 'held in tension'.

Not unlike Coleridge, MacQuarrie distinguishes between religious symbols, analogues, and images, which call from us a 'response of commitment', and metaphor, which is 'used mostly in literary contexts' and which elicits an aesthetic response.[66] Although limiting in its sharp separation of the credal from the aesthetic, and of the religious from the literary, this distinction is helpful with reference to language which attempts to describe God's nature. F. W. Dillistone, in his study on

Christianity and Symbolism (1955), distinguishes between analogy, which has links with the simile, and metaphor, which has links with the contrast. Metaphor, he observes, is the favourite tool of the great poets:

Through it the prophet leaps outside the circle of present experience, the realm of the factual and the commonsense, the typical and the regular. He parts company with those who are travelling the surer and steadier road of analogical comparison. By one act of daring he brings into creative relationship the apparently opposite and contrary and, if his metaphorical adventure proves successful, gains new treasure both for language and for life.[67]

Sallie McFague, who cites Dillistone in her *Metaphorical Theology* (1982), offers an 'amalgam' of the views of writers such as I. A. Richards, Max Black, Paul Ricoeur, and Nelson Goodman on metaphor, and particularly its 'tensive' character:

By retaining the interaction of *two* thoughts active in the mind, one recalls, as one does not with a simile, that the two are dissimilar as well as similar . . . A metaphor that works is sufficiently unconventional and shocking so that we instinctively say no as well as yes to it, thus avoiding absolutism . . . Religious metaphors, because of their preservation in a tradition and repetition in ritual, are especially prone to becoming idols.[68]

But we have seen that MacQuarrie makes very similar comments on symbols and analogues. Dillistone, who observes that when a metaphor is first presented we are 'surprised, even shocked, by the fact that this word does not really belong to the situation in which it is being used', adds that the same could be claimed to be true of the analogy, although in this case 'the transition is so gentle and so natural that we are not shocked: we are only conscious of a feeling of general approval and satisfaction'.[69]

Modern linguistic theory has, of course, shifted the whole ground of the discussion, and metaphor is now treated not only as a specific figure of speech but also, in its broader sense, as the foundation of language itself. Whereas nineteenth-century Evangelicals such as Bickersteth thought in terms of a 'heavenly' figurative language which was as immutable as the Word, Sallie McFague characterizes a metaphorical theology as 'open-ended, tentative, indirect, tensive, iconoclastic, *transformative*' (my emphasis),[70] and we saw earlier that in Matthew Arnold's view, Jesus's new language 'transformed' the materialist Jewish notions concerning the resurrection of the body. It is in similar terms and in a similar context that Michael Edwards begins his study on the language of literature and religion, entitled *Towards a Christian Poetics* (1984). Basing his theory on what he calls the 'cosmology of Christianity', namely 'creation, fall and re-creation', Edwards cites St Paul's teaching in 1 Corinthians 15 that the 'natural body' will be raised at the end as a 'spiritual body', and argues that 'the function of language and literature is to strain towards that spiritualising of the body'.[71] What follows is a late-twentieth-century reworking of materials (drawn from Bishop Butler) that were very familiar to the eighteenth and nineteenth centuries.[72]

It seems, then, that the theology of a future life is still fertile ground for the student of religious language. As we move towards understanding the Christian poetics of death, we will find that the boundaries between 'literary' and 'non-literary' writing, and between the metaphoric and the analogical, are far from clear. We need working definitions, however, and perhaps the best way to distinguish between metaphor and analogy for the purposes of this study is to see analogy as a parallel relation based upon similarity, whereas metaphor, being contrastive, functions through substitution. Thus the Christian analogy of 'sleep' is based upon the parallel relation, or analogue, sleep:awakening / death:resurrection. The breakdown of communication associated with this analogy in the kind of Victorian consolatory discourse relating to the deathbed and the grave which I will examine in Chapter 1 is uncannily anticipated in a prototypical New Testament narrative: the story of the raising of Lazarus in John 11.

'OUR FRIEND LAZARUS SLEEPETH': A TEST CASE

The eleventh chapter of the fourth gospel, a crucial passage in a New Testament which contains little specific teaching on the nature of resurrection, provided a fascinating test case in relation to the questions of biblical authority and language in the nineteenth century. Matthew Arnold noted in *God and the Bible* (1875) that every detail of the account of the raising of Lazarus had been 'canvassed with elaborate minuteness'.[73] No part of the narrative had received closer attention than verses 11–14:

he saith unto them, Our friend Lazarus sleepeth [*kekoimētai*]; but I go, that I may awake him out of sleep. Then said his disciples, Lord, if he sleep, he shall do well.

Howbeit Jesus spake of his death [*thanatou*]: but they thought that he had spoken of taking of rest in sleep [*koimēseōs touhupnou*].

Then said Jesus unto them plainly, Lazarus is dead [*apethanen*].

(John 11.11–14)

This is one of several examples in the fourth gospel of the disciples' failure immediately to comprehend or rightly interpret Jesus's sayings. One question posed by the passage touches upon the issues of the gospel's authorship and its relationship to the synoptic gospels: Why did the disciples fail to recognize a figure of speech which they might reasonably have been expected to remember from earlier usages, and particularly from the other two recorded miracles in which Jesus recalled the dead to life – the raising of Jairus's daughter (Mark 5, Luke 8, and Matthew 9, where the father is not named) and of the son of the widow of Nain (Luke 7)? E. H. Bickersteth addressed the question in *The Shadowed Home* (1875), where he explained the biblical context of the opening sentence of the burial service – 'I am the Resurrection and the Life, saith the Lord: he that believeth in Me, though he were dead, yet shall he live: and whosoever liveth and believeth in Me shall never die':

when His hour was come, Jesus arose to go into Judaea again . . . And as they were going, He said, Our friend Lazarus sleepeth, but I go that I may awake him out of sleep. In heaven's language the death of saints is sleep; but this language was not here understood by the disciples. The lofty freedom of the Divine style is excellent beyond compare; but man's dull apprehension makes Scripture often stoop to our more sombre way of speaking. Christ, on an earlier occasion, had interpreted this celestial dialect, when, ere He raised Jairus' daughter, He said, The maiden is not dead, but sleepeth [*katheudei*]. But, probably, from misunderstanding His words, This sickness is not unto death, but for the glory of God [John 11.4], the disciples were persuaded that Lazarus would not actually die; and therefore when He afterwards said, Our friend sleepeth, they thought that the Lord had given His beloved sleep, – that at His command Lazarus had fallen into that long, refreshing, peaceful sleep, which so often marks a favourable crisis in dangerous illness. Jesus therefore drops heaven's figurative language, and speaks in that of men: Lazarus is dead . . .[74]

The casualness with which Bickersteth equates the terms 'dialect' and 'style' betrays a lack of precision in his treatment of religious language, although this is hardly surprising in a popular book of meditations on the burial service. More significantly, he considers Christ's 'heavenly' language to be a mark of his divinity, and thus ignores the critical question of how this language was mediated to us in the writing of the gospel.[75] Like his use of the language of the Victorian sick-bed, however ('that long, refreshing, peaceful sleep, which so often marks a favourable crisis in dangerous illness'), Bickersteth's references to heaven's language provide a clue to his method in his own writing on death. At the end of the section headed 'I am the Resurrection and the Life', for example, he refers to the corpse as 'the sacred tabernacle' and the burial-ground as 'God's acre',[76] and we will see that in the deathbed scene in his epic poem, *Yesterday, To-Day, and For Ever*, his favourite figure is that of euphemism.

Interestingly, the first example in the *OED* of *euphemism* in the sense of 'an instance of this figure' is from the second volume of James Beattie's *Elements of Moral Science* (1793), where he quotes Acts 7.60: 'When it is said of the martyr St Stephen, that "he fell asleep," [*ekoimēthē*] instead of – he died, the euphemism partakes of the nature of metaphor, intimating a resemblance between sleep and the death of such a person.'[77] A hundred years after Beattie, John Hutchison, DD, writing on the disciples' 'slowness of apprehension' in the Lazarus narrative, explained that 'the figure of sleep, – the blessed euphemism for death, – though not unknown to Jewish and Gentile modes of thought, was far from being then in common use, as it is now', and describes the words 'Lazarus is dead' as a translation into 'plain, direct, prosaic words'.[78] Like Bickersteth, then, Hutchison thought of Jesus as an interpreter or translator, although unlike Bickersteth he acknowledged that the 'figure of sleep' was generated in a this-worldly rather an other-worldly plane.

F. D. Maurice, in his discourses on John, passed over the problem of the provenance and currency of the word 'sleep' as applied to death in the New Testament, and, in much sharper contrast to Bickersteth, wrote of Jesus as a teacher of a new language:

Our Lord is evidently teaching His disciples a new language; a language drawn from nature and experience; one which had mixed itself with other forms of speech in the dialect of all nations; but yet which was not easy for them to learn, and which we understand very imperfectly yet.[79]

Maurice had developed this last point more fully two years previously, in 1855, when he explained his reservations about some of the euphemisms in common currency at mid-century. His text in *Death and Life*, a sermon delivered at a memorial service for C. B. Mansfield at Lincoln's Inn, where he was chaplain, was I Thessalonians 4.14: 'For if we believe that Jesus died and rose again, even so them also which sleep [*koimēthentas*] in Jesus will God bring with Him.' Maurice argued here that the death and resurrection of Jesus Christ caused a change in Paul's 'mode of speech', and he asked the congregation to recollect

the synonyms which we have adopted for the words – 'That man is dead.' All point to some aspects of death; all are felt, at some point or other, to fail. We say, sometimes, 'He sleeps in the grave,' – 'After life's fitful fever he sleeps well!' There is something in such language which harmonizes with our feelings; there is something which jars with them. You remember the bodily pain, the restlessness of mind, you have seen in some one you have known well. The thought that he is in repose is the one you fly to most eagerly. But oh, that dreary, earthly repose! can it ever accord with the activity and energy which you knew were in him, which were expressed in his words, which you saw in his countenance? Was this all to end in a dull stagnation? You task yourself to discover some better form of thought than that: – 'He has departed this life.' . . . 'He has yielded to the inevitable destiny of man.' . . .

Now compare these expressions with St. Paul's; 'He sleeps in Jesus.' There is the rest which you were longing to claim for him, the termination of uneasy struggles, of doubts, of sufferings. But it is rest in Him from whom all his energies and activities were derived, in Him who was the secret spring of his soul's life and his body's life.[80]

Although Maurice's use of the word 'synonym' glosses over the question of the difference between death and sleep, his subsequent comments directly address the problem that confronted not only preachers and theologians, but also poets and novelists: namely, working with the analogy of sleep without falling into literalism. Maurice's own comments on the aptness of St Paul's 'He sleeps in Jesus' flow from his uneasiness with the material associations evoked by such language, and are reminiscent of Schleiermacher's observation that the only 'essential thing in every conception [the Christian] may form of existence after death' is the 'persistent union of believers with the Redeemer'.

Returning to the passage from John 11, I have so far considered a number of interpretations which are in one sense uncritical: that is, they comment upon the exchange between Jesus and his disciples as if it were a verbatim record of an actual conversation. D. F. Strauss, whose *Life of Jesus* was first published in England in 1846, in Marian Evans's translation, takes a quite different approach:

The alleged conduct of the disciples . . . is such as to excite surprise. If Jesus had represented to them, or at least to the three principal among them, the death of the daughter of Jairus as a mere sleep, how could they, when he said of Lazarus, *he sleeps, I will awake him*, . . . think that he referred to a natural sleep? One would not awake a patient out of a healthy sleep; hence it must have immediately occurred to the disciples that here sleep (*koimēsis*) was spoken of in the same sense as in the case of the maiden. That, instead of this, the disciples understand the deep expressions of Jesus quite superficially, is entirely in the fourth evangelist's favourite manner, which we have learned to recognise by many examples. If tradition had in any way made known to him, that to speak of death as a sleep was part of the customary phraseology of Jesus, there would immediately spring up in his imagination, so fertile in this kind of antithesis, a misunderstanding corresponding to that figure of speech.[81]

Comparisons between the 'resuscitations of the dead' in the Old Testament and that of Lazarus had, in Strauss's view, long ago persuaded theologians of more 'enlarged' views that 'the resurrections in the New Testament are nothing more than mythi, which had their origin in the tendency of the early Christian church, to make her Messiah agree with the type of the prophets, and with the messianic ideal'.[82]

Within the parameters of his historicist exegesis, Strauss seems to ignore the fact that memories are unreliable. More significantly, the words of misunderstanding in verse 12 – 'if he sleep, he shall do well' (*ei kekoimētai sōthēsetai*) – reveal, when read figuratively, the very secret of salvation itself, and the possibility of dying into life.[83] One modern commentator argues that sleep in the passage from John 11 is not simply a euphemism for death, and that the ambiguous word *kekoimētai* in verse 11 'points us to the deeper background of actual death': 'The theological statement which relativises the power of death by the reality of salvation moves on from the Old Testament and apocalyptic basis beyond the assertions of Hellenistic religion . . . proclaiming the basic powerlessness of death in the light of the resurrection.'[84]

This piece of commentary might have appealed to Matthew Arnold, who considered that Strauss's explanation of the miracles in the New Testament as a reiteration of the miracles of the Old was too systematic. For Arnold, 'every miracle has its own mode of growth and its own history, and the key to one is not the key to others'.[85] Arnold also disagreed with Strauss about the relative importance of the authorship of the fourth gospel: 'Not whether or no John wrote it, is for us the grand point, but whether or no Jesus said it.'[86] When he himself turns to John 11, therefore, he argues that the miracle story probably grew out of the *logion*, 'I am the resurrection and the life', and effaced the very truth which Jesus wished to convey.[87] In questioning the authenticity of the miracle story, Arnold ignores the misunderstanding under discussion and concentrates instead upon Jesus's initial statement in verse 11:

To the eye of Jesus, the kingdom of God, the reign of the saints, the introduction and triumph of everlasting righteousness, – that triumph in which re-live all the saints who are dead, and the saints who are yet alive live for evermore, – was at this moment beginning.[88]

Arnold's idealist interpretation of the *logion* can be compared with 'inaugurated eschatology',[89] and is based upon a suspicion of literalism that is reminiscent of his contemporary F. W. Farrar. We have seen that F. D. Maurice was also concerned about the possible materialist associations of the analogy of sleep, as in the idea of sleeping in the grave, for example, but that he laid special emphasis upon the raising of Lazarus because it specifically addresses the very issue of the physical (or material) reality of death.

The physical and the spiritual, the this-worldly and the other-worldly, the literal and the figurative: each category becomes problematic when applied to a miracle story that also contains a crucial *logion*, as we have seen in the work of nineteenth-century commentators. At one extreme Bickersteth blithely invokes 'the lofty freedom of the Divine style', while at the other Strauss and Arnold question the authenticity of the miracle. Only Maurice, in his uneasiness concerning the danger of misapplying Jesus's 'new language' in the clichés of the Victorian epitaph, comes close to acknowledging that it is at the very point of stress or fracture in the discourse of consolation that both the provisional nature of language and communication *and* the grounds of Christian faith are laid bare. It is to that discourse of Christian consolation in Victorian literature and theology that I now turn.

PART ONE

THE FOUR LAST THINGS

CHAPTER I

Death

Death and its two-fold aspect! wintry – one,
Cold, sullen, blank, from hope and joy shut out;
The other, which the ray divine hath touched,
Replete with vivid promise, bright as spring.
(Wordsworth, *The Excursion*, v.554–7)[1]

Evidence of the Victorians' obsessive interest in death is as widely available in the imaginative literature of the period as it is in the theology. The deathbed scene, for example, was a familiar literary convention not only in prose fiction but also in narrative poetry and biography;[2] and a remarkably high proportion of the lyric poetry of the period, particularly by women writers, addressed the themes of death and dying, bereavement and mourning.[3] Deathbed scenes and anthologies of poems for mourners are features of the 'Victorian cult of death', together with mourning costume and jewellery, the elaborate plumes and other trappings of the Victorian funeral, black-edged mourning paper and envelopes, the gravestone and the pious epitaph, and 'God's acre', whether small country churchyard or vast urban necropolis.[4]

The existence of a Victorian cult of death implies a measure of social and intellectual homogeneity. So too does the fact that a cluster of key ideas and symbols associated with death and the future life provided writers with a shared vocabulary which can be described as characteristically Victorian. The variety, however, of images of death itself in nineteenth-century literature reflects the wide range of responses to the subject that one would expect to find in any period. The traditional figure of death the Reaper, for example, plies his scythe in Bailey's *Festus*.[5] Charlotte Brontë describes death as 'that dread visitant before whose coming every household trembles', and Newman's Gerontius announces that a 'visitant / Is knocking his dire summons'.[6] But death is also often described as a friend. Death calls to Tennyson's Elaine 'like a friend's voice from a distant field / Approaching through the darkness' ('Lancelot and Elaine', 992–3).[7] Elizabeth Stone observes in *God's Acre; or, Historical Notices Relating to Churchyards* (1858) that

> The much-suffering look on Death not as the destroying angel on the pale horse, not as the ghastly spectre whose unerring dart bears on its point the annihilation of all their joys and pleasures, but as the friend who is to give them release and repose, as the guide who is to lead them home.[8]

More grimly, in a *Punch* cartoon of the Hungry Forties entitled *The Poor Man's Friend*, the skeletal figure of death stands over the bed of a pauper who is praying for his release from a life of hardship and squalor (illustration 1). Through the window of his hovel can be seen the 'Union' or workhouse to which he would have been taken if his prayer had remained unanswered.[9] (The idea of death as the leveller, incidentally, familiar to readers of eighteenth-century graveyard poetry, was rather less prominent in the nineteenth century, when the elaborate funeral and mourning customs of the middle classes reinforced in death the subtle gradations of social hierarchy established in life.)

My main concern is with a hope which was popularized in the consolatory euphemism, 'Not lost, but gone before', and in such conventions as calling the earthly death-day of the departed his or her heavenly birthday.[10] Again, however, examples of a quite different perspective can be cited, such as the sense of death as a terminus (a fitting analogy in the railway age), which is reflected in the frequent references in the nineteenth century to Hamlet's 'undiscovered country, from whose bourn / No traveller returns'.[11] Whereas E. H. Bickersteth sees death as a new beginning, and writes of a 'veil' between mortals and departed spirits sometimes being lifted by God, who separates time from eternity,[12] Pater's Marius reflects that death 'must be for every one nothing less than the fifth or last act of a drama' (*Marius the Epicurean*, 1885; 28). A. O. J. Cockshut adopts the same analogy as Pater when he argues that Victorian biographers seldom distinguished clearly between two ideas of the moment of death: 'the curtain line, and the adumbration of the future'.[13]

What Wordsworth called 'death and its *two-fold* aspect' in *The Excursion* (1814) was, however, directly addressed by many theologians and preachers, poets, novelists, and painters in the nineteenth century.

Frederick W. Robertson, for example, the famous Brighton preacher, argued that our difficulty in coming to terms with death results from the fact that our lives are dedicated to being, and surviving in order to be:

Talk as we will of immortality, there is an obstinate feeling that we cannot master, that we end in death; and *that* may be felt together with the firmest belief of a resurrection. Brethren, our faith tells us one thing, and our sensations tell us another. When we die, we are surrendering in truth all that with which we have associated existence.[14]

The double consciousness of faith, which holds the this-worldly and the other-worldly in tension, finds in death and the future life a subject which is at once fitting and unaccommodating.

Like Frederick Robertson, F. D. Maurice acknowledged that the most devout of men and women know the anguish of doubt, and he valued greatly his friend Tennyson's treatment of 'honest doubt' in *In Memoriam* (1850). Maurice also argued in his discourses on the fourth gospel (1857) that the raising of Lazarus, in John 11, provides comfort to the bereaved because it meets the very question which they ask when a loved one dies: 'Can light ever penetrate into that darkness?'[15] We have seen that Maurice confessed in the second edition of his *Theological Essays* (1853) that he did not dare lose faith in an 'abyss of love'. The words that followed – 'I sink into death, eternal death, if I do so' – almost proved to be prophetic, as he suffered doubts and 'nervous fears' on his own deathbed, before affirming: 'I am not going to *Death* . . . I am going into *Life!*'[16]

These conflicting ideas and emotions associated with death in its two-fold aspect or paradoxical nature – as the first of the four last things, as terminus and point of departure, or as loss and gain – often focused upon two *loci* in the nineteenth century: the deathbed and the grave. Social and literary conventions relating to the deathbed included the visit from a doctor or priest, the presence of a loving attendant to whom a dying confession could be made or of a family on whom a dying blessing could be bestowed, the laying out of a corpse in a darkened room, the 'last visit' of the bereaved, and the closing of the coffin. Those associated with the grave included the funeral procession, the funeral itself, the burial, the erection of a memorial stone, and subsequent visits to the grave made by the bereaved.[17] These conventions formalized the different stages of death and bereavement, giving shape and thus possibly some meaning to a transitional phase between one state and another.[18]

Such transitions, whether physical (from living body to corpse) or spiritual ('from this world to the next'), are characteristically difficult and ambiguous. Victorian writing on death is frequently ambiguous, and in deathbed scenes and graveyard scenes – key sites of communication and interpretation – alternative discourses are often either conflated or confused, as in the Lazarus story. The function of analogy, for example, is often problematic in these contexts. By examining the naming of death as sleep, and, by extension, of the grave as a bed, as crucial examples of the conflation or confusion of discourses in Victorian writing on death, we can approach the nineteenth-century debates concerning judgment and the future life (the subject of Chapters 2–4) via the problematics of language attached to the subject.

THE DEATHBED: CONSOLATION AND COMMUNICATION

To sum up . . . in a few words the circumstances in which most people seem to think a happy death consists . . . ; – if a man has had distinct notice some considerable time before hand that his end was approaching, and has thus been enabled to occupy that interval in what is usually termed, preparation for death; – if he has been attended by a minister, and has received the sacrament of the Lord's Supper a little before his departure; – if, though he may have suffered considerably in the course of the disease, he at last dies calm and easy both in body and mind, in full possession of his faculties, and professing the most perfect confidence of his acceptance with God; and finally, if his body receives what is called christian burial in consecrated ground, and especially if a handsome monument is erected over it; – this person's death is thought to combine all the circumstances which are usually reckoned the most desirable, important, and satisfactory.

Now if such opinions, such cases, and such feelings as I have been describing, are rational and christian, we may expect to find them agreeable to the christian *Scriptures*; if otherwise, they cannot be unattended with danger . . .[19]

Richard Whateley, Professor of Political Economy at Oxford and later Archbishop of Dublin, was perhaps the best known of the Oriel 'Noetics', and his rational approach to what he calls 'A Christian Departure' in *A View of the Scripture Revelations Concerning a Future State* (1829) contrasts with that of the Evangelical who looked for signs of grace in a departing brother or sister in Christ, or of the Roman

Catholic who arranged for the last rites to be administered to the dying. Conventions associated with the *ars moriendi*, familiar to the educated English reader from Jeremy Taylor's *Holy Dying* (1651), were deeply rooted in the corporate memory of the faithful, and provided nineteenth-century novelists with excellent material on which to work. Like Whateley, however, although not always on such strictly scriptural grounds, writers of many different persuasions questioned both the validity and the efficacy of these conventions.

Take, for example, the desire to be 'attended by a minister'. Whereas Charles Reade assumed that the visit to the deathbed was the essential priestly function,[20] the 'spirit' who records a recent visit to earth 'to see and assist the passing away of a young girl' in the Spiritualist *Glimpses of a Brighter Land* (1871) holds different views. Although the visitant from the other side reports that she successfully 'unwound the threads of life that bound [the girl's spirit] to the earthly husk or covering', her efforts are not made easier by the presence of a clergyman, whose 'cold ignorant attempts at comfort' are ineffective, both for the dying child and her mother:

Yet the man was sincere, he preached that which he had learnt, and knew no more. Oh how I longed to flood his brain with truth divine, celestial truth, to open and expand the narrow portals of his mind, to let him see and feel the Father's love, to enable him to progress and teach others while yet on earth![21]

The inadequacy of the clergyman as a comforter of the dying was also the subject of Samuel Butler's black humour in his treatment of Christina Pontifex's death in *The Way of all Flesh*, which was begun in the early 1870s, but remained unpublished until 1903.[22] F. W. Farrar, who considered that the common Protestant view of judgment and damnation was abhorrent, and might therefore have agreed with Butler, was equally sceptical about deathbed conversions. In *Mercy and Judgment* (1881), the sequel to his sermons on *Eternal Hope*, he stated that in recent years he had been called to many deathbeds:

Those scenes have left on my mind the deep conviction that a death-bed very rarely makes any observable difference in the general habit of mind of the dying . . . very frequently I find the strongest possible disinclination to speak of religious subjects, or the habit of fencing off all approach to anything like a heart-searching intercourse . . . And, so far as I have seen, they die, in nine cases out of ten, exactly as they have lived.[23]

H. N. Oxenham, who wrote against Farrar during the controversy which followed the publication of *Eternal Hope*, shared his doubts about dying conversions, but saw the issue from the quite different perspective of Catholic eschatology:

Take . . . the case of what are called death-bed conversions. I am far from denying that such cases are possible, and may be not uncommon, though there is not, perhaps, much evidence to show for it . . . But the habits and associations of a lifetime are not so easily unlearnt, and the work of sanctification has still to be accomplished. The soul . . . must be cleansed, and braced, and perfected in the fires of God's righteous correction, before it can bear the unclouded sunshine of His love.[24]

The last words of the dying, however, had a special significance for the Victorians, and became something of a literary convention in their own right. Kingsley's *Alton Locke* (1850) ends with a poem entitled 'My Last Words', and Owen Meredith's poem, 'Last Words', appeared in an early volume of the *Cornhill*.[25] Thomas Hardy, whose use of place in his fiction and poetry reflects an agnostic's reverence for sites of painful human emotion, wrote of the 'sacredness of last words' in *The Mayor of Casterbridge* (1886; 45). When a large number of such words are brought together, as in the American F. R. Marvin's *The Last Words (Real and Traditional) of Distinguished Men and Women* (1900), a high degree of cultural shaping is revealed. The poet Mrs Hemans, for example, is reported to have said: 'I feel as if I were sitting with Mary at the feet of my Redeemer, hearing the music of his voice, and learning of Him to be meek and lowly.'[26] After that it is tempting to focus on more mundane, but also, ironically, more moving examples, such as Dickens's last words: because he was losing his balance and was afraid of falling, he said, 'On the ground'. But last words which convey spiritual experiences, including deathbed visions of some kind, also deserve serious attention. Elizabeth Barrett Browning's last words – 'It is beautiful' – typify the numberless beatific visions which have been recorded down the centuries, and which in the nineteenth century were often associated with the 'smile of death' which suggested a glimpse of future glory.

Nineteenth-century physiology was aware that contractions of the facial muscles sometimes follow death,[27] but a more interesting challenge to the sentimental tradition of the smile of death was Emily Brontë's, in *Wuthering Heights* (1847). When Cathy dies, Nelly Dean tells Heathcliff that she 'lies with a sweet smile on her face; and her latest ideas wandered back to pleasant early days' (16). Heathcliff's response is extremely violent, and he curses Cathy as a 'liar to the end', who would certainly not go to some conventional heaven. When Nelly later finds Heathcliff himself lying dead in the coffin-like bed at the Heights, the smile on his face is unnerving:

Mr. Heathcliff was there – laid on his back. His eyes met mine so keen and fierce, I started; and then, he seemed to smile.

I could not think him dead – but his face and throat were washed with rain; the bed-clothes dripped, and he was perfectly still.
. . .
I tried to close his eyes . . . They would not shut – they seemed to sneer at my attempts, and his parted lips, and sharp, white teeth sneered too! Taken with another fit of cowardice, I cried for Joseph. (34)

Nelly's repeated 'seemed' indicates that this is one of the many problems of interpretation that she encounters as a narrator. *Wuthering Heights*, a classic of narrative indeterminacy, thus provides a suitable context for a Gothic critique of the interpretation of the dying process.

Another convention associated with the Victorian deathbed was the presence of a comforter, usually a woman, who ministered to the dying. Priscilla Maurice, editor of *Sacred Poems for Mourners* and the author of manuals for sick-visitors, also published *Prayers for the Sick and Dying* (1853), the second part of which includes 'Texts Suited to be Read to Dying Persons', to be read '*very* slowly, *very* distinctly, and with pauses between; longer or shorter, according to the state of the person'.[28] The patient figure who looked to the spiritual as well as the physical needs of the dying was often described as 'angelic'. Thackeray, for example, uses this stock epithet in *Vanity Fair* (1847–8): 'When women are brooding over their children, or busied in a sick-room, who has not seen in their faces those sweet angelic beams of love and pity?' (61). Discourses can be confused, with unintended comic effect, however, where religious language is used in a realistic novel. In Dinah Craik's *John Halifax, Gentleman* (1856), for example, Phineas Fletcher, the narrator, describes the moment when the hero breaks the news to his future wife, Ursula March, that her father is dying:

One thing I can tell, for she said it to me herself afterwards, that he seemed to look down upon her like a strong, pitiful, comforting angel; a messenger sent by God.

Then she broke away, and flew up-stairs. (13)

A word like 'angel', of course, has considerable potential for ambiguity. When Elizabeth Stone asserts in *God's Acre* that angels 'do most especially minister' at a deathbed, it is not immediately clear whether the signified is other-worldly or this-worldly, a guardian angel or an 'angelic' human being.[29] E. H. Bickersteth exploits this kind of ambiguity in a different way in *Yesterday, To-Day, and For Ever*, when the Seer describes the period in which he seemed to be hovering (a favourite word in deathbed scenes) between life and death:

> Six days I lay
> In that strange borderland, so she, who watch'd
> Unwearied as an angel day and night
> Beside my pillow, told me when I woke
> From the fruition of celestial love
> To drink in, like a thirsty traveller,
> The sweetness of her human love once more: –
> Never so sweet as now. They sin who deem
> There can be discord betwixt love and love.   (1.100–8)[30]

During this transitional phase, the Seer found in love the continuity between his experience on earth and the existence that was promised him, and that he is now enjoying, in heaven. His wife's angel-like 'watching' was an earnest both of his guardian angel's watching of his 'footsteps from the wicket gate of life' (1.464–5), and of the couple's reunion in paradise. Characteristically, Bickersteth idealizes where he might have attempted a negotiation between the real and the ideal. There is no hint here of the physical realities of the comforter's role beside a sick-bed, and no awareness of the potential irony in references to 'human love' where a man is dying with his sexual partner beside him.[31] Rather, it is as if the pair were already in heaven, where there is no marriage or giving in marriage.

Philippe Ariès, a leading authority on the history and sociology of death, characterizes the post-Romantic deathbed as being charged with emotion and sexuality, and death as an event that is witnessed by a family who are now active participants in the drama.[32] In his sweep through the history of the West, Ariès draws other equally significant conclusions from a mass of data. He finds in the nineteenth-century cult of death, for example, a sense that death was unacceptable, and argues that it came to be thought of as 'Thy death'. (This tendency is reflected in the emphasis upon the bereaved person in Romantic English elegy.)[33]

Many aspects of Victorian culture cry out for Ariès's psycho-sexual analysis. In everyday life, as well as in religious epic poems, the bed in which a woman died might well have been that in which she had conceived and given birth to her children. In a less mobile society than our own, this same bed might even have been a family heirloom, in which she herself had been conceived and born. The apogee of the public deathbed scene in the period is probably W. I. Walton's *The Last Moments of HRH The Prince Consort*, in which doctors and statesmen, as well as the grieving royal family, are gathered in the state bedchamber (illustration 2). John Morley contrasts this formal, establishment picture with a crude 'cut out' version of the event, in which Albert's children hurry to his embrace.[34] Walton's picture, however, not only suppresses emotion, but also conceals a potential for sexual irony, with the children of a fruitful marriage gathered near the bed. The overt analysis of the relationship between *eros* and *thanatos*, however, was largely the preserve of the Gothic in the nineteenth century, where the 'normal' (and safe) compartmentalizing of birth, marriage, and death was disrupted. The marriage-bed is shown to be a deathbed, for example, in *Wuthering Heights*, and in Sheridan Le Fanu's terrifying story, 'Schalken the Painter'.

Of more immediate relevance to my central theme, however, are the less sensational but equally important associations with the bed, to which Ariès pays little attention: namely, the bed as a place of rest, and of sleep from which we rise again each day to new life. When applied analogically to death and resurrection, in the novel, for example, the idea that the dead person 'sleeps' is fraught with technical difficulties. Bickersteth's poem, quoted above, is narrated by a Seer who has passed through death, and who views the earth and the universe, past, present, and future, from the 'other side'. Thus his description of waking from sleep to find his wife ('as an angel') beside him, is, from heaven's perspective, a type of that waking to new life (with a guardian angel) that is death. As such a privileged narrative perspective, however, was not normally adopted by the Victorian novelist or poet, the deathbed was generally viewed from a limited, this-worldly perspective in which the question of a future state was a matter of faith and hope. Set firmly in a temporal context, but perceived within the larger horizon of the eternal, the deathbed scene was the perfect site for an investigation through language of the problems of interpretation associated with death and its two-fold aspect.

The most basic problem of interpretation in Victorian death scenes is diagnostic: is the dying person alive or dead? In Browning's dramatic monologue, 'The Bishop Orders his Tomb at Saint Praxed's Church' (1845), the dying person himself is not always sure about this:

> As here I lie
> In this state-chamber, dying by degrees,
> Hours and long hours in the dead night, I ask
> 'Do I live, am I dead?' Peace, peace seems all.[35]

Many of Browning's most successful monologues work on what his Bishop Blougram calls 'the dangerous edge of things', where the paradoxes of human nature are most vividly displayed: 'the honest thief, the tender murderer, / The superstitious atheist'.[36] The worldly Bishop at Saint Praxed's does not anticipate transcendence through death, but rather perpetuity in the peaceful church that represents the nearest he has come to a glimpse of heaven:

> And up into the aery dome where live
> The angels, and a sunbeam's sure to lurk . . .

Newman, preaching on 'Holiness Necessary for Future Blessedness', argued that heaven would not be like this world, but much more like a church. Thus heaven, where every man must do '*God's* pleasure', would be 'hell to an irreligious man'.[37] Browning's Bishop, whose eye stops at the dome of the church, reverses the simile (his church is like heaven), and thus puts off the question of judgment, heaven, and hell. Through the workings of his imagination, his deathbed becomes his tomb. Shaping himself into his own effigy ('I fold my arms as if they clasped a crook') he prepares for the sleep of death. Eternity, however, is understood from the this-worldly viewpoint of the monumental mason:

> And 'neath my tabernacle take my rest,
> With those nine columns round me, two and two . . .

The word 'tabernacle' (for Bickersteth a euphemism for the corpse) is here an architectural feature, and the effigy reposing beneath it – the Bishop's idealized self – substitutes for the immortal soul as the antithesis of and emotional defence against the corruption of the flesh:

> Gritstone, a-crumble! Clammy squares which sweat
> As if the corpse they keep were oozing through . . .

In 'The Bishop Orders his Tomb', the nature of the confusion of death with life reveals the spirituality of the dying person. In Hood's poem 'The Death-Bed' (1831) the confusion is of the more familiar kind – that shared by attendants at the bedside, who are interpreters:

> We watch'd her breathing thro' the night,
> Her breathing soft and low,
> As in her breast the wave of life
> Kept heaving to and fro!
>
> So silently we seem'd to speak –
> So slowly moved about,
> As we had lent her half our powers
> To eke her living out!
>
> Our very hopes belied our fears,
> Our fears our hopes belied –
> We thought her dying when she slept,
> And sleeping when she died!
>
> For when the morn came dim and sad –
> And chill with early showers,
> Her quiet eyelids closed – she had
> Another morn than ours![38]

The chiasmus at the heart of the poem, and of my present theme – 'We thought her dying when she slept, / And sleeping when she died' – is worked for from the opening line of the poem, where a gentle pressure is first applied to the simple but ambiguous words associated with the deathbed. 'Watch'd her breathing' suggests more than 'observed her respiration'. Other senses of 'watch' are present – to be vigilant or careful, and to stay awake – and 'breathing' also means, metonymically, living. As so often in nineteenth-century writing on death, the wave metaphor that follows, and that Tennyson used in *In Memoriam* (lyrics 11 and 19), barely suppresses the more familiar associations with death that it contains: life is said to 'ebb away', for example, and a dying person 'goes out with the tide'. In the second stanza, the emphasis shifts to those who 'watch'. They are no longer tensely passive, but, through an act of will, attempt the impossible: a transfusion of energy to the dying woman. Whereas the antithesis we/she cannot be resolved, the reversal of the antitheses in the third stanza (hope/fear, die/sleep) prepares for the collapse of this-worldly categories in the unwilled transcendence of the final stanza, when eyes that, against nature, close at daybreak, open to that other morn which is beyond the horizon of those who watch but cannot see. A problem of interpretation (is she asleep or dead?) has given way to an affirmation of transcendence through the analogy between sleep:awakening and death:resurrection.

To put this another way, the last two stanzas of 'The Death-Bed' bring together two kinds of interpretation: reading signs and making sense. Both are particularly challenging to the children who figure in many deathbed scenes. Bickersteth introduces the theme in *Yesterday, To-Day, and For Ever*, and shows how the questions of frightened children can be answered by referring them to the Bible. The Seer's children are summoned to his deathbed:

> They were but learners in the infant school
> Of sorrow, and were scarcely able yet
> To spell its simplest signs. But when they caught
> The meaning of their mother's words, and knew
> That I was going to leave them, one low sob
> Broke from them, like the sighing of the wind
> That frets the bosom of a silver lake
> Before a tempest.
> . . .
> I raised my head upon the pillow, saying,
>
> 'Weep not, my children, that your father's work
> Is over, and his travelling days are done.
> For I am going to our happy home,
> Jerusalem the golden, of which we
> On Sabbath evenings have so often sung,
> And wish'd the weary interval away
> That lay betwixt us and its pearly gates.'   (1.190–210)

The Seer's reference to family hymns supplies the children with a firm point of reference from which they can make sense of what is going on. It provides the key not only to Bickersteth's favourite methods in his writing on death, but also to the most characteristic Victorian response to bereavement. For the Seer's use of biblical language when he reminds his children of what they have been taught concerning death and the future life – 'The Bridegroom cometh quickly/', 'Let your loins / Be girded', 'the sleep of death', 'Your Father's house', and so on (1.220–9) – is taken up by the children themselves as they read, one by one, 'in a low voice most musical / Some fragments of the book of life' (1.306–7). Publishing his epic poem shortly after Newman's *Dream of Gerontius*, Bickersteth substitutes the family of a married clergyman for Gerontius's 'Attendants', and portions of scripture for the last rites in the *Rituale Romanum*.

Whereas the grief of the Seer's children's parting from their father (1.374–85) is absorbed into a consolatory religious discourse, George Eliot's handling of a similar episode in 'Amos Barton', one of her *Scenes of Clerical Life* (1857), is stark and uncompromising. The Revd Amos Barton's wife, Milly, is dying. When she sends for her children, each responds according to his or her age – the eldest, Patty, bursting into sobs, while little Walter stretches out his arms and smiles (8). The children are led away before their mother dies, and they do not witness their father shrieking 'She isn't *dead*?' and being 'dragged out of the room'. Even at the beginning of her career as a novelist, George Eliot overtly treats the children's bemused sense of loss as a problem of interpretation, which she takes up in a reprise of the deathbed scene, with the children this time gathered around the grave:

Patty alone of all the children felt that mamma was in that coffin, and that a new and sadder life had begun for papa and herself . . . Fred and Sophy, though they were only two and three years younger, and though they had seen mamma in her coffin, seemed to themselves to be looking at some strange show. They had not learned to decipher that terrible handwriting of human destiny, illness and death. Dickey . . . stood close to his father, with great rosy cheeks, and wide open blue eyes, looking first up at Mr Cleves and then down at the coffin, and thinking he and Chubby would play at that when they got home.   (9)

The only continuity between the deathbed and the grave in 'Amos Barton' is that of sustained grief and an inability to make sense of events. Amos's consolation is limited to 'outward solace', in the form of acts of human kindness from a formerly hostile congregation, and these cannot 'counteract the bitterness of this inward woe'. Whereas Bickersteth bathes the wounds of bereavement in a warm solution of consolatory texts, the bleakness of George Eliot's treatment of the subject is relieved only by a solitary, and thus highly charged use of religious language:

There were men and women standing in that churchyard who had bandied vulgar jests about their pastor, and who had lightly charged him with sin; but now, when they saw him following the coffin, pale and haggard, he was consecrated anew by his great sorrow, and they looked at him with respectful pity.

The ordinal is emptied of sacramental mystery in the humanist consecration of the sufferer through sympathy. Two years earlier George Eliot had fiercely attacked Revd Edward Young, author of *Night Thoughts* (1742–5), whose description of the Last Judgment she described as 'a compound of vulgar pomp, crawling adulation, and hard selfishness, presented under the guise of piety'. In the same essay she referred, in contrast, to an ideal that was to be her own as a writer: 'the widening and strengthening of our sympathetic nature'.[39]

Returning, however, to the theme of the child's failure fully to grasp the meaning of death, I wish briefly to consider the death of Helen Burns in *Jane Eyre*, a *locus classicus* of its kind, and too well known to require detailed description. It begins with an exchange in which Jane is precipitated into knowledge of a reality which she attempts to efface:

'Why are you come here, Jane? It is past eleven o'clock: I heard it strike some minutes since.'

'I came to see you, Helen: I heard you were very ill, and I could not sleep till I had spoken to you.'

'You came to bid me good-bye, then: you are just in time probably.'

'Are you going somewhere, Helen? Are you going home?'

'Yes; to my long home – my last home.'

'No, no, Helen:' I stopped, distressed.   (9)

Earlier, Jane has defeated Mr Brocklehurst by refusing to engage with him in the formal religious discourse of the catechism, answering his questioning on the avoidance of hell with the famous response: 'I must keep in good health, and not die' (4). Now, her down-to-earth interpretation of the word 'good-bye', which is uncannily reminiscent of the disciples misunderstanding Jesus's reference to Lazarus falling asleep, defers her recognition of the most common contemporary ideas of death and heaven: namely, parting, or departure, and the long, or last home. The two girls discuss the question of a 'future state', with Jane, as usual, questioning Helen at every point, until they fall asleep. They are discovered in one another's arms in the morning: 'I was asleep, and Helen was – dead.' The pause gives added weight to the contrast between their states, or, more accurately, that antithesis which Strauss located in John 11. Within this pause, however, there is also a trace of the word 'asleep', perhaps from Helen's description in an earlier chapter of eternity as 'a *rest* – a mighty home' (6), or from the words that are almost her last: 'I feel as if I could sleep' (9). By a kind of unconscious association, the words 'dead' and 'asleep' are superimposed. Thus the reality revealed in the cold light of day, and conveyed through antithesis, contains the germ of a hope of a future life through a potential synonymy of the kind F. D. Maurice discussed in the funeral sermon quoted earlier. Fifteen years after Helen's death, the adult Jane has a gravestone made for her. It is inscribed with her name, and the word 'Resurgam' (9).[40]

Jane meditates upon Helen's ideas on death later in the novel, and her youthful rejection of her friend's total denial of the world in favour of a heavenly reward is tempered in adulthood by her respect for her universalist creed. Jane's thoughts go back to Helen when she is called to her Aunt Reed's deathbed at Gateshead-hall. The deathbed scenes contrast sharply in their emotional content:

> In pondering the great mystery, I thought of Helen Burns: recalled her dying words – her faith – her doctrine of the equality of disembodied souls. I was still listening in thought to her well-remembered tones – still picturing her pale and spiritual aspect, her wasted face and sublime gaze, as she lay on her placid deathbed, and whispered her longing to be restored to her divine Father's bosom – when a feeble voice murmured from the couch behind: 'Who is that?'   (21)

This is one of several moments in the novel when Jane is brought back from a dream-like state to a present reality, and here she has to re-establish her identity with her aunt, who has summoned her so that she can 'ease her mind' before she dies – a familiar desire among the dying. Aunt Reed veers alarmingly between discourses:

> 'Well: I must get it over. Eternity is before me: I had better tell her. Go to my dressing-case, open it, and take out a letter you will see there.'

The awkward contiguity of the lofty private thought about eternity and the prosaic instruction concerning a letter in a dressing-case reflects not only the tension in *Jane Eyre* between the demands of the novel and those of romance, but also that between the other-worldly and the this-worldly in all Victorian writing on death.

When Jane returns to Thornfield from Gateshead-hall, quietly, and in the evening, Rochester plays with the very sentiments which, if Jane had loved her aunt, would have been sacrosanct:

> 'Yes – just one of your tricks: not to send for a carriage . . . but to steal into the vicinage of your home along with twilight, just as if you were a dream or a shade. What the deuce have you done with yourself this last month?'
> 'I have been with my aunt, sir, who is dead.'

'A true Janian reply! Good angels be my guard! She comes from the other world – from the abode of people who are dead; and tells me so when she meets me alone here in the gloaming!'   (22)

Rochester's characteristically irreverent use of the language of the death-bed, and the touch of Gothic which he adds for effect, disperse any minimal emotion which had been attached to the cold, inflexible Aunt Reed in her dying.[41]

Although adult responses to death and bereavement are, of course, just as harrowing as those of children, they are often held in tension with a mature faith in some kind of life after death. As a result, a blurring effect is frequently to be detected in the language of consolation. The correspondence of the Hares, a prominent Broad Church family, provides several interesting and characteristic examples. Like many other works of its kind, Augustus Hare's pious family record entitled *Memorials of a Quiet Life* (1872–6) is littered with references to the deaths of friends and relations. The context in which these are described is captured in Hare's thumb-nail sketch of his adoptive mother, Maria, the inspiration of and main correspondent in the *Memorials*. The writer's loving memory, Maria's own fervent religious beliefs, and, possibly, the influence of Baron Bunsen (a family friend), combine to create an idealized vision:

During the early years of her life at Lime my dearest mother seemed to live so completely in heaven that all outward times and seasons were so many additional links between it and her. Spring came to her as the especial season of the Resurrection, and in the up-springing of each leaf and flower she rejoiced as typical of the rising again of all her loved and lost ones.[42]

Closer to the complexity of reality than this prose version of *The Christian Year* are the mourning letters that Hare reproduces in the *Memorials*. Here, for example, Lucy Hare (née Stanley), wife of Marcus Hare, writes to Maria Hare, her sister-in-law, on 28 March 1842:

Our beloved Mary Grey has entered into her Rest, on the evening of yesterday, Easter Sunday, the same day *our* mother entered into hers; at six o'clock she fell asleep. All she had so dreaded of the struggle between soul and body was spared her; there was no struggle, she slept most of the day, all pulsation seemed to cease at four, and she breathed her last sigh two hours after, so peacefully, they scarcely knew when she was gone . . . We had heard on Saturday she was so much better, we did not think how near she was – that the gate of Everlasting Life was opening for her, and that in a few hours she was to be with the Lord.[43]

The juxtaposition of the mundane and the supramundane is similar to the Aunt Reed deathbed scene in *Jane Eyre*. In the first sentence, 'fell asleep' is part of a religious discourse, and reinforces the words, 'entered into her Rest' (Hebrews 4). Yet in the next sentence, which describes the last hours of the dying person, the word 'sleep' is used in the purely secular and commonplace sense: 'she slept most of the day'. It seems, then, that like the disciples in John 11, the writer of the letter can separate the two senses to the extent of forgetting the existence of the other. When the two discourses are brought together, however, in the third sentence, the effect is one that is becoming familiar. The prosaic 'she was so much better' prepares for the plain 'how near she was [to death]', which is elided into the euphemistic 'the gate of Everlasting Life was opening for her'.

In private correspondence of this kind, rational thought tends to be subordinated to the emotional needs of the writer and the recipient, and, even in a learned clerical family such as the Hares, the profound theological implications of affirming that the dead person is meeting the Lord in a few hours are silently passed over in order to draw consolation from familiar pieties. Indeed, it is for the same reason that precisely the opposite of this separation of two senses of 'sleep' occurs in a letter of 1845 from Maria Hare, where she describes the death of her brother-in-law, Marcus: 'At five o'clock, on Wednesday morning, our beloved Marcus gave up his spirit into his Father's hands, and literally "fell asleep" without a struggle.'[44] The quotation marks around the familiar biblical phrase contradict the word 'literally'. Under the pressure of emotion, the writer conflates an actual physical death which looked like falling asleep, and the spiritual transcendence of death promised in the New Testament.

Returning to prose fiction, we can examine the effect of emotion attached to death on the treatment of the subject in *John Halifax, Gentleman*, quoted earlier. Mr March's transition from sleep to death, at the aptly named Enderley, is concisely and conventionally marked:

We both ran through the empty kitchen to the foot of the stairs that led to Mr. March's room.
Mr. March's room! Alas, he owned nothing now on this fleeting, perishable earth of ours. He had gone from it: the spirit stealing quietly away in sleep. He belonged now to the world everlasting.   (13)

It is concern for the dead man's daughter, Ursula, that proves to be the controlling emotion in this episode, and the word 'sleep' is made to do no work here. Later in the novel, John Halifax's own daughter, Muriel, who is blind, dies in the same house. Phineas Fletcher records that the night seemed very like that on which Mr March had died. In the morning, long before it is light, Phineas is greeted by Guy, one of Muriel's young brothers, who plans to go out and gather beech-nuts and fir-cones for her:

'It's her birth-day to-day, you know.'
   It was, for her. But for us – Oh, Muriel, our darling – darling child!
   Let me hasten over the story of that morning, for my old heart quails before it still.
   John went early to the room up-stairs. It was very still. Ursula lay calmly asleep, with baby Maud in her bosom; on her other side, with eyes wide open to the daylight, lay, – that which for more than ten years we had been used to call 'blind Muriel.' She saw, now.   (28)

Again we find the use of dashes to indicate elisions: 'But for us [it was her death-day]'; 'lay, [Muriel's dead body].' The sense that Muriel has passed into a new life (it is her heavenly as well as her earthly birthday), and into a light which for her is indeed new and glorious, is heightened by the presence of the quietly sleeping figures of her mother and baby sister, in a way that is reminiscent of Helen Burns's death in *Jane Eyre*. When the adults of the family later gather around her bed, Phineas Fletcher reports: 'One could almost fancy the little maid had just been said "good-night" to, and left to dream childish dreams on her nursery pillow, where the small head rested so peacefully.' By a clumsy plot device the narrator is left to witness the grief-stricken John Halifax 'alone' with his daughter and imploring her to return to him. The chapter ends with a plaintive comment from Phineas, itself like an echoing call: 'But thou wert with the angels, Muriel – Muriel!' This part of the narrative is rounded off in the opening sentence of the following chapter, which carries the metaphor of sleep over from the deathbed to the bed that is the grave: 'We went home, leaving all that was mortal of our darling sleeping at Enderley underneath the snows' (29). The snow loses none of its chill through the association with the white sheets of the child's nursery bed, but its whiteness reinforces the sense of her innocence which had been established in the preceding chapter.

   In contrast, then, to the death of Mr March, Muriel's is described with intense emotion, and her passing from this world to the next is softened, or blurred, through the use of a discourse that slips between literal and metaphorical usages: birthday, lay . . . asleep, eyes . . . saw, daylight, good night, dreams, rested . . . peacefully, sleeping. Phineas Fletcher, as a retrospective narrator, controls this ironic slippage from the beginning of the passage quoted, where the elided 'death-day' is antithetical to two senses of 'birthday', which are themselves mutually antithetical in a different plane. It is often through such misunderstandings and ambiguities that the pain of bereavement is accommodated in a consolatory discourse in Victorian writing on death.

Victorian deathbed scenes involving children have been the subject of much adverse criticism. In a letter of 1881, Gerard Manley Hopkins commented in detail on Robert Bridges's poem 'On a Dead Child', which Bridges himself considered to be the best he had written. Hopkins argues that although it is a 'fine poem', neither the rhythm nor the thought is 'flowing enough', and the diction is 'not exquisite', but belongs to

a familiar commonplace about 'Reader, have you never hung over the pillow of . . . pallid cheek, clammy brow . . . long, long night-watches . . . surely, Sir Josiah Bickerstaff, there is *some* hope! O say not all is over. It cannot be.' You know. [Hopkins's ellipses.][45]

By this date the 'death of the child' has become so conventionalized and sentimentalized that Hopkins's amusing parody is aimed at a large target. Early in Bridges's poem, an uncanny moment of recognition reverses the usual sequence from life to death:

> To me, as I move thee now in the last duty
> Dost thou with a turn or gesture anon respond;
> Startling my fancy fond
> With a chance attitude of the head, a freak of beauty.

Here is a subject fit for Thomas Hardy, who would have drawn out the irony of this 'freak of beauty'. Bridges, however, maintains the idealizing tone:

> So I lay thee there, thy sunken eyelids closing, –
> Go lie then there in thy coffin, thy last little bed! –
> Propping thy wise, sad head,
> Thy firm, pale hands across thy chest disposing.[46]

Much twentieth-century criticism on the treatment of the death of children in Victorian fiction – little Paul in *Dombey and Son* (1846–8), for example, or Eric in F. W. Farrar's *Eric; or, Little by Little* (1858), or William in Mrs Henry Wood's *East Lynne* (1861) – is hostile. Peter Coveney discusses the deathbed scenes in *East Lynne* in a chapter entitled 'Reduction to Absurdity', arguing that 'William's death is the one last, careful, twist of the knife of the sadist masquerading as moralist': 'It is part . . . of what might be called the "death-wish" of the whole work.'[47] It is certainly true that the punishment of Lady Isabel for her adultery, and for her abandonment of her husband and family, borders on the sadistic. The infuriated Coveney, however, passes over interesting features of the episode, such as the confusion of discourses that I have noted elsewhere. The dying William's question, 'Papa . . . is the trial over?', at first elicits no reply from his father, who does not know whether the boy refers to his last illness or to the current trial of a murderer (III.20). William's sister, Lucy, mistakes his 'Good-bye' in the same way that Jane mistakes Helen's in *Jane Eyre*. The most significant example of misinterpretation, however, and the most ambitious, is that on which the whole episode is based: Madame Vine, the governess who weeps at the bed side, is in fact Lady Isabel, the boy's disguised and disfigured mother. Left alone with her dying son, she flings up her arms 'in a storm of sobs':

> 'Oh, William, darling! in this dying moment let me be to you as your mother!'
> Again he unclosed his weary eyelids. It is probable that he only partially understood.
> 'Papa's gone for her.'
> 'Not *her*! I – I – ' Lady Isabel checked herself, and fell sobbing on the bed.

Her self-disclosure to her son, who cannot take it in, prepares for her deathbed confession to her husband, which soon follows (III.21). In both cases the hope of reunion where they neither marry, nor are given in marriage, and where the bond between the mother and her children can in some way be renewed, underpins both deathbed scenes.

Coveney, however, is particularly incensed by the opening paragraph of the chapter, which is somewhat gruesomely entitled 'The Death Chamber':

> By the side of William Carlyle's dying bed knelt the Lady Isabel. The time was at hand, and the boy was quite reconciled to his fate. Merciful indeed is God to dying children! It is astonishing how very readily, where the right means are taken, they may be brought to look with pleasure rather than fear, upon their unknown journey.

Coveney exaggerates when he states that 'one might excusably feel more kinship with the mutterings of savagery', and that the word '"pleasure" gives the whole emotional facade away'.[48] Mrs Henry Wood has, in Coveney's view, 'perhaps said too much'. Perhaps Coveney would prefer the child to die in fear? We have seen that in *Yesterday, To-Day, and For Ever* the Seer's children are buoyed up in their grief by consolatory hymns and Bible readings that affirm the resurrection of the body and the life everlasting. William Carlyle and his parents discuss the description of heaven in the Revelation, and John Martin's famous painting, *The Plains of Heaven* (illustration 8). The boy is certain that he will be fetched in a boat, as in the picture, and is only concerned to know whether Jesus can be in all the boats. Mrs Wood, like E. H. Bickersteth, draws on a shared cultural resource in her treatment of William's consolation which cannot be brushed lightly aside.

Perhaps the most moving and painful example of this kind of consolation in the nineteenth century is recorded in Mrs Catharine Tait's narrative of the death through scarlet fever of five daughters, aged between one and ten years, between 6 March and 10 April 1856, in the Deanery at Carlisle. Catharine Tait, the youngest daughter of Archdeacon Spooner, and her husband Archibald, who later became Archbishop of Canterbury, survived this ordeal only through faith, and in the knowledge of the widespread sympathy aroused by their bereavements, including that of the Queen herself. Both they and their children drew upon hymns and Bible passages to sustain them at this time. Three weeks after the birth of baby Lucy, who survived (together with a son, Crauford), 'Chatty', aged five, died. The eldest daughter, 'Catty', chose a hymn for the remaining children to sing in the schoolroom:

> Here we suffer grief and pain,
> Here we meet to part again,
> In heaven we part no more.
>   Oh! that will be joyful,
>   Joyful, joyful, joyful!
>   Oh! that will be joyful,
> When we meet to part no more.[49]

This children's hymn, which Catharine Tait quotes in full, was one of many of its type sung in Victorian homes, as well as in Sunday Schools.[50] So the language of these hymns, and the themes to which they repeatedly return – Jerusalem the Golden, families meeting in heaven, Jesus the good shepherd – were not reserved for Sundays and church, but were part of everyday life, particularly for clerical families like the Bickersteths or the Taits. They therefore provided a genuinely consolatory discourse at such times of crisis.

Like the story of the raising of Lazarus, the death of a child is a stern test of faith, and the two are brought together in Mrs Tait's narrative after the third death, that of Frances, aged three. The parents did not tell their firstborn child, 'Catty', who was already ill, that her sister had died:

We had not dared to tell you, but I believe that God Himself had revealed to you the tidings of joy. She slept, but as the coffin which contained the form of her beloved Frances crossed the threshold of our door, she raised herself in her bed, and with a loud voice said, 'Jesus cried, Lazarus, come forth. And he that was dead came forth, bound hand and foot with grave-clothes; and Jesus said, Loose him, and let him go.' When she had said this, she lay quite still in a deep sleep.[51]

When Catty herself is dying she looks 'upward towards heaven' and points there 'distinctly with her finger':

While pointing upward I said, 'She sees in heaven her Chatty, her Susan and Frances.' When I mentioned the name of the latter, of whom before we had not spoken to her as taken from us, a brighter light came upon her, and again she pointed clearly and distinctly, and then with an earnestness no words can convey, stretched forth both her hands to be taken also.[52]

Two acts of interpretation are going on here: the daughter's and the mother's. Both are informed by faith that is grounded in scripture. Significantly, however, Catharine Tait does not, like Bickersteth, pass over the terrible reality of a painful death. She writes of the death of little Susan:

The little body was quite stiff, the arms and legs twitching . . . It was a sight full of agony; the conflict with death was long. Between six and seven more hours we kept our sad watch, expecting every moment that all would be over. It was between one and two when our darling little Susan left our poor home on earth to join her Chatty in the Fold above . . . I never saw my little lamb again.[53]

As in the correspondence of the Hare family, death itself is marked by a transition from a descriptive to a consolatory religious discourse, in this case the language of children's hymns: 'Fold above', 'little lamb'. Even in the earlier, descriptive sentence, however, the words 'agony' and 'conflict' place the child's suffering in the context of Christ's passion, through which the hope of resurrection was won.

Coveney's critique of *East Lynne* takes no account of the fact that for a girl like Mary, aged eight, the last of the five Tait daughters to die, death had from her earliest babyhood seemed 'a great and blessed reality, the way by which she was to attain her real life'.[54] Dean Tait wrote in his diary, five months after these tragic weeks of illness and death: 'May the memory of these afflictions help to sanctify my heart.'[55] He also recorded at this time that he had been reading Trench's introduction to *Sacred Poems for Mourners*, and found his analysis of the burial service 'very striking'.[56] A culture which throws up volumes such as Priscilla Maurice's may seem quaint, morbid, or even sinister to late-twentieth-century eyes. To Archibald Tait or to Edward Henry Bickersteth (who himself published memorials of a daughter who died at the age of nineteen),[57] such volumes were aids to understanding death and its two-fold aspect within the horizon of eternal life.

THE GRAVE, AND THE ANALOGY OF NATURE

Whereas Richard Whateley's critique of people's idea of a 'happy death' and a good burial was grounded in scripture,[58] Wordsworth's critique of early-nineteenth-century customs and attitudes in his 'Essay upon Epitaphs' (1810) was based upon the authority of nature. The poet's description of the traditional 'parish-church, in the stillness of the country', as a 'visible centre of a community of the living and the dead', and his comments on 'the soothing influences of nature', could be cited as examples of the 'Victorian Wordsworth' – the Wordsworth of John Keble and of Matthew Arnold.[59] Earlier in the essay he contrasts the burial grounds in modern towns and cities with the Greek and Roman practice of interment by the wayside, asking the reader to imagine the impact of the 'lively and affecting analogies' such as 'death as a sleep overcoming the tired wayfarer' on ancient monuments:

These, and similar suggestions, must have given, formerly, to the language of the senseless stone a voice enforced and endeared by the benignity of that nature with which it was in unison. – We, in modern times, have lost much of these advantages; and they are but in a small degree counterbalanced to the inhabitants of large towns and cities, by the custom of depositing the dead within, or contiguous to, their places of worship . . .

In moving the site of burial – and thus the memorial stone – from the wayside to the interior of a church, the immediacy of certain analogies is lost. The Victorian cult of the rural or semi-rural burial site, in the country churchyard or tree-lined suburban cemetery, represents an attempt to restore something of that immediacy by placing the memorial stone in a context which is redolent of the 'soothing influences of nature'. In this section I hope to demonstrate that, as in Victorian deathbed scenes, language comes under great pressure in what can broadly be described as graveyard scenes, when analogies drawn from different scriptural and secular sources conflict or collide with each other. And Wordsworth provides a fitting starting point, as some of the contradictions and difficulties encountered by Victorian writers are at least partly attributable to him.

Wordsworth's 'Essay upon Epitaphs' was later reprinted as an appendix to Books v–vii of *The Excursion* (1814), a work which has been described as 'almost the Bible' of the early-Victorian poetry-reading public.[60] His description in Book v of Grasmere church, 'screened by tufted trees' (81) and with rafters like 'leafless underboughs, in some thick wood' (148), and of its incumbent, who loves his 'native soil' (116), emphasizes their naturalness. Stephen Prickett has argued that Wordsworth's organicist aesthetic profoundly influenced Keble, Newman, and F. D. Maurice, among others, in their thinking on the nature of the Church of England.[61] The portrayal of the Anglican clergyman in *The Excursion* suggests that these churchmen were indebted to Wordsworth for his treatment of feeling and moral truth rather than of theology, for the Pastor is notoriously vague on matters of doctrine. Of special interest here is Wordsworth's avoidance of the problems associated with death and the future life which Victorian writers were later to address.

As in Gray's 'Elegy', the grander monuments within Grasmere church ('all / Ending in dust', 174–5) are briefly described and then left in favour of the graves in the 'green churchyard' (229). The latter, however, proves to be the site of conflicting interpretations. For the sceptical Solitary it is a 'subterraneous magazine of bones' (345). For the Poet this 'pregnant spot of ground' (371) gives rise to mixed emotions and thoughts. The most significant interpretation, however, and the most surprising, is that of the Pastor himself, for although he refers to Christ as Saviour (and Wordsworth made various 'Christianizing' additions to the poem in later years), he says nothing about judgment, and emphasizes human solidarity rather than resurrection in his references to the dead:

To a mysteriously-united pair
This place is consecrate; to Death and Life,
And to the best affections that proceed
From their conjunction; consecrate to faith
In Him who bled for man upon the cross;
Hallowed to revelation; and no less
To reason's mandates; and the hopes divine
Of pure imagination; – above all,
To charity, and love, that have provided,
Within these precincts, a capacious bed
And receptacle, open to the good
And evil, to the just and the unjust;
In which they find an equal resting-place:
Even as the multitude of kindred brooks
And streams, whose murmur fills this hollow vale,
Whether their course be turbulent or smooth,
Their waters clear or sullied, all are lost
Within the bosom of yon crystal Lake,
And end their journey in the same repose!

And blest are they who sleep; and we that know,
While in a spot like this we breathe and walk,
That all beneath us by the wings are covered
Of motherly humanity, outspread
And gathering all within their tender shade,
Though loth and slow to come!   (v.903–27)

The Pastor's subtext is from the Sermon on the Mount: 'Thou shalt love thy neighbour, and hate thine enemy . . . for he maketh his sun to rise on the evil and on the good, and sendeth rain on the just and on the unjust' (Matthew 5.43, 45). His speech, however, draws more heavily upon 'reason' and 'imagination' than upon the revealed Word in scripture. Consciously or unconsciously he takes the rain in the gospel passage into the natural simile of the streams which debouch into the adjacent lake. The Poet, the Wanderer and the Solitary have followed the same track as both a funeral procession (down from the fells to the church), and a stream (down to the lake).

For the Pastor, then, the graveyard by the lake is a 'capacious bed', a communal resting-place rather than the orthodox 'God's acre' of individual 'narrow beds'. The absence of discussion on the subject of judgment and a future life partly explains why Evangelicals attacked the

laxity of the representation of faith in *The Excursion*.[62] Death and life
are 'mysteriously-united' in the Pastor's existential interpretation of the
churchyard because death defines the finished shape of the lives of those
whose 'authentic epitaphs' or epitomes (650–1) he is about to narrate.
Those lives are characterized by obscure suffering and resignation, and it
has been suggested that the 'primacy of mind over faith' makes the poem
a meditative rather than a devotional work.[63]

Evidence of this is supplied by the epigraph to this chapter, in which
the Pastor speaks of 'death and its two-fold aspect', and by a passage
that precedes it, where he affirms that human life is 'either fair and
tempting' or 'a forbidding tract of cheerless view', depending on how it is
'looked at, or approached' (526–30). The 'contrast' he draws is, however,
on his own account even more appropriate to death than to life:

> Thus, when in changeful April fields are white
> With new-fallen snow, if from the sullen north
> Your walk conduct you hither, ere the sun
> Hath gained his noontide height, this churchyard, filled
> From east to west, before you will appear
> An unillumined, blank, and dreary plain,
> With more than wintry cheerlessness and gloom
> Saddening the heart. Go forward, and look back;
> Look, from the quarter whence the lord of light,
> Of life, of love, and gladness doth dispense
> His beams; which, unexcluded in their fall,
> Upon the southern side of every grave
> Have gently exercised a melting power;
> *Then* will a vernal prospect greet your eye,
> All fresh and beautiful, and green and bright,
> Hopeful and cheerful: – vanished is the pall
> That overspread and chilled the sacred turf,
> Vanished or hidden; and the whole domain
> To some, too lightly minded, might appear
> A meadow carpet for the dancing hours.   (v.531–51)

The 'lord of light' is the beneficent God who works through his creation
rather than the incarnate Son of John 1 (conflated with the forces of
nature and thus erased in a submerged pun on sun/Son). Although
Wordsworth's use of place and of natural analogy in *The Excursion*
provided a model for Victorian writers (and the passage quoted above
was particularly well known),[64] he did not address the specific problem

of accommodating the 'lively hope' of the gospel within his scheme of resignation in life and memorializing through epitaphs in death. Rather, the Solitary's 'slighted Hope' (III.459) and the Wanderer's 'Admiration, Hope, and Love' (IV.763) are left in dialectical opposition in the poem, as the Pastor, whose title emphasizes his role as ministering shepherd rather than administering priest, recounts the lives of the flock who lie in his green churchyard.

The relationship between the Wordsworth of *The Excursion* and his Victorian successors is complex. Certainly his powerful influence can be traced in the emphasis upon natural process in Victorian graveyard scenes. Unlike in Book v of *The Excursion*, however, the grave is often portrayed in these later scenes as the site of a transition from the death-bed to a future state, and of a hope of resurrection. I have suggested that the contradictions and difficulties encountered by Victorian writers are partly attributable to Wordsworth, but we have also seen already that contradictions and difficulties associated with death and burial abound in New Testament theology itself. Similarly, the burial service in the Book of Common Prayer, far from reinforcing the manageable stages of separation enshrined in Victorian mourning customs, consoled the bereaved through affirmations of faith which are based upon some of the most challenging paradoxes and contraries in the New Testament. The priests and clerks 'meeting the Corpse at the entrance of the Church-yard, and going before it, either into the Church, or towards the Grave, shall say, or sing',

I am the resurrection and the life, saith the Lord: he that believeth in me, though he were dead, yet shall he live: and whosoever liveth and believeth in me shall never die.   (*St. John* xi.25, 26)

The lesson, from 1 Corinthians 15, teaches that the resurrection of the dead is sown in corruption, dishonour, and weakness, and is raised in incorruption, glory, and power. It is sown a natural body, and raised a spiritual body, in St Paul's natural analogy. And in the supremely earthly and earthy rite of committal itself, when the body is lowered into the ground, earth to earth, ashes to ashes, dust to dust, the priest shall say:

in sure and certain hope of the Resurrection to eternal life, through our Lord Jesus Christ; who shall change our vile body, that it may be like unto his glorious body, according to the mighty working, whereby he is able to subdue all things to himself.

The scriptural language of the burial service speaks of a resurrection that is as miraculous as the *hidden and mysterious* workings of nature: of life in death, of incorruption in corruption, of rising in descending. Joseph Butler, in the *Analogy of Religion*, cites not only the dramatic transformations which occur in the chrysalis, but also the scarcely discernible changes which are continually taking place in trees and in human body tissue. Similarly, graveyard scenes in Victorian literature seek to draw consolation not only from St Paul's description of the miraculous transformation of the spiritual body 'in the twinkling of an eye', but also, and simultaneously, from natural analogies such as diurnal and seasonal cycles which speak of an organicist gradualism that is also available to secular forms of consolation.

Like the deathbed, then, the grave is a site of conflicting ideas. It is also a site of strong and often confused emotions, not least because the mourner will naturally meditate on his or her own 'end' as well as that of the 'departed'. Tennyson shaped his 'Supposed Confessions of a Second-Rate Sensitive Mind', written before the death of Arthur Hallam, around lugubrious meditations which are not dissimilar to those of the mid-eighteenth-century 'graveyard' tradition. In Tennyson's poem, however, the separation of the speaker from the community of the faithful is registered in the subjunctive mode:

> How sweet to have a common faith!
> To hold a common scorn of death!
>   And at a burial to hear
>   The creaking cords which wound and eat
>   Into my human heart, whene'er
>   Earth goes to earth, with grief, not fear,
> With hopeful grief, were passing sweet!   (33–9)

The alienation of the sensitive mind anticipates that of the narrator of *Maud* (1855), Tennyson's 'little *Hamlet*'. From the effect of the 'creaking cords' on 'my heart', the poem moves finally to an imaginative projection to 'my' grave and the inevitable decay of 'my' body:

>   Oh teach me yet
>   Somewhat before the heavy clod
> Weighs on me, and the busy fret
> Of that sharp-headed worm begins
> In the gross blackness underneath.

> O weary life! O weary death!
> O spirit and heart made desolate!
> O damnèd vacillating state! (183–90)

The weight of the 'heavy clod' seems to betray a fear of burial as the final, irreversible separation of the dead from the world of the living, although it could also be argued that because only a living and conscious being could register such a weight, the passage also reveals an unconscious fear of premature interment, a phenomenon which occurred frequently enough in the nineteenth century to encourage the more nervous to ask for alarm systems to be rigged up in their graves.[65] The 'sharp-headed worm' has more complex associations. Most obviously the work of the worm on the corpse reminds us of the corruption of the body. It also, however, recalls the worm that 'dieth not' (Mark 9.44), and thus reinforces the association of the grave with hell (or Hades), as in the burial and descent 'into hell' of Christ, affirmed in the creeds. Swinburne's poem, 'After Death', which begins with the ambiguous lines 'The four boards of the coffin lid / Heard all the dead man did', ends with the dead man asking the boards,

> 'What good gift shall God give us?'

> The boards answered him anon:
> 'Flesh to feed hell's worm upon.'[66]

Swinburne gleefully plays with the biblical idea, often discussed in the nineteenth century, of death as Adam's curse (Romans 5.12), and of the corruption of the body after death as a mark of man's fallen state, and of his utter reliance upon God's mercy. Thus fears associated with death and burial were closely linked with the fear of judgment and hell. This complex of anxieties was exploited by preachers and teachers of many different persuasions, as we shall see in Chapter 4. In his notorious series of 'Books for Children', for example, Father Furniss described for his young readers the bloated and stinking state of the exhumed corpse of a drunkard, and recommended that they said the Hail Mary for their drunken parents every day, lest they themselves were taken to hell with their parents.[67] At the other extreme, however, secularists boasted that with the shedding of fears of hell and judgment it was possible to lose the fear of death. Austin Holyoake, for example, published a burial service in 1870 which contained a statement to be read at the grave side of a male secularist who had 'long been free from the fears and misgivings of superstitious belief'.[68] Whereas the Burial Service in the Book of Common Prayer emphasizes the hope of a future resurrection, Holyoake's somewhat laboured order of service ends with this wooden dismissal: 'Peace and respect be with his memory. Farewell, a long farewell!'

Holyoake is buried in the same grave as his intimate friend, James Thomson, who wrote of death as release from a world without hope:

> The certitude of Death, which no reprieve
> Can put off long; and which, divinely tender,
> But waits the outstretched hand to promptly render
> That draught whose slumber nothing can bereave.[69]

Later in *The City of Dreadful Night* (1874) a funeral oration, reminiscent of Holyoake's, modifies the Christian perspective on death as sleep:

> This little life is all we must endure,
> The grave's most holy peace is ever sure,
>   We fall asleep and never wake again;
> Nothing is of us but the mouldering flesh,
> Whose elements dissolve and merge afresh
>   In earth, air, water, plants, and other men.   (XIV)

Because of the corruption of the flesh, the grave requires some kind of purification or cleansing, and here the agent is nature, through the absorption of the body into the earth. The corruption of the body is confronted directly in the New Testament, of course. The raising of Lazarus initiates the sequence of events which leads to Christ's own death and burial, and his victory over death in John 11 anticipates his own resurrection:

> Jesus said, Take ye away the stone. Martha, the sister of him that was dead, saith unto him, Lord, by this time he stinketh: for he hath been dead four days.
> Jesus saith unto her, Said I not unto thee, that, if thou wouldest believe, thou shouldest see the glory of God?   (John 11.39–40)

Martha's blunt reference to the corruption of the body reinforces the connection (John 11.2) between the raising of Lazarus and Mary's anointing of Jesus with spices (John 12.3), which itself looks forward to his death and burial. The raising of Lazarus is one of the lessons used in Christian burial services. In the Roman Catholic Church the ritual cleansing of the body and the grave by the priest re-enacts the sanctify-ing act of Jesus Christ who, in the words of one of the prayers in the ancient order of Compline, 'didst rest in the sepulchre, and didst sanctify the grave to be a bed of hope'. This theme is taken up in an aphorism in Coleridge's *Aids to Reflection*, where the grave is described as 'thy bed of rest': 'thy Saviour has warmed it, and made it fragrant'.[70]

These ideas were reinforced and popularized in the thousands of tracts, sermons, and hymns which poured from the religious presses during the Victorian Age. Elizabeth Stone in *God's Acre* reminded her readers that the first Christians called their places of burial '*coemeteria*, "dormitories" or "sleeping places," because they looked on death as a sleep merely, and the departed only as it were laid to rest until the resurrection should awaken them'.[71] Although many popular treatments of 'God's Acre' tended towards sentimentality, some religious writers saw that the claims of Christianity with respect to the dead who peopled the graveyard were in fact unsentimental and uncompromising. Mrs Alexander, author of 'Once in royal David's city' and 'All things bright and beautiful', uses words from the Apostles' Creed – 'descended into hell; The third day he rose again from the dead' – as the epigraph to another of her popular *Hymns for Little Children* (1848) entitled 'The rich man did of Pilate crave', in which the reality of death is sharply conveyed:

> There are short graves in churchyard ground,
>   Where little children buried lie,
> Each underneath his narrow mound,
>   With stiff cold hand, and close shut eye;
> Bright morning sunbeams kiss the spot,
> Yet day by day, they open not.
>
> But surely as our SAVIOUR rose
>   On Easter morn from Joseph's cave,
> Shall all those mounds at last unclose,
>   And Christian people leave the grave.
> He died, He slept, He rose to be
> An earnest of our victory.
>
> Lord, Who for us so cold and deep
>   Down in that garden grave hast lain,
> When we like Thee must fall asleep,
>   Be with us in our hour of pain,

> That strengthened by Thy Grace Divine,
> Alive or dead we may be Thine.[72]

Late-twentieth-century sensibilities may be shocked by the first verse quoted here. The image of the dead infant lying in the grave, however, is identical to one which many children who first sang the hymn would actually have seen: namely, that of a child lying (or 'sleeping') in its coffin (or 'bed') in the days immediately following its death, and before the physical corruption to which the hymns cannot, perforce, refer, sets in. The body of Christ, perfect and incorruptible, was raised from 'sleep' on the third day, an earnest of the resurrection of the 'Christian people' of the hymn, and Mrs Alexander's description of the dead children in their graves implies that their bodies will be raised incorruptible (1 Corinthians 15.52). Thus the grave is treated as the site of a transition from the deathbed, which it resembles, to the heaven to which it points.

This idea is also hinted at in the exchange between the fading William Carlyle and his mother, Lady Isabel (disguised as 'Madame Vine'), in *East Lynne*:

'When you are very, very tired, William, does it not seem a luxury, a sweet happiness, to lie down at night in your little bed, waiting for sleep?'

'Yes. And I am often tired; as tired as that.'

'Then, just so do we, who are tired out with the world's cares, long for the grave in which we shall lie down to rest. We *covet* it, William; long for it; almost pray for it: but you cannot understand that.'

'*We* don't lie in the grave, Madame Vine.'

'No, no, child. Our bodies lie there, to be raised again in beauty at the last day. We go into a blessed place of rest, where sorrow and pain cannot come. I wish – I wish,' she added with a bursting heart, 'that you and I were both there!'

'Who says the world is so sorrowful, Madame Vine? I think it is lovely . . . '

(III.10)

Mercifully, Lady Isabel's death-wish is not understood by William, but his correction – '*We* don't lie in the grave' – elicits from her a description of a place which sounds like a familiar Victorian euphemism for the grave: 'a blessed place of rest'.

Such conflations of the deathbed, the grave, and heaven (the place of eternal rest) are the literary equivalent of the work of the monumental masons whose angels and cherubic effigies of children were designed to make the Victorian graveyard a heaven upon earth. But Lady Isabel's emphasis upon a place of *rest* is a product of the context in which she speaks: she holds out the hope of an end to sickness and fever while also suggesting a continuity between this world (William lies in bed) and the next (he will enter into his rest). Keble's *The Christian Year* (1827), the most popular volume of verse in the nineteenth century, also adapts the idea of rest to the homiletic context in this way. 'Morning', the first poem in the series, includes lines that are familiar from the popular hymn:

> New every morning is the love
> Our wakening and uprising prove;
> Through sleep and darkness safely brought,
> Restored to life, and power, and thought.
>
> New mercies, each returning day,
> Hover around us while we pray;
> New perils past, new sins forgiven,
> New thoughts of God, new hopes of Heaven.[73]

In 'Morning' Keble emphasizes the call to work to the glory of God which each day brings. He therefore describes heaven, in the final stanza, as 'perfect Rest above', a fitting reward after the long day that is our mortal life. In 'Burial of the Dead', however, heaven is the 'new heaven' of the *parousia*, in contrast to the place of rest (or sleep) which follows death:

> Far better they should sleep awhile
>   Within the church's shade,
> Nor wake, until new heaven, new earth,
> Meet for their new immortal birth
>   For their abiding place be made,
>
> Than wander back to life, and lean
>   On our frail love once more.[74]

This idea of the grave as a place of sleep 'within the church's shade' combines a sense of place (in the shade of a church) and a sense of membership (in the Catholic and Apostolic Church). Both literally and metaphorically, the emphasis is upon peace: the dead sleep undisturbed in God's acre. We have seen, however, that F. D. Maurice was troubled by the familiar euphemism, 'He sleeps in the grave', because although it is comforting in the context of former pain and illness, the thought of a long, dreary sleep in the grave is disturbing. Again, the problem with figurative language is that although it may suit a specific context or spiritual need, other extraneous and purely physical associations can be evoked. This is a particularly frequent occurrence in writing on death and burial, where the other-worldly perspective of a bereaved person is all too likely to be interrupted by the physical reality of this world. Consider, for example, the first verse of Edward Caswall's hymn:

> Days and moments quickly flying
> Blend the living with the dead;
> Soon will you and I be lying
> Each within our narrow bed.[75]

As in Gray's 'Elegy' ('Each in his narrow cell'), the grave contains and limits what in life had freedom of movement in space. 'Narrow bed', however, also suggests a chaste solitariness. What, then, of graves in which husbands and wives are buried together? Interestingly, Elizabeth Stone in *God's Acre* cites Edmund Burke's reflections on Westminster Abbey, and his preference, like Gray's, for a country churchyard: 'The good old expression, "family burying-ground," has something pleasing in it, at least to *me*.'[76] She continues:

> When in earlier times it was forbidden to inter two bodies in one grave, exception was always made in the case of husband and wife – the most touching and most reverent acknowledgment of the sanctity of the marriage tie that it is possible to conceive.

Macabre alternatives, however, to Mrs Stone's sentimental view of the subject are suggested by one of the most appropriate biblical texts in this context: Adam's description of Eve as 'bone of my bones, and flesh of my flesh' (Genesis 2.23). *Eros* and *thanatos* are brought into grotesque juxtaposition in Heathcliff's account in *Wuthering Heights* of his arrangement with the sexton to prepare Cathy's grave as a kind of double bed for him, from which Edgar, her lawful husband, is to be excluded (29). Nelly Dean is shocked that Heathcliff should have 'disturbed' the dead, but he claims that he 'disturbed nobody'. Like Cathy's substitution of the heath for an orthodox Christian heaven which, in her dream, did not seem to be her 'home' (9), Heathcliff's idea of bodies dissolving into each other displaces a 'vertical' spiritual transcendence in favour of a consolation which is rooted in natural process. Following Nelly's account of local reports that the spirits of Cathy and Heathcliff 'walk', and Lockwood's reference to the disintegration of the kirk, the pieties of Lockwood's final sentence are profoundly ironic: 'I . . .

wondered how anyone could imagine unquiet slumbers, for the sleepers in that quiet earth' (34).

The churchyard in which Edgar Linton, Cathy, and Heathcliff are buried ('next the moor') is the site of word-play ('heath and hare-bells') rather than Christian analogy: the moths that flutter are merely moths. Indeed, Emily Brontë's rejection of analogy is an aspect of her radicalism. For whereas *Wuthering Heights* seeks for explanations in nature alone, much mainstream Victorian literature and art drew upon the analogical tradition which came down from Bishop Butler and his *Analogy of Religion*, and which drew parallels between nature and the revealed truths of scripture. James Buchanan, whose treatise on *Analogy* (1864) was quoted earlier, believed that 'the future resurrection of the body has its natural analogue in the annual resurrection of Nature from the death-like torpor of winter'.[77] St Paul's analogy of the body as a seed which is buried in the ground (1 Corinthians 15) was often cited in this context. Similarly, the tree was a favourite organic analogy in the religious writings of Coleridge and Newman, both of whom drew upon Butler. These analogies were used in a nineteenth-century painting which illustrates the tension between the feeling that we end in death and the hope of a future life. Henry Bowler's *The Doubt: 'Can These Dry Bones Live?'*, a genre painting in the Pre-Raphaelite style, was exhibited at the Royal Academy in 1855 (illustration 3). A young lady leans over a gravestone, contemplating the exhumed remains of one 'John Faithful' which lie exposed on the earth. The painting was intended as an illustration to *In Memoriam*, although the reviewer in the *Art Journal* no doubt had quite other reasons for suggesting that the question should have been posed by a man rather than a woman! Apart from the sentimental effect achieved by having a charming young lady as a subject, a sharper contrast is also achieved by juxtaposing her fresh and blooming cheek with the brown skull of the late lamented Faithful. Unlike Christina Rossetti, who applies the text from Ezekiel to the Conversion of the Jews,[78] Bowler interprets the question 'Can these dry bones live?' in individualistic terms. The neutrality of the lady's expression suggests that from her own perspective (which, in literal terms, is less privileged than that of the viewer), the stark reality of death which the skull and bones signify throws the claims of religion into momentary doubt.

For the viewer, however, the painting contains a surplus of signs of hope of resurrection over signs of death: the message of the inscriptions on the two gravestones in the foreground ('I am the Resurrection and the Life' (John 11.25) and 'Resurgam') is reinforced by two symbols of new life and resurrection – the germinating chestnut on the flat stone, and the butterfly which sits on the skull.[79] The parallel visual relationship between the standing stone and the skull, and between the tree and the open chestnut reinforces the analogical relationship between the hope of resurrection revealed in the Word (John 11) and the promise of new life embodied in the cycle of nature.[80]

Whateley's caricature of a 'happy death' included 'christian burial in consecrated ground, and especially if a handsome monument is erected over it'. Such ideas were not 'agreeable to the christian *Scriptures*'. The nineteenth-century ideal of a quiet death in one's own bed, followed by interment in the charming 'natural' setting of a country churchyard, was certainly far from the experience of the early church. Bultmann has argued that nowhere in the New Testament is the attempt made to 'interpret death as a natural occurrence and thus to neutralise it':

Even where its abolition through resurrection is thought of and dying and rising again are described according to the analogy of a natural process (1 Cor.xv.36; John xii.24), it is not conceived of as a natural occurrence any more than the resurrection. That event, used as an analogy, is not in the biblical sense to be understood as a natural process in the Greek scientific sense.[81]

At first sight, Bowler's placing of Faithful's grave in the proximity of a church and beneath a spreading chestnut tree would seem to be 'unscriptural' in emphasis. Yet the analogical tradition within which he works is more effective in its presentation of Christian truth claims than such an interpretation would allow. *The Analogy of Religion* opens with a chapter entitled 'Of a Future Life', in which Butler argues the 'presumption or probability' of a future existence for man in the light of the 'analogy of nature, and the several changes which we have undergone', and other examples of *transformation* such as that of the worm turning into the fly.[82] Like St Paul's analogy of the grain of wheat, that of the worm (or lava) and the fly, while 'natural', does not soften death or domesticate resurrection. Rather, it challenges the faithful in the way that the Burial Service does in the Book of Common Prayer: these things are mysteries. *The Doubt* confronts the reality of physical decay, and the exhumed bones exposed to public view remind us of the radical binary *opposition* between the deep grave below ground (corruption, darkness, and death) and the gravestone inscription above ground (incorruption, light, and new life). The mysterious transformation of the small chestnut into the tree, the dimensions of which can only be guessed at, is an adequate if limited analogy to the mysterious transformation that is the resurrection of the body. But then the transformation of chestnuts into trees, like that of worms into flies, is, after all, no more than an analogy, and human souls are neither worms nor chestnuts. Indeed, the interest of Bowler's *The Doubt* as a 'problem picture' lies in the way in which its analogical parallelism is presented to the viewer in such a way that the stark reality of the exhumed bones is not erased, or explained away, but rather held in tension with the hope of resurrection offered by the text from John 11 on the gravestone (a *logion* that exercised the biblical critics, as we have seen). Thus the viewer is driven back to the ultimate question of *faith* that confronts the mourner, such as Lazarus's sister, and the lady in Bowler's picture. Natural analogies are not proofs, but aids to reflection for those who already believe.

Whereas Faithful is buried in a green English churchyard, Lazarus's tomb (Gk. *mnēmeion*) was made in rocky terrain: it is described as a 'cave' (*spēlaion*) with a stone covering the entrance. Although Christ's tomb was also cut out of rock, it was situated in a 'garden' (*kēpos*) which, to an English ear, has helpful organic associations. Mrs Alexander's hymn for children refers to Christ's rising 'from Joseph's cave'. In contrast, the little children of the hymn are buried in 'churchyard ground'. In a later verse, however, the two forms of burial are conflated in the lines 'Lord, Who for us so cold and *deep* / *Down* in that garden grave has lain'. In the nineteenth century, God's acre was thought of as a garden in which each body was sown in its own 'plot'. Millais's paintings provide a particularly interesting example of such associations. *Autumn Leaves* (1856; illustration 4), which, unusually for Millais, he intended to 'awaken by its solemnity the deepest religious reflection', is set in the garden of Annat Lodge in Perth, where he and his wife Effie had settled after their marriage in 1855.[83] Meanwhile he was planning to paint 'a picture with nuns in it', and two years later he completed *The Vale of Rest* (1858; illustration 5), which was to be his favourite among his own works.[84] The background to this picture was taken from the walled garden at Effie's family home in Perth, and the graveyard portion in the foreground from an old churchyard in Perth. In the painting, however, the burial ground is simply part of a convent garden. Other symbols in the picture, such as the bell, the ivy, the death's head on the rosary, and the ring-like wreaths that remind us of the spiritual marriage of a nun, encourage an analogical interpretation of the garden/ graveyard. This is supported by the fact that the poplars silhouetted against the sunset clearly refer to the garden scene of *Autumn Leaves*. Like the Bowler, however, Millais's picture with its open grave presents the viewer with a challenging question: it is mute, or unstated, but is to be found in the steady gaze of the sister on the right, who has dedicated her life (and death) to Christ.

Apart from parallels between burial in a plot of consecrated ground and the planting of seeds in a garden, God's acre is also a place where both wild and cultivated flowers grow, and Mrs Stone devotes a whole chapter of her book to 'Flowers on Graves'. Tennyson writes in *In Memoriam* of Hallam's burial:

> 'Tis well; 'tis something; we may stand
> Where he in English earth is laid,
> And from his ashes may be made
> The violet of his native land.   (18)

Tennyson himself compared the stanza with these lines from *Hamlet*:

> Lay her i' th' earth,
> And from her fair and unpolluted flesh
> May violets spring!   (v.1.232–4)[85]

Flowers growing on graves are a familiar convention in classical as well as Christian elegy, and they figure in Shelley's 'Adonais': 'The leprous corpse, touched by this spirit tender, / Exhales itself in flowers of gentle breath.' The butterfly in God's acre, however, is a specifically Christian analogy, which we have seen in Bowler's painting. It is used on the illustrated cover of E. H. Bickersteth's *The Shadowed Home*, which epitomizes the popular treatment of such ideas in the Victorian period (illustration 6). The butterfly above the grave and the rays of the morning sun (associated with the resurrection hour) are embossed in gilt on purple cloth. The epitaph on the grave board is from the *Pilgrim's Progress*:

THE PILGRIM THEY LAID IN A CHAMBER
WHOSE WINDOW OPENED TOWARD THE SUN RISING
THE NAME OF THE CHAMBER WAS PEACE
WHERE HE SLEPT TILL BREAK OF DAY.

The idea of the churchyard as a garden also has comforting domestic associations, and thus strengthens the link between the grave and heaven as a place of rest or peace, or as our last home. Great efforts were often made in the nineteenth century to bring those who died abroad home to their 'native soil', as in the case of Arthur Hallam. In Charlotte Yonge's best-selling novel, *The Heir of Redclyffe* (1853), however, the hero, Sir Guy Morville, dies in Roman Catholic Italy and is buried there, at sunrise, in the 'stranger's corner' of a graveyard: 'for of course the church did not open to a member of another communion of the visible church' (36). An English clergyman, however, reads the English rite over his grave:

> The blessing of peace came in the precious English burial-service, as they laid him to rest in the earth, beneath the spreading chestnut-tree, rendered a home by those words of his Mother Church – the mother who had guided each of his steps in his orphaned life. It was a distant grave, far from his home and kindred, but in a hallowed spot, and a most fair one; and there might his mortal frame meetly rest till the day when he should rise, while from their ancestral tombs should likewise awaken the forefathers whose sins were indeed visited on him in his early death; but, thanks to Him who giveth the victory, in death without the sting.   (36)

Displaced from the garden of home (an English churchyard), by the sins of the fathers, Guy finds a true spiritual home in the indivisible one Catholic and Apostolic Church, via the liturgy of the Church of England to which he has always remained true.[86] The 'spreading chestnut-tree', reminiscent of Bowler's painting of an English churchyard exhibited two years later, domesticates the promise of resurrection.

Anxieties concerning the 'natural' resting place of the dead are reflected in similar strategies in the poetry of Matthew Arnold, who fell into a necessary error in his elegy on Charlotte Brontë when he wrote of the sisters who had died before her:

> Round thee they lie – the grass
> Blows from their graves to thy own![87]

Arnold wrote 'Haworth Churchyard' shortly after Charlotte Brontë's death on 31 March 1855. Although he had been in Haworth three years earlier, he had evidently not discovered that the Brontë graves were in a vault in the church, and not in the churchyard 'next the moors'. When Elizabeth Gaskell informed him of this in a congratulatory letter, he replied:

I am almost sorry you told me about the place of their burial. It really seems to me to put the finishing touch to the strange cross-grained character of the fortunes of that ill-fated family that they should even be placed after death in the wrong, uncongenial spot.[88]

Revealing as this comment is about Arnold's idea of a congenial spot for burial, he might also have added that he needed a more congenial site for his 'pindarics'.

In 'Rugby Chapel: November, 1857', however, which is written in the same form as 'Haworth Churchyard', Arnold's negative emotional response to his father's burial within the walls of a church is worked out and transcended within the poem itself:

> Coldly, sadly descends
> The autumn-evening. The field
> Strewn with its dank yellow drifts
> Of withered leaves, and the elms,
> Fade into dimness apace,
> Silent; hardly a shout
> From a few boys late at their play!
> The lights come out in the street,
> In the school-room windows; but cold,
> Solemn, unlighted, austere,
> Through the gathering darkness, arise
> The chapel-walls, in whose bound
> Thou, my father! art laid.

Although his father's body is pent in the grave within the unlit chapel, the poet stands in what both he and Wordsworth would have considered a more congenial site of mourning: an autumnal scene of withered leaves and elm trees that one might find in a country churchyard. The lights in the school-room windows and in the street prepare for later stanzas in which compensation for loss is achieved through the poet's memory and the recognition that those whom Dr Arnold influenced for good in the school are now working in the 'sounding labour-house vast / Of being'. Unlike the hero of Thomas Hughes's *Tom Brown's Schooldays* (also 1857), who finds inspiration at the end of the novel by praying at the chapel altar under which Dr Arnold was buried, Matthew Arnold's meditations spring from standing in the autumnal evening scene and thinking of 'bygone autumns' with his father.

Eighteen years later, in *God and the Bible* (1875), Arnold was to claim that Jesus's words to Martha – 'I am the resurrection and the life' – were intended to 'transform' the materialist Jewish concept of the resurrection of the body, but that his words provided the basis for the evolution of a miracle story 'exactly effacing the truth which [he] wished to convey'.[89] Our 'hope of immortality', he wrote, our 'common materialistic notions about the resurrection of the body and the world to come', are 'in direct conflict with the new and loftier conceptions of life and death which Jesus himself strove to establish'. The position of Arnold (the critical spirit incarnate) in the grounds outside the chapel in which his father is buried allows him to avoid the question which, in F. D. Maurice's view, the story of the raising of Lazarus answered for mourners with a will to believe: 'Can light ever penetrate into that darkness?' Or as the Lord said to Ezekiel: 'Can these dry bones live?'

Arnold was one of several writers in the last thirty years of the nineteenth century who challenged or subverted mid-Victorian themes and conventions associated with deathbed and graveyard scenes. Hopkins's comments on Bridges's poem, 'On a Dead Child', have been cited. In Samuel Butler's Utopian satire, *Erewhon* (1872), the Victorian cult of the dead child is quietly set aside in the Erewhonians' concealment of the fact that a child has died, in a country where illness is a crime:

Should the child unhappily die, a coroner's inquest is inevitable, but in order to avoid disgracing a family which may have been hitherto respected, it is almost invariably found that the child was over seventy-five years old, and died from the decay of nature.   (13)

At the end of *Jude the Obscure* (1894–5), Arabella is inconvenienced by Jude's dying just when she wants to join in the celebrations that are going on in Christminster (VI.11). She decides to leave the body unattended, however, and rejoins the revellers, announcing that Jude is 'sleeping quite sound' and that he 'won't wake yet'. The language of religious consolation – 'Not dead, but sleeping', and 'The dead shall awake' – becomes in Arabella's mouth a casual deception.

   Hardy, of course, was to write some of the most grotesquely ironical poetry on the subject of death and bereavement in the language, and I will return to this. For the moment, however, an earlier example of a grimly satiric treatment of the Victorian way of death should be cited: part of Mr Herbert's lecture in Mallock's *The New Republic* (1877). Mr Herbert – Mallock's parody of Ruskin – outlines his ideas for the sanitary disposal of the dead in a Utopian city. A 'sincere advocate for cremation', he would have corpses turned into gas, which could be collected in small separate gasometers:

There is not one amongst you who, watching a dead friend flickering for the last time before you in the form of a gas-flame, and seeing how a little while and this flame was with you, and again a little while and it was not with you, would be at all sure whether this was really because, as your hearts would suggest to you, it went to the Father, or because, as your men of science would assert to you, it went simply – out.   (v.1)

Black humour can be therapeutic, and to laugh in death's face was, of course, not unknown to the Victorians. The passage quoted culminates in a playful version of the main linguistic feature I have been considering, in that two alternative interpretations reflect the two-fold aspect of death: 'went to the Father' or 'went simply – out'. The disposal of the body after death, then, dramatized the antithesis between physical and spiritual interpretations of death as sharply as did the deathbed in the nineteenth century.

Three years before the publication of *The New Republic*, Bishop Christopher Wordsworth of Lincoln preached a sermon in Westminster Abbey entitled 'On Burning of the Body; and on Burial'. Christianity, he argued, had extinguished the flames of the funeral piles which blazed throughout the Roman Empire. If, as was now being proposed in certain quarters, their piles should be rekindled in London and other great cities, popular belief in the resurrection of the body would be weakened. When Bishop Wordsworth turned, however, to the effect on the individual mourner of committing a loved one to the flames, as if for 'penal execution', his defence of Christian burial was grounded in traditional organic symbolism drawn from New Testament eschatology and the Book of Common Prayer:

No, – rather you will consign that beloved form to the bosom of the earth in Christian faith, hope, and love, as the husbandman commits the seed to the ground, in full reliance on God's mercy, and with a joyful foresight of the great day of harvest, when Christ, the Lord of the Harvest, will send His Reapers, the Angels, to gather together His elect from the four winds of heaven.[90]

Other conservative clergymen were to continue the defence of burial and its associated natural eschatological analogies via a rearguard action against cremation, but the arguments of the sanitary reformers could not be set aside. Following a vigorous campaign, supported, incidentally, by Anthony Trollope, cremation was finally legalized in 1885. At the end of the century the Catholic Modernist theologian, George Tyrrell, affirmed in the year in which he wrote his notorious article on hell entitled 'A Perverted Devotion' that the question of cremation was a 'purely disciplinary matter', and that

To try and connect the practice with the doctrine of the Resurrection as though the disintegration and dispersion of our dust presented any greater difficulty in one case than the other, is too ridiculous to think of. There would be more faith – more intelligent faith, in cremation, from that point of view. Custom and the sentiment founded on it, is doubtless the root-reason.[91]

Interestingly, however, he added that for himself he liked the idea of 'quietly mouldering away under the green sod in some quiet Catholic Churchyard with those *qui dormiunt in somno pacis*' (in the event he was refused a Catholic burial), and considered that there was something 'violent and unrestful' in the mechanics of cremation. The only argument for cremation to which Tyrrell would listen was 'the sanitary one', and even Christopher Wordsworth had acknowledged in his sermon of 1874 that the danger to public health of overcrowded burial grounds could not be ignored. 'The Burial of the Dead', he observed, 'ought never to be the cause of injury to the living.'[92]

While the cremation question opened up a rift between the modern rational arguments of the sanitary reformers and old-fashioned sentiment inherited from traditional 'Christian' practice, Thomas Hardy's poetry probed the conventions of that sentimental tradition and its inscription in Victorian consolatory verse. The final stanza of 'In Tenebris I' is characteristic:

> Black is night's cope;
> But death will not appal
> One who, past doubtings all,
> Waits in unhope.[93]

Like Swinburne, Hardy makes the hallowed ground of God's acre a space in which he can explore death's little ironies. In 'The Levelled Churchyard', dated 1882, the dead cry out to the passing 'passenger', complaining that they are 'Half stifled in this jumbled patch / Of wrenched memorial stones!':

> Here's not a modest maiden elf
> But dreads the final Trumpet,
> Lest half of her should rise herself,
> And half some sturdy strumpet!

Whereas earlier Victorian writers we have examined try to reconcile the physical reality of death and the Christian hope of resurrection, Hardy deconstructs the other-worldly language of transcendence by inserting it into the jocular this-worldly discourse of the popular lyric. 'In Death Divided', a poem of the 1890s, denies that most common Victorian hope of reunion after death by limiting the subject to the topographical. The lovers of the poem are buried in different graveyards:

> The simply-cut memorial at my head
>> Perhaps may take
> A rustic form, and that above your bed
>> A stately make;
> No linking symbol show thereon for our tale's sake.

Perhaps the most painful poems, however, are those in which Hardy examines the human need, strongly felt in the nineteenth century, to honour the dead by visiting the grave. Mothers squabble over their children's graves in 'In the Cemetery' ('Satires of Circumstance in Fifteen Glimpses', v; 1911), ignorant of the fact that the gravediggers have 'moved the lot' to make way for a new main drain. In the familiar 'Ah, Are You Digging on My Grave', which ends with the dead woman's dog admitting that he had simply buried his bone here, but had 'quite forgot' it was her 'resting-place', we have come a long way from the breathless solemnity of Bowler's *The Doubt: Can These Dry Bones Live?* Only a few years later the war that was to end all wars in fact precipitated the West into a new way of thinking about death in the mass. And for the war poets the challenge was to be a new one: to write meaningfully of death in the trenches, in a desert landscape far from the green church-yards of home and the consolations associated with the Victorian graveyard tradition.

CHAPTER 2

༣༡༡༢

Judgment

Day of Wrath! O day of mourning!
See fulfill'd the prophets' warning!
Heav'n and earth in ashes burning!
Oh, what fear man's bosom rendeth
When from Heav'n the Judge descendeth,
On Whose sentence all dependeth!

(Dies Irae)

Victor Turner cites Van Gennep's definition of *rites de passage* as 'rites which accompany every change of place, state, social position and age', and then explains the three phases that Van Gennep identified in these rites:

The first phase (of separation) comprises symbolic behavior signifying the detachment of the individual or group either from an earlier fixed point in the social structure, from a set of cultural conditions (a 'state'), or from both. During the intervening 'liminal' period, the characteristics of the ritual subject (the 'passenger') are ambiguous; he passes through a cultural realm that has few or none of the attributes of the past or coming state. In the third phase (reaggregation or reincorporation), the passage is consummated.[1]

Turner's interest as an anthropologist is in rites of passage which involve a withdrawal from and a subsequent return to society, such as fertility rituals in primitive African tribes or pilgrimages in Roman Catholic countries. Interpreted broadly, these ideas also have a useful application to the subject of death and bereavement.

In figure 1, the concept of liminality is applied to the deathbed as the passenger's site of transition, seen from a this-worldly perspective:

Fixed state   *Liminal phase*   *Fixed state*

Life $\rightarrow$ Recognition: death is anticipated $\rightarrow$ Dying process $\rightarrow$ Moment of death $\rightarrow$ Death

Figure 1

But for the bereaved person who attends to the body after death, the diagram can be drawn like this:

Deathbed → Moment of death → Period of transition → Burial → Grave

Figure 2

The concept of liminality can also help us to relate Victorian ideas concerning death and dying to the theology of the period which focused upon judgment. For in both the transition from the deathbed to the 'bed' that is the grave, and the 'intermediate state' between the moment of death and the last judgment, the characteristics of the passenger and the language applied to him or her are often ambiguous. Christ's death and resurrection conforms to Turner's model in this way:

Life on earth → Death → Three days in the tomb → Resurrection → Life in heaven

Figure 3

The passive humility which Turner associates with liminality is epitomized in the passion and burial of Christ: humbled for a season, he ceases to act after the arrest and is simply acted upon. During the three days after the crucifixion his body lies in the tomb. Meanwhile, according to tradition, his spirit 'descends into hell', or Hades, to save the saints of ancient Israel.[2]

The three days in the tomb have, of course, exercised a profound influence on ritual and culture in the West, particularly as a subject of penitential meditation and practice. St Patrick's Purgatory, for example, the three-day pilgrimage at Lough Derg in Ireland, is organized as a ritual 'death' to the world, a descent into a 'purgatory', and a final rising to new life in the spirit on the third day.[3] In the nineteenth century, the three days in the tomb provided writers with a model on which to base teaching on death and the future life. In *The Blessed Dead*, for example, first read as a paper before a private 'prophetical society' in 1862, E. H. Bickersteth addressed the question of 'those now sleeping in Jesus': 'What . . . says the Scripture regarding the intermediate state of departed saints, who are absent from the body and present with the Lord?'[4] In Bickersteth's view the Bible says that the intermediate state is the period between the death of the 'saint' and the second coming. He argues that it is a state of rest, and comments on the word 'sleep',

which is so frequently used of death, relating perhaps first to the body, which is laid in the grave as in a bed, but also, when used of the saints, to the calm rest of the spirit when the day's work is over.[5]

Although a state of rest, it is also a state of 'consciously living to God', and here he draws an important parallel with Christ, whose body rested in the tomb until the resurrection, but whose spirit 'gained new powers of motion, and travelled . . . on a blessed mission to the region of departed spirits'.[6] We can therefore gather that our spirit shall acquire new life in losing the burden of the flesh.

From Bickersteth's other-worldly perspective, lying in the grave does not represent the final state of the body. Rather, the earthly or 'natural' body lies in the grave (another kind of bed) only for a season, and is raised a 'spiritual' body (1 Corinthians 15.44) when it is reunited with the soul at the general resurrection. Meanwhile the soul exists in a (diminished) 'intermediate state':

Earthly state $\xrightarrow{}$ Death $\xrightarrow{}$ Intermediate state $\xrightarrow{}$ Resurrection $\xrightarrow{}$ Final state

Figure 4

As a 'premillennial' thinker, Bickersteth believed that there was a further transitional period between the intermediate state and the last judgment:

Intermediate state $\xrightarrow{}$ Resurrection $\xrightarrow{}$ Millennial sabbath $\xrightarrow{}$ Last judgment $\xrightarrow{}$ Final state

Figure 5

As we will see later, in *Yesterday, To-Day, and For Ever* the *parousia*, the inauguration of the millennial sabbath, and the last judgment are the most significant events in a complex scheme of repetitions and deferrals which create a sense of steadily increasing anticipation.

This combination of anticipation and *deferral* will figure prominently in this chapter, where the relationship between judgment (whether 'particular', 'private' and immediate, at the moment of death, or 'general' and final, at the last judgment) and the 'intermediate state' in nineteenth-century theology, and the relevance of this to Victorian literature, are to be discussed. The 'lively hope' of the New Testament is affirmed in the context of eschatological expectation and the delayed *parousia*. In the midst of persecution and injustice the early Christians looked forward in confidence to the coming of the kingdom. Christ's death and resurrection as the 'first fruits', or as an 'earnest' of a 'lively hope'; the looked-for *parousia*; the anticipated inauguration of Christ's kingdom on earth: all are part of a scheme in which those who wait and hope in the here-and-now look forward in lively expectation to that which is to be revealed. As St Gregory of Nyssa taught, 'all holy desires grow by delays'.[7] On Bultmann's analysis, however, the apostles also lived *in* the end-time, as Christ had already been raised, and, paradoxically, the 'lively hope' is already an 'eschatological blessing'. Another way of expressing this is in the terms *chronos* and *kairos*, adopted by Frank Kermode in *The Sense of an Ending* (1966). Although not always contrasting in New Testament Greek, these words can be said to maintain 'a certain polarity'. While waiting in consecutive time (*chronos*) which passed without bringing the anticipated *parousia*, the apostles saw their own time or season (*kairos*) as 'filled with significance, charged with a meaning derived from its relation to the end'.[8]

The kind of apocalyptic thinking that Kermode traces from the Middle Ages to Lawrence is associated with both hope and fear, and reflects Christ's paradoxical nature as both saviour and judge. New Testament teaching on judgment, upon which both the intermediate (or 'pareschatological')[9] and final (or eschatological) states of the soul turn, also has a temporal dimension. Kermode writes:

Already in St. Paul and St. John there is a tendency to conceive of the End as happening at every moment; this is the moment when the modern concept of *crisis* was born – St. John puns on the Greek word, which means both 'judgment' and 'separation.' Increasingly the present as 'time-between' came to mean not the time between one's moment and the *parousia*, but between one's moment and one's death.[10]

This change in the concept of the present as 'time-between' also threw into strong relief other aspects of the four last things, and particularly that future and *post-mortem* 'time-between' which begins with one's death and ends with the last judgment. Anticipation of the *parousia* in the earthly life was thus taken up into doctrines relating to a future state in which the faithful wait or are prepared for God's final judgment upon all mankind.

Eschatology is grounded in concepts of judgment, and perhaps the clearest modern account of this aspect of Christian tradition is S. G. F. Brandon's in *The Judgment of the Dead* (1967), where he discusses the attempts made in the early church to harmonize what appeared to be conflicting beliefs: Christ as both saviour and judge, his message being for Jew and for Gentile, and his judgment being of a group (or nation) and an individual. Brandon argues that with the continuing delay of the *parousia* the church went through a process of eschatological re-interpretation, and that this was already evident in the Lucan and Johannine gospels: 'From that of the essentially eschatological figure who was about to intervene catastrophically in the cosmic process, and gather to their eternal reward his Elect, they being already incorporated into him, Christ now began to be imagined as dwelling in heaven as the mediator between God and men.'[11]

A number of difficulties arose, however, in the process of accommodating these developments in a scheme that preserved the primitive eschatology inherited from Jewish apocalyptic (the last day, the general resurrection, and the last judgment): Where were the dead until the last day? In what condition? Were they conscious or unconscious? A further complication originates in the parable of Dives and Lazarus (Luke 16.22) and Jesus's promise to the penitent thief on the cross (Luke 23.43), both of which imply some kind of immediate post-mortem judgment and entry into paradise.[12] These issues were central to the development of doctrine concerned with the four last things in the early church; they were still live and, indeed, highly contentious issues in the nineteenth century, which drew heavily upon patristic theology. In order, then, to gain some purchase on these doctrinal questions and their treatment in our period, I can turn to F. W. Farrar and his summary in the preface to the first edition of *Eternal Hope* of the four main views of eschatology prevalent in the 1870s, and then consider both the doctrine of an intermediate state and millenarianism in the nineteenth century. For it is in the context of these doctrines and forms that I wish to discuss judgment in Victorian poetry and fiction.

JUDGMENT, THE INTERMEDIATE STATE, AND THE MILLENNIUM

Farrar's analysis of what he calls the 'common view' of eschatology is similar to that of his mentor and former tutor, F. D. Maurice, who believed that the main weakness of Protestantism was its assumption that the saved were the exception to a rule:[13]

> The *Common* view, which, to the utter detriment of all noble thoughts of God, and to all joy and peace in believing, except in the case of many who shut their eyes hard to what it really implies – declares (i.) that at death there is passed upon every impenitent sinner an irreversible doom to endless tortures, either material or mental, of the most awful and unspeakable intensity; and (ii.) that this doom awaits the vast majority of mankind.[14]

Farrar wanted his own Church of England to remove 'the greatest of all stumbling-blocks from the path of faith' by, among other things, restoring 'the ancient belief in an intermediate state' and emphasizing God's love and mercy.[15] Although the main thrust of his argument was against a literalist view of hell as a place of everlasting physical torment, the concept of an 'irreversible doom' (or judgment) at death also troubled him profoundly.

An alternative to the common view was annihilationism, or 'conditional immortality': 'the opinion that after a retributive punishment the wicked will be destroyed'.[16] Drawing on a handful of proof texts such as Romans 6.23 ('For the wages of sin is death') and 2 Timothy 1.10 ('Our Saviour Jesus Christ, who hath abolished death'), conditionalists held that a sentence of death passed on man at the fall had been mercifully withheld, that those who believed in Christ were saved and thus immortal, and that those who did not were annihilated. Exponents of such views were mainly Congregationalists and Anglican Evangelicals, and included in the second half of the nineteenth century adventists and millenarians.[17] Geoffrey Rowell discerns two varieties of conditionalists: those who emphasized the biblical language of the 'second death' (Revelation 20.14, 21.8) and argued that annihilation occurred after the wicked had been punished, and those who, influenced by Darwinism, believed in annihilation at death, while the saved (or fittest) survived. Henry Constable, one of the latter group, quoted Tennyson's lyric 56 in *In Memoriam* ('"So careful of the type?" but no') in drawing an analogy between the 'whole races of living things', which, as the fossil record showed, God had destroyed, and God's purpose for sinners.[18] Although the idea of annihilation, at death or after a period of punishment, was for many preferable to the common belief in everlasting punishment for sinners, it seemed to challenge New Testament teaching on our sharing Christ's risen life (e.g. 1 Corinthians 15). Schleiermacher wrote in *The Christian Faith*: 'if the soul of the Redeemer were imperishable, but our souls perishable, it could not justly be said that as man He was like us in all points, except sin'.[19]

Thirdly, there is purgatory:

the view that besides Heaven, the final state of the blessed, and Hell, the final doom of the accursed, there is a state wherein those souls are detained and punished which are capable of being purified, – an intermediate purification between death and judgment.[20]

The maturation from the fourth century of doctrine relating to some kind of trial after death to the general acceptance of belief in purgatory in the late twelfth century and beyond has been traced in a recent study. Jacques Le Goff shows how purgatory is an 'intermediate place' in two senses:

the souls there are neither as happy as the souls in Paradise nor as unhappy as the souls in Hell, and Purgatory comes to an end at the time of the Last Judgment. All that remained to make it truly intermediary was to assign it a location between Paradise and Hell.[21]

Temporally and spatially 'in-between', purgatory is hope.[22] With purgatory, however, the state of the soul at death is crucial. Indeed, Le Goff argues that purgatory was one of the main reasons for the 'dramatization of the moment of death' in the thirteenth century,[23] as purgatory, like the 'intermediate state', can be explained only in terms of an immediate 'private' or 'particular' judgment at death. Moreover, as purgatory comes to an end at the last judgment it is both delimited and defined by acts of divine judgment. It thus retains the sense of a (catastrophist) ending within a (gradualist) scheme of purification. I will examine nineteenth-century ideas on purgatory in some detail in Chapter 7 (on *The Dream of Gerontius*). Meanwhile the obvious attraction of such an accommodation to nineteenth-century thinkers should be noted, as catastrophist and gradualist (or 'uniformitarian') models conflicted in many spheres, including political theory, historiography, and biology, as well as theology.[24]

Belief in some kind of purgation in a future state was not restricted to
Roman Catholics in the nineteenth century. The views of Anne Brontë's
heroine in *The Tenant of Wildfell Hall* (1848), for example, have been
related to Patrick Brontë's reticence about hell: 'through whatever purging fires the erring spirit may be doomed to pass – whatever fate awaits
it, still it is not lost, and God, who hateth nothing that He hath made,
will bless it in the end!'[25] Like Helen Burns's views in *Jane Eyre*, Helen
Huntingdon's reflect the Brontë sisters' leanings towards the fourth view
of eschatology defined by Farrar: '*Universalism*, or, as it is now
sometimes termed Restorationism: the opinion that all men will be
ultimately saved.'[26] Although Origen's universalist eschatology of
'restoration' (*apocatastasis*) was rejected as unorthodox in the Eastern
Church in the third century, his influence and that of other early Hellenistic Fathers survived down the ages, offering an alternative to the
doom-laden Augustinian tradition of mainstream western theology. The
dominant view of the fall, for example, was questioned by
Schleiermacher in the early nineteenth century, when, following
Irenaeus, he emphasized man's development towards a future perfection, rather than man's falling away from a pre-lapsarian ideal state in
the past.[27] Some liberal Victorian theologians, such as F. D. Maurice,
may at first appear to be broadly universalist in their views, and the
sympathies of many poets and novelists of the period, including Tennyson, Philip Bailey (author of *Festus*), Browning, George MacDonald,
and Olive Schreiner, also tended in this direction. Considerable care
must be exercised here, however. Although a dividing line was carefully
drawn by F. W. Farrar, for example, between universalism and his own
theology of hope, he was accused by his critics of having used universalist arguments while repudiating universalist conclusions in *Eternal
Hope*, and had to write *Mercy and Judgment* in order to clarify his
position.[28]

The minutiae of the doctrinal issues involved in this debate are discussed by Rowell, and do not concern us here.[29] It is worth noting,
however, that one of Farrar's major objections to universalism is its
potential impact on moral behaviour. For in many debates in the
nineteenth century on the range of views that he outlines – the common
view, conditionalism, purgatory, and universalism – there is a tension
between a longing for a more hopeful and less dark eschatology, and a
fear lest the weakening of belief in judgment and some kind of punish-

ment should have a damaging effect on the morals both of believers and unbelievers. Gladstone, for example, writing at the end of the century, expressed his anxiety lest the moral efficacy of the 'terrors of the Lord' be lost.[30] More positively, however, belief in God's judgment was also sustained in the nineteenth century by an acute sense both of man's fallen condition and of the injustices of this world. The doctrine of a 'Judge and Judgment to come' was in Newman's view a 'development of the phenomenon of conscience',[31] and the belief that God's judgment would finally correct injustice is summed up in the words of Edmund Gurney: if 'the present iniquitous distribution of good and evil was . . . final, I should . . . desire the immediate extinction of the race'.[32]

We have seen, then, that all four views referred to by Farrar are based upon the interpretation of doctrine relating to God as judge. Farrar is less concerned in *Eternal Hope* with the temporal significance of the Greek word *krisis*, discussed by Kermode, than with what he considered to be its mistranslation and doctrinal application as 'damnation'.[33] He never denied what he called the 'doctrine of a retribution',[34] but directed his argument against those who accepted the 'common view' of damnation and who appeared to gloat over the idea of the wrath of God, expressed, for example, in the Dies Irae on which the epigraph to this chapter is based. He regretted that the Reformers, in rejecting the 'Romish doctrine' of purgatory which had become over-systematized and associated with such corruptions as indulgences, did not preserve the ancient and perhaps necessary belief in some kind of intermediate state. 'There is hope for you', he declared in one of his sermons, 'though you . . . may have to be purified in that Gehenna of aeonian fire beyond the grave'.[35] Belief in some kind of spiritual *progress* in an intermediate state was remarkably widespread among nineteenth-century Protestants of widely differing theological positions. H. B. Wilson, for example, whose liberal views on hell were challenged in the ecclesiastical courts, suggested an organicist model of post-mortem development in his article in *Essays and Reviews*:

we must . . . entertain a hope that there shall be found, after the great adjudica-tion, receptacles suitable for those who shall be infants, not as to years of terrestrial life, but as to spiritual development – nurseries as it were and seed-grounds, where the undeveloped may grow up under new conditions – the stunted may become strong, and the perverted be restored.[36]

For H. M. Luckock, a Tractarian and Canon of Ely, progress after death

is a corollary (by analogy) of the consciousness of the soul in the intermediate state:

> If it be admitted that the soul exists after death, and is conscious, it seems
> almost impossible to believe that it remains altogether unchanged.
> Conscious life by all analogy involves progress or retrogression, growth or
> decay . . .
> . . . is not progress, steadily advancing progress, a very law of God's
> kingdom?[37]

Gladstone also believed in what he called the 'progressive state' of the
'Christian dead', but argued that, as pain is one of God's instruments of
restoration in the earthly life, by analogy we have no right to assume
that the progressive state after death will not involve 'an admixture of
salutary and accepted pain'.[38]

These commentators wrestled with difficulties that nineteenth-century
Protestantism had inherited from the Reformation, when, as Brandon
shows, the Reformers found that in abandoning purgatory they were
faced with the problems which that doctrine had been designed to solve.
Calvin, unlike Luther, rejected the idea that souls sleep until the last
judgment (*psychopannychia*) and stated that they are 'gathered into rest,
where they await with joy the fruition of their promised glory; and thus
all things remain in suspense until Jesus Christ appears as the
Redeemer'.[39] Such a view assumes an immediate judgment but is unspecific about the paradisal intermediate state, emphasizing instead the
deferral of 'glory' until after the *parousia*. In the nineteenth century,
paradise was often distinguished from heaven (the final state of the
saved) by those who believed in some kind of intermediate state. Meanwhile the damned also know their eternal doom from the time of their
death. H. P. Liddon, a conservative High Churchman, and Canon and
Chancellor of St Paul's, wrote in a Passiontide sermon of 1887:

> We know that those who die in a state of grace enter not heaven as yet, but
> Paradise – an intermediate state in which they are gradually becoming more and
> more ready for the fully unveiled Beauty of the Most Holy. We know that just as
> the lost enter upon a fearful looking for of judgment and fiery indignation
> [Hebrews 10.27], which is not yet the place of punishment: so the saved are in
> an antechamber of heaven, the door of which will open for them at the last great
> day. Of this truth the supreme Revelation was made by our Lord upon the
> cross.[40]

Similarly, the Evangelical E. H. Bickersteth thought of paradise as one division of Hades, separated from the prison of the lost by the 'great gulf fixed' between Dives and Lazarus (Luke 16.26).[41] Unlike Liddon, however, Stewart Salmond, Professor of Theology at the Free Church College, Aberdeen, argued that there is too little evidence in the gospels to give us grounds for saying that Christ taught any doctrine of an intermediate state.[42]

Nevertheless, Geoffrey Rowell can argue at the end of *Hell and the Victorians* that the growing importance of the doctrine of the intermediate state in the nineteenth century was the one notable common feature which contrasted with the eschatology of earlier generations. The term 'intermediate state' itself, he believes,

was characteristic of the nineteenth century, and, whether it took the form of a tentative reappraisal of purgatory, or of a fore-shortened hell, or as a place of moral progress and expansion of the mind, it represented a move away from a predominantly Calvinist eschatology . . . It fitted better with a dynamic, evolutionary picture of the universe, than the conception of fixed and unalterable states into which men entered at death.[43]

Unlike what Farrar calls the 'common view' of eschatology, any scheme which includes an intermediate state, however defined, also offers some degree of *deferral* of God's final judgment upon mankind. In the case of progressive models the idea of an intermediate state also holds out the hope either of salutary purgation or of spiritual growth in preparation for the deferred final state that is heaven.

When we look back, however, to early-nineteenth-century schemes that most late-Victorian thinkers rejected, we find that different kinds of anticipation and deferral also characterize millenarianism, to which Rowell devotes comparatively little attention, incidentally. 'Premillennial' thinking, which commanded serious attention in the 1820s and 1830s, and enjoyed a revival as late as *c.* 1867–73, places great emphasis on the time between death (or the *parousia* in the case of those who are still alive when that event occurs) and the last judgment. The second coming of Christ represents a 'glorious hope' because it will inaugurate the millennium, when Christ will reign upon earth, and is therefore anticipated with joy and fervent expectation.

Narrower and more exclusive than most late-nineteenth-century schemes, millenarianism has deep historical roots. The sub-title to Norman Cohn's study, *The Pursuit of the Millennium* (1957), also reflects another kind of radicalism: 'Revolutionary millenarians and mystical anarchists of the Middle Ages'. According to Revelation 20 it was the Christian martyrs who were to 'live and reign with Christ a thousand years', although early sects soon interpreted this as including themselves as the suffering faithful who could anticipate the second coming in their lifetime. Cohn, like most modern commentators, interprets the word 'millenarianism' in the still broader sense of a particular type of salvationism, which he describes as collective, terrestrial, imminent, total, and miraculous.[44] Although Augustine had taught that the millennium was not a physical state, but a spiritual state accessible to believers through the sacraments and other means of grace, outbreaks of apocalyptic millenarianism recurred in the Middle Ages, when Joachite prophecy added a further dimension to the movement's history.[45] Interestingly, Victor Turner draws parallels between the properties of liminality in tribal rituals and in millenarian movements, including homogeneity, equality, anonymity, absence of property, abolition of rank, and acceptance of pain and suffering.[46]

J. F. C. Harrison's study on popular millenarianism 1780–1850 focuses upon the prophecies of Richard Brothers in the 1790s and of Joanna Southcott in subsequent decades until the 'virgin birth' fiasco and her death in 1814.[47] During this post-revolutionary period of war between England and France, many 'believers' became convinced that they were living in the last days, and English poets who were of millenarian persuasion later looked back on the French Revolution and the rise of Napoleon as critical 'signs of the times'.[48] Unlike 'postmillennialists', whose world-view was gradualist, progressive, and reformist in orientation, as for them the second coming was to *follow* the millennium, 'premillennialist' ideas were revolutionary and catastrophist, seeing Christ's second coming as the sudden inauguration of his kingdom on earth. (Some believed that the second coming had already occurred and that the millennium had begun.) The attractiveness of premillennialism to working-class radicals of the time is obvious.[49] Unusually, however, in both England and America in the early nineteenth century, and particularly *c.* 1820–35, it also drew support from well-off and even wealthy believers.[50] In England the years preceding the First Reform Act of 1832 were fraught with anxiety for the Evangelicals and nonconformists who dominated the millenarian movements of the day. The repeal of the old Test and Corporation Acts in 1828 and the introduction of the Catholic Emancipation Act in 1829 led to fears of disestablishment among Churchmen.[51] Ernest R. Sandeen cites a summary of the beliefs of millenarians at this time in the form of a six-point statement published in 1829 as the conclusion of a series of conferences held under the auspices of Henry Drummond, an Irvingite millenarian and a Member of Parliament:

1 The 'dispensation' or age will not end 'insensibly' but cataclysmically in judgment and destruction of the church in the same manner in which the Jewish dispensation ended.
2 The Jews will be restored to Palestine during the time of judgment.
3 The judgment to come will fall principally upon Christendom.
4 When the judgment is past, the millennium will begin.
5 The second advent of Christ will occur before the millennium.
6 The 1,260 years of Daniel 7 and Relevation 13 ought to be measured from the reign of Justinian to the French Revolution. The vials of wrath (Revelation 16) are now being poured out and the second advent is imminent.[52]

It was generally believed in English millenarian circles that the next important events would occur between 1843 and 1848, and that the end of time would occur between 1866 and 1873.[53] E. H. Bickersteth specifically referred to his treatment of the second coming, the 'millennial sabbath' and the last judgment when he wrote in the preface to the first edition of *Yesterday, To-Day, and For Ever* (1866),

The design of the following poem has been laid up in my heart for more than twenty years. Other claims, however, prevented me from seriously undertaking the work until little more than two years ago. But then the deep conviction that those solemn events, to which the latter books of my poem relate, were already beginning to cast their prophetic lights and shadows on the world, constrained me to make the attempt.[54]

This sense of urgency was shared by preachers such as William Ker, Vicar of Tipton, Staffordshire, whose discourses on '*The Things which must Shortly come to Pass*' (1868) included two entitled 'The Advent of "The Avenger"' with a text from Revelation 16.15: 'Behold, I come as a thief.'[55]

Bickersteth's epic poem and Ker's sermons are only two examples of a kind of writing which characterized the period of social and political crisis in which the Second Reform Act was introduced and George Eliot wrote *Middlemarch*, a 'novel of crisis' set in that earlier period of apocalyptic expectation, the late 1820s and early 1830s.[56] Like the idealists of George Eliot's novel whose ambitions are thwarted by the realities of provincialism in an unheroic century, those who looked for the imminent return of Christ to earth, there to reign with his saints for a thousand years, had to come to terms with various degrees of disappointment, especially when what appeared to be the last days brought no *parousia*. Edmund Gosse sardonically describes a stronger response than this particular kind of disappointment in his father, Philip, a member of the Plymouth Brethren and a fervent Adventist:

> He waited, with anxious hope, 'the coming of the Lord,' an event which he still frequently believed to be imminent. He would calculate, by reference to prophecies in the Old and New Testament, the exact date of this event; the date would pass, without the expected Advent, and he would be more than disappointed, – he would be incensed. Then he would understand that he must have made some slight error in calculation, and the pleasures of anticipation would recommence.[57]

Edmund Gosse's strong antipathy to the more extreme beliefs which his father forced upon him in his youth made mature reflection upon the potential spiritual value of such 'pleasures of anticipation' impossible. In his view, to turn to miscalculation as an explanation was to rationalize an absurdity. On this argument it could be claimed that the 'millennial sabbath', that paradisal but earthly time-between which defers the last judgment and entry into the full joys of heaven (and thus sustains a sense of expectation and of hope deferred), is simply an idealized projection from the time-between that is the present life of one who looks to the second coming and the inauguration of that sabbath. A more sympathetic but critical approach to prophecies in the Revelation such as the millennium would, on the other hand, emphasize that the Revelation was written specifically for Christians suffering under Roman persecution; that the book's author drew heavily upon Jewish apocalyptic; and that the enduring value of the Revelation lies in its spiritual content and the message that Christians should live as if Christ's second advent were imminent, their lamps trimmed, awaiting the Bridegroom. Christina Rossetti discusses these traditional types and symbols at length in her devotional commentary on the Apocalypse, *The Face of the Deep* (1890),[58] and uses them extensively in her own poetry. A particularly striking example is the opening of 'Advent', written in 1858, later read at her own funeral, and regarded by Swinburne as 'perhaps the noblest of all her poems'.[59] Here, however, the sense of 'hope deferred' refers to a lack of 'signs' rather than to disappointment that signs have failed to bear fruit:

> This Advent moon shines cold and clear,
>   These Advent nights are long;
> Our lamps have burned year after year
>   And still their flame is strong.
> 'Watchman, what of the night?' we cry
>   Heart-sick with hope deferred:
> 'No speaking signs are in the sky,'
>   Is still the watchman's word.[60]

What, then, is the relationship between adventist and millenarian 'hope deferred' and judgment? Whereas the doctrine of an intermediate state takes a number of different forms which reflect a variety of beliefs, the theology of the 'millennial sabbath' tends to conform quite closely to that of Farrar's deprecated 'common view' of eschatology: the separation of saints from sinners during the millennium anticipates the division of the sheep and goats at the last judgment. Whereas the 'saints' who are alive at the inauguration of the millennium never experience death, the damned are imprisoned and await the 'second death' in store for them at the last judgment. As we turn to the poetry and fiction of the period, however, and consider the ways in which writers treat the subject of judgment and the last things in the epic, or the dramatic monologue, or the novel, we must attend not only to such broad questions as God's nature as judge and the extent of his ultimate forgiveness, but also to the ways in which models of judgment can be related to literary form. For whereas the religious epic, an extended form, can attempt a cosmological explanation in and through time, shorter poetic forms accommodate a more this-worldly and experiential treatment of the subject. Meanwhile the development of the Victorian novel is marked by a decline in the use of the judgmental ending, that secularized last assize.

POETIC FORMS AND APOCALYPTIC VISIONS

Having first paid homage to the great Turner collection in the Tate Gallery, London, many modern visitors move on to three massive paintings, each measuring about six and a half feet by ten feet: the famous 'judgment paintings' of John Martin, executed between 1851 and 1854. Perhaps it is the thought of the labour which went into these canvases that attracts viewers; or the lurid colours; or the sensational effects which influenced the historical epics of early Hollywood. Martin's subjects – *The Last Judgment*, *The Great Day of His Wrath* (originally named *The End of the World*), and *The Plains of Heaven* – also appeal to the contemporary taste for the apocalyptic, reflected in post-modernist versions of the sublime, for example, and in one of the cinema's most popular forms, the disaster movie. An interest, however, in the subject of death and the future life, is perennial.

John Martin was never accepted into membership of the Royal Academy. Ruskin attacked his work on several occasions, contrasting it unfavourably with Turner's.[61] Martin's judgment paintings, however, caused a sensation when they went on tour in Britain and America after his death in 1854: engravings of his work hung in the Parsonage at Haworth; and Mrs Henry Wood referred to *The Plains of Heaven* in *East Lynne* (1861), one of the most popular novels of the century. The sharp separation of the saved from the damned in the paintings also invites comparison with popular millenarianism in the mid-nineteenth century, a period in which both the hell-fire sermon and the pious volume on the recognition of friends in heaven flourished. Significantly, however, Martin's attempt to portray the saved, the damned, and the heavenly host in one painting, *The Last Judgment*, failed (illustration 7). The eye cannot take in both the picture's design, with its complex perspectives and disturbing vertical hierarchy, and the mass of details which clamour for close attention. Similar problems confronted those nineteenth-century writers who emulated Dante and Milton in epic poems on the subject of the 'four last things', while liberal Protestant theologians challenged the common view of hell and the idea that the vast majority of mankind would suffer everlasting physical torments, and be viewed by the elect in heaven from the other side of a 'great gulf fixed'.

Martin's paintings epitomize the 'apocalyptic sublime'[62] which became fashionable in English painting and poetry in the 1820s and 1830s, depicting biblical and historical subjects which combine what Tennyson described in 'Armageddon' as 'vast sights' and 'inconceivable visions' with a sense of imminent ending, or of God's sudden and dramatic intervention as judge in the course of time. Martin's *The Fall of Babylon* and *Belshazzar's Feast* were exhibited in 1819 and 1821 respectively. *The Destruction of Pompeii and Herculaneum* (1822) was the subject of a poem of the previous year by his friend Edwin Atherstone, with whom he enjoyed a friendly rivalry, as well as of Edward Bulwer's more famous novel, *The Last Days of Pompeii* (1834). Similarly, Martin's *The Fall of Nineveh* (1828) appeared in the same year as the first six books of a poem by Atherstone which was to grow to thirty books by 1868, and *The Last Man* (1833) was preceded by literary works on the same subject by Thomas Campbell and Mary Shelley.

The best known literary treatment of judgment itself in this pre-Victorian era, however, is Byron's *The Vision of Judgment* (1822), a brilliantly playful satiric riposte to Southey's *A Vision of Judgment* (1821), in the preface to which the laureate had scored some cheap points against him. Neither poet treats the last judgment, of course, but rather the coming to ('immediate') judgment of old King George, who had died in 1820. Southey, however, in the opening passage of his poem, adopts the convention, often also followed by those who wrote on the second coming and the last judgment, of introducing his portrayal of last things with a description of an evening scene:

> 'Twas at that sober hour when the light of day is receding,
> And from surrounding things the hues wherewith day has adorn'd them
> Fade, like the hopes of youth, till the beauty of earth is departed:
> Pensive, though not in thought, I stood at the window, beholding
> Mountin and lake and vale; the valley disrobed of its verdure . . .
>
> Earth was hush'd and still; all motion and sound were suspended . . .
>
> Pensive I stood and alone, the hour and the scene had subdued me,
> And as I gazed in the west, where Infinity seem'd to be open,
> Yearn'd to be free from time, and felt that this life is a thraldom.[63]

A passing bell for the late king then induces in the poet a longing for release from the 'thraldom' of this life.

In describing the vision that follows, Southey uses prophetic language associated with the Holy Spirit ('a sound like the rushing of winds, or the roaring of waters') and invokes Dante as his precursor: 'to thy mortal sight shall the Grave unshadow its secrets; / Such as of yore the Florentine saw'. The overweening ambition of *A Vision of Judgment* that so infuriated Byron, and the vast vagueness of such phrases as 'where Infinity seem'd to be open', were also characteristic of the eighteenth-century tradition of meditative-descriptive poetry to which the opening of the work is indebted. Edward Young's *Night Thoughts* (1742–5), together with Blair's *The Grave* (1743) and Thomson's *The Seasons* (1726–30), was still one of the most widely read poems in the late eighteenth century.[64] George Eliot's description of Young's treat-

ment of the last judgment as 'a compound of vulgar pomp, crawling
adulation, and hard selfishness, presented under the guise of piety' was
quoted earlier.[65] During the hundred years that separate Young and
Eliot, however, many other ambitious religious poets had invoked the
Holy Spirit as their spiritual muse and described the last things in all
their awesome glory. Macaulay, whose comparative analysis of Dante
and Milton (1825) was a significant contribution to critical discussion
on religious symbolism in poetry, attacked the work of his contemporary, Robert Montgomery, on grounds that were similar to George
Eliot's in her critique of Young:

> The Day of Judgment is to be described, and a roaring cataract of nonsense is
> poured forth upon this tremendous subject. Earth, we are told, is dashed into
> Eternity. Furnace blazes wheel round the horizon, and burst into bright wizard
> phantoms . . . The red and raging eye of Imagination is then forbidden to pry
> further. But further Mr Robert Montgomery persists in prying . . .
>   And this is fine poetry! . . . This is what has been described, over and over
> again, in terms which would require some qualification if used respecting
> Paradise Lost![66]

Macaulay's   distaste   for   the   'puffing'   of   Montgomery's   *The
Omnipresence of the Deity* (1828) is matched by his abhorrence of the
poetaster's vaunting ambition. Montgomery's 'prying' into the mysteries
of the four last things certainly contrasts with Macaulay's own more
humble approach in a poem of 1826, written four years before his
review. 'Dies Irae' includes these lines:

> *Jesus*, hast *thou* borne the pain,
> And hath all been borne in vain?
> Shall thy vengeance smite the head
> For whose ransom thou hast bled? . . .
>
> Mercy, mercy, save, forgive,
> Oh, who shall look on thee and live?[67]

'Dies Irae', however, is a short meditative poem which avoids the
problems that confronted those who were inspired to write on the grand
scale, like Montgomery. Robert Pollok's hugely ambitious epic, *The
Course of Time* (1827), is perhaps the most interesting of many attempts
in this period to narrate the unnarratable, and to tread where the writers
of the Revelation, the *Divine Comedy*, and *Paradise Lost* had already
trodden. The publishers paid Pollok the huge sum of £2,500 for the
poem, much more than was given for the poems of Scott or Campbell.

Its continued popularity in the mid-Victorian period is reflected not only in the number of editions published – the twenty-fifth edition appeared in 1867 and the 'seventy-eighth thousand' in 1868, when millenarian expectations were again intense – but also in Blackwood's publication of an attractive illustrated edition in 1857, for which Birket Foster and John Tenniel provided designs. This edition is prefaced by an anonymous Memoir in which the genesis of the poem is described. While training for the Secessionist ministry in Scotland, Pollok was inspired by the thought that no previous poet had done justice to the subject of the general resurrection. He thereupon took up his pen and wrote part of what he originally intended to be the first book of a long poem on the subject. As time went on, however, other subjects presented themselves, and he began to reorder his materials until finally, in another moment of inspiration, 'the idea of the poem struck him, and the plan of it, as it now stands, stretched out before him; so that, at one glance, he saw through it from end to end like an avenue, with the Resurrection as only part of the scene'.[68] The general resurrection of the dead thus became the subject of Book VII in a poem of ten books, roughly equivalent in its placing to Milton's climactic Book IX (the description of the fall) in his epic of twelve books. In other respects, however, Pollok's narrative strategies are very different from Milton's. They are principally those of deferral and suspense combined with repetition, allowing the poet to dwell on the sinfulness of man at great length, and thus to justify the sharp separation of the sheep from the goats at the last judgment, which is delayed until the final books.

The poem opens in paradise after the last judgment, and therefore after the end of time when the earth was destroyed. Two 'youthful sons of Paradise' (here not distinguished from heaven) welcome a newly arrived stranger from another world who has seen hell on his journey, and who asks them for an explanation. They take him to an 'ancient bard of Earth' who answers his questions by narrating the history of man from the creation. The bard's lengthy description of man's fallen state on earth continues to the beginning of Book V, where he takes stock of the course of time:

> The span of Time was short, indeed; and now
> Three-fourths were past, the last begun, and on
> Careering to its close, which soon we sing.
> But first our promise we redeem, to tell
> The joys of Time, her joys of native growth;
> And briefly must, what longer tale deserves.[69]

The celebration of the innocent joys of life on earth which follows has the double function of balancing the gloomy account of man's wretchedness which has preceded it and deferring the promised description of time's 'close'. After thirty pages there follows a description of the 'evil state of society that preceded the Millennium'. This catalogue of signs of the times includes the inevitable attack on the Roman Catholic Church, the 'scarlet-coloured Whore, / Who on the breast of civil power reposed / Her harlot head'.[70] The great battle of three days, however, comes suddenly and with devastating effect, as 'the Lord, clad like a man / Of war', presides over the fall of Babylon, the divorce of Church and State, the binding of Satan, and the inauguration of the millennium, when 'Messiah reigned; / And Earth kept jubilee a thousand years'.[71]

Significantly, the millennium itself is described in only a few pages at the end of Book v, for Pollok's true subject is the depravity of sinners, and it is to this that he returns in the following book, where Satan is unbound and, in the words of the Argument, 'violence and crime prevail over all the earth, now ripe for final doom'.[72] This doom is not to be described until much later in the poem, however, and what follows is a repetition of the great battle before the millennium, as 'God in his car of vengeance comes', and the last night begins – 'the long, dark, dark, dark night'.[73] The bard falters as he approaches the subject of the damned:

> What harp of boundless, deep, exhaustless woe,
> Shall utter forth the groanings of the damned,
> And sing the obsequies of wicked souls,
> And wail their plunge in the eternal fire? –
> Hold, hold your hands! hold, angels! – God laments,
> And draws a cloud of mourning round his throne:
> The organ of Eternity is mute,
> And there is silence in the heaven of heavens.[74]

This cosmic pause (cf. Revelation 8.1), of which there are several in the poem, is reflected in the narrative itself, which pauses in order to recapitulate:

> But we have overleaped our theme: behind,
> A little season waits a verse or two –
> The years that followed the Millenial [sic] rest.[75]

So another opportunity is provided to describe the sinful nature of man and to anticipate God's judgment, thus extending, in narrative terms, the suffering of those sinners in the liminal state which precedes the last judgment. Then the end of the world seems to have come:

> O earth! thy hour was come: the last elect
> Was born, complete the number of the good,
> And the last sand fell from the glass of time.[76]

But the narrative is again interrupted, this time by the call to the heavenly equivalent of Evensong.

This established pattern of deferral and repetition is continued in Book VII, where the bard returns to the last day (when 'suddenly, alas, fair Earth! the sun / Was wrapped in darkness'), and there is another cosmic pause:

> and beasts of every kind stood still.
> A deep and dreadful silence reigned alone . . .
>
> In horrible suspense all mortals stood;
> And, as they stood and listened, chariots were heard
> Rolling in heaven . . .
>
> Earth, arrested in her wonted path,
> As ox struck by the lifted axe, when nought
> Was feared, in all her entrails deeply groaned.[77]

What Pollok in his Argument calls the 'universal pause of Nature' precedes the trumpet call which heralds the resurrection: 'Awake ye dead!' The twenty pages that follow were presumably the first that Pollok wrote, and they represent the first major summit towards which the poem has been labouring. When the dead are raised, old men regain their prime, a mummy comes to life as the 'brown son of Egypt' who stands beside the 'European, his last purchaser', and there is much busy sorting out of 'essential organs' and 'fellow particles', particularly in the graveyards:

> The doors of death were opened; and in the dark
> And loathsome vault, and silent charnel-house,
> Moving, were heard the mouldered bones that sought
> Their proper place.[78]

Meanwhile the damned are also raised in order to suffer 'the second death'.

Although one might have expected the last judgment to follow immediately, the whole of the lengthy subsequent book (VIII) is devoted to the 'last pause of expectation' as every member of the human race dwells on his or her follies and sins, again allowing the poet to make *his* judgments upon mankind and to warn the reader against the temptations of the world. For the third time in the poem, God's sudden (and almost identical) intervention follows a long period of anticipation and delay:

> and suddenly
> In heaven appeared a host of angels strong,
> With chariots and with steeds of burning fire . . .[79]

Like the millennium earlier in the poem, the last judgment itself is described briefly: as in Matthew 25, the sheep are separated from the goats, and families are divided, never to meet again. Significantly, however, whereas the saved are described in only half a page, six pages are devoted to Satan, and at the end of the book the heavens are divided by a bow on which are written words that might have served as Pollok's epigraph to *The Course of Time*: 'As ye have sown, so shall ye reap this day!'[80]

The final book (x), as the Argument reveals, amounts to a rewriting of Book IX, following a crisis of narrative confidence:

Prayer and thanksgiving of the Author. – Solemn dedication of his labours. – Supplication for the Divine Influence. – The Bard resumes. – The Judgment-day – what it really was. – The redeemed and the reprobate still standing as described in Book IX. – Universal calm of Earth waiting her doom. – The trumpet sounded by Michael. – Gathering of the heavenly hosts . . .[81]

The poem ends with Christ the Judge passing sentence on the damned ('Depart from me, ye cursed, into the fire, / Prepared eternal in the gulf of hell'),[82] destroying the 'guilty earth' with fire, and inviting the blessed to join him at God's right hand.[83] The bard's last lines are those of a celestial (and thus omniscient) narrator who has gone the second mile with the new arrival from earth:

> Thus have I sung beyond thy first request,
> Rolling my numbers o'er the track of man,
> The world at dawn, at mid-day, and decline:
> Time gone, the righteous saved, the wicked damned,
> And God's eternal government approved.[84]

The order and closure celebrated here, however, mask the unsatisfactory nature of Pollok's vision of judgment, which fails not least because the earlier descriptions of divine intervention in the poem make the last judgment itself virtually redundant in narrative terms.

The problem, then, for the writer of this kind of Christian epic is to sustain a sense of anticipation within a providential scheme of repetition and reinforcement that can easily become static and closed. This problem confronted Edward Henry Bickersteth in *Yesterday, To-Day, and For Ever* (1866), probably the last poem of its kind in English letters. Published during the last major period of heightened millenarian expectation in the nineteenth century, the work went through seventeen editions by 1885, and had sold 27,000 copies in England and 50,000 in the United States by 1907.[85] (Bickersteth's biographer, Aglionby, however, commented in 1907 that in future the poem was more likely to be studied than read.) The poem is of greater significance and interest than Pollok's, largely because Bickersteth emphasizes personal spirituality rather than corporate guilt in his treatment of death and the future life. Beginning with the Seer describing his own death, surrounded by his family,[86] the poem goes on to develop the relationship between the Seer and his guardian angel, Oriel, the life, death, and final judgment of the damned Theodore, and the inner torment and self-abasement of Satan, in ways that are closer to Milton than to Pollok and his more generalized treatment of human types. Bickersteth's interpretation of scripture, explained in detail in his end-notes, also differs from Pollok's, as, for example, in his belief that the earth is not to be destroyed by fire on the last day, but will be purged and renewed to become the site of God's 'many mansions' – the final state that is heaven itself.[87] Like Pollok, however, Bickersteth was a premillennialist, and at least one contemporary reviewer believed that it was in the last four books of the twelve-book poem, where he described 'The Bridal of the Lamb', 'The Millennial Sabbath', 'The Last Judgment', and 'The Many Mansions', that Bickersteth was most impressive, as this was 'more untrodden' ground.[88] The circumspect Aglionby, on the other hand, writing forty years later, emphasized that Millenarianism represented a minority view.[89]

Like Pollok's, Bickersteth's title emphasizes the temporal while also providing a clue to the poem's structure. Hebrews 13.8 was a favourite and often quoted text in the nineteenth century: 'Jesus Christ the same yesterday, and to day, and for ever'.[90] In the central books of the poem the Seer's guardian angel, Oriel, tells him 'the story of the great To-day of Time' (v.956), and explains God's providential scheme since the 'yesterday' that was before the creation. The later books convey their teleological argument by representing the lot of the 'Risen Saints' as a preparation for, and a series of ascents towards the 'Many Mansions' of heaven (Book XII). Thus as God's 'Last Judgment' (Book XI) brings the saved to the highest heaven, the distance between them and the damned in the lowest deeps of hell is infinitely great.

A sense of ascent and separation later in the poem is heightened by its beginning with a 'Descent to Hades' (Book I), following the Seer's death. In the nether 'Paradise of the Blessed Dead' the Seer meets Oriel, who explains that he shall see 'greater things than these' (I.872). The presence of Enoch and Elijah in this intermediate state of paradise, rather than the final state of heaven, which Bickersteth justifies in an end-note, provides a focus for the anticipation which is generated at the end of Book II:

> their presence here
> Is pledge and earnest to the Blessed Dead
> Of that great resurrection day, whose dawn
> Already gilds the Easter of the world:
> They with the saints who rose when Jesus rose
> Are wave-sheafs of the harvest.   (II.1011–16)

Like Pollok, Bickersteth tries to convey a feeling of adventist expectation through narrative suspense, as in Oriel's closing words:

> But of these
> And other mysteries in earth and heaven
> Conversing, on the range of yonder hills,
> Whose summits bound these beatific fields,
> And look far off into the waste beyond,
> If such thy pleasure, let us wait the end.   (II.1016–21)

The plot of the 'blessed dead' in paradise – the subject of Bickersteth's tractate of 1862, cited earlier – is left in suspense while Oriel shows the Seer 'The Prison of the Lost' (Book III) and relates the story of Theodore, one of the 'lost souls' in hell who 'wait their sentence' at the judgment which is 'beyond' (III.594). The first three books of the poem are thus anticipatory, like the intermediate states in Hades that they describe, and that are explained by Oriel later in the poem in terms of God's foreknowledge of the fall:

> He, foreseeing all this ruin, had form'd,
> Deep in the unfathomable depth that lies
> Beneath the ocean veiling things unseen,
> Two vast receptacles *sunder'd though near*;
> One luminous, one dark: the first He named
> After this lovely Eden, Paradise,

Henceforth the outer court of heaven itself;
The other, precinct to the fiery lake
Of dread Gehenna, Hell: and, ever as death
Touch'd with his icy spear the sons of men,
Thither their spirits dismantled should descend,
And there await His judgment-bar, when they
And rebel angels should receive their doom.

(v.669–81; my emphasis)

The central books of the poem are devoted to Oriel's account of 'The Creation of Angels and of Men' (IV), 'The Fall of Angels and of Men' (V), 'The Empire of Darkness' (VI) – Satan's council after the flood – and 'Redemption' (VII), which describes Christ's life, death, descent into Hades, and resurrection. Book VIII, 'The Church Militant', is reminiscent of Pollok's *The Course of Time* in its anti-Roman Catholic excesses. Oriel then invites the Seer to recount his 'spirit's life' (VIII.982–3). With the end of their colloquy and a sudden trumpet call – 'the first / Of the three trumpet signals fore-announced, / That usher in the long-expected close' (VIII.1016–18) – the narrative enters a new phase in which Oriel and the Seer together witness the unfolding of God's final purpose for man and the earth. That purpose is enacted through judgment and the infinitely wide separation of those who in Hades were 'sunder'd though near'.

As in Pollok's poem, the resurrection of the dead (in Book IX, 'The Bridal of the Lamb'), is the fulcrum on which Bickersteth's epic turns. The Seer's 'sainted wife', who is now rapturously greeted by him, is both antitype and type: as one of the blessed dead she is 'Not consort, but what consort typifies' (IX.68), but her reunion with her earthly husband in paradise is only a 'precious foretaste of the feast at hand' (49). Oriel announces that 'The time is short' (92) and the blessed dead *rise* to the earth, where the resurrection occurs in the twinkling of an eye (321). Avoiding the pitfalls of *The Course of Time*, where the resurrection is described in too much literalist detail, Bickersteth follows Pollok in making the resurrection the occasion of another preliminary judgment. Joined by the 'thousand times ten thousand living saints, / Changed and transfigured, from all lands and seas' (335–6) (with whom, incidentally, all Adventists wished to be numbered), the 'soaring multitudes' witness the 'Bridal of the Lamb' with his church. Babylon falls (372), Elijah completes the restoration of the Jews (411), and Christ inaugurates 'The Millennial Sabbath', the subject of the subsequent book (X). Here again the typology of the sabbath – 'The memory of a bygone Paradise, / The earnest of a Paradise to come' (x.29–30) – underlines the transitional nature of this part of God's providential plan, where the end of the millennium is seen as 'the golden eve of everlasting day' (x.594). Characteristically, the sense of fulfilment in the inauguration of the millennium at the beginning of Book x – 'It dawn'd at last' (45) – has been displaced by a sense of continued anticipation by the end, for all has now been prepared for the final transitional phase which separates the damned and the risen saints from their final states: 'The Last Judgment' (Book XI).

While the risen saints have enjoyed the first fruits of the millennium on earth, the damned in hell have broken an 'oppressive silence' only to bemoan and confess past sins (XI.19). As in earlier books, there are several pauses in Book XI – narrative lacunae that suggest the awesomeness and the unnarratability of the separation of the damned from the Logos, and that, unnervingly, make it possible to hear the slightest murmur of the damned. During Satan's confession, for example, he acknowledges that he and the 'lost' are 'damn'd for evermore':

> Again was silence for a space in hell,
> So terrible, that only the quick breath
> Of spirits in pain was heard like tongues of flame
> Sibilant in the sultry atmosphere.   (XI.123–6)

Released from their bondage, the fallen angels return to the 'renovated earth' (209), where Satan's envy prompts him to comment that 'this is worse than hell' (256). A final rebellion is planned as the millennium draws to its close and 'fiendish malice' is loosed upon the earth. Again a sense of anticipation is expressed in the language of adventism:

> Watchman, what of the night? Night is far spent:
> Morn is at hand, the morn of endless day.
> Broods yet a tempest? Yet the last, hell's last
> Expiring struggle, heaven's last victory:
> Beyond is cloudless light and perfect peace.   (353–7)

A sense of heightened anticipation is justified here, as the last battle between God and Satan, and the last judgment itself, are the final narratable events of the epic: the final state of 'cloudless light and perfect peace' is ineffable, and cannot be written.

Narratable events therefore serve as types of that which will follow.

When the conspiracy of 'devils and men' is put down, for example, the Lord himself lays on Satan the 'right hand of Omnipotence':

> The touch
> Alone was foretaste of the second death,
> Such death as damned spirits for ever die.   (482–4)

His hosts, now manacled, wait 'in speechless horror' for the last judgment, while the prison of the damned is emptied and destroyed. Like Pollok, Bickersteth gives much more space to the damned than to the risen saints here, emphasizing 'the terrors of the wrath to come' (511) rather than the hope of heaven. The description of the judgment itself follows Matthew 25, with Christ calling his own to inherit 'the royalties and realms' prepared and destined for them before 'the foundations of the world were laid' (637–40):

> So saying, He drew us nearer to His side,
> And placed us on his glorious right. O scene
> Of solemn unimaginable awe!   (646–8)

This 'unimaginable' spectacle is of the Messiah on his judgment-throne, surrounded by the thrones of the saved who are to witness the judgment of the damned:

> Each in its order'd place, tier above tier,
> Rank above rank, so marvellously set,
> Or such the virtue here of sight and sound,
> We saw the shades that pass'd on every brow,
> We heard the whisper of the faintest sigh.   (658–62)

'Face to face' with the elect, the 'apostate spirits' acknowledge the righteousness of a Lord whose 'tones of wrath' are 'so strangely blent with grief':

> And, as the awful sentence fell on each
> Of chains and everlasting banishment
> To his own portion in the lake of fire,
> As by the Spirit of holiness compell'd
> We and the blessed angels said, Amen.   (701–5)

Satan is then crushed under the 'burning heel' of his 'Conqueror', the 'crystal empyrean' opens beneath him, and he and his rebel armies fall into a 'yawning gulf':

> Standing upon its rugged edge we gazed
> Intently' [sic] and long down after them; and there
> They sank and sank, the forms more indistinct,
> The cries more faint, the echoes feebler, till
> The firmamental pavement closed again:
> And silence was in heaven.   (740–5)

The 'millions of the dead', the lost, are then also judged, beginning with Cain and including Theodore, and are finally dismissed to everlasting fire 'Beneath Gehenna's burning sulphurous waves / In the abyss of ever-during woe' (879–80).

Bickersteth in his consolatory writings used a euphemistic religious discourse which excludes the this-worldly: the dead body is a 'tabernacle' but not also a corpse; the graveyard is 'God's acre' but not also a burial ground. In order to continue with a text of this kind the reader must suspend his or her knowledge of the tension between the this-worldly and the other-worldly which is the ground of incarnation theology and the subject of more complex imaginative literature on death and the future life. In his description of the last judgment in *Yesterday, To-Day, and For Ever*, Bickersteth implicates the reader in a sense of exclusive Calvinist solidarity through the Seer's narrative in the first-person plural. With the benefit of a perfect view and perfect acoustics, the spectators at the last assize miss not a single detail. The privileged perspective of the Seer from his vantage point among the company of the saved at God's right hand is validated by the acquiescence in the faces of the damned which his gaze meets, and by their reinforcement of his sense of Christ as 'Almighty Love'. Indeed, this climactic justification of the ways of God to men dramatizes what has been present in the text from the beginning. For whereas the damned in hell (the 'Prison of the Lost') are truly in a liminal phase (humble, ground down, vulnerable, passengers uncertain of their destination after the '*unknown* wrath to come' (III.982; my emphasis), the blessed dead in paradise (Book II) are assured of God's purpose for them, and the Seer himself is provided with Oriel as a divine interpreter and guide on a safe journey which leads ever upwards towards unspeakable glory.

This imbalance in Bickersteth's depiction of the damned and the saved is maintained in his portrayal of the last judgment when he applies a favourite Victorian text (Revelation 7.17, 21.4) in an unusual way. The elect see that Christ weeps 'tears / Of grief and pity inexpressible' over the damned (890–1):

And straightway we remember'd who had wept
Over Jerusalem, and is the same
For ever as to-day and yesterday;
And in full sympathy of grief the springs
Gush'd forth within us; and the angels wept:
Till stooping from the throne with His own hand
He wiped the tears from every eye, and said,
'My Father's will be done; His will is Mine;
And Mine is yours: but mercy' [*sic*] is His delight,
And judgment is His strange and dreadful work.
Now it is done for ever. Come with me,
Ye blessed children of my Father, come;
And in the many mansions of His love
Enjoy the beams of His unclouded smile.' (892–905)

The familiar prophetic utterance, 'And God shall wipe away all tears from their eyes', normally taken to refer to the consoling of those who have come out of 'great tribulation', are here used to underline the continuity between 'us' and 'him', and between our will, his will, and the will of his Father in the unpleasant duty of dispatching the lost to everlasting torments. As time collapses ('the same / For ever as to-day and yesterday') so too do the defining (earthly) polarities of man and God. 'We' weep not for 'them', but for him whose will is also 'ours'. The reader is allowed no imaginative freedom within a closed soteriological system.

Christ then rises majestically towards the heaven of heavens, and the torments of a contrite Satan and the damned are described, again with reference to the power of the divine eyesight: 'His Eye, who is consuming fire, / Unintermittently abode on them' (XI.923–4). Book XI ends with a hymn of praise to God from the depths of hell: 'Glory to God who sitteth on the throne, / And to the Lamb for ever and for ever' (XI.1019–20). For the damned, God is 'there'. For the elect, in the words of the last line of the poem, 'God is here' (XII.653). The last book tells of 'our' final ascent, with Christ, to the 'Many Mansions' of the Father, where God is 'all in all' (XII.292). Interestingly, Bickersteth emphasizes that heaven is not static, and that not all its delights are revealed at once:

Hence they err'd, who taught
That in His presence faith and hope are lost
Who is the God of patience and of hope.
Things once invisible were visible;

> Things hoped for present: but beyond them all
> Illimitable fields untravelled lay . . .   (393–8)

Thus even in the final state of the saved there is a sense of anticipation of further bliss.

Although unorthodox in its millenarianism, Bickersteth's eschatology typifies in most other respects what Farrar called the 'common view': the 'vast majority of mankind' is condemned to everlasting punishment, and God is ultimately 'all in all' only to the saved. Whereas Pollok deploys narrative techniques such as suspense and repetition in order to foreground his own judgments on sinful man, Bickersteth uses the same techniques to emphasize the widening of the great gulf fixed between the saved and the damned under the providence of a loving God. Much of the intellectual energy of liberal theologians who wrote on eschatological subjects in the nineteenth century, such as F. D. Maurice and F. W. Farrar, was directed against this common view. In dedicating *Mercy and Judgment* to Tennyson, Farrar described him as the 'poet of "the larger hope"'. Hallam Tennyson's gloss on the famous phrase from *In Memoriam* (55) also describes the hopes of many other writers who, if not strictly universalist in their views, were at least sympathetic to that position: 'he means by "the larger hope" that the whole human race would through, perhaps, ages of suffering, be at length purified and saved'.[91]

Philip James Bailey's *Festus* (1839), the best known work by the 'Spasmodic School' of poets, was frankly universalist in its otherwise confused theology. The poem was admired, albeit with reservations, by several eminent contemporaries, including Tennyson, particularly after the appearance of the second edition in 1845.[92] The first, anonymous edition of Bailey's eccentric reworking of the Faust legend contained a little over 8,000 lines; the second, which was attributed, nearly 13,000; and the last – the eleventh (1901) – just under 40,000.[93] Although the numerous and increasingly redundant additions to the poem reflect changes in Bailey's conception, his theological position is always liberal:

> *Festus.*
> We dare to ask for all things in Thy name;
> We dare to pray for all that live or die.
> Man dies to man; but all to Thee, God, live.
> We pray Thee, therefore, for the general dead. . .[94]

In *Festus*, God is not 'all in all' only for the elect. Indeed, the kind of position taken by Pollok and Bickersteth is parodied by Bailey in the 'Market-place' scene, where Lucifer, assuming the role of a ranting Evangelical, preaches a sermon. 'Beginnings are alike', he declares, 'it is ends which differ', and he goes on (in a passage marked by Tennyson in his copy of the second edition)[95] to warn his listeners that they shall 'perish sudden and unsaved':

> The counsellor, wise fool!
> Drop down amid his quirks and sacred lies.
> The judge, while dooming unto death some wretch,
> Shall meet at once his own death, doom, and judge.
> The doctor, watch in hand and patient's pulse,
> Shall feel his own heart cease its beats – and fall.[96]

This reference to the judge prepares for Bailey's judgment scene at the end of the poem, as does Festus's lengthy public prayer which follows Lucifer's sermon, and which Bailey added in the second edition:

> for all,
> Quick, dead, we ask Thy boundless mercy, more
> Than all sin, all defect, as infinite
> O'erlaps all finites. But by us be none
> Condemned. Shall culprits take the Judge's seat?
> Christ's lesson of forgiveness mote not we
> Forget . . .

> To whom shall mercy hope deny?[97]

If Pollok's key word is 'sin', Bailey's is 'hope'.[98]

Whereas Pollok's and Bickersteth's epic poems are narrated from an other-worldly and post-mortem perspective, Bailey's poetic drama adopts a Goethean model in which earthly scenes ('A Mountain', 'A Metropolis', and so on) are interspersed with visits to other worlds ('A Better World', 'Heaven', 'Hell'). Significantly, however, the last scenes of *Festus*, which follow the death of the hero, conform to a pattern which is similar to those of the Evangelical epic writers. In the first of these final scenes, which is very brief and is set in 'The Skies', God dismisses Lucifer to Hades, 'there / To wait my will while the world's Sabbath lasts'.[99] Typically, Bailey devotes much more space (over forty pages in later editions) to the 'Angel World', in which the angels and saints praise God. This worship continues in 'The Millennial Earth', where Hope exclaims,

> How sweet, how sacred now, this earth of man's,
> The prelude of a yet sublimer bliss![100]

and the Archangel explains to Festus the nature of the intermediate state:

> God works by means. Between the two extremes
> Of earth and Heaven there lies a mediate state, –
> A pause between the lightning lapse of life
> And following thunders of eternity; –
> Between eternity and time a lapse,
> To soul unconscious, though agelasting, where
> Spirit is tempered to its final fate . . .[101]

This interpretation of the intermediate state would have met with the approval of Tennyson, F. D. Maurice, and F. W. Farrar, although they would have queried the soul's *unconscious* state. In the following scene, however, entitled 'Hades', Death's announcement that 'the end's at hand', his removal of Lucifer, the resurrection of the dead, and the Archangel's announcement that the 'general judgment is at hand' would seem to prepare for an orthodox ending.[102] Similarly, in 'Earth' the Angel reports the last battle against Lucifer.[103] It is in the Son of God's speech in 'The Judgment of Earth' that Bailey subverts the Evangelical position by substituting Matthew 7 ('Judge not, that ye be not judged') for Matthew 25 ('Depart from me, ye cursed, into everlasting fire'):

> *Son of God.* I come to repay sin with holiness,
> And death with immortality; man's soul
> With God's Spirit; all evil with all good.
> All men have sinned: and as for all I died,
> All men are saved. Oh! Not a single soul
> Less than the countless all can satisfy
> The infinite triumph which to me belongs,
> Who infinitely suffered. Ye elect!
> And all ye angels, with God's love informed,
> Who reign with me o'er earth and Heaven, assume
> Your seats of judgment. Judge ye all in love,
> The love which God the Father hath to you –
> For His Son's sake, and all shall be forgiven.[104]

The last judgment itself is not described. Instead, the scene ends on the Son of God's words:

> The Book of Life is opened. Heaven begins.

And the final scene ('The Heaven of Heavens') opens with Festus being saved:

> *The Recording Angel.* All men are judged save one.
> *Son of God.*   He too is saved.
> Immortal! I have saved thy soul to Heaven.
> Come hither.[105]

The future of the baffled Lucifer is then discussed, and God himself decrees his restoration:

> This day art thou
> Redeemed to archangelic state. Bright child
> Of morning, once again thou shinest fair
> O'er all the starry armaments of light.[106]

Thus in the final triumphal pages of the poem, God is proclaimed not only as 'all in all' but also as being for all:

> *Son of God.* Now all in all are one; and Deified
> All nature as in God.
> *Holy Ghost.*   God, all in all.
> *Son of God.* All God hath made are saved. Heaven is complete.
> *Angel of Earth.* Be glad, O world of worlds! Rejoice, all life,
> And mourn no more. Death, evil, suffering, cease.[107]

Where Bickersteth emphasizes the unity of God and his elect by showing the latter weeping in sympathy with Christ, Bailey includes all mankind, and thus all sinners, in an *eschaton* which could be described as the 'one far-off divine event, / To which the whole creation moves' (*In Memoriam*, Epilogue).

Bailey's *Festus*, first published in 1839, was very much a product of its time. The work that Bailey himself described as a 'dramatic poem' owed much to Byron, whose verse dramas have always enjoyed a higher reputation on the Continent than in Britain. *Festus* also appeared at the end of a decade which had witnessed a revival in (mainly historical) verse drama, with plays by Bulwer, Knowles, Landor, Talfourd, and Sir Henry Taylor. In retrospect, however, it is to Browning's contributions to this revival, in *Strafford* (1837) for example, that literary historians have turned with most interest, in order to chart the poet's development from the early, and unsuccessful experiments with a purely 'reading' drama to the dramatic monologue.[108] One aspect of that development –

the move towards experiential 'incarnations' of individual consciousnesses undergoing some kind of spiritual crisis – is of relevance here, with respect to nineteenth-century ideas on divine judgment. For in Browning's *Christmas-Eve and Easter-Day* (1850) we find a vision of judgment which differs radically from those in the extensive forms of the epic and the verse drama.

Whereas Pollok's, Bickersteth's, and Bailey's concepts of judgment are integral to their grandiose cosmological explanations of God's whole providential scheme, before, during, and after 'the course of *time*' (*chronos*), Browning's *Easter-Day*, which takes the form of a one-sided dialogue, turns upon a privileged moment of vision in an individual life at a specific time or 'season' (*kairos*) – the climax of the Christian year. Instead of Milton or Dante, Browning's precursors are St Augustine and Bunyan, perhaps the most influential writers of 'spiritual autobiography'. In both the *Confessions* and *Grace Abounding* the relationship between Christ and the individual sinner is direct, immediate, personal, and unique. In a famous passage from *Grace Abounding* (1666), for example, which recalls the New Testament accounts of the conversion of St Paul, Bunyan records a moment of revelation on the 'Sabbath-day' when God breaks into time suddenly, catastrophically, and unignorably:

> the same day, as I was in the midst of a game at Cat, and having struck it one blow from the Hole, just as I was about to strike it the second time, a Voice did suddenly dart from Heaven into my Soul, which said, *Wilt thou leave thy sins and go to Heaven, or have thy sins and go to Hell?* At this I was put to an exceeding Maze. Wherefore, leaving my Cat upon the ground, I looked up to Heaven, and was as if I had, with the Eyes of my understanding, seen the Lord Jesus looking down upon me, as being very hotly displeased with me, and as if he did severely threaten me with some grievous Punishment for these and other my ungodly Practices.[109]

The impact of the 'crisis-autobiography', and particularly the *Confessions*, on English Romantic literature is central to M. H. Abrams's argument in *Natural Supernaturalism* (1971).[110] Victorian autobiographical and pseudo-autobiographical writing shares the same inheritance. Tennyson's lyric 95 in *In Memoriam*, for example – 'By night we linger'd on the lawn' – can be read in relation to a mystical tradition which came down from Augustine.[111] Teufelsdröckh's account of his spiritual crisis in Carlyle's *Sartor Resartus* (1833–4) represents a more radical revision of the spiritual autobiography in the *absence* of the divine 'voice', and the professor's consequent reliance upon the self and the will. As in Tennyson's roughly contemporary 'Supposed Confessions' (1830), this absence is registered in the subjunctive mode:

Had a divine Messenger from the clouds, or miraculous Handwriting on the wall, convincingly proclaimed to me *This thou shalt do*, with what passionate readiness, as I often thought, would I have done it, had it been leaping into the infernal Fire . . .

To me the Universe was all void of Life, of Purpose, of Volition, even of Hostility . . .

Full of such humour . . . was I, one sultry Dog-day, after much perambulation, toiling along the dirty little *Rue Saint-Thomas de l'Enfer* . . . when, all at once, there rose a Thought in me, and I asked myself: 'What *art* thou afraid of? . . . Well, Death; and say the pangs of Tophet too, and all that the Devil and Man may, will or can do against thee! . . . Let it come, then; I will meet it and defy it!' And as I so thought, there rushed like a stream of fire over my whole soul; and I shook base Fear away from me forever.[112]

Carlyle's treatment of 'The Everlasting No' would have been of interest to Browning, not only as an account of the purging of Calvinist paranoia in a 'Baphometic Fire-baptism', but also in its narrative technique, whereby personal experience is mediated through the two filters of the Teufelsdrockh persona and the Editor persona.[113] Like Carlyle and Tennyson, Browning understood the kind of Protestant tradition in which dreams and visions, and prophetic voices and writings were taken to be admonitory signs of the imminent danger of being judged and found wanting on the last day. All three writers adapt apocalyptic language and conventions to their own specific purposes. Browning, however, moved and influenced by the nonconformist piety of both his wife and his mother (who had recently died),[114] is in *Christmas-Eve and Easter-Day* unusually direct in his treatment of the Christian faith and sympathetic towards Evangelical doctrine.[115]

In the first poem, *Christmas-Eve*, the speaker tells how he came to witness the different responses of three religious traditions to the mystery of the incarnation. First, having hovered 'irresolute' in the porch, 'Partitioned off from the vast inside' (line 18), he joins the strange assortment of frail humanity who make up the 'elect' of Mount Zion chapel. Unable, however, to listen patiently to the dissenting 'preaching man's immense stupidity' (144), he escapes to the freedom of the common where, in his 'own church' of nature (272), the sudden appearance of a moon-rainbow in the sky heralds a firsthand encounter with Christ himself: 'All at once I looked up with terror. / He was there' (430–1). Christ then takes him to see the midnight mass at St Peter's in Rome, but he finds himself 'left outside the door', sitting 'on the threshold-stone' (596–7). Again, while the Straussian 'hawk-nosed high-cheek-boned Professor' delivers his Christmas-Eve discourse in Göttingen, he is left 'Alone, beside the entrance-door' (784). The speaker eventually finds himself back in the chapel again, having in reality fallen asleep and dreamt during the sermon (1238–45). An outsider in Rome and Göttingen, and, as he believed, in Mount Zion, he discovers that he has in fact been inside all the time. For all the limitations of dissent, he can now affirm, 'I choose here!' (1341), and the poem ends with his putting up his pencil and joining the congregation in a hymn, thus marking his membership through a communal act of worship.

Like Bunyan in the middle of his game of cat and Tennyson seated alone in the garden at night, the speaker in *Christmas-Eve* is transported – freed from the limits of space and time in a moment of spiritual crisis. Having crossed the threshold of organized religion, he is open to an unmediated 'Vision' which he can claim to be 'true', and in which he encounters the Christ who is 'Very man and very God' (586). When he has effected the transition from outsider to insider he can see that Christ is indeed present where two or three are gathered together, and that the 'veil' which conceals him from sight is thin even where the human material which embodies his Church is least physically attractive:

> I then, in ignorance and weakness,
> Taking God's help, have attained to think
>   My heart does best to receive in meekness
> That mode of worship, as most to his mind,
> Where earthly aids being cast behind,
> His All in All appears serene
> With the thinnest human veil between,
> Letting the mystic lamps, the seven,
>   The many motions of his spirit,
> Pass, as they list, to earth from heaven.   (1301–10)

What the speaker describes in *Christmas-Eve* is his passage through a classic liminal phase: he moves from the threshold of Mount Zion chapel (cf. Revelation 14.1) to membership of its elect via a vision which reduces him to a state of ignorance, weakness, and meekness. The function of the vision in such a passage is familiar to readers of the great mystics: it is theophanic rather than epiphanic.[116] The unmediated personal encounter with God, the emphasis laid upon making a decision for Christ, and the rejection of rationalism in favour of the leap of faith are also strongly reminiscent of Browning's contemporary, Kierkegaard, as Philip Drew has shown.[117] William De Vane rightly argues that the revelation of divine love in the life and death of Christ links *Christmas-Eve* and *Easter-Day*.[118] Equally important, however, is the shared theme of the (Kierkegaardian) paradox of incarnation, which in *Easter-Day* is conveyed through an apocalyptic vision of judgment.

The main speaker in *Easter-Day* makes the poem's central statement in the opening lines: 'How very hard it is to be / A Christian!' Having developed this theme in conversation with his more shadowy 'easy Christian' interlocutor, he prepares to relate a 'dread' event – an encounter with God which, he implies, is as 'solemn' and 'strange' as Moses's on Sinai:

> I still
> Stand in the cloud and, while it wraps
> My face, ought not to speak perhaps;
> Seeing that if I carry through
> My purpose, if my words in you
> Find a live actual listener,
> My story, reason must aver
> False after all – the happy chance!   (350–7)

Three years ago this Easter-night he crossed 'The common, where the chapel was, / Our friend spoke of, the other day' (374–5). Turning over in his mind the kind of problem he has just been discussing, he asked himself a question that would not be out of place in *Grace Abounding*:

> 'How were my case, now, did I fall
> Dead here, this minute – should I lie
> Faithful or faithless?'   (396–8)

Behind this question lies a biblical text that was often cited in nineteenth-century eschatological debates: 'if the tree fall toward the south, or toward the north, in the place where the tree falleth, there it shall be' (Ecclesiastes 11.3). Newman, for example, refers to the text in the *Essay on Development* when discussing what Coleridge and Farrar deprecated as the 'wresting of texts':

In religious questions a single text of Scripture is all-sufficient with most people
. . . to prove a doctrine or a duty in cases when a custom is established or a
tradition is strong . . . 'Where the tree falleth, there shall it lie,' shows that our
probation ends with life.[119]

That our probation ends with life is to be a central theme in *Easter-Day*.

For the moment, however, the speaker relates how he merely toyed
with such profound matters as the contingency of mortal life, the wish
that 'God's kingdom come', and the possibility that that time or season
(*kairos*) might coincide with Easter:

> And it shall dawn, that day,
> Some future season; Easter may
> Prove, not impossibly, the time –
> Yes, that were striking – fates would chime
> So aptly! Easter-morn, to bring
> The Judgement!   (461–6)

In putting flesh on his idle speculations, the speaker playfully adopts the
kind of traditional apocalyptic language beloved of Robert Pollok and
E. H. Bickersteth: the skylark, 'taken by surprise', shall 'recognize /
Sudden the end' (471–3); '"At night it cometh like a thief"' (476); 'I
fancy why the trumpet blows' (477); and so on. But one of his ideas
suggests a further parallel between Browning, the mystics, and Kierkegaard – the 'father of Existentialism':

> From repose
> We shall start up, at last awake
> From life, that insane dream we take
> For waking now, because it seems.   (478–81)

At the very moment, however, in which he dismissed this train of
thought (which had finally led him into childhood reminiscences) it was
authenticated in an outward and visible form:

> And as I said
> This nonsense, throwing back my head
> With light complacent laugh, I found
> Suddenly all the midnight round
> One fire . . .
>
>   Sudden there went,
> Like horror and astonishment,

> A fierce vindictive scribble of red
> Quick flame across, as if one said
> (The angry scribe of Judgment) 'There –
> Burn it!'   (501–14)

When he felt the 'Judgement-Day' begin, he knew that he could not go back: 'There, stood I, found and fixed, I knew, / Choosing the world. The choice was made' (552–3). In his own defence he pointed out that to have rejected utterly the world in all its beauty would have been 'too hard' (575), but in a final universal conflagration a voice beside him said:

> 'Life is done,
> Time ends, Eternity's begun,
> And thou art judged for evermore.'   (594–6)

He looked up, saw only the common and the sky as before, and tried to dismiss the 'waking dream' (609) by recalling that not all the features of the last judgment described in the Revelation had been present: 'And where had place the great white throne? / The rising of the quick and dead?' (615–16). As in *Christmas-Eve*, however, an unmediated vision of God himself silenced all doubts:

> HE stood there. Like the smoke
> Pillared o'er Sodom, when day broke, –
> I saw Him . . .
>
> Motionless, thus, He spoke to me,
> Who fell before His feet, a mass,
> No man now.   (640–55)

God reminded the speaker that in the 'probation' that is mortal life he had chosen the world of his own free will, and that now, 'Judgement done', he could have the world but was 'shut / Out of the heaven of spirit' (696–7). In a radical reversal of the 'threshold' theme in *Christmas-Eve*, God said of the world:

> 'Expend
> Eternity upon its shows,
> Flung thee as freely as one rose
> Out of a summer's opulence,
> Over the Eden-barrier whence
> Thou art excluded. Knock in vain!'   (729–34)

Again the speaker found himself on the common, and consoled himself, first with the thought that nature's delights are inexhaustible, then those of art, and then those of the mind. The 'voice', however, unsettled him by saying that the earth is only 'God's antechamber' (752), while 'royalties' are in store 'one step past the entrance-door' (754–5), and that all 'displays / Of power and beauty intermixed' are merely 'needful furniture / For life's first stage' (816–20). Finally, the speaker acknowledged his error:

> 'Behold, my spirit bleeds,
> Catches no more at broken reeds, –
> But lilies flower those reeds above:
> I let the world go, and take love!'   (931–4)

He cowered before God, pleading to be allowed to go on, 'Still hoping ever and anon / To reach one eve the Better Land!' (1002–3), and, after a final revelation of divine love, 'lived again' in the Easter dawn on the common. As in most mystical experiences, his first thought was to dismiss the vision as a mere dream. Three years later, however, and back in the poem's narrative present, his closing comments leave the question open:

> 'Condemned to earth for ever, shut
> From heaven!'
>   But Easter-Day breaks! But
> Christ rises! Mercy every way
> Is infinite, – and who can say?   (1037–40)

Whereas Pollok adopts a narrative device whereby 'the course of time' is viewed retrospectively from the privileged (other-worldly) perspective of heaven, Browning's *Easter-Day* begins and ends within the (this-worldly) horizon of the present. From an opening statement of difficulty and limitation, however – 'How very hard it is to be / A Christian' – the speaker has moved back in time through a retrospective narrative, to return to a changed present in which continued uncertainty ('and who can say?') is held in tension with a truth claim ('Christ rises') which, being both specific and universal, of this time and of all eternity, is as all-embracing as the epic scope of Bickersteth's title: *Yesterday, To-Day, and For Ever*. But unlike in Bickersteth's poem, that truth claim has been worked for in the text. Within the narrative past, an apocalypse enacted in the name of divine love precipitated the speaker into a liminal phase from which he emerged in a new state of knowledge.[120] The speaker's former defensive rhetorical strategies, whereby God was kept at bay and his judgment deferred to a distant end-time ('it shall dawn, that day, / Some future season'), reserved as only a possibility ('How were my case, now, did I fall'), or ironized ('This nonsense'), were dissolved in the simple present of a vision in which the 'season' was now: 'thou art judged for evermore'. The teleological is displaced by the immanent, *chronos* disrupted by *kairos*. It is only, of course, in the recalled present (which in this-worldly terms is past, absent) that the full presence of God is described. The collapse, however, of temporal categories at the end of the poem releases the concept of divine judgment from the teleological limit of 'last' into the immanent 'present' of life as a period of probation or a 'preparatory state'.

Both *Christmas-Eve* and *Easter-Day*, then, describe moments of choice in a spiritual crisis. Only in the latter poem, however, are the several meanings of *krisis* – separation, judgment, turning-point – brought into ironic interplay. In *Christmas-Eve* an ambiguous vision reveals some of the disturbing paradoxes of the kingdom.[121] *Easter-Day* is even more challenging, drawing upon a Protestant tradition of authority in which the individual has direct access to the divine, and yet mediating its vision of judgment through the indeterminate form of narrative recollection. Most modern critics of Browning have found these transitional 'problem poems' an embarrassment, and have gratefully moved on to the securer ground of *Men and Women*.[122] One of the first reviewers of *Christmas-Eve and Easter-Day* has thus been proved wrong in his prophecy that, although essentially different from *In Memoriam*, which was published in the same year (1850), they were 'both destined to an earthly immortality'.[123] Read as a linked pair of mid-nineteenth-century crisis poems, however, they are central rather than marginal works.

FICTION AND THE SENSE OF AN ENDING

For those mid-Victorian critics who emphasized the moral function of fiction, the authorial narrator was a God-like judge within the realist novel's horizon of the this-worldly, who not only proposed but also disposed through the deaths of characters and through narrative endings.[124] The concluding chapter of Trollope's *The Warden* (1855) – a one-volume novel – begins in a self-conscious manner that is reminiscent of Jane Austen:

Our tale is now done, and it only remains to us to collect the scattered threads of our little story, and to tie them into a seemly knot. This will not be a work of labour, either to the author or to his readers; we have not to deal with many personages, or with stirring events, and were it not for the custom of the thing, we might leave it to the imagination of all concerned to conceive how affairs at Barchester arranged themselves.   (21)

While promising closure here, the authorial narrator shared with the contemporary reader the embarrassment of ending, although that reader was not to know that a sequel was in prospect. In the previous chapter, the narrator declares of Archdeacon Grantly that 'we have seen only the weak side of the man', and thus prepares the ground for the character to be developed in a more complex way in later novels. Mr Harding and his friends are not declared fictionally dead or brought to judgment at the end of *The Warden*; rather they are left in a kind of limbo, from which they are later to be rescued in *Barchester Towers*.

   In *The Last Chronicle of Barset* (1866–7), however, some kind of last judgment is appropriate, and it takes the form of 'dealing' with various characters in their dying. Deliberately to die standing up, as Patrick Brontë did for example, can signify stoic fortitude or stubborn wilfulness. Mrs Proudie's grotesque sudden death, however – she is found standing with one arm clasped round a bed-post, the mouth rigidly closed, the eyes open and apparently staring (66: 'Requiescat in Pace') – represents in a final tableau her ultimate isolation from her husband the Bishop, with whom she has just had a distressing argument. Dying at the margin of the site in which, it is hinted in an earlier novel, she dominated her husband, Mrs Proudie provides a foil against which Mr Harding's peaceful deathbed scene can be written towards the end of the novel. With those he loved alongside him, he 'seemed to sleep' near the end, and finally 'he was praying' (81). Mrs Proudie's funeral is not described. Mr Harding's represents the ideal easy transition from deathbed to grave:

They buried him in the cathedral which he had loved so well . . . and all Barchester was there to see him laid in his grave within the cloisters. There was no procession of coaches, no hearse, nor was there any attempt at funereal pomp. From the dean's side door, across the vaulted passage, and into the transept, – over the little step upon which he had so nearly fallen when last he made his way out of the building, – the coffin was carried on men's shoulders. It was but a short journey from his bedroom to his grave.

Whateley's strictures upon the popular idea of the 'happy death' were based upon the perception that it was unscriptural.[125] For the novelist, however, working in a secular form, it provided excellent material.

Turning to overt references to post-mortem judgment in Victorian fiction, we find in Thackeray's novels, which Trollope much admired, that the death of a character can draw the reader into a recognition of a shared and fallen humanity. Old Sedley in *Vanity Fair* (1847–8) dies a broken man, supported by his daughter Amelia who is comforted by her father's 'resignation, and his future hope' (61). To die in debt, 'helpless and humble', praying for forgiveness 'with a contrite heart, at the feet of the Divine Mercy', is a 'better ending' than that of the worldly, the prosperous, and the famous. The sense of a common humanity which will finally come into the divine presence is also foregrounded at the end of *The Newcomes*, where three generations of the family pray together before the little boy is – in an ambiguous phrase – 'laid to rest' for the night (41). Old Colonel Newcome's day is approaching 'when he should be drawn to the bosom of the Eternal Pity', and in the following and final chapter of the novel his death at Grey Friars, his old school, is described in schoolboy terms:

At the usual evening hour the chapel bell began to toll, and Thomas New-come's hands outside the bed feebly beat time. And just as the last bell struck, a peculiar sweet smile shone over his face, and he lifted up his head a little, and quickly said, 'Adsum!' and fell back. It was the word we used at school, when names were called; and lo, he, whose heart was as that of a little child, had answered to his name, and stood in the presence of The Master.

Thackeray's emphasis upon God's mercy and pity in his references to the future life is typical of the major Victorian novelists, who were all liberal or agnostic on the question of divine judgment. The more extreme liberal views, however, could raise difficulties for the novelist, who was expected to 'judge' characters. Elizabeth Gaskell, for example, as a Unitarian who did not believe in hell or the last judgment, was criticized for her failure finally to condemn even her more reprehensible characters. (I discuss *Mary Barton* and hell in Chapter 4.) Dickens, like Thackeray, often exploits the tension between Christian values and those worldly values upon which many aspects of Victorian plotting are based, such as ownership, land, power, and physical attractiveness. At Magwitch's trial, for example, the divide between the 'innocent' and the 'guilty', the 'judge' and the 'criminal' is dissolved in a reference to the 'greater Judgement that knoweth all things and cannot err' (*Great Expectations*, 56). Trials in courts of law figure in many novels, including *Paul Clifford*, *Pickwick Papers*, *Bleak House*, *Mary Barton*, *Alton Locke*, and *Felix Holt*. In most cases a critique of the law serves to strengthen the authority of the novelist; and even where characters are handed over to the higher authority of divine mercy, as in Dickens and Thackeray, a large measure of authorial control is in play.

The whole project of serious fiction in the early- and mid-Victorian periods is judgmental, both of individuals and of the society in which they live and die. The rejection of this moral function of fiction in later generations of novelists is reflected in the handling of the biblical language of judgment, and particularly from the Revelation. Whereas in *Hard Times* (1854) Dickens's use of apocalyptic symbolism is as central to his vision as Blake's or John Martin's, Hardy's ironic reference to a 'Last Day luridness' in the confession scene in *Tess of the d'Urbervilles* (1891; 34) is as marginal as the teaching of the church itself to the novel's judgment of Tess as 'A Pure Woman'. Samuel Butler's revisionary account of English religious practice in *The Way of all Flesh* (1903) was written mainly in the 1870s, soon after the publication of *Middlemarch* and the last major revival of millenarian expectation in England. Overton, the narrator, recalls how things were back in 1811, when the bell tolled for old Mrs Pontifex and his nurse terrified him by saying that he too could be struck with paralysis and 'taken straight off to the Day of Judgment':

The Day of Judgment indeed, according to the opinion of those who were most likely to know, would not under any circumstances be delayed more than a few years longer, and then the whole world would be burned, and we ourselves be consigned to an eternity of torture, unless we mended our ways more than we at present seemed at all likely to do . . .

. . . we were astonished to find that Napoleon Buonaparte was an actually living person. We had thought such a great man could only have lived a very long time ago, and here he was after all almost as it were at our own doors. This lent colour to the view that the Day of Judgment might indeed be nearer than we had thought, but nurse said that was all right now, and she knew.   (3)

Theobald Pontifex, who comforts a dying and frightened old woman by informing her that she will be 'lost' if she doubts that 'we shall all appear before the Judgment Seat of Christ, and that the wicked will be consumed in a lake of everlasting fire' (15), is himself brought to another kind of (Butleresque) judgment when his wife Christina is dying and, being afraid of the day of judgment, seems to question his efficacy as a clergyman (83). In Ernest Pontifex's final rejection of his parents' narrow Evangelical religion, Butler represents his own, and the century's coming of age.

Returning, however, to the mid-century period in which many writers of the former generation – including Tennyson, Browning, Dickens, the Brontës, and Ruskin – were producing their most significant work, and in which the influence of Carlyle's prophetic writings was probably at its height, we find that the language of apocalypse is an aspect of their shared culture and a potent force in their writing. For Romantic novelists, such as Dickens, and Charlotte and Emily Brontë, the language of the Revelation was an aspect of their 'poetry'.

One of the main limitations of realist fiction in the nineteenth century was that, unlike the heavenly spectators in Evangelical epic poems, for example, narrators could not penetrate the veil which separates 'this side' from 'that side': even their so-called 'omniscience' is restricted to time and space. Yet many of the key passages in realist Victorian fiction are precisely those in which the gradual uncovering of events in an orderly and chronological sequence in the narrative is displaced by the kind of catastrophist structures and language normally associated with Romantic forms such as the Gothic novel or the 'sensation' novel. George Eliot's sensational treatment of the Bulstrode/Raffles plot in *Middlemarch*, for example, is reminiscent of Dickens or Charlotte Brontë in its demonstration that at moments of crisis, when a man is judged, the reality of a concealed past is illuminated with an unrelieved, unaccustomed, and lurid brilliance. Furthermore, as in experiential or confessional poetry in which the horizon is ostensibly this-worldly, such moments of stress or fracture in the narrative can also allow the other-worldly to be issued in, usually through visionary or some other spiritual experience. It is, however, in the romances of Charlotte and Emily Brontë that this 'vertical' dimension of narrative is exploited most fully, and the theme of judgment explored.

The third and final volume of *Jane Eyre* (1847), for example, which is to focus upon last things, begins with Jane's internal dialogue after the wedding fiasco: 'What am I to do? . . . Leave Thornfield at once' (27). It is not until the end of this chapter, however, in which Rochester gives his account of his married life with Bertha Mason in the 'bottomless pit' of hell (Revelation 9.1), and tries to persuade Jane to live with him on the Mediterranean, that a visionary figure directs her to leave Thornfield:

I dreamt I lay in the red-room at Gateshead . . . The light that long ago had struck me into syncope, recalled in this vision, seemed glidingly to mount the wall, and tremblingly to pause in the centre of the obscured ceiling. I lifted up my head to look: the roof resolved to clouds, high and dim; the gleam was such as the moon imparts to vapours she is about to sever. I watched her come – watched with the strangest anticipation; as though some word of doom were to be written on her disk. She broke forth as never moon yet burst from cloud: a hand first penetrated the sable folds and waved them away; then, not a moon, but a white human form shone in the azure, inclining a glorious brow earthward. It gazed and gazed on me. It spoke, to my spirit: immeasurably distant was the tone, yet so near, it whispered in my heart –

'My daughter, flee temptation!'

'Mother, I will.'

So I answered after I had waked from the trance-like dream.

Unlike the moon-rainbow in Browning's *Christmas-Eve*, which heralds the subsequent appearance of Christ beside the speaker, this moon resolves itself into a figure who represents the 'feminine principle' in the novel, and who is akin to the Great Mother, the lunar goddess of pagan religions.

Having escaped from Thornfield and the threatening male domination of Rochester, Jane is 'as hard beset' by his polar opposite, St John Rivers, whose reading of Revelation 21 has a powerful influence upon her:

never did his manner become so impressive in its noble simplicity, as when he delivered the oracles of God; and to-night that voice took a more solemn tone – that manner a more thrilling meaning – as he sat in the midst of his household circle (the May moon shining in through the uncurtained window, and rendering almost unnecessary the light of the candle on the table): as he sat there, bending over the great old Bible, and described from its page the vision of the new heaven and the new earth – told how God would come to dwell with men, how he would wipe away all tears from their eyes, and promised that there should be no more death, neither sorrow nor crying, nor any more pain, because the former things were passed away.   (35)

Rivers, a more intelligent Evangelical than Brocklehurst, implicitly repeats the warnings of that earlier oppressor as he subtly directs at her the verse on the 'lake which burneth with fire and brimstone, which is the second death'. In the prayers that follow, he claims 'the boon of a brand snatched from the burning', and then lays his hand on Jane's head:

> I stood motionless under my hierophant's touch. My refusals were forgotten – my fears overcome – my wrestlings paralyzed. The Impossible – *i.e.* my marriage with St. John – was fast becoming the Possible. All was changing utterly, with a sudden sweep. Religion called – Angels beckoned – God commanded – life rolled together like a scroll – death's gates opened, shewed eternity beyond: it seemed, that for safety and bliss there, all here might be sacrificed in a second. The dim room was full of visions.

Jane's temporary submission to St John is marked by her entry into his own religious discourse and mute acceptance of his eschatology. As the candle dies out, however, and the moon floods with moonlight, her own prayers are answered by Rochester's cry. Escaping from the house, and also from St John's discourse, she interprets the cry as 'no miracle', but 'the work of nature', and seems to penetrate 'very near a Mighty Spirit' when she hurries upstairs to pray in a 'different way' from St John's.

Jane Eyre re-enters St John's discourse, but now as the narrator, in the last paragraphs of a 'Conclusion' which has promised closure in its famous opening: 'Reader, I married him.' While she and a chastised Rochester (he thanks the God who 'judges not as man judges') find an earthly paradise in family life, Jane anticipates for St John the inevitable end for the missionary in India, and the equally certain reward:

His is the ambition of the high master-spirit, which aims to fill a place in the first rank of those who are redeemed from the earth – who stand without fault before the throne of God; who share the last mighty victories of the lamb; who are called, and chosen, and faithful.

. . . No fear of death will darken St. John's last hour: his mind will be unclouded; his heart will be undaunted; his hope will be sure; his faith steadfast. His own words are a pledge of this: –

'My Master,' he says, 'has forewarned me. Daily he announces more distinctly, – "Surely I come quickly;" and hourly I more eagerly respond, – "Amen; even so come, Lord Jesus!"'

Jane Eyre ends with St John Rivers's 'last words', which are almost the last words in the Bible (Revelation 22.20). In a work of contraries – between novel and romance, spiritual autobiography and Gothic fiction, Evangelicalism and Byronic excess – two kinds of final judgment are held in tension in this Conclusion: a this-worldly ending for Jane Eyre and Rochester which promises male–female equipoise in an earthly future life, and an other-worldly ending for St John which anticipates his dying into eternal life with Christ.

Wuthering Heights, published in the same year as *Jane Eyre* and drawing on similar materials at several points, is more radical in its treatment of traditional teaching on the last judgment. Lockwood's first nightmare in the coffin bed at the Heights is uncannily similar to Browning's *Christmas-Eve*. This dream draws upon Lockwood's reading of the young Cathy's diary, inscribed in a book of sermons, where she describes her and Heathcliff's Sunday services under the direction of the fanatical Calvinist, Joseph, who provided them with books on 'Th' Helmet uh Salvation' and 'T' Broad Way to Destruction' (3). But Lockwood, too, like Nelly Dean before him, is strongly judgmental in his initial response to the inhabitants of the Heights, including the child ghost who visits him in his second dream, and this characteristic, together with his physical and psychological disorientation and his sexual anxieties, is reflected in the paranoid first nightmare. The last words he reads, however, before falling asleep, are the title of Jabes Branderham's sermon on 'Seventy Times Seven, and the First of the Seventy-First' (Matthew 18.22), which Branderham (a brand plucked from the burning?) preaches in the Chapel of Gimmerden Sough in the dream. As Trollope reminds his readers in *Barchester Towers* (6), those who attend a church service are trapped during the sermon, and have to hear it out. Lockwood is 'condemned' to hear Jabes interpret Christ's teaching on forgiveness as if there had been no new dispensation and he were preaching the old Jewish law, until he reaches the *'First of the Seventy-First'*. At this 'crisis', Lockwood 'denounces' Branderham, who in turn 'accuses' him with the words of Nathan to the adulterous David:

'Thou art the Man!' . . . Brethren, execute upon him the judgment written! Such honour have all His saints!

The rapping of the pilgrim staves in the battle that ensues is resolved into the rapping of a branch on the window, which is to resolve itself again into the ghost's tapping as Lockwood drifts back into sleep.

Unlike Browning's linked poems and *Jane Eyre*, this judgment dream deconstructs itself, revealing its sources – both theological and psychological – as it is narrated. Whereas Jane Eyre and Browning's speakers hold in tension a vision of divine judgment and a sense of earthly

limitation, Lockwood's dream is self-reflexive, like the retrospective narrative which it precedes and which is to make up the bulk of the novel.
Its language of judgment – 'condemned', 'crisis', 'execute', and so on –
and the participation of the 'saints' in the act of judgment, are other-
worldly counters in a dream of a this-worldly event. The effect of this
and the second dream on the subsequent narrative is similar to that of
Cathy's dreams, as she describes it to Nelly Dean: 'they've gone through
and through me, like wine through water, and altered the colour of my
mind' (9). Like Lockwood's, the dream that she presses upon an unwilling listener, in which she finds that heaven is not her 'home' and that she
is expelled like the fallen angels, back to her beloved moors,
deconstructs itself as it reverses the oracles of religion. These disruptions
of 'normal' behaviour and judgment, of course, prepare for the famous
and much debated ending of the novel, where Lockwood passes a now
delapidated kirk to examine the gravestones on the edge of the moors,
and to say over them: 'I . . . wondered . . . how anyone could ever
imagine unquiet slumbers for the sleepers in that quiet earth' (34). Like
Nelly's earlier attempts to understand Cathy and Heathcliff, Lockwood's analysis falls short of the revisionary nature of their idea of
heaven. Caught up in the bonds of orthodox judgmental thinking, he
cannot comprehend how they have transcended both death and judgment. Here, surely, is one explanation for the failure of most contemporary critics to understand the radical indeterminacy of *Wuthering
Heights*, although many acknowledged its strange power. Like Nelly
Dean and Lockwood, but most especially Joseph, critics generally
assumed that Heathcliff was damned.[126]

Of the ninety-nine English translations of the hymn Dies Irae made
between 1621 and 1895, eighty-eight are dated after 1800.[127] *Wuthering
Heights*, like the other novels and poems I have been considering, was
written in a period in which God's wrath and the possibility of imminent
judgment were central to orthodox Christian teaching, and were widely
accepted commonplaces of popular belief. They were also the subject of
debate. The Victorian novel, a fundamentally secular form, engaged in
this debate, most obviously in the portrayal of characters such as Joseph
or St John Rivers. The Brontës' special significance, however, lies in the
fact that, like Browning, they also drew upon literary traditions in which
spiritual *experience* is conveyed through dreams and visions. Reference
has been made to Augustine and Bunyan as precursors, but both the

Divine Comedy and *Paradise Lost* (to which Pollok and Bickersteth were indebted), are also 'visions'. And behind all of these is the Revelation itself:

> I was in the Spirit on the Lord's day, and heard behind me a great voice, as of a trumpet,
>
> Saying, I am Alpha and Omega, the first and the last: and, What thou seest, write in a book, and send it unto the seven churches which are in Asia . . .
>
> And I turned to see the voice that spake with me. And being turned, I saw seven golden candlesticks . . .   (Revelation 1.10–12)

Like the speaker in Browning's *Easter-Day*, Jane Eyre lifts up her head, sees, and then hears. In both cases the vision is conveyed within a dream, although, unlike in *Wuthering Heights*, where Lockwood remains an inadequate exegete, both figures enter a new state of knowledge through these apocalypses. Whereas the large structures of the epic poem allowed Pollok and Bickersteth to attempt a cosmological explanation of God's judgment upon man through time, the novel and the crisis poem proved to be better vehicles for more provisional and experiential visions of judgment in the nineteenth century.

CHAPTER 3

Heaven

Holy, Holy, Holy! all the Saints adore Thee,
  Casting down their golden crowns around the glassy sea;
Cherubim and Seraphim falling down before Thee,
  Which wert, and art, and evermore shalt be.
Bishop Heber (1826)[1]

Divine judgment, the subject of the last chapter, is perceived in the nineteenth century as process, either cosmically, as part of a providential plan for mankind which is to be fulfilled in the last days, or experientially, via unmediated moments of *krisis* (both turning-point and separation/judgment). In the former case, judgment is enacted in, through, and at the end of time. Features of the formalized rites of passage associated with the dying process, such as deferral, anticipation, and hopeful expectation, also characterize the process of judgment and the movement towards the final or fixed state. Other kinds of liminal experience too, such as intimations of judgment where a figure is taken out of this-worldly limits into an other-worldly state and precipitated back to the this-worldly, are described as journeys, but in a 'vertical' dimension. Although often problematic as a subject for the writer, either theologically or in terms of the numinous quality of visionary experience, judgment is narratable as process or journey.

Heaven comes into the picture as the reward of the blessed; it is the goal, the fulfilment, the consummation of the Christian's 'lively hope'. The writer of 1 Peter refers to 'an inheritance incorruptible . . . reserved [*tetērēmenēn*: lit. having been kept] in heaven [*ouranois*: lit. heavens] for you, Who are kept [*phrouroumenous*: lit. being guarded] by the power of God through faith unto salvation ready to be revealed in the last time' (1.4–5). For the Jewish mind, the commentators remind us, endings are inextricably associated with beginnings. Thus 'when the Jew wished to designate something as predestined, he spoke of it as already existing in heaven', and the perfect tense in verse 4 'brings out the thought that the custody of the inheritance has been from all time'.[2] E. H. Bickersteth wrote in his commentary on the New Testament: 'This heritage – which is nothing less than the fruition of the favour of God for ever, in his likeness, in his service, in his presence – is safely stored in the heavens for the saints.'[3] Such an inheritance, however, reserved in heaven for some, implies the exclusion of others, and we have seen how in *Yesterday, To-Day, and For Ever*, for example, Bickersteth involves the risen saints in the judgment of the lost.

All this is suggestive of completion and narrative closure. Heaven is a place or a state (which, is a matter of debate) rather than a process; and, being a final place or state with traditional eirenic associations, it is often thought of in static rather than dynamic terms. Heaven is sometimes defined as or characterized by the beatific vision of the deity, which is in itself unnarratable. Another model of heaven is as a place of everlasting songs of praise, where saints 'cast down their golden crowns'. Here again, the subject does not lend itself readily to narrative, although it has lyrical possibilities. Both major movements in the religious revival of the early nineteenth century – Evangelicalism and Tractarianism – developed a typological understanding of heaven as the eternal sabbath; as the future blessedness of which holiness in this life is an earnest; as the eucharistic feast of which the worshipper has a foretaste in this life. And in their hymns – the most enduring and widely familiar form of Victorian lyric verse to this day – heaven is treated as a transcendant spiritual dimension rather than a projection of earthly desires.

Although there are potential contradictions between heaven as beatific vision and heaven as worship,[4] for example, all the models mentioned so far are theocentric, and emphasize both the eternal nature of the church as the body of Christ and the continuity of the kingdom 'from this world to the next'. Other models, however, are anthropocentric, and stress the continuity of personal identity and thus of interpersonal relationships. As Colleen McDannell and Bernhard Lang have shown, from the mid eighteenth century, when Swedenborg began to record his visions of heaven and hell, the anthropocentric heaven of human love and spiritual progress steadily gained ground on the more static theocentric heaven which had been in the ascendant in Western European theology since the Reformation.[5] Perhaps the most characteristic Victorian ideas of heaven are of a place in which family reunions and 'the recognition of friends' are to be achieved after death, and (more radically Romantic) of a site in which lovers are reunited as couples. Worked upon by imaginations less powerful than Blake's, such heavens are often more like a middle-class suburb in the sky than the city of God; less like the mystical marriage of Christ with his church than the consummation of erotic desire in an idealized form of safe sex. It is not difficult to see why such individualistic and exclusive heavens were scorned as pie-in-the-sky by working-class radicals in the social-problem novels of the period, and provided Feuerbach and Marx with easy targets in their critiques of religious belief and practice in the mid nineteenth century.[6]

Whereas a modern theologian who believes in a post-mortem existence can acknowledge without embarrassment that all the traditions relating to it 'cannot be fitted together',[7] it was difficult to adopt such a position in the nineteenth century, when many Christian writers clearly felt obliged to attempt an account of the heavenly state that was both coherent and complete. For there was strong popular interest in 'what heaven is like'. Robert Weaver, a Congregational minister, distinguished between two readerships in his sub-title to a book published in the year of Victoria's accession: *Heaven: A Manual for the Heirs of Heaven; Designed for the Satisfaction of the Inquisitive, as well as for Assistance to the Devout. Also, on Angels and their Ministry* (1837). In reality the devout were also all too often inquisitive. Questions which were often asked, even after the publication of Weaver's ostensibly definitive 'manual', included several that were of general interest and concern: Are we to be conscious in heaven? Will we be reunited with friends and family? How will we spend our 'time'? In joining the heavenly choir, are we to give up our earthly assumption that all forms of life are associated with growth and change?

The Victorians' obsessive interest in post-mortem existence has of course been widely ridiculed in our own century. Although the activities of the Society for Psychical Research have been the subject of serious scholarly study in recent years, the broader subject of spiritualism is generally treated as a somewhat quaint aspect of the Victorian cult of death.[8] Ulrich Simon, in *Heaven in the Christian Tradition* (1958), is scornful of the 'uncosmic celestialism' which was a product of the subjectivization and secularization of heaven in the West after Goethe. A socially useful refuge from appalling conditions in this life, heaven came to mean 'anything from unusual happiness to the life after death', and Victorian hymns brought themes of consolation and reward to the fore.

As in Pre-Raphaelite art, Simon argues, the greater the effort of 'descriptive realism', the emptier the result: 'The verbiage of "angel faces, hosts of light, and stars upon their way" fails miserably.'[9]

Now as Simon points out, one solution to the problem of accommodating the ancient Christian heaven in a modern scientific world-view is to 'ignore and even to refuse to state it', as Schleiermacher did in abandoning the 'original, cosmic claims' of Christianity.[10] In the light of the 'indefinite' or 'purely figurative' nature of the Redeemer's teaching on the future life, Schleiermacher argued, Christians can gather only that it is essentially 'the persistent union of believers with the Redeemer'.[11] Yet in England some theologians continued to attempt a reconciliation between science and a traditional biblical cosmology, and in both theological and imaginative writings two ideas of the heavenly state – as worship and as community – proved to be particularly resilient to cultural change. For heaven still fulfilled its traditional function of providing a site in which love, both sacred and profane, could be said to find its perfection, or completion, or consummation. At the very least it was possible to mount a defence of writing about heaven in a scientific age by treating it as an expression of the highest spiritual and moral priorities in this life. The interest in the nineteenth century in guardian angels, the recognition of friends in heaven, and the singing of hymns in the heavenly choir reflect a longing for different *kinds* of continuity between this world and the next. Such interest in that which lies beyond the veil raises questions of religious language that are by now familiar. Rather surprisingly, however, we will see that even some of the Evangelical writers who solemnly plotted the topography of heaven were sensitive to the question of the provisionality of the figurative language they used.

Having first reviewed some of the traditional concepts and terms related to this area of Christian eschatology, I will examine Victorian ideas and descriptions of heaven, with special reference to religious language. I will then focus upon devotional and literary works in which these themes are treated in a particularly significant way: first, Victorian hymns which convey a synchronic heaven – the site of perpetual worship; and secondly, the poetry of Dante Gabriel and Christina Rossetti, Coventry Patmore, and Francis Thompson in which heaven is the site of a final reconciliation between sacred and profane love.

HEAVEN, PARADISE, AND THE KINGDOM

Although 'heaven' is occasionally used as a periphrasis for God in the Judaeo-Christian tradition,[12] it is generally taken to be God's realm, created by him, subject to him, and thus distinguished from him.[13] Heaven is above us, both physically, as a synonym for the sky, and metaphysically, as the abode of God who is above all things. In the Old Testament, God's interventions are from 'above', and prophecies in Isaiah of a cosmic collapse and the creation of a new heaven and a new earth draw heaven increasingly into 'soteriological ideas'.[14] Christ's saving mission can be represented in mythic terms as that of a sky god whose incarnation, death, burial, and ascension describe a great circle which begins and ends in heaven.[15] During his ministry on earth he teaches his disciples to pray to 'Our Father, which art in heaven'. The creeds describe the Father as 'maker of heaven and earth', and the Son, Jesus Christ, as he who 'ascended into heaven' and 'sitteth on the right hand of God the Father Almighty'.

Bultmann comments on the fact that in the twentieth century we 'no longer believe in the three-storied universe which the creeds take for granted'.[16] The cosmological framework within which the New Testament writers worked had, of course, been displaced long before the nineteenth century, during which the findings of science and the Higher Criticism raised new questions concerning the creation of the universe and the mythic nature of biblical cosmology.[17] We will see, however, that there was serious discussion in the nineteenth century on the question of the location of heaven: perhaps it is *below* the earth? When this and other issues, such as the nature of the spiritual body in heaven, are discussed, reference is often made to the tension between the literal and the metaphorical, or the physical and the metaphysical, or the this-worldly and the other-worldly in religious language. Only in heaven itself could such tensions be resolved, it is assumed. For Ulrich Simon, however, an imaginative reading of the Bible is the soundest basis for discussion of such questions, as in the Bible 'extremes of literalism are balanced by extremes of metaphorical symbolism'.[18] We ourselves, he argues, 'oscillate between literal fanaticism and liberal vagueness', and we must bear in mind the freedom behind the scriptures (which we have lost) in order 'to understand the immense richness to be found there with respect to Heaven'.

'Richness' in the Bible, as Simon knows, is often synonymous with complexity, and we can see this in one of the key passages in the New Testament concerning heaven. Paul's account of his 'visionary rapture to paradise' brings several of the issues mentioned above into sharp relief, raises the important question of the distinction between heaven and paradise, and is of further interest as another prototype of the kind of visionary experience described in Browning's *Christmas-Eve and Easter-Day*, for example:

> I knew a man in Christ above fourteen years ago, (whether in the body, I cannot tell; or whether out of the body, I cannot tell: God knoweth;) such an one caught up to the third heaven [*hēos tritou ouranou*].
> And I knew such a man, (whether in the body, or out of the body, I cannot tell: God knoweth;)
> How that he was caught up into paradise [*paradeison*], and heard unspeakable words, which it is not lawful for a man to utter. (2 Corinthians 12.2–4)

'Paradise' derives from a Persian word meaning an enclosure, and thence a nobleman's park, which was borrowed by both the Hebrew and Greek languages.[19] Andrew Lincoln comments: 'Most frequently [paradise] is heavenly in character but it can also be earthly . . . or even combine elements of both.'[20] In nineteenth-century literature the tradition of the 'earthly paradise' was exploited by Romantic and Utopian writers, ranging from Coleridge to William Morris, whose dreams were of a new order in the here-and-now.[21] The millennium was generally understood as Eden (or 'paradise') reinstated upon earth.[22] (Such thinking helps to explain the concept of the kingdom, to which I will turn in a moment.) Newman, in his Oxford sermons, also considered the intermediate state (or 'paradise') to be like Eden, that other paradise which, 'though pure and peaceful, visited by angels and by God Himself, was not heaven'.[23] The *garden* of Eden also reinforces the helpful organicist symbolism of the graveyard in the nineteenth century.

The Eden parallel is to be found in Revelation 2.7, one of only three texts in the New Testament in which the word 'paradise' is used: 'To him that overcometh will I give to eat of the tree of life, which is in the midst of the paradise of God.' The second usage is in Christ's promise on the cross to the penitent thief (Luke 23.43), and the third is our present text, where Paul refers both to 'paradise' and the 'third heaven'. Modern commentators offer a variety of glosses on the third heaven, some of which allow the term to be synonymous with paradise.[24] The Anglican

Newman and others in the nineteenth century distinguished between paradise, meaning the intermediate state, and heaven, meaning the final state of glory. In other contexts, however, paradise and heaven were equated.[25]

Finally, turning to the ineffable nature of the experience described by Paul, it has been claimed that the event 'may be thought of as an anticipation of the final transference of believers to heaven, or Paradise'.[26] The conclusion that can be drawn from this is highly significant in relation to the visions described in Browning's *Christmas-Eve and Easter-Day* and Tennyson's *In Memoriam*: 'Mystical and apocalyptic-eschatological religion are not as far apart as is sometimes supposed.' The difficulty of finding words to describe such experiences is a common theme in mystical writing, and the repetitive and halting manner of the passage in 2 Corinthians 12 probably reflects this as much as any private embarrassment to which it has been attributed.[27] Verse 4, however, also indicates that Paul is restrained from describing such a sacred event, and commentators have disagreed about the degree to which this is usual in such cases.[28]

Heaven- and paradise-language, then, were problematic in early Christian tradition, and by the nineteenth century an accretion of conventions and interpretation had complicated matters still further. Kingdom-language, on the other hand, could be applied to a wide range of nineteenth-century beliefs concerning the nature of eternal life, and is still widely used in contemporary theology. This is perhaps partly because the kingdom is less cosmological than heaven in its associations. Although the phrase 'the kingdom of heaven' (which is virtually unique to Matthew) might be thought to underline the contiguity between the Father and heaven (his special creation and domain), a modern authority informs us that the essential meaning is 'reign' rather than 'realm', and that by definition this reign does not arise by human effort.[29] The ambiguity of the 'reverential periphrasis' as explained in the *Catholic Dictionary* (1884) suggests parallels with the several different meanings of 'paradise':

the phrase 'Kingdom of the Heavens' does not necessarily imply a kingdom in another world than this. Nevertheless the expression lends itself of its very nature to a certain ambiguity and the context will have to decide the exact formality of its use in any given passage. Sometimes it is the Messianic kingdom of God on earth, sometimes the apotheosis of that kingdom in heaven, sometimes the recognition of God's royal rights by the individual soul. The perspectives will often merge since the kingdom on earth is designed as the antechamber to the kingdom in heaven, e.g. 8:11–12.[30]

Messianic expectation in the Old Testament that the kingship of God was imminent prepared the ground for the more spiritual and inward kingdom-language of Christ, who described the kingdom through parables. Unlike the term 'paradise', however, which can mean Eden, the intermediate state, and the final state of glory, the several meanings of 'kingdom' all proclaim the eternal divine king-ship.

The two most important models of heaven in the nineteenth century – heaven as worship and heaven as community – were in many respects difficult to reconcile. F. D. Maurice's emphasis, however, in *The Kingdom of Christ* (1838; rev. 1842) upon love and fellowship offered a means of drawing these concepts together, through kingdom-language. With reference to the epistles of Peter and the doctrine of John, Maurice writes:

For that men are not to gain a kingdom hereafter, but are put in possession of it now, and that through their chastisements and the oppositions of their evil nature they are to learn its character and enter into its privileges, is surely taught in every verse of the one; and that love has been manifested unto men, that they have been brought into fellowship with it, that by that fellowship they may rise to the fruition of it, and that this fellowship is for us as members of a family, so that he who loveth God must love his brother also, is affirmed again and again in express words of the other.[31]

The 'dynamic dialectic' of Maurice's idea of the church which shaped his Christian Socialism is beyond the scope of this study.[32] There are, however, important parallels between *The Kingdom of Christ* and Maurice's later ideas on the nature of the heavenly reward. In a lecture of 1861 on the Revelation, for example, he anticipates objections to the millennium by focusing upon its value in emphasizing that the earth is redeemable:

'We have been taught to look for a heavenly state; you want us,' they say, 'to fix our hope upon an earthly paradise. We have been looking forward to a reward which is to greet those who have served God faithfully here when they have passed the boundary of death; you point us to a blessed condition which may befall this world generally. . .'

. . . To me it seems that the hope of good for this earth is essentially involved in all the promises of God; that we must suppress the most obvious statements in Scripture, and kill the best wishes in our own hearts, if we refuse to cherish it.

> . . . The deliverance of the earth is assuredly [the Apocalypse's] subject – but the deliverance of the earth, from the sensual masters who had degraded it, by its true spiritual Lord. The idea of a Kingdom of Heaven, which has been developing itself through every part of the New Testament, now reaches its completion.[33]

Maurice's argument that the kingdom is continuous between this world and the new heaven and earth that are to be revealed is compatible with Paul's 'paradise now and not yet', which implies that there is no break between an order already established in heaven but as yet only immanent on earth, and that which is to be fulfilled. Similar negotiations between past, present, and future revelations are transacted in Protestant and Roman Catholic liturgies of the eucharist, and in Victorian hymns. Liturgy and hymnody will be discussed later in this chapter. For the moment, however, I must examine in some detail the content of the popular views cited by Maurice: 'We have been taught to look for a heavenly state . . . We have been looking forward to a reward which is to greet those who have served God faithfully here when they have passed the boundary of death.' In the Victorian period there was great interest in and much discussion on the nature of heaven. After what was known as the 'spirit-rapping' craze of mid-century,[34] much popular interest in the subject was channelled into various aspects of parapsychology. 'Glimpses of a Brighter Land' via 'Spiritual Intercommunion' were not, it was believed by some spiritualists, incompatible with Christian teaching on heaven.[35] The 'reluctant doubters' who founded the Society for Psychical Research aimed not only to prove that there is spiritual 'survival', but also to investigate the nature of existence on the 'other side'.[36]

The recurrent implied question, then, was: What is heaven like? A prior question for the theologian, however, was: Is heaven a state or a place? Roman Catholicism regarded heaven as a place without claiming to know anything of its spatial characteristics or its relation to the physical universe. The theological argument as presented in the *Catholic Dictionary* is that as 'the sacred humanity is not omnipresent, heaven is a definite place in which Christ and the Blessed Virgin exist, and in which the angels and blessed souls are gathered together'.[37] Whereas this account set aside the question of the location or locality of heaven, some of the books on heaven recommended to Protestant millenarian readers in the late 1850s and 1860s acknowledged a difficulty here even as they skirted around it. The aptly named John Angell James of Birmingham, for example, argued in 1859 that

> we are accustomed to think of heaven more under the idea of a state than a place, because we can render it more apprehensible to ourselves under the former, than under the latter; but some place there is, unvisited perhaps by human imagination, unthought of, where the King of Glory dwells, and gathers round His throne His chosen and redeemed people.[38]

Two years later William Branks, Minister of Torpichen, began the first of his three popular (but anonymous) books on heaven with a chapter entitled 'Heaven a Locality'.[39] (This book, entitled *Heaven our Home*, was said to have been read by Queen Victoria and Albert in the last six months of the Prince Consort's life.[40]) Similarly, in 1866 the view that heaven 'is not a particular locality, designed as the final residence of the pious; but merely that equable and blessed state of mind to which men are brought by the spirit of holiness' was attacked in an anthology of writings on *The Recognition of Friends in Heaven*.[41]

To argue against the idea that heaven is merely a state of *mind* is to address only a narrow, and probably untenable part of the case for heaven as a state.[42] Having claimed, however, that heaven is a specific, if unknown place, the author, who is not identified, goes on to discuss the various 'allusions by which heaven is represented to our faith': Mount Zion, a magnificent temple, the 'green pasture', and so on. He implies, then, that the 'Divine Word' refers or alludes to earthly things, using our limited earthly language, in order to make heavenly things accessible to us through the scriptures. 'By such *metaphors*', he suggests, 'is the place of our future rest described' (my emphasis).[43] E. H. Bickersteth comes to a similar conclusion about biblical symbolism in his prose discourse on the 'Estate and Employments of the Risen Saints', written at the same time as his epic poem. Heaven is defined as a state. It is a state of personal perfection, both of body and spirit; of eternal rest and refreshment; of combined royalty and service; of social perfection; of perfected communion with God in Christ; of perpetuity and yet of progression; and saints 'will there receive the reward of the inheritance'. The Bible, he argues, exhausts 'all the images of the purest and the deepest human joy' in describing the heavenly state. When he tested whether 'all the happiest scenes of earth' are used in the Bible to 'prefigure the good things to come', he 'found that in every case Holy Scripture had appropriated the figure'.[44] These scriptural 'figures' included several that Victorian writers of hymns and consolatory verse made their own: a happy home, rural delights, the joy of harvest, the 'social pleasures of a well-ordered city', and so on. Bickersteth, however, is aware not only of the intrinsic limitations of language in relation to heavenly things, but also of the dangers of literalism in the appropriation of biblical language. He himself believes, for example, that the 'almost uniform testimony of Scripture points to Hades as a region below'. But those who think that it is 'actually situate within the crust of our terrestial globe' should remember that the Bible's 'Divine language may only be an accommodation to our earthly thoughts of height and depth'.[45]

Bickersteth's caveats about figures of speech and the dangers of literalism clear the ground for his own writing project, both in prose and poetry: to interpret what the Bible reveals of the estate and employments of the risen saints. With or without such caveats, however, this and similar projects were open to the kind of attack mounted by the secularist Austin Holyoake, whose pamphlet *Heaven & Hell: Where Situated?* (1873) appeared at the end of the last major revival of popular interest in the subject:

What is the Christian's Heaven? Where is it situated? In what part of the so-called Sacred Writings shall we find a clear and intelligible description of this abode of bliss – this promised land of never-ending pleasures, which is to be the reward of all true believers? It appears to be situated, by common consent, up above – beyond the clouds – beyond immeasurable space – and yet in the clouds. Whether in the torrid or the frigid zone, we are not informed. What its climate will be no man knoweth . . . How will the Englishman live and be happy, where the African can thrive, or the Russian of the wilds of Siberia will be at home? Are we to be dumb there, or are all to speak one language?[46]

The argument is crude and can easily be demolished. (It ignores, for example, the whole question of religious language and its function of mediating an established system of belief in a transcendent reality.) Yet Holyoake's short pamphlet touches upon several of the major issues considered so far in this study, including the nature of the resurrection of the body and the question of authority in Roman Catholic and Protestant traditions. By adopting a literalist approach to scripture, however, Holyoake draws the debate about the future life into the only arena in which secularism can and wishes to fight, namely within the horizon of this world and our mortal life. He exploits the fact that Christian apologetics draw upon scriptural 'figures' which attempt to describe heaven in this-worldly terms, but ignores the fact that apologists themselves recognize the limits of language.

Like the Roman Catholic definition of heaven as a 'place', quoted earlier, Tractarian writing on the subject of the 'unseen world' was cautious, reflecting a reserve which was intended partly to protect revealed doctrines from 'human judgment'. Both Newman and Keble emphasized the 'mystery' of the 'hidden truth' in the scriptural revelation concerning the 'unseen world'.[47] Tractarians also attached great significance to the holiness of those who are to enter heaven – a secret hidden with God.[48] Whereas the Tractarians emphasized the relationship between holiness and religious discipline, liberal Protestantism took a broader view. Thomas Erskine of Linlathen, for example, whose work influenced F. D. Maurice and initially impressed Newman,[49] argued in *The Unconditional Freeness of the Gospel* (1828) that heaven is 'the joy of God', and that we 'cannot enter into the joy of God without entering into the character of God': indeed, heaven is 'the name for a character conformed to the will of God'.[50] Fifty years later, F. W. Farrar mounted a very similar argument in *Eternal Hope*: 'Is it not a state rather than a place? . . . is it not *to be something* rather than to *go somewhere*? Yes, this, this is Heaven.'[51] 'To go *there*', he added, 'you must *be thus*', and we should not think of heaven as 'some meadow of asphodel beside the crystal waters, or golden city in the far-off blue'.[52]

The note of impatience here, which is also to be found in other writers in the 1870s, perhaps reflects the extent to which such symbolic language had been over-used, and indeed misused, during the third quarter of the nineteenth century.[53] That images of heaven will always fall short of its perfection is a commonplace in the nineteenth century.[54] One corollary of this is the argument put forward by Branks: 'It is not *one* type alone, but the *various figures* of the Scriptures *combined*, that give us the truest view of heaven.'[55] A second addresses the question of the nature of these figures which, in Robert Weaver's view, 'all have a spiritual signification'.[56] A third, expressed by Christina Rossetti in a poem entitled 'Paradise', takes the view that what are now images (here in a dream) will in heaven be wonderful realities.[57]

The dream images described in 'Paradise' are flowers, songs, the 'Fourfold river', the 'Tree of Life', the 'gate called Beautiful', and glimpses of the heavenly city. The reconciliation of rural and urban

images that Christina Rossetti achieves in her dream poem by drawing
upon the Revelation is more problematic in some other contexts. Indeed,
the organic associations of country churchyards spoke to an increasingly
urban society not least because they pointed to a heaven that was rural,
and that thus represented an ideal which *contrasted* with prevailing
conditions in the world.[58] Heavenly 'views' or 'landscapes', however, are
often those of the illustrated family Bible, with the inevitable palm trees
to shade those who are 'at rest'.[59] Traditional symbolism which
represents the dying as passing over a great sea to the 'eternal shore'
beyond is widely adopted in Victorian poetry and hymnody.[60] It is
difficult, however, to hold both of these images *and* images of the
heavenly Jerusalem in the consciousness together. Characteristically,
John Martin made the attempt in his painting, *The Plains of Heaven*
(illustration 8). Here the faintness of the mirage-like heavenly city in the
background is the visual equivalent of Pollok's and Bickersteth's sketchy
accounts of the 'many mansions' or the 'highest heaven' at the end of
their epic poems.[61] Jerusalem, with its vast domes that could be mistaken
for clouds or, as in Jewish tradition, the highest mountain,[62] is thus
accommodated in a vision of heaven which is predominantly rural by
having its city-like features disguised.

Difficulties in interpreting the heavenly Jerusalem were recognized by
Augustine.[63] E. H. Bickersteth saw 'the heavenly Jerusalem' as 'both real
and typical – an actual city, of which every part typifies the spiritual
temple of living stones'. He also believed that the details of the celestial
city in the Revelation 'awaken conceptions of delight which we cannot
always define or describe'.[64] In *Yesterday, To-Day, and For Ever* the city
which the Messiah has built for his Bride, the Church, is described as 'A
city, or a temple, or a home, / Or rather all in one' (XII, 298–9). In
drawing together traditional Jewish ideas concerning Jerusalem as the
final home of Israel, when paradise will come again, and the eschatology
of the Revelation, he grounds the most common Victorian idea of
heaven – 'the long home' – in biblical typology.[65]

In its popular conception, heaven as home often had materialist
associations, yet the home/house/city nexus seems to have been more
helpful than rural associations for those writers who saw heaven as the
site in which all earthly types are fulfilled, and who emphasized what
Isaac Taylor called the 'correspondence between the present and the
future employment of the active principle of human nature'.[66] The question, What is heaven 'like'? could be said in the strictest sense to invite an

analogical answer, and William Branks, like Taylor, commented upon the centrality of analogy to his argument that 'a state of grace upon earth is a state of glory begun'.[67] Clough wrote of the hope that 'What here is faithfully begun / Will be completed, not undone.'[68] Kant's emphasis upon 'moral improvement' had led him to think in terms of a state in 'the course of things to come' where 'the creature who has remained true to his nature and who has made himself worthy of happiness through morality will actually participate in this happiness'.[69] For Robert Pollok, happiness in heaven would be impossible without activity in 'meet pursuit',[70] and when Archibald Tate lost his son, then a young clergyman, he drew consolation from the thought that God wanted him 'for some work elsewhere, that [he] might serve in His own immediate Presence in the Heavenly Sanctuary'.[71]

Each of the different states or activities implied in these descriptions reflects an idea of progress, or development, or completion. Such thinking raises a number of difficulties. Tennyson expressed his concern lest the soul of Arthur Hallam should in some way develop in heaven to the point at which reunion was no longer a possibility.[72] It is not easy to imagine continued identity without continued sexuality, or to reconcile the idea of family reunions with New Testament teaching on there being no marrying in heaven.[73] The idea that heaven is 'greatly made up of little children'[74] represents a limited interpretation of the kingdom of heaven described in Matthew 19.14, and was the subject of many popular hymns.[75] To foreground children in heaven (as John Martin literally does in *The Plains of Heaven*) is to emphasize innocence and thus to defer the question of adult sexuality. Children, it was generally agreed, would not somehow grow to 'adulthood', and those who wrote on the 'recognition of friends in heaven' consoled bereaved parents by stating that their children would be 'among the first to welcome' them on their arrival.[76]

A hope of reunion in heaven was frequently expressed in nineteenth-century literature and theology, and treatises discussing this particular kind of continuity between earthly and heavenly existence were taken seriously by many educated readers.[77] Isaac Taylor's *The Physical Theory of Another Life* (1836), which deeply impressed the young Marian Evans,[78] includes a chapter entitled 'The Survivance of Individual Character, and of the Moral Consciousness', in which he develops his argument on the mutual dependence of the physical and moral nature. After the 'passage from the present, to another mode of existence', there will naturally be a settling-in period, and here the book begins to read like one of Murray's guides: 'A short season probably, will be enough to impart to us an easy familiarity with our new home, a ready use of our corporeal instruments, and a facility in joining in with the economy around us.'[79] William Branks saw his own argument that heaven would be social above all, a 'home' with a *great and loving family in it*, as a counterbalance to the negative and unsocial views of heaven given by most divines.[80] Similar ideas were preached in a novel by the American writer Elizabeth Stuart Phelps entitled *The Gates Ajar* (1868),[81] which proved to be so popular in Britain that an irate, but unnamed Dean of the Church of England felt compelled to denounce it as unscriptural, sensational, and spiritualist in its teaching.[82] Other approaches to the topic were more reserved. Keble, for example, wrote in *The Christian Year* of the 'store' of 'friends out of sight',[83] while F. D. Maurice, who, as we have seen, thought of the kingdom as a family, recorded that he could not read the account of the raising of Lazarus 'without feeling that, among those things in heaven and earth that are so to be restored, the sympathies and affections of the family are some of the chief'.[84]

I argued earlier that for E. H. Bickersteth, Christ's use of 'heaven's language', or 'the Divine style', or a 'celestial dialect' in the story of the raising of Lazarus was a mark of his divinity.[85] On the widely accepted view that entry into heaven is also entry into knowledge of God and his will, many Victorian commentators argued that the saved would immediately and without difficulty acquire 'heaven's language', which was before Babel and will be for evermore. Interestingly, however, Pollok in *The Course of Time* emphasized the continuity between *personal* earthly and heavenly existence by having the Bard of Earth explain that although all languages can be understood in heaven, as all are 'perfect here in knowledge', traces of earthly languages remain in a form of dialect:

> for each in heaven a relish holds
> Of former speech, that points to whence he came.
> But whether I of person speak, or place . . .
>
> . . . the meaning still,
> With easy apprehension, thou shalt take.[86]

This aspect of what Isaac Taylor called the 'economy' of another life emphasizes heaven as community, the site of idealized interpersonal relations in which love of neighbour is apotheosized. Is it to be assumed, however, that the perfected strains of the celestial choir of angels and risen saints mask any traces of earthly dialects, as heavenly worship (or love of God apotheosized) is in 'one voice'? In this as in other respects, the two main Victorian models of heaven as community and heaven as worship are no more compatible than the rural and urban imagery used to describe heaven. Kingdom-language, however, can be applied meaningfully to both traditions, while also suggesting earthly–heavenly continuities such as that of fellowship. It is in relation to continued fellowship that the communion of saints also accommodates both models, taking love of neighbour up into the corporate expression of love of God in worship.

As a doctrine, the communion of saints is particularly cherished by those clergy and religious for whom the daily round of work and worship is a divine office understood in relation not only to the church visible but also to the church invisible. Some sense of this is conveyed in a letter of condolence from B. F. Westcott, then Bishop of Durham, to William Michael Rossetti, concerning the death of Christina Rossetti in December 1894. No overt reference is made to the communion of saints, but the doctrine clearly shapes Westcott's thinking:

Not a week passes, I think, when I do not find some real pleasure from fragments of your sister's works. And my experience is, I am sure, that of very many. Those who so teach us and reveal themselves to us cannot be lost. However hard it is to realise as yet that the fact that they pass out of sight makes them unchangeable, at least I know – this house with its Chapel tells me so every day – that some of the friends who are dearest to me and help me most have entered on a fuller life. May you feel the consolation of this eternal companionship which *knows no break* in the presence of God [my emphasis].[87]

Sixty years earlier, Newman preached a sermon on the communion of saints in which he affirmed that the 'heavenly Jerusalem is the true Spouse of Christ and virgin Mother of Saints', and that 'this *invisible* body is the *true* Church, because it changes not, though it is ever increasing'.[88] In another sermon entitled 'The Invisible World' he wrote of the 'world of spirits', though unseen, being 'present': 'It is not above the sky, it is not beyond the grave; it is now and here; the kingdom of God is among us.'[89] Thus a 'world of Saints and Angels, a glorious world, the palace of God, the mountain of the Lord of Hosts, the heavenly

Jerusalem, the throne of God and Christ, all these wonders, everlasting, all-precious, mysterious, and incomprehensible, lie hid in what we see'.[90] Among the great divines of the nineteenth century, Newman had the strongest sense of the ministry of angels, those 'inhabitants of the world invisible' about whom, on his argument, we know more than about the faithful departed, as they are active, rather than resting from their labours. Although they are so wonderful that we could not bear to look at them, if that were possible, they are 'our "fellow-servants" and our fellow-workers, and they carefully watch over and defend even the humblest of us, if we be Christ's'.[91]

It is important to emphasize that although Newman wrote of the kingdom of heaven being among us and of angels as our fellow-workers, the 'invisible world' is by definition hidden and utterly *different* from this world, in which we can discern only signs of its presence. Heaven for Newman 'is not like this world', but much more like a church, 'because both in the one and the other, there is one single sovereign subject – religion – brought before us'.[92] Heaven 'would be hell to an irreligious man', because in heaven every man must 'do *God's* pleasure' rather than 'choose and take his *own* pleasure'.[93] Other writers of different religious persuasions put forward similar arguments in the nineteenth century, but no teaching was more influential than Newman's on 'Holiness Necessary for Future Blessedness'.[94] Perhaps the most interesting counter-argument was F. D. Maurice's in his lecture on 'The Vision of Heaven' in the Revelation:

Oftentimes it has been said in Christian pulpits, that heaven is but the continuance of the worship upon earth. Those who have found that worship on earth very dreary and unsatisfactory, have said that they should prefer any Greek Elysium or Gothic Walhalla to such a heaven. I think if we take St. John as our guide – if we accept his revelation as the true revelation – we may see a meaning in the assertion of the divine, and a meaning in the protest of the layman. All is worship there, because all are pursuing the highest good in contemplation and action; because all are referring their thoughts and acts to one centre, instead of scattering and dispersing them by turning to a thousand different centres; because each thinker and each doer is forgetting himself in the object which he has before him, in the work which is committed to him.[95]

'Work is Worship', that favourite tag of Thomas Carlyle, Maurice's sceptical fellow-worker in the labouring house of the world, here finds its apogee in a Christian Socialist heaven where worship and work know no division.[96]

Maurice's subsequent description of Hooker's announcement on his deathbed that he was going to 'a world of order' as a 'thrilling statement' reflects a deep sense of what Matthew Arnold in 'The Scholar-Gipsy' called the 'sick hurry' and 'divided aims' of modern life.[97] Although in danger of suggesting a tidy, somewhat claustrophobic heavenly state, talk of 'order' is characteristic of a period in which heaven as a state of 'harmony' and completion was commonplace.[98] Only in Victorian hymnody, however, to which I now turn, were such ideas conveyed in a liturgical context which proclaimed heaven as worship.

HYMNODY: HEAVEN IN THE PRESENT TENSE

A formal act of public worship constitutes a corporate rite of passage in and through time. Following a general confession of sins committed in time past, for example, forgiveness or reconciliation may be declared in time present, before a congregation is sent back into the world of time future with a blessing and the saying of the grace. Lessons from the Old Testament, the epistles, and the gospels may be linked typologically, and the fulfilment of history-like events in later history-like events related to the lives of a congregation in time present and time future via a sermon or homily. Although diachronic, however, in its internal dynamics and its engagement with a revelation that is historical, an act of worship is synchronic in relation both to the divine reality and to the universal church, each of which is in a different sense 'present'. This is reflected in the dominance of the present tense in liturgy, as in the words 'I believe in God', 'Give us this day our daily bread', and 'We are not worthy so much as to gather up the crumbs under Thy Table.' Victorian hymns exploit both the diachronic and the synchronic potentialities of liturgical language in order to speak of heaven within the present of an act of worship.[99] Heaven may be now, or not yet, or now and not yet.[100] I wish to argue that the continuities and discontinuities between this fleeting world and heaven are conveyed in the language of hymnody through special uses of tense and syntactic construction.

Within the dominant present tense of hymnody, three kinds of present can be distinguished: first, what I will call the 'eternal' present of heaven as an affirmed transcendental reality; secondly, the 'locutionary' present in which the hymn is sung; and thirdly, the 'existential' present of a mortal lifespan, as opposed to a future post-mortem existence. All three are to be found in this short version of one of J. M. Neale's *Hymns for Children* (1842):

> Around the Throne of God a band
> Of glorious Angels ever stand;
> Bright things they see, sweet harps they hold,
> And on their heads are crowns of gold.
>
> Some wait around Him, ready still
> To sing His praise and do His will;
> And some, when He commands them, go
> To guard His servants here below.
>
> Lord, give thy Angels every day
> Command to guide us on our way,
> And bid them every evening keep
> Their watch around us while we sleep.
>
> So shall no wicked thing draw near,
> To do us harm or cause us fear;
> And we shall dwell, when life is past,
> With Angels round Thy throne at last.[101]

The transition in verses 2 and 3 from the evoked eternal present of heaven (cf. Revelation 5) to the locutionary and existential present is characteristic of Victorian hymnody. Here it is effected through reference to the dual role of angels: in verses 1 and 2, some 'ever' (or, in a later version, 'always')[102] stand in heaven ready 'still' (in the sense of 'always') to obey God's will; in verses 2 and 3, some are sent 'here below' to guard us day and night, and, by analogy, in life and death. In the first two verses, traditional items in heaven are simply and directly described in the authoritative tone of hymnic affirmation. Then the petitionary form of 'Lord, give' in the third verse briefly establishes the hymn's locutionary present, which modulates into the continuous existential present of time future in the construction 'give . . . every day . . . bid . . . every evening', as in H. F. Lyte's 'Abide with me'.[103] Finally, the fourth verse affirms a blessed future in both this world and the next, where, as the hymn ends where it began, we will dwell 'at last' with angels who always stand around the throne of God.

The use of the first person singular can enhance the sense of immediacy in the locutionary present of Victorian hymnody, although the characteristic unction of pious ejaculations on the subject of heaven can be excessive:

> O Paradise! O Paradise!
>   I want to sin no more,
> I want to be as pure on earth
>   As on thy spotless shore;
>   Where loyal hearts and true
>   Stand ever in the light,
>   All rapture through and through,
>   In God's most holy sight.[104]

Like Newman, F. W. Faber, who wrote this hymn fifteen years after his conversion to Roman Catholicism in 1846, placed great emphasis upon holiness being necessary for future blessedness. Heaven is attainable only after a lifelong struggle against sin, which is dramatized in the repeated words 'I want' in the locutionary present.

James Montgomery, like Faber, believed that the existential present of a human lifespan should be dedicated to expectant preparation, as expressed in his hymn 'Songs of praise the Angels sang' (1819):

> Saints below, with heart and voice,
> Still in songs of praise rejoice;
> Learning here, by faith and love,
> Songs of praise to sing above.[105]

On a universal scale, however, the whole of creation, past, present, and to come, looks forward to the end of the present order which Montgomery's contemporary, Robert Pollok, called the 'course of time'. For it is not until the last day that the blessed will enter into the full glory of heaven:

> Heav'n and earth must pass away,
> Songs of praise shall crown that day;
> God will make new heavens and earth,
> Songs of praise shall hail their birth.

Thus the worshipper's expectation in the existential present is taken up into a universal eschatological vision of God's providential plan for mankind.

Having defined and illustrated terms with which to describe different aspects of the present in Victorian religious language, I will now apply them to the strategies whereby the spiritual qualities of the heavenly state are conveyed in hymns. As we have seen, kingdom-language was less problematic than heaven- or paradise-language in the nineteenth century. A hymn by F. T. Palgrave, editor of the *Golden Treasury*, entitled 'Kingdom of God within', begins with these words:

> O Thou not made with hands,
>   Not throned above the skies,
> Nor walled with shining walls,
>   Nor framed with stones of price,
> More bright than gold or gem,
> God's own Jerusalem!
>
> Where'er the gentle heart
>   Finds courage from above;
> Where'er the heart forsook
>   Warms with the breath of love;
> Where faith bids fear depart,
> City of God, thou art.[106]

The Pauline source, 'an house not made with hands' (2 Corinthians 5.1), refers, in Andrew Lincoln's view, to the 'heavenly resurrection body'.[107] For Palgrave, however, the negative form of the famous phrase simply provides a suitable scriptural basis for a hymn which marginalizes transcendental interpretations of the kingdom of heaven in order to earth the kingdom in the 'gentle heart', and to emphasize the locutionary and existential present of his final verse:

> Not throned above the skies,
>   Nor golden-walled afar,
> But where Christ's two or three
>   In his name gathered are,
> Be in the midst of them,
> God's own Jerusalem!

Palgrave's hymn was published in 1867, when the publication of books describing heaven, often in literalist terms, was at its height. In internalizing the Book of Revelation, however, it denies the otherworldly side of the familiar liturgical parallel between worship in church and worship in heaven, in sentences such as 'Therefore *with* Angels and Archangels, and *with* all the company of heaven, we laud and magnify Thy glorious Name.' This kind of synchronic parallelism was exploited by hymnists of several different traditions in the nineteenth century. The revised (1827) version of Bishop Reginald Heber's Advent hymn, 'Hosanna to the living Lord', for example, celebrates the continuity between heaven, the 'house of prayer', and the human heart, via the workings of the Holy Spirit in 'God's temple':

> Hosanna to the living Lord!
> Hosanna to the Incarnate Word,
> To Christ, Creator, Saviour, King,
> Let earth, let heaven Hosanna sing,
>   Hosanna in the highest!
>
> O Saviour, with protecting care
> Abide in this Thy house of prayer,
> Where we Thy parting promise claim,
> Assembled in Thy sacred Name.
>   Hosanna in the highest!
>
> But, chiefest, in our cleansed breast,
> Eternal, bid Thy Spirit rest;
> And make our secret soul to be
> A temple pure and worthy Thee.
>   Hosanna in the highest![108]

The repetition of 'Let' in the fourth line brings earth and heaven into synchronic harmony: 'Let earth, let heaven Hosanna sing'. The subsequent movement from verse to verse, however, is inwards, and it is possible that the second verse in the original (1811) version was later omitted in order to clarify this. What the missing verse brings out though is the continuity between the church militant and the church triumphant, and the synchrony between the eternal present of heaven and the locutionary present of the hymn as sung in church. Again this is achieved through repetition, although here the effect in the first two lines is antiphonal:

> Hosanna, Lord! thine angels cry;
> Hosanna, Lord! thy saints reply;
> Above, beneath us, and around,
> The dead and living swell the sound;
>   Hosanna! Lord! Hosanna in the highest![109]

Similar techniques are adopted in the opening verses of L. B. C. L. Muirhead's hymn, published in his friend Robert Bridges's *Yattendon Hymnal* of 1899:

> The Church of God a kingdom is,
>   Where Christ in power doth reign;
> Where spirits yearn till, seen in bliss,
>   Their Lord shall come again.

> Glad companies of saints possess
>   This Church below, above:
> And God's perpetual calm doth bless
>   Their paradise of love.[110]

From the eschatological perspective of the first verse, the hymn moves into a confident affirmation of the transcendent in the second, and the directness of description which is continued in subsequent verses could be read (if not sung) as a description of the altar piece on which it is said to be based.[111] The delicate equipoise in the second verse between the church militant here on earth and the church triumphant in heaven is achieved by a contiguity ('This Church below, above') which suggests a coincidence of opposites and accommodates all three kinds of present currently under discussion.

Such strategies were well adapted to the aims of hymnists who wished to emphasize the sacramental in their treatment of the heavenly state, as we can see in three hymns from different traditions, but all written in 1854–5. Horatius Bonar, a member of the Free Church of Scotland, treats the eucharist as a direct encounter with the divine in his communion hymn:

> Here, O my Lord, I see Thee face to face;
>   Here would I touch and handle things unseen;
> Here grasp with firmer hand th'eternal grace
>   And all my weariness upon Thee lean.
>
> Here would I feed upon the Bread of God;
>   Here drink with Thee the royal Wine of heaven;
> Here would I lay aside each earthly load;
>   Here taste afresh the calm of sin forgiven.[112]

Following the confident affirmation of the first line, which is in the existential present and the first person singular, present and future are conflated in the 'would' which acknowledges that the bread and wine are no more than first fruits. To drink *with* Christ the 'royal Wine of heaven' suggests partaking of the heavenly feast. Hedged about with cautious Protestant modifiers that emphasize the binary opposition of 'my' sin and 'thy' grace, Bonar's hymn ends, as it began, in the present tense: 'Here is my robe, my refuge, and my peace, – / Thy Blood, Thy righteousness, O Lord my God'.

As the earthly sabbath is a type of the 'eternal sabbath' of the millennium or of heaven itself as a state of repose, so the eucharist is a foretaste of a heaven that is future. Faber's communion hymn, 'Jesu, gentlest Saviour', which is often sung to Stainer's 'Eucharisticus' (1875), begins in the locutionary present:

> Jesu, gentlest Saviour,
>   Thou art in us now,
> Fill us with Thy Goodness,
>   Till our hearts o'erflow.[113]

'Till' already hints at future development in the spiritual life, and this is emphasized in subsequent verses where the gift of the eucharist is seen as a taste of the heavenly bliss for which we must wait in the existential present:

> Oh, how can we thank Thee
>   For a Gift like this,
> Gift that truly maketh
>   Heav'n's eternal bliss!
>
> Ah! when wilt Thou always
>   Make our hearts Thy home?
> We must wait for Heaven;
>   Then the day will come.

Finally, in William Bullock's 'We love the place, O God', revised by Sir Henry Baker for *Hymns Ancient and Modern* (1861), each aspect of church worship reflects God's presence among his flock: the two major sacraments of the Church of England, in 'the sacred Font', where the 'Holy Dove' pours out 'His blessings from above' (verse 3), and 'Thine Altar', where 'We find Thy Presence near' (4); and the 'Word of life', that tells of peace and ceaseless joys (5).[114] In the fifth and penultimate verse, however, an exclamation dramatizes the fact that these earthly forms fall short of heavenly worship:

> We love to sing below
>   For mercies freely given;
> But, oh, we long to know
>   The triumph-song of Heav'n.

And the final verse is a simple prayer for grace:

> Lord Jesus, give us grace
>   On earth to love Thee more,
> In Heav'n to see Thy Face,
>   And with Thy Saints adore.

These sacramental hymns, then, proclaim a heaven that is now and not yet, seen or tasted in the eucharist but to be enjoyed fully only after the last day. Newman's view that heaven would be like a church became a commonplace in Victorian hymnody, where the 'courts' of earth and heaven are often compared, as in Lyte's famous hymn:

> Pleasant are Thy courts above
> In the land of light and love;
> Pleasant are Thy courts below
> In this land of sin and woe:
> Oh, my spirit longs and faints
> For the converse of Thy Saints,
> For the brightness of Thy face,
> For Thy fulness, God of grace.[115]

As in Bullock's hymn, the emphasis falls upon 'longing' for heaven as the fulfilment of that to which earthly worship points. An alternative strategy is to set a hymn in the eternal present itself, as in Frances Cox's translation from the German of H. T. Schenk. The question posed in the first verse is based upon Revelation 7, where the past tense of the narrative account of the vision ('And one of the elders answered') gives way to the present in the reply ('What are these which are arrayed in white robes?'):

> Who are these like stars appearing,
>   These before God's Throne who stand?
> Each a golden crown is wearing,
>   Who are all this glorious band?
>   Alleluia, hark! they sing,
>   Praising loud their heavenly King.[116]

The answers explain the present in relation to the past: 'These are they who have contended / For their Saviour's honour long'; 'These are they whose hearts were riven, / Sore with woe and anguish tried.' The final verse celebrates the special kind of continuity between a priest's earthly vocation and heavenly reward by making two durative verb forms rhyme:

> These, the almighty *contemplating*,
>   Did as priests before Him stand,
> Soul and body always *waiting*
>   Day and night at His command:
>   Now in God's most holy place
>   Blest they stand before His Face.

The immediacy of the eternal present brings 'these' into the locutionary present, in the same way that constructions such as 'See . . .' and 'Hark . . .' can make angels 'present' in Victorian hymns.

Perhaps the most impressive triumphalist vision of the period, however, is Matthew Bridges's great hymn of praise to the risen Christ, written three years after his conversion to Roman Catholicism in 1848:

> Crown Him with many crowns,
> The Lamb upon His Throne;
> Hark! how the heavenly anthem drowns
> All music but its own:
> Awake, my soul, and sing
> Of Him Who died for thee,
> And hail Him as thy matchless King
> Through all eternity.[117]

Here synchrony between the eternal present and the locutionary present is established through the ambiguity of 'heavenly' in the third line: the anthem that is sung in heaven, *and* this earthly hymn which is like that in heaven. Thus the worshipper enacts the crowning (cf. Revelation 19.12; Hebrews 2.9) as he or she has been enjoined, and in the third verse emulates the angels' heavenly reserve:

> Crown Him the Lord of love:
> Behold His Hands and Side,
> Those Wounds yet visible above
> In beauty glorified:
> No Angel in the sky
> Can fully bear that sight,
> But downward bends his burning eye
> At mysteries so bright.

'Crown Him with many crowns' is suitable for Ascensiontide, the season in which the nature of heaven as the realm 'above' and the separation of the risen Christ from his disciples are major themes. The Victorians inherited Charles Wesley's great hymn, 'Hail the day that sees Him rise', for example, where Christ's entry into glory and his preparation of our 'place' is described in the eternal present as 'the first-fruits of our race'.[118] The translation in the nineteenth century of ancient ascension hymns from the Latin or Greek made it possible to sing of the old three-storied universe, as, for example, in the third verse of J. M. Neale's 'O Lord most High, Eternal King':

> To Thee the whole creation now
> Shall, in its threefold order, bow,
> Of things on earth, and things on high,
> And things that underneath us lie.[119]

Bishop Christopher Wordsworth's highly scriptural ascension hymn, 'See the Conqueror mounts in triumph' (1862), is characteristically conservative in its typological and cosmological treatment of the subject:

> While He lifts His Hands in blessing, He is parted from His friends;
> While their eager eyes behold Him, He upon the clouds ascends;
> He Who walk'd with God, and pleased him, preaching truth and doom to come,
> He, our Enoch, is translated to His everlasting home.[120]

In contrast, Emma Toke's 'Thou art gone up on high' (1852), represents a simple and highly personal plea:

> Thou art gone up on high,
> To mansions in the skies;
> And round Thy Throne unceasingly
> The songs of praise arise;
> But we are lingering here,
> With sin and care oppress'd;
> Lord, send Thy promised Comforter,
> And lead us to Thy rest.[121]

It is fitting, however, to end this section with a brief examination of the hymn which was liked by Tennyson better than most,[122] and which supplied the epigraph for this chapter: Bishop Heber's 'Holy, Holy, Holy', appointed for Trinity Sunday. Like Frances Cox in her translation of Schenk's hymn, Heber adapts passages from the Revelation to his own purposes. The use of tenses in the Authorized Version reflects a difficulty which confronted the translators. Their additions to the original Greek are marked with square brackets in the following quotation:

And immediately I *was* in the spirit: and, behold, a throne was set in heaven, and [one] sat on the throne . . .

And before the throne [there was] a sea of glass like unto crystal: and in the midst of the throne, and round about the throne [were] four beasts full of eyes before and behind

. . . and [they were] full of eyes within: and they *rest* not day and night, saying, Holy, holy, holy, Lord God Almighty, which was, and is, and is to come.

And when those beasts *give* glory and honour and thanks to him that *sat* on the throne, who *liveth* for ever and ever,

The four and twenty elders *fall* down before him that *sat* on the throne, and worship him that liveth for ever and ever, and cast their crowns before the throne, saying,

Thou art worthy, O Lord, to receive glory and honour and power: for thou hast created all things and for thy pleasure they *are* and *were* created.

(Revelation 4.2, 6, 8–11; my emphases)

Some idea of the problem can be conveyed by comparing the Authorized Version with a literal translation of verse 9:

Kai hotan dōsousin ta zōa doxan kai timēn kai eucharistian tō kathēmenō epi tō thronō tō zōnti eis tous aiōnas tōn aiōnōn . . .

And whenever shall give the living creatures glory and honour and thanks to the [one] sitting on the throne[,] to the [one] living unto the ages of the ages . . .[123]

And when those beasts give glory and honour and thanks to him that sat on the throne, who liveth for ever and ever . . .

Thus both 'give' *and* 'sat' (AV) are durative, conveying the sense of what I have identified as the eternal present of heaven.

Having put the words of the four living creatures in the mouth of the worshipper in the locutionary present of his first line, Heber suggests a promise of continued and regular earthly worship through the durative 'shall' in his second:

> Holy, Holy, Holy! Lord God Almighty!
>   Early in the morning our song shall rise to Thee:
> Holy, Holy, Holy! Merciful and Mighty!
>   God in Three Persons, Blessed Trinity![124]

Continuity between the locutionary and eternal present is established in the second verse:

> Holy, Holy, Holy! all the Saints adore Thee,
>   Casting down their golden crowns around the
>   glassy sea;
> Cherubim and Seraphim falling down before Thee,
>   Which wert, and art, and evermore shalt be.

In the Revelation it is the *elders* who cast down their crowns, and the elders are differentiated from the transfigured saints and the angels.[125] Heber's adaptation, however, strengthens the parallel between the earthly congregation and the heavenly 'host' of the redeemed. Several of the hymns quoted earlier invoke the various senses of 'crown' and 'crowning' in the Revelation: 'Songs of praise shall crown that day' (Montgomery); 'on their [the angels'] heads are crowns of gold' (Neale); 'Each [of the redeemed] a golden crown is wearing' (Cox); 'Crown Him with many crowns' (Bridges). The line 'Casting down their golden crowns around the glassy sea' is, however, one of the most vivid and memorable lines in nineteenth-century hymnody, and one that epitomizes the sense of synchronic worship in heaven that I have tried to illustrate. The rhyming of the durative 'casting' and 'falling' reinforces the effect of the thrice repeated 'Holy, holy, holy', which is itself given temporal universality in the echoing triple structure of the line, 'Which wert, and art, and evermore shall be.'

Verse 3 returns to the locutionary present, and in the final verse a universal song of praise to the Trinity broadens to a *benedicite* offered on behalf of the three-fold creation of 'earth, and sky, and sea':

> Holy, Holy, Holy! though the darkness hide Thee,
>   Though the eyes of sinful man Thy glory may not see,
> Only Thou are Holy, there is none beside Thee
>   Perfect in power, in love, and purity.
>
> Holy, Holy, Holy! Lord God Almighty!
>   All Thy works shall praise Thy Name, in earth, and sky,
>   and sea;
> Holy, Holy, Holy! Merciful and Mighty!
>   God in Three Persons, Blessed Trinity!

HEAVEN IN POETRY OF SACRED AND PROFANE LOVE

The binary opposition earth/heaven, which in secular contexts suggests mutual separateness and inaccessibility (earth *or* heaven), takes on the sense in some Victorian hymns of mutual interaction and continuity (earth *and* heaven). In Muirhead's lines, 'Glad companies of saints possess / This Church below, above', for example, the comma signifies addition, both by substituting for 'and' (below and above) and by bringing opposing signs (below/above) into contiguity. In a liturgical context, Victorian hymns which 'spoke' of the kingdom could affirm the communion of saints as being at once below and above by establishing a continuity between the locutionary present and the eternal present. Similar effects could be achieved in non-liturgical writing, such as E. H. Bickersteth's epic poem, for example, by introducing an angel visitant –

a messenger of God who can speak in the narrative's present tense of that other angelic vocation, the endless worship of God in the eternal present of heaven. In other narrative forms such as the dramatic monologue, access to the eternal present is often via descriptions of dreams and visions, inserted into a standard past tense narrative. Traditional religious dream or vision narratives (the *Commedia*, *Piers Plowman*, the *Pilgrim's Progress*), like the New Testament sources upon which they draw (Paul's account of the third heaven, the Book of Revelation), are framed in the past tense, but can move into the present tense via dialogues between earthly and heavenly voices. This convention is followed by Browning in *Christmas-Eve and Easter-Day*.

The poetry to be considered in this section explores the major traditional *topos* of sacred and profane love, using not only some of the techniques I have shown to be characteristic of Victorian hymnody, but also some of those associated with dream narratives. Dante Gabriel Rossetti adapts Edgar Allan Poe's narrative technique in 'The Raven' to his own purposes in 'The Blessed Damozel', that ambiguous vision of lovers separated by death, yet able, even if fleetingly, to communicate across the bar of heaven. In contrast, three other poets write of earthly love in specifically theological terms: Christina Rossetti, in her fervent poems of renunciation and Christian hope; Coventry Patmore, in his bereavement odes which attempt to harmonize remarriage and the heavenly reward; and Francis Thompson, in his odes on unmediated religious experience, interpreted in relation to platonic human love. Although these four writers' treatments of sacred and profane love are different, each of them uses subtle modulations in tense and mode to convey intimations of a heaven which is both now and not yet.

Poe's 'The Raven' (1845) produced a sensation in England, and clearly impressed the young Gabriel Rossetti. Whether or not he planned 'The Blessed Damozel' (1847) as a companion piece, parallels between the two poems are too strong to be ignored.[126] At the end of the first stanza of 'The Raven', which opens in the traditional past tense of a Gothic narrative ('Once upon a midnight dreary'), the present tense comes through in the conventional form of a reported statement: '"'Tis some visiter," I muttered, "tapping at my chamber door – / Only this and nothing more".'[127] At the end of the second stanza, however, the modulation from past to present has the quite different effect of placing the 'lost Lenore' in the eternal present of heaven:

> Eagerly I wished the morrow; – vainly I had sought to borrow
> From my books surcease of sorrow – sorrow for the lost Lenore –
> For the rare and radiant maiden whom the angels name Lenore –
> Nameless here for evermore.   (9–12)

The last word of the stanza prepares for the Raven's only word, 'Nevermore', the varied contextualizing of which in later stanzas registers a deepening disturbance in the mind of the narrator – Poe's real subject.[128] The possibility that the bird will leave the narrator 'nevermore' (60), suggesting an apparently endless earthly future, contrasts with the poem's central fact – the lover's presence nevermore, registered in the future tense: the 'cushion's velvet lining' she 'shall press, ah, nevermore!' (76–8). The narrator's later use of the present tense in his interrogation of the creature he takes to be some kind of supernatural visitant ('"Is there – *is* there balm in Gilead? – tell me – tell me, I implore!"', 89), is ominously fragile in this penultimate line of the stanza, as the last word immediately evokes the expected rhyme of 'Nevermore' from the Raven (90). The subsequent construction in future and (eternal) present tenses, where the narrator asks the Raven to tell 'this soul' if it shall 'clasp a sainted maiden whom the angels name Lenore', by now seems shaped to draw out the only possible answer, 'Nevermore' (93–6). His last use of the past tense, in describing his 'upstarting' and shrieking at the bird ('"Take thy beak from out my heart, and take thy form from off my door!" / Quoth the Raven, "Nevermore"', 101–2), leads into the continuous present of a fixed state in the final stanza, where is sketched a ghastly and, to the narrator, hellish mockery of an 'evermore':

> And the Raven, never flitting, still is sitting, *still* is sitting
> On the pallid bust of Pallas just above my chamber door;
> And his eyes have all the seeming of a demon's that is dreaming,
> And the lamp-light o'er him streaming throws his shadow on the floor;
> And my soul from out that shadow that lies floating on the floor
> Shall be lifted – nevermore!   (103–8)

Rossetti's pencil and ink sketches of 'The Raven' (*c.* 1847) experiment with different ways of conveying a sequence of events in a single scene – a problem that was to be central to Victorian narrative painting. The most Dantesque treatment of the subject is that in which Lenore leans yearningly towards the narrator as she passes underneath the Raven in a procession of angels (illustration 9).[129] Whereas in the poem, which moves through time, the narrator's separation from Lenore is conveyed partly through play with two different and, here, irreconcilable kinds of present tense – the existential present of the bereaved narrator and the eternal present of Lenore in heaven – the sketch conveys the idea of separation by bringing the Raven and the two figures together in the same scene (as they are in the narrator's imagination), but with the central figures separated spatially at the point of her departure. Heaven itself, as other and elsewhere, is only *in posse*. During Rossetti's subsequent career as a poet-painter he explored the ironic relationship between *eros* and *thanatos* through the use of both narrative/temporal and pictorial/spatial mediums. The resulting contiguity of human beings and angels, the mortal and the immortal, makes his treatment of heaven profoundly ambiguous.

'The Blessed Damozel' is a highly problematic poem for critical analysts, not only because of the numerous changes that Rossetti introduced in the different versions which appeared during his lifetime, but also because no one version is stable in its perspectives on life and death, earth and heaven. According to D. M. R. Bentley, for example, the early Pre-Raphaelite version, published in *The Germ* in 1850, justifies Swinburne's conception of the implied Pre-Raphaelite poet as a Christian.[130] For Bentley, the reader-spectator 'comes to participate in an awareness of the Catholic Middle Ages' in this early version.[131] Yet even this critic acknowledges that a 'mercurial amalgam' can be sensed behind the 1850 version, written by a poet who 'knew about religious doubt as well as medieval faith, about personal misgiving as well as idealistic vision, about despair as well as hope'.[132]

This and later versions, including those of the 1870s, when Rossetti was working on the famous painting of the same name, reflect a radical insecurity in his thinking on the subject of heaven.[133] The poem's structure suggests that Rossetti attended not only to Poe's treatment of a disturbed mind at work but also to his handling of tense. Again the poem is framed in the past tense of traditional narrative forms ('The blessed Damozel leaned out / From the gold bar of Heaven', 1856), although here the place is apparently other-worldly – the matter being in some doubt initially because of the fleshly qualities of the damozel, with her hair 'yellow like ripe corn' and bosom that 'must have made / The bar she lean'd on warm'.[134] Between these two uses of the word 'leaned' in the main narrative is its second use in the poem, where the interpolated voice of the lover states – parenthetically, in the present tense, and in a specific earthly site – that whereas to those the damozel left what seemed her 'day' in heaven had counted as ten years,

> (To *one* it is ten years of years.
> . . . Yet now, and in this place,
> Surely she lean'd o'er me – her hair
> Fell all about my face . . .
> Nothing: the autumn fall of leaves.
> The whole year sets apace.)

For the moment a very recent and transient sense of the damozel's presence is denied, the experience being explained away in terms of nature's annual and thus unremarkable signs of decay and death – important symbols for Keats, Tennyson, and the Pre-Raphaelites – autumn leaves.

Back in the main narrative the damozel's heavenly site is described in more detail, first in the past tense ('It was the rampart of God's house / That she was standing on'), and then in the (eternal) present:

> It lies in Heaven, across the flood
> Of ether, as a bridge.
> Beneath, the tides of day and night
> With flame and darkness ridge
> The void, as low as where this earth
> Spins like a fretful midge.

Here the sense of the separation of heaven from earth suggested by 'rampart' (an improvement on the too modern and domestic 'terrace' in *The Germ*, 1850) is greatly intensified by the modulation from past tense to present, whereby the contrast between the monumental stability of the bar of heaven and the restless mobility of the earth seems to be eternally ordained. Yet while the damozel leans over the fixed bar, looking longingly towards the earth from which her lover's soul will journey, all around her is life and movement in heaven. The final (1881) version of the relevant stanza reads:

> Around her, lovers, newly met
> 'Mid deathless love's acclaims,
> Spoke evermore among themselves
> Their heart-remembered names;
> And the souls mounting up to God
> Went by her like thin flames.

This version of the stanza opens up the poem's central dichotomy between a Romantic idea of heaven as the site of erotic reunion between lovers and a more 'spiritual' idea implied in the 'thin flames'. Rossetti's preliminary sketch (1876) for the background of his painting *The Blessed Damozel* (illustration 10) shows a number of couples meeting, two women in the left foreground in a sisterly kiss-of-peace embrace, the remaining man/woman couples in a variety of amatory embraces. The version of the fourth line of the stanza as quoted at the foot of the sketch, in which the lovers speak 'Their rapturous new names' (1872, 1873), emphasizes the idea of heaven as erotic bliss. For the lovers are enraptured by each other (heaven as reunion and community), not by the experience of the divine presence (heaven as worship). The more pietistic 1850 version in *The Germ* was different in emphasis:

> Heard hardly, some of her new friends,
> > Playing at holy games,
> Spake, gentle-mouthed, among themselves,
> > Their virginal chaste names;
> And the souls, mounting up to God,
> > Went by her like thin flames.

The contrast cannot be explained simply in terms of Rossetti's conscious secularizing of his early work, as 'virginal chaste names' was kept in until 1870. In all versions, however, without her lover the blessed damozel still leans out, not unlike Cathy in her dream in *Wuthering Heights* (9), published in the year that the poem was written, although Cathy's longing was to return to earth. The damozel's sense of longing is expressed in her opening words:

> 'I wish that he were come to me,
> > For he will come,' she said.
> 'Have I not pray'd in Heaven? – on earth,
> > Lord, Lord, has he not pray'd?
> Are not two prayers a perfect strength?
> > And shall I feel afraid?

> 'When round his head the aureole clings,
> > And he is clothed in white,
> I'll take his hand and go with him
> > To the deep wells of light,
> And we will step down as to a stream,
> > And bathe there in God's sight.'   (1856)

Although she is already 'one of God's choristers', her heaven is not a place of worship in Newman's sense. Her prayers are not expressions of praise or thanksgiving, as Beatrice's are in Dante, but petitions for reunion with her lover. Her anthropocentric and Romantic vision of how heaven will be then is that of a virgin ('She had three lilies in her hand') who is still unfulfilled. The eroticism which in a Christian poem might be of the kind expressed in the Song of Songs, and directed towards Christ the Bridegroom, is here channelled into the thought of 'lying' with the lover in heaven. The continuity for which the damozel longs is that between an earthly and a heavenly *paradise*, rather than that of the kingdom as expressed in, say, the doctrine of the communion of saints.

The crucial transition in the final (1881) version of the poem is reminiscent of Tennyson's *In Memoriam*, lyric 41. When the lover actually hears the damozel's words, his interpolated response to her talk of 'we two' being in heaven together in the future is anxious, as he doubts whether their former earthly union could ever be regained:

> (Alas! We two, we two, thou say'st!
>   Yea, one wast thou with me
> That once of old. But shall God lift
>   To endless unity
> The soul whose likeness with thy soul
>   Was but its love for thee?)[135]

In the main narrative the damozel then continues her description of an imagined future bliss for 'we two' in the presence of Christ and of Mary (who, like some tolerant 'Mother' will 'approve' her 'pride' in her lover), after which there are two concluding stanzas in the poem:

> 'There will I ask of Christ the Lord
>   Thus much for him and me: –
> Only to live as once on earth
>   With Love, – only to be,
> As then awhile, for ever now
>   Together, I and he.'

> She gazed and listened and then said,
>   Less sad of speech than mild, –
> 'All this is when he comes.' She ceased[.]
>   The light thrilled towards her, fill'd
> With angels in strong level flight.
>   Her eyes prayed, and she smil'd.

> (I saw her smile.) But soon their path
>   Was vague in distant spheres:
> And then she cast her arms along
>   The golden barriers,
> And laid her face between her hands,
>   And wept. (I heard her tears.)   (1881)

Whereas the apocalyptic prayer of the church militant is for Christ's presence ('Even so, come, Lord Jesus', Revelation 22.20), the damozel's last words in heaven, where Christ is already present, apply to the lover, and have erotic overtones. Her longing to be 'As then awhile, for ever now / Together I and he' is for a future that is not to be realized. For the earthly lover's final parenthetical statements, registering his seeing as well as hearing her, are in the past tense, quietly suggesting that there is no future for them. The damozel is left in a tragic gap between past and future, on the very margin of eternal bliss. Desire remains unfulfilled, heaven, in all versions of the poem, ambiguous.

Rossetti's career as a painter is characterized by an obsessive interest in the idealized female form which signifies the transforming, or perhaps transfiguring power of eroticism which issues in death. The different versions of the seventh stanza of 'The Blessed Damozel' (37–42) reflect a lifelong struggle with this ideal/real paradox, now openly confronted, now suppressed. In the famous oil painting, executed in the 1870s, paradoxes abound (illustration 11). Heaven is presented as a place of life and sexuality, with a deadly-alive damozel who is unsmiling. But then so too are the angels beneath her (only potential mediators between heaven and earth, sited in the space between the bar of heaven and the parallel framing bar beneath them), the lovers behind her, and the figures in Rossetti's other paintings. In March 1878 he deliberately 'brightened' the picture with 'flowers in hedges, aureoles round heads etc.'.[136] The tomb-like arrangement of the predella, however, is suggestive of death, the male figure (like Adam associated with the earth) in a recumbent position, his weapon sheathed (he will not 'come'), the landscape dark and bloomless.

That the idea of a transcendental heaven was problematic for Rossetti is also reflected in his treatment of the nativity in the triptych commissioned for Llandaff Cathedral, and entitled *The Seed of David* (1858–64; illustration 12). Technical problems in executing decorative art of this kind delayed him for years, but the finished design of the central canvas reflects a sympathy with the subject of God made flesh, with angels walking on the earth. Rossetti himself described the arrangement

of the angels who figure in three of the canvas's four vertical divisions
(marked by three characteristically bold horizontal lines) in these terms:

An Angel . . . leads by the hand a King and a Shepherd, who are bowing
themselves before the manger on which the Virgin Mary kneels, holding the
infant Saviour. . . other Angels look in through the opening round the stable,
or play on musical instruments in the loft above.[137]

It is instructive to contrast the cramping of his angels, and the narrow
limits within which Rossetti set what he himself described as 'not a
literal reading of the event of the Nativity, but rather a condensed
symbol of it',[138] with, say, Botticelli's apocalyptic *Mystic Nativity* (*c.*
1500; illustration 13). Here both the enlarged figure of the madonna,
and the strong vertical hierarchy which elevates the angels in heavenly
glory above the earthly scene, privilege the transcendent. Through the
spatial equivalent of the eternal present, Botticelli's mystic nativity folds
earthly time and space into a vision of that new heaven and new earth
when 'we shall see clearly'.[139] Rossetti's vertical hierarchy, on the other
hand, follows earlier models in stopping at the level of the loft, itself
more a prototypical musicians' gallery or organ-loft than a glimpse of
heaven. (One recalls Browning's Bishop at Saint Praxed's.) Rossetti's
nativity scene signifies incarnation but not resurrection, earth as the site
of 'heavenly' love but not of a new heaven and a new earth. Rather it
was his sister Christina who looked for the coming of the kingdom, and
whose cry was 'Come, Lord Jesus.'

   Christina Rossetti commented that 'The Blessed Damozel' fell short of
expressing the 'highest view'.[140] The contrast between her theological
perspective on heaven and her brother's more fleshly view is reflected in
their different experiments with tense. Like the Victorian hymnists,
Christina Rossetti uses what I have called the locutionary present, the
existential present, and the eternal present in her poetry which treats of
heaven. One of her most important forms of syntactic play in this
context (as in the poetry of Coventry Patmore and Francis Thompson) is
her future constructions. Here she exploits the fact that terms such as
'will' or 'shall', 'when' and 'then' can be omitted in English after their
first use in a sentence or clause, thus allowing subsequent verbs which
are primarily to be read as future also to suggest or establish some kind
of present reality, in this case the eternal present. The nearest that one
finds to the effect in 'The Blessed Damozel' is in the second and last lines
of this stanza:

> 'When round his head the aureole clings,
>   And he is clothed in white,
> I'll take his hand and go with him
>   To the deep wells of light;
> We will step down as to a stream,
>   And bathe there in God's sight.'   (73–8)

The first and fifth lines contain strong future constructions ('When . . . clings', 'We will'), whereas in the second and sixth lines, which are syntactically and typographically separated from the initial 'when' or 'will', the sense of future is weakened, although not sufficiently to suggest a secondary reading of these lines as if they stood alone; that is, as if written in the present tense. In the work of Christina Rossetti, however, this syntactic feature is used to make the anticipated heavenly consummation that is not yet, also now.

Whereas Gabriel Rossetti's blessed damozel undergoes no form of judgment, but, soon after death, leans on the bar which divides heaven from the void and the restless world, Christina Rossetti writes of the bar to which the soul will be brought at the last judgment, beyond which heaven is possible. This is the subject of her poem 'After this the Judgment' (MS title 'In Advent'), written during Advent in 1856 and published ten years later. The poem (the first of three of Christina Rossetti's I will examine in some detail) explores the nature of its own art as heavenly song (the speaker longing to 'take up her part' in harmony with the heavenly choir), and is grounded syntactically in present tense constructions similar to those of hymnody and scripture. It begins with a series of familiar analogies of the spiritual quest for heaven, the doors of which are described (as in Newman, cf. Revelation 21.25) standing open for all who would enter:

> As eager homebound traveller to the goal,
>   Or steadfast seeker on an unsearched main,
> Or martyr panting for an aureole,
>   My fellow-pilgrims pass me, and attain
> That hidden mansion of perpetual peace
>   Where keen desire and hope dwell free from pain;
> That gate stands open of perennial ease;
>   I view the glory till I partly long,
> Yet lack the fire of love which quickens these.   (1–9)

The existential present of the first four lines ('pass', 'attain') modulates into the eternal present of heaven ('dwell', 'stands') before returning to the existential ('long', 'lack', 'quickens') via the ambiguous 'view', which only hints at the eternal present. Unlike in 'The Blessed Damozel', it is in the existential present of this mortal life that desire and hope are felt, whereas in heaven they 'dwell free from pain'.

It is through the mediation of a heavenly messenger that the existential and the eternal are to be unified:

> O passing Angel, speed me with a song,
> A melody of heaven to reach my heart
>   And rouse me to the race and make me strong;
> Till in such music I take up my part
>   Swelling those Hallelujahs full of rest,
> One, tenfold, hundredfold, with heavenly art,
>   Fulfilling north and south and east and west,
> Thousand, ten thousandfold, innumerable,
>   All blent in one yet each one manifest;
> Each one distinguished and beloved as well
>   As if no second voice in earth or heaven
> Were lifted up the Love of God to tell.   (10–21)

Taken up into the theocentric heaven that is everlasting worship, the speaker's 'voice' will ultimately remain unique and yet be 'blent in one', as it never can be within the limits of earthly language. Indeed, the merging of the future construction after 'Till' (13) into the eternal present represents no more than a foretaste of a heaven that is not yet.

Divine love, which subsumes the highest expressions of profane love ('Be Husband, Brother, closest Friend to me; / Love me as very mother loves her Son', 28–9), also includes judgment, without which heaven is impossible (36ff.). Within the projected future of that judgment ('Shall meet me at the inexorable bar', 44) the omission of later 'shalls' also suggests that it is a present spiritual reality:

> How shall I then stand up before Thy face . . .
>
>   . . . when no rock
>   Remains to fall on me, no tree to hide,
> But I stand all creation's gazing-stock,
>   Exposed and comfortless on every side,
> Placed trembling in the final balances
>   Whose poise this hour, this moment, must be tried? –   (40, 49–54)

The judgment 'after this' of the title, expressed in terms of future time (*chronos*), is also experienced now, in the season of penance that is Advent (*kairos*).

The final section of the poem draws upon the farewell discourses in the fourth gospel in which the present tense is that of the 'hour' which 'was come that he should depart out of this world unto the Father' (John 13.1) and of the season in which the disciples are to be tested:

> This is my commandment, That ye love one another, as I have loved you.
> Greater love hath no man than this, that a man lay down his life for his friends.
> Ye are my friends, if ye do whatsoever I command you.
>
> (John 15.12–14)

A poem of petitions ('speed me with a song', 'Draw Thou mine eyes') now concludes with a prayerful meditation on the passion which is reminiscent of Hopkins in its spiritual intensity:

> Ah Love of God, if greater love than this
>   Hath no man, that a man die for his friend,
> And if such love of love Thine Own Love is,
>   Plead with Thyself, with me, before the end;
> Redeem me from the irrevocable past;
>   Pitch Thou Thy Presence round me to defend;
> Yea seek with piercèd feet, yea hold me fast
>   With piercèd hands whose wounds were made by love;
> Not what I am, remember what Thou wast
>   When darkness hid from Thee Thy heavens above,
> And sin Thy Father's Face, while Thou didst drink
>   The bitter cup of death, didst taste thereof
> For every man; while Thou wast nigh to sink
>   Beneath the intense intolerable rod,
> Grown sick of love; not what I am, but think
>   Thy Life then ransomed mine, my God, my God.   (55–70)

This prayer draws both past and future into the urgent immediacy of its present tense: pleading for the redemption of past sins at the future judgment, it recalls both the historical reality and the eternal efficacy of Christ's death and passion. The voice which addresses God in the present of a projected future judgment is also located in the poem's locutionary present. Thus specific petitions such as 'Pitch Thou Thy Presence round me to defend' are for today, but also for yesterday, and for ever.

This theme of judgment is also central to a poem which has been described as making up a pair with 'The Blessed Damozel', namely 'The Convent Threshold', written in July 1858 and published four years later.[141] The poem opens with a reference to yet another bar:

> There's blood between us, love, my love,
> There's father's blood, there's brother's blood;
> And blood's a bar I cannot pass:
> I choose the stairs that mount above,
> Stair after golden skyward stair,
> To city and to sea of glass.   (1–6)

While her lover looks 'earthward' and sees a pagan earthly paradise (30–7), the speaker, acknowledging that her 'lily feet are soiled with mud' (7), looks up to the heaven of the martyrs:

> I see the far-off city grand,
> Beyond the hills a watered land,
> Beyond the gulf a gleaming strand
> Of mansions where the righteous sup . . .   (18–21)

This contrast between the sacred and the profane becomes more pressing, however, when the poem takes on a strongly Adventist note: 'The time is short and yet you stay' (46).

It is in a later passage that 'The Convent Threshold' most clearly locates itself in relation to 'The Blessed Damozel':

> How should I rest in Paradise,
> Or sit on steps of heaven alone?
> If Saints and Angels spoke of love
> Should I not answer from my throne:
> Have pity upon me, ye my friends,
> For I have heard the sound thereof:
> Should I not turn with yearning eyes,
> Turn earthwards with a pitiful pang?
> Oh save me from a pang in heaven.   (69–77)

The dramatic impact of the locutionary present in this last line is prepared for in line 73 ('Have pity upon me'), where the present is that of a projected future paradise and heaven, the provisionality of which is indicated by the use of the subjunctive mode. Other projections follow, this time in the past tense of a remembered series of dreams, the second of which brings *eros* and *thanatos* into contiguity through Gothic play with the idea of the grave as a bed (110–25). Having prayed for her lover in words she cannot write (130), the speaker has emerged from this dark night of the senses with pinched face and grey hair, and with frozen blood on the sill (134–5).

This shuffling of tenses, which is characteristic of dream narratives, prepares for the remarkable final section, where the eternal present of heaven is brought into the locutionary present of the poem, more in the manner of hymnody:

> If now you saw me you would say:
> Where is the face I used to love?
> And I would answer: Gone before;
> It tarries veiled in paradise.
> When once the morning star shall rise,
> When earth with shadow flees away
> And we stand safe within the door,
> Then you shall lift the veil thereof.
> Look up, rise up: for far above
> Our palms are grown, our place is set;
> There we shall meet as once we met
> And love with old familiar love.   (137–48)

In the first lines quoted it is a present, earthly meeting rather than a future, heavenly reunion that is imagined in the subjunctive mode. Within that present the lover's looking back into the past ('the face I used to love') contrasts with the speaker's 'Gone before'. This elegant use of the familiar consolatory euphemism opens up both the present and future constructions which alternate in the subsequent lines (141–4), in a manner which is reminiscent of the Revelation, the subject of Christina Rossetti's devotional commentary, *The Face of the Deep* (1892).[142] It also prepares for the conflation in line 140 ('It tarries veiled in paradise') of the existential present of the liminal conventual life referred to in the poem's title and the eternal present of the intermediate state of paradise in which, after death, she will wait for the last judgment and eventual reunion in heaven. For the speaker, the reconciliation of sacred and profane love is possible only when the God of love is all in all, at the end of time. Only through renunciation in this life, the speaker believes, can she and her lover avoid the danger of sin, and thus anticipate in certain hope the 'safe' reward that is reserved for them even now in heaven. Only through her grappling with past and future realities, as in the poem's penultimate line, can the anticipated eternal present of the final line speak of the love that is ultimately to be expressed only in heaven.

Four months after writing this poem, Christina Rossetti produced one of her most fully developed dramatized accounts of heaven in verse. The title 'From House to Home' sends us back to that favourite Victorian idea of heaven which provided material for consolatory manuals by writers such as William Branks and E. H. Bickersteth, and which Jane Eyre misinterpreted at Helen Burns's deathbed. As in 'After This the Judgment', the poem rejects an 'earthly paradise supremely fair' (7), although here the 'pleasure-place', which is within her soul, is described in wonderful detail, rivalling that of Tennyson in 'The Palace of Art', to which it clearly refers. Continuing in the narrative past tense, the speaker describes her 'angel' companion and how he left her when she denied his 'Tonight' with 'Tomorrow' (65–8). Again her renunciation of sexual love changes her overnight (78), but 'something' whispers, 'You shall meet again, / Meet in a distant land' (91–2).

It is through the speaker's vision of a woman 'in a certain place', however, again described in the past tense, that this distant land is mediated in the poem. As she suffers, voices call out on her behalf, the last of which answers, 'Rend the veil, declare the end, / Strengthen her ere she goes' (159). In the description of the apocalypse which follows, all the stages of the last days to which Pollok and Bickersteth devote whole books in their epic poems are drawn together in one mighty consummation – of the world, of the mystic marriage of Christ with his church, and, it is implied, of all profane love. The past tense in which the vision is recalled complements the intertextuality of a passage which draws upon the Revelation and, in a beautifully weighted pun on 'rose', the *Paradiso*:

> Multitudes – multitudes – stood up in bliss,
>   Made equal to the angels, glorious, fair;
> With harps, palms, wedding-garments, kiss of peace,
>   And crowned and haloed hair.
>
> They sang a song, a new song in the height,
>   Harping with harps to Him Who is Strong and True:
> They drank new wine, their eyes saw with new light,
>   Lo, all things were made new.

> Tier beyond tier they rose and rose and rose
>   So high that it was dreadful, flames with flames:
> No man could number them, no tongue disclose
>   Their secret sacred names.
>
> As tho' one pulse stirred all, one rush of blood
>   Fed all, one breath swept thro' them myriad-voiced,
> They struck their harps, cast down their crowns, they stood
>   And worshipped and rejoiced.   (165–80)

In 'After This the Judgment', unity in difference, when voices are 'All blent in one yet each one manifest', remains future. Here, through the use of the narrative past tense and through simile ('As tho' one pulse stirred all'), it is already achieved.

From 'all' the speaker moves to 'each':

> Each face looked one way like a moon new-lit,
>   Each face looked one way towards its Sun of Love;
> Drank love and bathed in love and mirrored it
>   And knew no end thereof.   (185–8)

F. D. Maurice, that other admirer of Dante and commentator on the Revelation, defends the idea of heaven as worship by arguing that 'all is worship' there, 'because all are referring their thoughts and acts to one centre'.[143] Where Maurice strives to reconcile work and worship in heaven, the vision in 'From House to Home' points to a reconciliation between sacred and profane love:

> Glory touched glory on each blessèd head,
>   Hands locked dear hands never to sunder more:
> These were the new-begotten from the dead
>   Whom the great birthday bore.
>
> Heart answered heart, soul answered soul at rest,
>   Double against each other, filled, sufficed:
> All loving, loved of all; but loving best
>   And best beloved of Christ.
>
> I saw that one who lost her love in pain,
>   Who trod on thorns, who drank the loathsome cup;
> The lost in night, in day was found again;
>   The fallen was lifted up.   (185–96)

Some of the favourite clichés of the writers of sacred poems for mourners, and of novelists such as Mrs Henry Wood in England and

Elizabeth Stuart Phelps in America – 'hands locked dear hands', 'the great birthday', 'heart answered heart' – here regain vigour and authority in their true eschatological context: an apocalyptic discourse in which profane love is fulfilled in the consummation that is a theocentric heaven of everlasting worship, and in which the language of *eros* ('Double against each other, filled sufficed') is taken up into the mystical language of heaven's *agape* – precisely the opposite of Dante Gabriel Rossetti's 'transvaluation' of the Christian idea of divine love.[144] Like the woman who has 'fallen' on thorns, the fallen language of this world is here 'lifted up'.

In the poem's closing section the speaker makes this vision the basis for her argument to her lover, in the here-and-now of the existential present: 'Therefore in patience I possess my soul' (205). The biblical metaphor of the vine with which the poem ends is here sacramental in emphasis:

> Altho' today He prunes my twigs with pain,
>   Yet doth His blood nourish and warm my root:
> Tomorrow I shall put forth buds again
>   And clothe myself with fruit.
>
> Altho' today I walk in tedious ways,
>   Today His staff is turned into a rod,
> Yet will I wait for Him the appointed days
>   And stay upon my God.

The eucharist at once anticipates and partakes in the feast of the heavenly reward. As in 'After This the Judgment', that reward is for those who have been 'pruned' and who have felt the 'rod' which signifies the love of God as judge. Yet will the speaker wait for Him the appointed days, and stay(s) upon her God.

Through subtle changes of tense and mode, then, Christina Rossetti's eschatological poetry folds present renunciation into future judgment, future heaven into present vision. Where her brother looked for the transfiguration of the body through the erotic in the here-and-now, she anticipated the transformation of the spiritual body described by St Paul, and the deferred consummation of all earthly longings in the mystical marriage of Christ with his church in the *eschaton*. Coventry Patmore, an associate of the Pre-Raphaelites from the beginning of the movement, attempted in his most important poetry a reconciliation of ideas which are broadly similar to these two positions. I Corinthians

15.46, a verse which is often overlooked, was a favourite text: 'that was not first which is spiritual, but that which is natural; and afterward that which is spiritual'.[145] Like, in my view, two friends of his early years in the British Museum library – Dante Gabriel Rossetti and Alfred Tennyson – he thought of the incarnation as the greatest 'secret' of all: 'an event which is renewed in the body of every one who is in the way to the fulfilment of his original destiny'.[146] He is perhaps closest to Gabriel Rossetti when he argues that the 'spiritual body, into which the bodies of those who love and obey God perfectly are from time to time transfigured, is a prism'.[147] Yet although this Victorian laureate of married love, who believed in the chastity of marriage, was strongly influenced by Swedenborg, he was aware with Aquinas that, in J. C. Reid's words, 'the sacramental quality of marriage does not lie in intercourse'.[148] A major shift in his thinking in later life brought him closer to the position of the Rossetti whose name was taken by his daughter when she became a nun:

In Patmore's progress beyond and through the sanctified analogy of married love to a wider acceptance of love in which, mystically, the body is made holy through rejection of the pleasures of the body, and in which, while married love is still accepted as a great and holy love, a foreshadowing of the union with God, dedicated celibacy is a love of at least equal and perhaps higher virtue, Sister Mary Christina's example was paramount.[149]

Whereas much of Christina Rossetti's poetry resists autobiographical readings,[150] Patmore's bereavement odes almost invite them. The death of his first wife Emily in 1862 proved to be the fulcrum around which both his life and work turned, occurring after the completion of *The Angel in the House*, which she had inspired, and releasing in him much of his best writing, in a way which anticipates Thomas Hardy's development as a poet fifty years later.[151] Yet two years after Emily's death, Patmore converted to Roman Catholicism, as she had prophesied he would, and remarried, as she had wanted him to. His change of project from the spiritualizing of human love in *The Angel in the House* to the humanizing of divine love in *The Unknown Eros*[152] represented not only a reversed perspective on the same subject, as the incarnation might be treated in a theological treatise, but also an attempt to justify (primarily to himself) his remarrying so soon after the wife he had idealized, and who was now in heaven, had 'departed' with 'sudden, unintelligible phrase'.[153]

One of the most successful of Patmore's early bereavement odes, which was to be placed immediately before 'Departure' in *The Unknown Eros* (1877), was 'The Azalea', a poem based upon an actual experience.[154] A number of familiar elements of Victorian domestic elegiac writing are present: a misinterpretation as the central narrative event; a dream; a letter written by the dead person. So too is the domestic interior, in this case the married couple's bedroom:

> There, where the sun shines first
> Against our room
> She train'd the gold Azalea, whose perfume
> She, Spring-like, from her breathing grace dispersed.
> Last night the delicate crests of saffron bloom,
> For this their dainty likeness watch'd and nurst,
> Were just at point to burst.   (1–7)

The sense of daily recurrence in the first four lines, brought quietly into question by the shift from the present tense to the past, is interrupted in the specificity of 'last night' and the expectancy of 'just at point to burst'. The line that follows echoes Wordsworth's 'Lucy' poem:

> At dawn I dream'd, O God, that she was dead,
> And groan'd aloud upon my wretched bed,
> And waked, ah, God, and did not waken her,
> But lay, with eyes still closed,
> Perfectly bless'd in the delicious sphere
> By which I knew so well that she was near,
> My heart to speechless thankfulness composed.   (8–14)

Ironically the scent which the speaker associates with his wife is described in line 12 in terms which would better describe his wife's fixed state in heaven than his fool's paradise in a liminal phase between sleep and consciousness:

> Till 'gan to stir
> A dizzy somewhat in my troubled head –
> It *was* the azalea's breath, and she *was* dead!
> The warm night had the lingering buds disclosed,
> And I had fall'n asleep with to my breast
> A chance-found letter press'd
> In which she said,
> 'So, till to-morrow eve, my Own, adieu!
> Parting's well-paid with soon again to meet,
> Soon in your arms to feel so small and sweet,
> Sweet to myself that am so sweet to you!'   (15–25)

Following the descent from a dream state to waking reality with which the past narrative had to end, the epistolary form in lines 22–5, grounded in the present, introduces a future dimension which, in this context, can be read off as hope of (erotic) reunion in heaven, thus reversing the flow of the irony in line 12.

Whereas the subtext in 'The Azalea' is suggestive of the Romantics' heaven of reunion, the second of the three Patmore odes I wish to consider overtly draws upon New Testament eschatology in relating this bereavement and the possibility of remarriage to Christ's passion and resurrection, a central *topos* of Roman Catholic devotions.[155] In 'Tired Memory', one of the odes originally printed for private circulation in 1868, three of the poem's four turns from the past tense of the narrative to the present tense of direct speech foreground this intertextual relationship. The speaker's prayers to keep his 'vows of faith' having proved empty, he has also failed to find an outlet for 'duteous love':

> But, kneeling in a Church, one Easter-Day,
> It came to me to say:
> 'Though there is no intelligible rest
> In Earth or Heaven,
> For me, but on her breast,
> I yield her up, again to have her given,
> Or not, as, Lord, Thou wilt, and that for aye.'

Just as the women and the eleven had to 'yield him up' on the first Good Friday, and again after the resurrection, so the speaker must let his first wife go. He must also leave in God's hands the mystery embodied in the problem text with which Patmore most frequently wrestled: 'they which shall be accounted worthy to obtain that world, and the resurrection from the dead, neither marry, nor are given in marriage' (Luke 20.35).

Having for the first time dreamt of 'possessing' his 'most Dear' in 'gay, celestial beauty nothing coy', and experienced 'fresh despair' on waking, the speaker records his further attempt to pray in his own Gethsemane:

> In agony, I cried:
> 'My Lord, if Thy strange will be this,
> That I should crucify my heart,
> Because my love has also been my pride,
> I do submit, if I saw how, to bliss
> Wherein She has no part.'
> And I was heard,
> And taken at my own remorseless word.

In a radical reversal of the norm, the 'bliss' that primarily signifies the other-worldly (marriage in heaven) is here to be 'submitted to' in this world, through remarriage. (Where Christina Rossetti's way of the cross involved renouncing the love of two men on religious grounds, Patmore's led to two further marriages.)

The final passage of direct speech is the first wife's reply to her husband's question:

> O, my most Dear,
> Was't treason, as I fear?
> 'Twere that, and worse, to plead thy veiled mind,
> Kissing thy babes, and murmuring in mine ear,
> 'Thou canst not be
> Faithful to God, and faithless unto me!'
> Ah, prophet kind!
> I heard, all dumb and blind
> With tears of protest; and I cannot see
> But faith was broken.

The simplicity of the wife's words, suggestive in their eternal present of life with and in God, has great authority for the speaker in his troubled and confused state, following his intimations of Gethsemane and Golgotha. The speaker's Lucan parallels now reach their logical culmination in a road-to-Emmaus event, when, 'Dead of devotion and tired memory', he recognizes 'a strange grace' of his dead wife in a 'fair stranger', whom he describes as her 'Sister sweet':

> So that I lived again,
> And, strange to aver,
> With no relapse into the void inane
> For thee;
> But (treason was't) for thee and also her.

Already in parenthesis, the sense of betrayal in the poem's final line will, it is suggested, fade in the resurrection life of his 'living again'.

Like the followers of Jesus after his death and burial, the speaker, caught between despair and hope, is given a sign. With extraordinary boldness, Patmore relates the speaker's spiritual renewal to the resurrection life of the early church, when men and women held all things in common, in anticipation of the coming of the kingdom. Thus, on a biographical reading, the possibility that conversion to Roman Catholicism would eternally separate Patmore from his first wife is gently denied in the speaker's description of the 'fair stranger' as his dead wife's 'sister'. The theology which informs this description is more overtly spelt out in Patmore's devotional odes such as 'Deliciae Sapientiae de Amore', also printed in the anonymous volume of 1868, and later placed in Book II of *The Unknown Eros* (IX). Here the speaker is not in a domestic setting where he can perceive only intimations of heaven. Sited instead 'by the Porch / Of the glad Palace of Virginity', he invites all to 'behold / The dainty and unsating Marriage-Feast'. Again reversing the norm, heavenly music in praise of 'the Husband of the Heavens' is played upon 'the harps they bore from Earth, five-strung', thus sanctifying the profane. The Blessed Virgin Mary is then seen in glory:

> And how the shining sacrificial Choirs,
> Offering for aye their dearest hearts' desires,
> Which to their hearts come back beatified,
> Hymn, the bright aisles along,
> The nuptial song,
> Song ever new to us and them, that saith,
> 'Hail Virgin in Virginity a Spouse!'
> Heard first below
> Within the little house
> At Nazareth;
> Heard yet in many a cell where brides of Christ
> Lie hid, emparadised,
> And where, although
> By the hour 'tis night,
> There's light,
> The Day still lingering in the lap of snow.

'The Azalea' explores the ironies of loss and bereavement via the perfume which the dead wife's 'breathing grace dispersed'. 'Tired Memory' records a moment of uncanny recognition through a 'strange grace' of the wife in a 'fair stranger'. Here hymnody in the eternal present of the heavenly 'nuptial song' echoes for ever both the yesterday of the first Ave (Luke 1.28) and the today of the sisters who repeat it ('Hail Mary, full of grace') in their hidden lives as brides of Christ, their condition on earth akin to the intermediate state of paradise, their convent cells reminiscent of the humble little house at Nazareth.

Patmore's belief in the chastity of marriage is reflected in the lines that follow:

> Gaze and be not afraid
> Ye wedded few that honour, in sweet thought
> And glittering will,
> So freshly from the garden gather still
> The lily sacrificed
>
> . . .
>
> 'Tis there your Hymen waits!

In heaven the limits of earthly language fall away, and 'each to other' sighs, 'Twas this we meant!' Similarly, wholeness in the form of virginity could in Patmore's view be regained through penitence and turning to God in love.[156] Thus of the holy virgins, none 'Save One' looks 'fairer' than Mary Magdalene, and all who love God are, in the poem's final lines,

> Heirs of the Palace glad,
> And inly clad
> With the bridal robes of ardour virginal.

'Deliciae Sapientiae de Amore' is not about progress or development in heaven but rather the heavenly state as the consummation of the earthly life. Indeed, 'consummation', or the relationship between its different kinds of completion – of marriage, of earthly life, of the temporal world – is often the implicit subject of his and the Rossettis' writing. In Patmore's Marian 'Deliciae', the other-worldly consummation is mediated through a vision described by a speaker located in a privileged site 'above'. In other poems the perspective is this-worldly, and heaven is mediated through a variety of means: in Dante Gabriel Rossetti by making heaven 'fleshly'; in Christina Rossetti via the sacraments, or the seasons of the Christian year which formalize the 'seasons' of God's relationship with man, or visions seen in the here-and-now; in Coventry Patmore through the 'grace' of a perfume, or of a physical likeness which indicates sisterhood. Like these precursors, Francis Thompson adapts the syntactic resources of tense and mode to his own special purposes in writing different kinds of mediating vision of heaven. For Thompson, however, it is primarily the *kingdom* of heaven which the incarnation has inaugurated, and which perfectly expresses the love of God for man, or the grace which operates from God's side to man's, from the other-worldly to the this-worldly.

It was on the basis of *The Unknown Eros* that Francis Thompson became a respectful admirer of Coventry Patmore.[157] Alice Meynell (the Roman Catholic poet who pointed out that Patmore's 'Angel' was not his wife Emily, but rather Love) and her husband Wilfrid brought the two men together in Patmore's last years, when he shared his 'secret self' with Thompson.[158] As Patmore aged, in the early 1890s, a group of young Capuchin Franciscans came to see Thompson, their contemporary, as the natural heir to their former 'prophet'.[159] If this reflects the poets' shared opinions concerning the interrelationship between the spiritual and material worlds, other aspects of their writing reveal differences between them. Compared to Patmore's domestic bereavement odes, which, like much of the Rossettis' poetry, are somewhat claustrophobic in atmosphere, Thompson's poetry is positively bracing. Patmore could not have described marriage as '*mere* knocking at the gates of union', as the bachelor Thompson did:

Therefore sings Dante, and sing all noble poets after him, that Love in this world is a pilgrim and a wanderer, journeying to the New Jerusalem: not here is the consummation of his yearnings, in that mere knocking at the gates of union which we christen marriage, but beyond the pillars of death and the corridors of the grave, in the union of spirit to spirit within the containing Spirit of God.[160]

Nor does Patmore's poetry convey a strong sense of the kingdom of heaven that is within and among us, a sign of God's king-ship in the world, as Thompson's does.

Indeed, Francis Thompson's genius – like Gerard Manley Hopkins's – was to internalize what other poets earlier in the nineteenth century had attempted to describe as some kind of external reality. The classic example is, of course, 'The Hound of Heaven' (1890):

> I fled Him, down the nights and down the days;
> I fled Him, down the arches of the years;
> I fled Him, down the labyrinthine ways
>   Of my own mind; and in the mist of tears
> I hid from Him, and under running laughter.
>   Up vistaed hopes I sped;
>   And shot, precipitated,
> Adown Titanic glooms of chasmed fears,
>   From those strong Feet that followed, followed after.   (1–9)[161]

Thompson's late Victorian Catholic baroque internalizes the kind of sublime landscape that the nineteenth-century Protestant epic had located as external, remotely 'above' or 'below', other-worldly. As in Augustine and the medieval mystics, Thompson's subject is the I/Thou relationship between man and God, whose love pursues its 'prey'.[162] Heaven itself is only 'dimly guessed' (143), the 'battlements of Eternity' rarely emerging from the mists (145). So intimate is the love expressed to the speaker in the present tense of the poem's closing lines that the favourite Victorian idea of heaven reads quite naturally as a homely sign of what is 'stored' for him (cf. 1 Peter 1.4). In contrast to the haunting 'shadow' of Poe's Raven, it is God's hand that will shade him:

> 'All which thy child's mistake
> Fancies as lost, I have stored for thee at home:
> Rise, clasp My hand, and come!'
> Halts by me that footfall:
> Is my gloom, after all,
> Shade of His hand, outstretched caressingly?
> 'Ah, fondest, blindest, weakest,
> I am He Whom thou seekest!
> Thou dravest love from thee, who dravest Me.'   (174–82)

Line 181 recalls Mary Magdalene's recognition of her risen Lord ('Woman, whom seekest thou?', John 20.15) and Peter's self-identification after his vision, when he hears the voice of the Lord ('I am he whom ye seek', Acts 10.21). It is in the now of God's presence that what has been a pursuit becomes a completion or consummation, here marked by the past tense of the poem's final line.[163]

Thompson himself thought that 'The Hound of Heaven' was the greatest of his odes because it 'embodies a world-wide experience in an individual form of that experience: the universal becoming incarnated in the personal'.[164] Although more culturally specific, two of the odes which explore the mystery of the passion of the incarnate Son also 'incarnate' the subject in the personal, treating it with a vigorous excess reminiscent of seventeenth-century religious verse. 'Ode to the Setting Sun' (1890) reflects Thompson's reading of Crashaw for an essay he completed shortly before writing the poem.[165] The 'Prelude' establishes in the present tense a specific moment in time – 'The wailful sweetness of the violin / Floats down the hushed waters of the wind' (1–2) – and earths the poem in a specific place, based on the 'Field of the Cross' at the Praemonstratensian Priory at Storrington (at this time his home), where the cross is actually 'planted' (17). Taking up Patmore's theme in 'Winter' (*The Unknown Eros*, I.III), whose 'dim cloud' has 'less the characters of dark and cold / Than warmth and light asleep', the ode announces that 'It is the falling star that trails the light, / It is the breaking wave that hath the might' (8–9). From its initial claim that 'The fairest things in life are Death and Birth, / And of these two the fairer thing is Death' (3–4), the ode works towards its last words – 'and Death is Birth' (238) – via meditations on the setting sun/Son, the hill, like the cross, standing 'black as life against eternity' (203). The universal is made personal in the poem's 'After-Strain', where the poems' spatial and temporal setting is again made vividly present – 'One step, and lo! the Cross stands gaunt and long / 'Twixt me and yet bright skies, a presaged dole' (3–4). Yet the first-person plural of line 6 is both specific (of this community) and universal (of all humankind): 'Even so, O Cross! thine is the victory. / Thy roots are fast within our fairest fields' (5–6).

Thompson began work on the 'Ode to the Setting Sun' in the Field of the Cross at Storrington, and finished it 'ascending and descending Jacob's Ladder' – the local name for a steep path built into the side of the downs.[166] This other favourite symbol of mediation between earth and heaven figures prominently in one of his later poems, written in the early years of the twentieth century, which should be quoted in full:

> O world invisible, we view thee,
> O world intangible, we touch thee,
> O world unknowable, we know thee,
> Inapprehensible, we clutch thee!
>
> Does the fish soar to find the ocean,
> The eagle plunge to find the air –
> That we ask of the stars in motion
> If they have rumour of thee there?
>
> Not where the wheeling systems darken,
> And our benumbed conceiving soars! –
> The drift of pinions, would we hearken,
> Beats at our own clay-shuttered doors.
>
> The angels keep their ancient places; –
> Turn but a stone, and start a wing!
> 'Tis ye, 'tis your estranged faces,
> That miss the many-splendoured thing.

But (when so sad thou canst not sadder)
Cry; – and upon thy so sore loss
Shall shine the traffic of Jacob's ladder
Pitched betwixt Heaven and Charing Cross.

Yea, in the night, my Soul, my daughter,
Cry, – clinging Heaven by the hems;
And lo, Christ walking on the water
Not of Gennesareth, but Thames!
                    ('The Kingdom of God: "In no Strange Land"')

The subtitle is a quotation from Coventry Patmore's poem 'The Three Witnesses'. As Brigid Boardman points out, however, Thompson does not 'commit the error which he had feared in Patmore's too-ready identification between the natural and the supernatural, carried dangerously further by his Capuchin friends'.[167] Like Newman in the 1830s, Thompson writes of the kingdom of God 'now and here', and 'among us', but also as other, and ultimately mysterious.[168] The poem's immediacy, reminiscent now of Vaughan, now of Blake, is achieved through the use of an existential present which presses towards the eternal present of the penultimate stanza, where the constant mediatory 'traffic' of the angels (in the old sense of commerce) between earth and heaven promises to break through into the modern world of London with its 'traffic' (in the new, nineteenth-century sense of vehicular movement). This imagined future mediation prepares for the revelation in the final stanza, where the durative present of 'clinging' and 'walking' is reminiscent of the eternal present of the Apocalypse and of Victorian hymnody. As in the sacrament of the eucharist, the mystery of the incarnation is constantly renewed in each generation.

In Francis Thompson's 'Ode for the Diamond Jubilee of Queen Victoria, 1897', the 'long Victorian line that passed with printless tread' is headed by the 'holy poets, two on two' (17–18). Along with Tennyson, Robert and Elizabeth Barrett Browning, and Matthew Arnold are three other poets. Dante Gabriel Rossetti comes on 'disranked', his heart stirring within his breast 'like lightning in a cloud, a Spirit without rest' (48–50). Elizabeth Barrett's 'fervid breathing' breaks on Christina Rossetti's 'gentle-taken breath' (46–7). Coventry Patmore, Thompson's friend and co-religionist, is honoured above all, walking alone as the 'throngs' give room to him (57–8), until he turns away to find his 'station in the dim, / Where the sole-thoughted Dante waited him' (70–1).

It would be misguided to look for clues to Thompson's idea of a future life in this highly formalized processional ode, which goes on to celebrate a wide range of Victoria's pantheon of departed national heroes. His choice and treatment of the 'holy poets' I have discussed in this section is, however, of some interest. That he should have associated only Patmore with Dante, for example, and not the Rossettis, is suggestive of partiality. What Thompson himself shared with these poets was a sense of the centrality of the incarnation to the theology of heaven, paradise and the kingdom in the nineteenth century. Whereas Victorian hymns tended to work within a comparatively narrow syntactic range, being grounded in the locutionary present which a liturgical context dictated, the odes and dramatic monologues of these poets modulate from past to future tense, from existential to eternal present, from indicative to subjunctive mode, as they explore the relationship between sacred and profane love within the horizon of eternal life.

CHAPTER 4

Hell

And is there in GOD's world so drear a place,
   Where the loud bitter cry is rais'd in vain?
Where tears of penance come too late for grace,
   As on th'uprooted flower the genial rain?
         John Keble, *The Christian Year*[1]

Edward Henry Bickersteth, that most prolific of Evangelical writers on the four last things, held firmly to what F. W. Farrar described as the 'common view' of salvation, and would have responded as the High Churchman Keble did to his own rhetorical question in the epigraph above: ''Tis even so.' Written in the middle of a period in which belief in everlasting punishment declined, Bickersteth's epic poem *Yesterday, To-Day, and For Ever* (1866) again provides a helpful point of reference, reflecting in its treatment of the subject the kind of views which fuelled fierce theological controversy during much of Victoria's reign.[2]

Having made his 'Descent to Hades' (Book I), the Seer is shown the 'Paradise of the Blessed Dead' (II) by Oriel, who then leads him to 'The Prison of the Lost' (III). This 'realm of night' (98), the 'awarded prison / Of darkness, till the judgment trumpet sounds' (171–2), is grave-like in its subterranean position, its darkness, and its transitional nature. A 'world o'ershadow'd with the pall of death, / The sepulchre of life' (103–4), it will be emptied on the last day. Crucially – and here was a stumbling-block for many in the nineteenth century – there is no possibility of avoiding the ultimate doom that is Gehenna after the last judgment. Thus 'there is no path / From hell to heaven, from heaven to hell direct' (158–9).

Later in Book III, Oriel relates the story of one of the lost souls, Theodore, who in the fourth century renounced his Christian faith, married a pagan, and was almost immediately killed in battle. Citing Matthew 16.18 and Dante's *Inferno*, many nineteenth-century writers invested the gates of hell with particular symbolic significance, and here Bickersteth makes Oriel describe his leading Theodore up to the great 'iron gates' (499) which 'recoil'd / Back, slowly back, with ponderous noise' (513–14). These gates and the walls of hell are, as Bickersteth's precursor Robert Pollok emphasized in *The Course of Time* (1827), 'Above all flight of hope'.[3] Thus when Theodore asks for Christ's mercy, Oriel tells him that his plea cannot possibly be answered: the only way in which he can serve his maker is in 'passive submission' (592). Now he and the other lost souls 'wait their sentence' at the judgment which is 'beyond' (594).

When he first entered the prison of the lost, Theodore caught a glimpse, 'permitted him by God', of paradise in the distance (624), and Oriel had to remind him of 'the deep inexorable gulf' (650) described in the parable of Dives and Lazarus (Luke 16). Fifteen centuries later, Theodore, who has always had paradise in view (809), has undergone a 'solemn change'. But here Oriel makes an important general observation:

> Lost souls of every type were there: and yet
> The hell of one was not another's hell.
> Nor needed separate prisons to adjust
> The righteous meed of punishment to each.
> As they had sinn'd, they suffer'd . . .   (906–10)

and the 'native idealities of men' remain 'immutable for ever' (987).

The first three books of *Yesterday, To-Day, and For Ever* are anticipatory, like the intermediate states in Hades that they describe (v.669–81). Before, however, the description of the last judgment and the dismissal of the damned to Gehenna in the poem's final books, Bickersteth's treatment of the 'Redemption' (VII) reflects the close identity between hell and the atonement that one would expect to find in the work of a nineteenth-century Evangelical. He criticized Milton elsewhere for describing the war in heaven as taking place before the creation of man, instead of after Christ's ascension.[4] For Bickersteth, the focus of the battle between God and Satan, good and evil, love and death, in human history was Christ's redemptive act upon the cross (VII.777–94). Even before the deposition, Christ 'traversed the dark avenue that leads / Straight to the adamantine doors of hell' (844). When those detained in the prison of the lost, seeing him without strength, tried to detain him in order to secure their own release, he was drawn by his Father across the gulf that separates the two halves of Hades. The awful final destination of the damned was then disclosed, when fissures opened up to reveal 'A lower depth of fire unquenchable, / Gehenna's lake, soon hidden' (888–9).

In 'The Last Judgment' (XI), the prison of the lost is emptied and destroyed, falling 'sheer into the bottomless pit':

> But huge
> As was that ruin, loom'd more huge, more vast
> That shoreless fathomless abyss of fire,
> Which swallow'd up in its remorseless waves
> Whatever lay beyond the mighty gulf
> Coasting the triple wall of Paradise.   (XI.534–9)

Like Pollok, Bickersteth gives much more space to the damned than to the risen saints in his account of the last judgment, emphasizing 'the terrors of the wrath to come' (511) rather than the hope of heaven. The description of Gehenna follows Matthew 25: even Satan's 'apostate spirits' could only answer,

> 'Thou art righteous, Lord:'
> And, as the awful sentence fell on each
> Of chains and everlasting banishment
> To his own portion in the lake of fire,
> As by the Spirit of holiness compell'd
> We and the blessed angels said, Amen.   (700–5)

Satan is then crushed under the 'burning heel' of his conqueror, the 'crystal empyrean' opens beneath him, and he and his rebel armies fall into a 'yawning gulf':

> Standing upon its rugged edge we gazed
> Intently' and long down after them; and there
> They sank and sank, the forms more indistinct,
> The cries more faint, the echoes feebler, till
> The firmamental pavement closed again:
> And silence was in heaven.   (740–5)

(Again there are parallels with the grave, the angels looking down as if into the deepest of graves.) The 'millions of the dead', the lost, are then also judged, beginning with Cain and including Theodore, and are finally dismissed to everlasting fire 'Beneath Gehenna's burning sulphurous waves' (879). Sounds of wailing subside as 'His Eye, who is consuming fire' (923) quells the damned into silence, broken only when Satan leads them in praise of God. They are not forgotten in heaven, however, as the 'smoke of their great torment' rises, and is 'in the presence of the Lamb of God, / For ever and for ever' (918–19). (Unending cremation and final burial from which there will be no rising again are thus uncannily combined.)

On Bickersteth's scheme, then, those who are 'lost' go straight to their separate prison in Hades after death, where, beyond hope themselves, they can nevertheless see paradise, which is also in Hades. After the last judgment they will suffer everlastingly in the fires of Gehenna, the smoke from which will always be smelt in heaven. In thus sharply differentiating between Hades and Gehenna, Bickersteth avoids some of the problems of translation associated with the use of the word 'hell' in the Authorized Version. It was via this and other problematic key words, however, and particularly those associated with the idea of everlasting punishment, that such traditional schemes were challenged in the second half of the nineteenth century, from the early 1850s (Maurice) to the late 1870s (Farrar) and beyond. While popular religious forms such as Evangelical tracts, Roman Catholic mission sermons, and Salvationist hymns continued to stoke the fires of hell, the Broad Churchmen who questioned the doctrine of *poena sensus* in theological essays were often anticipated in the more informal medium of the novel – in the fiction of the Brontë sisters, for example, and of their contemporary, J. A. Froude.

Complicated as it is by sectarian divisions and variations, the plot of the theology of hell in the nineteenth century has certain clearly discernible lines of development, and these are examined in the third section of this chapter. By 1890 the idea of endless physical punishment had been discredited in the more liberal Protestant traditions, and even moderated in English Roman Catholic circles. (When Gladstone comments in the 1890s, however, that the traditional hell has been relegated to the 'far-off corners of the Christian mind', one assumes that he is referring to the Protestant mind; in our own time David Lodge has placed the disappearance of the traditional hell of Roman Catholics 'at some point in the nineteen-sixties'.)[5] By 1890 an Archbishop of Canterbury had declared that the damnatory clauses in the Athanasian Creed were not taken literally by anybody in the Church of England, and cremation had been legalized, suggesting that those who associated the committal of the body to the flames with hell-fire were becoming a minority. Belief in hell as a spiritual reality, however, was still widespread. Was not the separation from God, who is love, the only possible final state of those who in this life set their faces against divine grace? Thus although belief in everlasting punishment declined, a fear of some kind of hell remained for many, and this is the subject of the second section of the chapter. In the fourth section I will show how language traditionally associated with hell continued to provide Victorian writers – including Kingsley, Gaskell, and Gissing, Meredith, Swinburne, and James Thomson – with a vocabulary with which to describe painful spiritual experiences in this world, and particularly in the treatment of two kinds of 'hell on earth'.

THE FEAR OF HELL

In modern secular societies in the West, fear of death is focused more upon the dying process than what might follow. If there is some kind of life after death, it is often assumed, that life will be wonderful, heavenly. If not, then the future is simply oblivion and, as we will know nothing about it, we will not suffer. In the century of the Shoa, it is often said, hell is experienced by the living. But if there really were to be a post-mortem state of hell, it would be for those who have no belief in or desire for God. It may not necessarily take the form of eternal punishment or pain, but perhaps we all experience something of hell in divine judgment? For most people in the late twentieth century, however, 'hell' has come to be used as a 'metaphor based on another metaphor', referring to 'painful states of consciousness, to despair or to alienation'.[6]

Although some humanist and secularist intellectuals held advanced views on these matters in the second half of the nineteenth century, the fear of hell was alive elsewhere. Thomas Hardy, for example, describes Tess Durbeyfield as being 'well grounded in the Holy Scriptures', like all village girls, but he also suggests that other influences contributed to the fears of such girls:

She thought of the child [her baby Sorrow] consigned to the nethermost corner of hell, as its double doom for lack of baptism and lack of legitimacy; saw the arch-fiend tossing it with his three-pronged fork, like the one they used for heating the oven on baking days; to which picture she added many other quaint and curious details of torment sometimes taught the young in this Christian country.   (*Tess of the D'Urbervilles*, 1891; 14)

But not only village girls were vulnerable to the fear of hell. Mark Pattison recalls in his memoirs how an Oxford professor was converted to Christianity unexpectedly, 'not by the seduction of piety, but by the terrors of hell'.[7]

Behind these instances, and indeed behind the fact that the 'decline of hell' was extremely slow (it can be traced from the seventeenth century), lies the use of hell as a moral deterrent.[8] A traditional justification for such practice is that in holding over us the threat of hell, God must have had a moral purpose for us in this life:

If we are always thinking of Hell, we shall not easily fall into it. For this cause God has threatened punishment, for He would not have done so, if there was not great advantage in thinking of it.[9]

The specific nature of that punishment could also be explained on these grounds. Father Furniss, for example, whose penny booklet, *The Sight of Hell* (1861), was designed to save children through pure terror, puts the following words into the mouth of Christ addressing the damned in hell:

It was a mercy that the punishment of Hell was made everlasting. If so many broke my law, knowing that the punishment would be everlasting, how would it have been, if the punishment had not been everlasting? There are millions in Heaven who would not have been there but for the everlasting pains of Hell. They were wise . . .[10]

When hell is seen in this light, the need to save people, and especially young people, from everlasting torment becomes urgent, and Father Furniss devoted much of his ministry to missions to children and the production of booklets which sold in their millions.[11] Furniss drew upon the tradition of St Alphonsus Liguori, the founder (1732) of the Redemptorist order of which he was a member, and the author of devotional writings which were widely read on the Continent in the early nineteenth century, and in Britain after their translation into English by R. A. Coffin.[12] Other models were also available, such as the source of the famous hell-fire sermon in Joyce's *Portrait of the Artist as a Young Man* (1914–15): Pinamonti's *Hell Opened to Christians to Caution them Entering It*, reprinted in 1807 with terrifying woodcuts, and available for most of the nineteenth century.

Furniss chooses as an epigraph for *The Sight of Hell*, however, this quotation from Father Faber's *The Creator and the Creature* (1858):

The false delicacy of modern times in keeping back the searing images of Hell, while in the case of children, it has often marred a whole education, is a formidable danger to the sanctity as well as to the faith of men.

No such false delicacy afflicts Father Furniss, as he addresses the 'little child' with the words,

> if you go to Hell, there will be a devil at your side to strike you. He will go on striking you every minute for ever and ever, without ever stopping.[13]

He then invites his young reader to accompany him on a visit to a series of 'dungeons of hell'.[14] In the first is a girl of about eighteen, wearing a terrible dress of fire which burns and scorches her, but can never destroy her. (Similarly Robert Pollok in *The Course of Time* described 'most miserable beings', 'Burning continually, yet unconsumed'.)[15] Furniss has an eye for the unnerving detail. The girl in the dress of fire

> counts with her fingers the moments as they pass away slowly, for each moment seems to her like a hundred years. As she counts the moments she remembers that she will have to count them for ever and ever.

Her crime was to have gone to 'dancing-houses and all kinds of bad places' to show off her dress, instead of going to mass. Similarly, a young prostitute, who died aged sixteen as a result of the 'bad life she led', is doomed to stand for ever on a red hot floor, while a young man who on earth frequented 'dancing-houses, public-houses, and theatres' stands immobile in hell, the blood in his veins and the brain in his skull boiling like a kettle. God is 'terrible to sinners in Hell', he says, 'but He is just!' And so the subterranean tour continues.

To read *The Sight of Hell* is to see how Furniss held the attention of his young audiences during missions. Whereas a sophisticated contemplative tradition such as St Ignatius Loyola's is designed to stimulate the adult reader's imagination by asking a limited number of questions in a 'Meditation on Hell',[16] Furniss fills his young readers' minds with detailed descriptions of hell and evokes a strong sense of place, answering every possible question they might have and thus leaving little space for doubt or uncertainty. As well, however, as playing upon the child's emotions by dwelling upon physical pains and repulsive physical properties of hell such as choking smoke and continual noise, Furniss also tackles the more abstract concept of 'everlasting' punishment by using the traditional rhetorical technique of turning the limits of language and cognition to his own advantage, offering a series of analogies which fail to convey the idea:

> Think of a great solid iron ball, larger than the Heavens and the Earth. A bird comes once in a hundred millions of years and just touches the great iron ball

with a feather of its wing. Think that you have to burn in a fire till the bird has worn the great iron ball away with its feather. Is this Eternity? No.

. . . How long, then, will the punishment of sinners go on? For ever, and ever, and ever![17]

Having thus established a sense of the vastness of eternity, and therefore of everlasting punishment, he later illustrates the 'badness of mortal sin' by explaining that if it is put into one scale and the pains of hell into the other 'you will see that the balance stands equal': '*A mortal sin of one moment deserves the everlasting pains of Hell.*'[18]

Disturbing as it is, the avidity with which Father Furniss contemplates the torments of hell and the awesome idea of everlasting punishment is representative of a strand of Christian tradition which goes back to the second century, and cannot be lightly dismissed.[19] In the modern era, frightening children with hell had long been common practice among English Protestants too, as Isaac Watts's *Divine Songs for Children* (1715) reveals. Like some Roman Catholics, some Victorian High Churchmen used hell as a means of pointing their congregations to heaven. As Pusey wrote, the 'dread of hell peoples heaven: perhaps millions have been scared back from sin by the dread of it'.[20] Wisely, though, Pusey added that the appropriateness of hell-fire preaching depended upon the nature of the congregation. This perhaps helps to explain the success of William Booth, founder of the Salvation Army, who saw the need of such preaching among the people he was called to save.[21]

Why, though, should the fear of hell be so powerful a weapon, at least when used in the appropriate circumstances? As with heaven, there is a problem of language associated with hell. In Pollok's *The Course of Time*, for example, the bard falters as he approaches the subject of the damned: 'What harp of boundless, deep, exhaustless woe, / Shall utter forth the groanings of the damned . . . ?'[22] Yet, like Dante and Milton, Victorian epic writers have more to say about the physical properties of hell than of heaven, and about the condition of those who inhabit hell. For whereas contradictory models of heaven could be said to destabilize the idea of a place of perfect harmony, the contradictoriness of traditional descriptions of hell – a place of fire and water, crowdedness and solitude, noise and silence – is itself an aspect of its horror. Heaven is also more obviously 'other' than hell. Although one can talk of heaven on earth, or of glimpses of heaven in human experience, and although models of heaven as community or worship are necessarily based upon earthly experience, heaven is fundamentally that which is beyond and above earthly experience, as it is the dwelling place of God. Hell, on the other hand, is not only understood, perforce, in anthropocentric terms, but is also the site of God's absence, where the soul is trapped in the damnation that is its own unredeemed nature and those of other lost souls. Just as it is easier to see hell on earth than heaven on earth, so it is easier to see earth in hell than in heaven.

Although specialist writers such as E. H. Bickersteth conceived of an intermediate paradise in Hades, which is beneath the earth, most of the imaginative and descriptive effort of Victorian writers of pious consolatory literature, including Bickersteth's, was focused upon the difficult and mysterious subject of the resurrection of the dead to new life in heaven, which is above. The use of traditional analogies such as the transformation of the worm into the butterfly, and of the dead seed into the ear of corn, proved to be problematic in the nineteenth century, requiring elaborate symbolic reinforcement in Bowler's painting *The Doubt: 'Can These Dry Bones Live?'*, for example (illustration 3). In contrast, parallels between hell and the grave, our common destination, are easy and natural, and would seem to have biblical authority. Where in the Authorized Version the Psalmist is rendered 'if I make my bed in *hell*, behold, thou art there' (Psalm 139.8), modern translators have *Sheol* (RV and NEB) or *the grave* (ASB Liturgical Psalter). Death and the descent to Sheol, or Hades, are often synonymous in the Bible, and the Authorized Version's use of the word 'hell' brings the symbolism of hell and the grave into contiguity: 'Yet thou [Lucifer] shalt be brought down to hell [Sheol NEB], to the sides of the pit [depths of the abyss]' (Isaiah 14.15). Both hell and the grave are 'below' and loathsome, and the two senses of 'hell' – the pareschatological Hades and the eschatological Gehenna – parallel the dual nature of the grave, which is at once transitional (as the site of the resurrection of the body to judgment) and permanent (as the fixed state of physical corruption).

Both death and damnation are traditionally thought of as a downward movement, a descent into the depths. F. D. Maurice, for example, writes of the 'abyss of death', and of 'sinking' into eternal death.[23] Bickersteth refers to the '*crypt* / Which overarch'd the fiery gulf below', and describes how 'the *vault* . . . / Fell sheer into the bottomless *pit*'

(XI.530–4; my emphases). Characteristically, however, it is Swinburne who, in the final stanza of 'Dolores', published in the same year as Bickersteth's epic, draws attention to the ambiguity that he exploits:

> We shall know what the darkness discovers
> If the grave-pit be shallow or deep. . .[24]

In Victorian poetry, I have argued, references to worms strengthened an association between the fear of death and burial, and the fear of judgment. Bickersteth, in his paper on *The Second Death* (1869), focuses upon the 'undying worm' of scripture (Isaiah 66, Matthew 18), which he interprets as the individual sinner's 'accusing conscience' that torments him in the unquenchable fire of Gehenna.[25] Father Furniss's parallels between the grave and hell are more explicitly repulsive. Worse than the smell of a living body suffering from cancers or ulcers, he reminds his young readers, is the 'smell of death coming from a dead body lying in the grave'. But

St. Bonaventure says that if one single body was taken out of Hell and laid on the earth, in that same moment every living creature on the earth would sicken and die. Such is the smell of death from one body in Hell. What then will be the smell of death from countless millions and millions of bodies laid in Hell like sheep?[26]

Father Furniss's exploitation of parallels between hell and the grave in order to reinforce fears associated with damnation with those associated with death is characteristic of writers who considered that it was their duty to warn their readers of the perils of living in a state of mortal sin. The tide of opinion in the Victorian period turned against this kind of teaching, however. The sources of public criticism are in the main fairly predictable. In Charles Kingsley's Broad Church novel *Yeast* (1848), for example, the authorial narrator offers this aside:

The New Testament deals very little in appeals *ad terrorem*; and it would be well if some, who fancy that they follow it, would do the same, and by abstaining from making 'hell fire' the chief incentive to virtue, cease from tempting many a poor fellow to enlist on the devil's side the only manly feeling he has left – personal courage.   (16)

In the 1870s, the secularist Austin Holyoake argued that the doctrine of hell 'brutalises all who believe in it', and that it 'does *not* make men good';[27] F. W. Farrar concluded that the 'virtue which has no better basis than fear of Hell is no virtue at all';[28] and Samuel Butler began work on his brilliant satire of Evangelical clergy and their use of threats of hell in *The Way of All Flesh* (published posthumously in 1903).

Those who took the high ground, however, on the broad issue of punishments and rewards were themselves vulnerable to criticism. Matthew Arnold rejected the idea of Christianity as nothing but a promise of paradise to the saint and a threat of hell-fire to the worldly man.[29] Similarly, in *Culture and Anarchy* (1869), he commented sadly that Mr Smith, whose suicide had been reported, and who was said to have 'laboured under the apprehension that he would come to poverty, and that he was eternally lost', was 'a kind of type . . . of all the strongest, most respectable, and most representative part of our nation'.[30] H. N. Oxenham's response to Arnold's position in the preface to the first edition of *Catholic Eschatology* (1876) is telling:

It is currently asserted that the doctrine of eternal punishment, and indeed of future retribution altogether, is peculiarly repugnant to the spirit of the age; and I quite believe it. There is something uncongenial to an atmosphere of high intellectual culture and elaborate artificial refinement in an ethical system, like the Christian, based on the acknowledgment of what the Apostle calls the exceeding sinfulness of sin. The conviction of sin, whether original or actual, is abhorrent alike to the pride and sensuality – or sensuousness, if that term be preferred – of the dominant 'Zeitgeist'.[31]

It was upon the 'sinfulness of sin' that the question of whether it was right to inculcate the fear of hell in believers turned. For although many high-minded people deprecated the methods of popular preachers such as Father Furniss or William Booth, some shared Gladstone's concern, expressed in the 1890s, lest the relegation of hell to 'the far-off corners of the Christian mind' might adversely affect morals, as a sense of the 'terrors of the Lord' could thus be lost.[32] The High Church theologian, J. B. Mozley, for example, wrote in response to Maurice's *Theological Essays*, in 1854:

the belief in eternal punishment is the true and rational concomitant of the sense of moral obligation. Destroy the punishment and you destroy the sin; limit it, and you make sin a light thing.[33]

F. W. Farrar acknowledged that one of his major objections to universalism was its potential impact upon moral behaviour.[34]

Farrar knew, however, from his pastoral experience, that extreme measures such as hell-fire preaching or deathbed calls to repentance were not necessarily effective in the fight against sin, as they took no account of the fact that genuine change in people is usually gradual, and that most die in the manner in which they live. Indeed, one of the most effective defences against the terrors of hell would seem to have been the kind of stubborn resistance that George Eliot portrays in 'Amos Barton' from *Scenes of Clerical Life* (1857).[35] The Revd Barton, a 'university-taught clergyman', has neither a 'flexible imagination' nor an 'adroit tongue', and, when preaching in the workhouse, fails to convey his message to the unlettered poor who sit before him. After the service he notices that old Mrs Brick's snuff box is empty. Whereas a more tactful and broad-minded man might have quietly supplied her with a refill, and thus warmed her heart towards him and his office, Barton simply says in a brusque manner, 'So your snuff is all gone, eh?':

> Mrs Brick's eyes twinkled with the visionary hope that the parson might be intending to replenish her box, at least mediately, through the present of a small copper.
>
> 'Ah, well! you'll soon be going where there is no more snuff. You'll be in need of mercy then. You must remember that you may have to seek for mercy and not find it, just as you're seeking for snuff.'
>
> At the first sentence of this admonition, the twinkle subsided from Mrs Brick's eyes. The lid of her box went 'click!' and her heart was shut up at the same moment.   (2)

When he then turns his attention to a boy of seven who has misbehaved during the service, he is equally ineffectual, again resorting unthinkingly to the stock threats traditionally employed by clergymen as a means of gaining control over rebellious spirits:

> 'Do you like being beaten?'
>
> 'No-a.'
>
> 'Then what a silly boy you are to be naughty. If you were not naughty, you wouldn't be beaten. But if you are naughty, God will be angry, as well as Mr Spratt; and God can burn you for ever. That will be worse than being beaten.'
>
> Master Fodge's countenance was neither affirmative nor negative of this proposition.

As so often in George Eliot's fiction, references to invisible things have little or no impact upon her ordinary simple folk, who are of the earth, earthy.

It is recorded in a defence of Father Furniss against some of the strong criticism which his work received that the children who attended his missions showed many signs of affection towards him.[36] Several possible explanations for this present themselves, including the debt which the children might have felt they owed to the priest who showed so much concern for their salvation. Some no doubt remained impervious to what was said, or, like Jane Eyre, resolved to keep in good health, and not die. Others, while possibly accepting that they would go to hell if they did not attend mass regularly, probably found Furniss's vivid narrative so extreme and foreign to their own experience that they could not fix hell in their minds, and therefore dismissed it as something remote and, in present terms, unreal. It would seem that it is later in life, and specifically during transitional phases such as adolescence, or child-bearing, or the dying process, when a sense of past sins is awakened, that the fear of hell is most acute. Mrs Brick and Master Fodge are less vulnerable to the threat of hell than are Joyce's Stephen Dedalus, or Hardy's Tess Durbeyfield, or the dying cottager's wife in whom the Revd Theobald Pontifex induces a 'paroxysm of fear', in Butler's *The Way of All Flesh* (15). It was through their satirical treatment of this kind of ministry that writers such as Eliot, Hardy, and Butler focused their critiques of a religion which seemed to play cruelly upon the hopes and fears of vulnerable people, and all in the name of a loving God.

THE THEOLOGY OF HELL

Turning from pastoral to more specifically theological questions associated with hell in the nineteenth century, we should first remind ourselves of the two kinds of punishment traditionally believed to be reserved for the damned: the *poena sensus* (the punishment or pain of sense) and the *poena damni* (the punishment or pain of loss). Much of the opposition to hell-fire preaching was grounded in a repulsion from teaching on physical torments, and opinions on the validity and effectiveness of such teaching varied widely. Before the middle of the century the liberal preacher F. W. Robertson of Brighton could state in a sermon that 'we have learned to smile' at the idea of a 'bodily hell', and that 'in bodily awful intolerable torture we believe no longer'.[37] Such ideas were still being disseminated at the end of the century, however, when Gladstone comments that the 'fashion' of describing details of the pains of hell, 'sometimes even approaching to the loathsome', has 'continued, within narrowing limits, down to the present day'.[38] Gladstone cites one Mr Trapp, an English clergyman, as an example of 'a strong element of pure vulgarity' in such writing:

> Doomed to live death, and never to expire,
> In floods and whirlwinds of tempestuous fire,
> The damned shall groan . . .

The idea of *poena damni*, however, was much more widely acceptable in the Victorian period. The loss of heaven, and thus the absence of God, seemed for most who believed in a post-mortem judgment to be the inevitable consequence of a willed rejection of Christ in this life. (Universalists and Unitarians, of course, held different views, and the question remained of limbo, and what happened to those who had never heard the name of Christ.) If heaven is to be with God, hell is to be without him, and with the loss of God goes the loss of his spiritual gifts: in hell, 'tears of penance come too late for grace' (Keble epigraph). 'What is Perdition but a loss?', asked Maurice, and Tennyson would quote with approval his friend's view that the 'real Hell was the absence of God from the human soul'.[39] It was easier for liberals to accept what could be thought of as internalized spiritual pain which resulted from man's sinful nature, than some kind of physical pain more obviously inflicted from without by an avenging and punitive God. And here was material with which the novelist or poet for whom the inner life and a sense of the absence of God were primary themes could work.

Again, the great literary precursor was Dante, whose vision of the perpetuation of our sinful nature in death is the subject of A. C. Charity's study:

by making his shades 'alive' with their human character undiminished, and with real names . . . attached to them, Dante has taken a bold step already. But he has presented them as dead too, inescapably: they no longer have what is essential to *Dasein*, real human being: they are without a future . . . Their death is the direct subject, and only through death is life seen. But it is seen; life and death are shown as typologically related.[40]

Commenting in the mid nineteenth century on Dante's hell, Maurice makes a slightly different point. 'Men are in eternal misery', he writes, 'because they are still covetous, proud, loveless', and he adds that 'the thought of His ceasing to punish them, of His letting them alone, of His leaving them to themselves, is the real, the unutterable horror'.[41] Indeed, in purely temporal terms, *poena damni* can be more daunting than *poena sensus*, which is sometimes conceived of as diminishing. In a fascinating letter addressed to Hallam Tennyson, Aubrey de Vere reports a visit he made to the eighty-nine-year-old Newman, saying that he wished Hallam's father could have been present to hear the Cardinal's words on a religious subject which was of interest to him:

Eternal Punishment, respecting which he remarked that though the 'Pain of Loss' (that of the Vision and Fruition of God) never ceased, yet *Catholic* Theology allowed of a belief entertained by many Theologians, that the '*Poena Sensus*' does not share that Eternity, but gradually diminishes and may wholly cease, as is implied by the expression 'beaten by few *stripes*'. This is wholly opposed to the Calvinist Theology, especially when combined with the teaching that the 'Fire' like the 'Worm' is a *figure*, that Eternity includes no sense of *Succession*, and that the gates of Heaven are always open; so that the reason that the reprobate and impenitent does not enter is because he has no love for God and *does not desire* His presence.[42]

This last point is crucial, and is often made in relation to the *poena damni* in both the Victorian Age and our own. Hans Küng, for example, rejects a mythological understanding of hell, which still implies a place in the upper or lower world, and instead favours a purely theological interpretation as 'an exclusion from the fellowship of the living God', while John Bowker argues that everlasting punishment is impossible in our universe, where time is a statistical effect of entropy, but hell as the absence of God is possible.[43]

The cruder attempts in the nineteenth century to locate hell as a place in the lower world – to Father Furniss, for example, it seemed likely that it is in the middle of the earth[44] – provided easy targets for Austin Holyoake, who asked how hell could be both within the earth and bottomless.[45] In contrast the *Catholic Encyclopedia* was more cautious, stating that 'the Church has decided nothing on this subject; hence we may say hell is a definite place; but where it is, we do not know'.[46] Like heaven, hell could be seen as a state rather than a place, a view which was favoured by spiritualists among others,[47] and this position was again more compatible with the traditional *poena damni* than with the *poena sensus*.

Whereas Roman Catholics referred to 'Holy Church' for their authority on such matters and spiritualists to their sources on the other side, Evangelical Protestants like E. H. Bickersteth naturally turned to the Bible on the subject of the condition of the lost, and it was on this ground that the great theological battles on the subject were fought in the nineteenth century. In his paper on *The Second Death* (1869), for example, Bickersteth uncritically cites Old Testament texts on what he calls 'these eternal verities'.[48] He then quotes Josephus on the beliefs of the Jews before the fall of Jerusalem, explaining the 'orthodox' position of the Pharisees on the existence of an 'everlasting prison', and the Sadducees' denial of any future state or punishments and rewards in Hades.[49] Moving on to the New Testament, he begins with John the Baptist as one of the strongest sources of evidence, quoting texts on 'the wrath to come' and 'unquenchable fire' (Matthew 3.7,12), and 'the wrath of God' (John 3.36).[50] In the Sermon on the Mount, Bickersteth argues, 'the Truth' preaches 'the Pharisaic creed of the everlasting prison and of a burning Gehenna'.[51] And at the end of his ministry Jesus said, 'Depart from Me, ye cursed, into everlasting fire, prepared for the devil and his angels' (Matthew 25):

But can this word *everlasting* possibly have a limited meaning in their case? With what can you compare it? – the duration of the bliss of the saved – 'These shall go away into everlasting punishment: but the righteous into everlasting life.' It is, as you know, the same word in both clauses [*aiōnion*] . . . and these were the last accents of the Saviour's voice, ere He retired to prepare to suffer and to die.[52]

(A few years later the mistranslation of the word *aiōnion* was to be a major plank in Farrar's argument against everlasting punishment.) Having then quoted from the doubtful verses at the end of Mark (16.16) as a post-resurrection statement on damnation, Bickersteth finally goes through the rest of the New Testament, culminating in Revelation 21 and 'the lake which burneth with fire and brimstone: which is the second death'.[53]

Among the many theological problems with which liberal churchmen struggled, that of '*everlasting* punishment' was primary: hell and heaven are fixed states (there are no escalators between them), and the vast majority of mankind are doomed to go to hell. Such a view was incompatible with their idea of a loving God, and could be challenged on ethical grounds. Whereas hell had traditionally been explained as an expression of God's justice, it came to be seen more as an injustice, and thus not of God, especially as an expanding empire brought home to people the existence in the world of vast numbers of adherents to other faiths.[54] Long before Farrar was writing on the subject in the 1870s, however, J. A. Froude used Markham Sutherland's letters in his novel *The Nemesis of Faith* (1849) as a means of expressing his repugnance from the 'doctrine so horrible':

the largest portion of mankind . . . are to be tortured for ever and ever in unspeakable agonies. My God! and for what?[55]

People are 'thrown into life' unformed, Markham argues, and if man is forgiving, how much more must God be. Heaven would be hell if one knew that even one soul was suffering in hell. Christ went down to hell, but it was 'to break the chains, not to bind them'.[56] Like most doctrinal issues, these go back to the question of early Christian sources, and Markham refers to the early creeds and devotes a letter to the authority of the Bible. Again, however, it is with a reminder of the 'sinfulness of sin' that a new note is introduced, and in a highly dramatic manner. Like Rochester in *Jane Eyre* (27), published the same year, Markham in his despair comments that hell could not be worse than this life: 'not that dark sulphurous home of torture . . . hell itself, could be less endurable than the present'.[57] When he prepares to commit suicide, however, in order 'to lighten others' sorrows' and to end his own, he is suddenly interrupted by a voice that at first he does not recognize:

'Die without *hope* – the worst sinner's worst death – to bear your sin, and your sin's punishment, through eternity!' (my emphasis)[58]

Frederick Mornington is the Newman figure in a novel in which, unusually, the original is himself described:

sin with Newman was real; not a misfortune to be pitied and allowed for; to be talked of gravely in the pulpit, and forgotten when out of it; . . . but in very truth a dreadful monster, a real child of a real devil . . .[59]

The question of hell, then, turns upon our idea of hope, and upon whether, as for Newman, a suicide for example loses all hope of eternal life, or, as for Farrar, 'eternal hope' would embrace even the worst of sinners in the possibility of purgation in an intermediate state.

Markham Sutherland's cast of mind contrasts strongly with that of Charles Reding in Newman's own novel *Loss and Gain* (1847):

He [Charles] had had some difficulty in receiving the doctrine of eternal punishment; it had seemed to him the hardest doctrine of Revelation. Then he said to himself, 'But what is faith in its very notion but an acceptance of the word of God when reason seems to oppose it? How is it faith at all if there is nothing to try it?' This thought fully satisfied him.   (15)

Charles cannot, however, get satisfactory answers from Mr Upton, a High Churchman, on the articles and the creeds. Did the anathemas of the Athanasian Creed, for example, apply to all its clauses? It was on the Athanasian Creed that a major debate within the Church of England concerning hell and everlasting punishment was to focus in the 1870s. The significance of the debate is reflected in the fact that in the monumental *Life* of Archbishop Tait, which includes separate chapters on major ecclesiastical issues of the day such as the controversies surrounding *Essays and Reviews* and Bishop Colenso, another whole chapter (22) is entitled 'The Athanasian Creed (1870–1873)', and records that among Tait's books were, 'besides scores of pamphlets, eight separate volumes devoted to this single subject, all of them published between the years 1868 and 1872'.[60] Why was this creed so contentious?

The rubric of the Book of Common Prayer stated that on certain major feast days, including Christmas Day, the Epiphany, Easter Day, Whit Sunday, and Trinity Sunday, the Athanasian Creed was to be sung or said at Morning Prayer instead of the Apostles' Creed. The creed includes 'damnatory clauses' concerning, first, the 'Catholick Faith' – 'Which Faith except every one do keep whole and undefiled: without doubt he shall perish everlastingly' – and, secondly, the last judgment: 'And they that have done good shall go into life everlasting: and they that have done evil into everlasting fire.' In the early nineteenth century many easygoing parish churches had let this command slip, but the Oxford Movement changed this, and congregations were both surprised by the unfamiliar words and annoyed when clergymen defended the action by pointing to the rubric.[61] As Anthony Trollope observed in 1866, the question was viewed differently by different generations, the 'old rector' having been ready enough with his belief (and 'he believed that he believed what he said that he believed'), whereas 'the new parson has by no means so glib an answer ready to such a question' because he is 'ever thinking of it'.[62]

The whole question became the subject of a major controversy in the early 1870s, following the timely appointment of a Royal Commission to inquire into the rubrics and rituals of the Church of England in 1867. It preoccupied many clergy for a number of years of largely tedious debate, and Tait, as Primate, was put in the difficult position of being lobbied by brother bishops with strongly held but widely differing views. At the heart of the question lay the corollary that those who had never heard the gospel preached were condemned to everlasting punishment. Opinion divided over whether the creed should be excluded from the prayer book altogether, or some explanatory note should be inserted

to the effect that 'nothing in this creed is to be understood as condemn-
ing those who by involuntary ignorance or invincible prejudice are
hindered from accepting the faith therein declared', as Pusey and his
fellow professors in Oxford proposed. The intensity of feeling over this
issue is reflected in Pusey and Liddon's avowed intention to retire from
the ministry even if there were to be a rearrangement of the days on
which the creed was compulsorily to be said.[63]

Significantly, Archbishop Tait's own speech in Convocation on the
matter addressed the difficult question of religious language, and specifically of literalism. His comments were to be quoted against him for the
rest of his life:

The Bishop of Peterborough [W. C. Magee] . . . says every clause is to be taken
in the absolute literal sense, and that of all the words of the creed none are so
explicit as the damnatory clauses. Very well. We are to take them, then, in the
plainest and most literal sense. But we do not. There is not a soul in the room
who does. Nobody in the Church of England takes them in their plain and
literal sense.[64]

In the end a Convocation of 1873 agreed on a statement that 'the
Church in this confession [doth] declare the necessity for all who would
be in a state of salvation of holding fast the Catholic faith, and the great
peril of rejecting the same'.[65]

It is illuminating to contrast Tait's approach in his speech with that of
E. H. Bickersteth in his paper on *The Second Death* (1869), where he
argues that the 'Word of God has spoken' on everlasting punishment:

and we have all affirmed that the doctrine of the Athanasian Creed, 'They that
have done good shall go into life everlasting, and they that have done evil into
everlasting fire,' '*ought thoroughly to be received and believed: for it may be
proved by most certain warrants of Holy Scripture*' [Article 8].[66]

Bickersteth no doubt had the creed in mind when he argued in the same
paper that the theme of everlasting punishment was 'deeply exercising
many minds at this time'.[67] Characteristically, the path that he himself
beat through this particular thicket of ecclesiastical argument was narrow and undeviating.

By the 1870s the Athanasian Creed had become something of a litmus
test of people's religious views. In 1875 we find Newman, for example,
rejoicing in Charles Kingsley's defence of the creed, and 'in his views
generally nearing the Catholic view of things'.[68] Several leading Victorian writers, however, held liberal positions on the subject. Anthony

Trollope provides an interesting gloss on the Bickersteth position in his perception that the 'fulminating clause of the Athanasian Creed' was an example of the discrepancy between actual beliefs and declarations of faith, pointing out that although few of the clergy believed it, each clergyman declared aloud that he did 'a dozen times every year of his life'.[69] Tennyson followed the lead of his father, who refused to read the creed in church, and Charlotte Brontë described it as 'profane'.[70]

The 'common view' on 'life everlasting' and 'everlasting fire' had traditionally been based upon the Athanasian Creed and a number of scattered proof texts, including Isaiah 33.14, Daniel 12.2, and Matthew 25.46. The parable of Dives and Lazarus (Luke 16) was also a key text, often cited quite uncritically as 'evidence', including in popular religious literature. In an Evangelical miscellany entitled *The Traveller's Guide, from Death to Life* (n.d.), for example, which was reprinted at least fifty-one times, the following is presented as 'A Solemn Fact':

> There is a way for any sinner to *keep* out of hell. There is no way to *get* out of hell. Jesus says, 'I am the Way.' But the rich man in hell was told that there was 'a great gulf fixed.'[71]

As late as the 1890s, Gladstone, a keen student of eschatological controversies of the period, simply cited the passage in Luke against an argument for the possibility of spiritual development after death.[72] Yet sixty years earlier Whateley had argued that although such a parable '*may* chance to agree in every point with matter of fact . . . there is no necessity that it should'.[73] A larger question concerning the parable is that of translation. The Authorized Version translates the Greek *hadēs* (Luke 16.23) as 'hell', whereas the emphasis changes if it is understood that both Dives and Lazarus go to Hades. In the preface to the first edition of his Westminster Abbey sermons, *Eternal Hope* (1878), F. W. Farrar shows how the word 'hell' is used to translate three different words in the New Testament: first, the one instance of the Greek version of *tartarus* (2 Peter 2.4), which refers to an intermediate state previous to judgment; secondly, *hadēs*, which is the exact equivalent of the Hebrew *sheol*, and means 'the unseen world', as a place both for the bad and the good, and which again refers to an intermediate state of the soul previous to judgment; and thirdly, *gehenna*, a word for the common sewer of a city where the bodies of the worst criminals were dumped, and which came to mean punishment, but *never* endless punishment, beyond the grave.[74]

The major crux in relation to translation, however, was the word *aiōnios*. Bickersteth comments on the matter in *The Second Death*:

some have in all ages tried to evade or escape the force of these Scriptures by affirming that the word (*aiōnios*) translated eternal or everlasting, does not mean *unending*, but coextensive with that age or dispensation (*aiōn*) to which it refers. To this our simple answer must be, not what may be the possible etymological meaning of the word, or what its use by uninspired authors, but what is its actual meaning as employed in the New Testament.[75]

Having begged the question of authority by referring to 'uninspired authors' and 'actual meaning', he goes on to cite a number of New Testament 'Scriptures' which seem to him 'absolutely decisive against any theories either of universalism or of annihilation: they declare in no ambiguous terms that the punishment is without end, and the penal suffering to continue for ever and ever'.[76]

Precisely the opposite interpretation informs Farrar's main argument in *Eternal Hope*, published nine years later:

The word *aiōnios*, sometimes translated 'everlasting,' is simply the word which, in its first sense, means *agelong* or *aeonian*; and which is in the Bible itself applied to things which have utterly and long since passed away; and is in its second sense something 'spiritual' – something above and beyond time, – as when the knowledge of God is said to be eternal life. So that when, with your futile billions, you foist into this word *aiōnios*, the fiction of endless time, you do but give the lie to the mighty oath of that great angel, who set one foot upon the sea, and one upon the land, and with hand uplifted to heaven sware by Him who liveth for ever and ever that 'Time should be no more.'[77]

Interestingly, he illustrates his argument in a footnote with a quotation from Newman's verse drama *The Dream of Gerontius* (1865), which includes the lines 'For spirits and men by different standards mete / The less and greater in the flow of time'. As in Newman's comment in old age, cited earlier, on Roman Catholic teaching 'that Eternity includes no sense of *Succession*', the theological debate turns upon the limits of our this-worldly ideas of time and eternity. Farrar's former tutor F. D. Maurice had suggested in *Theological Essays* (1853) that 'Eternity in relation to God has nothing to do with time or duration', a view which was to impress Tennyson.[78] Farrar himself was to comment on the first page of *Mercy and Judgment* (1881) that he did not deny 'the eternity of punishment', but that he understood 'the word eternity in a sense far higher than can be degraded into the vulgar meaning of endlessness'.[79]

More traditional interpretations continued to be expounded until the
end of the nineteenth century. Professor Salmond, for example, stated in
1895 that the phrase 'eternal fire' conjures up 'a sufficiently appalling
picture of the retributive future, and . . . in using it Christ Himself gives
no hint of a termination of the penalty meant by it'.[80] Once the ground
had been loosened, however, around these key biblical terms, the decline
of hell as a place of everlasting physical pain was accelerated, and by
1879 G. Somers Bellamy could claim that 'thank God, very few of us
remain today' who believe in 'endless punishment'.[81]

'FROM FEARFUL HOPE INTO FEARLESS DESPAIR': SOME VERSIONS OF HELL ON EARTH

While the theologians wrangled over key words and doctrines, the leading novelists and poets, most of whom held liberal or radically revisionary views on the subject, continued to find in the language traditionally
associated with hell a repertoire of resonances and associations through
which to describe spiritual experience in the here-and-now, and particularly in the treatment of two versions of hell on earth. One is associated
with the Industrial Revolution and the growth of the great cities, and is
to be found mainly in the social-problem novels of the middle of the
century and, later, in the fiction of George Gissing. The other is
diametrically opposed to the conventionalized 'heaven' of profane love:
the 'hell' of love which is dead, or betrayed, and particularly associated
with sex where there is no love – a secularized version of the theologians' *poena damni*, perhaps most poignantly explored in George
Meredith's sonnet sequence, *Modern Love* (1862), and most ambig-
uously in Swinburne's 'Laus Veneris' (*Poems and Ballads*, 1866).
Whereas for liberal theologians the decline of hell as everlasting punishment is associated with a new emphasis upon the 'lively hope' of a future
life with Christ, the more radical secular writers of the 1860s and 1870s
deny that hope and argue the need for stoic endurance in a world of
pain. This kind of movement 'from fearful hope into fearless despair'
(Swinburne)[82] is epitomized in James Thomson's *City of Dreadful Night*
(1874).

I begin, however, with the first of the two versions of hell on earth
which provide a context for reading Thomson, namely that associated
with industrialization and urbanization in the early nineteenth century.

If the Blake who wrote of England's dark satanic mills is the strongest literary precursor of Victorian writings on the subject, it is John Martin's apocalyptic paintings which provide some of the most illuminating contemporary parallels in the graphic arts. Martin's treatment of 'wonderful subjects', mainly from the Bible, in the late 1820s and 1830s coincided with one of the peaks of millenarian activity in the nineteenth century. It was also in this period, of course, that the demand for political and social reform in the context of frighteningly rapid urban development during the Industrial Revolution came to a head. In one of Martin's late 'judgment' paintings, *The Last Judgment* (1853; illustration 7), a railway train – that potent symbol of the new age of steam – crashes down a ravine into the abyss of hell. The fears and suspicions concerning the advent of the railway train, which seemed to express in its fire and steam, its weight and apparently resistless energy, a force greater than nature and therefore suggestive of satanic power, are thus embodied in this classic example of the apocalyptic sublime, in which the doomed train conveys a multitude of sinners into the pit.

In his apocalyptic paintings and his illustrations to *Paradise Lost*, Martin was strongly influenced by the shapes and colours of the industrial landscape of the North-East of England where he was brought up, as were other artists included in Francis D. Klingender's classic study on *Art and the Industrial Revolution* (1947). The relationship, however, between such landscapes and hell also works the other way, as Klingender suggests: 'If Martin gave Hell the image of industry . . . contemporary illustrators often gave industry the image of Hell.'[83] Klingender cites as an example of this W. Read's aquatint entitled 'Drawing the Retorts at the Great Gas Light Establishment, Brick Lane' (in London), which provided the frontispiece of the 1821 volume of *The Monthly Magazine* (illustration 14). Remove some of the details such as the products and machinery depicted here, and it would be easy to mistake the picture for a vision of hell. Even the slatted air vent, through which a moonlit sky can be seen, is suggestive of the traditional belief that it is possible for those who suffer in the stifling fires of hell to see heaven in all its glory.

According to his son Leopold, Martin's 'judgment' paintings were inspired partly by a journey through the Black Country at dead of night:

The glow of the furnaces, the red blaze of light, together with the liquid fire, seemed to his mind truly sublime and awful. He could not imagine anything more terrible even in the regions of everlasting punishment. All he had done or attempted in ideal painting fell far short, very far short, of the fearful sublimity.[84]

This statement contains a clue to one of the principal reasons for the decline in the power of images of hell as *poena sensus* in the nineteenth century, for during the Industrial Revolution reality began to exceed the bounds of the imagination, even in the most dramatic visual or poetic versions of hell. This theme was taken up by social commentators on the appalling squalor of the urban slums in the 1830s and 1840s, and by the end of the nineteenth century had become conventionalized. William Booth's ironic response to Stanley's account of his African journeys – *In Darkest England and the Way Out* (1890) – is typical in this respect:

Talk about Dante's Hell, and all the horrors and cruelties of the torture-chamber of the lost! The man who walks with open eyes and with bleeding heart through the shambles of our civilisation needs no such fantastic images of the poet to teach him horror.[85]

Again, the horror of reality at home exceeds the horror of hell, or indeed of darkest Africa, which the Victorian reader can imagine only with the help of the poet or the travel writer.

As in the case of industrial scenes, images of the city were often as suggestive of hell as images of hell were suggestive of the city. In Gustave Doré's illustrations for Jerrold's *London* (1872), for example, published six years after his *Paradise Lost* and *The Vision of Hell* (Dante), the huddled figures in plates depicting the docks and the surrounding brothels, pubs, and opium dens adopt the postures of the damned.[86] Of the many features of urban deprivation and alienation to which social commentators drew their readers' attention, several were reminiscent of hell. Friedrich Engels, for example, focused upon that sense of isolation in a crowd which had always been a traditional feature of hell, as in Dante, in his description of London,[87] and described the Old Town of Manchester as a 'Hell upon Earth'.[88]

Engels was one of several visitors to Britain who were like modern Dantes, penetrating the Inferno of a new industrial age, but without a Virgil at their side. De Tocqueville, for example, when writing on Manchester in 1835, described the polluted streams that wound their way between and beneath the town's appalling slum dwellings as 'the Styx of this new Hades'.[89] Whereas classical allusion in the original Dante reflected the writer's Catholic world view and was central to both his learning and his technique, by the middle of the nineteenth century in England it can have the effect of weakening the specifically Christian connotations of references to hell. Alexander Welsh argues that Dickens's London is like the classical hell, and draws a parallel with S. E. Finer's quotation frolm *The Times* of 1847:

To investigate the source of a malaria or stench Mr. Chadwick would swim through the stagnant pools of Avernus and enter the pestiferous jaws of Orcus itself: *per loca foeda situ* he would track the secrets of the nether world, to rescue his Eurydice from the reign of Black Dis.[90]

Interestingly, Charles Kingsley's working-class hero, Alton Locke, says '*Facilis descensus Averni!*', when describing as narrator how the tailoring trade was forced to put work out at contract prices, and thus caused unemployment (10). It is the prophetic note of Carlyle's writing, however, that can be heard most clearly in a passage in the previous chapter, where Locke describes the atmosphere of London, bringing together disparate elements of the city as hell on earth:

that was uncongenial enough; crime and poverty, all-devouring competition, and hopeless struggles against Mammon and Moloch, amid the roar of wheels, the ceaseless stream of pale, hard faces, intent on gain, or brooding over woe; amid endless prison walls of brick, beneath a lurid, crushing sky of smoke and mist. It was a dark, noisy, thunderous element that London life; a troubled sea that cannot rest, casting up mire and dirt; resonant of the clanking of chains, the grinding of remorseless machinery, the wail of lost spirits from the pit. And it did its work upon me; it gave a gloomy colouring, a glare as of some Dantean 'Inferno', to all my utterances.   (9)

These are the same materials with which Dickens worked in his social novels of mid-century: the prison walls; the urban desert of resistant brick; the smoke and mist hanging over the city; the grinding machinery of the works; the glare of the furnaces.

Kingsley's application of the language of hell to the city is most fully developed in the chapter entitled 'The Lowest Deep' (35), in which Jemmy Downes's wife and children are found dead, their bodies already gnawed by rats, in a slum dwelling at 'the very mouth of hell', where a dirty gas-lamp just serves to make 'darkness visible'. Downes himself drowns in the 'hell-broth' of a stream that runs under the floor of this room. And who are to blame? The rich, who turn a blind eye to this squalor, and who 'leave the men who make their clothes to starve in such hells on earth' as Locke's workroom (5)? For a Christian commentator, however, there was always a danger that this kind of loose application of the language of hell to social conditions could not be supported theologically. Consider, for example, this passage from William Booth's *In Darkest England*, where he attacks those who 'ruin' girls by forcing them into prostitution:

> Her word becomes unbelievable, her life an ignominy, and she is swept downward, ever downward, into the bottomless perdition of prostitution. But there, even in the lowest depths, excommunicated by Humanity and outcast from God, she is far nearer the pitying heart of the One true Saviour than all the men who forced her down, aye, and than all the Pharisees and Scribes who stand silently by while these fiendish wrongs are perpetrated before their very eyes.[91]

Milton's 'bottomless perdition' must be metaphoric here, but what follows is at best ambiguous and at worst blasphemous, hinting at a separation between God and the one true saviour. Booth posed the question: 'Why all this apparatus of temples and meeting-houses to save men from perdition in a world which is to come, while never a helping hand is stretched out to save them from the inferno of their present life?' The relationship between the suffering of sinners on earth, however, and their hope of heaven, remains unclear. For the prostitute who lives in the lowest depths of depravity; the wife of a drunkard who lives at the mouth of hell; the stoker who works near the heat of a furnace; the tailor who labours in a sweat-shop; or the weaver in the mill, deafened by the noise of the machines and with fluff on the lung, to whom it seemed that hell had come on earth, escape was possible only in the respite of limited leisure hours, and in the hope of heaven. A cultural product partly of middle-class guilt and partly of a Christian reformist agenda, the social-problem novelists' hell on earth often fails to resolve or even address the theological issues which its sources in Christian tradition would seem to raise.

An exception to this is Elizabeth Gaskell's *Mary Barton* (1848), in which images of hell on earth are consistent with a Unitarian theology that denies everlasting punishment.[92] The worst fear of the prostitute in this novel, Esther, whose life in this world seems to be lived in 'outer darkness' (22), is that she will be separated from her dead daughter, born out of wedlock, in the world to come. She says to Jem Wilson:

> 'I've done that since, which separates us as far asunder as heaven and hell can be.' Her voice rose again to the sharp pitch of agony. 'My darling! my darling! even after death I may not see thee, my own sweet one! She was so good – like a

little angel. What is that text, I don't remember, – that text mother used to teach me when I sat on her knee long ago, it begins "Blessed are the pure"'' –   (14)

The whole thrust of the novel is towards forgiveness, and ideas of the future life are grounded in 'texts of comfort': 'Where the wicked cease from troubling, and the weary are at rest'; 'The tears shall be wiped away from all eyes', and so on (19). When Esther is buried with John Barton, a confessed murderer who has been forgiven by his victim's father, the epitaph is from Psalm 103: 'For He will not always chide, neither will He keep His anger for ever' (38).

The novel's non-judgmental ending, then, suggests that Esther's anxious reference to the parable of Dives and Lazarus was misplaced. In the case of John Barton, however, his perversion of the parable in his set-piece speech in the opening chapter is shown to be blasphemous:

'. . . we pile up their fortunes with the sweat of our brows; and yet we are to live as separate as if we were in two worlds; ay, as separate as Dives and Lazarus, with a great gulf betwixt us: but I know who was best off then,' and he wound up his speech with a low chuckle that had no mirth in it.[93]

Whateley was sceptical about the possible coincidence between this parable and fact, and later in the century F. W. Farrar focused on the problem of translating *hadēs*. Elizabeth Gaskell's handling of the parable is consistent with her Unitarianism. In a sermon on the Gadarene, for example, Theophilus Lindsey (one of the founders of English Unitarianism) attempted to explain how the 'great gulf' of the parable of Dives and Lazarus is part of Jewish tradition, and that the concept of everlasting torment has no place in the New Testament. Discussing the Gadarene's 'devils', he wrote:

St. Luke has it, 'that he would not command them to go out into the deep,' *i.e.* the abyss, the supposed place of wicked spirits betwixt death and the resurrection, in the vulgar estimation . . . Hence Dives, in the parable, is made to talk of a great gulf betwixt him and Abraham, consistently with these Jewish notions; but the scriptures teach no such thing, speak of no such state.[94]

While Esther's anxiety concerning the future state is shown to be misplaced and Barton's misapplication of the parable of Dives and Lazarus is corrected by the novel's theology of forgiveness, Elizabeth Gaskell can still fall back upon a parallel between industry and hell which is very close to that of W. Read and other artists of the Industrial Revolution. Seen through the eyes of three policemen who have never been in a foundry before, Jem Wilson's workplace makes a deep impression:

> Dark, black were the walls, the ground, the faces around them, as they crossed the yard. But, in the furnace-house a deep and lurid red glared over all; the furnace roared with mighty flame. The men, like demons, in their fire-and-soot colouring, stood swart around, awaiting the moment when the tons of solid iron should have melted down into fiery liquid . . .   (19)

That the reference to demons is purely aesthetic perhaps reflects Elizabeth Gaskell's lack of belief in hell, but such references were to become more common with the erosion of belief in everlasting punishment in the second half of the century.

The freedom with which George Gissing treats ideas of hell on earth in his social fiction of the 1880s is explained partly by his agnosticism. It also reflects the fact that by then the major doctrinal battles over everlasting punishment had been fought and won by the more progressive forces in the Established Church of England, and thus the subject had become less problematic in the public mind. Freed from the complications associated with their former doctrinal significance, images of hell take on a new life in his early novels, and from the opening paragraph of *Workers in the Dawn* (1880) to the last paragraph of *The Nether World* (1889) hell is a recurrent controlling metaphor. His close examination of physical conditions in the slums of late-nineteenth-century London, and his more impressive analysis of psychological impoverishment in the depressing environment of mean streets, broadly correspond to the *poena sensus* and *poena damni* of the theologians. Like most of them he sees the *poena damni* as the greater suffering, being a state in which the individual human being is cut off from love and hope.

Dante, the presiding genius of nineteenth-century social commentary, is present here too, where the author-narrator in *Workers in the Dawn* writes like a Henry Mayhew in the role of Virgil in the *Inferno*: 'Walk with me, reader, into Whitecross Street' (1). Flames and a 'reddish light' contrast with 'deep blackness' overhead; through a 'yawning archway' are 'unspeakable abominations'. Whereas in Kingsley, however, the reader tries to relate such language to the writer's Christian Socialist programme, there is no question of discovering in Gissing some kind of providential scheme for mankind, or even any hope of reform. Indeed, there is in *The Nether World* a new sense of hopelessness concerning the masses of the urban poor in London, the 'city of the damned':

Over the pest-stricken regions of East London, sweltering in sunshine which
served only to reveal the intimacies of abominations; across miles of a city of the
damned, such as thought never conceived before this age of ours; above streets
swarming with a nameless populace, cruelly exposed by the unwonted light of
heaven; . . . the train made its way at length beyond the utmost limits of dread,
and entered upon a land of level meadows.   (19)

What John Martin said of the sublime power of industry fifty years
earlier, Gissing now writes of the enormously expanded East End of
London, where reality has surpassed what was formerly imaginable, and
where the light of heaven, now only the sky, shines remorselessly upon
the damned, now only on this earth.

Peter Keating has suggested that Gissing's metaphor of the abyss in his
social fiction reflects a new fear of the masses in the last decades of the
century, and that the metaphor recurs with this connotation in the work
of H. G. Wells, C. F. G. Masterman, and E. M. Forster.[95] Just as central
to Gissing's writing is the idea of the circle of hell, here secularized in the
careful grading of the levels of poverty on each floor of depressing
lodging-houses, for example, in the city of the damned. The circular
structure of his early novels – *Workers in the Dawn* begins and ends in
an abyss, the famous 'Io Saturnalia' chapter in *The Nether World* almost
literally revolves around the pawnshop (12) – suggests the vicious circle
or downward spiral that we now call the poverty trap. In Gissing's
world only a madman could experience an angel visitation, and even this
sole angel can offer no hope of transcendence: 'This life you are now
leading', it announces to Mad Jack, 'is that of the damned; this place to
which you are confined is Hell!' (*The Nether World*, 37).

The haunting portrayal in Gissing's fiction of marriages or liaisons
under intolerable pressure, largely for financial reasons, and of the
psychological 'hell' in which couples find themselves trapped, reflects the
unhappiness of his two disastrous marriages to women of a lower social
class than his own. George Meredith's experience was closer to
Ruskin's: by June 1857 he knew that his young (and probably sexually
frustrated) wife Mary Ellen and the painter Henry Wallis were lovers;
less than a year later she had a child by Wallis. The focus of his creative
effort at this time is summed up in the subtitle of David Williams's
informal biography, *George Meredith: His Life and Lost Love* (1977).
First, only two years after he and his wife separated, Meredith published
The Ordeal of Richard Feverel: A History of a Father and Son (July
1859). With his high style, which is liberally embellished with allegory,

classical allusion, and synecdoche (his favourite figure of speech), Meredith is the only novelist who can write at mid-century of hell and the devil in a relaxed and assured manner, treating them figuratively but without sacrificing a sense of the profound moral significance attached to them in European culture. His early work represents the most significant exploration in the Victorian period of our second kind of hell on earth: the secularized version of *poena damni*, in which love is dead or betrayed.

Two of Meredith's most familiar metaphors – the devil and the mask – recur in the key chapter (33) in which Sir Austin Feverel, whose wife ran off with a poet, confronts the fact that the famous educational 'System' which he applied to his son Richard has failed. Meredith himself explained the chapter in a letter to Samuel Lucas, the journalist and reviewer: 'The "System", you see, had its origin not so much in love for his son, as in wrath at his wife, and so carries its own Nemesis.'[96] In what one reviewer called Richard Feverel's 'fall' into the 'perilous regions of the "demi-monde"'[97] in the extraordinary chapter entitled 'An Enchantress' (38), Meredith marshals the forces of the melodrama in order to dramatize his young hero's temptation by the fascinating Bella Mount – herself seduced at sixteen and an experienced woman of the world at twenty-one, and described as receiving 'the devil's wages'. As she moves through a bewildering series of role changes – now masquerading as the dandiacal 'Sir Julius', a raffish member of the fast set and a stock 'gentleman seducer', now as a witch, now as her usual social persona – a 'lurid splendour' glances about her like 'lights from the pit', and Richard, drinking a couple of glasses of champagne in succession, stares about: 'Was he in hell, with a lost soul raving to him?' In the seductress's boldest *coup de théâtre*, when she looks 'beautiful and devilish' in the role of a witch, the chapter's play on the idea of hell comes to a bizarre climax as she spills burning spirits onto the carpet, which catches fire, creating a miniature domestic inferno which Richard extinguishes, but which presages judgment. As the couple finally come together, an intimation of the desolation which is to ensue (after his wife Lucy loses her mind and dies) is conveyed in the language of lost souls and the echo of *Richard III*:

'Lost, Richard! lost for ever! give me up!'

He cried: 'I never will!' and strained her in his arms, and kissed her passionately on the lips.

She was not acting now as she sidled and slunk her half-averted head with a kind of maiden shame under his arm, sighing heavily, weeping, clinging to him. It was wicked truth.

> Not a word of love between them!
> Was ever hero in this fashion won?

'Not a word of love between them': sex without love is one of the most difficult and dangerous areas of an already taboo subject in the mid Victorian period, and it was one which haunted the cuckolded George Meredith, for whom it seems to have represented hell on earth. Indeed, the close parallels between the satanic language of *Richard Feverel* and of *Modern Love*, published three years later, suggest an obsessive mind at work. Meredith's description of Bella Mount, for example – 'There was sorcery in her breath; sorcery in her hair: the ends of it stung him like *little snakes*' (my emphasis) – is echoed in the familiar opening lines of the sequence:

> By this he knew she wept with waking eyes:
> That, at his hand's light quiver by her head,
> The strange low sobs that shook their common bed,
> Were called into her with a sharp surprise,
> And strangled mute, like *little* gaping *snakes*,
> Dreadfully venomous to him.   (I; my emphases)[98]

Similarly, the wife in the poem is described as a 'star with lurid beams' which 'seemed to crown / The *pit* of infamy' (II; cf. XXIII), and as a 'devilish malignant *witch*' (IX; my emphases). The tone of the 'Enchantress' chapter in *Richard Feverel* is also to be heard in *Modern Love*. Keith Hanley suggests of the husband's expression of feeling towards his wife that in 'a welter of maniacally melodramatic imagery accompanied by Biblical diction he conveys the moral repulsiveness of his attraction to this snake-like witch, who brings out in him the demon and the beast'.[99]

As Hanley also points out, *Modern Love* derives ironically from the Renaissance sonnet sequence tradition of amatory courtship.[100] That Petrarchan tradition, of course, continued the medieval courtly love convention of applying the language of divine love to the experience of profane love. Thus Meredith's description of the death of love as hell represents another aspect of that ironical relationship between his sonnet sequence and the tradition upon which it is formally based. In the first phase of the poem (I–XXVI),[101] 'death' (*thanatos*) and the death wish are closely associated with 'love' (*eros*) and its breakdown, and the two words seem increasingly to coil around each other in serpentine movements:

> Like sculptured effigies they might be seen
> Upon their marriage-tomb, the sword between;
> Each wishing for the sword that severs all.   (I)

In later sonnets the husband refers to 'Love's corpse-light' (XVII), and says, 'Shamed nature, then, confesses love can die' (VI). When in earlier, happier days he caused her to weep by saying (though not thinking), 'Ah, yes! / Love dies!' (XVI), the 'red chasm' which grew 'among the clinking coals' proved to be prophetic, for now he gets 'a glimpse of hell' in guessing that his wife may have something to confess:

> She will not speak. I will not ask. We are
> League-sundered by the silent gulf between.   (XXII)

Traditional biblical imagery relating to the separation of the saved from the damned, and of man from God (who is love), here conveys a sense of a secularized and existential *poena damni* – the pain of loss of the vision and fruition of (profane) love. At Christmas time, the husband's dream inverts the hope embodied in the incarnation:

> I dreamed a banished angel to me crept:
> My feet were nourished on his breasts all night.   (XXIII)

Love betrayed becomes a 'subtle serpent' with which he is 'cursed' henceforward (XXVI).

In the second phase, concerning the husband's subsequent affair, the devil seems kind when 'not a soul' will comfort his distress (XXVII), and he feels 'the promptings of Satanic power' (XXVIII). In his illicit relationship with the blonde 'Lady', he is acutely aware of their mortality – 'But, as you will! we'll sit contentedly, / And eat our pot of honey on the grave' (XXIX; cf. XXX) – and of the reality of temptation, as he indicates in his criticism of Raphael's portrayal of a 'too serene' St Michael conquering the devil:

> 'Oh, Raphael! when men the Fiend do fight,
> They conquer not upon such easy terms.
> Half serpent in the struggle grow these worms.
> And does he grow half human, all is right.'   (XXXIII)

Earlier in the poem he has scorned both those 'miserable males' who 'sniff at vice and, daring not to snap, / Do therefore hope for heaven'

(XX), and the man who 'would burden the poor deuce / With what ensues from his own slipperiness'. The real moral battle must be fought out and the repercussions suffered in the here-and-now.

The attempted reconciliation with his wife in the third and final phase (XL–L) is ill-fated, for his confession of his own affair prompts her to leave him free to go to his Lady:

> She has gone forth, I know not where.
> Will the hard world my sentience of her share?
> I feel the truth; so let the world surmise.   (XLVIII)

Whether her going forth is a departure, possibly with her lover, or her death, is unclear until the end of the following sonnet, which Meredith may have added as an afterthought, together with the final sonnet in the sequence: the husband 'knows all' when he kisses his wife – 'Lethe had passed those lips' (XLIX). She has taken poison.

In June 1862 Swinburne defended *Modern Love* in the *Spectator* by answering those who denigrated the sequence for not preaching the bourgeois gospel of marriage: the time had come, he argued, for the age to accommodate itself to a new and bolder species of poetry which dealt with art rather than morality.[102] Ironically, when Swinburne himself was preparing his *Poems and Ballads* for the press four years later, it was Meredith, the scourge of Grundyism, who encouraged him to establish a 'firmly grounded' reputation by expurgating passages from the volume.[103] In the event the publication of *Poems and Ballads* proved to be one of the sensations of the decade, deeply offending the conservative majority of readers and commentators, and delighting the younger generation. (Undergraduates shouted the morally offensive stanzas of 'Dolores' on the pavements of Cambridge, shocking their elders.)[104] Like the Decadents of the 1890s, several of whom were deeply impressed by *Poems and Ballads* as adolescents, Swinburne's style of life and style of writing were similar: both were outrageously extravagant, and both were frequently associated with the satanic by opponents and supporters alike.

Struggling to come to terms with *Poems and Ballads*, John Morley in his review in the *Saturday Review* itemized features of what sounds like an extreme version of Meredith's psychic melodrama in *Modern Love*:

We are in the midst of fire and serpents, wine and ashes, blood and foam, and a hundred lurid horrors. Unsparing use of the most violent colours and the most intoxicated ideas and images is Mr. Swinburne's prime characteristic.[105]

Swinburne's religious position seemed equally puzzling, and, to some critics, no less lurid. Robert Buchanan announced in a review in the *Athenaeum* that Swinburne had clearly 'never thought at all on religious questions', but imagined that 'rank blasphemy' would be esteemed very clever, while W. M. Rossetti, in his preface to the poems, argued that Swinburne had never 'enacted the act of faith'.[106] In the *London Review*, however, an anonymous reviewer commented that 'the strangest and most melancholy fact in these strange and melancholy poems is, not the *absence* of faith, but the presence of a faith which mocks at itself, and takes pleasure in its own degradation'.[107] Swinburne speaks of a hell, for example, but 'says he would gladly encounter it for one minute's hot enjoyment' ('Les Noyades'). The ambivalence of Swinburne's religious position is reflected in the fact that Henry Morley's reading in the *Examiner* is diametrically opposed to the *London Review*'s, locating in the poetry a 'terrible earnestness':

He sings of Lust as Sin, its portion Pain and its end Death. He paints its fruit as Sodom apples, very fair without, ashes and dust within. In dwelling on their outward beauty he is sensual. Men see that and say that he is a licentious writer. But again and again when he has dwelt as proper folk object to dwell on the desire of the flesh, the beauty drops away and shows the grinning skeleton beneath with fires of hell below.[108]

Swinburne himself stated that he had never mocked what the English held most sacred, unlike Shelley and Byron, and it is worth recalling here that in 1872 Benjamin Jowett was to commission him to assist in the production of a *Children's Bible*.[109] He may have lost his faith as an undergraduate at Balliol, but he never lost his remarkable ability, developed in childhood, to quote extensively from the Bible.[110] That the reviewers found it difficult to judge Swinburne's moral position and to interpret his religious references is hardly surprising. He was pleased with Henry Morley's review while not entirely agreeing with its point of view, yet had himself read Baudelaire in a similar way, claiming in 1861 that

there is not one poem of the *Fleurs du Mal* which has not a distinct and vivid background of morality to it. Only, this moral side of the book is not thrust forward in the foolish and repulsive manner of a half-taught artist . . .[111]

Baudelaire's response to Swinburne's review anticipated Swinburne's response to Morley's: he mildly demurred.[112]

This parallel is particularly striking because *Poems and Ballads* reveals a profound debt to Baudelaire, more in the treatment of sexuality rather than of urban life. One of the most significant similarities between the poets, however, is in their use of the language of hell and damnation. Baudelaire rejected the liberal position on hell – that it was incompatible with a beneficent creator – and thought of his own life as irredeemably 'damned', from the beginning and for ever. F. W. J. Hemmings argues that 'damnation' can almost be equated with 'vocation' here: in the nineteenth century it was 'almost a commonplace that a vocation for art or poetry was inseparable from moral suffering and only too often entailed desperate material privation as well'.[113] The nature of Baudelaire's damnation

was that he could have said 'yes' to his better promptings, but he could not help constantly saying 'no' or 'not yet'. In this sense, in a purely theological if not Christian sense, he was damned.[114]

In Hemmings's view the clearest example of this sense of damnation is in 'Le Rebelle', a sonnet in which the response of 'the damned' to his good angel – a threateningly powerful figure – remains the same: 'Je ne veux pas.' Another side, however, to Baudelaire's treatment of hell and damnation is typified in the final lines of 'Le Gouffre':

> Plonger au fond du gouffre, Enfer ou Ciel, qu'importe?
> Au fond de l'Inconnu pour trouver du *nouveau*![115]

For Robert Hughes these lines reflect the way in which the imagery of hell shifted into the realm of aesthetics during the nineteenth century, 'thanks to the Satanists and Decadents':

Hell, by their implication, is an antidote to vulgarity. Its terrors exist to produce an unexpected *frisson* for poets and painters; and so they are, in reality, neutralised.[116]

The last part of this statement is too sweeping, as references to hell and Satan, far from being neutral, carried a powerful charge for many English Decadents, from Swinburne to Wilde. Moreover, Swinburne's apparent relishing of the prospect of hell and revulsion from bourgeois ideas of heaven, like Baudelaire's, is often in fact expressed by a dramatized persona, and cannot be read as a personal statement of the poet's. Take, for example, the final stanza of 'Dolores (Notre-Dame des Sept Douleurs)':

> We shall know what the darkness discovers
>   If the grave-pit be shallow or deep;
> And our fathers of old, and our lovers,
>   We shall know if they sleep not or sleep.
> We shall see whether hell be not heaven,
>   Find out whether tares be not grain,
> And the joys of thee seventy times seven,
>   Our Lady of Pain.[117]

Swinburne's defence of his work in *Notes on Poems and Reviews* (1866) is grounded in the statement that 'the book is dramatic, many-faced, multifarious; and no utterance of enjoyment or despair, belief or unbelief, can properly be assumed as the assertion of its author's personal feeling or faith'.[118] Thus 'Dolores' is to be read not as a 'study in the school of realism', but as a 'distinctly symbolic and fanciful' expression of

> that transient state of spirit through which a man may be supposed to pass, foiled in love and weary of loving, but not yet in sight of rest; seeking refuge in those 'violent delights' which 'have violent ends', in fierce and frank sensualities which at least profess to be no more than they are.[119]

Swinburne's further observation in the *Notes* that suffering and passion are 'indeed the same thing and the same word' reflects a 'terrible earnestness', but not of the moralizing kind that Henry Morley discerned where 'the beauty drops away and shows the grinning skeleton beneath with fire of hell below'. It is 'Laus Veneris', however – for Morley an exposure of 'rottenness within' – which best illustrates the slipperiness of Swinburne's language of hell and damnation where he investigates the nature of passion/suffering.

One way of approaching this poem is via Swinburne's *Notes on Poems and Reviews*, where he explains his treatment of the Tannhäuser legend:

> my first aim was to rehandle the old story in a new fashion. To me it seemed that the tragedy began with the knight's return to Venus – began at the point where hitherto it had seemed to leave off. The immortal agony of a man lost after all repentance – cast down from fearful hope into fearless despair – believing in Christ and bound to Venus – desirous of penitential pain, and damned to joyless pleasure – this in my eyes was the kernel and nucleus of a myth comparable only to that of the foolish virgins and bearing the same burden. The tragic touch of

the story is this: that the knight who has renounced Christ believes in him; the lover who has embraced Venus disbelieves in her. Vainly and in despair would he make the best of that which is the worst – vainly remonstrate with God, and argue on the side he would fain desert. Once accept or admit the least admixture of pagan worship, or of modern thought, and the whole story collapses into froth and smoke.[120]

Swinburne's commentary, like his poem, is reminiscent of Browning, whom he admired. 'Laus Veneris' is a dramatic monologue in which an old legend is reworked in its original setting, providing a vehicle for the exploration of the central persona's ambiguous position within a traditional system of belief. Although he has repented, inspired by his love of God, he believes himself to be beyond the means of grace, as an unwilling outcast from the Church whose pontiff holds St Peter's keys of heaven and hell. Yet ironically, in spite of his repulsion from his own lust for Venus, which was at one time love, he finds himself to be once more an insider in her abode: 'Inside the Horsel here the air is hot.' Located in the consciousness of the suffering narrator, the poem moves with disturbing agility between memories, present reality, and an anticipated future state, and blurs the boundary between the orthodox hell of Catholic doctrine and the hellish experience that is the narrator's present experience.

Ambiguous from the start ('Asleep or waking is it?'), the poem's shifting perspective unsettles traditional theological categories. The narrator speaks of 'the gold bars of the gates', which are suggestive of purgatory, the 'Golden Prison'. Yet although in Swinburne's words 'desirous of penitential pain', he remains unpurged. 'Damned to joyless pleasure', he tries to make Venus and himself believe that they should not envy the saved, 'High up in barren heaven'. It is the language of hell which predominates in the poem, the subject of which – burning lust without love – is an extreme version of the second kind of hell on earth, in which love is dead or betrayed. Yet the narrator's state is less a secularized version of Gehenna than of Hades, or more specifically of the intermediate Prison of the Lost in Hades described in Bickersteth's *Yesterday, To-Day, and For Ever*, published the same year. For 'Laus Veneris', like the parable of the foolish virgins, is about exclusion from the kingdom, and is eschatological in its anticipation of the last judgment. Parallels between the narrator's state and hell are of several kinds, each of which is problematic. First, the hellish quality of the poem's inner, psychic landscape is comparable to *poena sensus*, in its references to fire and heat for example – 'the air is hot', 'the salt burnt sands', 'Night falls like fire', 'the flame shakes' – and in the physicality of the metaphors applied to Venus:

> I dare not always touch her, lest the kiss
> Leave my lips charred. Yea, Lord, a little bliss,
>   Brief bitter bliss, one hath for a great sin;
> Nathless thou knowest how sweet a thing it is.
>
> Sin, is it sin whereby men's souls are thrust
> Into the pit? yet had I a good trust
>   To save my soul before it slipped therein,
> Trod under by the fire-shod feet of lust.
>
> For if mine eyes fail and my soul takes breath,
> I look between the iron sides of death
>   Into sad hell where all sweet love hath end,
> All but the pain that never finisheth.
>
> There are the naked faces of great kings,
> The singing folk with all their lute-playings;
>   There when one cometh he shall have to friend
> The grave that covets and the worm that clings.

The second stanza quoted here is ambiguous, the tenses – 'yet *had* I a good trust / To save my soul before it *slipped* therein' – suggesting on a first reading that the speaker has already been damned, but then, in the light of the vision of hell which follows, suggesting that hell is elsewhere, as is confirmed in later references to the 'fire of hell' and the 'heat of hell'.

Secondly, the narrator's suffering in the poem is akin to that of *poena damni*, as he feels himself to be cut off from what Newman called the 'Vision and Fruition of God'. He sees his former escape from the Horsel as God's saving act:

> So that God looked upon me when your hands
> Were hot about me; yea, God brake my bands
>   To save my soul alive, and I came forth
> Like a man blind and naked in strange lands . . .

His pilgrimage to Rome, however, was abortive, as the Pope refused to accept his penance, thereby precipitating his return to Venus. But the Vicar of Christ, in rehearsing the role of the divine judge on the last day, added what appeared to be an empty limiting clause to the excommunication:

> 'Until this dry shred staff, that hath no whit
> Of leaf nor bark, bear blossom and smell sweet,
>   Seek thou not any mercy in God's sight,
> For so long shalt thou be cast out from it.'

In the original legend the staff breaks into blossom after three days, signifying, presumably, the power of God's grace as revealed most fully in the resurrection. When the Pope tries to recall the knight, however, it is too late: he has returned to the Horsel. Now for Swinburne the tragedy begins here, and therefore the narrator's account of his journey to Rome is introduced only at the end of 'Laus Veneris', the main body of which is devoted to the description of a state approximating to *poena damni*, experienced by a man 'believing in Christ and bound to Venus'. By writing a dramatic monologue in which the protagonist's view is limited to the this-worldly, Swinburne explores the '*immortal* agony of a man lost after all repentance' (my emphasis) within the horizon of an earthly life extended until the end of time. Thus the referential status of the poem's eschatological language remains profoundly ambiguous.

Thirdly, and finally, the narrator's frequently expressed longing for extinction is characteristic of those who suffer the torments of hell.[121] In some of the poem's loveliest lines he yearns to be dead and buried:

> Ah yet would God this flesh of mine might be
> Where air might wash and long leaves cover me,
>   Where tides of grass break into foam of flowers,
> Or where the wind's feet shine along the sea.

The mingling of the elements here, as the air and grass imitate the action of the sea, associate his imagined physical dissolution with a soothing coolness after the heat of the Horsel. For the knight is the sole survivor of Venus's sinister 'little chambers' which 'drip with flower-like red':

> Yea, all she slayeth; yea, every man save me;
> Me, love, thy lover that must cleave to thee
>   Till the ending of the days and ways of earth,
> The shaking of the sources of the sea.
>
> Me, most forsaken of all souls that fell;
> Me, satiated with things insatiable;
>   Me, for whose sake the extreme hell makes mirth,
> Yea, laughter kindles at the heart of hell.

Hell, then, is elsewhere, and death in some distant future, as the poem's final stanzas confirm.

When Rochester contemplates suicide in *Jane Eyre* (1847; 27), arguing that 'there is not a future state worse than this present one' in the 'bottomless pit' that is his married life in Jamaica, Hope prevents him by persuading him to return to England. *Modern Love* (1862), a later realist narrative, ends with a death-wish fulfilled, through suicide. 'Laus Veneris' (1866), however, takes the idea of the death of love as hell on earth to its limit, applying the language of orthodox eschatology, descriptive of an intermediate state of the lost which will be followed by judgment and hell, to the present agony of one who finds himself doomed until the end of time to be outside the community, cut off from God, and enduring the passion/suffering of his lust. Swinburne's inheritors were the late-nineteenth-century Decadents, whose work lies beyond the scope of this study. The story of the man who 'killed the thing he loved' in *The Ballad of Reading Gaol* (1898), with its references to the Tannhäuser legend, its portrayal of the condemned man being watched in case he takes his own life, and its treatment of the other prisoners, 'each in his separate Hell' where 'Hope' is dead and 'all but Lust is turned to dust', probably owes something to Wilde's reading of Swinburne. Like Wilde's, Arthur Symons's life led directly to imprisonment and pain which, as Barbara Charlesworth puts it, 'lies at the end of the mind's darkest passages'.[122] Symons, in his essay on Beardsley (1898), celebrated the fact that evil, 'carried to the point of a perverse ecstasy, becomes a kind of good, by means of that energy which, otherwise directed, is virtue', and went on, in a sentence that would have appealed to Swinburne:

The devil is nearer to God, by the whole height from which he fell, than the average man who has not recognised his own need to rejoice or to repent.[123]

Between the first edition of *Poems and Ballads* and the poetry of the 1890s, however, came James Thomson's masterpiece, *The City of Dreadful Night* (1874), in which a descent from 'fearful hope into fearless despair' is *celebrated* as the means to stoic resistance in a godless universe. Earlier in this chapter I argued that the question of hell turns upon our idea of hope: does Farrar's 'eternal hope' embrace suicides, for example? It is precisely this theological relation between hope and the doctrine of damnation with which Thomson plays in *The City*, where his critique of hell is closely associated with his secularist rejection of

Christianity's 'lively hope'. An atheist with an intimate knowledge of the
Bible, Thomson had been brought up in the strictest Presbyterian doctrines, and had not altogether lost his Christian faith when he first began
writing.[124] Significantly, however, it was after the death of the young
Irish girl whom he hoped to marry – a lock of whose hair is buried with
him in the same grave as Austin Holyoake in Highgate Cemetery – that
he moved first into a 'doubtful' phase in early adulthood, then into the
melancholia and sporadic alcoholism which afflicted him as an army
schoolmaster, and finally the declared atheism of his London period.[125]
After T. R. Wright had read an adapted version of Holyoake's *Secularist
Burial Service* over Thomson's grave, he gave a tribute which included
these words: 'it would have given him pleasure to know that his ashes
would mingle with those of his old friend and fellow-worker in the great
cause of the *redemption* of humanity from the bondage of superstition'
(my emphasis).[126] Hatred of that bondage fuels the speaker's 'cold rage'
in *The City*, and informs the poem's critique of hell.[127] As in Wright's
secularist eulogy, however, the language of that critique cannot finally
free itself from the theological categories it denies.

Many of the poem's most striking episodes and images, however,
subvert received religious ideas and the conventionalized consolatory
strategies of the period. The speaker in the cathedral, for example, states
that 'We fall asleep and never wake again; / Nothing is of us but the
mouldering flesh', and concludes: 'Lo, you are free to end it when you
will, / Without the fear of waking after death' (XIV.51–2, 83–4). This
theme is developed later, in the River of the Suicides section (XIX), where
received ideas of the 'good' death (quietly, in one's own bed) and the
'bad' death (violently, in the river) are deconstructed. Social critics such
as Hood and Dickens had lamented the conditions which caused the
destitute and the 'fallen' to throw themselves into the Thames, while the
churches had taught that suicides were 'lost souls'. Neither view is
expressed here. Rather, the speaker regards suicide as a rational act in a
world of pain, and death as a 'sweet sleep' precisely because it is the 'one
best sleep which never wakes again' (34–5). Whereas hope is invoked in
the rescue of both Edward Rochester and Markham Sutherland from the
brink of suicide, Thomson's speaker associates hope with a religion of
fear which he denies. Indeed, his strongest argument against suicide
seems to be that stoic resistance is better than escape from a life that is
but 'one brief night of dreary pain' (30).

Thomson liked to think of himself as a Job figure, and Melville called

The City 'the modern Book of Job'.[128] For Thomson, Sheol, as described in a verse from Job which he thought of using as an epigraph for his poem, offers no false hope of transcendence, as the despised Christian scheme does: 'A land of darkness, as darkness itself, and of the shadow of death; without any order, and where the light is as darkness'.[129] The speaker's rage is vented in the attempt to express the woe which only the reader whose 'faith and hope are dead' can understand (Proem, 28). Like, it could be argued, the very gospel which the poem rejects, 'None uninitiate by many a presage / Will comprehend the language of the message' (40–1). Thus the speaker's description of this true opposite of the City of God[130] reads like a coded anti-gospel: 'Where Death-in-Life is the eternal king' (III.25); 'And he is verily as if new-born' (V.14); 'Good tidings of great joy for you, for all: / There is no God' (XIV.39– 40); and so on. The denial of the cardinal virtue of hope is dramatized early in the poem.[131] First, the speaker follows a man who endlessly revisits the sites of his desolation: 'Perpetual recurrence in the scope / Of but three terms, dead Faith, dead Love, dead Hope' (II.47–8). Then the 'stalwart shape' who has come from the desert declaims to the city: 'But I strode on austere; / No hope could have no fear' (IV.14–15, etc.).

A religion of hope, it is argued, is also a religion of fear, so to die without hope of a future life is a blessing. The speaker says of the City:

> They leave all hope behind who enter there:
>   One certitude while sane they cannot leave,
> One anodyne for torture and despair;
>   The certitude of Death, which no reprieve
> Can put off long; and which, divinely tender,
> But waits the outstretched hand to promptly render
>   That draught whose slumber nothing can bereave.   (I.78–84)

Thomson had a profound respect for Dante, agreeing with Ruskin's estimate that he is 'the central intellect' of the world.[132] In section VI of *The City*, a 'stranger' adopts Dante's triplets in relating to one who was to follow him how a 'demon warder' prevented him from passing through the gates of hell on which is written 'Leave hope behind, all ye who enter here', as he had no hope to leave in the chest which stood open there (25–36).[133] Following this radical revision of the traditional soul-at-heaven's-gate narrative, the couple bemoan their lot in this 'limbo' of an earthly life, and begin looking for 'some minute lost hope' to gain entrance to hell. Through this bitterest of ironic subversions, they find themselves in the ultimate marginal state.

Thomson, then, goes beyond those Victorian writers who describe this life as hell on earth: it is worse than that. Yet both kinds of hell on earth that I have been examining are present in the subtext of the poem – that associated with the Industrial Revolution and the city most consistently, but also the hell of love which is dead. When the orator in section IV states, for example, that 'hell is mild / And piteous' matched with the 'accursed wild' of the desert from which he has come, he is describing the pain experienced in his encounter with a woman, 'Bareheaded and barefooted on that strand', which revived hope that 'travailed with such fear' (65–81). Half of him dies with her, losing all hope and fear; 'But I, what do I here?' (106). In the City a different kind of isolation is experienced, more reminiscent of Engels's analysis of the 'dissolution of mankind into monads' in the urban throng, cited earlier. As in 'some necropolis', each isolated mourner is 'wrapt in his own doom' (1.50–4). On William Sharpe's argument, however, Thomson's poem 'also attempts to overcome the very isolation and despair it so vividly conveys': 'by sharing, though not necessarily in conventional consolations like hope, men can eventually forge identity through unflinching consciousness of their situation'.[134] In contrast to the submissiveness of the damned in Bickersteth's Evangelical epic poem, for example, the several voices of *The City* gradually build up a vague sense of solidarity based upon citizenship. A *polis*, however, with no discernible history and no politics, the City seems to represent a world that is post-holocaust, as well as post-Christian. In revolutionary Paris, as Dickens recalls in *A Tale of Two Cities* (1859), the cemetery gates bore the secularist legend, 'Here is eternal sleep.'[135] Whereas Dickens's second city is a hellish site of conflict and bloody anarchy, Thomson's City is a limbo, an 'insufferable inane', empty of meaning and direction, its permanent public monuments (described in the last two sections of the poem) the sphinx which outfaces the angel, and the massive statue of 'Melencolia'. Its people can endure to the end or, less admirably, take their own lives. The choice marks out the limits of their freedom. A world without God, it is a world without hope (of heaven), without fear (of hell), and without transcendence (through love). One begins to understand how the children who heard Father Furniss preach on hell could say they loved him.

In this chapter I have cited the responses of two men of sharply opposed beliefs to the literal interpretation of religious language associated with hell. First there was James Thomson's friend and fellow secularist,

Austin Holyoake, who asked in 1873 how hell could be both within the earth and bottomless. Secondly, there was Archbishop Tait, who stated in the previous year that nobody in the Church of England took the damnatory clauses in the Athanasian Creed in their plain and literal sense. Whereas Holyoake's aim was to expose the illogicalities of traditional religious language to a simple, broadly scientific-materialist critique, Tait's was to remind his audience of the figurative nature of religious, as of all, language. In drawing attention to the limitations of the English translators, churchmen like Maurice and Farrar opened up discussion on the dangers of a literal interpretation of words such as 'everlasting damnation' and 'hell' in the Authorized Version. It is no coincidence that in their apologetical writings, both Maurice and Farrar refer to the poets of their generation – in Farrar's case frequently. For it was the Victorian poets whose writing explored its own metaphorical nature. Thus hell came to be written, by poet and theologian alike, as a state rather than a place, a spiritual condition rather than a physical torment, a theological reality rather than a polemical threat.

THE POOR MAN'S FRIEND.

1 *The Poor Man's Friend*, from *Punch*, 1845

2 W. I. Walton, *The Last Moments of HRH The Prince Consort*, lithograph, 1862

3 Henry Bowler, *The Doubt: 'Can These Dry Bones Live?'*, 1855

4 John Everett Millais, *Autumn Leaves*, 1856

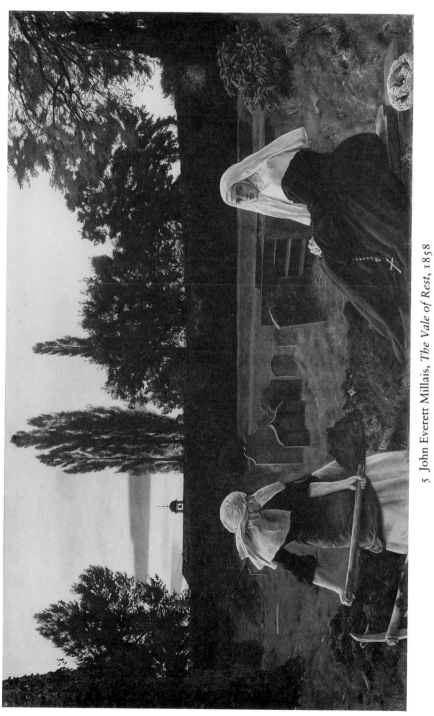

5 John Everett Millais, *The Vale of Rest*, 1858

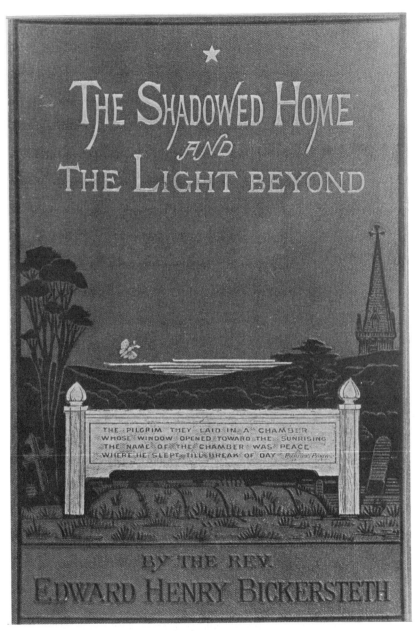

★

THE SHADOWED HOME
AND
THE LIGHT BEYOND

THE PILGRIM THEY LAID IN A CHAMBER
WHOSE WINDOW OPENED TOWARD THE SUNRISING
THE NAME OF THE CHAMBER WAS PEACE
WHERE HE SLEPT TILL BREAK OF DAY *Pilgrim's Progress*

BY THE REV.
EDWARD HENRY BICKERSTETH

6 Cover design for Edward Henry Bickersteth, *The Shadowed Home*, 1875

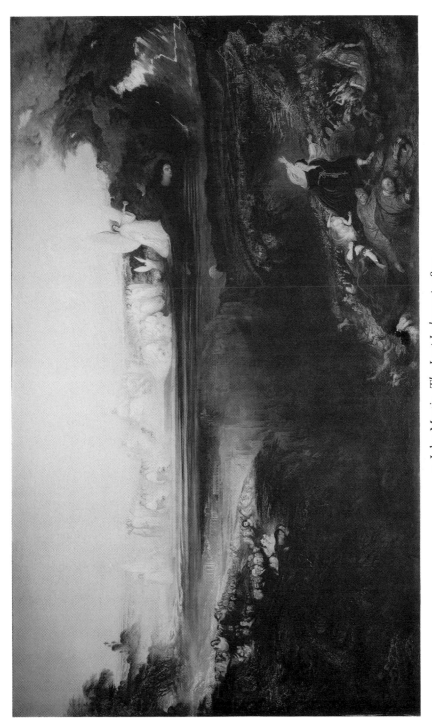

7 John Martin, *The Last Judgment*, 1853

8 John Martin, *The Plains of Heaven*, 1853

9 Dante Gabriel Rossetti, sketch for illustration to *The Raven*, *c.* 1847

10 Dante Gabriel Rossetti, preliminary sketch for *The Blessed Damozel*, 1876

11 Dante Gabriel Rossetti, *The Blessed Damozel*, 1878

12 Dante Gabriel Rossetti, centrepiece from *The Seed of David*, 1864

13 Sandro Botticelli, *Mystic Nativity*, c. 1500

14 W. Read, *Drawing the Retorts at the Great Gas Light Establishment, Brick Lane, from The Monthly Magazine*, frontispiece, 1821

15 Marcus Stone, wrapper for the monthly numbers of *Our Mutual Friend*, 1864

16 William Blake, *Death's Door*, from Robert Blair, *The Grave*, 1808

The Bathing of the Heart with the Bloody Sweat.

Christ's bloody sweat immortal blessings gives,
As by its daily sweat man's body lives.

JOEL III. 21.

I will cleanse their blood, that I have not cleansed.

EPIG. 41.

THIS bath thy Saviour sweat with drops of blood,
  Sick heart, on purpose for to do thee good.
They that have tried it can the virtue tell ;
Come, then, and use it, if thou wilt be well.

17 Francis Quarles, *The Bathing of the Heart with the Bloody Sweat*, from *The School
of the Heart*, 1638; reprinted 1866

Contrast.

HE was crowned with thorns Who crowns the martyrs with eternal flowers; He smitten on the face with palms Who yields true palms to them that conquer; He stripped of His earthly raiment Who clothes others with the robe of Immortality; He received gall for food Who gave the food of Heaven; and He had vinegar to drink Who instituted the Cup of Salvation.

St. Cyprian.

THe obsequies of Him that could not die,
And death of life, end of eternity,
How worthily He died, that died unworthily.

Giles Fletcher.

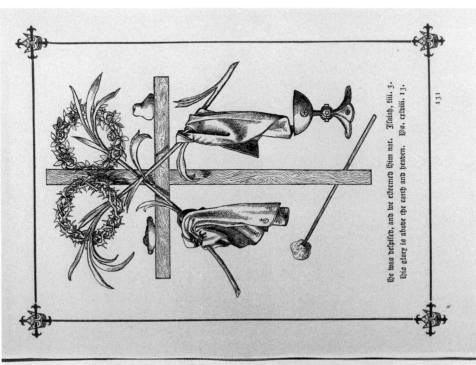

He was despised, and we esteemed Him not. Isaiah, liii. 3.
His glory is above the earth and heaven. Ps. cxlviii. 13.

18 W. Harry Rogers, *Contrast*, from *Spiritual Conceits, Extracted from the Writings of the Fathers, the Old English Poets, etc.*, 1862

PART TWO

FOUR LITERARY TEXTS

Tennyson, *In Memoriam*

At the desire of a most afflicted family, I write to you because they are unequal from the grief into which they have fallen to do it themselves. Your friend, sir, and my much-loved nephew, Arthur Hallam, is no more. It has pleased God to remove him from this, his first scene of existence, to that better world for which he was created. He died at Vienna, on his return from Buda, by apoplexy, and I believe his remains come by sea from Trieste. Mr. Hallam arrived this morning in 3 Princes Buildings. May that Being in whose hands are all the destinies of man, and who has promised to comfort all that mourn, pour the balm of consolation on all the families, who are bowed down by this unexpected dispensation! . . .[1]

Henry Elton's letter to Tennyson is the first of several acts of substitution associated with this most literary of bereavements. It reveals a practised hand: the deferred periphrasis 'is no more' is prepared for by references to family grief in the first two sentences, and even the awkward contiguity of the this-worldly and the other-worldly – of news of the father's movements, and restrained consolatory sentiments which draw upon the Bible and the burial service – is somehow fitting in the context of strained emotion. Within days of receiving the letter, at the beginning of October 1833, Tennyson echoed it in writing of '[his] Arthur's loved remains', in one of the first elegiac lyrics 'In Memoriam, A.H.H.' to be written: 'Fair ship, that from the Italian shore' (9). When Hallam's *Remains in Verse and Prose* were privately circulated in the spring of 1834, his father referred quite unselfconsciously to the fact that the 'remains of Arthur were brought to England, and interred on the 3rd of January, 1834, in the Chancel of Clevedon Church'.[2] If the iron box buried with the coffin did indeed contain Hallam's heart, the plural 'remains' was in this case grotesquely accurate.[3] That the word also served to describe the writings left by one who might have produced so much more in a brilliant future which had been erased, is also sadly appropriate. But the *Remains* also provide a simple illustration of the kind of tension between literal and figurative signification that Tennyson was to exploit in a complex and sophisticated way in *In Memoriam*.

Tennyson apparently changed his mind about attending the funeral at Clevedon, and remained in Somersby entertaining a visitor. Several reasons for his absence have been suggested,[4] but he was probably 'unequal' to it, particularly as he was already three months into the bereavement process. He survived the emotional crisis not only by writing the first of his elegiac stanzas, but also by reading the letters, reminiscences, and miscellaneous literary remains which substituted for the direct encounter with the reality of Hallam's death that would have occurred, say, on a last visit to his deathbed in the case of a prolonged terminal illness, or at the burial of his physical remains. The many-voiced quality[5] of *In Memoriam* (1850) is partly the result of its genesis over a number of years as a series of acts of memory in which disparate reminiscences, both personal and literary, were drawn together and made present in the imagination. The poem memorializes Hallam, for example, by echoing his words and thoughts; and close editorial work has only recently revealed the great range of literary and biblical allusion and parallelism in the work.[6] A variety of classical elegiac forms, for example, provided specific models for many of the early lyrics. Matthew Arnold in his elegy on Charlotte Brontë described a more congenial spot for her burial place, and thus for his 'pindarics', than she had in reality.[7] Tennyson as elegist fell into a similar necessary error in lyric 18 of *In Memoriam*, written in 1834, which refers to the burial of Hallam:

> 'Tis well; 'tis something; we may stand
>   Where he in English earth is laid,
>   And from his ashes may be made
> The violet of his native land.

Even before the private circulation of the *Remains*, Tennyson probably knew that Hallam was buried inside the church rather than in the graveyard.[8] Although interment inside the church would be 'among familiar names to rest', however, the 'ashes' of the poem had to be buried where a violet could grow, and thus where the traditional resources of elegy could be exploited:

> I sing to him that rests below,
>   And, since the grasses round me wave,
>   I take the grasses of the grave,
> And make them pipes whereon to blow.   (21)

The universalizing effect of literary modifications and substitutions such as these subserves a larger movement in the poem from the specific to the general, both emotionally and intellectually: from the death of the poet's friend (to take the most significant example) and his post-mortem existence in heaven, to the 'larger hope' for humanity. Throughout the long lyric sequence, however, its many themes and voices are mediated through a unifying persona (I will call him the 'lyrist'), whose emotional states, felt along the heart, are registered in the poem's characteristic iambic pulse and regular stanzaic form. The Prologue (introductory stanzas written for the trial issue of March 1850) is in part an act of contrition – 'Forgive these wild and wandering cries'; and the therapeutic value of the subsequent lyrics for the 'unquiet heart and brain' are anxiously acknowledged (5). From the early lyrics of bereavement and loss, of the dark house 'where my heart was used to beat' (7), through the central lyrics of spiritual trial, where 'the heart is sick' (50), to the point at which

> My heart, tho' widow'd, may not rest
>   Quite in the love of what is gone,
>   But seeks to beat in time with one
> That warms another living breast   (85)

the heart's pain is written out, in both senses, in a kind of diary form.[9] The heart, traditionally the seat of feeling and of love, is Tennyson's ultimate authority, and not only provides the most important conceit in the poem, but also informs both its stanzaic structure and its overall design. Tennyson's belief in a life after death, for him the 'cardinal point of Christianity',[10] was grounded in belief in a God of *love* (reflected, for example, in his response to Dante in *In Memoriam*) and a hope for 'the Christ that is to be' (reflected in the Johannine emphasis upon incarnation in the poem).

   T. S. Eliot's famous observation that the poem's faith is a 'poor thing', but its doubt 'a very intense experience'[11] has proved to be influential.[12] His argument, however, that the '"Strong Son of God, immortal Love"', with an invocation of whom the poem begins, has only a hazy connexion with the Logos, or the Incarnate God', perhaps reflects the anti-pathy of a High Churchman to Tennyson's liberal treatment of religious experience. In contrast to the scientist, Tennyson regarded evidence as material with which to corroborate the position that he already held, and in my view this habit of mind is reflected in his emphasis upon incarnation in *In Memoriam*. His eclectic mind drew upon those aspects of Christianity which he felt to be true, selecting, as it were, what was most helpful to him spiritually, from a position on the margin of the Church of England and its disciplines. Thus although some ideas concerning the future state explored in the poem are specifically Christian, others are closer to classical traditions. Eliot argues that Tennyson craves for renewal that is at best a 'continuance', or a 'substitute for the joys of friendship upon earth', and that 'his desire for immortality never is quite the desire for Eternal Life; his concern is for the loss of man rather than for the gain of God'.[13] This last distinction is too sharply drawn, taking no account, for example, of Tennyson's theomorphic conception of man in the poem. Nevertheless, it is highly significant that of the main nineteenth-century models of heaven, as worship, or as reunion and community, only the latter figures in *In Memoriam*.

Having first examined in more detail his appeal to the authority of the heart, I propose to discuss Tennyson as the poet of the 'larger hope', whose perceptions on the controversial subjects of hell and judgment were consonant with those of Broad Church opinion. I will then consider the treatment of the heavenly state in the poem, or what Hallam's uncle called that 'better world for which he was created'.

THE AUTHORITY OF THE HEART, AND THE GOD OF LOVE

Tennyson, who had a general knowledge of physiology, would surely have shared Wordsworth's interest in the physiology of the heart, its physical reality as well as its analogical potential for his elegies.[14] A post-mortem examination of Hallam after the fatal apoplectic 'rush of blood to the head' of 15 September 1833 revealed 'a want of sufficient energy in the heart'.[15] Tennyson might naturally have consulted books on the subject in 1833, or later. Whether he did or not cannot be proved, and is of only marginal interest, although the nature of Hallam's death may be reflected in the structure of Tennyson's *In Memoriam* stanza. More significantly, Tennyson's heartfelt response to that death most certainly

is. The ABBA stanza has been much discussed, and particularly the effect
of the rise at the end of the third line and the dying fall of the fourth,[16]
described by Charles Kingsley as a return to the 'mournful minor key'.[17]
To my ear the most characteristic effect of the third line is one of filling,
expanding or swelling to the anticipated second B rhyme. Another way
of describing this would be dilation, or diastole, and indeed the four-line
stanzas are often not unlike the four-chambered heart in their systolic–
diastolic movements.[18] The most fundamental opposition in the poem is
based upon the I/he relation in life of Alfred to Arthur: the beating,
suffering 'unquiet heart' (5) in the 'labouring breast' (15) of the 'I', and
the 'dead calm in that noble breast / Which heaves but with the heaving
deep' (11) of the 'he'. In Romantic elegy the mourner displaces the
mourned as the principal subject,[19] and it is the poet's heart's events
which inform the *In Memoriam* stanza.

Every individual lyric in the poem includes some binary opposition –
I/he, here/there, life/death, light/dark – and what has been described as
the 'diastolic–systolic rhythm' in the work[20] is registered through
seasonal change, the passing of the years, and the stages of bereavement.
The poem's deep pulsations are also discernible in its larger organization. Indeed, Tennyson's suggestion to James Knowles that there were
nine natural groups or divisions in the poem makes more sense than is
generally recognized in modern criticism when seen in this light.[21]
'Groups' is perhaps the more appropriate term in relation to a poem that
imitates the unpredictable ebb and flow of emotion associated with
bereavement in its loose construction and frequent repetitions. For, as in
Tennyson's approach to intellectual difficulties, the organization of the
poem reflects a method rather than a system. The transitions between
the first five groups establish a pattern of opposition or polarity which
accommodates both the traumatic first stage of bereavement and the
opening out of the lyrist's thoughts on the larger themes of the future life
and the question of God's providential scheme for mankind. In the first
group (lyrics 1–8) the lyrist describes his lonely earthly existence as a
mourner, meditating upon the 'Old Yew, which graspest at the stones /
That name the under-lying dead' (2), where earth is committed to earth,
and describing the sense of desolation felt in the 'long unlovely street',
the resistance of which is conveyed in the repetition of the word in the
final line: 'On the bald street breaks the blank day' (7). Lyric 9 ('Fair
ship, that from the Italian shore') moves the poem's imaginative focus

from mourner to mourned in the second group (9–20), and from earth to water: the sea on which the fair ship carries the 'precious relics' (17) to the 'pleasant shore' where 'twice a day the Severn fills' (19).

Variations on this earth/sea binary opposition in the third and fourth groups broaden the central theme of separation, placing it in relation to time and eternity. Thus lyrics 21–7 look back to the four years of a shared earthly pilgrimage, 'And all the secret of the Spring / Moved in the chambers of the blood' (23); while lyrics 28–49 look forward to a shared future existence in the 'deep' of eternity, the elements of which are air and fire. The central, fifth group (50–8) returns once more to the lyrist on earth who falters where he firmly 'trod' and gathers 'dust and chaff' as he meditates on the findings of geology (55), the science of the origin and structure of the earth.

In the remaining four groups of lyrics, these pulsations (earth/heaven, I/he, life/death) quicken or shorten, until a visionary unity is achieved in the Epilogue and the mystical marriage of the 'one far-off divine event, / To which the whole creation moves'. This process begins in the sixth group (59–71), where Hallam is imagined in a 'higher height, a deeper deep' (63), and the question of communication between earth and heaven, particularly through dreams, is considered. The boundaries between earth and heaven are broken down in the seventh group (72–98), conditionally in the lyrics on the earthly fame that Hallam would have achieved had he lived (73–5) and experientially in the climactic spiritual communion achieved in lyric 95. The eighth group (99–103), which records the departure from the old home with all its associations, is transitional. It repeats in little the earlier earth/sea, earth/heaven oppositions, beginning with the earthbound lyrist firmly placed in the diurnal round ('Risest thou thus, dim dawn, again') and ending with his dream of reunion with Hallam on a 'great ship', in which the categories of earth and heaven are finally dissolved: 'We steer'd her toward a crimson cloud / That landlike slept along the deep.' This short reprise prepares for the ninth and final group, where the poem's themes are reviewed in a 'higher' key (the word recurs several times in the final lyrics), and love is described as 'vaster' and Hallam as 'mix'd with God and Nature' (130).

My argument, then, is that the pulse or heart-beat informs the structures of *In Memoriam* at every level of its organization: its lines, stanzas, lyrics, and groups of lyrics. This reflects Tennyson's inheritance of his Romantic precursors' respect for the authority of the heart, and, more significantly in relation to my present theme, of a broader tradition of Protestant religious authority. The appeal to the heart and to feeling in matters of religion has a venerable history, of course, from the Psalmist's 'harden not your heart' (Psalm 95.8) and St Paul's 'fleshy tables of the heart' (2 Corinthians 3.3) to Pascal's *Pensées*: 'We know Truth not only through reason, but also by the heart; it is in this way that we have knowledge of first principles.'[22] It was European Romanticism, however, a movement of radical 'reformation', that apotheosized the heart and feeling as the inner or internal authority in both theology and literature. In Germany, for example, Schleiermacher argued that authority lies in religious experience, which he defined as 'Feeling and Self-consciousness' – equivalent terms which he juxtaposed in order to avoid misrepresentation of his word 'feeling' as simply emotion, or even unconscious states. The 'essence of piety' is defined by him as 'the consciousness of being absolutely dependent, or, which is the same thing, of being in relation with God'.[23] Hegel's reported comment on this is well known: if the essence of religion consists in the feeling of an absolute dependence, 'then the dog would be the best Christian'. Early in his career, however, Hegel himself had defined a 'religious man' as one whose 'heart feels the activity, the awe and presence of the Godhead . . . he bows before Him, utters thanks and praise'.[24]

In England, Coleridge found in the heart's function an analogy for the living principle of Christianity. The word 'heart' recurs again and again in his *Aids to Reflection*, where he writes, 'Too soon did the Doctors of the Church forget that the *Heart*, the *Moral* Nature, was the beginning and the end; and that Truth, Knowledge, and Insight were comprehended in its expansion.'[25] Almost as early as Coleridge and Schleiermacher, and without being indebted to either, Thomas Erskine of Linlathen was in Scotland 'an apostle of the "Christian consciousness"', in the view of John Tulloch, author of the first survey of nineteenth-century religious thought in Britain.[26] Erskine's religion was '*all heart*', and appealed to 'internal evidence': 'the revelation of Love to love, of Life to life, – of God to man, raising him to divine communion, and reflecting upon him the divine likeness'.[27] F. D. Maurice, whose theology has been compared to Erskine's,[28] wrote in *The Kingdom of Christ*: 'By acting in concert with each of them a man shall find that the feeling of God's universal love in himself does not clash with the feeling of God's eternal and unchangeable law.'[29] And Jowett, another liberal who became a friend of Tennyson's in the 1850s, used similar terms when developing a Kantian argument concerning our 'sense of a future life': 'We feel that God cannot have given us capacities and affections, that they should find no other fulfilment than they attain here.'[30]

Jowett's words would serve as a broad summary of Tennyson's position in *In Memoriam*, and when one compares the comments of these liberals on feeling with the language of lyric 124, where the lyrist's chronicle of the heart's events is related most directly to the question of belief in a future life, it is easy to understand how Tennyson came to be seen as the laureate of the Broad Church:

> If e'er when faith had fall'n asleep,
>   I heard a voice 'believe no more'
>   And heard an ever-breaking shore
> That tumbled in the Godless deep;
>
> A warmth within the breast would melt
>   The freezing reason's colder part,
>   And like a man in wrath the heart
> Stood up and answer'd 'I have felt.'
>
> No, like a child in doubt and fear:
>   But that blind clamour made me wise;
>   Then was I as a child that cries,
> But, crying, knows his father near;
>
> And what I am beheld again
>   What is, and no man understands;
>   And out of darkness came the hands
> That reach thro' nature, moulding men.

Like Coleridge, Tennyson was weary of Christian 'evidences'.[31] Although Bishop Butler in *The Analogy of Religion* provided him and his contemporaries with many of their arguments for the existence of a future state, grounded in probabilities rather than demonstrations or proofs, Tennyson was no more satisfied with the argument from design than with the appeal to reason.[32] The third stanza quoted above was not in the trial issue of March 1850.[33] In the first (June 1850) and later editions the effect of this modifying stanza is characteristic of the poem as a whole: in describing the moment when the grounds of belief in feeling are at last found, the authoritative statement is qualified. Yet in this case the qualification is actually closer to a Schleiermachian feeling of absolute dependence, in that image of the child whose wisdom is more precious than knowledge (the theme of lyrics 108–13), and which has been compared to Charles Wesley's 'A poor blind child I wander here'.[34] The added stanza thus validates the renewed sense in the final stanza of a personal identity ('what I am') in contradistinction from God ('What is'), echoing the mystical climax of the poem in lyric 95 ('And came on that which is'). The idea of God as father-creator ('The Power in darkness whom we guess') is necessary to define a sense of self.

In relation to God the Son, the hope for 'the Christ that is to be' (106) was particularly attractive to F. D. Maurice, who befriended Tennyson after the publication of *In Memoriam*. Maurice cites lyric 106 in his dedicatory letter in *Theological Essays* (1853), when referring to his young godson, Hallam Tennyson, who might one day read the essays:

they may tell him what meaning some of the former generation attached to words, which will be familiar and dear to his generation, and to those that follow his, – how there were some who longed that the bells of our churches might indeed

> Ring out the darkness of the land,
> Ring in the Christ that is to be.[35]

Lyric 106 ('Ring out, wild bells, to the wild sky') follows the description of the last of the three Christmases in the poem, and thus marks a point of new growth via a number of transitions: from the old home to 'the stranger's land' (105); from a bereaved state to a more settled and hopeful frame of mind; from a sense of Arthur Hallam as an individual to one in which he represents the highest aspirations for the future of mankind; from an awareness that Christian doctrine as preached in the early nineteenth century could not answer the profoundest doubts, to the hope that 'the true Christianity' (as Tennyson later paraphrased Maurice),[36] which teaches a gospel of love, may be inaugurated in the future.

The invocatory form of lyric 106 is anticipated in the last stanza of lyric 30, where the movement in *In Memoriam* from despair to hope begins with the first Christmas:

> Rise, happy morn, rise, holy morn,
>   Draw forth the cheerful day from night:
>   O Father, touch the east, and light
> The light that shone when Hope was born.

This early lyric, which describes the Christmas that followed Hallam's death but preceded his funeral, is the first in which the nature of the future state is directly addressed, and I will return to it later with this in view. For the present I want to draw attention to its movement from initial sorrow in bereavement ('And sadly fell our Christmas-eve'), to an affirmation of belief which strengthens through shared *feeling* ('a gentler feeling crept / Upon us') and ends in the reference to the birth of Christ ('when Hope was born'). This movement, which is repeated in *In Memoriam* as a whole, associates feeling and love with the incarnation, as Hallam himself does in the formal theological discourse of the 'Theodicaea Novissima', for example:

now that we know [Christ] as an Elder Brother, a being of like thoughts, feelings, sensations, sufferings, with ourselves, it has become possible to love as God loves, that is, to love Christ and thus to become united in heart to God . . . when then by affection towards Christ we have become blended with his being, the beams of Eternal Love falling, as ever, on the one beloved object will include us in him, and their returning flashes of love out of his personality will carry along with them some from our own, since ours has become confused with his, and so shall we be one with Christ and through Christ with God.
   Thus then we see the great effect of the Incarnation, as far as our nature is concerned, was to render human love for the Most High a possible thing.[37]

Several words and phrases in this passage from the essay that Tennyson specifically asked to be included in the *Remains* indicate how extraordinarily 'echo-like' *In Memoriam* is, but Hallam's comments on human and divine love in relation to the incarnation, and his idea of the 'confusion' of our personality with Christ's, are particularly relevant here. His argument, as he frequently states, is based upon analogy, and the systematizing of the doctrine of analogy, itself grounded in man's creation in God's image, was partly to justify the anthropomorphic language of the Bible. At the end of the nineteenth century, J. R. Illingworth contributed to a movement back towards the confident use of the analogy between the creator and his creation, arguing that the apparently damaging effect of admitting to an anthropomorphic element in theology is neutralized by the assertion of a theomorphic doctrine of human nature.[38] (Interestingly, a similar argument has been advanced more recently by Michael Edwards in relation to a 'Christian poetics': 'Rather than our vision of God and of heaven being anthropomorphic, isn't it a man who is theomorphic, and the world which is, so to speak, ouranomorphic?')[39] It is mistaken to claim, as some critics have,[40] that Hallam is Tennyson's substitute for Christ in *In Memoriam*, for the description of Hallam as 'half-divine' (14) and the reference to the 'Known and unknown; human, divine' (129) are closer to Hallam's own thinking on the *effects* of the incarnation than to the doctrine itself – that Christ is both wholly man and wholly God. Indeed, it could be argued that Tennyson anticipates Illingworth in reversing the 'analogical leap' from man to God, and seeing Hallam theomorphically in the later lyrics of the poem.[41]

The substitution of the words 'Hope' (30), 'the Life' (32), 'the Word' (36), and 'Love' (Prologue) for the name of Jesus Christ is more specifically referential than is generally recognized, and reflects the Johannine orientation of both his and Hallam's theology.[42] Tennyson places little emphasis upon the life and ministry of Jesus in the poem; or upon Christ as saviour and judge; or, crucially, Christ's death and resurrection (the ground of hope for Coleridge and Schleiermacher, for example). Whereas Maurice believed that the story of the raising of Lazarus directly addressed and answered the most pressing questions of the mourner, lyric 31 (which immediately follows the Christmas lyric quoted above) focused upon what remained 'unrevealed' in the narrative of the Evangelist. For Tennyson, resurrection seems to have been a less secure ground for belief in a future life than the revelation of God's love in the incarnation, and this is reflected in the structural and thematic significance attached to the three Christmases in the poem. For Hallam too, as we have seen, the essence of God was love, and in the 'Theodicaea Novissima' he capitalizes the statement 'GOD IS LOVE', in Coleridgean style.[43] The opening stanza of the hymnic Prologue to *In Memoriam*, 'Strong Son of God, immortal Love', is perhaps best read as a frame to the main body of the poem, in which echoes of Hallam's voice, as well as of the poet's, are heard.[44] And behind Hallam and the Apostles stood Maurice, for whom the '*starting-point* of the Gospel' was the 'absolute Love of God'.[45]

The great *literary* precursor whose writing on divine love shaped the minds and sensibilities of Maurice, Hallam, and Tennyson was Dante. In 1899 Edward Moore, Principal of St Edmund Hall, Oxford, and a leading authority on Dante, looked back on an 'extraordinary revival in the study of his works' in the nineteenth century.[46] In the Victorian Age, he argued, all sects, including even the Swedenborgians, had claimed Dante for themselves, whereas for the greater part of the seventeenth and eighteenth centuries he had been largely neglected in Britain. This neglect partly explains why the Revd Francis Cary's translation of the *Inferno* into English blank verse received little attention when it was first published in 1805–6. The *Inferno* was later reprinted at Cary's own expense and published with the recently completed *Purgatorio* and *Paradiso*, but again there was little critical response. It was largely through the acclaim of Coleridge (who had met Cary on the beach at Littlehampton), and the subsequent publication of a new, corrected edition in 1819, that Dante came to be widely read in English.

Although Dante was never to appeal to the narrower English Protestant mind, his works were key texts for those liberal Anglicans who looked to Coleridge as their mentor. For as Moore explains, Dante's theology was unusual: his purgatory was not that of orthodox Catholicism, either medieval or modern, and his emphasis upon love rather than satisfaction was unique.[47] Maurice referred to Dante in the expanded concluding essay on 'Eternal Life and Eternal Death' in the second edition of his *Theological Essays* (1853):

> What is Perdition but a loss? . . . The noblest Doctors of the Middle Ages . . . did believe . . . that Love was at the root of all things, and that to lose Love, was to lose all things . . . It was this inward conviction which made them tolerant of the idea of Purgatory . . . They were afraid to limit the love which they felt had been so mighty for them and for the world . . . They would rather think of material punishments which might, elsewhere as here, be God's instruments of acting upon the spirit to awaken it out of death. The great poem of the Florentine brings out this deeper theology of the Middle Ages, in connexion with all the forms in which it was hidden.[48]

Earlier in the essay, however, he put the following interpretation of Dante's hell into the mouths of those 'Unitarians and multitudes who are not Unitarians' who object to his church's doctrine of everlasting punishment after death: 'Even in the Inferno of the Florentine poet, though all hope was to forsake those who entered it, what traces there are of recollection and affection, what hints of a moral improvement through suffering!'[49] Maurice's own position is very close to Tennyson's in *In Memoriam*:

> if you take from me the belief that God is always righteous, always maintaining a fight with evil, always seeking to bring His creatures out of it, you take everything from me, all hope now, all hope in the world to come . . .

> . . . I am obliged to believe in an abyss of love which is deeper than the abyss of death: I dare not lose faith in that love. I sink into death, eternal death, if I do so. I must feel that this love is compassing the universe. More about it I cannot know. But God knows. I leave myself and all to Him.[50]

A brief account of the Apostles in the Tennyson *Memoir* is immediately followed by a reference to the poet's great interest in Arthur Hallam's work on a translation of Dante's *Vita Nuova* in 1830.[51] The Victorian critic Richard Simpson compared *In Memoriam* to the sonnet sequences of Dante, Petrarch, and Shakespeare, commenting that the poem's subject 'is always the scale or ladder of love'.[52] Hallam was strongly attracted to Dante's philosophy based on the analogical relation between divine love and human love, and on the divine origin of erotic love.[53] He was said to have admired particularly the 'peculiar sweetness and tenderness' of so much of Dante's poetry, and his father recorded that, 'like all genuine worshippers of the great Florentine poet, he rated the Inferno below the two later portions of the Divina Commedia; there was nothing even to revolt his taste, but rather much to attract it, in the scholastic theology and mystic visions of the Paradiso'.[54]

The private association of Hallam with Dante in the writing of *In Memoriam* is reflected in Tennyson's famous description of the work: 'The poem concludes with the marriage of my sister Cecilia. It was meant to be a kind of *Divina Commedia*, ending with happiness.'[55] The influence of the *Vita Nuova* and the *Commedia* on *In Memoriam*, and Hallam's intermediary role as a student and translator of Dante, has been examined by Gordon D. Hirsch, and more briefly discussed elsewhere.[56] Hirsch argues that the broadening effect in *In Memoriam* to which I referred earlier can be explained partly in terms of this influence, as a departure from the structure of the English elegy and a return to the 'elegies' (in Hallam's view) of Dante.[57] One can also say that Tennyson's emphasis on 'the larger hope' is compatible with his reading of Dante, copies of whose works he carried with him everywhere, including at the time of Hallam's death.[58] For although the famous words inscribed on the gates of hell – 'All hope abandon, ye who enter here' (Cary)[59] – presented difficulties to all those with liberal views on the question of hell and eternal punishment, the numerous other references to hope in the *Commedia*,[60] including Dante's reply to St James, where he defines hope as 'of the joy to come a sure expectance / The effect of grace divine and merit preceding', are central to the work's theology.[61] In the *Memoir*, Tennyson's son comments on the previous lines of Dante's inscription over the gates of hell:

> 'Fecemi la divina potestate
> La somma sapienza, e 'l primo amore,'

'were words which he was fond of quoting in this relation, as if they were a kind of unconscious confession by Dante that Love must conquer at the last'.[62]

For the poet of the larger hope, as for the author of *Theological Essays*, the doctors of the Middle Ages taught that love was at the root of all things.

THE POET OF 'THE LARGER HOPE'

'They are always speaking of me as if I were a writer of philosophical treatises.'[63] Although Tennyson speaks for all poets who have been misread or misinterpreted in this way, his complaint had a special resonance in an age in which the laureate was assessed as a sage. At the end of the nineteenth century, Gladstone, who had been Hallam's friend at Eton seventy years earlier, wrote of the 'great philosophical insight, with which the *In Memoriam* is charged throughout'.[64] In this case, the emphasis on the poem's philosophical content probably reflects uneasiness in a High Churchman concerning Tennyson's liberal theology, which Gladstone goes on to criticize. J. A. Froude's account of the reception in his own circle of Tennyson's early poetry and *In Memoriam* as 'what the "Christian Year" was to orthodox Churchmen' was typical of more liberal mid-Victorian responses.[65] 'We read them', Froude recalled, 'and they became part of our minds, the expression in exquisite language of the feelings which were working in ourselves.' At the turn of the twentieth century, Tennyson's poems were disparagingly described by Frederic Harrison as 'exquisitely graceful re-statements of the current theology of the broad-Churchmen of the school of F. D. Maurice and Jowett – a combination of Maurice's somewhat illogical piety with Jowett's philosophy of mystification'.[66]

A review of *In Memoriam* by one member of this school, Charles Kingsley, has been cited as an example of the explicit appropriation of Tennyson's poetry to 'the age and its specific causes'.[67] Maurice's dedication of his *Theological Essays* to Tennyson three years later would seem at first sight to provide similar evidence.[68] Before the publication of *In Memoriam*, however, it was Tennyson who had been indebted to Maurice, even if indirectly, as the 'mysterious, awesome figure' and shaping spirit behind the Cambridge Apostles of the 1830s, and the leading proponent of the Coleridgean tradition of liberal Anglican thought.[69] Similarly, F. W. Farrar might be accused of having appropriated Tennyson to his cause in dedicating the sequel to *Eternal Hope*, entitled *Mercy and Judgment* (1881), to 'Alfred Tennyson, Esq., Poet Laureate, &c., &c., who, among his many high services to all that is pure in conduct and great in thought, will also be remembered by posterity as the poet of "the larger hope"'.[70] For although in his religious views Farrar's position was described as being between Broad Church and Evangelical schools of thought,[71] his controversial books on eschatology reflect the influence of Maurice (who taught him at King's College, London), and he clearly used 'the larger hope' as something of a rallying cry to liberal opinion on the question of divine judgment. It would be mistaken, however, to see the relationship of Farrar to Tennyson as being purely appropriative. Farrar dedicated *Mercy and Judgment* to Tennyson 'by his own kind permission', and we know that the poet often talked of Farrar's, and Maurice's, ideas on eternal punishment with Arthur Coleridge.[72]

Tennyson's main concern was that his works should not be read as *systematic* philosophical, or indeed religious statements. Significantly, he placed his defence of his formal strategy in *In Memoriam* – 'If these brief lays, of Sorrow born' (48) – immediately after the group of lyrics concerned with the nature of the future life. His unwillingness to 'part and prove', to close 'grave doubts and answers here proposed', not only made *In Memoriam* particularly attractive to readers like Maurice and Farrar who disliked 'little systems' (Prologue) in the church and in theology.[73] It also reflects an imaginative freedom which was denied even to these Christian apologists, whose essays and sermons were highly controversial. It was Farrar who, as we have seen, referred to Tennyson and Browning when claiming that the 'intuitions of the poet like those of the saint, may contain more essential truth than the limitless inferences of theologians from dimly-apprehended metaphors'.[74] F. W. Robertson of Brighton, who, like Maurice, belonged to 'every party and to none' but was generally regarded as a Broad Churchman,[75] wrote of Tennyson's answering 'doubts, and worse' in *In Memoriam*, 'not as a philosopher would answer them, nor as a theologian, or a metaphysician, but as it is the duty of a poet to reply, by intuitive faculty, in strains in which Imagination predominates over Thought and Memory'.[76]

Tennyson's comparative freedom as a poet rather than a theologian or metaphysician is exemplified in his informal treatment of hell and judgment, subjects to which Farrar was to devote over seven hundred printed pages. In the lyric describing the fear that the spirit of Hallam may progress so far in the 'secular to-be' that the lyrist will be 'evermore a life behind', for example, the question of hell is marginalized through the use of periphrasis and a negative construction in what is merely a subordinate clause:

> For tho' my nature rarely yields
>   To that vague fear implied in death;
>   Nor shudders at the gulfs beneath,
> The howlings from forgotten fields;
>
> Yet oft when sundown skirts the moor
>   An inner trouble I behold,
>   A spectral doubt which makes me cold,
> That I shall be thy mate no more . . .   (41)

Various sources for the 'gulfs' and 'forgotten fields' have been proposed, but Tennyson himself commented: 'The eternal miseries of the Inferno'.[77] Hellish nightmares and visions in the poem, as for example in lyrics 70 and 127, are 'stilled' by a sense of Hallam's tutelary presence: 'And thro' a lattice on the soul / Looks thy fair face and makes it still'; 'O'erlook'st the tumult from afar, / And smilest, knowing all is well.' Tennyson's 'intuitive faculty' is in full play here, as he sets aside what in any attempt at a complete account of eschatology – as in a cosmological epic like the *Commedia*, for example, or a formal theological argument – would have to be addressed.

In contrast, Maurice's liberal views on hell in *Theological Essays* cost him his chair at King's College, London.[78] In later years Tennyson would quote with approval Maurice's view that the 'real Hell was the absence of God from the human soul'.[79] His own views on hell are also revealed in one of his son's reminiscences in the *Memoir*:

> One day towards the end of his life he bade me look into the Revised Version and see how the Reviser had translated the passage 'Depart from me, ye cursed, into everlasting fire.' [Matthew 25.41] His disappointment was keen when he found that the translators had not altered 'everlasting' into 'aeonian' or some such word: for he never would believe that Christ could preach 'everlasting punishment.'[80]

Although in 1884 Tennyson referred his friend William Allingham to 'Farrar's book', which 'proves from original sources that no such doctrine [of everlasting damnation] existed in the early days of Christianity',[81] Farrar only confirmed what he himself had always felt, or 'known', and thus believed. Where Farrar produces batteries of sources to support an argument, Tennyson simply records the promptings of inner experience: his 'nature', or very being, does not 'shudder at the gulfs beneath'.

The terrors of judgment are neutralized in lyric 51 ('Do we indeed desire the dead') through further references to Hallam's guardianship:

> Shall he for whose applause I strove,
>   I had such reverence for his blame,
>   See with clear eye some hidden shame
> And I be lessen'd in his love?
>
> I wrong the grave with fears untrue:
>   Shall love be blamed for want of faith?
>   There must be wisdom with great Death:
> The dead shall look me thro' and thro'.
>
> Be near us when we climb or fall:
>   Ye watch, like God, the rolling hours
>   With larger other eyes than ours,
> To make allowance for us all.

These last lines, which gave particular comfort to Queen Victoria after the death of the Prince Consort,[82] soften what otherwise would be a terrifying picture, and one not unlike the scene at the last judgment in Bickersteth's *Yesterday, To-Day, and For Ever*, when the saved have a perfect view of those who are to be damned.[83] Here, however, it is 'the dead' who are foregrounded, so that those who were themselves imperfect are thought to look him 'thro' and thro''. Similarly, in the final stanza, attention is focused on the apotheosized loving friend rather than the all-seeing eye of God. But Hallam is not simply substituted for God. Nor is the phrase 'like God' merely a token reference to the deity. Rather, in reversing the normal direction of the 'analogical leap' from man to God ('God makes allowances for us in the same way that a loving friend does') and stating that Hallam watches him as God does, the lyrist suggests with great economy that Hallam has partaken of God's loving nature in heaven.

This lyric comes near the beginning of the fifth group of nine in the scheme suggested by Tennyson to Knowles.[84] Lyrics 50–8 are thus centrally placed in the poem.[85] They are also the most frequently discussed in modern criticism, and have come to be seen as central to the poem's larger themes, being the group in which the impact of science is explored. As Alan Sinfield suggested, however, in his study on the language of *In Memoriam*, it is possible to overestimate the importance of scientific imagery in *In Memoriam*.[86] It is also possible to overlook the fact that this central group of lyrics contains statements about sin, divine judgment, and God's providential scheme for mankind which were quoted almost as holy writ during Tennyson's lifetime.

Lyrics 52 and 53 address the question of personal morality. In the former, the 'Spirit of true love', acknowledging that human frailty will always make mankind fall short of the ideal of 'the sinless years / That breathed beneath the Syrian blue', promises never to leave the lyrist, and assures him that 'thy wealth is gather'd in, / When Time hath sunder'd shell from pearl'. A liberal line taken on youthful folly and sin in the opening stanzas of lyric 53 preserves the final moral appeal from stridency:

> Hold thou the good: define it well:
>   For fear divine Philosophy
>   Should push beyond her mark, and be
> Procuress to the Lords of Hell.

The placing, however, of this reminder of the moral imperative immediately before lyric 54 proves to be significant, as the major objection to the broadly universalist position adopted there is thus anticipated:

> Oh yet we trust that somehow good
>   Will be the final goal of ill,
>   To pangs of nature, sins of will,
> Defects of doubt, and taints of blood;
>
> That nothing walks with aimless feet;
>   That not one life shall be destroy'd,
>   Or cast as rubbish to the void,
> When God hath made the pile complete . . .   (54)

If the last two lines quoted are a critique of the 'common view' of everlasting punishment, or even a veiled parody of judgment scenes like Bickersteth's, in which the completion of the number of the elect is the signal for the closing of the mouth of hell, the line 'That not one life shall be destroy'd' would seem to reject the 'annihilationist' position, or conditional immortality. (Ironically, Tennyson unwittingly supplied illustrative material for Henry Constable's Darwinian conditionalist argument in the subsequent lyric 56 – '"So careful of the type?" but no'.)[87]

When quoting these first two stanzas of lyric 54, however, in the preface to the first edition of *Eternal Hope* (1878), Farrar added a cautionary note to his accurate summary of Tennyson's position in *In Memoriam*:

But however deep may be our desire that this should be the will of God; however beautifully it may seem to accord both with His mercy and His justice, that sin, after bringing its own punishment, should be turned to holiness, and so forgiven; however much we may cling to the hope that some such meaning may underlie the broad and boundless promises of a future Restitution, – I dare not lay down any dogma of Universalism; partly because it is not clearly revealed to us, and partly because it is impossible for us to estimate the hardening effect of obstinate persistence in evil, and the power of the human will to resist the law and reject the love of God.[88]

It is instructive to set these comments alongside Tennyson's own private thoughts on the question of sin and judgment in a letter of 1839, addressed to his future wife:

It is a hard thing that if I sin and fail I should be sacrificed to the bliss of the Saints . . . there is no answer to these questions except in a great *hope* of universal good: and even then one might ask, why has God made one to suffer more than another, why is it not meted equally to all? Let us be silent, for we know nothing of these things, and we trust there is One who knows all . . . Who knows whether revelation be not itself a veil to hide the glory of that Love which we could not look upon without marring our sight, and our onward progress? If it were proclaimed as a truth 'No man shall perish: all shall live, after a certain time shall have gone by, in bliss with God'; such a truth might tell well with one or two lofty spirits, but would be the hindrance of the world.[89]

Tennyson and Farrar agree on the moral dangers of proclaiming universal salvation to a sinful world. They differ, however, in their approach to the question of revelation, for whereas Farrar emphasizes its indefiniteness in relation to eschatology, Tennyson adopts a position that looks surprisingly close to that of Tractarian reserve, while indicating the possibility that the hidden message of the gospel is even more glorious than its outward manifestation. Whereas Farrar looked for the restitution of the ancient belief in a purifying intermediate state and an emphasis upon God's love and mercy, Tennyson as the poet of 'the larger hope' could go further, expressing intuitions, feelings, and aspirations which were beyond the bounds of Christian orthodoxy. In referring to our 'clinging' to hope of a future restitution, Farrar echoes a characteristic Tennysonian note in a poem which is full of references to grasping and holding, and which speaks for all those who have experienced periods of spiritual aridity:

> I stretch lame hands of faith, and grope,
>   And gather dust and chaff, and call
>   To what I feel is Lord of all,
> And faintly trust the larger hope.   (55)

Tennyson told Bishop Lightfoot of his belief that 'the cardinal point of Christianity is the Life after Death', and he searched throughout his life for corroborative evidence to support his intuitive sense that he himself would experience it.[90] Yet on the same page of the *Memoir* as the Lightfoot anecdote, his son records his remark that

he 'would rather know that he was to be lost eternally than not know that the whole human race was to live eternally'; and when he speaks of 'faintly trusting the larger hope' he means by 'the larger hope' that the whole human race would through, perhaps, ages of suffering, be at length purified and saved, even those who now 'better not with time' . . .

For Tennyson, then, the argument derived from Kant (partly from reading Goethe and listening to Hallam) that the 'immortality of the soul' is necessary for man to realize the full potential of his moral nature through eternal striving was inseparable from this larger hope for the whole human race.[91] The broadening of *In Memoriam* from the anxieties of an individual mourner in the early lyrics about his friend's and his own future life in heaven, to the future of 'that great race, which is to be' (103), of which Hallam is a type, could be described as a development towards a larger hope for mankind that is, in Farrar's view, truly Christian.

'THAT BETTER WORLD FOR WHICH HE WAS CREATED'

Earlier I suggested that the incarnation seems to have provided Tennyson with his surest grounds for hope as he explored his own feelings and beliefs concerning the future life. Lyric 28 ('The time draws near the birth of Christ') introduces not only the first of the three Christmases in the poem, but also, on the Knowles scheme, the fourth group of lyrics (28–49), in which the nature of 'that better world for which he was created' is the major theme. I intend to examine the way in which

Tennyson broadens his treatment of this theme in *In Memoriam*, from the speculative lyrics of the fourth group, through the later dream lyrics in which some kind of contact with Hallam is achieved, and towards the eventual universalizing of the theme in the latter part of the poem.

Lyric 30 ('With trembling fingers did we weave') proves to be 'echo-like' not only in its treatment of the family's memories of Hallam's presence with them the previous year, but also in voicing ideas which are to be echoed in subsequent lyrics. Voice is very important in this lyric, where a pause in the noisy gambolling at 'old pastimes' follows a reference to the '*mute* Shadow watching all' – the liminal 'shade' of the dead but still unburied Hallam, who has entered the 'shadow' of death. The circle listening to the winds in the beech waits in attentive silence, before the 'merry song we sang with him' is sung 'impetuously', and again the group falls into silence. Written twenty years before the vogue for spiritualism in the 1850s, this is not a description of a seance. Rather, the family finds the true voice of feeling for which it is searching through the ambiguous and unspoken perception that 'surely rest is meet': for only when the circle rests from the vain rehearsal of former celebrations can it be stated that the dead 'rest' and that their 'sleep is sweet'. Tears follow this shared statement of faith, and the voices take a 'higher range', or key, as they sing of the 'higher' state of the blessed dead. Here the ideas and beliefs which are to be examined in detail later in the fourth group of lyrics are simply affirmed: the future state, which from a limited this-worldly perspective is fundamentally paradoxical, must be progressive, opening up worlds of experience which are beyond the grasp of our mortal imaginations, yet remaining somehow in 'sympathy' (an important concept for Hallam)[92] with mortal existence.

Being somewhat abstract, and drawing on no single religious or philosophical tradition, the song lacks the kind of immediacy and confidence conveyed in the 'eternal present' of Victorian hymnody: 'Pleasant are Thy courts above', 'Hark! how the heavenly anthem drowns', 'Casting down their golden crowns', and so on. Whereas in the first edition of *In Memoriam* the final stanza of lyric 30 ('Rise, happy morn, rise, holy morn') is part of the song, it is separated from it in the second and subsequent editions:

> 'Rapt from the fickle and the frail
>   With gather'd power, yet the same,
>   Pierces the keen seraphic flame
> From orb to orb, from veil to veil.'

> Rise, happy morn, rise, holy morn,
> > Draw forth the cheerful day from night:
> > O Father, touch the east, and light
> The light that shone when Hope was born.

Is this, then, the same inner or mute 'voice' – possibly the lyrist's, possibly that of shared feeling in the group – which says 'surely rest is meet' in the fifth stanza? With the inverted comma placed at the end of the penultimate rather than the final stanza, it would appear that the final invocation ('rise', 'draw', 'touch', 'light') is the lyrist's. Tennyson himself declared in a statement that is often quoted that '"I" is not always the author speaking of himself, but the voice of the human race speaking thro' him.'[93] Characteristically, then, it is through the very indeterminacy of the final stanza that something like the eternal present of hymnody is achieved. For if the stanza's present tense is that in which the act of writing is performed, it is also a locutionary present, recalled, like the song, from the Christmas Eve in the past. The eternal present is thus opened up, as the prayer recalls to mind (*anamnēsis*) the birth of the Christ child that was and is the birth (and dawn) of the Christian hope.

Incarnation and resurrection are mutually dependent in Christian theology, and the reference to 'gather'd power' in lyric 30 anticipates the clearest affirmation of Christ's resurrection, near the end of the poem: 'The love that rose on stronger wings, / Unpalsied when he met with Death' (128). The lyrics that immediately follow the first Christmas, however, and describe the raising of Lazarus, are equally unspecific. The miracle itself is treated as an extraordinary and wonderful event, with no attempt made at analysis: 'The rest remaineth unreveal'd' (31). Rather, the emphasis falls upon events that followed the miracle, and particularly Mary's response to the restoration of her brother to life:

> Then one deep love doth supersede
> > All other, when her ardent gaze
> > Roves from the living brother's face,
> And rests upon the Life indeed.   (32)

Mary experiences in her lifetime the fullness of revelation which, following Christ's death and resurrection in the next few days, will be possible only in heaven. The subsequent lyrics convey a number of recurrent anxieties, including that relating to the lyrist's fitness to write of the mysteries of faith. The simplicity of 'thy sister's' faith – 'Her early Heaven, her happy views' (33) – reflects that of a gospel which 'he may read that binds the sheaf' (36), and which was not so much written as lived when

> the Word had breath, and wrought
> With human hands the creed of creeds
> In loveliness of perfect deeds,
> More strong than all poetic thought . . .

The lyrist's 'earthly Muse' has, however, brooded on 'the dear one dead, / And all he said of things divine' (37), and so the lyrics concerning the state of the 'spirit' after death (40–7) have a special authority. Yet these lyrics have been said to leave the modern reader at a loss,[94] and critics have tended either to ignore them or to describe them as parochial and misguided.[95] I consider that they not only represent a necessary stage in the process of bereavement; they also maintain in their 'short swallow-flights of song' a provisionality which suggests that those who seek for final answers concerning the future life are asking the wrong kind of question.

Although John D. Boyd is correct in his claim that these lyrics are 'built upon examination of a series of analogies', his definition of the second of three varieties of 'immortality' in the poem as 'immortality in the ordinary Christian sense', namely 'survival of a man's spirit and personal identity after death', is simplistic.[96] The Greek concept of the immortality of the soul, or spirit, entered the Christian tradition in early patristic theology, but has always proved difficult to reconcile with biblical teaching on the unity of body and soul in the resurrection of the dead.[97] The future state of the blessed, far from being an 'ordinary' and settled matter of doctrine, was the subject of controversy throughout the nineteenth century. Indeed, taken together, the lyrics concerning heaven offer a critique of a wide range of nineteenth-century views on the subject. Boyd's definition does, however, reflect the centrality of Tennyson's most fundamental belief that 'our individuality endures'.[98] While rejecting the possibility that any one model of a future state is in itself satisfactory or complete, the lyrist explores the paradoxical nature of that state, and particularly what for him were the crucial questions of spiritual development and communication with the living, in the light of this belief.

The conditional opening of lyric 40 ('Could we forget the widow'd hour') sets the tone for the lyrics that follow, suggesting both the emotional response of the bereaved, in statements that begin 'if only', and the limits of analogy, here illustrated in the inadequacy of the analogy of the bride leaving home. In contrast, the kind of 'work' for 'each thinker and each doer' in heaven that Maurice was later to describe in his *Lectures on the Apocalypse* – the pursuit of the 'highest good in contemplation and action'[99] – is here confidently affirmed:

> And, doubtless, unto thee is given
> A life that bears immortal fruit
> In those great offices that suit
> The full-grown energies of heaven.

The characteristic emphasis in the last line on development in heaven, and the contrast between Hallam's state in 'undiscover'd lands' and the lyrist's in the fields he knows, are also the subject of lyric 41, where the fear of being 'evermore a life behind' displaces the more common fear of hell and judgment. This contrast between their states is again marked grammatically, but here, as in subsequent lyrics, the subjunctive (a mode of will) expresses the lyrist's desires and conveys the fragility of his imagined ideal:

> Deep folly! yet that this could be –
> That I could wing my will with might
> To leap the grades of life and light,
> And flash at once, my friend, to thee.

Until the lyrist has lost his will to understand that which is ultimately mysterious, he cannot be open to the kind of unwilled experience that 'flashes' upon him later in the poem. In the meantime, lyric 42 ('I vex my heart with fancies dim') completes the first train of thought, offering reassurance in the idea of heaven as 'place', as in formal theological arguments: 'And so may Place retain us still.'

A new line of speculation, which recalls the song on the first Christmas Eve, is opened in lyric 43 ('If Sleep and Death be truly one'), where the flower analogy of 'every spirit's folded bloom' develops into the strange idea of a kind of universal memory, enrolled in 'many a figured leaf'. In contrast to transformative analogies of resurrection, such as those of the seed, the chrysalis, or the worm, which assume a unity of the resurrected body and soul, the flower analogy points to a vaguer, spiritualized consummation: 'And at the spiritual prime / Rewaken with the dawning soul.' An immediate return in lyric 44 ('How fares it with the happy dead?') to the assumption that the spirit is conscious after death, and enjoys some kind of communal existence, points up the unsatisfactoriness of the idea of death as sleep for the lyrist, and allows the crucial argument concerning the post-mortem memory to be restated. In *Heaven our Home* (1861), which emphasizes the social nature of heaven, William Branks devotes the whole of Part III to 'The Interest those in Heaven feel in Earth', drawing upon evidence from philosophy, scripture, and 'events'.[100] Such a sympathetic interest requires memory, without which the 'Recognition of Friends in Heaven' – the subject of Branks's Part II – would be impossible. These issues are crucial in *In Memoriam*, where the hope of reunion with Hallam is paramount. In order to express this hope, however, not only is there a return to the subjunctive mode, but a guardian angel is introduced as a heavenly mediator:

> If such a dreamy touch should fall,
>   O turn thee round, resolve the doubt;
>   My guardian angel will speak out
> In that high place, and tell thee all.

The issue of post-mortem memory is again the subject of both lyric 45 ('The baby new to earth and sky'), which reinforces the idea that death (rather than resurrection) is a 'second birth', thus erasing the possibility that there is some kind of intermediate state, and lyric 46 ('We ranging down this lower track'), in which it is argued that the dark areas of forgetfulness in our mortal life will be illuminated after death: 'But clear from marge to marge shall bloom / The eternal landscape of the past.' 'Bloom' is not a dead metaphor, but an example of the kind of verbal echo which makes this particular sequence of lyrics most obviously reminiscent of the sonnet sequences of Dante, Petrarch, and Shakespeare. In picking up the flower analogy of lyric 43, it suggests a Dantesque 'mystic hint' in the last lines of lyric 46: 'Look also, Love, a brooding star, / A rosy warmth from marge to marge.'[101] The opening out of horizons here threatens the very sense of the endurance of individuality upon which the mourner's current thinking is based, and this is taken up in lyric 47 ('That each, who seems a separate whole'), the last in the heaven sequence. As in the first (40), the authority of its affirmations – 'And I shall know him when we meet', 'And we shall sit at endless feast' – is achieved through the contrastive effect of moving into the indicative mode from the subjunctive in which the lyric begins ('Should move his rounds'). The lyric ends in a moving projection of the kind of parting denied to Hallam and Tennyson in life into a future separation before 'the spirits fade away': '"Farewell! We lose ourselves in light."' Thus while completing a circle in returning to the theme of separation introduced in lyric 40, the sequence has raised the argument to the level of the 'last and sharpest height'.

The sequence is followed, as it is prefaced, by lyrics in which the provisionality of poetry and of its sources is acknowledged: 'If these brief lays, of Sorrow born' (48) and 'From art, from nature, from the schools' (49). Each lyric, and thus also the fourth group of lyrics which they complete, ends 'in tears' which drown the 'bases of my life', dissolving the will to understand and to organize rational thoughts on the nature of the future state. The relationship between the individual will and formative unwilled spiritual experience is to be explored in the key dream lyrics later in the poem. It is an important theme, however, from the beginning: 'To Sleep I give my powers away; / My will is bondsman to the dark' (4). The nautical image of the next line – 'I sit within a helmless bark' – anticipates the sea imagery of the second group of lyrics, and particularly lyric 12 ('Lo, as a dove when up she springs'), in which the lyrist describes the first trance state in the poem:

> Like her I go; I cannot stay;
>   I leave this mortal ark behind,
>   A weight of nerves without a mind,
> And leave the cliffs, and haste away . . .

Thus Tennyson's emphasis in the 'heaven' lyrics upon the immortality of the soul, or 'spirit', rather than the resurrection of the body, and upon the 'continuance' of the self in a conscious existence immediately after death, rather than the sleep of the dead or some kind of intermediate state, has an experiential basis in the early lyrics, where the separation of the spirit from the body is described.

It is in the last five lyrics in the sixth group (59–71), however, that the relationship between sleep, dreams, and death becomes a major theme. Sleep is 'Death's twin-brother', yet 'knows not Death', and allows access to images of the dead as they were in life, through dreams (68). It is 'kinsman' not only to death, but also to trance and madness (71). Several of these strands of thought are brought together in lyric 67:

> When on my bed the moonlight falls,
>   I know that in thy place of rest
>   By that broad water of the west,
> There comes a glory on the walls:

Thy marble bright in dark appears,
    As slowly steals a silver flame
    Along the letters of thy name,
And o'er the number of thy years.

The mystic glory swims away;
    From off my bed the moonlight dies;
    And closing eaves of wearied eyes
I sleep till dusk is dipt in gray:

And then I know the mist is drawn
    A lucid veil from coast to coast,
    And in the dark church like a ghost
Thy tablet glimmers to the dawn.

In this, one of the finest lyrics in *In Memoriam*, Tennyson skilfully accommodates a narrative, which moves through time, entirely within the present tense. Whereas in lyric 12 the present is that of a unique experience in the here-and-now ('Like her I go; I cannot stay'), in lyric 67 it is continuous, conveying a sense of recurrent experience ('When on my bed the moonlight falls'). The characteristic 'I know' in the second line draws the uninvoked and unwilled appearance of the 'glory on the walls' in the fourth into a synchrony which is not unlike that achieved in the eternal present of Victorian hymnody and the poetry of Christina Rossetti. And through the authority of 'I know', the words 'comes' and 'swims' convey a sense of an observed experiential reality that cannot be examined or analysed: it can only be accepted or rejected.

The narrative of lyric 67 repeats the circular pattern of lyric 12, creating movement in imagined space rather than time, while play upon the conventional idea of the grave as a bed, or euphemistic 'place of rest', collapses the actual spatial separation of the mourner from the mourned.[102] The first 'glory', in the fourth line, can be taken as a purely natural phenomenon: either the radiance of moonlight in a general sense, or, more specifically, the halo or nimbus associated with the moon. Having passed, however, across Hallam's memorial stone, itself a kind of glorification, in the dark church, it is a 'mystic glory', broadly suggestive of spiritual exaltation, or splendour, as well as, more specifically, the glory or halo that surrounds the heads of the blessed, or the beauty and bliss of heaven, where they reside. In the final stanza, where the pattern of the first ('I know . . . There comes a glory') is repeated in the opening line, a return to the daylight world of consciousness is marked by the sympathetic action of nature in covering both the lyrist and his dead friend with mist. This 'lucid veil', however, at once transparent and opaque, is also paradigmatic, suggesting the thinness of the divide between the this-worldly and the other-worldly.[103] Whereas the reference to 'that broad water of the west' in the first stanza can be read purely topographically, the words 'from coast to coast' suggest not only the stretch of land between the lyrist's bed and his friend's grave, but also the divide between earthly life and existence on that 'other shore'.

Poised between, say, Milton's mystical treatment of the 'saintly veil of maiden white' with which nature hides 'her guilty front' in 'On the Morning of Christ's Nativity' (1629), and Joyce's epiphanic treatment of the snow which covers 'all the living and the dead' at the end of 'The Dead' (1914), Tennyson's 'lucid veil' is profoundly ambiguous. For as the lyrist passes through the liminal phase between consciousness and sleep, his mind explores the ambiguous crepuscular boundaries between day and night, life and death, the this-worldly and the other-worldly. Liminal states are also the subject of the next group of lyrics (72–98), where the boundaries between earth and heaven are gradually broken down. In lyric 84, for example, the subjunctive mode is used to describe what might have been had Hallam lived, culminating in an extraordinary description of his being taken into heaven with the lyrist as a single soul:

> Thy spirit should fail from off the globe;
>
> What time mine own might also flee,
>   As link'd with thine in love and fate,
>   And, hovering o'er the dolorous strait
> To the other shore, involved in thee,
>
> Arrive at last the blessed goal,
>   And He that died in Holy Land
>   Would reach us out the shining hand,
> And take us as a single soul.

In the final stanza, the lyrist regrets this 'backward fancy', although the ideal of achieving some kind of unity in heaven (without, incidentally, undergoing a particular or individual judgment at death) is to prove important in later lyrics.

In the subsequent lyric (85), the first, shorter version of which had been completed in 1833–4, the pressing nature of the problem of separation – 'We cannot hear each other speak' (82) – is reflected in the additional stanzas that Tennyson wrote on the subject, probably in 1841.[104] First a retrospective account is given of Hallam's death, based upon Henry Elton's fateful letter, and his post-mortem existence is described in conventional terms, drawing freely, as in Dante, Spenser, and Milton, upon biblical and classical sources.[105] A summary of the changes in the lyrist's emotional state since the death of his friend then brings the poem into the more problematic present, where although the lyrist's 'pulses' now 'beat again / For other friends', every 'pulse of wind and wave' recalls his 'prime passion in the grave'. In the additional stanzas that follow, the lyrist, having achieved what is said to be an impossible act of communication with the dead, dismisses it as a rhetorical strategy:

> And lightly does the whisper fall;
>   ''Tis hard for thee to fathom this;
>   I triumph in conclusive bliss,
> And that serene result of all.'
>
> So hold I commerce with the dead;
>   Or so methinks the dead would say;
>   Or so shall grief with symbols play
> And pining life be fancy-fed.

Whereas in lyric 84 the ideal of entering heaven as one soul is interrogated via a transition from the subjunctive to the indicative, here the same effect is achieved through the reverse process ('the dead *would* say'). Ironically, however, in exercising the kind of imaginative freedom that Maurice and Farrar celebrated in *In Memoriam*, Tennyson has written the very words that cannot be spoken. As Peter Allan Dale has shown, Tennyson, like his fellow Apostles, believed in the hiddenness of the power of words, which, through the mysterious workings of the Holy Spirit, could convey divine truth through the 'spirit' of Hallam.[106] By the end of the poem, the lyrist can look back on the kind of 'contradiction on the tongue' that I have been considering, and say:

> Yet Hope had never lost her youth;
>   She did but look through dimmer eyes;
>   Or Love but play'd with gracious lies,
> Because he felt so fix'd in truth . . .   (125)

In lyrics 90–5, however, where the theme of the communion between the living and the dead is developed, the process of affirmation and interrogation continues. The invocatory form at the end of lyric 91 – 'Come, beauteous in thine after form' – gives way first to the subjunctive at the beginning of lyric 92 – 'If any vision should reveal / Thy likeness, I might count it vain' – and then to the firm negative in the opening line of lyric 93: 'I shall not see thee.' Like other negative statements in the poem, however, such as 'We cannot hear each other speak' (82), these words prove to be the means, through dialectical opposition, whereby positive assertions can be made. For, anticipating the climactic lyric 95, the lyrist declares that it is through the *spirit* rather than some kind of outward and visible 'bodily' form that the dead might communicate with the living:

> No visual shade of some one lost,
>   But he, the Spirit himself, may come
>   Where all the nerve of sense is numb;
> Spirit to Spirit, Ghost to Ghost.

Thus the lines that most excite those who read *In Memoriam* as a poem of homosexual love – 'Descend, and touch, and enter; hear / The wish too strong for words to name' – can be located in a tradition of inspirational language associated with the coming of the Holy Spirit, which, as Dale has argued, is central to the language and meaning of *In Memoriam*.[107]

Lyric 94, which marks the final stage in the careful preparation for the description of the 'communion with the dead' that follows, is eirenic in emphasis, like lyric 30, where spiritual communion within the circle of the family was possible only when they fell into peaceful silence:

> In vain shalt thou, or any, call
>   The spirits from their golden day,
>   Except, like them, thou too canst say,
> My spirit is at peace with all.

Although Tennyson was later to take an interest in spiritualism, he could not abide, according to his son, 'the thought of the souls of dead men manifesting themselves by table-rappings'.[108] Even in its less crude forms, spiritualism was to base its claims upon physical manifestations of various kinds, whether visual, as in spirit sightings, the production of ectoplasm, and automatic writing, or aural, in the voices of those who had 'passed over' being heard by the living. Although the reference to calling the spirits from their golden day seems to suggest the occult, the last line quoted is more reminiscent of the priest's invitation in the Communion service in the Book of Common Prayer to those who are in love and charity with their neighbours.

I argued earlier that lyric 30 ('With trembling fingers did we weave') is 'echo-like' in the special sense of voicing ideas which are to be echoed and developed in the fourth group of lyrics, and also later in the poem. In contrast, lyric 95 ('By night we linger'd on the lawn'), the climactic lyric in a many-voiced poem, gathers together several of the main strands of thought and feeling expressed earlier in *In Memoriam*. Its narrative method, for example, which is securely placed in the past tense, and its description of a social gathering at which old songs are sung, are reminiscent of lyric 30 itself; its circular structure, and the reference to the 'silvery haze of summer drawn', recall lyric 67, in which the mist is 'drawn / A lucid veil from coast to coast' at dawn; the moment of 'strange' communion, although generally referred to by critics as a 'vision', is actually described in terms of touch, for which the previous lyrics, and especially lyric 93, have prepared. More significantly, however, earlier themes and images are here transposed into a higher key. Although the brooding of the lyrist's earthly muse on all the 'dear one dead' said of 'things divine' (37) gave the fourth group of lyrics a special authority, those lyrics provided no final answers to the poem's deepest questions. In lyric 95, on the other hand, it is reading the dead man's thoughts on 'doubts that drive the coward back' that induces the moment of communion. And whereas in previous lyrics communication was possible only through the 'silent-speaking words' generated through rhetorical strategies, here the dead man's words initiate a communion of spirit with spirit that reveals a higher reality.

This privileged moment in lyric 95, for which so much that has come before in the poem seems to be a preparation, can be read simply as a modern literary epiphany.[109] Certain key phrases in its central section, however, suggest that a larger field of religious reference is in play. Left alone in the darkened garden, the lyrist turns to written testimony of his dead friend's past existence:

> A hunger seized my heart; I read
> Of that glad year which once had been,
> In those fall'n leaves which kept their green,
> The noble letters of the dead . . .

In the Lincoln manuscript and all editions up to 1870, the lyric
continues:

> So word by word, and line by line,
>   The dead man touch'd me from the past,
>   And *all at once* it seem'd at last
> His *living soul* was *flash'd* on mine,
>
> And mine in his was wound, and whirl'd
>   About empyreal heights of thought,
>   And *came on that which is*, and caught
> The deep pulsations of the world,
>
> Aeonian music measuring out
>   The steps of Time – the shocks of Chance –
>   The blows of Death. At length my trance
> Was cancell'd, stricken thro' with doubt.   (My emphases)

The much discussed crux, 'His living soul' (1850), and Tennyson's
substitution in 1872 of 'The' for 'His', presents several problems of
interpretation that are characteristic of *In Memoriam*. Tennyson himself
commented to Knowles:

The living soul – perchance of the Deity. The first reading was 'His living Soul
was flash'd on mine' – but my conscience was troubled by 'his.' I've often had a
strange feeling of being wound and wrapped in the Great Soul.[110]

Several possible explanations for the conscience-stricken emendation
present themselves, including Tennyson's anxiety concerning the nature
of his relationship with Hallam, and the danger that, read in 1872,
twenty years after the table-rapping craze had been imported from
America, the event described might have been interpreted in spiritualist
terms. Some critics argue that the version we now have ('The living
soul') is preferable to the original, being suitably mysterious and ambiguous, and suggesting both Hallam and the deity.[111] What few of the
commentators have considered, however, is the question of the provenance of the collocation 'living soul'.

Possible literary sources for the phrase include Coleridge's 'Dejection'
(1802) – 'To her may all things live, from pole to pole, / Their life the
eddying of her living soul!' – and the familiar lines from Wordsworth's
'Tintern Abbey', written four years earlier: 'we are laid asleep / In body,
and become a living soul'. The subject-matter of lyric 95, however, is
closer to that of Bailey's *Festus*:

> *Faith.*   The dead sleep as yet;
> But their time cometh, and the bonds of death
> Already slacken round the living soul . . .[112]

'*The* living soul' is as ambiguous here as in Tennyson's revised version, but in both cases the context would seem to suggest the primary biblical source, in Genesis, to which Beatrice refers in the *Paradiso* when she describes Adam as 'the first living soul'.[113] St Paul cites Genesis 2.7 in 1 Corinthians 15, where he writes of Christ as a 'quickening spirit', by whom 'shall all be made alive': 'And so it is written, The first man Adam was made a living soul; the last Adam was made a quickening spirit.' Coleridge's interpretation of 'living soul' in *Aids to Reflection* – 'It was [man's] proper *being*, his truest *self*, *the* man *in* the man'[114] – would probably have appealed to Tennyson, whose elegiac lyrics also draw upon the mythic account of man becoming a living soul when God 'breathed into his nostrils the breath of life'.[115] In lyric 95, however, the quickening effect of his/the living soul being 'flash'd' on 'mine' is that of a new creation which can best be described as mystical, and not only in the rather vague Tennysonian sense.

  Such a reading is supported by other key phrases in the passage. The critical moment in which the lyrist is touched (and we speak of being touched emotionally, in the heart) is reminiscent of that 'self-same moment' in which the Ancient Mariner can pray: 'A spring of love gushed from my heart, / And I blessed them unaware.' Again, however, a much older Christian text provides the more significant parallel: the passage in the *Confessions* where, reading books by the Platonists, St Augustine passes in his meditations

from bodies to the soul, and . . . thus with the flash of one trembling glance it arrived at THAT WHICH IS. And then I saw Thy *invisible things understood by the things which are made.* But I could not fix my gaze thereon; and my infirmity being struck back, I was thrown again on my wonted habits, carrying along with me only a loving memory thereof, and a longing for what I had, as it were, perceived the odour of, but was not yet able to feed on.[116]

(This last metaphor puts one in mind of the words 'a hunger seized my heart'.) Shatto and Shaw gloss 'that which is' as 'an expression in Greek philosophy for the supreme Truth of things'.[117] The close structural and verbal parallels, however, between lyric 95 and Pusey's translation of Augustine, published three or four years before the lyric is thought to have been written (1841–2), suggest that the *Confessions* might have been a specific source for Tennyson. The question of whether the Augustine passage is a source or a parallel must remain unresolved, but, in either case, the shaping and phrasing of the central stanzas place lyric 95 in a specifically mystical tradition, upon which the famous passage from the *Confessions* had a formative influence.[118]

The phrase 'all at once' is also significant in this context. Descriptions in Carlyle and Browning of critical moments of vision that occur 'all at once' are written in the same tradition as Bunyan's *Grace Abounding* – one that comes down from the Book of Revelation and passages such as St Paul's account of being caught up into paradise: 'I knew a man in Christ above fourteen years ago, (whether in the body, I cannot tell; or whether out of the body, I cannot tell: God knoweth;) such an one caught up to the third heaven' (2 Corinthians 12.2).[119] Tennyson himself referred to this passage when commenting on the 'kind of waking trance' that he had experienced since boyhood, saying that 'this might be the state which St. Paul describes, "Whether in the body I cannot tell, or whether out of the body I cannot tell"':

This has generally come upon me thro' repeating my own name two or three times to myself silently, till *all at once*, as it were out of the intensity of the consciousness of individuality, the individuality itself seemed to dissolve and fade away into *boundless being*, and this not a confused state, but the clearest of the clearest, the surest of the surest, the weirdest of the weirdest, utterly beyond words, where death was an almost laughable impossibility, the loss of personality (if so it were) seeming no extinction but the only true life. (My emphases)[120]

Tennyson's son adds that in such 'phases of thought and feeling his idealism tended more decidedly to mysticism'.

The last stanza from lyric 95 quoted above ('Aeonian music measuring out') is strongly reminiscent of Dante's vision of heaven in the *Paradiso*, XII.[121] Of equal significance, however, is Cary's version of a passage from the first verse paragraph of the *Paradiso*:

> In Heaven,
> That largeliest of his light partakes, was I,
> Witness of things, which, to relate again,
> Surpasseth power of him who comes from thence;
> For that, so near approaching its desire,
> Our intellect is to such depth absorb'd,
> That memory cannot follow.[122]

For not only does this passage conform, as do those from St Paul and St Augustine cited earlier, to a familiar convention in mystical writing whereby the transience of heightened spiritual experience (which often throws the mystic into doubt) and the limits of language and understanding are acknowledged and lamented. It also seems to be specifically recalled in the subsequent stanza:

> Vague words! but ah, how hard to frame
>   In matter-moulded forms of speech,
>   Or ev'n for intellect to reach
> Thro' memory that which I became . . .[123]

In the 'doubtful dusk' that follows, however, a spiritual event that can be described only in terms of revelation is corroborated in nature through the action of the 'breeze', which,

>   gathering freshlier overhead,
>   Rock'd the full-foliaged elms, and swung
>   The heavy-folded rose, and flung
> The lilies to and fro, and said
>
> 'The dawn, the dawn,' and died away;
>   And East and West, without a breath,
>   Mixt their dim lights, like life and death,
> To broaden into boundless day.

A parallel relation that is akin to analogy is thus established between two consecutive events, one revealed, the other natural, so that the 'mixing' of east and west, dawn and dusk (a word already applied to the dawn), '*without* a breath', enacts in the landscape a broadening into boundless day which serves as a sign or earnest of the ultimate unity of all the living and the dead for which the lyrist yearns.

Lyric 95 is therefore not only climactic; it is also pivotal in relation to the broadening of the central theme in *In Memoriam* that I am tracing, from an anxious emphasis upon the continuity of personal identity and one-to-one relationship towards the affirmation of a 'larger hope' of universal perfection. Grounded in mystical experience, and described in terms of the 'Great Soul' and 'boundless being', this broadening movement is specifically religious rather than vaguely spiritual, although its characteristics are not exclusively Christian. John Hick's panoptic study on *Death and Eternal Life* (1976) is particularly illuminating here. Hick differentiates between the self as ego, which is 'essentially finite because bounded', and the self as personal, which is 'in principle infinite', as a part of the totality of interpersonal life'.[124] He adopts the term 'atman' (used here as an English word) in the eschatological sense of 'the ideal state of human consciousness which waits to be realized through the negating of individual egoity', and argues that while the great world religions differ in their pareschatologies, or ideas of what occurs immediately after death, they are similar in their eschatologies, or tentative ideas of the final state, all of which point to a final passage from egoity to atman.[125] Whereas in lyric 47 ('That each, who seems a separate whole') the idea of 'remerging in the general Soul' seemed 'faith as vague as all unsweet', the later lyrics of *In Memoriam* treat the apotheosis of the interpersonal as a means of effecting that passage.

In terms of the personal 'plot' of *In Memoriam*, the eighth group of lyrics (99–103) is transitional, describing the departure from the old home. Its positioning in the poem underlines the significance of this rite of passage, and whereas in earlier lyrics the lyrist's out-of-body experiences are described in terms of a circular journey, lyric 103 ('On that last night before we went') relates a dream journey that is open-ended:

> And while the wind began to sweep
> A music out of sheet and shroud,
> We steer'd her toward a crimson cloud
> That landlike slept along the deep.

Through the transforming power of ambiguity, the very sheet and shroud which wrap the corpse are also the means by which the 'great ship' is propelled towards the wide horizon. The accuracy and consistency of the nautical language – 'wind', 'sheet', 'shroud', 'steer'd', 'deep' – grounds the stanza in an observed reality which has been wholly taken up into a transcendent realm through dream logic.

Voyaging across the deep are not only the lyrist and Hallam, but the maidens who have accompanied the former on his journey. When the interpersonal life of the hall was disrupted by 'a summons from the sea', the maidens 'wept and wail'd, but led the way / To where a little shallop lay', and accompanied the lyrist on a journey in which both 'they' and 'I myself' gathered 'strength and grace / And presence, lordlier than before',

> As one would sing the death of war,
> And one would chant the history
> Of that great race, which is to be.
> And one the shaping of a star;

> Until the forward-creeping tides
> Began to foam, and we to draw
> From deep to deep, to where we saw
> A great ship lift her shining sides.

Tennyson emphasized continuities between this life and the next in his two glosses on the maidens, telling Knowles that they were 'all the human powers and talents that do not pass with life but go along with it', and annotating the Eversley edition of his works with the comment: 'They are the Muses, poetry, arts – all that made life beautiful here, which we hope will pass with us beyond the grave.'[126] The profound and universal *subjects* of their songs, however, both open up ultimate horizons of beginning and ending, creation and final consummation, and reflect the aims of an age of progress which Hallam in his lifetime had epitomized. Thus when the ship was reached, and 'The man *we* loved was there on deck, / . . . To greet *us*', the personal reunion ('I . . . fell in silence on his neck'), which robs the lyrist of both speech and responsibility, is followed by Hallam's invitation to 'go with us' – and 'they enter'd in'.

A sense of renewal following these rites of passage is registered in the early lyrics of the ninth and final group (104–31). The poem's third Christmas, on 'new unhallow'd ground' (104), is followed by the famous New Year lyric 106 ('Ring out, wild bells, to the wild sky') discussed earlier, the last stanza of which was quoted by F. D. Maurice in his dedicatory letter to Tennyson in *Theological Essays*:

> Ring in the valiant man and free,
> The larger heart, the kindlier hand,
> Ring out the darkness of the land,
> Ring in the Christ that is to be.[127]

In lyric 108 ('I will not shut me from my kind'), interpersonal life and the cultivation of 'wisdom' (the subject of lyrics 109–14) are embraced, while the ego's introspection and 'vacant yearning' are rejected in an extraordinary self-parody:

> What profit lies in barren faith,
> And vacant yearning, tho' with might
> To scale the heaven's highest height,
> Or dive below the wells of Death?

> What find I in the highest place,
>> But mine own phantom chanting hymns?
>> And on the depths of death there swims
> The reflex of a human face.

The first stanza quoted is reminiscent of Romans 10, where St Paul locates faith in the believing heart (verse 9) rather than the questioning mind which asks 'Who shall ascend into heaven?' (verse 7),[128] while the second finds in the lone phantom chanting hymns – in heaven as on earth a corporate act – and the reflection of his own face, paradigms of the bounded nature of egoity. Interestingly, however, one of the most hymnic lyrics in *In Memoriam*, but one that is seldom quoted, is to be found in this final group of lyrics.[129] It expresses the basis in love of the 'true Christianity', for which Hallam, Maurice, and Tennyson yearned:

> Love is and was my Lord and King,
>> And in his presence I attend
>> To hear the tidings of my friend,
> Which every hour his couriers bring.
>
> Love is and was my King and Lord,
>> And will be, tho' as yet I keep
>> Within his court on earth, and sleep
> Encompass'd by his faithful guard,
>
> And hear at times a sentinel
>> Who moves about from place to place,
>> And whispers to the worlds of space,
> In the deep night, that all is well.   (126)

The use here of the present tense and of repetition, and the references to 'his court on earth' and the guardian angel, are all reminiscent of the treatment of heaven in Victorian hymnody. Tennyson beautifully adapts these features to his own purposes, however, by making traditional kingdom language both personal and immediate within the limited perspective – 'at times', 'whispers' – of the this-worldly.

The assurance that 'all is well', suggestive as it is of Dame Julian of Norwich's *Revelations of Divine Love*,[130] is sustained in the extraordinary lyric that follows – 'And all is well, tho' faith and form' (127) – in which Tennyson's version of the apocalyptic sublime reflects the social and political anxieties that he and Hallam had shared in the early 1830s, a period of millenarian activity in Britain:[131]

But ill for him that wears a crown,
   And him, the lazar, in his rags:
   They tremble, the sustaining crags;
The spires of ice are toppled down,

And molten up, and roar in flood;
   The fortress crashes from on high,
   The brute earth lightens to the sky,
And the great Æon sinks in blood,

And compass'd by the fires of Hell;
   While thou, dear spirit, happy star,
   O'erlook'st the tumult from afar,
And smilest, knowing all is well.

Opening up an other-worldly perspective from which the end of the world is part of a providential scheme, this lyric conflates the language of science and religion, geology and apocalypse, as Rosenberg has shown.[132] Rosenberg's view, however, that the last line is 'very nearly incredible' can be answered by citing Ricks's observation that 'such sentiments as Hallam's and Tennyson's may now sound complacent but they were in line with serious geological study'.[133] Lyell, Ricks reminds us, placed cataclysmic subterranean upheaval in the larger perspective of what he called the 'conservative principle', insisting that 'the general tendency of subterranean movements, when their effects are considered from a sufficient lapse of ages, is eminently beneficial'.

Although the Book of Revelation also ends well, it is the preceding vision of division and judgment that is evoked in lyric 127:

And the seventh angel poured out his vial into the air; and there came a great voice out of the temple of heaven, from the throne, saying, It is done.

And there were voices, and thunders, and lightnings; and there was a great earthquake, such as was not since men were upon the earth, so mighty an earthquake, and so great.   (Revelation 16.17–18)

As in lyric 51, however, the terrors associated with the last day and with judgment are neutralized through references to Hallam's guardianship: he is a sign of ultimate harmony and unity. Unlike in Robert Pollok's *The Course of Time* or E. H. Bickersteth's *Yesterday, To-Day, and For Ever*, the 'fires of Hell' are not a theological reality for the poet of the larger hope, whose treatment of judgment, though not so overtly universalist, is closer to that of Philip James Bailey.

These late lyrics, in which Tennyson draws together many of the strands from earlier sections of *In Memoriam*, develop an idea of the future life – for the individual and for all humankind – which is grounded in unity, signified in a 'mingling' (129) of elements, a 'diffusing' (130) of paradoxes, a 'mixing' (130) of beings. The difference between earth and heaven, mourner and mourned which was interpreted as a sign of tragic separation and loss in the early sections of the poem now becomes a cause for celebration in lyric 129 ('Dear friend, far off, my lost desire'), as the 'strange friend' is apotheosized through love as 'past, present, and to be'. In place of the voice from the throne in Revelation 16, it is the voice of Hallam that is heard in lyric 130:

> Thy voice is on the rolling air;
>   I hear thee where the waters run;
>   Thou standest in the rising sun,
> And in the setting thou art fair.

We have moved on two chapters in the Book of Revelation, to the description of the 'marriage of the Lamb', with the 'voice of many waters' (19.6) and the angel 'standing in the sun' (19.17), in which the lyrist, like St John, can 'rejoice' (19.7).

The final lyric before the Epilogue contains an unusually high proportion of biblical allusions, and is similar in tone to the Prologue:

> O living will that shalt endure
>   When all that seems shall suffer shock,
>   Rise in the spiritual rock,
> Flow thro' our deeds and make them pure . . .   (131)

This prayer-like opening is, however, deceptive, for Tennyson's insistence that the 'living will' was 'free will in man' rather than the 'divine will' encourages a reading of the lyric as a statement of hope for man rather than as a prayer to God.[134] 'All that seems' is the opposite of 'that which is' (95),[135] and lyric 131 anticipates the complete encounter with the divine of which the lyrist's experience in the garden at night had been a foretaste. Tennyson altered the manuscript version of the last two lines of the lyric – 'And come to look on those we loved / And That wh made us, face to face'[136] – which preserves an opposition between God and man in St Paul's words 'face to face', to the published version which folds the past, present, and future of yesterday, today, and forever into a more generalized deferred closure: 'Until we close with all we loved, / And all we flow from, soul in soul'. Whereas Arthur Hallam in the 'Theodicaea Novissima' wrote of our becoming 'blended' with Christ's being, and 'confused' with his personality, and F. D. Maurice stated his preference for speaking of the dead as sleeping 'in Jesus', as St Paul does,[137] the second person plural and the euphonious assonance of 'close . . . flow . . . soul . . . soul' suggest a less culturally or theologically specific completion of the passage from ego to atman.

Tennyson's mixing of Christian themes and classical forms, which can be a source of ambiguity in *In Memoriam*, reflects his syncretic intellect and his refusal to be bound by cultural or theological systems. The Epilogue, while conforming closely to the conventions of the classical epithalamium, is very English and, one might say, very Anglican in the narrative subject on which its later meditations are based. Beginning with a funeral, *In Memoriam* ends with a marriage service in a country church, based upon the wedding of the poet's sister Cecilia and his friend Edmund Lushington in 1842. The theme of growth and development which becomes more insistent in the later lyrics of the poem is sustained in the Epilogue, where the lyrist measures the time since Hallam announced his love for another 'daughter of our house' in terms of the human body's system of self-renewal:

> Tho' I since then have number'd o'er
> > Some thrice three years: they went and came,
> > Remade the blood and changed the frame,
> And yet is love not less, but more . . .

As well as being aware of the fact of these physiological changes, Tennyson would probably have interpreted them as analogous to the endurance of personal identity after the great change that is death, in the tradition of Bishop Butler and his *Analogy of Religion* to which he and his contemporaries were heirs.[138] Just as, on Butler's argument, the adult is the same being that inhabited the much smaller frame of the child he or she once was, so love has both remained the same and grown through changes over 'summers that are flown': 'For I myself with these have grown / To something greater than before.' This growth is reflected in the mature love the lyrist feels for the sister who is to be parted from him now that she is joined to her husband in holy matrimony:

> O happy hour, behold the bride
> > With him to whom her hand I gave.
> > They leave the porch, they pass the grave
> That has to-day its sunny side.
>
> To-day the grave is bright for me.

Clearly based on the Pastor's famous analogy in the fifth book of *The Excursion* for 'death and its two-fold aspect',[139] the reference to the graves outside the church continues the juxtaposition of living and dead which is established a few stanzas earlier, during the service itself:

> Now waiting to be made a wife,
>   Her feet, my darling, on the dead;
>   Their pensive tablets round her head,
> And the most living words of life
>
> Breathed in her ear. The ring is on,
>   The 'wilt thou' answer'd, and again
>   The 'wilt thou' ask'd, till out of twain
> Her sweet 'I will' has made you one.

The marriage service in the Book of Common Prayer locates matrimony in a divine economy which embraces the couple's future lives both here and hereafter, in 'life everlasting'; and in the poem the couple's vows represent ideally the 'living will that shalt endure' invoked in lyric 131.

The 'pensive tablets' in this passage recall the distant memorial 'tablet' of a 'stiller guest', across which the moonlight stole in lyric 67. Following the conventions of the epithalamium, the lyrist invokes the moon again in the Epilogue, that it may

> touch with shade the bridal doors,
> With tender gloom the roof, the wall;
> And breaking let the splendour fall
> To spangle all the happy shores
>
> By which they rest, and ocean sounds,
> And, star and system rolling past,
> A soul shall draw from out the vast
> And strike his being into bounds. . .

This is only part of the remarkably long verse sentence with which *In Memoriam* ends, and in which the lyrist's consciousness, elated and inspired by the images of the day, moves freely through time and across an imagined landscape, as in those earlier nocturnal lyrics 67 and 95. Beneath the this-worldly hope for a 'crowning race' of which Hallam was a type and the new baby will be a 'closer link', there is an eschatological subtext which surfaces only in the final stanza ('And one far-off divine event, / To which the whole creation moves'). I am thinking here not of the Adventist note struck in the penultimate stanza – 'Appearing ere the times were ripe' – or the references to gestation and the 'seed / Of what in them is flower and fruit', or indeed the 'crowning race' itself, suggestive of the crown of the heavenly reward in the Book of Revelation, but of the word which is present yet never voiced in the poem's final stanzas: 'consummation'. Consummation, or the relationship between its different kinds of completion – of marriage, of earthly life, of the temporal world – is often the implicit subject of Coventry Patmore's and the Rossettis' poetry.[140] In the Epilogue these three fields of reference are drawn together in one of *In Memoriam*'s boldest fusions, rather than confusions.[141] For the couple are also types, the consummation of their marriage inaugurating in their personal lives a new era in the conception of their unborn child, as the mystical marriage that is the one far-off divine event is for Tennyson to complete a cosmic union of all the living and dead in which individuality endures.

Like Maurice, Tennyson looked forward to the Christ that is to be. Like Farrar, who hailed him as the poet of the larger hope, he longed for the salvation of all mankind, and could not contemplate a future life in heaven which excluded those in everlasting punishment. Like Arthur Hallam, he believed that mankind could partake of God's loving nature, and that this was made possible in the incarnation. Claims that his hopes for the development of mankind are confused with his Christian hope of personal immortality take no account of his theomorphic conception of mankind, of which Hallam was the principle exemplum. The better world for which Hallam was created – and here was the final and most fruitful ambiguity associated with his death – is both here and elsewhere. He was taken before the time was ripe from a world which he would have made better had he survived, but he represented to Tennyson a sign of God's loving nature, made in God's image, which gave the poet hope for the future of the race and for continued development in heaven. Tennyson's larger hope was for the endurance of individuality after death, for the eventual salvation of the whole world, and, linked with the latter, a broader kind of Christianity, grounded in love.

When read in relation to Tennyson's engagement with the eschatological questions which exercised his contemporaries, *In Memoriam* is a far more resonant work than that to which some modern readers try to reduce it – a pseudo-scientific treatise caught in the toils of what is loosely called the Victorian problem of 'faith and doubt'. Although Peter Levi argues that Tennyson was 'too riddled with doubt' to be a

'Christian poet', he believes that *In Memoriam* is more Christian, if less orthodox, than the poetry of Pope, who was 'consciously a Christian' and a 'very great poet'.[142] The poetry of Pope does not figure in Levi's anthology of *English Christian Verse* (1984). *In Memoriam* is allotted the same amount of space as *Paradise Lost*.

CHAPTER 6

✣

Dickens, *Our Mutual Friend*

The marriage service from which Tennyson quotes at the end of *In Memoriam* begins with these words:

Dearly beloved, we are gathered together here in the sight of God, and in the face of this congregation, to join together this Man and this Woman in holy Matrimony: which is an honourable estate, instituted of God in the time of man's innocency, signifying unto us the mystical union that is betwixt Christ and his Church; which holy estate Christ adorned and beautified with his presence, and first miracle that he wrought, in Cana of Galilee . . .

(Book of Common Prayer)

Tennyson's 'one far-off divine event, / To which the whole creation moves' embraces this 'mystical union' (Epilogue). The married couple in the poem who 'leave the porch' and 'pass the grave / That has to-day its sunny side' have just received a blessing for their future lives both here and hereafter: 'and so fill you with all spiritual benediction and grace, that ye may so live together in this life, that in the world to come ye may have life everlasting'. On their way out of church they have also passed the font. Like the form of the Solemnization of Matrimony, the ministration of 'Publick Baptism of Infants' in the Book of Common Prayer looks forward to the last things, and to the inheritance of the kingdom by the brother or sister here named, in this case in the closing words of the final prayer:

And humbly we beseech thee to grant, that he [or she], being dead unto sin, and living unto righteousness, and being buried with Christ in his death, may crucify the old man, and utterly abolish the whole body of sin; and that, as he is made partaker of the death of thy Son, he may also be partaker of his resurrection; so that finally, with the residue of thy holy Church, he may be an inheritor of thine everlasting kingdom; through Christ our Lord. Amen.

Like Tennyson and some of the genre painters of the period, Dickens adapted to his own artistic purposes the liturgical and domestic drama

265

of the common round of christenings, marriages, and funerals which was regularly played out in the parish churches of England, when christening and wedding parties would often gather after the service in the graveyard where they were one day to be buried themselves. In *Our Mutual Friend* (1864–5), which contains an allusion to *In Memoriam*,[1] references to the baptismal service, the marriage service, and the burial service draw attention to the relationship between these rites of passage. As in John's gospel – the only gospel to describe both the first miracle, at Cana (the water into wine) and the greatest, at Bethany (the raising of Lazarus) – death and eternal life are closely related to baptism in Dickens's last complete novel, for which Christ's mysterious words to Nicodemus would have provided a fitting epigraph: 'Except a man be born again, he cannot see the kingdom of God' (John 3.3).

Our Mutual Friend continues Dickens's exploration in his later works of the inner or spiritual life, and of the hope of salvation and transcendence in a fallen world which threatens to return to its original primeval state, expressed in the novel's insistent symbolism of rising and falling. Although much less knowledgeable than Tennyson about science, theology, and philosophy, Dickens read more of the key documents of the early 1860s than is generally realized. Tennyson's urbane contribution to Broad Church liberalism was considered to be that of the poet, the intellectual, the reader of Dante in the original; whereas Dickens's populist agenda was that of the Broad Church social reformer. Their positions, however, on the teachings and practices of the Church of England, were not dissimilar. Both longed for a broader Christianity, and they held similar views on a number of major doctrinal issues of the day. There are further similarities in their shared hesitancy about making overt statements of or about the Christian faith in their work, preferring to convey their beliefs indirectly through the medium of their different forms of writing. Here is one source of their difficulty, some would say slipperiness, for the modern reader in terms of their religious beliefs, another being their play with key terms in their writing – Tennyson's usually solemn, Dickens's frequently jocular. Dickens would have understood Tennyson's thinking on the authority of feeling and the heart in matters of religion, while Tennyson would have been interested in Dickens's treatment of the margins of consciousness and unconsciousness, of day and night, life and death in his later novels.

Before examining *Our Mutual Friend* in detail, I would like to pursue some of these matters by addressing, first, the vexed question of Dickens and Christian doctrine, particularly on revelation, baptism, and eschatology, and then the significance of the Book of Common Prayer and John's gospel in relation to this body of doctrine. For it was upon this religious groundwork that the redemptive scheme of loving relationships in his last completed novel was constructed.

DICKENS AND CHRISTIAN DOCTRINE

Dickens's religious beliefs, and his treatment of religious themes in the fiction, have often posed problems for his critics. In the twenty years since the Dickens centenary – a period of major revaluation – criticism which emphasizes the novelist's more sceptical and 'demythologizing' side has generally been in the ascendancy. An example is Alexander Welsh's *The City of Dickens* (1971), which ends with the statement that 'today it is easier to believe that the holy city in the book of Revelation was made to appear like a bride from heaven because of our human trust in brides, than to believe in the divine truth of John's vision'.[2] In Dickens's novels, Welsh argues,

the promise of the heavenly city is muted or even denied. The same must be concluded of Christian concepts generally as they inform Dickens's work: they are inescapably there and yet finally elusive. The principle of grace is wishfully operative in the fiction yet not formally admitted; Christianity apparently contributes more to the complexity of social questions than it does to their solution; the teachings of Christ on charity and forgiveness run into unforeseen contradictions . . . As so often, Dickens's Puritan ethic fails to come to grips with Christ's teaching. The fault is not Dickens's alone; that teaching was hard enough to comprehend even before the rapid ebbing of the sea of faith in the nineteenth century.[3]

Dickens may sometimes 'write vaguely of far-away places', but he does not believe in 'supernatural powers'.[4] Thus if there is no longer a Christian heaven or hell, the 'sojourners in the city are biding their time in vain'.[5] For other critics in the early 1970s, too, the Christian symbolism in Dickens's novels simply lacks power and authority.[6]

By 1981 Dennis Walder could claim in his major study on *Dickens and Religion* that the weakness of Dickens's position had been 'more than sufficiently remarked': it was the strengths which now needed emphasizing.[7] Rightly, he argued that Dickens's beliefs are 'rarely explicit, they are embodied in the texture of his work'.[8] Walder's sense of Dickens's development as a novelist is broadly in line with most modern criticism, when he suggests, for example, that the process of conversion or change becomes increasingly important after *Barnaby Rudge*, and that from *Little Dorrit* on he turns to a 'more subjective, indeed spiritual, concern'.[9] Andrew Sanders, in *Charles Dickens, Resurrectionist* (1982), was even more concerned to correct an imbalance in criticism, claiming of Dickens that

At no point does he seem to have doubted basic Christian teachings, or to have been troubled by the phenomenon which modern writers have styled 'the Victorian crisis of faith' . . . his attitudes to dying, death and bereavement derive from his reading and understanding of the Gospels; he expresses not a conventional piety as a sop to his readers, but a comfort derived from a scheme of beliefs to which he genuinely adhered.[10]

Sanders's study on Dickens's treatment of death and resurrection includes an important chapter on *Our Mutual Friend* which identifies and analyzes the novel's dominant symbolism of baptism and regeneration. He prefers, however, not to pursue the theological implications of what he rather sweepingly describes as the 'baptism/resurrection idea' in the novel.[11] Thus a more specific question concerning Dickens and religion remains: how much did he actually know about Christian doctrine, and the theology which underpins it? Walder argues, *pace* Quiller-Couch, that Dickens was in fact aware of what was 'agitating men's thoughts' in his day: movements such as Tractarianism and Unitarianism, the claims and counter-claims of Wiseman, Newman, Gorham, and Colenso, and the ideas of Darwin and Huxley.[12] Walder illustrates the point by quoting from a letter of 21 May 1863 (when, incidentally, *Our Mutual Friend* was already forming in Dickens's mind), in which the novelist replies to an enquiry from his Swiss friend Cerjat concerning the 'Colenso and Jowett matter', as controversy raged over liberal ideas on hell and the Old Testament. H. B. Wilson expressed liberal opinions on judgment at the end of his contribution to *Essays and Reviews* (1860). We 'shrink from Calvinism and Augustinianism', he argued, because of the inferences which they draw respecting the majority of mankind, 'whom they comprehend in one mass of perdition'.[13] We must rather 'entertain a hope that there shall be found, after the great adjudication, receptacles suitable for those who shall be infants, not as to years of terrestial life, but as to spiritual development'.[14] 'Development' was a key-word in *Essays and Reviews*, and Dickens's letter concerns development in a broader sense which was of interest to several of Wilson's fellow contributors:

The position of the writers of Essays and Reviews is, that certain parts of the Old Testament have done their intended function in the education of the world *as it was*; but that mankind, like the individual man, is designed by the Almighty to have an infancy and a maturity, and that as it advances, the machinery of its education must advance too. For example . . . it is contended that the science of geology is quite as much a revelation to man, as books of an immense age and of (at the best) doubtful origin, and that your consideration of the latter must reasonably be influenced by the former. As I understand the importance of timely suggestions such as these, it is, that the Church should not gradually shock and lose the more thoughtful and logical of human minds; but should be so gently and considerately yielding as to retain them, and through them, hundreds of thousands . . . What these bishops and such-like say about revelation, in assuming it to be finished and done with, I can't in the least understand.[15]

The idea of mankind, like the individual man, having an infancy and a maturity, is worked out most fully by Frederick Temple, Headmaster of Rugby and a future Archbishop of Canterbury, in his essay on 'The Education of the World'.[16] Like other contributors he takes a liberal line on the impact of geology and the Higher Criticism on the interpretation of the Bible:

If geology proves to us that we must not interpret the first chapters of Genesis literally; . . . if careful criticism shall prove that there have been occasionally interpolations and forgeries in that Book, as in many others; the results should still be welcome . . . The substance of the teaching which we derive from the Bible will not really be affected by anything of this sort.[17]

Benjamin Jowett stated in his famous essay 'On the Interpretation of Scripture' that the 'growth or development' from the Old Testament to the New 'may be regarded as a kind of progress from childhood to manhood'.[18] As development has continued to this day, he argues, the educated who enjoy 'freedom of thought and inquiry' in modern society have a crucial role to play in maintaining the 'healthy tone of religion among the poor'.[19] Biblical criticism, Jowett acknowledges, 'is not for the multitude': 'Yet, indirectly passing from the few to the many, it has borne a great part in the Reformation of religion.'[20]

Dickens's incomprehension, then, of 'what these bishops and such-like say about revelation' reflects not only his own agnostic position on the incarnation, but also, more positively, a belief in the development and growth of mankind which he shared with the authors of *Essays and Reviews*. His emphasis in the novels upon finding Christ in other people, and upon the 'redemptive' role of a few enlightened people in society, suggests further parallels with these Broad Churchmen, and with Arthur Hallam's ideas on the 'confusion' of our personality with Christ's, which informed Tennyson's thinking in *In Memoriam*.[21] He would also have found in his own copy of *Essays and Reviews*[22] an essay by Charles Goodwin 'On the Mosaic Cosmogony', the main aim of which was to show that the kind of reconciliation that some scientific clergymen sought to make between Genesis and geology was untenable. *Essays and Reviews* and *Our Mutual Friend* were published in the first half of a decade in which, in Owen Chadwick's words, 'the anthropologists confronted religious men with a new kind of conflict – the fall of man versus the rise of man'.[23] Traditional teaching on the fall and on man's prelapsarian state is embodied in the mystical language of the prayer book, as in the passage cited earlier in which matrimony is described as an 'honourable estate, instituted of God in the time of man's innocency'. How could this view of man's origins be reconciled with the new perspectives of science which challenged Dickens and his generation in what are described in the opening sentences of *Our Mutual Friend* as 'these times of ours'?

For the reader of Dickens's last completed novel, talk of the fall of man versus the rise of man brings to mind its most powerful symbolic language, so that the river mud at Limehouse Hole and the slippery sides of Plashwater Weir Mill Lock begin to suggest primeval slime. Of more specific interest, however, is the terminology used in the debate associated with the various attempts of scientific clergymen and laymen to reconcile science and Genesis. Over twenty years before Samuel Wilberforce's famous review of the *Origin of Species* (1859), Thomas Chalmers and William Buckland had addressed the issue in their Bridgewater Treatises. Other Treatises, by Babbage (1837) and Kirby (1852), were in Dickens's library, together with a presentation copy of his friend Hugh Miller's *The Testimony of the Rocks; or, Geology in its Bearings on the Two Theologies, Natural & Revealed* (1857).[24] Miller admired the German *Naturphilosophe* Lorenz Oken for his 'peculiarly nice eye for detecting those analogies which unite the animal world into a *harmonious* whole' (my emphasis).[25] Dickens could have read in *Essays*

and Reviews Charles Goodwin's quotation from the tenth edition
(1856) of a standard work by Thomas Hartwell Horne entitled *An
Introduction to the Critical Study and Knowledge of the Holy Scriptures*: 'Geological investigations, it is now known, all prove the perfect
harmony between scripture and geology, in reference to the history of
creation.'[26] Goodwin found what he called the 'conciliators' to be 'at
variance with each other and mutually destructive', and to bend with the
wind of scientific advance in their manipulation of biblical evidence.
While it was true that if Genesis was not about the origin of the world,
modern discovery could not contradict it, Goodwin pointed out that it
was 'absurd to call this harmony'.[27]

This and similar other passages in Goodwin's essay and elsewhere
may well have caught Dickens's eye not long before he wrote *Our
Mutual Friend*; so too may the description (not unlike Hugh Miller's) of
the waters which at one stage of evolution 'abounded with monsters,
half-fish, half-crocodile, the well-known saurians, whose bones have
been collected in abundance'.[28] More central to the novel's scheme than
Mr Venus, however, is Mr Nicodemus Boffin and 'Harmony Jail', that
site of other kinds of reconciliation, most obviously between a formerly
'widowed' man and woman in holy matrimony. Whereas Goodwin's
article in *Essays and Reviews* questioned comparatively recent attempts
at harmonizing Genesis and science, much of the rest of the volume
challenged the assumptions behind a more traditional kind of harmony.
Many harmonized 'Lives of Our Lord and Saviour' were published in
the nineteenth century, and Dickens himself wrote *The Life of Our Lord*
in 1849 for his children, attempting to harmonize the four gospels in a
single narrative.[29] More specifically, biblical harmonies, in which passages from each of the four gospels are arranged in a reconstructed
chronological order, were widely used by both clergy and laity in the
Victorian period.[30] Whereas passages from the synoptic gospels are
frequently arranged side by side in columns in these harmonies, showing
variations in their accounts of the same event, John's gospel is strikingly
different, generally supplying long passages which stand alone on the
page. Modern commentators assume that it is impossible to harmonize
John,[31] but in the middle of the nineteenth century the attempt was still
being made, as a lack of harmony between the gospels threatened traditional ideas on their divine inspiration and thus authority.

Unlike the synoptics, John's gospel is highly selective in its account of
Jesus's ministry, subordinating breadth of narrative coverage to depth of

theological interpretation, and proclaiming throughout that Jesus is the Christ, the Son of God, full of power and might. Following a proem which announces the mystery of the incarnation, the account of Jesus's work in the world in the first half of John is grounded in his teaching on baptism and eternal life, and culminates in the raising of Lazarus, the fulcrum around which the whole gospel turns. The Lazarus narrative in chapter 11 and the triumphal entry into Jerusalem in chapter 12, when Jesus repeats his words to Nicodemus (3.14) in speaking of being 'lifted up from the earth' (12.32), lead into the farewell discourses and the passion narrative which form the second half of the gospel, concerning Jesus's return to his Father in heaven.

The symbolism of John foregrounds what Frank Kermode calls its 'threshold quality'. After the proem, he suggests,

the liminality of the poem is . . . deepened into myth, and the myth is dressed in representations of actuality. Jordan is an archetypal threshold. Crossing over its water is baptism: the dove that descends is a figure not only of the spirit from above but also of that *pneuma* that brooded over the formless waste of waters in the beginning, at the great threshold between darkness and light. The ladder by which angels will descend and reascend (as Jesus tells Nathaniel) is another bridge between chaos and spirit. Being can cross over or descend into becoming; it will participate in becoming until it reaches its end, a death which restores it to its former unencumbered state.[32]

Similarly, the first Cana miracle is a threshold for Jesus, when, abruptly, his hour has come; and Nicodemus's three appearances are an example of John's 'matches between narrative sequence and abstract pattern': 'for the first appearance of Nicodemus is used to make a point about birth and the last to mark with appropriate ritual the threshold between life that is death and death that is life'.[33] It is hardly surprising, then, to find that passages from John are included in the three major liminal ceremonies formalized in the Book of Common Prayer. While Nicodemus's visit to Jesus by night in chapter 3 is set as the lesson for the Ministration of Baptism to such as are of Riper Years, and the marriage at Cana in chapter 2 forms the theological groundwork for the Solemnization of Matrimony, the *logion* 'I am the resurrection and the life' in chapter 11 provides the sentence at the threshold of both the service and the church or churchyard in the order for the Burial of the Dead.

Later in this chapter I will argue that John's gospel and the orders of Baptism, Matrimony, and the Burial of the Dead in the prayer book shape Dickens's treatment of the baptism and resurrection themes in *Our Mutual Friend*, and that the reconciliation of the hero, John, with his identity as a Harmon, represents the most important word-play in a novel which constantly scrutinizes and interprets baptismal and family names. From the first or threshold number of *Our Mutual Friend* to the last, parallels with John's gospel frequently suggest themselves. Even the novel's treatment of the identity of 'our mutual friend' is illuminated by the role in John of the beloved disciple, who has always exercised the gospel's interpreters, as the author of *The Genesis of Secrecy* reminds us: 'He is in general a producer of enigmas; he is also a movable narrative focus, lending credit to the detail of places, acts, or speeches provided by the narrator; at once the instrument of explanation and of reticence.'[34]

Above all, however, it is the mysterious relationship in John between the 'new birth' of death and of baptism which seems to have seized Dickens's imagination in the writing of the novel. Infant baptism had been the focus fifteen years earlier in Dickens's career of the kind of sectarian dispute that he detested. The High Churchman who held fast to the prayer book's description of the baptized infant as 'regenerate' could not be reconciled with his Evangelical brother in Christ who feared that such a position threw into question the need for conversion and moral regeneration later in life.[35] Sectarian differences had come to a head in the famous Gorham case of the late 1840s, when Bishop Philpotts of Exeter refused to install the Evangelical G. C. Gorham in a parish he had been offered in the diocese, a decision which was eventually overturned by a judicial committee of the privy council. Dickens had little time for either wing of the Church of England, or for the issues which divided them. His novels, however, including *Our Mutual Friend*, reveal clear liberal views on the issues of baptism and conversion, and of judgment and eternal punishment, which were in line with mainstream Broad Church opinion. They also reveal an awareness of some of the theological implications behind those issues.

The Public Baptism of Infants reconciles individuation, in the naming of the child, with membership of a community, in the infant's being 'received into the ark of Christ's Church', thus anticipating his or her inheritance of the 'everlasting kingdom' with the 'residue' of God's 'holy Church'. The marriage service, too, brings together two named individuals 'in the face of this congregation'. It was the language of the burial service, however, which figured in one of Dickens's few overt references to a contemporary theological debate in his fiction, at the beginning of the chapter of *Our Mutual Friend* in which he describes little Johny's funeral:

Some of the Reverend Frank Milvey's brethren had found themselves exceedingly uncomfortable in their minds, because they were required to bury the dead too hopefully. But, the Reverend Frank, inclining to the belief that they were required to do one or two other things (say out of nine-and-thirty) calculated to trouble their consciences rather more if they would think as much about them, held his peace.

Indeed, the Reverend Frank Milvey was a forbearing man, who noticed many sad warps and blights in the vineyard wherein he worked, and did not profess that they made him savagely wise. He only learned that the more he himself knew, in his little limited human way, the better he could distantly imagine what Omniscience might know.   (II.10)

The words spoken over the dead in the burial service – 'in sure and certain hope of the Resurrection to eternal life' – were the subject of much debate in the 1860s during a prolonged series of ecclesiastical exchanges on the subject of liturgical reform. Frank Milvey, Dickens's ideal working clergyman, takes the standard liberal line on the matter, being willing to err on the side of charity in the kinds of difficult case cited by C. J. Vaughan, where the minister 'must give thanks to God for the sure and certain hope of another world by the grave of the drunkard or the adulterer'.[36]

Dickens would also have sympathized with the liberal position on the question of eternal punishment taken by H. B. Wilson in *Essays and Reviews*, which drew a hostile response from the nearly eleven thousand clergy, both Tractarian and Evangelical, who appealed to the articles of religion in declaring that the inspired scripture does indeed teach that the punishment of the cursed is everlasting.[37] Both Victorian versions of hell on *earth* – the first associated with the Industrial Revolution and the growth of the great cities, the second a 'hell' of love which is dead, or betrayed, or of sex without love – figure in Dickens's social novels of the 1850s, where hell is experienced in the here-and-now. In *Hard Times* (1854), for example, Dickens's version of the apocalyptic sublime which describes an industrial townscape in terms of the fires of hell also reflects in outward and visible form Louisa Gradgrind's inner hell associated with the absence of love.[38] In Dickens's novels of the 1860s this second, psychological version of hell on earth is more dominant, and is exemplified in the portrayal of Bradley Headstone's torments in *Our Mutual Friend*, for example. Whereas in the highly schematized plot of *Hard*

Times, Stephen Blackpool, who takes his Christian name from the first Christian martyr, is beatified in his descent into Old Hell Shaft and ascent into heaven (III.6), the descents and ascents of *Our Mutual Friend*, while signifying regeneration, are represented as a *prelude* to the working out of John Harmon's and Eugene Wrayburn's salvation through love in human relationship.

This emphasis upon the here-and-now is present from the beginning of Dickens's career, as Steven Marcus suggests when he claims that no novel could move further than *Pickwick Papers* (1836–7) 'toward asserting not only that the Kingdom of God is within each man but that it is possible to establish something that resembles the Kingdom of God on Earth'.[39] Also present from the beginning, however, and recurring later as the idea of establishing the kingdom on earth becomes problematized, is a transcendent post-mortem heaven. In the interpolated tale of the goblins and the sexton in *Pickwick*, for example, the sexton is shown a living 'picture' of a deathbed scene in which the dead child's brothers and sisters believe that he immediately becomes 'an Angel looking down upon, and blessing them, from a bright and happy Heaven' (29). In *Bleak House* (1852–3), Richard Carstone in his death 'begins the world' – 'the world that sets this right' (65). This other, compensatory world conforms in its broad characteristics to contemporary assumptions about the heavenly state, particularly in the early novels. In *Oliver Twist* (1837–9) it is assumed to be rural: town-dwellers are said to yearn to see nature before they die, as 'a foretaste of heaven itself' (32). In *Pickwick*, as in *In Memoriam*, Christmas is associated with heaven in its family reunions and the renewal of friendships,

that happy state of companionship and mutual good-will, which is a source of such pure and unalloyed delight, and one so incompatible with the cares and sorrows of the world, that the religious belief of the most civilised nations, and the rude traditions of the roughest savages, alike number it among the first joys of a future condition of existence, provided for the blest and happy!   (28)

The emphasis on 'mutual' good will in Dickens's first novel is also present in the title of the last completed novel, where heaven is still assumed to be a reality.

Unlike Tennyson, however, Dickens disliked speculation on the nature of the heavenly state, although he was equally open-minded on the subject of spiritualism.[40] For Dickens the Christian hope of heaven is associated mainly with peace and with rest, after 'the restless struggles of life' (*Pickwick*, 28). Both John's gospel (14.27; 20.19, 26) and the burial service, in which 'our hope' is that our brother or sister 'rests' in Christ, provide authority for such an emphasis, which is typified in the closing words of *The Life of Our Lord*. If we try to 'do right in everything', Dickens tells his children, 'and remember the life and lessons of Our Lord Jesus Christ, and try to act up to them, we may confidently hope that God will forgive us our sins and mistakes, and enable us to live and die in Peace'.[41] Sidney Carton's last words in *A Tale of Two Cities* – perhaps the best-known last words in English Literature – speak of a 'far, far better rest' at the end of a work that marks the transition from the social novels of the 1850s to the fiction of the 1860s in which Dickens explores the themes of individual guilt and redemption.

A highly emotional writer, Dickens was sensitive to what has since come to be known as the 'ministry of tears' in relation to death. He wrote to a bereaved lady in August 1852:

> May all those compassionate and hopeful lessons of the great Teacher who shed divine tears for the dead [Lazarus] bring their full comfort to you! I have no fear of that, my confidence is certainty.[42]

A letter to the novelist Emily Jolly, written three years later, reflects Dickens's emphasis upon the affective power of fiction. He is critical of the way in which his correspondent ends a story with the retributive deaths of a wronged husband and his children, and suggests that the erring wife should

> suppose [her husband] dead . . . but bring her round at last to the blessed surprise that her husband is still living, and that a repentance which can be worked out, *in the way of atonement for the misery she has occasioned to the man whom she so ill repaid for his love, and made so miserable*, lies before her. So will you soften the reader whom you now as it were harden, and so you will bring tears from many eyes, which can only have their spring in affectionately and gently touched hearts.[43]

Dickens himself writes movingly about 'atonement' (III.10) – and 'redemption' (III.7) and 'expiation' (III.4) – in *A Tale of Two Cities*, a novel frequently criticized for its over-explicitly Christian framework.[44] In *Our Mutual Friend* the challenge was not only to conceal the identity of John Harmon, but also to avoid making his 'baptism' to new life too schematized. In the 'Postscript in lieu of Preface' to *Our Mutual Friend*, Dickens described his own monumental task of concealment in the plot as the most difficult part of his 'design':

Its difficulty was much enhanced by the mode of publication; for, it would be very unreasonable to expect that many readers, pursuing a story in portions from month to month through nineteenth months, will, until they have it before them complete, perceive the relations of its finer threads to the whole pattern which is always before the eyes of the story-weaver at his loom.

As an attempt to emulate Wilkie Collins in the art of complex 'sensation novel' plotting, *Our Mutual Friend* is something of a failure, for Dickens was eventually forced to insert a chapter in which John Harmon explains his 'own' plot, the clarification of which had hitherto been subordinated to the demands of concealing his true identity (II.13). Dickens did succeed, however, in weaving together the John Harmon/Bella Wilfer plot with the Eugene Wrayburn/Lizzie Hexam plot. In both plots the male figure is brought back from the dead and redeemed through love. The link between the two is first made through the Boffins' adoption of Little Johny, and later strengthened through the efficacy of the burial service at his great-grandmother's (Betty Higden's) funeral. As in John's gospel, however, the increasing light in the novel is accompanied by increasing darkness, here the Bradley Headstone section of the Wrayburn plot. Unlike in John, it is a darkness which is upon the face of the deep in the beginning.

THE FIRST NUMBER AS PROEM

Nowhere did Dickens, the self-styled story-weaver at his loom, perceive more clearly the relations of a novel's finer threads to the whole pattern than in the opening, or threshold number of *Our Mutual Friend*. The imaginative effort of conceiving the novel's broad outline had proved to be unusually demanding and protracted. Having tried unsuccessfully to get started as early as 1861, Dickens settled on the title by October 1862. It was another year, however, before he could report that he saw his 'opening perfectly, with the one main line on which the story is to turn'. Three months later, on 25 January 1864, he announced that he had 'done the first two numbers', and was beginning the third. He described the book as

a combination of drollery with romance which requires a great deal of pains and a perfect throwing away of points that might be amplified; but I hope it is *very good*.[45]

The first number is certainly 'very good', a creation with which its creator could be pleased. Each of the number's four chapters provides commentary on the others, and together they announce the central themes which are to be worked out in the novel as a whole. Although the contrast between the primeval world of the Thames in chapter 1 and the 'bran-new' Veneerings' dinner-party in chapter 2 is characteristically sharp, it is what these worlds have in common that 'strikes the key-note' of the first number. In *Pickwick* Dickens located common ground between 'the religious belief of the most civilised nations, and the rude traditions of the roughest savages' in the idea of heaven as reunion. In *Our Mutual Friend* it is the dead mammonism of the advanced 'civilization' of 'these times of ours' that is anticipated in the words of the 'half savage' Gaffer Hexam to Rogue Riderhood:

'Had a dead man any use for money? Is it possible for a dead man to have money? What world does a dead man belong to? T'other world. What world does money belong to? This world. How can money be a corpse's?'   (1.1)

An unregenerate fisher of men who moves over the sur-face of the deep like a 'bird of prey', Gaffer represents in his trade a demonic version of the gospel's promise of life coming out of death.[46] For all its polished surface, the unredeemed world of the Veneerings is as fascinated by stories of death and burial as is the half savage Gaffer, with his primitive idea of another world. The Analytical Chemist having invited the dinner guests to table in the tone of one who would say 'Come down and be poisoned, ye unhappy children of men', and offered Eugene Wrayburn, 'buried alive in the back of his chair',[47] a 'champagne chalice' which lacks the efficacy of the eucharist, Mortimer Lightwood holds the company's attention with the story of old Harmon, which ends with the dead man's instruction in his will that he was to be buried 'with certain eccentric ceremonies and precautions against his coming to life' (1.2).[48]

News from the deep breaks the surface in the last words of chapter 2: 'Man's drowned.' Mortimer's question to Charley Hexam at the beginning of chapter 3 concerning any means that were taken to 'ascertain if it was possible to restore life' in the drowned man receives a weighty response:

You wouldn't ask, sir, if you knew his state. Pharaoh's multitudes that were drowned in the Red Sea, ain't more beyond restoring to life. If Lazarus was only half as far gone, that was the greatest of all the miracles.

Although able to read, unlike his father, Charley is unable properly to interpret these Bible stories. He emphasizes what Northrop Frye has called the 'demonic image' of the crossing of the Red Sea, associated with the shedding of blood in the destruction of Pharaoh's army (Exodus 14), when he might have focused upon the rescue of Israel – a type of baptism (1 Corinthians 10.1–2) and an image of salvation also associated by Christian commentators with Jesus's baptism and divine recognition, and with his resurrection.[49] And Charley's reference to the raising of Lazarus entirely misses its significance.

Charley Hexam's riverside world, from which a mechanical education offers a means of escape, threatens to regress to a state of primeval chaos, as the 'accumulated scum of humanity' are 'washed from higher grounds, like so much moral sewage', and as vessels seem to have got ashore and houses to have got afloat (1.3). The area is suggestive of the grave and of burial, the Hexams' house, a 'low building', having a 'look of decomposition'. John Harmon's fleeting appearance at the doorway, and his agitated statement that he is 'lost', suggest that he is in a kind of limbo, while the shrieks of the woman incarcerated in police cells are the cries of the damned. All are caught up in man's fallen condition, and all, the Night Inspector reminds them as abbot of his little monastery, are 'up to' murder. In denying the possibility of the kinds of miracle associated with Roman Catholic tradition, this illuminator of missals shares Charley's scepticism:

Pity there was not a word of truth in that superstition about bodies bleeding when touched by the hand of the right person; you never got a sign out of bodies.

Many of the characters in these early chapters are interpreters. Gaffer Hexam stares at the surface of the river, while Lizzie earnestly watches his face (1.1). Whereas Lizzie averts her gaze when the corpse is taken on board, her brother and father, the Night Inspector, Eugene and Mortimer, and John Harmon himself, all examine it for clues to its identity when it is brought ashore. Indeed, much of the interpretative effort expended in the novel is related to identity, and specifically to names. Gaffer's boat, which has 'no inscription' and cannot be interpreted, is 'allied to the bottom of the river rather than the surface' by reason of the 'slime and ooze' with which it is covered. His clothes seem to be 'made out of the mud' that begrimes his boat – a sign of his fallen state as the old Adam (a name traditionally associated with the earth) – in a novel in which mud sticks to many of the characters, and in which dust heaps – great mounds of 'earth' and 'ashes' – rise and fall. Even when the novel's most insistent kind of question – 'What is your name?' or 'Who are you?' – elicits in the following chapters elusive answers surrounding the 'identification' of 'John Harmon' among a group of characters with the alliterative Old Testament names of Job, Jacob, and Jesse (1.3), and some exuberant play upon the 'R' of R. Wilfer (1.4), individuation is subordinated to a sense of a shared mortality as different worlds within London are brought into contact with each other through a violent death.

The attempt to establish people's names and to place their identities is an aspect of that broader function of interpretation – the 'harmonizing' of discrete data into a coherent whole – which the novel frequently examines. While the illiterate Gaffer claims to be 'scholar enough' to know all the handbills of 'bodies found' that are stuck up on his wall, his action with the lamp is one of harmonization: 'He waved the light over the whole, as if to typify the light of his scholarly intelligence' (1.3). The literate Night Inspector is found 'posting up his books in a whitewashed office, as studiously as if he were in a monastery on top of a mountain', and oblivious to the screaming drunken woman in a nearby cell. Such disharmonies can be ignored and thus suppressed, but important evidences also refuse to harmonize, as the Night Inspector reflects when he reports that two 'excellent surgical opinions' on the injuries sustained by the man found dead in the river contradict each other. The chapter ends with the Inspector lurking about in boats, 'putting this and that together':

But, according to the success with which you put this and that together, you get a woman and a fish apart, or a Mermaid in combination. And Mr Inspector could turn out nothing better than a Mermaid, which no Judge and Jury would believe in.

The following chapter, which begins with the words 'Reginald Wilfer is a name', takes up the theme in the shy R. Wilfer's unwillingness to use his full name, and his lack of a complete, and thus matching, new suit of clothes; in the 'principle which matrimonially unites contrasts', illustrated in Mr and Mrs Wilfer; and in Bella Wilfer's 'ridiculous mourning', worn as 'a kind of a widow who never was married' (1.4).

This fourth chapter, however, the last in the first number, also contains jocular hints of a kind of harmony which is at present only latent: Cecilia Wilfer writes three months after her marriage saying that in spite of trying circumstances she is determined to honour her marriage vows; and R.W.'s return with a rasher of ham which is 'coyly embraced' by a fresh cabbage leaf is followed by 'melodious sounds' rising from the frying-pan. But far more resonant, in the context of her rough riverside home, is the voice of Lizzie Hexam in the previous chapter, when she responds to Charley's comment that she is their father's favourite, and could 'make him believe anything':

> 'I wish I could, Charley! For if I could make him believe that learning was a good thing, and that we might lead better lives, I should be a'most content to die.'

Whereas her spiritual quest is to be for a 'better life', Charley's ambition is for 'learning' in the narrow sense of schooling which leads to social elevation. The contrast between brother and sister is developed in their different interpretations of the glow in the fire in the brazier, a scene which figures in Marcus Stone's illustrated cover for the monthly numbers of *Our Mutual Friend* (illustration 15):

> 'That's gas, that is,' said the boy, 'coming out of a bit of a forest that's been under the mud that was under the water in the days of Noah's Ark. Look here! When I take the poker – so – and give it a dig –'
> 'Don't disturb it, Charley, or it'll be all in a blaze. It's that dull glow near it, coming and going, that I mean. When I look at it of an evening, it comes like pictures to me, Charley.'
> 'Show us a picture,' said the boy. 'Tell me where to look.'
> 'Ah! It wants my eyes, Charley.'   (1.3)

As in his earlier interpretation of the crossing of the Red Sea, Charley's reference to Noah's ark, that other type of baptism (1 Peter 3.19–21 and the Public Baptism of Infants) has no spiritual content for him. Whereas Charley's hazy understanding of the findings of the geologists is later to inform a crude version of social Darwinism in his 'climbing up out of the mire' of his class (II.15), Lizzie is to retain a belief that it is the 'real world' she sees in the fire (II.1). As Lizzie, the spiritual interpreter with 'eyes', relates to Charley what she sees in the past and in the future, she moves naturally into the eternal present associated with descriptions of the kingdom: 'There are you and me', 'There am I.' Surrounded by savagery and materialism, she adopts a proto-Christian discourse as she addresses the task of turning her father 'to wish to do better things'.

The main drive of the opening number, however, like Marcus Stone's cover plate, is downwards, as people go down into the river and the grave, down to dinner, down through the geological strata of prehistory. This first number represents a demonic version of the proem in John's gospel, in which there is more darkness than light, and in which you never get a sign out of bodies. In the remaining eighteen numbers Lizzie's role is to prove central in the rescue of John Harmon from the shadow of the dust heaps, associated in the cover plate with the skeletal figure of death. For the novel's central conceit of rising and falling, worked out in social climbing and abrupt descents, the amassing and removal of dust, a cityscape of airy rooftops and dark labyrinthine streets, and a river of drownings and rescues, is underpinned with a theological understanding of the fall and of man's redemption through love, worked out in the here-and-now as an earnest of a future heavenly state.

'THE REDEEMING ACTION OF THE WORLD': THE HARMON PLOT

In *The Old Curiosity Shop*, the schoolmaster says to Little Nell:

There is nothing . . . no, nothing innocent or good, that dies, and is forgotten. Let us hold to that faith, or none. An infant, a prattling child, dying in its cradle, will live again in the better thoughts of those who loved it, and will play its part, through them, in the redeeming actions of the world, though its body be burnt to ashes or drowned in the deepest sea. There is not an angel added to the Host of Heaven but does its blessed work on earth in those that loved it here.   (54)

The double perspective of the last sentence is central to Dickens's understanding of a future life: it is both here, in the sense that the dead have a continuing effective presence among the living, and elsewhere, in heaven. This theme is still being reworked at the end of his career, in *Our Mutual Friend*, where the funerals of little Johny and his great-grandmother, Betty Higden, prove to be of great significance in the novel's overall scheme. Turning first to the John Harmon plot, I want to consider how these two minor characters play a crucial role in their obscure lives and deaths, because, like the Boffins, they are 'blessed' (Matthew 5.3–12).

Dickens's interest in the relationship between the three major liminal orders of service in the prayer book is reflected in some characteristic play with their confusion or grotesque juxtaposition in *Our Mutual*

Friend. Jenny Wren, for example, studies the surplice of the clergyman who reads 'the service in the Prayer-book' at her drunken father's funeral, so that she can make a doll clergyman to unite two of her 'young friends in matrimony' (IV.9). R. Wilfer's 'Innocent Elopement' with his daughter to Greenwich is perhaps the happiest day in his life, 'not even excepting that on which his heroic partner had approached the nuptial altar to the tune of the Dead March in Saul' (II.8). Whereas Wilfer triumphantly rises above the funereal aspect of matrimony in his unselfish devotion to those 'companions' his children, the 'muddy' complexioned Pleasant Riderhood's dark interpretation of the world is shaped entirely by 'her own unfortunate experience':

Show [her] a Wedding in the street, and she only saw two people taking out a regular licence to quarrel and fight. Show her a Christening, and she saw a little heathen personage having a quite superfluous name bestowed upon it, inasmuch as it would be commonly addressed by some abusive epithet . . . Show her a Funeral, and she saw an unremunerative ceremony in the nature of a black masquerade, conferring a temporary gentility on the performers, at an immense expense, and representing the only formal party ever given by the deceased.

(II.12)

She lacks Lizzie Hexam's eyes. Only she, however, can 'interpret' her father's 'discontented growl' when he comes back from the 'inexplicable journey' of the dying process later in the novel: it is a dismissal as 'Poll-Parroting' of the doctor's hope that his escape from drowning 'may have a good effect' upon him (III.3). Rogue Riderhood avoids the 'good effects' of both the burial service and a secularized 'baptism' to new life, remaining unregenerate. Gaffer Hexam is 'baptized unto Death' when he is 'brought down' in his drowning (I.14), but his son's later talk of 'compensation – restitution – never mind the word' (II.1) has nothing to do with his being baptized into Christ's death (Romans 6.3–4), or with the theology of baptism and the burial service.

So strong are these dark threads in *Our Mutual Friend*, and so frequently is the possibility of transcendence denied, that when the transforming power of love is experienced in the novel its effect and emotional impact are heightened. While John Harmon's birthright is the subject of wills, in both senses, his name and identity are restored to him through love, and in the most unpromising of circumstances. His concealment of his true identity and later rescue from a kind of limbo unfold during his residence in the house that used to be called Harmony Jail, the etymology of which is explained to Silas Wegg by the hoarse gentleman with the donkey:

> 'Not a proper jail, wot you and me would get committed to . . . they giv' it the name, on accounts of Old Harmon living solitary there.'
> 'And-why-did-they-callitharm-Ony?' asked Wegg.
> 'On accounts of his never agreeing with nobody. Like a speeches of chaff. Harmon's Jail; Harmony Jail. Working it round like.'   (1.5)

Mrs Boffin, however, 'christened' it 'Boffin's Bower' when they came into the property. The Boffins, who never quarrel, also never try to harmonize their different tastes in furnishings, her 'Fashion' coexisting with his simple tastes 'by *mutual* consent' (my emphasis). Mr Boffin has not fallen into (book) knowledge, until the wrong Silas comes into the jail as 'an official expounder of mysteries' to read Nicodemus the wrong book by night: Gibbon's *History of the Decline and Fall of the Roman Empire*, its eight volumes ranged flat on a table, 'in a row, like a galvanic battery'.[50]

In the opening number of the novel both John Harmon (alias Julius Handford) and Bella Wilfer, a 'kind of a widow who never was married' (1.4), find themselves in a liminal phase of their lives. Breathless and hardly able to speak – 'I am lost! . . . I – I – am a stranger, and don't know the way' – Harmon is a benighted pilgrim for whom the Night Inspector with his wicket gate proves to be of little help as Interpreter (1.3). I have already quoted the reference in the second chapter to old John Harmon's burial, and his precautions against coming to life again. The Boffins' plan to adopt a little John Harmon deeply disturbs the Secretary, 'John Rokesmith', who thinks Mrs Boffin is speaking of 'the Dead', that is, of himself (1.9). The Boffins, however, lovingly preserve this John Harmon's name in the form of the signature he inscribed as a child on a wall in Harmony Jail, when he was comforted in his misery by the Boffins. Mr Boffin insists that Harmon's and his sister's names 'shan't be rubbed out in our time' (1.15). Harmon's infant scrawl, a sign of life, contrasts with the dead, dusty shell of the house itself:

> A gloomy house the Bower, with sordid signs on it of having been, through its long existence as Harmony Jail, in miserly holding. Bare of paint, bare of paper on the walls, bare of furniture, bare of experience of human life. Whatever is built by man for man's occupation, must, like natural creation, fulfil the intention of its existence, or soon perish.

Darwinian principles are also extended to the inhabitants of the house through the novel's argument that grasping miserliness must soon perish as the 'intention' of human existence is love and mutuality.

Bella's fancies on her 'Innocent Elopement' with Pa Wilfer first raise John Harmon from the dead, then consign him to his grave again (II.8). In the following chapter little Johny Harmon is to die, destined never to enter the Bower. Nor is his great-grandmother, Betty Higden,

an active old woman, with a bright dark eye and a resolute face, yet quite a tender creature too; not a logically-reasoning woman, but God is good, and hearts may count in Heaven as high as heads.   (I.16)

When she first visited Betty and her small charges, Mrs Boffin had been delighted that the little orphan was 'already Johny! Only one of the two names left to give him!' (I.16) (Sloppy, a 'love child', has 'no right name'.) When little Johny falls ill, both Bella and the Secretary accompany Mrs Boffin to Betty Higden's, buying a Noah's ark and other gifts at a toyshop on the way (II.9). Betty interprets the infant's condition in spiritual terms: 'All others belonging to him have gone to the Power and the Glory, and I have a mind that they're drawing him to them – leading him away.' At the sick-bed, that classic site of interpretative difficulties, Mrs Boffin asks whether little Johny is asleep, while Johny asks the by now familiar kind of question: 'Who is the boofer lady?' In the children's hospital to which they take him there is a coloured picture at his 'bed's head', 'representing as it were another Johny seated on the knee of some Angel surely who loved little children', with whom the nurses, described as 'the ministering women *at his bed's head*' (my emphasis), are thus associated. Having no close family of his own, the orphan regards his fellow patients as 'brothers and sisters' in a sense that is reminiscent of the prayer book: they are described as the 'family' whom God has 'brought together'. Noah's ark, a type of the church in the prayer book, here serves to 'fortify' the boy in the next bed to Johny, on whose table 'all Creation' is arranged in pairs. The doctor, a good interpreter of sick children's broken words, understands Johny's last will and testament, passing the ark and other toys to his neighbour in a gesture which contrasts sharply with the 'clutching' old Harmon's loss of his 'grip on life' (I.15). Little Johny's final gift, however, made at the end of the chapter, is more precious:

With a weary and yet a pleased smile, and with an action as if he stretched his little figure out to rest, the child heaved his body on the sustaining arm, and seeking Rokesmith's face with his lips, said:

'A kiss for the boofer lady.'

Having now bequeathed all he had to dispose of, and arranged his affairs in this world, Johny, thus speaking, left it.

What follows little Johny's death suggests that, in terms of the schoolmaster's perspective in *The Old Curiosity Shop*, he will play his part, through John Harmon, in the redeeming actions of the world. The opening paragraphs of the subsequent chapter, entitled 'A Successor' (II.10), describe how Frank Milvey buries little Johny with fewer qualms than some of his brethren, who were anxious because they were required to bury the dead too hopefully. Here Dickens emphasizes the effect of the funeral on Milvey, who reads the service thinking 'of his own six children, but not of his poverty', and 'with dimmed eyes'. He and his wife look down into the small grave and walk home 'very seriously'. The Secretary's manner towards Mrs Boffin at this time is more that of 'a young man towards a mother than that of a Secretary to his employer's wife', and is powerfully reminiscent of the response of John the beloved disciple to the Blessed Virgin Mary after the crucifixion (John 19.27) in that archetypal bequeathing of love which also informs other episodes in *Our Mutual Friend*.[51]

The Boffins, Bella, and the Secretary all agree, however, that John Harmon is an 'unfortunate name', and that it should not be 'revived' again, but left to 'rest in the grave'. The real John Harmon has to make a great act of will in order to 'bury' his true identity at the end of the chapter entitled 'A Solo and a Duett' (II.13), thus deferring his restoration to wholeness. The wind blows across Limehouse Hole so hard that the natural order is reversed as water flies up from the earth and stable signification is unsettled, in a manner suggestive of the last day: 'Doors were slamming violently, lamps were flickering or blown out, signs were rocking in their frames, the water of the kennels, wind-dispersed, flew about in drops like rain.' John Harmon's recollection of being drugged and almost drowned reads like another 'baptism unto death', for 'with Heaven's assistance' he was sucked under a boat and came up, 'only just alive, on the other side', eventually to be washed up on the opposite shore. His decision to bury his true identity again recalls the schoolmaster's idea of the efficacy of the memory of the dead:

Dead, I have found the true friends of my lifetime still as true as tender and as faithful as when I was alive, and making my memory an incentive to good actions done in my name. Dead, I have found them when they might have slighted my name, and passed greedily over my grave to ease and wealth, lingering by the way, like single-hearted children, to recall their love for me when I was a poor frightened child.

And dead to the material world, he may inherit the earth.

His retirement to his room in the Bower, however, in order to bury John Harmon 'many additional fathoms deep', follows Bella Wilfer's spurning of his declaration of devotion to her. The change in their relationship begins only after Betty Higden's funeral, which touches Bella, and thus reconciles her with Harmon. When Betty left London, the epitome of resolution and independence, she gave Bella 'a kiss for the boofer lady', 'encircling' her in the same embrace that the dying little Johny had given John Harmon (II.14). The chapter entitled 'The End of a Long Journey' (III.8), which begins a new number (XIII), also introduces a new religious note after the description of Boffin's 'fall into bad company' and the carting away of the mounds. The poor laws which threaten Betty with the workhouse, and the blinkered 'Gospel according to Podsnappery', are here contrasted with 'the truth' which will endure 'until the foundations of the universe are shaken by the Builder'. Betty's approaching death is described in terms of transcendence: with 'the shadow of advancing Death' over her, 'all the Light that shone on Betty Higden lay beyond Death'. When her 'pilgrimage' led her to follow 'the upward course of the river' towards her 'last home', she had 'hovered' near her 'abandoned dwelling' before going on. The river now calls to her, and she has a vision of her dead children and grandchildren on a barge, before encountering 'the Samaritan in his latest accredited form' – Rogue Riderhood, who fleeces her before she can escape from him. Exhausted, she thanks 'the Power and the Glory' before sinking down gratefully at the foot of a tree: 'It brought to her mind the foot of the Cross, and she committed herself to Him who died upon it.'

What follows these least ambiguous of Christian references (*pace* Garrett Stewart)[52] is a death scene in which the passenger through the liminal phase between life and death, and from this world to the heaven in which she believes, is the person who asks the critical questions, and in a form which speaks of life after death. Betty wakes up to find a young woman bending over her:

The darkness gone, and a face bending down.

'It cannot be the boofer lady?'

'I don't understand what you say. Let me wet your lips again with this brandy. I have been away to fetch it. Did you think that I was long gone?'

It is as the face of a woman, shaded by a quantity of rich dark hair. It is the earnest face of a woman who is young and handsome. But all is over with me on earth, and this must be an Angel.

'Have I been long dead?'

'I don't understand what you say. Let me wet your lips again. I hurried all I could, and brought no one back with me, lest you should die of the shock of strangers.'

'Am I not dead?'

'I cannot understand what you say. Your voice is so low and broken that I cannot hear you. Do you hear me?'

'Yes.'

'Do you mean Yes?'

'Yes.'

The young woman wants to lift the old woman up, but the latter twice replies: 'Not yet.' Once Betty is assured, however, that the 'Parish' will never touch her, nor yet so much as look at her, she can ask the novel's recurrent question – 'What is your name, my dear?' – and let Lizzie Hexam lift her:

> 'I must be sore disfigured. Are you afraid to kiss me?'
>
> The answer is, the ready pressure of her lips upon the cold but smiling mouth.
>
> 'Bless ye! *Now* lift me, my love.'
>
> Lizzie Hexam very softly raised the weather-stained grey head, and lifted her as high as Heaven.

Whereas verbal communication is fragmented and difficult in this death scene, two simple physical gestures signify a human love between strangers that 'speaks' of transcendence.

Like little Johny's death, Betty Higden's is described at the end of a chapter which is immediately followed by Frank Milvey's reading of the burial service:

> '"WE GIVE THEE HEARTY THANKS FOR THAT IT HATH PLEASED THEE TO DELIVER THIS OUR SISTER OUT OF THE MISERIES OF THIS SINFUL WORLD."' So read the Reverend Frank Milvey in a not untroubled voice, for his heart misgave him that all was not quite right between us and our sister – or say our sister in Law – Poor Law – and that we sometimes read these words in an awful manner, over our Sister and our Brother too. (III.9)

Always aware of the danger of allowing an elevated religious discourse to suppress the voice of social protest, Dickens continues the reformist theme in his comments on unmarked graves, another question presented to 'my lords and gentleman and honourable boards'. Frank Milvey, who, we remember, holds his peace in disputes over the 'sure and certain hope of the Resurrection to eternal life' (II.10), and who is broad-minded in his attitude to Lizzie Hexam's Jewish employers, is Dickens's ideal Church of England clergyman. Betty Higden is his ideal good-hearted old woman, who believes in angels and in heaven.

The idea that Betty dies as if at 'the foot of the Cross' was sufficiently important to Dickens to figure in his working notes.[53] Out of her suffering and death there comes reconciliation as the funeral brings John Harmon and Bella to Lizzie, and thus the novel's two main plots together. In drawing attention to the significance of this meeting, which points to the reconciliation of John Harmon and Bella, Dickens emphasizes that it entails a shared act of interpretation:

Brought face to face for the first time with the daughter of his supposed murderer, it was natural that John Harmon should have his own secret reasons for a careful scrutiny of her countenance and manner. Bella knew that Lizzie's father had been falsely accused of the crime and her interest, though it had no secret springs, like that of the Secretary, was equally natural. Both had expected to see something very different from the real Lizzie Hexam, and thus it fell out that she became the unconscious means of bringing them together.

Written with elaborate care, this passage marks an important stage in the sequence Dickens planned in his working notes: 'Betty Higden's Flight and Death. / Lizzie finds her. / Lizzie and Bella come together. / . . . *Lizzie to work an influence on Bella's character, at its wavering point.* (This last sentence is underlined twice in Dickens's notes.)

The emphasis upon mediation continues when, left alone together, Bella and John Harmon agree that they are both 'commissioned' – a word often associated with angels, mediators between God and man[54] – to give a report on Lizzie Hexam. In the middle of their discussion on Lizzie, Bella asks Harmon's forgiveness with tears in her eyes, and holds out 'her little hand'. Betty's funeral has affected her profoundly, for after this 'serious scene' she feels that she is 'useless enough in the world'. Harmon's answer that 'No one is useless in this world . . . who lightens the burden of it for any one else' broadens the sense of their 'commission' to embrace the redeeming actions of the world. All this points up the significance of Bella's subsequent dialogue with Lizzie by a fire which is reminiscent of the 'old brazier' with its 'old hollow down by the flare', reminding the reader of Lizzie's ability to 'see' the 'real world'. These shared confidences, which turn on questions of identity such as Lizzie's 'Can you tell me who my unknown friend is?' , are couched in terms of love and of 'hope', a word which recurs frequently in their conversation. Lizzie's declaration of her love for Eugene Wrayburn has a profound effect upon Bella, who sits 'enchained by the deep, unselfish passion of this girl or woman of her own age'. The exchange, like the burial service earlier, leaves Bella looking and feeling 'serious', and as she travels back to London by train she is in John Harmon's eyes, as in little Johny's and Betty Higden's, the 'boofer lady'.

They return to a Bower which fast regresses to a Harmony Jail, as Boffin the Golden Dustman is 'at his worst' in his feigned aggression against the Secretary. By adopting a purely mercenary or materialist discourse, Boffin draws from Harmon a declaration of love for Bella (III.15), and initiates in her a rebellion which results in her marriage to Harmon. The language of transcendence associated with Betty's future life in heaven is here applied to Bella's future life on earth: 'Bella, after hanging her head for a moment, lifted it up and laid it on his breast, as if that were her head's chosen and lasting resting-place!' (III.16). When she breaks the news to an amazed and rather faint R. Wilfer, Bella adopts a specifically religious discourse, telling her father that Harmon 'saved her' from herself. Pa Wilfer then movingly gives his 'blessing on this engagement', and organizes an impromptu tea of a cottage loaf and a drink of milk. Through the efficacy of love it is the most 'delicious repast' that any of them have ever made – a kind of fairy tale *agapē*. Similarly, the wedding service is followed by a breakfast of fishes, and a glimpse of an earthly paradise which combines Christian and pagan traditions:

the dishes being seasoned with Bliss – an article which they are sometimes out of, at Greenwich – were of perfect flavour, and the golden drinks had been bottled in the golden age and hoarding up their sparkles ever since.   (IV.4)

Interestingly, the festive quality of the wedding allows a relaxed and playful treatment of the form of the service, with the attendance of 'Gruff and Glum', and later, at the breakfast, of a head waiter who is dubbed 'the Archbishop of Greenwich', and who looks 'much more like a clergyman than *the* clergyman'. In the same vein, the closing sentence of the chapter, and thus of the number (XVI), clothes its weighty commentary in the dress of festive comedy: 'O 'tis love, 'tis love, 'tis love, that makes the world go round!'

Entering the church to be married, Bella Wilfer is 'swallowed up . . . for ever and ever', to emerge 'into the happy sunlight, Mrs John Rokesmith'. During this wedding chapter the Secretary is named first as 'John Rokesmith' and then as simply 'John' by his future father-in-law. Still living under an assumed surname, he is always 'John', his name in the eyes of the church, and the name he would be called in the marriage service; now also his new name to the Wilfers as one redeemed through love. Bella as a new wife in charge of a dolls' house on Blackheath peppers her talk with her family with 'Johns' (IV.5). John Harmon describes her role in the marital home in terms of 'loves and graces' and 'a bright light in the house', while her catechism, intended as a playful introduction to the announcement that she is expecting a child, is also significant in terms of his identity. The first question, as set down in the prayer book – 'What is your name?' – naturally disturbs him, and he answers the second – 'Who gave you that name?' – with the first words of the response: 'My godfathers and my godmothers, dear love?'[55] He does so well, although he hesitates, that she lets him off the rest. But her religious references continue, when she talks of 'sermon-time' in childhood, as a 'very small-sized sinner at church'; of the 'Calendar' of her life; and of 'believing'. Bella's and John's domestic bliss is thus sanctified in a rhetorical move that typifies Dickens's idealization of young married bliss, which in this novel contrasts with the hell on earth experienced by the mercenary Mr and Mrs Lammles. When John Harmon finally takes possession of the Bower and the news is broken to Bella of his true identity, it is the appearance of their baby, and the kisses showered upon it by the Boffins, that keep her from fainting (IV.13). The nursery harks back to little Johny and his Noah's ark: a high, airy room, like the children's ward, it is 'garnished with rainbows' (cf. Genesis 9.13). When Bella goes to feed him, 'smiling Peace associated herself with that young olive branch' (cf. Psalm 128.3). Peace, I have argued, is Dickens's idea of heaven, and here he shows us heaven on earth.

'COME UP AND BE DEAD': THE WRAYBURN PLOT

In the Wrayburn plot, as in the Harmon plot, light comes out of darkness, and new life out of death. Whereas Harmon's baptism to new life is

achieved, however, partly through subterfuge on the part of a bene-
volent Nicodemus Boffin, Wrayburn's is a baptism of fire, precipitated
by the dark force of his declared enemy Bradley Headstone, for me the
most interesting character in *Our Mutual Friend*. Certain Carlylean
themes associated with 'the latest Gospel of Monotony' and 'mechanical' education, and Headstone's suppressed emotion, are reminiscent of
Hard Times.[56] His particular version of hell on earth, however, is closer
to Swinburne's than anything in Dickens's earlier fiction, and brings to
mind Swinburne's observation that suffering and passion are 'indeed the
same thing and the same word':[57]

It seemed to him as if all that he could suppress in himself he had suppressed, as
if all that he could restrain in himself he had restrained, and the time had come –
in a rush, in a moment – when the power of self-command had departed from
him. Love at first sight is a trite expression quite sufficiently discussed; enough
that in certain smouldering natures like this man's, that passion leaps into a
blaze, and makes such head as fire does in a rage of wind, when other passions,
but for its mastery, could be held in chains.   (II.11)

Shortly after this passage, Jenny Wren uses the words 'selfish' and
'mutual', suggestive of the two kinds of love which the novel analyzes.
Headstone's obsessive and selfish love for Lizzie Hexam contrasts with
the mutual love between her and Eugene towards which the Wrayburn
plot works. (Bella, we recall, is to sit 'enchained by the deep, unselfish
passion' of Lizzie Hexam for Eugene Wrayburn (III.9).) Similarly, Headstone's association with the dangerous depths of the unconscious
mind, and his final return to slimy depths associated with his primeval
ancestors, contrast with Wrayburn's baptism to new life through mutual
love. John Harmon's linking of Lizzie's and Wrayburn's names has the
effect of opening a channel of emotion in Headstone which is 'an unexpectedly dark and deep and stormy one, and difficult to sound' (II.14).
In the following chapter Headstone and Charley Hexam meet Lizzie in a
dismal area of the City which has 'an air of death' about it, and from
which 'the set of humanity outward . . . is as a set of prisoners departing from gaol'. When they come to a churchyard, Headstone's name
takes on a new significance: 'Here, conveniently and healthfully elevated
above the level of the living, were the dead, and the tombstones; some of
the latter droopingly inclined from the perpendicular, as if they were
ashamed of the lies they told' (II.15).[58] The phrase 'inclined from the
perpendicular' belongs to Headstone's mechanical educational dis-

course, and the reference to false epitaphs serves as commentary on the schoolmaster's decent external appearance, which never changes while he is in London. In place of the language of love which speaks of heavenly or paradisal bliss, Headstone's in his declaration to Lizzie is that of hell on earth: 'You are the ruin of me . . . It is my doom . . . I have been in torments . . . I love you.' As he 'heaves up' these words from the bottom of the 'raging sea' within his own breast, he becomes increasingly disturbed:

> The wild energy of the man, now quite let loose, was absolutely terrible. He stopped and laid his hand upon a piece of the coping of the burial-ground enclosure, as if he would have dislodged the stone.

The 'powdered mortar' from under the stone rattles on the pavement as he becomes increasingly impassioned, but when Lizzie tells him that she will never favour him, his response is violent:

> 'Then,' said he, suddenly changing his tone and turning to her, and bringing his clenched hand down upon the stone with a force that laid the knuckles raw and bleeding; 'then I hope that I may never kill him!'
>
> The dark look of hatred and revenge with which the words broke from his livid lips, and with which he stood holding out his smeared hand as if it held some weapon and had just struck a mortal blow, made her so afraid of him that she turned to run away. But he caught her by the arm.

More strictly a 'half savage' than Gaffer Hexam, being a split personality, Headstone reveals an unredeemed masculinity, which is characterized by brutish aggression and blood lust.

Whereas the Gadarene, whom Headstone resembles in breaking loose from his chains and cutting himself with stones (Mark 5.4–5), runs to worship Jesus and is healed, Bradley Headstone, mechanical without and primeval within, suffers the torments of one who rejects both law and gospel. Like some jealous fallen angel, he blames Wrayburn for his damned state as one for whom mutual love is unattainable, and for his being 'set aside' and 'cast out'. Like other Victorian writers, Dickens often associated stone with the 'tables of stone' of Old Testament law, in contradistinction from the 'fleshy tables of the heart' on which Christian, mutual love is written (2 Corinthians 3.3).[59] The episode in the graveyard also echoes the passage in Luke's gospel in which the chief priests, the scribes, and the elders question Jesus in the temple about 'the baptism of John'. Jesus answers them by telling the parable of the vineyard, and then asks a question of his own concerning Psalm 118.22

('The stone which the builders refused is become the *head stone* of the corner'):

> And he beheld them, and said, What is this then that is written, The stone which the builders rejected, the same is become the head of the corner?
>
> Whosoever shall fall upon that stone shall be broken; but on whomsoever it shall fall, it will *grind* him to *powder*.
>
> And the chief priests and the scribes the same hour sought to lay hands on him . . .
> (Luke 20.19; my emphases)

In the chapter entitled 'Scouts Out' (III.10), which follows Betty Higden's funeral and the meetings between Harmon, Bella, and Lizzie, Eugene Wrayburn explains to his friend Mortimer Lightwood how Headstone 'undergoes grinding torments' when he is led through the labyrinth of London streets in the hope of finding Lizzie. When the couple encounter him, Headstone looks 'like the hunted and not the hunter, baffled, worn, with the exhaustion of deferred hope and consuming hate and anger in his face'.

What follows Wrayburn's account of Headstone's grinding torments is one of Dickens's darkest statements on criminality. In implicitly questioning the assumptions of most Christian commentators on the question, he prepares the ground for R. L. Stevenson:

> The state of the man was murderous, and he knew it. . . Tied up all day with his disciplined show upon him . . . he broke loose at night like an ill-tamed wild animal. Under his daily restraint, it was his compensation, not his trouble, to give a glance towards his state at night, and to the freedom of its being indulged. If great criminals told the truth . . . they would very rarely tell of their struggles against the crime. Their struggles are towards it.
> (III.11)

How, then, are 'great criminals' to be saved from hell, or to be made channels of grace? These questions become pressing in relation to Dickens's treatment of Headstone's death.

If Dickens's heaven is peace and rest, Headstone's comment to Rogue Riderhood after the attempted murder of Eugene Wrayburn, that he has been 'so long in want of rest', suggest a hell on earth which Riderhood's pursuit of the 'doomed' man would seem to confirm (IV.7). Headstone's psychological sufferings are described in specifically Old Testament terms in this chapter, entitled 'Better to be Abel than Cain': a 'shedder of blood', he keeps the 'avenger', remorse, at bay, for example (cf. Ezekiel 18.10; Deuteronomy 19.6). Whereas Eugene Wrayburn used to toy with him in reversing the roles of pursuer and pursued, avenger and avenged, in the labyrinth of the city, it is now Rogue Riderhood (whom he makes his double through disguise) who dogs his steps towards a drowning from which there is to be no rescue:

> Bradley had caught him round the body. He seemed to be girdled with an iron ring. They were on the brink of the Lock, about midway between the two sets of gates.
>
> . . .
>
> Riderhood went over into the smooth pit, backward, and Bradley Headstone upon him. When the two were found, lying under the ooze and scum behind one of the rotting gates, Riderhood's hold had relaxed, probably in falling, and his eyes were staring upward. But, he was girdled still with Bradley's iron ring, and the rivets of the iron ring held tight.   (IV.15)

The iron ring with which he binds Riderhood in death is a demonic version of the encircling arm with which little Johny and Betty Higden bequeath their inheritance of love to John Harmon and Lizzie Hexam. Whereas good characters in Dickens, such as Little Nell, are promised eternal life in heaven after death, a villain such as Quilp, whose body is washed up on the shores of the indeterminate marshy regions of the Thames estuary, is not sent to hell, but is left in some kind of limbo (*The Old Curiosity Shop*, 67). One assumes that Quilp's body will not be recovered, and that therefore he will be given no funeral rites. Similarly, in *Our Mutual Friend*, Headstone's final descent into the 'smooth pit' of Plashwater Lock and the absence of reference to a funeral for Headstone and Riderhood at which a clergyman would have to speak hopefully over their coffins leave the question of future judgment and damnation open. For the novel has enacted its own judgment on Bradley Headstone in his living hell on earth, and whereas other characters have some kind of 'future life' projected for them, on earth or in heaven, he has none. Thus Dickens's moral scheme in *Our Mutual Friend*, which includes judgments worked out within the limits of the narrative, is not unlike what nineteenth-century theologians called annihilationism, or 'conditional immortality', and specifically its post-Darwinian version: a belief that those who do not believe in Christ are annihilated at death, while the saved (or fittest) survive.[60] Yet earlier in the novel, Rogue Riderhood's return from the 'inexplicable *journey*' of the dying process suggests otherwise (III.3).

Bradley Headstone's last words – 'Come down!' – express climactically that steady downward movement, associated with man's fallen condition as the old Adam, of the earth, earthy, which characterizes so many areas of the novel. Struggling in opposition to this tendency, however, is the kind of transcendent upward movement that is expressed in Jenny Wren's slanting rows of children, and in Riah's roof garden. Living under an assumed name, Jenny is first 'disclosed' in her parlour near St John the Evangelist's, Smith Square, as 'a child – a dwarf – a girl – a something' (II.1). This indeterminate 'person of the house', herself neither child nor adult, girl nor woman, deconstructs adult society's categories, inverting hierarchies by, for example, dubbing her alcoholic father a 'prodigal old son' (II.2). In *The Life of Our Lord*, Dickens exhorted his children never to forget in adult life that 'the most miserable, the most ugly, deformed, wretched creatures that live, will be bright Angels in Heaven if they are good here on earth'.[61] In the crippled Jenny Wren, he created a marginal figure whose visions of angels are an earnest of eternal rest.

Dickens's notes reveal that he wished to bring out in Jenny both 'her imaginative side, and Earthy side'.[62] The substitution of the 'imaginative' for the 'heavenly' (cf. 1 Corinthians 15.47–9) is a characteristic Romantic move, but one that in this case points to a negotiation between the this-worldly and the other-worldly, rather than a collapsing of traditional categories. In the chapter preceding that in which Jenny describes her visions, Lizzie Hexam has herself been accused of being a 'dreamer' by Charley, who encourages her to forget about the old days when they looked into the hollow down by the flare in the fire, saying that they are 'looking into the real world, now' (II.1). Lizzie's insistence that they were 'looking into the real world then' prepares for the episode in which she and Eugene Wrayburn witness Jenny Wren's transfiguration as narrator of her visions:

> There was something in the face and action for the moment, quite inspired and beautiful. Then the chin dropped musingly upon the hand again.
>
> 'I dare say my birds sing better than other birds, and my flowers smell better than other flowers. For when I was a little child,' in a tone as though it were ages ago, 'the children that I used to see early in the morning were very different from any others that I ever saw. They were not like me; they were not chilled, anxious, ragged, or beaten; they were never in pain . . . Such numbers of them too! All in white dresses, and with something shining on the borders, and on their heads, that I have never been able to imitate with my work, though I know it so well. They used to come down in long bright slanting rows, and say all together, "Who is this in pain! Who is this in pain!" When I told them who it was, they answered, "Come and play with us!" When I said "I never play! I

can't play!" they swept about me and took me up, and made me light. Then it was all delicious ease and rest till they laid me down, and said, all together, "Have patience, and we will come again."' (II.2)

Like Stephen Blackpool's apotheosis in *Hard Times* (III.6), this passage reveals the side of Dickens which is epitomized in the maudlin short story entitled 'A Child's Dream of a Star', published in *Household Words* in 1850 and in *Reprinted Pieces* eight years later. There a boy longs to join a 'train of people' he dreams are taken up the 'sparkling road' of a star's rays by angels, to join his sister's angel in the star.[63] Jenny's shining children are also reminiscent of popular Bible illustrations of nativity scenes or, more pertinently, Jacob's ladder (Genesis 28.12), in which slanting rows of angels mediate between earth and heaven, 'coming down' in a sense quite different from Bradley Headstone's.[64]

For Dickens the Romantic, however, these simple popular forms provided a vehicle for important themes, and Jenny's strange, awkward nature saves the visionary passage from sentimentalism. Her reference to the fact that she cannot imitate the children's glory in her art, even though she knows it so well, is the familiar complaint of the mystic and of the visionary poet.[65] As Kermode reminded us, Jacob's ladder is 'another bridge between chaos and spirit'; it is also the type to which Jesus refers in his promise to Nathaniel, the true Israelite, that hereafter he shall see 'heaven opened, and the angels of God ascending and descending upon the Son of man' (John 1.51). But Jenny was a 'little child', and saw like a child, her narrative conveying a classic liminal experience which occurred in the early morning, on the crepuscular margins of sleeping and waking, night and day, death and life. She describes her visions in the past tense, and the transfiguring effect of retelling them soon fades:

By degrees, as she progressed in this remembrance, the hand was raised, the late ecstatic look returned, and she became quite beautiful. Having so paused for a moment, silent, with a listening smile upon her face, she looked round and recalled herself.

The visionary or ecstatic has been 'dead to the world', an idea that Keats conveyed in the archaism 'all amort' (*The Eve of St Agnes*, 70). When Jenny's prodigal old son stumbles in, however, and she chastizes him, refusing to forgive him, the doll's dressmaker becomes 'a little quaint shrew; of the world, worldly; of the earth, earthy'. Often 'dragged down by hands that should have raised her up', she is also often 'misdirected when losing her way on the eternal road'. Thus the tensions in Jenny's life between the imaginative and the earthy, heavenly visions and sordid mundane reality, dramatize the larger conflicts in the novel as a whole.

Jenny is closely associated with her 'godmother' (another inversion, this time of gender and religion), Riah the Jew, who is as marginal a figure as Jenny, both socially and spiritually. Book the Third opens, for example, with Riah moving at his grave and measured pace through a fog-bound London which is 'divided in purpose between being visible and invisible, and so being wholly neither', towards the chambers of his employer, Fascination Fledgeby, where he sits down 'on the threshold' of the bedroom, awaiting his pagan master's pleasure. Earlier in the novel he has escorted a bemused Fledgeby up the stairs of Pubsey and Co., where he lives, to meet Jenny and Lizzie:

As he toiled on before, with his palm upon the stair-rail, and his long black skirt, a very gaberdine, overhanging each successive step, he might have been the leader in some pilgrimage of devotional ascent to a prophet's tomb. Not troubled by any such weak imagining, Fascination Fledgeby merely speculated on the time of life at which his beard had begun, and thought once more what a good 'un he was for the part.

Some final wooden steps conducted them, stooping under a low penthouse roof, to the house-top. Riah stood still, and, turning to his master, pointed out his guests.   (II.5)

The emergence of the beardless Fledgeby, and of Riah, whose long grey hair mingles with his beard, from under the low penthouse roof redraws one of Blake's best known engravings in the nineteenth century: 'Death's Door', a plate for Robert Blair's *The Grave* (1808, rpt. 1813; illustration 16). Blake suggests the spatial equivalent of the eternal present by synchronizing the movements of the stooping old body below, and the rising renewed body above a strong horizontal lintel. His strong reading of the lines by Blair that the plate illustrates – ''Tis but a Night, a long and moonless Night, / We make the Grave our Bed, and then are gone!' – erases their orthodox sense of temporal deferral. In Dickens's version, a venerable Jew, later described looking in his ancient dress like 'the ghost of a departed Time' (II.15), is accompanied by a despicable fledgeling of a man who cannot do the necessary 'imagining'. During the discussion on the roof-top, however, Jenny Wren describes Riah's previous emergence from below alone, before Fledgeby interrupted their

peace. She could almost be describing the Blake, although in her consecutive narrative a transformation is achieved within the single figure of
the Jew:

> 'Why it was only just now,' said the little creature, pointing at him, 'that I
> fancied I saw him come out of his grave! He toiled out at that low door so bent
> and worn, and then he took his breath and stood upright, and looked all round
> him at the sky, and the wind blew upon him, and his life down in the dark was
> over! – Till he was called back to life,' she added, looking round at Fledgeby
> with that lower look of sharpness. 'Why did you call him back?'

Jenny's inversions are in fact those of the Judaeo-Christian tradition,
challenging a materialist idea of 'life' and 'death'. Thus the unimagin-
ative Fledgeby's 'calling back' of the Jew to 'life' in the streets below
conforms to the dominant downward movement in the novel towards
spiritual death. Jenny's comment that 'such a chain' falls from you when
you escape from the streets where 'the people who are alive' are pitifully
'crying, and working, and calling to one another', recalls the enchained
Headstone, and his nocturnal bafflement in the labyrinth below.
Whereas from Riah's roof garden, a place of 'rest', you see 'the golden
arrows pointing at the mountains in the sky from which the wind comes,
and you feel as if you were dead'.

When Riah finally sees Fledgeby off the premises, he remounts the
stairs and 'looks above' to see Jenny

> looking down out of a Glory of her long bright radiant hair, and musically
> repeating to him, like a vision:
> 'Come up and be dead! Come up and be dead!'

As Riah re-enacted the Blakean transformation for Jenny in himself, so
Jenny now enacts for him the vision which sustained her in her pain as a
younger child. Later in the novel she is to make a casual ironic comment
to Riah about it being a pity his people 'ever got out of Egypt' (IV.9). Her
call to come up and be dead is more obscurely linked to the crossing of
the Red Sea as a type of baptism via parallels between the roof garden
episode and a difficult passage in the Revelation of St John the Divine
concerning the two witnesses. Here the sacked city of Jerusalem is described as metaphorically the same demonic city as the Sodom under the
Dead Sea and Egypt whose army is under the Red Sea:[66]

> And when they shall have finished their testimony, the beast that ascendeth
> out of the bottomless pit shall make war against them, and shall overcome
> them, and kill them.

And their dead bodies shall lie in the street of the great city, which spiritually is called Sodom and Egypt, where also our Lord was crucified.

. . .

And they heard a great voice from heaven saying unto them, Come up hither. And they ascended up to heaven in a cloud; and their enemies beheld them.

(Revelation 11.7–8, 12)

Scaled down to the domestic level of the premises of Pubsey and Co., the episode in *Our Mutual Friend* speaks of a death to the world which is not unlike baptism, but which transcends the church's exclusivity, parodied elsewhere in the novel in Mrs Frank Milvey's anxieties concerning Lizzie and her Jewish employers.

'Little Miss Peecher' is as narrow in her religious outlook as Frank Milvey's 'bright little wife' (II.10), upbraiding Mary Anne when she gives the despised Miss Hexam's Christian name as 'Lizzie', and commenting that it must be considered very doubtful whether there were 'any Lizzies in the early Christian Church' (II.11). In a novel which constantly plays with names, the pointed drawing together of three women's names associated with Christ's nativity – Mary, Anne, and Elizabeth – the last of whom was the mother of John the Baptist, hints at an important mediatory role for Lizzie, irrespective of her class and education. Her spirituality is reflected in her knowledge of the 'real world' which is not this world, and in her 'unselfish passion' for Eugene Wrayburn. It is her account of how she has 'never dreamed' of the possibility of Eugene's being anything to her 'on this earth' that 'enchains' Bella Wilfer (III.9). If Lizzie is associated with the imaginative or visionary side of Jenny Wren, Eugene Wrayburn is associated with the earthy or worldly side, and cannot respond to her spiritual discourse (II.2). In the chapter following the roof garden episode, he and Mortimer Lightwood also look down on people at street level, from their dismal second-floor chambers in the Temple. Himself 'buried alive in the back of his chair' at the beginning of the novel (I.2), Eugene now apes the burial service in his indolent game of dropping pellets of earth into the court below, one of which is aimed at the hat of Charley Hexam, who accompanies the tormented Bradley Headstone in 'the mazes of the law' (II.6). Eugene's preparation of two more pellets for the purpose of bringing them both 'down', however, confirms that, for all his antipathy to them, he is bound up in their and the novel's dominant downward movement.

In relation to this broad symbolic scheme, the river episodes at the beginning of Book the Fourth, 'A Turning', take on particular significance. Down at Plashwater Lock one˙ summer evening, Eugene Wrayburn in his skull rises 'like an apparition against the light', from the 'point of view' of the concealed and disguised Bradley Headstone; Eugene rises as from the grave (IV.1). The crisis for these antagonists, both of whom are in pursuit of Lizzie who works nearby, occurs on another evening when the light emphasizes margins and perspectives. Now, however, it is the boundary between earth and heaven that is foregrounded in a descriptive passage which speaks of plenitude and transcendence:

So, in the rosy evening, one might watch the ever-widening beauty of the landscape – beyond the newly-released workers wending home – beyond the silver river – beyond the deep green fields of corn, so prospering, that the loiterers in their narrow threads of pathway seemed to float immersed breast-high – beyond the hedgerows and the clumps of trees – beyond the windmills on the ridge – away to where the sky appeared to meet the earth, as if there were no immensity of space between mankind and Heaven. (IV.6)

This passage is reminiscent of scenes in works such as Southey's *A Vision of Judgment* (1821) and Pollok's *The Course of Time* (1827), in which the *krisis* of judgment or the last day is preceded by a quiet evening, a sign of millennial peace and unity, and a type of the cosmic pause which follows the opening of the seventh seal (Revelation 8.1).[67] It is on this quiet evening that Eugene has a rendezvous with Lizzie, who secretly loves him but threatens to emulate the doggedly independent Betty Higden if he insists on driving her away by his attentions. Her purity, and her expressions of love and suffering, make a deep impression on Eugene, who holds her 'almost as if she were sanctified to him by death', and kisses her once, 'almost as he might have kissed the dead'. He walks on alone beside the river, pondering his dilemma and having 'wicked' thoughts:

'Out of the question to marry her,' said Eugene, 'and out of the question to leave her. The crisis!'
    He had sauntered far enough. Before turning to retrace his steps, he stopped upon the margin, to look down at the reflected night. In an instant, with a dreadful crash, the reflected night turned crooked, flames shot jaggedly across the air, and the moon and stars came bursting from the sky.

The Greek *krisis* means both separation and judgment.[68] Headstone in his murderous assault is a demonic judge, usurping the divine role with the bloody hand of the avenger, and leaving Eugene Wrayburn hovering on the margin between life and death, as he struggles for air in the water. Lizzie hurries to help the unknown victim, as earlier she hurried to succour Betty Higden:

> Now, merciful Heaven be thanked for that old time, and grant, O Blessed Lord, that through thy wonderful workings it may turn to good at last! To whomsoever the drifting face belongs, be it man's or woman's, help my humble hands, Lord God, to raise it from death and restore it to some one to whom it must be dear!

In the first sentence quoted here she echoes the prayer of committal in the burial service – 'in sure and certain hope of the Resurrection to eternal life, through our Lord Jesus Christ; who shall change our vile body, that it may be like unto his glorious body, according to the mighty working, whereby he is able to subdue all things to himself' – but with reference to her *own past life* rather than the drowning man's present danger: may her former vile business with her father now be made glorious in a saving act. As in the Harmon plot, the emphasis falls upon the 'redeeming actions of the world', upon mediation through human agency:

And grant, O Blessed Lord God, that through poor me he may be raised from death, and preserved to some one else to whom he may be dear one day, though never dearer than to me!

When she recognizes the person in the water, which is streaked with blood, she cries out, but then acts 'as if possessed by supernatural spirit or strength'. A minister of the sacrament of baptism ('O merciful God, grant that the old Adam in this Child may be so buried, that the new man may be raised up in him'), she is also a minister of healing – a Good Samaritan in 'binding up' Eugene's wounds, and getting him to his 'inn', the nearest place of 'succour'.

What would have been Eugene's deathbed scene, if Dickens had kept to his original plan, draws together a number of strands I have been considering in the Wrayburn plot. Eugene asks Jenny Wren whether she has seen the children, for example – a 'pretty fancy' – and Mortimer Lightwood, who exchanges declarations of love with his friend, turns to Jenny when Eugene is unconscious, 'as if she were an interpreter between this sentient world and the insensible man' (IV.10). The change that the 'crisis' has induced in Eugene, now the passive sufferer entirely dependent on the ministrations of others, is towards a Christlike forgiveness of his attacker: 'Don't think of avenging me', he tells his devoted friend. When Frank Milvey sets off for the inn, Bradley Headstone is appalled to discover that he is going to 'perform the marriage service at [Lizzie's] wedding', and not the burial service that would have been his third in the novel (IV.11). The connection between the two services, made so often earlier in the novel, is now made explicit:

> Then, they all stood around the bed, and Mr Milvey, opening his book, began the service; so rarely associated with the shadow of death; so inseparable in the mind from a flush of life and gaiety and hope and health and joy. Bella thought how different from her own sunny little wedding, and wept.

Like John Harmon's after his wedding, Eugene's name is all important to him, as he asks Lizzie to call him back from unconsciousness by calling his name. The penultimate number of the novel ends with his three times using the word 'hope', but feeling that in all conscience he 'ought to die'. He lives to share something of Jenny Wren's condition, the doctors telling him that 'he might not be much disfigured by-and-by' (IV.16), like Rochester in *Jane Eyre*. One of the prayers in the Public Baptism of Infants begins, 'Grant that all carnal affections may die in him, and that all things belonging to the Spirit may live and grow in him.' Whereas the carnal affections do not die in Bradley Headstone, the Cain of the novel, the things belonging to the spirit live and grow in Eugene Wrayburn, through the mediation not only of Lizzie, but also of his loving friends.

In form, subject-matter, and tone, *In Memoriam* and *Our Mutual Friend* could hardly be more different Victorian texts. One only has to place the 'A.H.H.' of the poem alongside any of Dickens's male characters to see this. Even in terms of Christian eschatology, Dickens's idea of heaven is more static than Tennyson's; and whereas the poet emphasizes the incarnation in his treatment of the subject, the novelist stresses the relationship between resurrection and baptism. When *In Memoriam* and *Our Mutual Friend* are placed alongside each other, however, similarities between them prove to be as revealing as their more obvious differences. Both end in marriage, and in a celebration of love that has grown, of light that has come out of darkness. Both affirm the hope of a future life in Christ. Both identify signs of transcendence within the horizon of the present, particularly in the development through love of special individuals in a fallen world, and their ability to influence the lot of others for good. Both are Johannine in their theology and symbolism, and reflect a longing for a broader Christianity that can accommodate the findings of science. Both emphasize the importance of touch at the precise point at which language breaks down.

Above all, however, as I have tried to show in the last two chapters, Tennyson and Dickens both sympathized with Anglican Broad Church opinion on most of the major doctrinal issues of the day, and grounded their writing on the subject of death and the future life in *In Memoriam* and *Our Mutual Friend* on the authority of the heart and a liberal interpretation of scripture. I now turn, by way of contrast, to Newman and Hopkins, both Roman Catholic priests writing for English Catholics, who based their treatments of purgatory and martyrdom in *The Dream of Gerontius* and *The Wreck of the Deutschland* on the authority and theology of the church to which they had converted.

CHAPTER 7

❧

Newman, *The Dream of Gerontius*

After *In Memoriam*, Newman's *The Dream of Gerontius* (1865) was the best known and most frequently discussed literary work on the subject of death and the future life to be published during the Victorian Age. Both works were welcomed by readers and critics as helpful, and specifically hopeful, religious poetry, and it is possible to discern similarities between them, and between their authors. For example, Newman called the incarnation 'the central aspect of Christianity';[1] he was more indebted to Dante than is generally recognized; his emphasis upon feeling and the human heart reflected a sensibility shaped by the Romantic intellectual and cultural tradition of the early nineteenth century; and his treatment of psychological pain was highly emotional. Even with respect to these similarities, however, it is the contrasts between the two writers' minds that are striking. In following his statement on the centrality of the incarnation with the caveat that 'one aspect of Revelation must not be allowed to exclude or to obscure another', Newman could have pointed to *In Memoriam* as an example. Whereas Tennyson and his fellow Apostles regarded Dante as the greatest poet of sacred and profane love, as well as Christian hope, Newman's debt was more specifically doctrinal and liturgical. In both the *Purgatorio* and the *Dream*, which share common sources in patristic theology, purgatory is primarily a place of sanctification rather than satisfaction, and an antechamber to heaven; and Dante's use of hymns and the liturgy, marking the transitions between different stages of his journey through purgatory with Virgil as his guide, seems to have influenced Newman in his organization of the *Dream*. Although the dramatic tension in the *Dream* springs from feeling, the work's dramatic form is inherently less personal than Tennyson's lyrics, and expressions of psychological pain become generalized to the point of typicality. For Gerontius that pain includes the fear of eternal punishment, described by Newman as the 'turning point between Christianity and pantheism': 'it is the critical doctrine', he wrote, 'you can't get rid of it – it is the very characteristic of Christianity'.[2] For Tennyson the cardinal point of Christianity was 'the Life after Death'.

Behind these contrasts lies a fundamental difference between the two writers' views on religious authority. For Tennyson, the imaginative project of poetry is grounded in the authority of feeling rather than in external scriptural authority. Newman, on the other hand, writes from within a faith which, while retaining (on his argument) the possibility of independence of mind for the believer, rests on the authority of the Roman Catholic Church, to which the believer willingly submits. In 1865, the year of the *Dream*, the second edition of the *Apologia Pro Vita Sua* included a note on liberalism, written in response to a request for clarification. Newman's position was diametrically opposed to that of the Oxford liberals against whom his comments had been directed, but his words of explanation in the note were equally applicable to some of the Broad Churchmen who looked to Tennyson as their laureate:

Liberalism then is the mistake of subjecting to human judgment those revealed doctrines which are in their nature beyond and independent of it, and of claiming to determine on intrinsic grounds the truth and values of propositions which rest for their reception simply on the external authority of the Divine Word.[3]

Indeed, the ninth liberal proposition which Newman 'earnestly denounced and abjured' could be applied specifically to Tennyson on the Revised Version: 'There is a right of Private Judgment: that is, there is no existing authority on earth competent to interfere with the liberty of individuals in reasoning and judging for themselves about the Bible and its contents, as they severally please.'[4]

Tennyson's and Newman's sharply contrasting ideas on authority are reflected in the formal differences between *In Memoriam* and the *Dream*. Mediated through the unifying 'I' of the lyrist, *In Memoriam*'s short swallow-flights of song record the heart's events mainly within the limits of this-worldly experience. With its insistent iambic pulse, the poem registers past emotion and future hope in chronological time, recording memories of Hallam from the past and anticipating reunion with him in the future, recalling the birth of Christ and anticipating the Christ that is to be. Even the climactic moment of mystical union in lyric 95 – the major turning-point in the poem – is narrated as a past event, recorded and placed in time, and it is precisely because the poem's structure and development are largely horizontal that its few excursions

into the verticality of vision or spiritual crisis are foregrounded as privileged moments. In contrast, the unique qualities, as well as the limitations, of the *Dream* as a work of devotional literature are closely
associated with its heavy reliance on the Roman rite and scripture, and
the authority of the church. In Newman's verse drama, the immediacy of
a form which functions in what I have called the locutionary present is
exploited in ways which recall the origins of medieval drama in ritual
and liturgy. For the drama unfolds not only in the horizontal dimension
of chronological time, via Gerontius's journey through death and judgment, but also in the vertical dimension of the eternal present, or what
Newman himself called the 'eternal now', in which a larger divine providential scheme for mankind is revealed.

Newman's appeal to the authority of the church is perhaps most
obvious in his use of the Roman rite of the 'Commendation of the Soul'
in the first part of the *Dream*, where the journey motif in the horizontal
intersects with the vertical order of the heavenly hierarchy established in
the Litany. In contrast to *In Memoriam* and the indeterminacy of its
intertextual relations, the authoritative words of the *Rituale Romanum*
are interpolated in Newman's text, in substantial passages of translation
from the Latin. The sense of the eternal present evoked in these prayers
is realized dramatically in later sections through the synchronic effects of
parallelism and repetition, so that although no detailed description is
given of the purgatory that the Soul is finally to enter, the spiritual
reality of purgatory is explored throughout, and always in relation to
the resurrection hope. In terms of scriptural authority, the theological
basis of Newman's treatment of Gerontius's death struggle, or 'agony',
and the Soul's approaching purgatory, is Christ's 'double agony', and
most tellingly the Agony in the Garden, where an angel ministers to him
(Luke 22.43). Angels not only figure prominently in the *Dream* and its
theology, but also, I shall argue, provide the kinds of perspective from
which the story of the salvation of mankind, and of Gerontius as Everyman, can be told, and the nature of divine judgment and eternal life
revealed. One of Newman's most significant statements on the mysteries
and sacraments of the church, where he relates these to the limits of
language and cognition, is immediately followed in the *Apologia* by his
description of his angelology:

The visible world still remains without its divine interpretation; Holy Church in
her sacraments and her hierarchical appointments, will remain, even to the end
of the world, after all but a symbol of those heavenly facts which fill eternity.

Her mysteries are but the expressions in human language of truths to which the human mind is unequal. It is evident how much there was in all this in correspondence with the thoughts which had attracted me when I was young, and with the doctrine which I have already associated with [Butler's] Analogy and the Christian Year.

It was, I suppose, to the Alexandrian school and to the early Church, that I owe in particular what I definitely held about the Angels. I viewed them, not only as the ministers employed by the Creator in the Jewish and Christian dispensations, as we find on the face of Scripture, but as carrying on, as Scripture also implies, the Economy of the Visible World. I considered them as the real causes of motion, light, and life . . .[5]

The juxtaposition is revealing, for one of the major roles of the angels in the 'unseen world' to which Newman often refers is to say, or sing, that which fallen man cannot express.

With its numerous musical references, Newman's verse drama seems almost to invite a musical setting, and today the work is known principally through Elgar's oratorio of 1900, perhaps the greatest single piece of Victorian music. Having discussed Newman's treatment of Gerontius's 'agony' and the role of the angels in the *Dream* (from which I shall quote quite extensively, as it is the least familiar of the works examined in detail in this study), I will consider how Elgar interpreted the original work, extending Newman's limited technical range and augmenting his dramatic effects. First, however, I must consider Newman's theology in relation to the history of purgatory. For the literary and musical techniques to which I have referred are closely related to the way in which the *Dream* continues, in Geoffrey Rowell's words, 'the traditional split in Western theology between individual and cosmic eschatology, and is thus intensely individualist, following the pattern which had telescoped the "Day of Judgment" into the "day of death"'.[6]

PURGATORY: 'THE GOLDEN PRISON'

The doctrines upon which nineteenth-century debates on judgment and the intermediate state turned originated in the process of eschatological reinterpretation in the early church, in the light of the continuing delay of the *parousia*. Questions that originally arose from the attempt to accommodate belief in a particular judgment immediately after death within a traditional Jewish apocalyptic which was grounded in a universal last judgment continued to exercise nineteenth-century apologists:

Where were the dead until the last day? In what condition? Were they conscious or unconscious?[7]

The development of belief in purgatorial punishment after the particular judgment, beginning with the third-century Greek Fathers, St Clement of Alexandria and Origen, and later continuing with St Augustine and St Gregory the Great, is traced in detail by Jacques Le Goff, who goes on to examine the general acceptance of belief in purgatory in the late twelfth century.[8] In the thirteenth century, he argues, purgatory was to be one of the main reasons for the 'dramatization of the moment of death'.[9] Although it presented the prospect of pain, in both *poena sensus* and *poena damni*, purgatory was *hope*, and the fact that souls in purgatory were considered to be members of the church militant reflects a strong sense of continuity between pre- and post-mortem existence.[10] Other kinds of continuity were formalized in the teachings and practices of the medieval church. There was, for example, a close relationship between commutation in the practice of the sacrament of penance and the granting of indulgences in relation to purgatory. Abuses associated with the administration of indulgences in subsequent centuries were a major contributory factor in the Reformation, of course, although in its turn the Reformers' rejection of purgatory created further difficulties for later Protestant theologians.[11]

It is worth pausing here, however, to consider the relation between penance in this life and purgatory in the next, and particularly Dante's treatment of the subject in the *Purgatorio*. Medieval 'penitentiaries' offered guidance concerning the severity and duration of penalties. St Peter Damian, for example, an exemplary doctor of the church in the eleventh century who was later admired by Dante, and whose hymn *De die mortis rythmus* has been proposed as a source of Newman's *Dream*,[12] drew up, with others, mechanical tables of the equivalents for purgatorial penance: one day's penance in purgatory was equivalent to twenty strokes on the hand, or the recitation of fifty psalms; one year's penance might be redeemed by three thousand strokes, if accompanied by the recitation of psalms; and so on.[13] Edward Moore, the leading English Dante scholar of his generation, stated in 1899 that 'not only did Dante in his conception of Purgatory rise far above the beliefs and practice of his age generally, but also no less remarkably above those of some whom the Church has "delighted to honour" by canonization', including Peter Damian.[14] While recognizing the church's teaching that purgatory was both for purification and satisfaction, Dante went against normal practice in emphasizing the former and keeping the latter in the background.[15] Moore went on to illustrate this through an important point, hardly noted before, concerning the symbolism of the three steps of the gate of purgatory in canto IX.94–106. Whereas scholastic writers traditionally gave the three steps in the sacrament of penance as contrition, confession, and *satisfaction*, the white marble of Dante's first step clearly represents candid confession, the dark stone of the second step contrition, and the flaming red porphyry of the third, burning *love*, so that satisfaction is associated 'more with the inward condition of heart than with outward acts'.[16] Tennyson was fond of quoting the inscription over the gates of hell in the *Inferno*, as if, in the words of his son, 'they were a kind of unconscious confession by Dante that Love must conquer at the last'.[17] In contrast, Newman in the *Dream* writes, like Dante, of the kind of love which demands both self-surrender and penance, and of sanctification in a purgatory which is an inward and spiritual reality.[18]

While Tennyson, Hallam, and other Cambridge Apostles of the late 1820s were studying Dante, Newman in his Oxford sermons was laying the foundations upon which his contributions to the Oxford Movement, and later to Roman Catholic thought, were to be based. He turned to the fathers as his authorities, emphasized the reality of the 'unseen world' of angels and principalities, taught that personal holiness is necessary for future blessedness, and attacked the secularization and liberalism of his own age. Thus began a critique of post-Reformation tendencies in the West away from the very attitudes, such as *contemptus mundi*, that had made the development of the doctrine of purgatory possible. Later, in his controversial Tract 90 (1841), he carefully distinguished between the 'Romish doctrine concerning purgatory', described in article XXII of the Church of England as a 'fond thing', and 'Primitive doctrines', none of which, on his argument, is condemned in the article. These included a doctrine that 'none will fail under it who are built upon the right foundation', and one in which

the cleansing, though a punishment, was but a *poena damni*, not a *poena sensus*; not a positive sensible infliction, much less the torment of fire, but the absence of God's presence. And another purgatory is that in which the cleansing is but a progressive sanctification, and has no pain at all.[19]

None of these primitive doctrines was advocated by Newman himself, still a leading force in the Oxford Movement, but the way had been cleared for his acceptance of Catholic teaching on purgatory when he was received into the Church of Rome in 1845.

Newman included a short section on purgatory in his *Essay on the Development of Christian Doctrine*, which was already going through the press when he finally decided to convert. Here he touches upon Clement of Alexandria's teaching on post-mortem purification by a 'discriminating fire'; St Perpetua's account of her prayers for her brother, who died at the age of seven, being answered in a vision of his translation from his 'place of punishment'; and St Cyril's belief in the efficacy of prayers in the eucharist service for the faithful departed.[20] He also cites Cardinal Fisher's argument concerning the development of purgatory out of earlier points of faith: namely, that belief in purgatory was not so necessary in the early church as it was fifteen hundred years later, because 'love so burned, that every one was ready to meet death for Christ', and 'crimes were rare, and such as occurred were avenged by the great severity of the Canons'.[21]

Secular models of crime and punishment help to clarify the differences between purgatory and the other three main views of eschatology outlined by F. W. Farrar in the 1870s.[22] Whereas conditionalists, for example, stood for the equivalent of capital punishment in their argument that a sentence of death passed on man at the fall had been mercifully withheld, and that for all who did not believe in Christ, death was annihilation, those who believed in purgatory – in Farrar's words, 'a state wherein those souls are detained and punished which are capable of being purified' – stood for penal servitude. In the *Essay on Development*, Newman quotes from a letter of St Cyprian which he had previously cited in Tract 79:

It is one thing to stand for pardon, another to arrive at glory; one to be sent to prison (*missum in carcerem*) and not to go out till the last farthing be paid [Matthew 5.25–6], another to receive at once the reward of faith and virtue; one thing to be tormented for sin in long pain, and so to be cleansed and purged a long while by fire (*purgari diu igne*), another to be washed from all sin in martyrdom; one thing, in short, to wait for the Lord's sentence in the Day of Judgment, another at once to be crowned by Him.[23]

As Newman commented in Tract 79, the words *missum in carcarem* and *purgari diu igne* 'seem to go beyond any mere ecclesiastical, though virtually divine censure'.

Geoffrey Rowell argues that in contrast to Catholics brought up in the Continental tradition of Liguorian devotion, who spoke of the penal fires of purgatory, the more restrained English Catholics, like Newman, wished to emphasize a 'purificatory rather than a penal understanding of purgatory', and frequently referred to St Catherine of Genoa.[24] St Catherine's writings on purgation and purgatory certainly anticipate Newman's, and particularly in the spirituality which they reflect, although he knew only the broad drift of her teaching before he wrote the *Dream*. Both describe purgatory as a prison. In *Purgation and Purgatory* we find:

the soul
does not leave its prison or seek to do so
until God has done all that is necessary.
Its only pain
would be in being excluded from His ordinance,
which above all things it finds just and merciful.
And she [Catherine] would add:
All this I saw as clearly as if I touched them,
but I cannot find the words to express them.
These things that I speak about work within me
in secret and with great power.
The prison in which I seem to be
is the world, the body its bonds;
and they weigh upon the lesser me within,
which is impeded from making its way to its true end.[25]

To describe purgatory as a prison was commonplace for nineteenth-century Roman Catholics. Newman's Oxford friend, Father H. J. Coleridge, SJ, for example, who as editor of *The Month* first published the *Dream*, himself wrote a book of 'Thoughts on the Catholic Doctrine of Purgatory' entitled *The Prisoners of the King* (1878).[26] It is Newman's emphasis upon 'the *willing* agony', however, which confirms the parallel with St Catherine (as well as with Dante, incidentally). These words are taken from a Newman poem of 1853, the title of which also provides the title for this section. 'The Golden Prison' reveals that some of Newman's main ideas on purgatory were already worked out at least twelve years before he wrote the *Dream*.[27] Like St Catherine, he thought of the prison of purgatory as an inward and spiritual reality, golden because it is an antechamber to heaven. Towards the end of the *Dream*, the Angel leads the Soul through the gates of purgatory:

Now let the golden prison ope its gates,
Making sweet music, as each fold revolves
Upon its ready hinge. And ye, great powers,
Angels of Purgatory, receive from me
My charge, a precious soul, until the day,
When, from all bond and forfeiture released,
I shall reclaim it for the courts of light.   (6)[28]

Some years before his conversion, Newman had distinguished
between 'the actual state of belief and of usage in the countries which
were in communion with the Roman church, and her formal dogmas'.
The example he provides is revealing: that although 'sensible pain' in
purgatory was the tradition of the Latin Church, and he had seen 'the
pictures of souls in flames in the streets of Naples', it was not 'implied in
the Tridentine decree upon Purgatory'.[29] What Newman and St
Catherine have most in common, however, is their sense of purgatory as
a living reality, fulfilled in the 'unseen world', but begun in the here-and-
now. Newman's theory of development generally reflects in its examples
a movement from the more secular to the more religious, whether in the
broad sweep of human history or in personal experience. One such
argument is particularly germane to the subject under discussion,
namely that 'the doctrine of a Judge and Judgment to come is a development of the phenomenon of conscience'.[30] Similarly, in his sermons he
constantly reminded his congregations of the relationship between
present holiness and future blessedness, and nowhere more forcibly than
in the sermon of that title on Hebrews 12.14:

If holiness be not merely the doing a certain number of good actions, but is an
inward character which follows, under God's grace, from doing them, how far
distant from that holiness are the multitude of men! . . . It follows at once, even
though Scripture did not plainly tell us so, that no one is able to prepare himself
for heaven, that is, make himself holy, in a short time . . .

. . . To obtain the gift of holiness is the work of *a life*. No man will ever be
perfect here, so sinful is our nature.[31]

Newman's emphasis upon personal holiness, reflected in the Anglican
Oxford sermons, also influenced his choice of St Philip Neri as his
patron, after his conversion. For St Philip has been described as a 'new
renaissance man', who 'assisted in the process of transmuting a mere
individualism into personal responsibility'.[32] While criticizing the

'intensely individualistic' nature of the *Dream*, in that it continued the traditional split between individual and cosmic eschatology, Rowell argues that 'insofar as it removed eschatology from mechanical inter-pretations into the realm of *the personal relationship between man and God* it spoke powerfully to the needs of the nineteenth century, and enabled many Protestants troubled about eschatology to consider the possibility of purgatory' (my emphasis).[33] The drama of the *Dream* is the drama of that relationship.

THE POEM: 'THE DOUBLE AGONY'

In describing the long and often painful history of his religious opinions in the *Apologia*, Newman used two analogies which were to recur in the *Dream*: the journey and the deathbed. He records in a famous passage that for years he must have had a latent notion that 'in some sense or other [he] was on journey'.[34] In a memorandum of 1829, for example, he had described himself in his rooms in Oriel: 'slowly advancing &c. and led on by God's hand blindly, not knowing whither He is taking me'. This memorandum contains the seed not only of 'Lead, kindly light', written in 1833 and described by Wilfrid Ward in 1912 as 'perhaps the most popular modern hymn in the language',[35] but also of the passage in the *Dream* in which the Soul asks the Angel why he is blind (4). At the beginning of the next chapter of the *Apologia*, Newman develops the second analogy:

From the end of 1841, I was on my death-bed, as regards my membership with the Anglican Church, though at the time I became aware of it only by degrees . . . A death-bed has scarcely a history; it is a tedious decline, with seasons of rallying and seasons of falling back; and since the end is foreseen, or what is called a matter of time, it has little interest for the reader, especially if he has a kind heart.[36]

Whereas in the *Apologia* both analogies emphasize the long-drawn-out nature of Newman's severance from the Church of England, they serve a strikingly different purpose in the *Dream*, which was written only a year later. The journey towards purgatory portrayed in sections 2–7 is more like that which Newman imagined in a sermon: it would leave a soul 'breathless' before the judgment seat of Christ.[37] The first section of the poem shares few of the usual characteristics of Victorian deathbed scenes: here are no problems of communication or interpretation, and no discussion concerning reunion with friends and relations in heaven. Rather, it reflects the Roman Catholic tradition (related to the general acceptance of the doctrine of purgatory six or seven centuries earlier) of dramatizing the moment of death and placing it in relation to moments of rescue or salvation in biblical and Church history.

For Gerontius is already close to death in the poem's opening lines:

> Jesu, Maria – I am near to death,
>   And Thou art calling me; I know it now.
> Not by the token of this faltering breath,
>   This chill at heart, this dampness on my brow, –
> (Jesu, have mercy! Mary, pray for me!)
>   'Tis this new feeling, never felt before,
> (Be with me, Lord, in my extremity!)
>   That I am going, that I am no more.   (1)

The urgency of Gerontius's alternating personal statements and formal petitions underlines the contrast between his fallen, and thus frail humanity, and the power of Christ as both saviour and judge, with Mary, mother of God, as mediator between God and man. His main fear, that in death he might drop 'Into that shapeless, scopeless, blank abyss, / That utter nothingness, of which [he] came', reflects his total dependence in death upon the God who gave him life, and he asks his friends around his deathbed to pray for him. The sentiments, like the scene itself, were familiar to Roman Catholics, and were formalized in the 'Prayers for a Happy Death', for example:

When my imagination shall be sunk in an abyss of anguish . . .
R/   Merciful Jesus, have mercy on me.

When my friends and relatives, encircling my bed, shall be moved with compassion for me, and invoke thy clemency in my behalf,

R/   Merciful Jesus, have mercy on me.[38]

The prayers of the Assistants and the Priest, however, are drawn from the 'Commendation of a Departing Soul' in the Ritual.[39] In his vulnerability and weakness, Gerontius's request to his friends ('pray for me') is immediately answered in their recitation of the Kyrie and the Litany ('pray for him'):

ASSISTANTS

Kyrie eleïson, Christe eleïson, Kyrie eleïson.
Holy Mary, pray for him.
All holy Angels, pray for him.
Choirs of the righteous, pray for him.
Holy Abraham, pray for him.
St. John Baptist, St. Joseph, pray for him.
St. Peter, St. Paul, St. Andrew, St. John,
All Apostles, all Evangelists, pray for him . . .

Newman's several omissions from the Litany, including holy Abel, all holy Patriarchs and Prophets, and several saints, allow him to compress the rite without sacrificing its massive sense of spiritual support through the Communion of Saints and a sense of a gathered Church Triumphant, together with 'All holy Angels', who have a position of eminence in the Litany.

The dramatic tension of the opening section lies not only in Gerontius's attempt to rouse himself, to 'play the man' and 'use well the interval', but in the very real danger of his eternal damnation:

ASSISTANTS

Be merciful, be gracious; spare him, Lord.
Be merciful, be gracious; Lord, deliver him.
From the sins that are past;
    From Thy frown and Thine ire;
        From the perils of dying;
        From any complying
        With sin, or denying
        His God, or relying
    On self, at the last;
        From the nethermost fire . . .

Christ gave himself utterly to his tormentors in order to bring salvation to mankind, and Roman Catholic meditations upon death mark each stage of his passion, from the agony in the garden to the burial in the sepulchre. In order to achieve salvation, Gerontius must throw himself utterly upon the mercy of Christ and the ministration of his church, and Newman's treatment of the 'agony', or death-struggle, in Part I strongly emphasizes this.

After he has affirmed his faith in the Sanctus and the Creed, Gerontius finds that he 'can no more', for in his dying state he is overtaken by 'That sense of ruin, which is worse than pain' and a spiritual vertigo which anticipates Hopkins's terrible sonnets ('as though I bent / Over the dizzy brink . . .'). He is finally driven to despair through an intimation of evil which is later to be realized in the encounter with the Demons (4), and cries out,

> O Jesu, help! pray for me, Mary, pray!
> Some Angel, Jesu! such as came to Thee
> In Thine own agony . . .
> Mary, pray for me. Joseph, pray for me. Mary, pray for me.

> ASSISTANTS
>
> Rescue him, O Lord, in this his evil hour,
> As of old so many by Thy gracious power: –
>   (Amen.)
> Enoch and Elias from the common doom;
>   (Amen.)
> Noe from the waters in a saving home; (Amen.) . . .

The Assistants' 'Libera, Domine', from the Ritual, is based on Hebrews 11, which refers to God's rescue of his chosen people from bodily destruction or danger, mainly in the Old Testament, but including examples from the Apocrypha and the Acts of the Apostles ('And the two Apostles from their prison-thrall'). As we will see, Gerontius's reference in his deepest despair to the Angel of the Agony is of great structural and theological significance.[40] Its further local effect, however, is to alert the reader to the fact that in six of the cases cited in Hebrews – those of Isaac, Lot, Moses, Daniel, the 'Children Three' of Daniel 3, and the imprisoned apostles – angels, or the angel of the Lord, act as God's mediators and agents of salvation.

The angels have been described as taking a 'dynamic part' in the processes of salvation history as understood in the early church,[41] and Newman lays great stress upon this in the *Dream*. As Gerontius dies, repeating, as in the Ritual, Christ's last words in agony on the cross ('Into Thy hands, / O Lord, into Thy hands'), the Priest follows the rubric, which in the original Latin reads, '*Deinde, cum in* agone *sui exitus anima anxiatur, dicantur sequentes Orationes*' (my emphasis):

> Proficiscere, anima Christiana, de hoc mundo!
> Go forth upon thy journey, Christian soul!
> Go from this world! Go, in the name of God

The Omnipotent Father, who created thee! . . .

Go, in the name
Of Angels and Archangels; in the name
Of Thrones and Dominations; in the name
Of Princedoms and of Powers; and in the name
Of Cherubim and Seraphim, go forth! . . .

The ministry of the angels in the unseen world (as messengers, mediators, and worshippers), upon which the Roman rite places considerable emphasis, is analogous to that of the clergy in this world. Appropriately, then, the first section of the *Dream* ends with the Priest, on this side of eternity, completing Gerontius's break with the world, and handing him over to the ministration of the angels in the next.

The Profiscere, with its emphasis upon continuing the journey, crossing the barrier of death, and, eventually finding a place 'in peace', marks the first major point of transition in the poem, at the end of its opening section. A series of other transitions follow on the horizontal axis of the Soul's spiritual journey, each of which is distinguished by its different attendant angels. Following a period of apparent solitude, the Soul encounters his Guardian Angel (2), who leads him through, successively, the gate of the House of Judgment (5), the stairs and gate of the Presence-chamber (5), and the particular judgment (6), and finally into the 'penal waters' of purgatory itself (7). The last words of the Angel at the end of the poem take up the theme of the Soul's first words after death ('I went to sleep; and now I am refresh'd', 2):

Farewell, but not for ever! brother dear,
  Be brave and patient on thy bed of sorrow;
Swiftly shall pass thy night of trial here,
  And I will come and wake thee on the morrow.[42]

Thus the traditional analogy of death as sleep, here applied to purgatory, suggests a future reawakening to make the final journey beyond purgatory and the last judgment which, as the Angel informs the Soul, is 'rehearsed' in the particular judgment and in the 'presage' of judgment which the Soul senses immediately after death (3).

That the Soul will finally enter heaven is certain from the Angel's opening hymn ('Alleluia, / And saved is he', 2), for there can be no postmortem probation in Roman Catholic theology. That he must first

undergo the willing agony of purgatory is equally certain, although its
nature and duration are not dwelt upon. Rather, they are conveyed
through the Soul's spiritual experience in the liminal phase between
death and purgatory, and the agony of the particular judgment with
which it concludes. Gerontius asks the Angel why he now has no fear of
meeting the Judge, whereas in life he did:

> ANGEL
>
> It is because
> Then thou didst fear, that now thou dost not fear,
> Thou hast forestall'd the agony, and so
> For thee the bitterness of death is past.
> Also, because already in thy soul
> The judgment is begun.   (3)

Meanwhile the 'calm and joy' in his soul is 'first-fruit' of his
'recompense', and 'heaven begun'.

In focusing upon this phase in the spiritual journey of an individual
soul, Newman can use angelic narratives to unfold the (horizontal)
salvation history of mankind, from the War in Heaven to the last judgment, within the (vertical) eternal now of personal judgment. In
emphasizing the relativity of the inward and spiritual judgment of
individual souls in the 'immaterial world', where everyone is 'standard
of his own chronology',[43] he also frees the doctrine of purgatory from its
earthly, chronological associations, as in the obsessive calculation of
indulgences, for example. To convey, however, a sense of that eternal
now in words which move only in time, he has to construct a time
scheme of some kind in his portrayal of the unseen world. Thus immediately after waking from the sleep of death, the Soul intimates that he can
still hear the Priest saying the Subvenite (2) – a prayer in the Ritual to be
read when the soul has left the body. Later the Angel explains that
although the Soul is 'hurrying to the Just and Holy Judge' with
'extremest speed', he is scarcely 'disembodied' yet, and the Priest and
Assistants have 'scarcely yet' begun the Subvenite (3). Indeed, the
Subvenite is still being said around Gerontius's bed when the Soul goes
before his Judge towards the end of the poem (6). As the Angel says,
'spirits and men by different standards mete / The less and greater in the
flow of time'.[44]

More central, however, to the structure and meaning of the *Dream* is

Newman's attempt to convey a sense of the eternal now within the limits of language. In the first section of the poem, this is adumbrated in the parallelism of the Litany, whereby the anaphoric listing of saints, Old Testament patriarchs, and orders of angels, has the effect of telescoping long historical sequences into a single and present reality. In later sections, the perspective of the angels, to which we have privileged access through the convention of the spiritual journey, allows us to see what in this-worldly terms are only separate historical events also ordered in a kind of vertical series, which suggests coexistence in the present of eternal life with God. A key example is the Angel's reference to St Francis's miraculous stigmata in order to describe the combination of agony and joy which is to characterize the Soul's particular judgment. Like the angel who appeared to St Francis, he admonishes and encourages the Soul to prepare for that which God will give and do to him:[45]

> and, from the agony
> Which thrill'd through body and soul in that embrace,
> Learn that the flame of the Everlasting Love
> Doth burn ere it transform . . .
> (4)

So familiar is the story of St Francis's stigmata to Roman Catholics that he does not need to be named: the Angel refers to him as 'a mortal, who is now above / In the mid glory'. Both inheritor (of Christ's agony on the cross) and precursor (of the Soul's agony in the particular judgment), St Francis *is* in the mid glory. This sense of the eternal now which subsumes or transcends time is augmented when, with anticipation heightening as the Soul and the Angel pass into the House of Judgment, the First Choir of Angelicals sing the first verses of 'Praise to the Holiest in the height', celebrating Christ's past battle against sin in the world. As the personal is related to the universal, and the 'future' to the 'past', the Choir sing of the God who *is* 'Most sure in all his ways'.

Having passed the gate of the House of Judgment, the Soul and the Angel hear the Second Choir of Angelicals take up the hymn of praise. A sense of continual worship is conveyed through the repetition of the first verse ('Praise to the Holiest in the height'), whereas the verses that follow develop the narrative of the First Choir by describing the fall of man, who 'once had Angels for his friend' (5). The Third Choir brings man's salvation history up to the present of the Soul's own spiritual journey, and, as the Angel explains to him, sing of his 'approaching agony':

> Yet still between that earth and heaven –
>   His journey and his goal –
> A double agony awaits
>   His body and his soul.
>
> A double debt he has to pay –
>   The forfeit of his sins:
> The chill of death is past, and now
>   The penance-fire begins.

The Angel's further explanation brings us to the heart of Newman's conception of purgatory as the state which all who have seen the 'pensive eyes' of Christ at the particular judgment enter willingly:

>   for, though
> Now sinless, thou wilt feel that thou hast sinn'd,
> As never thou didst feel; and wilt desire
> To slink away, and hide thee from His sight:
> And yet wilt have a longing aye to dwell
> Within the beauty of His countenance.
> And these two pains, so counter and so keen, –
> The longing for Him, when thou seest Him not;
> The shame of self at thought of seeing Him, –
> Will be thy veriest, sharpest purgatory.

As the momentum of the verse drama increases, and the Soul's 'double agony' approaches, the two related themes which I have been tracing are foregrounded even more prominently as the work's major subjects of theological reference and spiritual meditation: Christ's agony in the garden and the ministry of the angels. Newman was never more aware of the smallness and sinfulness of man than when he compared him to the angels who worship God in endless songs of praise, and who, like the Choirs of Angelicals, can sing of universal history.[46] When the Angels of the Sacred Stair 'hymn the Incarnate God' in a 'grand, mysterious harmony', as the Soul and the Angel pass up the stairs towards the Presence-chamber, they sing of how it needs 'An Angel's deathless fire, an Angel's reach of thought' to tell of God's triumph:

> It needs that very Angel, who with awe,
>   Amid the garden shade,
> The great Creator in His sickness saw,
>   Soothed by a creature's aid,

> And agonized, as victim of the Law
> Which He Himself had made;
> For who can praise Him in His depth and height,
> But he who saw Him reel amid that solitary fight?

After the Fourth Choir has reinforced the theme of Adam's frailty in his fall, the crossing of the threshold to the Presence-chamber is marked by the 'glad responsive chant' of the Fifth Choir, who sing the words which J. B. Sykes was to set to music for the Appendix to *Hymns Ancient and Modern* three years after the publication of the *Dream*. Sykes left the words unchanged, but repeated the first verse of praise at the end. The ending of the original version, which also concludes the whole series of thirty-five verses sung by the five Choirs, is thus quite different in emphasis and effect:

> O generous love! that He who smote
> In man for man the foe,
> The double agony in man
> For man should undergo;
>
> And in the garden secretly,
> And on the cross on high,
> Should teach His brethren and inspire
> To suffer and to die.

As we have seen, the structure and symbolism of the *Dream* emphasize parallels between two major transitions: the agony and death of Gerontius, and the particular judgment and entry into purgatory of the Soul. It is therefore appropriate that as the Soul approaches the particular judgment, the Fifth Choir should sing of Christ's double agony, as it was to Christ in his own agony that Gerontius prayed on his deathbed. Gerontius's death and the Soul's judgment are thus brought into vertical rather than horizontal relationship, and it is at this point in the *Dream* that the 'echoes' of the Subvenite being said by Gerontius's friends and the Priest around his bed can be heard before the Throne, where the Angel of the Agony stands:

> ANGEL
> The same who strengthen'd Him, what time He knelt
> Lone in that garden shade, bedew'd with blood.
> That Angel best can plead with Him for all
> Tormented souls, the dying and the dead.

ANGEL OF THE AGONY

Jesu! by that shuddering dread which fell on Thee;
Jesu! by that cold dismay which sicken'd Thee;
Jesu! by that pang of heart which thrill'd in Thee. . .

Jesu! spare these souls which are so dear to Thee,
Who in prison, calm and patient, wait for Thee;
Hasten, Lord, their hour, and bid them come to Thee,
To that glorious Home, where they shall ever gaze on Thee.

SOUL

I go before my Judge. Ah! . . .   (6)

Thus the Angel of the Agony presides over both death and judgment,
and pleads for both the dying, in the agony of the death-struggle, and the
dead, in the prison of purgatory. The ministry of the Angel to Christ in
the garden, when his disciples fail to watch with him, is an earnest of the
ministry of the angels to the Soul in purgatory. For God will not leave
his own comfortless.

The Angel foretold that the particular judgment would be the Soul's
'veriest, sharpest purgatory', and now he describes the Soul 'scorch'd,
and shrivell'd' by the 'keen sanctity' of the Crucified: 'O happy, suffering soul! for it is safe, / Consumed, yet quicken'd, by the glance of God'.
Like many doctrines, that of purgatory is profoundly paradoxical:

SOUL

Take me away, and in the lowest deep
        There let me be,
And there in hope the lone night-watches keep,
        Told out for me.
There, motionless and happy in my pain,
        Lone, not forlorn, –
There will I sing my sad perpetual strain,
        Until the morn.

As the Angel hands his charge over to the guardianship of the Angels of
Purgatory, the Souls in Purgatory sing Psalm 90, a community lament:
'Lord, Thou hast been our refuge: in every generation.' After the fire of
the particular judgment, it is into the 'penal waters' of purgatory that the
Angel gently lowers the Soul. In the Angel's last lines, and the poem's,
the hope expressed by the Soul is reinforced through references to the

presence of the angels, through the parallel between this moment and the moment of death, and through the promise of reawakening to new life:

> Angels, to whom the willing task is given,
>   Shall tend, and nurse, and lull thee, as thou liest;
> And Masses on the earth, and prayers in heaven,
>   Shall aid thee at the throne of the Most Highest.
>
> Farewell, but not for ever! brother dear,
>   Be brave and patient on thy bed of sorrow;
> Swiftly shall pass thy night of trial here,
>   And I will come and wake thee on the morrow.

Making minimal reference to horizontal temporal associations with purgatory, the Angel emphasizes the verticality of the mass, during which, according to Catholic teaching, prayers mediated via the angels have a special efficacy.[47]

In its forward momentum, and its language of rehearsal, presage and first-fruits, the poem also enacts a series of returns – through the Choirs' salvation history, for example, and the Angel's account of Gerontius's mortal life, and the Soul's references to the sound of the Subvenite being said by those who still kneel around his deathbed. The Angel's closing reference to the mass not only earths what otherwise might become vapidly ethereal; in the best tradition of meditations upon death and the future life, it also gently reminds the reader that he or she is on the same spiritual journey, as are those who have died. For the *Dream* claims our attention not in its power of 'myth-making', as *The Prelude* does, for example,[48] but in its effectiveness as devotional verse, its ability to convey to the reader a sense of the eternal present where the spiritual journey of Everyman towards his God is now. As we turn to Elgar's interpretation of the *Dream* in the oratorio of 1900, we will see that he brilliantly augmented Newman's comparatively limited dramatic effects, having first heavily cut the text. His handling of the libretto, however, also reveals an awareness of the depth of Newman's unique spiritual insight into the nature of death, judgment, and purgatory, and an understanding of his theology, particularly in relation to the agony in the garden and the ministry of the angels.

THE ORATORIO: FROM VERSE DRAMA TO MUSIC DRAMA

The musical references in the *Dream* reflect the fact that Newman was himself an accomplished amateur musician. He enjoyed playing the violin in trios and quartets into old age, encouraged young Oratorians to work towards Beethoven (in his view the master), and attended public concerts, which he often found profoundly moving.[49] When he took St Philip Neri as his patron after his conversion, and founded the first English Oratory near Birmingham (his home for the rest of his life), Newman inherited not only a great religious tradition, but also a musical and artistic one. As he wrote in *The Scope and Nature of University Education*, Philip 'preferred to yield to the stream, and direct the current, which he could not stop, of science, literature, art, and fashion, and to sweeten and to sanctify what God had made very good and man had spoilt'.[50] Palestrina, he reminded his audience, 'had Father Philip's ministrations in his last moments'.[51] It is from the Congregation of the Oratory, begun informally by Philip Neri in Rome in the 1550s and approved in 1575, that the word 'oratorio' originates, for traditional *laude* – medieval precursors of the baroque oratorio – were performed during services in Neri's prayer-hall, or oratory, the first of which was simply a converted loft.[52]

It was therefore highly appropriate that Edward Elgar, himself a Roman Catholic, should have written for the Birmingham Festival of 1900 an oratorio based upon a poem by the founder of the Birmingham Oratory. The idea of writing the piece had been 'soaking' in his mind for at least eight years,[53] when, on his way to a performance of a new oratorio by the American composer Horatio Parker entitled *Hora Novissima* in September 1899, he was joined by Father Edward Bellasis, an old acquaintance of Newman's and author of *Cardinal Newman as a Musician* (1892).[54] Although the meeting was entirely coincidental, it must have seemed a good augury to Elgar.

Without a flourishing tradition of music festivals in late-nineteenth-century England, however, which encouraged the production of oratorios, Elgar's would almost certainly not have been written. For, as music historians have often pointed out, Elgar was naturally a *dramatic* composer, and would have written operas if he had been born on the Continent. Indeed, his oratorio of the *Dream* is best described as a music drama. Elgar's friend and editor at Novello's, A. J. Jaeger, described it as a 'great drama', and part of it as the most stirring thing he had encountered since Wagner's *Parsifal* (1882).[55] Like most musical libretti based on literary works, the *Dream* is much shorter than the original.[56] Whereas the 730 lines of Newman's sections 2–7 were reduced by Elgar to 300 in his Part II, partly by removing the Soul's and Angel's long speeches of detailed commentary, Part I contained almost the whole of Newman's opening deathbed section. Nevertheless, Elgar went further than Newman in cutting lines from the Litany, and used the polyphonic resources of choral singing to compress the Litany further by having different lines sung synchronically by soprano, alto, tenor, and bass voices.[57] Visually, in the vocal score, and aurally, in performance, 'All holy Disciples' (soprano), 'All Evangelists' (alto), 'All holy Martyrs' (tenor), and 'All holy Hermits' (bass) are thus ranged in a vertical rather than horizontal order. Later, in the Hebrews 11 section immediately before Gerontius's death, Elgar provided in turn a dramatic contrast to the semi-chorus's polyphonic harmonies by setting the lines (which are again abridged) to a simple chant based upon the Gregorian De Profundis (1, cue 64). Sung in unison, the words 'Noe from the waters in a saving home . . .' are foregrounded, as they come through clearly to a listening audience. Musical repetition in the chant refrain strongly emphasizes the parallelism of the passage, and the drama of the deathbed scene is intensified by having the solo tenor voice of Gerontius float

Example 1

in above those of the semi-chorus, a technique inherited from operatic tradition.

These effects are prepared for at the beginning of the deathbed scene, which follows a long introduction for orchestra in which the work's main musical themes are stated. Where Newman adopted parentheses to distinguish Gerontius's urgent formal petitions – '(Jesu, have mercy! Mary, pray for me!)' – from his private expressions of fear, Elgar could use the instruments of the orchestra to introduce at these points what Jaeger (under the composer's supervision) called the Prayer theme (I, cue 23, Example I).[58] In the poem, Gerontius's long opening speech, which ends 'So pray for me, my friends, who have not strength to pray', is followed by the Assistants' Kyrie and Litany. In the oratorio, Elgar omits eleven of Gerontius's lines, and writes the entry of the semi-chorus in such a way that their presence since the beginning of the scene is beautifully suggested. For as Gerontius holds the B flat on his last word ('pray'), which is marked *p*, the tenor line of the semi-chorus comes in on the same note with their first word ('Kyrie'), marked *ppp*, reflecting both the sympathy of friendship and the spiritual unity of the church militant (I, cue 28, Example 2).

Example 2

Example 2 (*cont*)

Like Newman in the poem, Elgar in the oratorio draws several parallels between Part I and Part II, and one of them is between the Assistants'
first entry on the same note as Gerontius's last, cited earlier, and the
Angel's first entry an octave above the G with which the Soul has
concluded his opening recitative (II, cue 11). More central to the meaning of the *Dream*, however, or my interpretation of it, is Elgar's imaginative response to Newman's development of the agony theme, via
parallels between Part I and Part II. Elgar's treatment of the solo part
immediately before Gerontius's death in Part I reveals his awareness as a
composer of the significance of the theme. For not only are the first three
words of the phrase 'in thine own agony' sung, quite uniquely and thus
emphatically, unaccompanied (I, cue 62, Example 3); the word 'own' is
also foregrounded by being set at the top of the tenor range and marked
fff. The top B flat registers the highest level of both pitch and emotion in
Part I,[59] bringing to a climax the series of passages since the first lower B
flat entry of the semi-chorus (I, cue 29), now again taken up in the
response of the tenor line – 'Rescue him'. As in the Hebrews 11 choral
passage, though through a different technique, the word 'own' is
allowed to come through more clearly than the words that surround it,
in this case underlining Gerontius's appeal to Christ who has suffered
before him, and who is his sole hope of salvation.

Example 3

Although Elgar omitted more than half the lines in Newman's sections 2–7 when writing Part II of the oratorio, he retained all but one of the passages I quoted earlier from the poem which refer to the double agony. He draws a parallel between Gerontius's death and judgment by setting the words 'that sight of the Most Fair' in the Angel's description of the Soul's impending particular judgment to the *Novissima hora* theme (II, cue 56).[60] When the Angel then refers to St Francis's agony, the playing of the Judgment theme by the strings section underlines the idea that the saint's stigmata are a type of the particular judgment, from which the Soul can 'Learn that the flame of the Everlasting Love / Doth burn ere it transform' (II, cue 58, Example 4). Celestial music for harp and strings, the latter suggesting angel wings, then immediately leads into the first verses of 'Praise to the Holiest in the height' (II, cue 60), where the Angel's words, 'They sing of thy approaching agony', describe what the semi-chorus and chorus are actually singing at the same time (II, cue 70). A series of crescendos prepares for the crossing of the threshold, and for Elgar's biggest set piece in the oratorio – his massive setting of the Fifth Choir's 'Praise to the Holiest' (II, cue 74f). Here he foregrounds the two verses on Christ's 'double agony' by moving from broken polyphonic part singing in the chorus to a synchronic homophony in which the words of the libretto can be heard clearly (II, cue 80, Example 5). These words are repeated, making the emphasis upon the double agony even stronger, before the final verse of Newman's original version is also sung in simple harmony.

Example 4

Example 5

It is in the section of the oratorio which portrays the Soul's particular judgment, however, that Elgar most effectively applies a wide range of musical techniques to his interpretation of Newman's text. Following

Example 5 (*cont*)

the great chorus, 'Praise to the Holiest', and as the Angel leads the Soul
into the presence of their God, they hear the voices of friends around
Gerontius's bed singing the Subvenite. The parallel between the deathbed and judgment scenes, which Elgar emphasizes by repeating the
Profiscere theme in the orchestra (II, cue 103), is further strengthened by
the common musical device of having the same bass soloist take the
parts of the Priest in Part I and the Angel of the Agony in Part II.
Moreover, the Angel of the Agony's entry – 'Jesu! by that shudd'ring
dread which fell on Thee' – is on the same top D that earlier introduced

the Priest's Profiscere. Elgar himself, however, noticed another parallel that is highly significant in relation to the agony theme. In August 1900, several months after composing this part of the work, he wrote to Jaeger pointing out that the 'appalling chord' which precedes the Angel of the Agony's entry (II, cue 105, Example 6) is a close development of the Agony figure in Part I (I, cue 62), which I quoted earlier.[61] 'I really do it without thought', he commented, 'intuitively I mean'. The eight years, however, in which the poem had been soaking in his mind bore fruit in a connection which was Newman's before it was his.

I argued earlier that the Angel of the Agony presides over both death and judgment in the poem, and in the oratorio Elgar emphasizes this by reintroducing the *Novissima hora* theme in the orchestral accompaniment to his prayer for those who wait in the prison of purgatory: 'Hasten, Lord their hour, and bid them come to Thee, / To that glorious Home, where they shall ever gaze on Thee' (II, cue 112, Example 7).[62] As in the poem, the parallel between death and purgatory emphasizes that both are rites of passage, and that purgatory is hope.

Following the Soul's statement, 'I go before my Judge', Elgar makes several bold changes to the original poem which not only make the moment of the particular judgment a great dramatic climax, but also relate it (vertically) to the agony of the deathbed in Part I. Where Newman has ellipses after the Soul's cry of 'Ah!' and before the Angel's

Example 6

Example 6 (*cont*)

subsequent words, 'Praise to His Name!', Elgar brings in the semi-chorus as 'Voices on Earth' (II, cue 115) to repeat part of the Litany ('Be merciful . . .', I, cue 35) to the music of the Kyrie (I, cue 29).[63] The

Angel's description of the moment of judgment ('The eager spirit has darted from my hold . . .') is cut, and only the last two lines of the speech, in which the paradoxical nature of the moment is stated, are retained: 'O happy, suffering soul! for it is safe, / Consumed, yet quicken'd, by the glance of God.' The omission allows the composer imaginative space in which to convey more than words ever could. The effect of the orchestral passage that follows is described in Jaeger's analytical notes on the oratorio:

The climax is prepared by the Judgment theme, given out, fully harmonised (and *what* harmonies!) at first over a pedal A, and rising with awe-inspiring steps, and, after a short pause, to one momentary *fffzp* on the chord of the thirteenth, which we must consider the composer's illustration of the Angel's promise to Gerontius: 'Yes, for one moment thou shalt see thy Lord'. At this point the composer's score contains this direction: 'for one *moment* must every instrument exert its fullest force'.[64]

Example 7

Example 7 (*cont*)

Jaeger does not mention that the composer's original treatment of this moment had been the one page of the score with which he, as music editor, had been dissatisfied; that in a series of letters exchanged in the last week of June 1900 he had goaded Elgar into writing a dramatic climax that would rank with those of Wagner; and that Elgar had finally agreed to substitute the passage we now have for his original quiet, melancholy description of one who has been shrivelled and scorched, and now wishes to be taken away, '*anywhere* – out of sight'. Elgar's biographer sees this capitulaton to the 'masculine' advice of 'Nimrod', that he should expand his powers by taking artistic risks, as characteristic: it had happened before with the *Enigma Variations*.[65]

The Soul's 'Take me away' speech (II, cue 120) is accompanied first by the *Novissima hora* theme, and then by no fewer than five other themes identified by Jaeger.[66] This effect of drawing several musical strands together in the work's closing pages conveys the way in which the particular judgment draws together in one critical moment the strands

Example 7 (*cont*)

of Gerontius's life on earth, and makes him long for purgatory where he can 'in hope the lone night-watches keep'. Elgar omits the Angel's speech ('Now let the golden prison ope its gates'), thus making it possible to repeat for the last time the effect of having the last words of the solo voice of the Soul overlap with the first words of the chorus in their spiritually supportive role – here the bass entry (reminiscent of the Priest and the Angel of the Agony) of the Souls in Purgatory (II, cue 125, Example 8).

This short chorus (Elgar uses only the first two verses of the Psalm) leads into the Finale, the main theme of which accompanies the Angel's final solo, and is perhaps the most beautiful in the work (II, cue 127, Example 9). Again, Elgar fully exploits the synchronic potential of the oratorio form by having the chorus sing verses from 'Lord, Thou hast been our refuge' beneath the Angel's second and subsequent verses (II, cue 129), and then adding a second chorus singing 'Praise to the Holiest' beneath the fourth verse ('Farewell, but not for ever! brother dear') (II, cue 132). With the faint sound of a final 'Praise to the Holiest' and a

Example 8

parting admonition from the Angel ('Be brave and patient, brother dear'), the oratorio ends with a sustained Amen.

Elgar's oratorio ends in the flowing manner which characterizes it

Example 9

throughout. Howard Smither, the leading historian of the form, comments that the *Dream* is 'an unusually continuous work; its music fuses the traditionally separate elements of narrative, dialogue and contemplation and is excellently suited to Newman's extended meditative poem'.[67] Through Elgar's skilled use of leitmotifs, counterpoint, and the overlaying of solo and choral parts, his music extends the range of effects that were available to Newman. His treatment of the agony theme reveals a remarkably sympathetic understanding of its centrality to Newman's theology in the poem, although his first thoughts concerning the particular judgment passage were strangely incompatible with the sustained tension between pain and anticipated joy associated with the agony of death, judgment, and purgatory. For the lyricism of his Finale, like the Angel's parting words in the original poem, is an earnest of life with the angels who sing praise to the holiest in the height, in the eternal now of heaven. It reveals, like other great passages in the music drama, the exceptional imaginative sympathy between its composer and Newman, author of the verse drama which formed the basis of Elgar's libretto.

CHAPTER 8

Hopkins, *The Wreck of the Deutschland*

John Henry Newman and Gerard Manley Hopkins had similar English middle-class backgrounds. (Their Anglican fathers were in banking and insurance respectively.) Both men showed a love of music from an early age, and both were exceptionally gifted intellectually. Both their early adult lives were strongly influenced by Oxford, but their vocations to the Roman Catholic priesthood estranged them from the university in which they might otherwise have passed their days. Hopkins's Oxford of the 1860s, however, was itself partly shaped by Newman, the presiding genius of the Oxford Movement who had finally converted to Rome in the year after the poet's birth in 1844; and the world of English Catholicism which Hopkins entered as an undergraduate in 1866 was even more strongly imbued with the spirit of its most famous convert. Having been received into the Roman Church by Newman, Hopkins taught for him at the Birmingham Oratory school for a year, and thereafter always kept in touch, sending him an annual note on his birthday. After the completion of *The Wreck of the Deutschland* in 1876, Hopkins naturally submitted it to Father Coleridge, his oldest Jesuit friend and editor of *The Month*. It was Coleridge, also a friend of Newman's, who had published *The Dream of Gerontius* ten years earlier.

The Dream of Gerontius and *The Wreck of the Deutschland*, then, were written by Catholics for Catholics. (The first person plural in Hopkins's letter to his Anglican mother concerning the *Wreck* – 'You forget that we have a magazine of our own, the *Month*' – is characteristic.)[1] As converts, both Newman and Hopkins were acutely aware of the fundamental differences of belief between English Catholics and Protestants in the nineteenth century. In Newman's discourse on 'The Glories of Mary for the sake of her Son', for example, which was read aloud in the refectory during Hopkins's Jesuit training,[2] he comments on belief in the incarnation:

340   few Protestants have any real perception of the doctrine of God and man in one

Person. They speak in a dreamy, shadowy way of Christ's divinity; but, when their meaning is sifted, you will find them very slow to commit themselves to any statement sufficient to express the Catholic dogma . . . They cannot bear to have it said, except as a figure or mode of speaking, that God had a human body, or that God suffered . . .[3]

It was this Catholic dogma, and the associated doctrine of 'presence' in the eucharist, that drew Hopkins into the Roman Church and later informed his theology of suffering in the *Wreck*.

Although both the *Dream* and the *Wreck* embody uncompromising statements of Catholic doctrine, their critical receptions as Catholic poems have been very different. Newman's treatment of purgatory was well received by his contemporaries, including some Protestants, but has been largely neglected in this century outside the Catholic journals. Hopkins's poem, on the other hand, remained unpublished until it appeared in Robert Bridges's edition of the *Poems* (1918), since when it has received an enormous amount of critical attention, much of which focuses upon the poet's technical innovations, and his theories of inscape and instress. The poem's specifically Catholic content has often been treated as a matter of regret, or, more recently, regarded as a means of sublimating frustrated sexual drives. In 1935 C. C. Abbott declared that

The poet is handicapped by the academic religious subject and by his determination to make the poem safe as doctrine. The work is marred by the something of propaganda and 'presentation-piece' that pervades it, and becomes definitely smaller – excited, violent, overpitched – as the main subject [stanza 20] is approached and the poet strives to justify his choice.[4]

Like F. R. Leavis, John Robinson dislikes the ending of the poem, where in his view 'the problems the disaster poses, and which till now have been so determinedly faced, are abandoned for pat answers'.[5] Tom Paulin, on the other hand, reads what he chooses to call 'the orgasmic stanza' in the *Wreck* (28), where 'Hopkins makes the tall nun's death resemble a combination of sexual intercourse and a cavalry charge', as an example of the baroque, and wonders whether future critics will 'pay more attention to the element of camp baroque in Hopkins's art'.[6]

Serious scholarly studies of Hopkins's Catholicism, such as David Downes's (1959) and Donald Walhout's (1981), are often cited, and the work of other American critics, such as Elisabeth Schneider and Jerome Bump, reflects an informed awareness of the centrality of the poet's

Catholic sensibility to an understanding of the poetry.[7] Nevertheless, the most detailed study on Catholic *doctrine*, namely James Finn Cotter's *Inscape: The Christology and Poetry of Gerard Manley Hopkins* (1972), is rarely cited by other critics. J. Hillis Miller, for example, in his chapter on the *Wreck* in *The Linguistic Moment* (1985), writes of the structural and thematic relationship between the poet and the tall nun without referring to Cotter's important analysis of the theology of that relationship.[8] He also argues that, like 'Lycidas', 'Adonais', or *In Memoriam*, the *Wreck* is 'only nominally about the dead whom it memorializes', and concludes that 'the poet's response to the death of another is the occasion for a personal affirmation about the poet's inner life and his sense of vocation'.[9] (Fifty years earlier, C. C. Abbott suggested that the two parts of the work could almost be regarded as two separate poems, and that the first is the more important.)[10] In its emphasis upon the 'underthought' of *In Memoriam* and *The Wreck of the Deutschland*, deconstructionist criticism has tended to marginalize the main themes of their 'overthought': the death and future life of 'A. H. H.' and of 'five Franciscan nuns / exiles by the Falck Laws / drowned between midnight and morning of / Dec. 7th, 1875'.[11]

Hopkins described *In Memoriam* as 'a divine work', and attributed its power to the fact that it was written from personal feeling.[12] In this chapter I will argue that the *Wreck*, too, was written from the 'heart', a key word in the poem, but that in this case the appropriate paradigm is Francis Quarles's *The Bathing of the Heart with the Bloody Sweat*, in *The School of the Heart* (illustration 17).[13] Of all the Victorian literature on death and the future life discussed in this study, *The Wreck of the Deutschland* articulates most fully a theology of death which is grounded in Christ's own death and passion. Hopkins's thinking on death, and on the 'beauty of suffering' in martyrdom (a stumbling block for many readers), is rooted in his Ignatian meditations on the passion, including, as in Newman's *Dream*, the agony in the garden. Whereas in the *Dream*, however, Gerontius, whose name is generic, is supported by the whole company of the church triumphant in a work which is full of names from Christian and Jewish tradition, Hopkins's sparing use of names in the *Wreck* reflects a more specifically typological treatment of death and the future life, and an eschatology that is internalized.

Having first examined the Catholic tradition upon which Hopkins drew in the poem, and particularly the repetitive organization of the works with which he was familiar as he trained to be a Jesuit, I will discuss the I/Thou relationship in Part I between the poet and the 'hero of Calvary', and the I/she relationship in Part II between the poet and the tall nun, whose 'agony' is that of the martyr of blessed memory, and who therefore both participates in the mystery of Christ's passion and shares in his eternal glory.

THE DOLOROUS PASSION

Hans Frei, in his study of the relationship between realist narrative and the 'Eclipse of Biblical Narrative', shows how in the second half of the eighteenth century (in England the period of the rise of the novel) a great reversal had taken place in German biblical criticism: interpretation had become a matter of 'fitting the biblical story into another world with another story rather than incorporating that world into the biblical story'.[14] Victorian Evangelicals like E. H. Bickersteth, however, continued to make the world fit into the biblical story, and so too did Roman Catholic writers like Newman and Hopkins. For Hopkins, human experience made sense in relation to the passion, rather than vice versa, and this was constantly reinforced in the disciplines of his order, the life of the Jesuit being an imitation of Christ, an interpretation of the way of the cross.

The passion provides Hopkins with more, however, than a model, or pattern for the religious life. In the mass, and in private devotions such as those of the five sacred wounds and the sacred heart, all Catholics are in some sense partakers of Christ's passion; and to those saints and martyrs, ecstatics and stigmatics to whom a special grace is granted, it may sometimes be revealed with unusual clarity, through spiritual or bodily signs, that they are also partakers *in* Christ's passion. (St Francis exemplifies this in both the *Wreck* and *The Dream of Gerontius*.) For Christ is both historic antitype, as the fulfilment of Old Testament hope, revealed in time, and eternal, living type, or archetype, as the way, the truth, and the life in all generations. In *The Teaching of the Types* (1854), a work which Hopkins knew, Robert Aitken chose to illustrate this with reference to Christ's passion, arguing that

we must regard the type as possessing a kind of living continuity of application, like the actions and words, the sufferings and death, of our blessed Lord, Who was once the Man of Sorrows, and is ever the Man of Sorrows, once the Crucified, and ever the Crucified.[15]

Hopkins, in his 'Comments on the Spiritual Exercises', constantly returns to the question of individuality – 'selfbeing', 'distinctiveness', 'selving' – in contradistinction from human nature and in relationship with God, where the self as absolute is to the absolute that is God as the infinitesimal is to the infinite.[16] He frequently refers to this mysterious I/Thou relationship in his writings on the passion: in the Ignatian commentary, in journal entries, and in his letters, as well as in his poetry.

For Hopkins as a Jesuit in training, the *Spiritual Exercises* of St Ignatius Loyola formalized a series of meditations in a repetitive sequence each year, twice over the full period of four weeks in retreat, but more often over a shorter space of time. The first exercise in the first 'week', for example, is a meditation upon the 'triple sin' of the angels, of Adam and Eve, and of any individual who has gone to hell for one mortal sin.[17] The second exercise is a meditation on 'my own sins' which begins with the same preparatory prayer and the same mental picture as in the first exercise, while the third exercise is described as 'A Repetition of the First and Second Exercises with Three Colloquies'. Thus the exercitant is constantly brought back to meditate anew upon his fallen nature, and upon the redemptive act of Christ in dying upon the cross for his sake.

These exercises are given focus through concrete 'pictures', which are generally firmly placed in spatial terms. St Ignatius explains in a note what he means by the picture or 'imaginative representation of the place' in a meditation:

For a visual contemplation or meditation, the picture is an imaginative representation of the physical place where the event to be contemplated occurs. By physical place I mean, e.g., a temple or mountain where Jesus Christ our Lord is, as demanded by the subject-matter. Where the subject-matter is not something visible, as in the present case of sins, the 'picture' will be the idea, produced by an effort of the imagination, that my soul is a prisoner in this corruptible body and that my whole self, body and soul, is condemned to live amongst animals on this earth, like someone in a foreign land.[18]

The imagination that is at work in the *Wreck* is characteristically Jesuit, not only in its tendency to return to the same object of meditation, but also in its ability to form a lively picture of a remote event. St Ignatius places particular emphasis upon spatial dimensions specifically in order to stimulate the imagination. Thus the picture in the fifth exercise of the first week – 'A Meditation on Hell' – is 'a vivid portrayal in the imagination of the length, breadth and depth of Hell', and in the second week the exercitant is instructed to study the place of the nativity: 'Is the cave spacious or cramped, low or high? How is it furnished?'[19]

For St Ignatius, as for Hopkins, the hardships of the nativity anticipate those of Christ's passion:

See and reflect on what they are doing. Here it is the journey they have to make, the hardships they have to put up with, before our Lord is born in utter destitution. After all His labours, after suffering from hunger and thirst, heat and cold, being treated with injustice and insulted, He is to die on the Cross — and all for me. Thinking of all this, I will derive some benefit for my soul.

The whole of the third week in the *Spiritual Exercises* is devoted to the last supper and the passion, the 'proper gift' of which is said to be 'sorrow in company with Christ in His sorrow, being crushed with the pain that crushed Christ, tears and a deep-felt sense of suffering, because Christ suffered so much for me'.[20] The exercitant is exhorted to enter imaginatively into each stage of Christ's suffering, drawing out the physical implications of the biblical narrative. Of the agony in the garden, for example, St Ignatius writes: 'And He sweated blood so abundantly that St Luke tells us: "His sweat fell to the ground like thick drops of blood", implying that His garments were already soaked.'[21]

Meditations upon Christ's passion were staples of Roman Catholic reading in the nineteenth century, and we know from the records of books read aloud in the refectory during Hopkins's Jesuit training that the poet was familiar with several of these. Passiontide readings at Stonyhurst, for example, included parts of F. W. Faber's *The Foot of the Cross; or, The Sorrows of Mary*, in March 1872, and Newman's discourse on 'Mental Sufferings of our Lord in His Passion', in April 1873; and at Manresa House, in April 1874, the sixth word on the cross from Luis de la Palma's *The History of the Sacred Passion*, translated by Father Coleridge.[22] It is in the journal kept by Hopkins during his Novitiate at Roehampton, however, that he describes a particularly powerful emotional response to one such reading:

One day in the Long Retreat (which ended on Xmas Day [1869]) they were reading in the refectory Sister Emmerich's account of the Agony in the Garden and I suddenly began to cry and sob and could not stop. I put it down for this reason, that if I had been asked a minute beforehand I should have said that nothing of the sort was going to happen and even when it did I stood in a manner wondering at myself not seeing in my reason the traces of an adequate cause for such strong emotion – the traces of it I say because of course the cause in itself is adequate for the sorrow of a lifetime. I remember much the same thing on Maundy Thursday when the presanctified Host was carried to the sacristy.[23]

Characteristically, Hopkins immediately applies his analytical mind to an outburst of emotion which took him unawares during a rigorous retreat, and goes on to theorize about the way in which the 'stress of sorrow' is not in itself enough to move us to tears, but requires a 'pathetic touch' to set it off. It is nevertheless highly significant that it should be a description of the agony in the garden that touched him in this way.

Sister Anne Catherine Emmerich (1774–1824) was an ecstatic, and a member of an Augustinian convent in Westphalia. (It was, incidentally, from Westphalia that the five nuns commemorated in the *Wreck* were expelled.) The narrative which she dictated to the poet Klemens Brentano on her sickbed, and which was published as *The Dolorous Passion of Our Lord Jesus Christ* in 1833 (in German), describes what she herself had seen in a series of visions. In her vision of the agony in the garden she saw 'the cavern in which he was kneeling filled with frightful figures; I saw all the sins, wickedness, vices, and ingratitude of mankind torturing and crushing him to the earth'. Among the 'sins of the world' she also saw her own.[24]

Two kinds of repetition can be discerned in *The Dolorous Passion*. First, to adopt St Ignatius's phrase, Sister Emmerich's 'sorrow in company with Christ in His sorrow' is a reliving of his agony, and her vision of the Blessed Virgin suffering during that agony is a paradigm of her own visionary experience: 'She fainted several times, for she beheld in spirit different portions of the agony of Jesus.'[25] Secondly, her meditations on the passion are a preparation for her own death. Having described the crucifixion in the most harrowing detail, she writes:

His sufferings were inexpressible; but it was by them that he merited for us the grace necessary to resist those temptations to despair which will assail us at the hour of death, – that tremendous hour when we shall feel that we are about to leave all that is dear to us here below.[26]

Newman observed that Protestants were unwilling to confess that God suffers. Catholics, brought up on writings like Sister Emmerich's, prepared for their own agony and death by meditating on Christ's sacred wounds and the sufferings of his sacred heart. These encounters with the saviour who, in Aitken's words, was once the man of sorrows, and is ever the man of sorrows, were stressful and painful spiritual exercises.

Sister Emmerich herself was part of a long Catholic tradition, as her biographer records:

Most of the phenomena of the ecstatic life which are shown us in the lives and writings of Saints Bridget, Gertrude, Mechtilde, Hildegarde, Catherine of Sienna, Catherine of Genoa, Catherine of Bologna, Colomba da Rieti, Lidwina of Schiedam, Catherine Vanini, Teresa of Jesus, Anne of St. Bartholomew, Magdalen of Pazzi, Mary Villana, Mary Buonomi, Marina d'Escobar, Crescentia de Kaufbeuern, and many other nuns of contemplative orders, are also to be found in the history of the interior life of Anne Catherine Emmerich. The same path was marked out for her by God.[27]

This 'same path' represents another kind of repetition: a spiritual way for those who are granted privileged access to the mysteries of Christ's life and death through visionary experience. Among her precursors listed here, St Gertrude (1256–1301/2) was a Benedictine nun and mystic of the monastery at Helfta in Saxony, who was famous for her special devotion to the sacred heart. The saint was said to be 'drawn in a miraculous manner *into* the Heart of Jesus' (my emphasis) as his mystical bride.[28] The anonymous author of St Gertrude's *Life*, published with the first English translation of her *Revelations* in 1865, relates this devotion to the problem of religious language in a way which sheds light on Hopkins's dramatic treatment of the 'heart' in the *Wreck*:

Tribulations and afflictions of heart are the Lord's language to His elect . . . that which is most pleasing to God is to maintain interior patience, and to desire that the entire will of God may be accomplished in them. Such an answer does not reach heaven in the usual manner of human communications, but resounds, as it were, through that sweetest Divine organ, the Heart of Jesus, which is the ecstatic joy of the entire Trinity and the heavenly host.[29]

St Gertrude wrote: 'I perceived in spirit that Thou hadst imprinted in the depth of my heart the adorable marks of Thy sacred Wounds, even as they are on Thy Body.'[30] With St Mechtilde, she was famous for her devotion to the five sacred wounds, a devotion which had been revived partly through the example of St Francis (1181/2–1226). (St Gertrude recited a prayer daily in honour of the 5,466 wounds which, according to a medieval tradition, were inflicted on Jesus during his passion.)[31] Sister Emmerich, however, was also a stigmatic, and this places her in another tradition of at least fifty people who had received the stigmata since St Francis.[32] Her biographer describes the stigmas as 'a source of indescribable suffering to her, down to the moment of her death', and adds: 'Her suffering body itself was to preach Jesus crucified.'[33] (She was frequently exposed to the public gaze, like a living crucifix, after the closure of her convent.)

Martyrdom is a third kind of participation in Christ's passion, and those who suffer martyrdom often glory in the fact. When St Carpus was put to the flames, for example, he prayed aloud, saying, 'Blessed are you, Lord Jesus Christ, Son of God, because you thought me, a sinner, worthy of having this share in you'; and Sts Perpetua and Felicitas rejoiced at the prospect of being scourged in the arena, 'that they had obtained a share in the Lord's suffering'.[34] This sense of sharing in Christ's suffering is reinforced in the very structure of the early accounts of the acts of the martyrs, which tend to repeat the sequence of the passion narrative: arrest, trial, torture, public execution. As well as daily readings during his Novitiate from the Roman Martyrology in Latin, Hopkins also heard accounts of terrible persecution in Japan, and of the 'Corean Martyrs' who in the 1860s suffered tortures of almost unbelievable cruelty before being executed. While acknowledging that some broke down and recanted their faith under extreme duress, the authors of these narratives emphasize the courage and faith of those martyrs who continued to welcome the fact that they were sharing in Christ's passion.[35] The history of the English martyrs was also of special interest and concern to Hopkins and his fellow Catholics around this time, for in the summer of 1874, a little over a year before Hopkins wrote the *Wreck*, formal moves were being made in London towards the beatification of the English confessors and martyrs.

The idea of the beauty of suffering in martyrdom is based upon the perception that the martyr's demeanour under torture and public execution reflects that of Christ, and that the martyr is to enjoy with Christ the heavenly reward. Martyrs are set apart in making the ultimate sacrifice, and their lives and testimonies thus have a special authority. Although each recorded martyrdom is unique in some way, accounts of martyrdoms tend to have titles such as *The Acts of the Christian Martyrs* or *The Corean Martyrs*, which, like *The Lives of the Saints*, emphasize the corporate identity of a particular group of martyrs in the life and history of the church. In the *Wreck*, Hopkins both treats the nuns as a group – 'five-livèd and leavèd favour and pride' – and isolates the 'tall nun', 'Christ's lily', whose wreck in the second part is interpreted in relation to the poet's in the first.

Hopkins was misled by an inaccurate report in *The Times* to the effect that the tall nun was the leader of the group. (In fact the leader's body was never recovered, and two of the four remaining sisters were tall.) To come upon the names of the five nuns in *The Times*, however – 'viz., Barbara Hultenschmitt, Henrica Fassbaender, Norbeta Reinkober, Aurea Badzinra, and Brigitta Damhorst' – is something of a revelation, so firmly has the poem established in one's mind the sense of a group of religious who are unnamed, and whose identity lies somewhere between his categories of 'self' and 'human nature', and between individuation and common humanity.[36] In the poem it is as if the 'N.' (or 'names') in the funeral mass of these 'handmaids' remained unspecific. Like St Gertrude and St Francis (who figures unnamed in *The Dream of Gerontius*), the 'tall nun' who has gone to her reward is now 'hidden' in Christ's wounds.

J. Hillis Miller finds in the *Wreck* a parallel between the 'tragedy of language in its inability to say the Word', and 'the mystery of the human situation': 'The more a man affirms himself, the more he affirms his eccentricity, his individuality, his failure to be Christ, or Christ-like, an "AfterChrist," as Hopkins puts it.'[37] It is precisely in the death agony, however, and in the eternal perspective of the future life, that this problem is resolved; and it is precisely that ground which we enter in the *Wreck*.

PART THE FIRST: 'TO HERO OF CALVARY'

The main parallels between the two parts of the *Wreck* have been described in a number of ways: as 'narrative doubling'; as two climaxes occurring four-fifths of the way through each section, both of which evoke a confession of faith; and as 'parallel wrecks' – the poet's own wreck on the *Spiritual Exercises*, and the tall nun's plight in the wreck of the Deutschland.[38] Perhaps the most important feature of the structure of the poem, however, is the order, or sequence, of the two parts. For the poet's treatment of the heroic tall nun in the second part, where his eschatology is externalized and conceived in terms of nature, is read in the light of his invocation of the (wrecked) 'hero of Calvary' in the first, where the I/Thou relationship between the poet and his God is described in terms of an eschatology that is internalized.

In Part the First, meditation upon this awesome relationship is brought to a climax in stanzas 6–8, where the poet meditates upon Christ's incarnation and passion, and describes the human heart as 'hard at bay' in responding to the bitter-sweet nature of the Christian revelation. The outer stanzas (1–5 and 9–10) explore the complex nature of man's encounter with God, initially via an account of the poet's own experience of God's mastery, and finally in a prayer for his mastery of the whole world.

The first stanza relates a past spiritual crisis to the poet's present sense that he again feels the finger of God the Father touch him:

> THOU mastering me
> God! giver of breath and bread;
> World's strand, sway of the sea;
> Lord of living and dead;
> Thou hast bound bones and veins in me, fastened me flesh,
> And after it almost unmade, what with dread,
> Thy doing: and dost thou touch me afresh?
> Over again I feel thy finger and find thee.

On second and subsequent readings, the parallelism between the two binary oppositions in the opening quatrain – strand/sea, and living/dead – anticipates the drama of the shipwreck in Part the Second. Its immediate local force, however, is more broadly eschatological, being suggestive of the four last things. The fourth line is reminiscent of the clause on the second coming in the Nicene Creed, as recited in the mass: '*Et iterum venturus est cum gloria judicare vivos, et mortuos*'. Hopkins would also have known the introduction to the so-called *Second Epistle of St Clement*: 'We are to think, brethren, of Jesus Christ as of God, that he is the "*judge* of the living and dead"' (my emphasis).[39] It is specifically the father, however, who is addressed in the poet's opening colloquy, and whose mastery is described in highly dramatic and personal terms in the second quatrain. Whereas for Tennyson in *In Memoriam* the physiology of the cardiovascular system provided a conceit through which to express his feelings towards the dead Hallam, who 'touched' him from the past, Hopkins's is a more Marvellian and specifically religious conceit, suggestive of what he was later to describe in the 'Comments on the Spiritual Exercises' as 'elevating' grace, which 'is truly God's finger touching the very vein of personality, which nothing else can reach'.[40]

The critical moment of affirmation described in apocalyptic terms in the second stanza ('I did say yes / O at lightning and lashed rod'), concerned an encounter of the poet, whose 'heart' swooned, with the second person of the Trinity – 'Thy terror, O Christ, O God'. Although they cannot be certain, most authorities believe that the passage refers to Hopkins's spiritual crisis leading up to his conversion, rather than that associated with his making his first retreat as directed by the *Spiritual Exercises*.[41] More important, however, is the fact that Hopkins's description of the ensuing spiritual *krisis* in the third stanza, where the Holy Spirit presides ('dovewinged', 'flame'), is also of a vision of judgment:

> The frown of his face
> Before me, the hurtle of hell
> Behind, where, where was a, where was a place?
> I whirled out wings that spell
> And fled with a fling of the heart to the heart of the Host.

This passage is Ignatian, not only in its physical sense of hell, as in the fifth exercise of the first week in the *Spiritual Exercises*,[42] but also in the drama of the poet's being caught between the twin terrors of an encounter with the living God and a vertiginous prospect of the absence of God, and in his searching for a saving object of devotion: 'where was a place [for my heart]?'

From the past tense of the last of the three stanzas on the Trinity,[43] the poem moves into the present in stanzas 4–6: 'I am soft sift / In an hourglass'; 'I kiss my hand / To the stars'; 'Not out of his bliss / Springs the stress felt'. The contraries in stanza 4 ([sand]/water) are held in the perpetual tension of the present tense: a constant 'fall', or fallen state, is countered and thus balanced by a constant grace, via the gospel. In stanza 5, where the focus shifts from scriptural to natural revelation, the present tense of the long final line – 'For I greet him the days I meet him, and bless when I understand' – enacts the poet's sense of God's constant, though often hidden presence 'under the world's splendour and wonder', a mystery to which both Newman and Keble often referred, and which must be 'instressed, stressed' by the poet himself. The crucial meditation on time in stanza 6 is thus securely placed in a present tense which can open out into what I have called the eternal present:

> Not out of his bliss
> Springs the stress felt
> Nor first from heaven (and few know this)
>   Swings the stroke dealt –

> Stroke and a stress that stars and storms deliver,
> That guilt is hushed by, hearts are flushed by and melt –
> But it rides time like riding a river
> (And here the faithful waver, the faithless fable and miss).

The meditation upon the Christian revelation in this and the subsequent two stanzas provides a theological foundation for the whole of the *Wreck*, including the poet's earlier descriptions of his encounter with God the Father, God the Son, and God the Holy Spirit, and of the sustaining virtues of the gospel and the natural creation. For here the poet rejects a supramundane model of God's agency in favour of a Scotist theology which speaks of the incarnation as being present before all time, and enduring until after the end of time.[44] One corollary of this unorthodox theology is that Christ's sacrifice actually *precedes* the creation of man.

Duns Scotus, then, provided a theological basis for Hopkins's meditations upon the beauty of suffering, and particularly as perfectly exemplified in the sacrifice of the passion. In the subsequent stanzas (7–8), however, the poet's treatment of the Christian revelation in relation to time also reflects a religious *imagination* that was influenced by the *Spiritual Exercises* of St Ignatius, and by devotional books such as Sister Emmerich's *The Dolorous Passion*:

> It dates from day
> Of his going in Galilee;
> Warm-laid grave of a womb-life grey;
> Manger, maiden's knee;
> The dense and the driven Passion, and frightful sweat:
> Thence the discharge of it, there its swelling to be,
> Though felt before, though in high flood yet –
> What none would have known of it, only the heart, being hard at bay,

> Is out with it! Oh,
> We lash with the best or worst
> Word last! How a lush-kept plush-capped sloe
> Will, mouthed to flesh-burst,
> Gush! – flush the man, the being with it, sour or sweet,
> Brim, in a flash, full! – Hither then, last or first,
> To hero of Calvary, Christ's feet –
> Never ask if meaning it, wanting it, warned of it – men go.

We have seen that in the *Spiritual Exercises* the hardships of the nativity are associated with those of Christ's passion – 'and all for me'. Similarly, it is recorded that in the last weeks of Sister Emmerich's life she was 'once more' by the child Jesus's manger at Bethlehem:

He was burning with fever, and showed me his sufferings and those of his mother. They were so poor that they had no food but a wretched piece of bread. He bestowed still greater sufferings upon me, and said to me: 'Thou art mine; thou art my spouse; suffer as I suffered, without asking the reason why.' I do not know what my sufferings are to be, nor how long they will last. I submit blindly to my martyrdom, whether for life or for death: I only desire that the hidden designs of God may be accomplished in me.[45]

In both the Ignatian meditation and Sister Emmerich's vision, the nativity is at once an historical and an eternally present revelation: Christ was once the man of sorrows, and is ever the man of sorrows. Moreover, in stanza 7 the shuffling of the sequence of events in the gospel story and the truncated syntax have the further effect of juxtaposing the womb and the grave, the manger and the passion, and thus draw out the full eschatological implications of the incarnation. For the swelling of the womb anticipates the birthpangs (Gk. *odines*) whereby Christ is to be delivered out of death in the resurrection (Acts 2.24), thus inaugurating a new order which is to be fulfilled in the last days (cf. Revelation 12.2).

The line, 'The dense and the driven Passion, and frightful sweat', captures succinctly the kind of harrowing picture of Christ's suffering which is drawn in minute detail in Sister Emmerich's *The Dolorous Passion*. Newman, in his discourse on 'Mental Sufferings of our Lord in His Passion', had commented that, in the agony in the garden, Christ in his sweat 'has bled before His time . . . His passion has begun from within'.[46] Hopkins, however, was to find a broader theological significance in the 'frightful sweat', in an interpretation which associates it with the 'swelling to be' in the following line. He writes on the incarnation in his later 'Comments on the *Spiritual Exercises*' that it is 'as if the blissful agony or stress of selving in God had forced out drops of sweat or blood, which drops were the world', and adds that the created world is marked with the 'confusion, clashing, and *wreck* which took place in the higher one' (my emphasis).[47] The word 'discharge' not only signifies the pouring out of the sweat and the blood in the passion, but also has electrical associations (cf. 'lightning' and 'storms'). Furthermore, in his death Christ is discharged or released from his suffering, so that the *plērōma*, or fullness of God, an active force charging all things, which is 'swelling to be', can be fulfilled in the *parousia*.[48]

Although the Christian revelation is eternally present, only the heart can respond fully to and, in Quarles's terms, be bathed with the bloody sweat:

> Christ's bloody sweat immortal blessings gives,
> As by its daily sweat man's body lives.[49]

Only the heart, when hard pressed, can taste the bitter-sweet experience of the revelation, and encounter the 'hero of Calvary' (stanza 8), whose beauty, as Hopkins expressed it later in a sermon, was 'wrecked'.[50] Such experiences are, however, beyond cognition and beyond words, and they demand the response of men, who 'go' to the foot of the cross without necessarily willing or fully understanding what they are doing. In stanza 9 the themes of the opening stanzas of the poem are rehearsed in the form of a prayer to the blessed Trinity, in which the poet restates his own encounter with God as both 'Father and fondler of *heart*' (my emphasis). As St Gertrude's biographer wrote in a passage quoted earlier: 'Tribulations and afflictions of heart are the Lord's language to His elect.'

PART THE SECOND: 'THOU MARTYR-MASTER'

News coverage of the wreck itself began in *The Times* on Wednesday 8 December 1875, with a brief report of telegrams received from Harwich. Lengthy daily reports on 'The Loss of the Deutschland' then followed, and on Monday 13 December began to appear under the title that was to be adopted by Hopkins: 'The Wreck of the Deutschland'. Having initially carried eye-witness accounts of the disaster and early evidence from the inquest, these reports, and their accompanying leaders, soon focused upon two matters of general concern: first, the shameful behaviour of the local 'smacksmen', who showed interest in the foundering ship only when it had become a source of booty; and secondly, the public scandal of there being no lifeboat stationed at Harwich. On Friday 10 December, however, a small item of 'human interest' strikes a new note in the middle of the day's report. A message in a bottle had been discovered, written by one D. J. Behring to his wife only an hour after the grounding of the ship on sandbanks: 'I believe we are lost. I depart in peace with my God and without any anxiety for you.'[51] Brief religious references then follow in subsequent reports: first, in a description of 'the chief sister, a gaunt woman 6ft. high, calling out loudly and often "O Christ, come quickly!" till the end came'; and secondly, in an account of the nuns lying in open coffins in a church in Stratford, East London, with vases of flowers and wreaths of immortelles at their heads and feet, being visited by their 'co-religionists', most of whom 'appeared to be prompted by feelings of devotion', before the solemn funeral mass at which Cardinal Manning was to deliver an oration.[52]

In Hopkins's poem, the proportions of secular and religious discourses are very different. For although the second part embodies a considerable amount of material gleaned from newspaper reports, the *Wreck* is essentially a religious poem into which documentary data are interpolated. Thus the parentheses in stanza 17 are paradigmatic:

> They fought with God's cold –
> And they could not and fell to the deck
> (Crushed them) or water (and drowned them) or rolled
> With the sea-romp over the wreck.

Written from within the Roman Catholic Church, unlike *The Times*'s report with its reference to those implicitly other 'co-religionists', Part the Second is closer to a funeral address than a news report in its structure and tone, and particularly in its treatment of the five nuns as if *sub specie aeternitatis*, and as members of a church of which martyrs are the seed. Hopkins concentrated upon the heroic figures in the wreck – principally the tall nun as 'lioness' and 'prophetess', but also the haunting figure of the brave sailor in stanza 16 – and did not refer to the sad cases of suicide and attempted suicide reported in *The Times*. Similarly, he could afford to ignore the scandalous aspects of the wreck, if only because they were already sufficiently well known to make his final call for the conversion of England seem timely to Catholic readers.

In terms of the poem's theology, however, Hopkins's avoidance of the theme of human frailty which emerged from contemporary newspaper accounts has several more significant effects. First, the elements become the main cause of the drownings, which thus appear to be a *natural* disaster, or what insurers such as Hopkins's father might have called 'an act of God'. Secondly, the main focus is upon the agony and death of the five nuns, and especially of the heroic tall nun who partakes in the mystery of Christ's passion as she suffers in 'God's cold'. Thirdly, the Protestant authorities in Germany who caused the nuns to be 'exiles by the Falck Laws' appear to be mainly responsible for events surrounding their deaths, thus making the nuns martyrs in the eyes of Catholic readers.

In the opening stanza (11) of a Part the Second which is apocalyptic both in its tone and its numerous echoes of the Book of Revelation,[53] the braggart figure of Death brings the fourth horseman of the Apocalypse ('Some find me a sword', cf. Revelation 6.8) into the age of steam, and of that recurrent Victorian nightmare, the railway accident ('some / The flange and the rail'). The nuns' extended agony in the shipwreck (itself a traditional apocalyptic symbol), and their violent deaths, are far from what Whateley ironically called 'the circumstances in which most people seem to think a happy death consists', namely a death free from pain, in one's own bed, and surrounded by a loving family or by friends.[54] Their deaths were more 'scriptural', in Whateley's terms. Like the martyrs of the early church, they died for the faith, having first found themselves beyond hope of human rescue, when 'Hope had grown grey hairs' and was 'twelve hours gone' in the wreck. Furthermore, rather than drawing upon the consolation of a 'lively hope by the resurrection of Jesus Christ from the dead', as in the burial service in the Book of Common Prayer, for example, Hopkins portrays the tall nun glimpsing, *in extremis*, something of the desolation of the cross, in also being beyond hope of *divine* rescue. Thus the affirmative ending of the *Wreck*, in which the poet can 'admire' God as 'master of the tides' (32) and can ask the drowned nun to 'Remember us in the roads, the heaven-haven of the reward' (35), but which offers no pat answers (*pace* Robinson), has to be worked for. It is achieved through a sequence of typological readings of the five nuns' agony in relation to the virgins, martyrs, and stigmatics of the church, and, finally, of the tall nun's agony as an ecstatic.

One of the ways in which the tall nun is foregrounded in the *Wreck* is by being introduced as a heroic lone figure in a sequence of stanzas in the very middle of the poem (17–19), before she is identified as one of a group of five sisters. In the previous stanza (16), the brave sailor's descent from the rigging, and his death in the '*burl* of the fountain of air' (my emphasis), suggestive for Hopkins of *plērōma*,[55] imitates Christ's *kenōsis* in the incarnation, when he took the form of a servant in a hostile world, and his later 'driven Passion' (7). This intimation of what Bump has called the 'sacrificial sublime'[56] prepares for the introduction of the tall nun in the following stanza (17): 'Till a lioness arose breasting the babble, / A prophetess towered in the tumult, a virginal tongue told'.

Whereas the muscular sailor's act of heroism is physical, the sister's is verbal. The emphasis upon sound in the stanza's long final polysyllabic line, which ends with a characteristic punning sound effect in 'tongue told' [tolled], is taken up in the musical metaphors in stanza 18:

> Ah, touched in your bower of bone,
>   Are you! turned for an exquisite smart,
> Have you! make words break from me here all alone,
>   Do you! – mother of being in me, heart.
> O unteachably after evil, but uttering truth,
>   Why, tears! is it? tears; such a melting, a madrigal start!
> Never-eldering revel and river of youth,
> What can it be, this glee? the good you have there of your own?

This public expression of surprise at the intensity of the heart's response is reminiscent of Hopkins's private record of his reaction to Sister Emmerich's account of the agony in the garden. Echoing the opening stanza of the *Wreck*, and written in the present tense of immediate feeling, the interpolation places the tall nun, and the poet's response to her, at the ode's emotional, as well as structural centre. God's 'melting' or softening of the heart (cf. Job 23.16) is another of Quarles's conceits in *The School of the Heart*.[57] The stanza's rhymes, however – 'turned for an exquisite smart', 'mother of being in me, heart', 'such a melting, madrigal start' (cf. Latin *matrix*, womb) – emphasize the poet's entry into what in Roman Catholic tradition is thought of as a feminine province of feeling, epitomized in that which the Blessed Virgin Mary kept 'in her heart' (e.g. Luke 2.19). Finally, having expanded the poem's emotional plot from the I/Thou relationship of the first part to the central triangle of relationships in the second – 'Sister, a sister calling / A master, her master and mine!' (19) – the poet completes the cycle begun with the sailor's descent in stanza 16 by describing the ascent of the sonorous 'call of the tall nun', which 'To the men in the tops and the tackle rode over the storm's brawling.'

In a poem of few names it is noticeable that the succeeding four stanzas, in which the unnamed tall nun and the four other members of her 'coifèd sisterhood' are identified with the sainted virgins, martyrs, and stigmatics of the church, contain no fewer than six names which serve a typological or more broadly symbolic purpose: Gertrude, Luther, Abel, Cain, Orion, and Francis. First, 'Gertrude, lily, and Luther', both of whom were associated with Eisleben in Saxony, serve as appropriate examples of good and evil coming out of the same source, as archetypally in the case of Abel and Cain (20). St Gertrude was famous not only for her special devotion to the sacred heart and the five sacred wounds, but also for her very literal interpretation of herself and her sisters as mystical brides of Christ.[58] Thus 'Christ's lily' (her distinguishing symbol) reminds a Catholic readership that she is a *representative* 'holy Virgin' of the church, in the words of the Litany. The anonymous writer of *The Life and Revelations of Saint Gertrude, Virgin and Abbess* records that after the interment of her corpse, 'the Saint appeared, with a troop of Virgins of admirable beauty', and that she 'held a lily and other flowers in her right hand'.[59] The saint was also said to have been visited during her lifetime by the Blessed Virgin Mary:

As Gertrude prayed, the Mother of God appeared to her, in the presence of the ever-adorable Trinity, under the form of a white lily, with three leaves; one standing erect, and the other two bent down. By this she understood that it was not without reason that the Blessed Mother of God was called the white lily of the Trinity.[60]

The relationship between sacrificial virginity and special signs of divine love (in this case after death) is to be a theme in the next stanza in the *Wreck* (21), where the exiles by the Falck Laws are portrayed as martyrs:

> Loathed for a love men knew in them,
> Banned by the land of their birth,
> Rhine refused them, Thames would ruin them;
> Surf, snow, river and earth
> Gnashed: but thou art above, thou Orion of light;
> Thy unchancelling poising palms were weighing the worth,
> Thou martyr-master: in thy sight
> Storm flakes were scroll-leaved flowers, lily showers – sweet
> heaven was astrew in them.

The poising palms are those of the divine judge of the Revelation, and the idea of imagining God looking down on the earth would have been familiar to Hopkins from the *Spiritual Exercises*.[61] As J. Hillis Miller has reminded us, however, Orion is connected specifically with the martyrs of the church (cf. Job 9.9; Amos 5.8): 'Orion is a harbinger of spring with its flowers, as well as a bringer of storms. The storms of persecution, and the martyrdom they cause, are necessary to the triumph of the Church in the spring.'[62] The flowers in stanza 21 are those associated with holy virgins, and particularly with religious as the brides of Christ, in a tradition based upon verses in the Song of Solomon (6.2–3): 'My beloved is gone down into his garden, to the beds of spices, to feed in the gardens, and to gather lilies. I am my beloved's, and my beloved is mine: he feedeth among the lilies.' St Gertrude's biographer, for example, records that Christ said these words to a 'favoured religious', and that this nun was a lily he held in his hand for eleven days before breaking it.[63] Sister Emmerich, for whom flowers were 'forerunners and figures of sufferings', saw many fresh flowers falling on her when she was dying, and called out, 'Come, O Lord Jesus.'[64] In the sight of Hopkins's 'martyr-master', however, the 'scroll-leaved flowers, lily showers' are signs of the martyrs' heavenly reward. In a Victorian version of the old emblem books, entitled *Spiritual Conceits* (1862; illustration 18), the epigraph of which reads 'No Cross, No Crown', W. Harry Rogers depicts the 'Contrast' drawn by the martyr Cyprian when he wrote: 'He was crowned with thorns Who crowns martyrs with eternal flowers.'[65]

The eternal present of the poet's affirmation in stanza 21 – 'but thou art above, thou Orion of light' – is sustained throughout the succeeding two stanzas, in which the five nuns are associated with the stigmata, first of Christ the eternal, living type, or archetype, and then of St Francis, who, as in *The Dream of Gerontius*, is both inheritor (of Christ's agony on the cross) and precursor (here of the five sisters in their deaths):

> Five! the finding and sake
> And cipher of suffering Christ.
> Mark, the mark is of man's make
> And the word of it Sacrificed.
> But he scores it in scarlet himself on his own bespoken,
> Before-time-taken, dearest prizèd and priced –
> Stigma, signal, cinquefoil token
> For lettering of the lamb's fleece, ruddying of the rose-flake.

> Joy fall to thee, father Francis,
> Drawn to the Life that died;
> With the gnarls of the nails in thee, niche of the lance, his
> Lovescape crucified
> And seal of his seraph-arrival! and these thy daughters
> And five-livèd and leavèd favour and pride,
> Are sisterly sealed in wild waters,
> To bathe in his fall-gold mercies, to breathe in his all-fire glances. (22–3)

In John Robinson's view, the 'ritual significance' which these stanzas give to the disaster 'further distances the poem from the reader who does not share Hopkins' preoccupation'.[66] The real problem, however, for critics such as Robinson (and it is one which leads him into a misreading of the last lines of stanza 23) lies not with Hopkins, as if he were idiosyncratic or obsessive in this regard, but with aspects of Roman Catholicism itself, and particularly with certain ways in which Catholic tradition interprets the world, in Frei's terms incorporating it into the story of the Bible. Take, for instance, this passage from Sister Emmerich's *The Dolorous Passion*, where she describes her vision of Calvary, which Christ and his executioners have just reached:

There was a fine view of the whole town of Jerusalem from the top of Calvary. This top was circular, and about the size of an ordinary riding-school, surrounded by a low wall, and with five separate entrances. This appeared to be the usual number in those parts, for there were five roads at the baths, at the place where they baptised, at the pool of Bethsaida, and there were likewise many towns with five gates. In this, as in many other peculiarities of the Holy Land, there was a deep prophetic signification; that number five, which so often occurred, was a type of those five sacred wounds of our Blessed Saviour, which were to open to us the gates of Heaven.[67]

Using a similar method of interpretation to Sister Emmerich's, but taking Christ's five sacred wounds as type and the five nuns as antitype, Hopkins commemorates the nuns' share in the passion, and the 'joy' reserved for them, as it was for St Francis (and later stigmatics), in being 'Drawn to the Life that died'. Like the Revelation which provides so much of the poem's symbolism, including, as Alison Sulloway has shown, its three emblematic colours of red, white, and gold, the *Wreck* can be read only within its own mythic world-view.[68]

It is in the context, then, of the sacrifice and reward associated with the church's virgins, martyrs, and stigmatics of happy memory that the tall nun's cry – 'O Christ, Christ, come quickly' (24) – becomes the object of the poem's most crucial act of interpretation, with the poet established in the 'here' of 'a pastoral forehead of Wales' and the now of the narrative present. Yet in a move of extraordinary boldness, made in a series of carefully and systematically argued stanzas (24–7), the cry is shown to be *beyond* interpretation within the limits of this traditional context. First, both the cross and the crown are offered as possible explanations:

She to the black-about air, to the breaker, the thickly
Falling flakes, to the throng that catches and quails
    Was calling 'O Christ, Christ, come quickly':
The cross to her she calls Christ to her, christens her wild-worst Best.

    The majesty! what did she mean?
    Breathe, arch and original Breath.
Is it love in her of the being as her lover had been?
    Breathe, body of lovely Death.
They were else-minded then, altogether, the men
Woke thee with a *We are perishing* in the weather of Gennesareth.
    Or is it that she cried for the crown then,
The keener to come at the comfort for feeling the combating keen? (24–5)

Like Christ's cry of desolation from the cross (Mark 15.34; cf. Psalm 22.1), the tall nun's petition is scriptural, drawing upon the penultimate verse in the Bible: 'He which testifieth these things saith, Surely I come quickly. Amen. Even so, come, Lord Jesus' (Revelation 22.20). This would seem to support Sulloway's reading of the *Wreck* as Victorian apocalyptic, and her claim that, like the apocalyptic martyrs who anticipate joining 'the heavenly hosts' at the end of the Book of Revelation, the nun desires death and 'escape from temporal horror into the bliss of eternal life'.[69] But neither of the poet's tentative answers to his own question in stanza 25 – that the tall nun might have longed to be one with Christ in his death, or to pass as quickly as possible from the cross to the crown – is broad enough to encompass the majesty of the event as he sees it:

    No, but it was not these.
    The jading and jar of the cart,
Time's tasking, it is fathers that asking for ease
    Of the sodden-with-its-sorrowing heart,
Not danger, electrical horror; then further it finds
The appealing of the Passion is tenderer in prayer apart:
    Other, I gather, in measure her mind's
Burden, in wind's burly and beat of endragonèd seas. (27)

The nun's experience of *krisis* at the heart of the storm is different from that of the generations of early Christian martyrs who lived and died under persecution, or of Sister Emmerich who suffered acutely in mind and body for most of her adult life, or indeed of Hopkins himself who meditated for days on the dolorous passion of our Lord during long retreats.

In the stanza that follows, the horizontality of chronological time is disrupted as the tall nun enters the vertical dimension of *kairos*. Although the first words ('But how shall I . . .') continue the sense of the previous stanza, the sentence fractures under the double stress of attempting both to share imaginatively in and to express linguistically the nun's miraculous visitation by Christ, in which she apprehends in her drowning and gasping for breath the *Ipse* or very self of her 'Master' (rather than 'martyr-master'):

> But how shall I . . . make me room there:
> Reach me a . . . Fancy, come faster –
> Strike you the sight of it? look at it loom there,
> Thing that she . . . There then! the Master,
> *Ipse*, the only one, Christ, King, Head:
> He was to cure the extremity where he had cast her;
> Do, deal, lord it with living and dead;
> Let him ride, her pride, in his triumph, despatch
> and have done with his doom there.   (28)

Like the 'poising palms' of stanza 21, the word 'doom' signifies divine judgment, present as a theme since the opening stanza of Part I ('Lord of living and dead'), so that Christ the King is at once judge and saviour as he breaks this lily, bringing to mind his own breaking on the cross, the extremity where he had been cast, and from which he rose again on the third day. For the nun in this life, Christ's sacrifice has been celebrated daily in the breaking of bread, and in the eucharist his coming again to judge the living and the dead has been powerfully anticipated. Oscar Cullman argues that 'all worship in early Christianity was considered an anticipation in the present of the Kingdom of God'; that the *Marana tha* ('Lord, come!') upon which Revelation 22.20 was almost certainly based, seems to be a *eucharistic prayer*; and that 'when we hear this prayer, we think first of an eschatological petition for the coming of the Lord at the end of days'.[70] Like the nun's cry, in which she repeats this ancient prayer, what Schneider has described as the 'supernatural event' in stanza 28 is specifically eucharistic, the word *Ipse* being associated with the minor elevation in the mass: '*Per ipsum, et cum ipso, et in ipso, est tibi Deo Patri omnipotenti, in unitate Spiritus Sancti, omnis honor, et gloria.*'[71] The measured language of the mass, however, cannot be heard across the storm. Rather, the stanza's aposiopesis is a classic example of the kind of breakdown of language found in the description and interpretation of deaths and 'last words' in the nineteenth century, where both the provisional nature of the writing project *and* the grounds of Christian faith are laid bare. Consecutive and completed sentences of a narrative which has functioned hitherto in a horizontal epistemological plane are violently disrupted. For the tall nun, the anticipation that is earthly worship is over, Christ the King is come, and she experiences his full presence in the now of her final agony.

In the following stanza – the last before the poem opens out into a concluding meditation on the broader significance of the wreck – the experience of the tall nun is described as itself an act of interpretation:

> Ah! there was a heart right!
> There was single eye!
> Read the unshapeable shock night
> And knew the who and the why;
> Wording it how but by him that present and past,
> Heaven and earth are word of, worded by? –
> The Simon Peter of a soul! to the blast
> Tarpeïan-fast, but a blown beacon of light.   (29)

All the disciples looked at the same Jesus, but only Peter saw the Christ: 'if therefore thine eye be single, thy whole body shall be full of light' (Matthew 6.22).[72] In Roman Catholic theology, however, it was because Peter *confessed* Jesus as the Messiah, that he became the rock upon which the church was built. The tall nun makes the same confession, and 'words' the incarnate son as *logos* (cf. John 1). This leads Cotter to counter Schneider's argument that Hopkins describes a miracle in stanza 28 with the claim that he dramatizes 'the moment of inscape': the nun 'knew the who and the why'.[73]

Perhaps the most significant aspect of this moment of *gnosis* in the tall nun, however, is that it occurs in the heart, as does that of the Blessed Virgin Mary, to whom much of the final section of the poem is addressed, in the annunciation. (As a High Anglican before his conversion, Hopkins would certainly have known Charles Collins's painting, *Convent Thoughts* (1850–1), in which a nun stands in a garden of lilies and roses with a missal in her hand, 'studying the significance of the passion flower'. The manuscript in her hand is open at a miniature of the crucifixion (a scene from the passion) and her finger marks another page with a miniature of the annunciation.)[74] Hopkins, however, was particularly devoted to the doctrine of the immaculate conception:

> Jesu, heart's light,
> Jesu, maid's son,
> What was the feast followed the night
> Thou hadst glory of this nun? –
> Feast of the one woman without stain.
> For so conceivèd, so to conceive thee is done;
> But here was heart-throe, birth of a brain,
> Word, that heard and kept thee and uttered thee outright.   (30)

In her death the nun re-enacts the 'conception' and 'delivery' of Christ, and the juxtaposition of the culmination of her martyrdom in her heavenly reward (she is not to experience purgatory) and the feast of the immaculate conception, celebrated on 8 December, effects a transition at the end of the poem from the sharply focused drama of her agony and death to the broader expression of its significance in relation to the corporate life of the Roman Church.

For the nun's death in the shipwreck – a traditional apocalyptic symbol – can itself be taken as a revelation, or sign, to the Catholic minority in England: 'is the shipwrack then a harvest, / does tempest carry the grain for thee?' (31; cf. Revelation 14.15). As in the *Spiritual Exercises*, the Roman Martyrology, Sister Emmerich's *Dolorous Passion*, and other works which shaped Hopkins's devotional life, a characteristically Catholic pattern of meditative recurrence can be discerned in the poem's circling back to its beginning as the language of its opening stanzas is reapplied to this broader eschatological context: 'Finger' (31/1); 'vein' (31/4); 'master of the tides' (32/1); 'wall' (32/1), and so on. The poet's 'hero of Calvary' and the tall nun's 'martyr-master' is both lord and *judge*:

> past all
> Grasp God, throned behind
> Death with a sovereignty that heeds but hides, bodes but abides;
>
> With a mercy that outrides
> The all of water, an ark
> For the listener; for the lingerer with a love glides
> Lower than death and the dark;
> A vein for the visiting of the past-prayer, pent in prison,
> The-last-breath penitent spirits – the uttermost mark
> Our passion-plungèd giant risen,
> The Christ of the Father compassionate, fetched in the storm of his strides.
>
> (32–3)

Just as Christ's own wreck in the crucifixion was a preparation for the building of the ark that is his church, so his descent into Hades signified that for the 'prisoners of the king' purgatory is hope.

The poet's meditations in the *Wreck* – on Mary and the nativity, Christ and the passion, Gertrude as a bride of Christ, the tall nun as a martyr – are drawn together in the final intercessory stanzas. For Hopkins the English convert, writing only a year after moves had begun to beatify the English Catholic confessors and martyrs, and Gladstone had written a 'political expostulation' on the Vatican decrees of 1870,[75] 'us' signifies both the Catholic minority, and the majority of unconverted English whose behaviour at the site of the wreck made the need for conversion seem the more urgent. He prays, however, that Christ's coming may be neither catastrophic, as in premillennialist apocalyptic, nor obscurely painful, as in his nativity, but mediated through grace. Far from being an unsatisfactory ending, it is a fine example of Hopkins's favourite technique of knotting different strands of his poetry together in a richly textured finale:

> Now burn, new born to the world,
> 　　Double-naturèd name,
> The heaven-flung, heart-fleshed, maiden-furled
> 　　Miracle-in-Mary-of-flame,
> Mid-numberèd he in three of the thunder-throne!
> Not a dooms-day dazzle in his coming nor dark as he came;
> 　　Kind, but royally reclaiming his own;
> A released shower, let flash to the shire, not a lightning of fire hard-hurled.
>
> 　　Dame, at our door
> 　　Drowned, and among our shoals,
> Remember us in the roads, the heaven-haven of the reward:
> 　　Our King back, Oh, upon English souls!
> Let him easter in us, be a dayspring to the dimness of us, be
> 　　a crimson-cresseted east,
> More brightening her, rare-dear Britain, as his reign rolls,
> 　　Pride, rose, prince, hero of us, high-priest,
> Our hearts' charity's hearth's fire, our thoughts' chivalry's throng's Lord.

In several ways the ending of *The Wreck of the Deutschland* is similar to that of *In Memoriam*. Both are affirmative, and expectant of some future revelation. Both draw together threads from earlier parts of the work which are here broadened and universalized. But whereas the Anglican Broad Church Tennyson ends his *Divina Commedia* with a wedding and the conception of a baby, Hopkins's perspective is that of the celibate Catholic priest, for whom the type of the mystical marriage of Christ with his church is the religious in her or his devotions. Whereas Tennyson, like Dickens, tends in Frei's terms to fit the biblical story into another world with another story, Hopkins, like Newman, incorporates that world into the biblical story, as interpreted by the conservative Church of Rome. Both Catholic writers laid great stress on the importance of the human heart in the spiritual life, Newman taking as his motto the words *Cor ad cor loquitur*, and Hopkins being touched in the heart by a reading, as the lyrist is in the garden in *In Memoriam*. Whereas such movements of the heart, however, are for Newman and Hopkins subordinated to and regulated by those of the sacred heart of Christ, Tennyson and Dickens make them their main authorities in their Romantic treatments of that central Victorian *topos*, death and the future life.

Appendix: the Old Testament as the book of hope

Having listed a number of Hebrew words for hope in the Old Testament, Rudolph Bultmann comments on their usage:

> for the Old Testament there is no neutral concept of *elpis*, which merely denotes expecting, so that an expectation would have to be qualified by the addition of good or bad as a hope or fear. On the contrary, to hope and to fear (with the future in view) are differentiated in the language from the first. To hope, as the expectation of what is good, is closely connected with confidence, and the expectation means at the same time being eagerly on the look-out, in which the idea of patient waiting as well as that of seeking refuge may be emphasised.[1]

This hope is 'fixed on God', and, indeed, God himself 'is the hope, the confidence of the godly'.[2] Bultmann examines the idea of waiting hopefully on God in stillness (as in the Psalms, a prayer-book for the Jewish community, and in Isaiah 30.15), and suggests that later in the Old Testament 'the attitude of confident waiting and trustful hope develops more and more into the awareness that all earthly things and those of the present time are entirely temporary, and becomes the hope for the eschatological future'.[3]

Read as the story of the Children of Israel, the Hebrew bible tells of the journey of the Jewish people towards a promised land that Moses can see but does not enter, a Jerusalem that is not yet, a Messiah who is still to be born. In the Victorian Age, which witnessed a remarkable revival of biblical typology in literature, art, and thought,[4] events in the Old Testament narrative were read as types of New Testament events. More broadly, the hopes expressed in the Old Testament were thought to have been fulfilled in Christ. In Charles Gore's controversial essay in *Lux Mundi* (1889), for example, entitled 'The Holy Spirit and Inspiration', the imperfections of the Old Testament are explained in terms of the 'gradualness of the Spirit's method': 'It is of the essence of the New

Testament, as the religion of the Incarnation, to be final and catholic: on the other hand, it is of the essence of the Old Testament to be imperfect because it represents a gradual process of education by which man was lifted out of depths of sin and ignorance.'[5] The outcome of what Gore calls 'Divine communication' in the Old Testament is 'to produce an organic whole which postulates a climax not yet reached, a redemption not yet given, a hope not yet satisfied'; and 'in this general sense at least no Christian ought to feel a difficulty in believing, and believing with joy, in the inspiration of the Old Testament'.[6] Significantly, the last word of the essay, in a quotation from Romans 15.4, is *hope*: 'For whatsoever things were written aforetime were written for our learning, that we through patience and comfort of the Scriptures might have hope.'[7]

The nature of hope in the Old Testament is also discussed by Gore's successor as Principal of Pusey House, R. L. Ottley, in the article on Christian hope in Hastings's *Encyclopaedia of Religion and Ethics* (vol. VI, 1913):

The Bible . . . is the book of hope. One strange book (Ecclesiastes) reflects the deep melancholy which was a pervading note of ancient literature; but hope cherished in the darkest times, hope continually kept alive by the labours of the prophets, hope of a future never abandoned and ever shining out anew in spite of every conceivable discouragement – this is the dominant note of the Old Testament . . . in a transfigured form, corresponding to the light shed upon the purpose and character of God by the Gospel, it re-appears in the New Testament . . . the gospel is the religion of the 'better hope' (Hebrews 7.19), because it is the religion 'through which men for the first time enter into intimate fellowship with God' . . .[8]

Hope in the Old Testament, then, is hope for the future for the Jewish nation; whereas the Christian hope is for the individual (salvation to eternal life through Jesus Christ), for the church (as defined, for example, in the doctrine of the communion of saints), and for the world (as Christ died for all mankind).

Furthermore, although it has been claimed that hope is the dominant note of the Old Testament, it is not until the later books that the apocalyptic writings which grew out of Jewish prophetic tradition held out the possibility of a 'desirable immortality'.[9] The ancient Hebrew Sheol, which is similar in conception to the Greek Hades, is a gloomy underworld in which the dead persist, in some kind of shadowy existence, cut off forever from the life of the nation and thus from the covenant between man and God.[10] None of the patriarchs of Israel, from

Abraham to Ezekiel, believed in a resurrection of the dead.[11] With the Babylonian conquest of Judah in the sixth century BC, however, and the subsequent exile, the emphasis on national life and identity gave way to individual self-consciousness; and by the time of the Maccabean wars in the second century, the question of the fate of the faithful martyrs after death had possibly become urgent. Daniel 12.2 reads: 'And many of them that sleep in the dust of the earth shall awake, some to everlasting life, and some to shame and everlasting contempt.'[12] The last judgment is described in Matthew's gospel in terms of traditional Jewish apocalyptic.[13] Thus not only the 'hope for the eschatological future' which Bultmann locates in the later books of the Old Testament, but also a Jewish idea of judgment, were carried over into the New Testament.

Notes

Place of publication is London, unless otherwise stated. For ease and economy of reference, and where there are no significant variants, locations of quotations from novels and from some well-known poetry are given in the main text (by chapter number and section/line numbers as appropriate), rather than by page number in these references. Details of all sources are, however, available in the Bibliography. Both in the main text and in the end-matter, obvious and insignificant printers' errors have been silently corrected.

Introduction

1 See J. H. A. Hart, 'The First Epistle General of Peter', in *The Expositor's Greek Testament*, edited by W. Robertson Nicoll, 5 vols. (1897–1910), V, 41–2.

2 See Geoffrey Rowell, *Hell and the Victorians: A Study of the Nineteenth-Century Theological Controversies Concerning Eternal Punishment and the Future Life* (Oxford, 1974), pp. 19–20. Cf. the debate between the 'orthodox' in the early church, who preached the bodily resurrection of Christ, and the gnostics, who denied it and were denounced as 'heretics': Elaine Pagels, *The Gnostic Gospels* (1980), p. 101. See also Appendix, 'The Old Testament as the book of hope' (pp. 367–9 above).

3 See Stephen H. Travis, *Christian Hope and the Future of Man*, Issues in Contemporary Theology series, edited by I. H. Marshall (Leicester, 1980), pp. 96–7. Travis adds, however: 'the doctrines of "resurrection" and "immortality" are not as opposed to each other as is commonly believed'. Cf. also Maurice Wiles, *The Remaking of Christian Doctrine* (1974), pp. 125–46, on immortality.

4 See Travis, pp. 13–14.

5 Rudolf Bultmann and Karl Heinrich Rengstorf, *Hope*, Bible Key Words series, 12 (1963), p. 38. On 'realized' and 'inaugurated' eschatology, see also A. T. Hanson, 'Eschatology', in *A New Dictionary of Christian Theology*, edited by Alan Richardson and John Bowden (1983), pp. 183–6.

6 See Patrick Sherry, *Spirits, Saints and Immortality*, Library of Philosophy and Religion, edited by John Hick (1984), pp. 51–63.

7 See Travis, pp. 13, 19–23, 63ff.

8 Cf. Sherry, pp. 62–3.

9 Ruskin quotes these verses when commenting approvingly on Veronese's portrayal of hope as aged and assured, rather than young and joyous, in *Modern Painters*, vol. V (1860), pt. IX, ch. 3, para. 20: *The Works of John Ruskin*, edited by E. T. Cook and Alexander Wedderburn, Library Edition, 39 vols. (1902–12), VII, 291.

10 See Andrew Lincoln, *Paradise Now and Not Yet: Studies in the Role of the Heavenly Dimension in Paul's Thought with Special Reference to his Eschatology*, Society for New Testament Studies Monograph series, edited by R. McL. Wilson and M. E. Thrall, 43 (Cambridge, 1981).

11 See, e.g., Stewart D. F. Salmond, *The Christian Doctrine of Immortality* (Edinburgh, 1895), p. 294. Henry Cadbury's helpful analysis of the question is cited in John Hick, *Death and Eternal Life* (1976), p. 181.

12 See S. G. F. Brandon, *The Judgment of the Dead: An Historical and Comparative Study of the Idea of a Post-Mortem Judgment in the Major Religions* (1967), pp. 100–1.

13 *In Memoriam* (1850), lyric 31: Tennyson, *In Memoriam*, edited by Susan Shatto and Marion Shaw (Oxford, 1982), p. 63.

14 See, e.g., Frank Kermode, *The Genesis of Secrecy: On the Interpretation of Narrative*, The Charles Eliot Norton Lectures, 1977–1978 (Cambridge, Mass. and London, 1979), pp. 23–7, 47.

15 *The Great Texts of the Bible: Revelation*, edited by James Hastings (1915), p. 291.

16 Salmond, pp. 423–5.

17 Northrop Frye, *The Great Code: The Bible and Literature* (1983), p. 135.

18 Friedrich Schleiermacher, *The Christian Faith*, edited by H. R. Mackintosh and J. S. Stewart (Edinburgh, 1928), p. 702.

19 See Arthur Stuart Duncan-Jones, 'The Burial of the Dead', in *Liturgy and Worship: A Companion to the Prayer Books of the Anglican Communion*, edited by W. K. Lowther Clarke (London and New York, 1932), p. 616; Ulrich Simon, *Heaven in the Christian Tradition* (1958), pp. 218–19.

20 Many Methodists, for example, used the Book of Common Prayer in their worship, and were buried by the Church of England incumbent. Nonconformists who objected to the burial service of the established church often maintained silence in the churchyard. The question of nonconformist burials became increasingly contentious until the Burials Act was passed in 1880. The prayer book service could now be replaced by other suitable forms. See Owen Chadwick, *The Victorian Church*, second edition, 2 vols., Ecclesiastical History of England, edited by J. D. Dickinson, vols. VII–VIII (1970), I, 370–1; II, 202–7. Roman Catholic prayers for the dead are discussed in Chapter 7, pp. 315–24 above.

21 See Duncan-Jones, p. 623.

22 Edward Henry Bickersteth, *The Shadowed Home, and the Light Beyond* (1875), p. 179.

23 *Sacred Poems for Mourners* [selected by Priscilla Maurice], introduced by R. C. Trench (1846), p. 123.

24 *The Illustrated Book of Sacred Poems*, edited by Robert H. Baynes (London and New York, 1867), p. 130.

25 On *Our Mutual Friend*, see Chapter 6, pp. 273–4 above. The British Library Catalogue lists twenty-seven tracts and books on liturgical reform published between 1859 and 1863 by individual named authors alone. Church reports, etc., must be added to this list.

26 Charles John Vaughan, *Revisions of the Liturgy: Five Discourses* (Cambridge and London, 1860), pp. 73–4.

27 *The Stones of Venice*, vol. II (1853), ch. 8, para. 85: *Works*, X, 399.

28 *Hymns Ancient and Modern, For Use in the Services of the Church; With Accompanying Tunes* [edited by Henry Williams Baker, *et al.*], Standard Edition (1916), p. 236. Cf. also Bishop Christopher Wordsworth's 'Gracious Spirit, Holy Ghost', p. 219.

29 *Hymns Ancient and Modern*, p. 242.

30 Bernard Ramm, *The Pattern of Religious Authority* (Grand Rapids, Mich., 1957), pp. 20, 63, 28, 29.

31 See John Henry Newman, *Lectures on the Prophetical Office of the Church, Viewed Relatively to Romanism and Popular Protestantism* (London and Oxford, 1837), pp. 152–201.

32 See Stephen Neill, *The Interpretation of the New Testament, 1861–1961*, The Firth Lectures, 1962 (1966), p. 31.

33 See James C. Livingston, *Modern Christian Thought: From the Enlightenment to Vatican II* (New York and London, 1971), p. 96.

34 Samuel Taylor Coleridge, *Confessions of an Inquiring Spirit*, edited by H. St J. Hart, Library of Modern Religious Thought (1956), p. 64.

35 Ibid., p. 59.

36 Benjamin Jowett, 'On the Interpretation of Scripture', in *Essays and Reviews*, seventh edition (1861), pp. 377, 383.

37 See Rowell, *Hell and the Victorians*, p. 121.

38 See Chadwick, II, 69.

39 Ibid., II, 74–5.

40 See Neill, pp. 33–60.

41 Matthew Arnold, *Dissent and Dogma*, edited by R. H. Super, Complete Prose Works, 11 vols. (Ann Arbor, Mich., 1960–77), VI, 362, 161.

42 Ibid., pp. 143–6.

43 Matthew Arnold, *God and the Bible*, edited by R. H. Super, Complete Prose Works, 11 vols. (Ann Arbor, Mich., 1960–77), VII, 350–1.

44 Ibid., pp. 371–2.

45 Arnold, *Dissent and Dogma*, p. 237.

46 Arnold, *God and the Bible*, p. 244.

47 *Lux Mundi: A Series of Studies in the Religion of the Incarnation*, edited by Charles Gore, eighth edition (1890), pp. 325–6.

48 Ibid., p. 357.

49 See, e.g., Chadwick, II, 100–11.

50 F. W. Farrar, *The Bible: Its Meaning and Supremacy*, second edition (1901), pp. 42, 98, 136.

51 Ibid., pp. 203–6.

52 Ibid., p. 214.

53 Ibid., p. 199.

54 Ibid., p. 52.

55 Chris Brooks, *Signs for the Times: Symbolic Realism in the Mid-Victorian World* (1984), pp. 3, 14. Like Brooks, W. David Shaw in his masterly study on Victorian poetics discusses the Victorian 'recovery of analogy' in terms of typology, in Keble's conservative hermeneutics and the poetry of Hopkins and Christina Rossetti, for example, but does not discuss the influence on these writers of Joseph Butler: see *The Lucid Veil: Poetic Truth in the Victorian Age* (1987), chapter 6. See also George P. Landow, *Victorian Types, Victorian Shadows: Biblical Typology in Victorian Literature, Art, and Thought* (1980).

56 On Butler's *Analogy*, see pp. 59–61 above.

57 *The Works of Joseph Butler*, edited by W. E. Gladstone, 2 vols. (Oxford, 1896), I, 19–24.

58 James Buchanan, *Analogy, Considered as a Guide to Truth, and Applied as an Aid to Faith* (Edinburgh and London, 1864), p. 354.

59 Ibid., p. 124.

60 S. T. Coleridge, *Aids to Reflection in the Formation of a Manly Character on the Several Grounds of Prudence, Morality and Religion*, edited by Thomas Fenby, New Universal Library (London and New York, [1905]), pp. 181–2.

61 Austin Farrer, *The Glass of Vision*, Bampton Lectures (1948), pp. 42, 109, 136.

62 Ibid., p. 74.

63 Ibid., p. 110.

64 See Michael Wheeler, 'Austin Farrer's *Glass of Vision*: A Literary and Theological Debate', *National Conference on Literature and Religion Newsletter*, 6 (April 1985), 14–21.

65 John MacQuarrie, *God-Talk: An Examination of the Language and Logic of Theology* (1967), p. 228.

66 Ibid., pp. 194–5.

67 F. W. Dillistone, *Christianity and Symbolism* (1955), p. 161.

68 Sallie McFague, *Metaphorical Theology: Models of God in Religious Language* (1983), p. 38.

69 Dillistone, p. 160.

70 McFague, p. 19.

71 Michael Edwards, *Towards a Christian Poetics* (London and Basingstoke, 1984), pp. 4–5.

72 Ibid., pp. 5–6.

73 Arnold, *God and the Bible*, p. 350.

74 Bickersteth, *Shadowed Home*, pp. 4–5.

75 During his time as Bishop of Exeter (1885–1900), however, Bickersteth acknowledged the role of biblical criticism 'when serious and reverent', and claimed that the Church of England stood on 'a far higher level than those who unconvinced, are compelled to submit, if not to subscribe, to the recent encyclical letter from the Vatican': Francis Keyes Aglionby, *The Life of Edward Henry Bickersteth, D.D., Bishop and Poet* (1907), p. 73.

76 Bickersteth, *Shadowed Home*, pp. 14–15.

77 James Beattie, *Elements of Moral Science*, 2 vols. (Edinburgh, 1790–3), II, 467.

78 John Hutchison, *Our Lord's Signs in St. John's Gospel: Discussions Chiefly Exegetical and Doctrinal on the Eight Miracles in the Fourth Gospel* (Edinburgh, 1892), p. 153.

79 Frederick Denison Maurice, *The Gospel of St. John: A Series of Discourses* (Cambridge, 1857), p. 306.

80 F. D. Maurice, *Death and Life: A Sermon Preached in Lincoln's Inn Chapel on the 25th March, 1855* (Cambridge and London, [1855]), pp. 9–11. Maurice intimated to his wife that his brother-in-law, Julius Hare, who had died only two months previously, was more 'present' to him than the man of whom he was more directly preaching: *The Life of Frederick Denison Maurice, Chiefly Told in his Own Letters*, edited by Frederick Maurice, 2 vols. (1884), II, 259.

81 David Friedrich Strauss, *The Life of Jesus, Critically Examined*, translated by Marian Evans, 3 vols. (1846), II, 371. Rudolf Bultmann argues, however, that the misunderstanding is not 'Johannine', for it 'has nothing to do with the confusion of the heavenly and earthly. Rather a primitive artificial device of the source lies behind this (cp. Mk.5.39)': *The Gospel of John: A Commentary*, translated by G. R. Beasley-Murray (Oxford, 1971), p. 399, n. 6; cf. p. 135, n. 1. Bultmann's position was in turn challenged by Cullmann: see *Theological Dictionary of the New Testament*, edited by Gerhard Kittel, translated and edited by Geoffrey W. Bromiley, 10 vols. (Grand Rapids, Mich., 1964–76), VIII, 555, n. 73.

82 Strauss, II, 383.

83 Cf. Edwyn Clement Hoskyns, *The Fourth Gospel*, edited by Francis Noel Davey, second edition (1947), p. 401.

84 *Theological Dictionary of the New Testament*, VIII, 555.

85 Arnold, *God and the Bible*, p. 171.

86 Ibid., p. 299.

87 Ibid., pp. 350–1.

88 Ibid., p. 350.

89 Cf. Bultmann and Rengstorf, p. 38. On 'realized' and 'inaugurated' eschatology, see also A. T. Hanson, 'Eschatology', in *A New Dictionary of Christian Theology*, edited by Richardson and Bowden, pp. 183–6.

1 Death

1 *The Poetical Works of William Wordsworth*, edited by E[rnest] de Selincourt and Helen Darbishire, 5 vols. (Oxford, 1940–9), V, 171. All further quotations from Wordsworth's poetry are taken from this edition.

2 See, for example, John R. Reed, *Victorian Conventions* (Athens, Ohio, 1975), chapter 7; A. O. J. Cockshut, *Truth to Life: The Art of Biography in the Nineteenth Century* (1974), chapter 3; Garrett Stewart, *Death Sentences: Styles of Dying in British Fiction* (Cambridge, Mass. and London, 1984), chapters 1–3. The best discussion on doctrinal questions related to deathbed conventions is Elisabeth Jay's in *The Religion of the Heart: Anglican Evangelicalism and the Nineteenth-Century Novel* (Oxford, 1979), chapter 3.

3 See, for example, the titles of poems in the collected works of Anna Barbauld (1743–1824), Felicia Hemans (1793–1835), Elizabeth Barrett Browning (1806–61) and Christina Rossetti (1830–94). See also Eric Smith, *By Mourning Tongues: Studies in English Elegy* (Ipswich and Totowa, N.J., 1977).

4 See John Morley, *Death, Heaven and the Victorians* (1971) and James Stevens Curl, *The Victorian Celebration of Death* (Newton Abbot, 1972).

5 '*Archangel*. Behold there, Death! / . . . his scythe, / Still wet out of its bloody swathe, one hand / Tottering sustains . . .': Philip James Bailey, *Festus: A Poem*, ninth edition (1875), p. 560.

6 Charlotte Brontë to W. S. Williams, 16 March 1850, in *The Brontës: Their Lives, Friendships & Correspondence*, edited by Thomas James Wise and John Alexander Symington, 4 vols., The Shakespeare Head Brontë (Oxford, 1932), III, 82; [John Henry Newman], *Verses on Various Occasions*, second edition (1869), p. 315.

7 *The Poems of Tennyson*, edited by Christopher Ricks, Longman Annotated English Poets, general editor F. W. Bateson (1969), p. 1,648. All further quotations from Tennyson's poems, other than *In Memoriam* (see note 85 below), are taken from this edition.

8 [Elizabeth] Stone, *God's Acre; or, Historical Notices Relating to Church-yards* (1858), p. 31. A nice cultural contrast to Mrs Stone's book in our own time is Francesca Greenoak's *God's Acre: The Flowers and Animals of the Parish Churchyard* (1985), a study of the churchyard as an 'unofficial nature reserve'. Whereas 'hell' is now often taken to be a metaphor of a metaphor, in this case the metaphoric has been emptied of significance and a 'natural' literalism has reclaimed the site.

9 *The Poor Man's Friend, Punch*, 8 (Jan.–June 1845), 93.

10 Following the burial of his eldest child, Philip Henry, the seventeenth-century nonconformist divine, wrote: 'My dear child, now mine no longer, was laid in the cold earth, not lost, but soon to be raised again a glorious body, and I shall go to him, but he shall not return to me. A few days after his dear friend, Mr. Lawrence . . . buried a daughter, that was grown up and very hopeful, and gave good evidence of a work of grace wrought upon her soul, how willing, saith he, may parents be to part with such when the Lord calls; they are not *amissi* but *praemissi*.' Matthew Henry, *The Life of the Rev. Philip Henry, A.M., with Funeral Sermons for Mr. and Mrs. Henry*, collected and enlarged by J. B. Williams (1825), p. 111. The saying which the Victorians turned into a cliché – 'Not lost, but gone before' – figured on many gravestones of the period, and was often used in popular books on the subject of death and the future life. See, for example, [Robert Bickersteth] *et al.*, *The Recognition of Friends in Heaven* (1866), pp. iv, 179, 250, 254–5. For an example of the convention of the 'heavenly birth-day', which is as old as Christianity itself, as we know from inscriptions in the Roman catacombs and from the Roman Martyrology, see 'The Three Birthdays' (1861) in Edward Henry Bickersteth, *The Two Brothers, and other Poems*, second edition (1872), pp. 211–13. The poem is dedicated to the memory of 'one who, in blindness and suffering, but in the full assurance of faith, said, a few hours before her death, that she had always heard that three birthdays were ours: – our natural birthday, our spiritual birthday, and our birthday into glory: and that she was sure the last was the brightest and the best'.

11 See, for example, *The Collected Letters of Thomas and Jane Welsh Carlyle*, Duke-Edinburgh Edition, general editor Charles Richard Sanders, 7 vols. (Durham, N.C., 1970–7), III, 34; and the painting entitled *The Bourne from which no Traveller Returns*, attributed to John Martin in Morley, plate 117, but not listed in William Feaver, *The Art of John Martin* (Oxford, 1975).

12 'Yet sometimes / The veil is lifted by His high behest / Who separates eternity from time, / And spirits have spoken unto men . . .' (1.630–3): Edward Henry Bickersteth, *Yesterday, To-Day, and For Ever: A Poem, in Twelve Books*, eighth edition (1873), p. 23. Tennyson adopts the tradi-

tional metaphor in *In Memoriam* (1850), 56: 'Behind the veil, behind the veil'. George Eliot subverts it in her short story 'The Lifted Veil' (1859).

13 A. O. J. Cockshut, *Truth to Life: The Art of Biography in the Nineteenth Century* (1974), p. 41.

14 Frederick W. Robertson, *Sermons, Preached at Trinity Chapel, Brighton*, third series (1857), p. 184.

15 Frederick Denison Maurice, *The Gospel of St. John: A Series of Discourses* (Cambridge, 1857), p. 307.

16 See *The Life of Frederick Denison Maurice, Chiefly Told in his Own Letters*, edited by Frederick Maurice, 2 vols. (1884), II, 640. Quoted in Cockshut, pp. 49–50.

17 Cf. Victorian genre paintings – Christopher Wood, *Victorian Panorama: Paintings of Victorian Life* (1976), chapters 13–14.

18 Cf. Victor W. Turner, *The Ritual Process: Structure and Anti-Structure* (1969), pp. 94–5. See also Arnold van Gennep, *The Rites of Passage*, translated by Monika B. Vizedom and Gabrielle L. Caffee (Chicago, 1960), pp. 10–13, 146–65.

19 [Richard Whateley], *A View of the Scripture Revelations Concerning a Future State: Laid Before his Parishioners, by a Country Pastor* (1829), pp. 246–9.

20 'A priest is never more thoroughly a priest than in the chamber of death' (97). Charles Reade, *The Cloister and the Hearth: A Tale of the Middle Ages*, Everyman's Library (London and New York, 1906), p. 694.

21 [A. M. H. W.], *Glimpses of a Brighter Land* (1871), pp. 122–3.

22 For discussion on *The Way of all Flesh*, see Chapter 2, pp. 112–13.

23 F. W. Farrar, *Mercy and Judgment: A Few Last Words on Christian Eschatology with Reference to Dr. Pusey's 'What is of Faith?'* (1881), pp. 159–61.

24 Henry Nutcombe Oxenham, *Catholic Eschatology and Universalism: An Essay on the Doctrine of Future Retribution*, second edition (1878), p. 45. (First edition, 1876.)

25 Owen Meredith [E. R. B. Lytton], 'Last Words', Cornhill Magazine, 2 (July–Dec. 1860), 513–17.

26 Frederic Rowland Marvin, *The Last Words (Real and Traditional) of Distinguished Men and Women, Collected from Various Sources* (Troy, N.Y., 1900), p. 76. Last words are also regarded as being of critical importance in Christian manuals on holy dying. See, for example, [Timothy East], *Death Bed Scenes; or, The Christian's Companion; On Entering the Dark Valley* (1825).

27 See J. A. Symonds, 'Death', in *The Cyclopaedia of Anatomy and Physiology*, edited by Robert B. Todd, 5 vols. (1835–9), I, 803.

28 [Priscilla Maurice], *Prayers for the Sick and Dying* (1853), p. 185.

29 Stone, p. 404.

30 Edward Henry Bickersteth, *Yesterday, To-Day, and For Ever: A Poem, in Twelve Books*, eighth edition (1873), pp. 4–5. Further references in the text are by book and line numbers.

31 Sex is idealized in the memory, and described in biblical terms:

> And then the plucking of the tree of life,
> With its ambrosial fruitage and fresh flowers,
> Upon our bridal day. We took and ate
> And lived – God's smile upon us.   (1.143–5)

32 Philippe Ariès, *Western Attitudes Toward Death: From the Middle Ages to the Present*, translated by Patricia M. Ranum (Baltimore and London, 1974), chapter 3. See also Ariès's more detailed study, *The Hour of Our Death*, translated by Helen Weaver (1981).

33 See Eric Smith, *By Mourning Tongues: Studies in English Elegy* (Ipswich and Totowa, N.J., 1977), chapters 1 and 4.

34 Morley, illustrations 25 and 30.

35 *The Complete Works of Robert Browning*, edited by Roma A. King, Jr, *et al.* (Athens, Ohio, 1969–   ), IV, 189. All further quotations from Browning's poetry are taken from this edition.

36 'Bishop Blougram's Apology'.

37 John Henry Newman, *Parochial and Plain Sermons*, new edition, 8 vols. (1868), I, 4–7. See also pp. 134–5 above.

38 *The Complete Poetical Works of Thomas Hood*, edited by Walter Jerrold (1906), p. 444. Cf. D. G. Rossetti's 'My Sister's Sleep', written in 1847 and published in 1850.

39 'Worldliness and Other-Worldliness: The Poet Young', in *Essays of George Eliot*, edited by Thomas Pinney (New York and London, 1963), pp. 377, 375.

40 Garrett Stewart believes that Jane's question ('Are you going home?') is disingenuous, and that in the inscription on Helen's tombstone 'it is as if the heroine herself, in a dead language recharged with feeling, has retrospectively engraved the tense of her own resurrection': Stewart, p. 104. The first comment is questionable; the second is more interesting, but takes no account of the fact that the mature Jane respects Helen's position on death and eternal life, and that the language of resurrection is not 'dead' to her.

41 For Stewart, Rochester's response again brings us back to writing and the limits of narrative: 'His ironic mistaking of her temporal grammar plays not only upon her supposed supernatural gifts but implicitly on her role as a narrator, harrowing death so as to strengthen her autobiographical record against recurrent instances of human closure.' Stewart, p. 31.

42 Augustus J. C. Hare, *Memorials of a Quiet Life*, 3 vols. (1872–6), II, 223. Bunsen's idea that spring is a 'type of the revival of the spirit after death' is quoted in the *Memorials*, II, 39. Augustus Hare's biographer, Malcolm Barnes, portrays Maria Hare as a warped and wilful woman who, even in the moment of death, could 'organise the proper gesture': *Augustus Hare* (1984), p. 115.

43 Hare, II, 236. Malcolm Barnes is scornful of such writing, and argues that 'the deeper their misery the more the Hare women resorted to pretentious clichés': Barnes, p. 95.

44 Hare, II, 293.

45 *The Letters of Gerard Manley Hopkins to Robert Bridges*, edited by Claude Colleer Abbot (1935), p. 122.

46 *Poetical Works of Robert Bridges, Excluding the Eight Dramas*, Oxford Edition (1914), pp. 267–8.

47 Peter Coveney, *The Image of Childhood, the Individual and Society: A Study of the Theme in English Literature*, revised edition (Harmondsworth, 1967), pp. 179, 182.

48 Ibid., p. 184.

49 *Catharine and Crauford Tait, Wife and Son of Archibald Campbell, Archbishop of Canterbury: A Memorial*, edited by William Benham (1879), pp. 302–3. For the full text of Thomas Bilby's hymn, see for example *Methodist Free Church School Hymns* (1888), no. 288. The hymn is sung by the Durbeyfield children, who learnt it 'at the Sunday-school': Thomas Hardy, *Tess of the d'Urbervilles* (1891; 51).

50 Hymns mentioned in Catharine Tait's narrative include 'Behold a stranger at the door', 'Jesus, Saviour, Son of God', 'Brother, thou art gone before', 'Away, thou dying saint, away', and 'How fair the day has been'. Consolatory hymns are also sung in F. W. Farrar's novels, for example: 'There is a calm for those who weep' (*Eric*, II.13); 'Nearer, my God, to Thee', 'Jerusalem the Golden', 'O for a closer walk with God', 'Rock of Ages', and 'My God, my Father, while I stay' (*St Winifred's*, I.19). The spirit and themes of Victorian consolatory hymns for children are conveyed visually in the memorial window dedicated to the memory of the Taits' children in Carlisle Cathedral.

51 *Catharine and Crauford Tait*, pp. 344–5.

52 Ibid., pp. 357–8.

53 Ibid., pp. 311–12.

54 Ibid., p. 372.

55 Randall Thomas Davidson and William Benham, *Life of Archibald Campbell Tait, Archbishop of Canterbury*, 2 vols. (London and New York, 1891), I, 192.

56 Ibid., I, 202.

57 See Francis Keyes Aglionby, *The Life of Edward Henry Bickersteth, D.D., Bishop and Poet* (1907), pp. 26, 117, 198.

58 See Whateley, pp. 246–9.

59 *Poetical Works of Wordsworth*, v, 449–50.

60 See Mary Moorman, *William Wordsworth, A Biography: The Later Years, 1803–1850* (1965), p. 183.

61 See Stephen Prickett, *Romanticism and Religion: The Tradition of Wordsworth and Coleridge in the Victorian Church* (Cambridge, 1976), chapter 3, *et seq*. Prickett does not discuss the main text of *The Excursion* in his study.

62 See Kenneth R. Johnston, *Wordsworth and 'The Recluse'* (New Haven and London, 1983), p. 286.

63 Ibid., p. 286.

64 Having quoted the passage, J. A. Froude can identify it simply by referring to 'the poet's churchyard visitor': 'The Spirit's Trials', in Zeta [James Anthony Froude], *Shadows of the Clouds* (1847), p. 92.

65 See *Encyclopaedia Britannica*, fifth edition, 20 vols. (Edinburgh, 1817), XI, 295–7; *Cyclopaedia of Anatomy*, I, 803–8; Curl, pp. 177–9.

66 *The Complete Works of Algernon Charles Swinburne*, edited by Edmund Gosse and Thomas James Wise, Bonchurch Edition, 20 vols. (1925; rpt. New York, 1968), II, 42.

67 J[oseph] Furniss, *The House of Death*, Books for Children and Young Persons, 7 (Dublin, 1860), pp. 16–17.

68 Austin Holyoake, *A Burial Service*, Secular Ceremonies [1870], p. 4.

69 *Poems and Some Letters of James Thomson*, edited by Anne Ridler (1963), p. 180. Further references in the text are by book numbers.

70 S. T. Coleridge, *Aids to Reflection*, sixth edition, edited by Henry Nelson Coleridge (1848), I, 245. Cf. J. M. Neale's Easter hymn, 'The foe behind, the deep before': 'No longer must the mourners weep, / Nor call departed Christians dead; / For death is hallow'd into sleep, / And ev'ry grave becomes a bed.' *Hymns Ancient and Modern, For Use in the Services of the Church; With Accompanying Tunes*, [edited by Henry Williams Baker, *et al*.], Standard Edition (1916), pp. 590–1. It was recorded that at Gladstone's burial, earth from the Garden of Gethsemane was mixed in with his native soil: *Black and White*, 4 June 1898, p. 743.

71 Stone, p. 52.

72 [Mrs Cecil Frances Alexander], *Hymns for Little Children* (1848), pp. 33–4.

73 [John Keble], *The Christian Year: Thoughts in Verse for the Sundays and Holydays Throughout the Year*, second edition (Oxford, 1827), p. 2.

74 Ibid., p. 354.

75 *Hymns Ancient and Modern*, p. 304.

76 Stone, p. 109.

77 Buchanan, p. 368. The literary critic R. P. Blackmur argues that 'collateral or analogical form is as near as we are likely to come to the organic' and that for poetry 'only in analogy are the opposites identical': *A Primer of Ignorance*, edited by Joseph Frank (New York, 1967), pp. 42–3.

78 See 'Christian and Jew: A Dialogue', written in 1858 and published in 1862: *The Complete Poems of Christina Rossetti*, Variorum Edition, edited by R. W. Crump, 2 vols. (Baton Rouge and London, 1979–86), I, 74.

79 Compare Hopkins's 'Fresh-firecoal chestnut-falls' ('Pied Beauty') with the last lines of 'The Windhover', also completed in the summer of 1877: '. . . and blue-bleak embers, ah my dear, / Fall, gall themselves, and gash gold-vermilion.' Hopkins wrote in his journal, 'Chestnuts as bright as coals or spots of vermilion': see *The Poems of Gerard Manley Hopkins*, fourth edition, edited by W. H. Gardner and N. H. MacKenzie (Oxford, 1967), p. 269. The analogy of the butterfly, fly, or winged insect of the spirit emerging from the chrysalis (or mortal flesh) at the moment of death is an ancient one. See, for example, Dante's *Purgatory*, x. Also compare the first chapter of Butler's *Analogy of Religion* (p. 60 above). For nineteenth-century examples see Paley's *Natural Theology* (1802), in *The Works of William Paley*, 4 vols. (Edinburgh, 1823), I, 383; Keble's Twenty-third Sunday after Trinity, in *The Christian Year*, p. 257; Mrs Gilman's 'Mother, What is Death?' in *Sacred Poems for Mourners*, [selected by Priscilla Maurice], introduced by R. C. Trench (1846), p. 151; Stone, p. 107; Ellice Hopkins, 'Life in Death' (1883), in *The Penguin Book of Victorian Verse*, edited by George MacBeth (Harmondsworth, 1969), p. 275.

80 Leslie Parris offers a different interpretation: 'Whether the young lady's doubts are answered, we are not told, though her expression suggests that they may not be. On the stone at the foot of the tree Bowler depicts a germinating chestnut: his own symbol, perhaps, of natural regeneration and an alternative to the supernatural resurrection proclaimed on the standing stone': *The Pre-Raphaelites*, Tate Gallery exhibition catalogue (1984), p. 130.

81 Rudolf Bultmann, *Life and Death*, Bible Key Words series, 14 (1965), pp. 86–7.

82 *The Works of Joseph Butler*, edited by W. E. Gladstone, 2 vols. (Oxford, 1896), I, 19–24.

83 See *The Pre-Raphaelites*, pp. 139–41. (Millais may have been inspired to paint such a scene after helping to sweep up and burn leaves during a visit to the Tennysons at Farringford.)

84 Ibid., pp. 175–7.

85 See Tennyson, *In Memoriam*, edited by Susan Shatto and Marion Shaw (Oxford, 1982), p. 180. (For further discussion on this lyric, see pp. 222–3 above.)

86 Charlotte Yonge's mentor, Keble, believed that the Church of England, the Church of Rome and the Orthodox Church 'are really one, though divided externally'. See Prickett, *Romanticism and Religion*, p. 102.

87 *Poems of Arnold*, edited by Kenneth Allott, second edition, edited by Miriam Allott, Longman Annotated English Poets, general editors F. W. Bateson and John Barnard (London and New York, 1979), pp. 427–8. All further quotations from Arnold's poetry are taken from this edition.

88 Ibid., p. 422.

89 Matthew Arnold, *God and the Bible*, edited by R. H. Super, Complete Prose Works, 11 vols. (Ann Arbor, Mich., 1960–77), VII, 350–1.

90 Chr[istopher] Wordsworth, *On Burning of the Body; and on Burial: A Sermon Preached in Westminster Abbey on Sunday July 5th, 1874* (Lincoln, 1874), p. 14.

91 *Letters from a 'Modernist'*, edited by M. J. Weaver (1981), pp. 20–1.

92 C. Wordsworth, p. 8.

93 *The Complete Poems of Thomas Hardy*, edited by James Gibson, New Wessex Edition (1976), p. 167. (Further quotations from Hardy's verse are taken from this edition.)

2 Judgment

1 Victor W. Turner, *The Ritual Process: Structure and Anti-Structure* (1969), pp. 94–5.

2 See S. G. F. Brandon, *The Judgment of the Dead: An Historical and Comparative Study of the Idea of a Post-Mortem Judgment in the Major Religions* (1967), pp. 114–15.

3 See Victor Turner and Edith Turner, *Image and Pilgrimage in Christian Culture: Anthropological Perspectives* (New York, 1978), p. 115.

4 E. H. Bickersteth, *The Blessed Dead: What Does Scripture Reveal of their State before the Resurrection?*, second edition, revised (1863), p. 5.

5 Ibid., p. 12.

6 Ibid., pp. 14–15. Bickersteth here draws upon 1 Peter 3.18–19 and Article III of the Church of England, 'as first published': 'That the body of Christ lay in the grave till his resurrection, but his spirit which He gave up was with the spirits which are detained in prison, or in hell, and preached to them, as the place in St. Peter testifieth.' Cf. Bickersteth's *Yesterday, To-Day, and For Ever: A Poem in Twelve Books*, eighth edition (1873), pp. 387–9.

7 These words are cited at the end of *The Cloud of Unknowing*. See *The*

Cloud of Unknowing and Other Works, translated by Clifton Wolters (Harmondsworth, 1978), p. 152. On Bultmann's analysis of the *eschaton*, see p. 2 above.

8 Frank Kermode, *The Sense of an Ending: Studies in the Theory of Fiction* (1967), pp. 46–7. For contrasting New Testament usages see, e.g., Revelation 1.3 and 10.6: 'the time (*kairos*) is at hand'; 'there should be time (*chronos*) no longer'. Kermode, however, cites James Barr, *Biblical Words for Time* (1962), in which the *kairos–chronos* distinction in the work of J. Marsh (1952), J. A. T. Robinson (1950) and others is strongly challenged. Kermode argues that 'the best one can hope for is that the words, in New Testament Greek, maintain a certain polarity' (p. 49). See also the article on 'time' in *The New International Dictionary of New Testament Theology*, edited by Colin Brown, 3 vols. (Exeter, 1978), III, 826, where the distinction is upheld.

 9 See John Hick, *Death and Eternal Life* (1976), p. 12.

10 Kermode, *Sense of an Ending*, p. 25.

11 Brandon, p. 109.

12 See Brandon, pp. 110–11. For a Tractarian treatment of the parable and of Christ's words on the cross as evidence for an intermediate state, see Herbert Mortimer Luckock, *After Death: An Examination of the Testimony of Primitive Times Respecting the State of the Faithful Dead, and their Relationship to the Living*, second edition (1880), pp. 26–31. See also notes 40 and 41 below.

13 Frederick Denison Maurice, *Theological Essays*, second edition (Cambridge, 1853), p. 468.

14 Frederic W. Farrar, *Eternal Hope: Five Sermons Preached in Westminster Abbey, November and December, 1877* (1904), p. xxii.

15 Ibid., pp. xxxiii–xxxv.

16 Ibid., pp. xxi–xxii.

17 See Geoffrey Rowell, *Hell and the Victorians: A Study of the Nineteenth-Century Theological Controversies Concerning Eternal Punishment and the Future Life* (Oxford, 1974), p. 181.

18 Ibid., p. 196.

19 Friedrich Schleiermacher, *The Christian Faith*, edited by H. R. Mackintosh and J. S. Stewart (Edinburgh, 1928), p. 701.

20 Farrar, *Eternal Hope*, p. xxii.

21 Jacques Le Goff, *The Birth of Purgatory*, translated by Arthur Goldhammer (1984), p. 226.

22 Ibid., p. 306.

23 Ibid., p. 293.

24 See, for example, A. Dwight Culler, *The Poetry of Tennyson* (New Haven and London, 1977), pp. 14–15.

25 See Elisabeth Jay, *The Religion of the Heart: Anglican Evangelicalism and the Nineteenth-Century Novel* (Oxford, 1979), pp. 84–5.

26 Farrar, *Eternal Hope*, p. xxi.

27 See Schleiermacher, p. 722, where he argues that the final 'universal restoration of all souls' deserves an equal claim to the 'ordinary view' of heaven and hell. See also Brandon, p. 118, and Hick, pp. 200, 208–10.

28 See F. W. Farrar, *Mercy and Judgment: A Few Last Words on Christian Eschatology with Reference to Dr. Pusey's 'What is of Faith?'* (1881), p. 7.

29 See Rowell, *Hell and the Victorians*, pp. 139–52.

30 See W. E. Gladstone, *Studies Subsidiary to the Works of Bishop Butler* (Oxford, 1896), p. 199.

31 John Henry Newman, *An Essay on the Development of Christian Doctrine* (1920), p. 48.

32 Edmund Gurney, *Tertium Quid* (1887), cited in Alan Gauld, *The Founders of Psychical Research* (1968), p. 158.

33 See Farrar, *Eternal Hope*, pp. xxxvi–xxxviii.

34 Ibid., p. xii.

35 Ibid., p. 88; cf. Farrar, *Mercy and Judgment*, pp. 11, 59, 158–75.

36 Henry Bristow Wilson, 'Séances Historiques de Genève – The National Church', in *Essays and Reviews*, seventh edition (1861), pp. 145–206 (p. 206).

37 Luckock, p. 36.

38 See John Morley, *The Life of William Ewart Gladstone*, 3 vols. (1904), I, 131, and Gladstone, pp. 253–4. The church had, in Gladstone's view, condemned the 'sleep of the soul' (*psychopannychia*) as unscriptural.

39 See Francois Wendel, *Calvin: The Origin and Development of his Religious Thought*, translated by Philip Mairet (London and New York, 1965), p. 287; cited in Brandon, p. 132.

40 H. P. Liddon, *Passiontide Sermons* (London and New York, 1891), pp. 278–9.

41 See Edward Henry Bickersteth, *The Shadowed Home, and the Light Beyond* (1875), p. 195.

42 See Stewart D. F. Salmond, *The Christian Doctrine of Immortality* (1895), p. 350.

43 Rowell, *Hell and the Victorians*, pp. 215–16.

44 Norman Cohn, *The Pursuit of the Millennium: Revolutionary Millenarians and Mystical Anarchists of the Middle Ages* (1970), p. 13.

45 See Ernest R. Sandeen, 'Millennialism', in *The Rise of Adventism: Religion and Society in Mid-Nineteenth-Century America*, edited by Edwin S. Gaustad (New York, 1974), pp. 104–18 (p. 107); Cohn, pp. 108–10; M. H. Abrams, *Natural Supernaturalism: Tradition and Revelation in*

Romantic Literature (New York and London, 1971), p. 58; Marjorie Reeves and Warwick Gould, *Joachim of Fiore and the Myth of the Eternal Evangel in the Nineteenth Century* (Oxford; 1987).

46 See Turner, *Ritual Process*, pp. 111–12.

47 J. F. C. Harrison, *The Second Coming: Popular Millenarianism, 1780–1850* (London and Henley, 1979).

48 See, for example, Bickersteth, *Yesterday*, pp. 94–5, 103–4.

49 See E. P. Thompson, *The Making of the English Working Class* (1963; rpt. Harmondsworth, 1968), pp. 52–5, 127–30, 420–31, 877–83.

50 See Sandeen, p. 111.

51 See Owen Chadwick, *The Victorian Church*, second edition, 2 vols., Ecclesiastical History of England, edited by J. D. Dickinson, vols. VII–VIII (1970), I, 7–47.

52 Sandeen, p. 109.

53 See John O. Waller, 'Christ's Second Coming: Christina Rossetti and the Premillennialist William Dodsworth', *Bulletin of the New York Public Library*, 73 (1969), 465–82 (pp. 476–7).

54 Bickersteth, *Yesterday*, p. v.

55 William Ker, *'The Things which must Shortly come to Pass': A Series of Discourses on the Prophecies of 'The Last Days,' Delivered in the Parish Church of Tipton, Staffordshire* (Dudley, 1868), discourses XI and XII.

56 Cf. Frank Kermode, 'Lawrence and the Apocalyptic Types', *Critical Quarterly*, Tenth Anniversary Number (1968), 26–35; extract reprinted as '*Middlemarch* and Apocalypse', in *George Eliot, 'Middlemarch': A Casebook*, edited by Patrick Swinden, Casebook series, general editor A. E. Dyson (London and Basingstoke, 1972), pp. 131–43.

57 Edmund Gosse, *Father and Son: A Study of Two Temperaments*, popular edition (1909), pp. 327–8.

58 Christina G. Rossetti, *The Face of the Deep: A Devotional Commentary on the Apocalypse* (1892).

59 Mackenzie Bell, *Christina Rossetti: A Biographical and Critical Study* (1898), pp. 244, 180–1.

60 *The Complete Poems of Christina Rossetti: A Variorum Edition*, 2 vols., edited by R. W. Crump (Baton Rouge and London, 1979), I, 68–9. See also Waller's article, cited in note 53 above.

61 See William Feaver, *The Art of John Martin* (Oxford, 1975), pp. 173–4, 181, 196.

62 See Morton D. Paley, *The Apocalyptic Sublime* (New Haven and London, 1986).

63 *The Poetical Works of Robert Southey*, 10 vols. (1837–8), X, 213–14.

64 See, for example, A. D. Harvey, *English Poetry in a Changing Society, 1780–1825* (1980), pp. 17–43.

65 See p. 38 above.

66 *Lord Macaulay's Essays, and Lays of Ancient Rome*, popular edition (1899), p. 132.

67 *The Miscellaneous Writings and Speeches of Lord Macaulay*, popular edition (1891), pp. 443–4.

68 Robert Pollok, *The Course of Time: A Poem*, Illustrated Edition (1857), pp. xvii–xviii.

69 Ibid., pp. 142–3.

70 Ibid., p. 174.

71 Ibid., pp. 176–84.

72 Ibid., p. 186.

73 Ibid., pp. 188–9.

74 Ibid., p. 190.

75 Ibid., p. 192.

76 Ibid., p. 205.

77 Ibid., pp. 221–2.

78 Ibid., p. 228.

79 Ibid., p. 317.

80 Ibid., p. 331.

81 Ibid., p. 334.

82 Ibid., p. 351.

83 Ibid., p. 357.

84 Ibid., pp. 358–9.

85 Francis Keyes Aglionby, *The Life of Edward Henry Bickersteth, D.D., Bishop and Poet* (1907), p. 112.

86 See pp. 36–7 above.

87 Bickersteth, *Yesterday*, pp. 362f., 429–30.

88 Extract from a review in *The Standard*, cited in 'Opinions of the Press', p. 1, printed after the main text of Bickersteth's *Yesterday, To-Day, and For Ever*.

89 Aglionby, p. 109.

90 In Elizabeth Gaskell's novel *North and South* (1854–5), for example, Margaret Hale exclaims: 'I begin to understand now what heaven must be – and, oh! the grandeur and repose of the words – "The same yesterday, today, and for ever"' (46).

91 [Hallam Tennyson], *Alfred Lord Tennyson: A Memoir* (1899), p. 269.

92 See John O. Waller, 'Tennyson and Philip James Bailey's *Festus*', *Bulletin of Research in the Humanities*, 82 (1979), 105–23.

93 See Robert Birley, *Sunk Without Trace: Some Forgotten Masterpieces Reconsidered*, The Clark Lectures, 1960–1961 (New York, 1962), pp. 173–6.

94 Philip James Bailey, *Festus: A Poem*, ninth edition (1875), p. 65. This passage first appeared in the second edition of 1845: see Birley, p. 184.

95 See Waller, 'Tennyson and *Festus*', p. 111.

96 Bailey, pp. 56, 60.

97 Ibid., p. 65.

98 Ibid., e.g. pp. 6, 8, 16, 63, 71, 75, 78, 165, 211, 212, 288, 290, 403, 503, 555.

99 Ibid., p. 507.

100 Ibid., p. 555.

101 Ibid., p. 557.

102 Ibid., pp. 560–1, 572.

103 Ibid., pp. 573–7.

104 Ibid., p. 578.

105 Ibid., p. 579.

106 Ibid., p. 582. In the first edition Lucifer is not restored.

107 Ibid., p. 585.

108 See, e.g., Michael Mason, 'Browning and the Dramatic Monologue', in *Robert Browning*, edited by Isobel Armstrong, Writers and their Background series, edited by R. L. Brett (1974), pp. 231–66.

109 [John] Bunyan, *The Pilgrim's Progress, Grace Abounding and A Relation of his Imprisonment*, edited by Edmund Venables, second edition, revised by Mabel Peacock (Oxford, 1900), p. 302.

110 Abrams, chapter 2.

111 See pp. 253–5 above.

112 Thomas Carlyle, *Sartor Resartus; On Heroes and Hero Worship*, Everyman's Library, 278 (London and New York, 1908), pp. 124–7.

113 The anonymous reviewer in *The Leader* compared Browning's mingling of 'the ludicrous with the intensely serious' in *Christmas-Eve and Easter-Day* with Carlyle: *Robert Browning: The Critical Heritage*, edited by Boyd Litzinger and Donald Smalley, Critical Heritage series, general editor B. C. Southam (1970), p. 140.

114 Augustine describes his own sorrow on the death of his mother, Monica, in the *Confessions* (IX. 12).

115 On Browning's sympathy towards Dissent and Evangelicalism see, e.g., William O. Raymond, *The Infinite Moment and Other Essays in Robert Browning* (Toronto, 1950), p. 24; Philip Drew, *The Poetry of Browning: A Critical Introduction* (1970), p. 222; William Irvine and Park Honan, *The Book, the Ring, and the Poet: A Biography of Robert Browning* (1975), p. 263.

116 His statement that 'This sight was shown me, there and then, — / Me, one out of a world of men' (405–6), for example, is reminiscent of Dame Julian

of Norwich. On the distinction between the theophanic and the epiphanic see Ashton Nichols, *The Poetics of Epiphany: Nineteenth-Century Origins of the Modern Literary Movement* (Tuscaloosa and London, 1988), pp. 27–9.

117 Drew, pp. 205, 206, 223–4, and 'Browning and Philosophy', in *Browning*, ed. Armstrong, pp. 104–7. (Drew believes that there is no evidence of *influence* on either side.)

118 William Clyde DeVane, *A Browning Handbook*, second edition (New York, 1955), p. 203.

119 Newman, *Essay on Development*, p. 114.

120 Cf. Abrams's definition of apocalypse as 'a vision in which the old world is replaced by a new and better world': Abrams, p. 41. (*Easter-Day* also conforms to what Abrams identifies as the characteristically circular structure of the Romantic journey narrative, of which Coleridge's 'The Ancient Mariner' is the paradigm.)

121 On ambiguity, see Phyllis J. Guskin, 'Ambiguities in the Structure and Meaning of Browning's *Christmas-Eve*', *Victorian Poetry*, 4 (1966), 21–8.

122 See, e.g., Ian Jack, *Browning's Major Poetry* (Oxford, 1973), pp. 133–4; Irvine and Honan, p. 266. Philip Drew is a notable exception in this respect.

123 Litzinger and Smalley, p. 144.

124 Cf. John Fowles's critique of the Victorian novel in *The French Lieutenant's Woman* (1969), chapters 12–13.

125 See pp. 28–9 above.

126 E. P. Whipple, writing in the *North American Review*, described Heathcliff thus: 'He is a deformed monster . . . to whom Dante would hesitate in awarding the honour of a place among those whom he has consigned to the burning pitch.' *The Brontës: The Critical Heritage*, edited by Miriam Allott, Critical Heritage series, general editor B. C. Southam (London and Boston, 1974), p. 248.

127 Charles F. S. Warren, *The Dies Irae: On this Hymn and its English Versions*, Part I, The Hymn (1897), pp. xii–xv.

3 Heaven

1 *Hymns Ancient and Modern, For Use in the Services of the Church; With Accompanying Tunes* [edited by Henry Williams Baker, *et al.*], Standard Edition (1916), p. 170.

2 Edward Gordon Selwyn, *The First Epistle of St. Peter* (1946), p. 124.

3 Edward Henry Bickersteth, *A Practical and Explanatory Commentary on the New Testament* [1868], p. 373.

4 See John Hick, *Death and Eternal Life* (1976), p. 202.

5 In a major survey of the history of heaven in the West, published after work on this chapter was completed, Colleen McDannell and Bernhard Lang show how medieval courtly love and a Renaissance conflation of the Christian and the pagan generated an anthropocentric heaven, the apex of which was to come in the nineteenth century: *Heaven: A History* (New Haven and London, 1988), pp. 353–8.

6 See, for example, George Eliot's *Felix Holt* (1866; 30). For Feuerbach, theology is in reality anthropology, and religion is 'the relation of man to his own nature . . . but to his nature not recognised as his own'; 'God is heaven spiritualised, while heaven is God materialised, or reduced to the forms of the senses': Ludwig Feuerbach, *The Essence of Christianity*, translated by Marian Evans, second edition, English and Foreign Philosophical Library, 15 (1881), pp. 197, 172. On Marx's response to Feuerbach, see Robert C. Tucker, *Philosophy and Myth in Karl Marx* (Cambridge, 1961), pp. 95–105; Arend Th. van Leeuwen, *Critique of Heaven* (1972), pp. 151, 174, 177–8.

7 See Hick, p. 206.

8 See Alan Gauld, *The Founders of Psychical Research* (1968) and Janet Oppenheim, *The Other World: Spiritualism and Psychical Research in England, 1850–1914* (Cambridge, 1985); John Morley, *Death, Heaven and the Victorians* (London and Pittsburgh, 1971), chapter 9.

9 Ulrich Simon, *Heaven in the Christian Tradition* (1958), pp. 31–2. Andrew Lincoln, author of a rigorous work of biblical scholarship in the area, considers that Simon provides in his broad overview 'some interesting, though often fanciful, insights': *Paradise Now and Not Yet: Studies in the Role of the Heavenly Dimension in Paul's Thought with Special Reference to his Eschatology*, Society for New Testament Studies Monograph series, edited by R. McL. Wilson and M. E. Thrall, 43 (Cambridge, 1981), p. 6.

10 Simon, p. 34.

11 See Introduction, note 18 above.

12 See, for example, William E. Addis and Thomas Arnold, *A Catholic Dictionary, Containing some Account of the Doctrine, Discipline, Rites, Ceremonies, Councils, and Religious Orders of the Catholic Church* (1884), pp. 736, 776, 853.

13 See Simon, pp. 52–5.

14 Gerhard von Rad, '*ouranos*', in *Theological Dictionary of the New Testament*, edited by Gerhard Kittel and Gerhard Friedrich, translated and edited by Geoffrey W. Bromiley, 10 vols. (Grand Rapids, Mich., 1964–76), V, 509.

15 See, e.g., Northrop Frye, *The Great Code: The Bible and Literature* (1982), p. 175.

16 In *Kerygma and Myth*, edited by H. W. Bartsch (New York, 1961), p. 4;

quoted in Lincoln, *Paradise Now and Not Yet*, p. 4, where he records that 'volumes could be and have been written on this'.

17 See, e.g., *Science and Religion in the Nineteenth Century*, edited by Tess Cosslett (Cambridge, 1984).

18 Simon, p. xii.

19 Lincoln, p. 79.

20 Ibid., p. 80; also cf. Simon, pp. 44–5.

21 See, e.g., Max F. Schulz, *Paradise Preserved: Recreations of Eden in Eighteenth- and Nineteenth-Century England* (Cambridge, 1985).

22 See, e.g., Oriel's description of Eden before the fall as 'heaven's miniature' in *Yesterday, To-Day, and For Ever: A Poem in Twelve Books*, eighth edition (1873), p. 153.

23 John Henry Newman, *Parochial and Plain Sermons*, new edition, 8 vols. (1891), III, 374.

24 See Lincoln, pp. 77–80. On Lincoln's own argument the third heaven cannot simply be equated with paradise, and Paul is granted an experience of an aspect of heaven which 'anticipates both "the intermediate state" and the glory of the final consummation'.

25 See, e.g., Arthur Penrhyn Stanley, *The Epistles of St. Paul to the Corinthians*, fourth edition (1876), p. 538. E. H. Bickersteth, who in *Yesterday, To-Day, and For Ever* clearly separates Paradise from the Many Mansions of Heaven, takes a different line on 'paradise' in 2 Corinthians 12 in his commentary on the New Testament, where he argues that it 'may here well describe the region of celestial glory': *The Holy Bible*, with a Devotional and Practical Commentary by R. Jamieson and E. H. Bickersteth, 3 vols. (London and New York, 1861–5), III, 299.

26 See C. K. Barrett, *A Commentary on the Second Epistle to the Corinthians* (1973), p. 309. Cf. also Christopher Rowland, *The Open Heaven: A Study of Apocalyptic in Judaism and Early Christianity* (1982), pp. 378–86.

27 See Lincoln, p. 77.

28 See, e.g., Lincoln, p. 82; Simon, p. 46.

29 Karl Ludwig Schmidt, '*basilea*', in *Theological Dictionary of New Testament*, I, 582.

30 Addis and Arnold, pp. 776, 853.

31 Frederick Denison Maurice, *The Kingdom of Christ; or, Hints to a Quaker Respecting the Principles, Constitution and Ordinances of the Catholic Church*, edited by Alec R. Vidler, 2 vols. (1958), I, 256–7.

32 Cf. Stephen Prickett, *Romanticism and Religion: The Tradition of Coleridge and Wordsworth in the Victorian Church* (Cambridge, 1976), p. 142. On the 'secularization of the kingdom idea in terms of notions of progress, development, evolution and material prosperity', for which Kant's, Schleiermacher's and Ritschl's view of the kingdom 'as the realm of

ideal human relations on earth' prepared the ground, see Eric J. Sharpe, 'Kingdom of God', in *A New Dictionary of Christian Theology*, edited by Alan Richardson and John Bowden (1983), p. 317.

33 Frederick Denison Maurice, *Lectures on the Apocalypse; or, Book of Revelation of St. John the Divine*, second edition (Cambridge and London, 1865), pp. 302–4.

34 See Anon., 'Spirits and Spirit-Rapping', *Westminster Review*, NS 13 (1858), 29–66.

35 A. M. H. W., *Glimpses of a Brighter Land* (1871), p. vii. The book is dedicated to Mary Howitt. See also the *Christian Spiritualist*, a weekly newspaper published by the Society for the Diffusion of Spiritual Knowledge in the middle of the nineteenth century. The Churches' Fellowship for Psychical and Spiritual Studies, founded in 1953, is still active today. Its president, Revd Dr Martin Israel, and chairman, The Venerable Michael Perry, have both published widely in the area.

36 See Gauld, p. 21.

37 Addis and Arnold, p. 394.

38 John Angell James, *Heaven; or, The Church Triumphant in its State of Celestial Repose* (1859), p. 6. Bailey had taken up the theme in *Festus*, where Lucifer states that

> Heaven is no place;
> Unless it be a place with God, allwhere.
> It is the being good – the knowing God –
> The consciousness of happiness and power.

Philip James Bailey, *Festus: A Poem*, ninth edition (1875), p. 36. (This passage first appeared in the second edition of 1845: see Robert Birley, *Sunk Without Trace: Some Forgotten Masterpieces Reconsidered*, The Clark Lectures, 1960–1961 (New York, 1962), p. 184.) A banal piece of Spasmodic theologizing, the passage hints at the poem's universalism but is difficult to reconcile with Bailey's placing of the action in the Skies, the Heaven of Heavens, Angel World, and so on. Such locations are suggestive of 'place', and for Bailey's *dramatis personae* to have some kind of identity, these locations have to be inhabited by beings who can speak a language of this world.

39 [William Branks], *Heaven our Home* (Edinburgh, 1861).

40 See Geoffrey Rowell, *Hell and the Victorians: A Study of the Nineteenth-Century Theological Controversies Concerning Eternal Punishment and the Future Life* (Oxford, 1974), pp. 9–10.

41 [Robert Bickersteth] *et al.*, *The Recognition of Friends in Heaven* (1866), p. 5.

42 The author himself, who is not identified, later writes of the everlasting blessedness of heaven as a state: R. Bickersteth, p. 8.

43 Ibid., pp. 6–8.

44 E. H. Bickersteth, *The Risen Saints: What does Scripture Reveal of their Estate and Employments?* (1865), p. 54.

45 E. H. Bickersteth, *Yesterday*, p. 387.

46 Austin Holyoake, *Heaven & Hell: Where Situated?: A Search after the Objects of Man's Fervent Hope & Abiding Terror* [1873], p. 2. Cf. Feuerbach's question, 'Where is the space in which individuals will live in the life after death?': see William B. Chamberlain, *Heaven Wasn't his Destination: The Philosophy of Ludwig Feuerbach* (1941), p. 89.

47 See, e.g., Newman, *Parochial and Plain Sermons*, III, 368.

48   But peace – still voice and closed eye
              Suit best with hearts beyond the sky,
              Hearts training in their low abode,
           Daily to lose themselves in hope to find their God.
    [John Keble], *The Christian Year: Thoughts in Verse for the Sundays and Holydays Throughout the Year*, second edition (Oxford, 1827), II, 82.

49 See Rowell, *Hell and the Victorians*, pp. 70–5.

50 Thomas Erskine, *The Unconditional Freeness of the Gospel: In Two Essays*, fourth edition (Edinburgh, 1831), pp. 24, 9.

51 Frederic W. Farrar, *Eternal Hope: Five Sermons Preached in Westminster Abbey, November and December, 1877* (1904), p. 19.

52 Ibid., pp. 21, 25. Cf. the contemporary theologian Hans Küng, who argues that the 'heaven of faith is not a place, but a mode of being; the infinite God cannot be localized in space, cannot be limited by time': *Eternal Life?*, translated by Edward Quinn (1984), p. 182.

53 Cf. also William Alger, an American Unitarian, who argued in 1878 that belief in a future life was possible and necessary in spite of the 'incongruous medley of physical imagery and gross imaginative pictures' that were to be found in the doctrine of some Christian believers. This whole 'suppositious mass' of 'mere poetry or superstition' is to be dismissed in favour of a 'calm confronting of the mystery of the future in its confessed secresy as it is, and a peaceful resignation to the will of God in conscious ignorance and trust': William Rounseville Alger, *The Destiny of the Soul: A Critical History of the Doctrine of a Future Life*, tenth edition (New York, 1878), pp. 727, 732.

54 See, e.g., Bailey, p. 73; R. W. Church, *Dante and Other Essays* (London and New York, 1901), p. 83.

55 Branks, *Heaven our Home*, p. 59.

56 [Robert Weaver], *Heaven: A Manual for the Heirs of Heaven; Designed for the Satisfaction of the Inquisitive, as well as for Assistance to the Devout. Also, on Angels and their Ministry* (1837), p. 34.

57 *The Complete Poems of Christina Rossetti*, Variorum Edition, 2 vols.,

edited by R. W. Crump (Baton Rouge and London, 1979–86), I, 221–2. All further quotations from Christina Rossetti's verse are taken from this edition.

58 See pp. 59–64 above.

59 Tennyson's *Enoch Arden* (1864) contains a famous example. Having looked for a sign in the Bible and found the words 'Under the palm-tree', Enoch's wife has a dream which leads her to believe that he must be in heaven, rather than shipwrecked, as in fact he is:

When lo! her Enoch sitting on a height,

Under a palm-tree, over him the Sun:

'He is gone,' she thought, 'he is happy, he is singing

Hosanna in the highest. . .'   (496–9)

Tennyson completed the set of associations in a description of Enoch's paradisal tropical island that Hopkins considered to be inspired: 'The mountain wooded to the peak, the lawns / And winding glades high up like ways to Heaven' (568–9).

60 One of the finest Victorian applications is H. F. Lyte's in 'Abide with me', where he conflates the fall of evening and the ebbing of the tide – two traditional analogies for death: 'Abide with me; fast falls the eventide; / The darkness deepens, Lord, with me abide'; 'Swift to its close ebbs out life's little day': *Hymns Ancient and Modern*, p. 26. For an excellent detailed account of the hymn, see J. R. Watson, *The Victorian Hymn*, Inaugural Lecture, 1981 (Durham, 1981), pp. 9–12. Where images of sea and shore become mere detached tokens, as so often in popular consolatory writing, the effect is banal sentimentalism. W. D. Smith's Minstrel ballad, 'Ring the Bell Softly', for example, has these immortal lines: 'Someone has gone to the bright golden shore, / Ring the bell softly, there's crape on the door': *The Parlour Song Book: A Casquet of Vocal Gems*, edited by Michael R. Turner (London and Sydney, 1972), p. 313.

61 See, e.g., E. H. Bickersteth, *Yesterday*, pp. 374–5.

62 See Eduard Lohse, 'Sion', in *Theological Dictionary of New Testament*, VII, 317.

63 See Augustine, *The City of God*, translated by Marcus Dods, introduced by Thomas Merton, Modern Library (New York, 1950), pp. 736–7.

64 E. H. Bickersteth, *Yesterday*, p. 431.

65 Examples include E. H. Bickersteth, *The Master's Home-Call: A Memoir of Alice Frances Bickersteth* (1872) and *The Shadowed Home, and the Light Beyond* (1875). E. H. Bickersteth wrote of his own daughter, who died at the age of nineteen, 'She always spoke of death as going home': *Master's Home-Call*, p. 31. Keble's *The Christian Year* (1827) contains numerous references to the 'eternal home above', the 'endless home', and so on. F. D. Maurice described the 'sleep in Jesus' as 'the rest of one who

has . . . reached his home after long wanderings': 'Death and Life', in *Christmas Day, and Other Sermons*, second edition (1892), p. 397. One of Christina Rossetti's most significant poems is 'From House to Home' (see pp. 161–3 above). Numerous examples from deathbed scenes in nineteenth-century fiction include *Jane Eyre* (see p. 38 above), The Revd Legh Richmond's *The Dairyman's Daughter* (1810), and F. W. Farrar's *Eric; or, Little by Little* (1858). Markham Sutherland in J. A. Froude's *The Nemesis of Faith* (1849) relates the idea to people's desire to be buried where they first worshipped and were brought up: 'We call heaven our home, as the best name we know to give it': *The Nemesis of Faith*, Victorian Fiction: Novels of Faith and Doubt (New York and London, 1975), pp. 101–2.

66 [Isaac Taylor], *Physical Theory of Another Life* (1836), pp. 181–2. On analogy he wrote: 'If once we relinquish the principle of analogy, as applicable to the divine operations and government, we abandon all means of extending our knowledge, and are left in a state of distressing incertitude, in relation to the most momentous subjects': p. 181.

67 Branks, *Heaven our Home*, p. 159.

68 'What we, when face to face we see', in *The Poems of Arthur Hugh Clough*, edited by A. L. P. Norrington (1968), p. 62.

69 Immanuel Kant, *Lectures on Philosophical Theology*, translated by Allen W. Wood and Gertrude M. Clark (Ithaca and London, 1978), p. 110.

70 Robert Pollok, *The Course of Time: A Poem*, Illustrated Edition (1857), p. 169.

71 *Catharine and Crauford Tait, Wife and Son of Archibald Campbell, Archbishop of Canterbury: A Memoir*, edited by William Benham (1879), p. 173.

72 *In Memoriam*, 41; see p. 244 above.

73 See Simon, pp. 217–18; Hick, p. 204; McDannell and Lang, pp. 217, 229, 257–64.

74 R. Bickersteth, p. 178.

75 See, e.g., A. Midlane's 'There's a Friend for little children', in *Hymns Ancient and Modern*, p. 381, and Mrs Cecil Frances Alexander's 'Once in royal David's city', in her *Hymns for Little Children* (1848), p. 31.

76 See, e.g., R. Bickersteth, pp. 32, 181–2.

77 Julius Hare held that consolation for the loss of friends 'lies in the thought, that, blessed as it is to have friends on earth, it is still more blessed to have friends in heaven': [Julius and Augustus Hare], *Guesses at Truth* (1867), p. 175. The young Thomas Carlyle wrote in a letter to Jane Welsh in 1823, 'With the hope of meeting in a brighter scene of existence, I look on Death as the most inestimable privilege of man': *The Collected Letters of Thomas and Jane Welsh Carlyle*, Duke-Edinburgh Edition, general editor Charles Richard Sanders, 7 vols. (Durham, N.C., 1970–7), II, 446. Froude records

in the *Life* that, after the death of his wife, Carlyle spoke 'of a life to come, and the meeting of friends in it as a thing not impossible': James Anthony Froude, *Thomas Carlyle: A History of his Life in London, 1834–1881*, new edition, 2 vols. (1897), II, 347.

78 See Rowell, *Hell and the Victorians*, pp. 5–6, n. 19.

79 Taylor, p. 170.

80 Branks, p. iv.

81 Elizabeth Stuart Phelps, *The Gates Ajar*, edited by Helen Sootin Smith, John Harvard Library, edited by Bernard Bailyn (Cambridge, Mass., 1964).

82 A Dean, *'The Gates Ajar' Critically Examined* (1871). See also Mark Twain's parody of the novel, entitled *Extract from Captain Stormfield's Visit to Heaven* (New York and London, 1909).

83 Keble, II, 195.

84 Frederick Denison Maurice, *The Gospel of St. John: A Series of Discourses* (Cambridge, 1857), p. 318.

85 See p. 17 above.

86 Pollok, p. 29.

87 Mackenzie Bell, *Christina Rossetti: A Biographical and Critical Study* (1898), p. 179.

88 Newman, *Parochial and Plain Sermons*, IV, 174–5.

89 Ibid., IV, 207.

90 Ibid., IV, 210.

91 Ibid., IV, 204.

92 Ibid., I, 5.

93 Ibid., I, 7, 3–4.

94 J. A. James, for example, argued that heaven, which is closed against the unpardoned, 'could in fact be no heaven to them; every view of the glory of "Him that sitteth upon the throne," that was attended with the consciousness that He had not forgiven their sins, and that they did not stand spotless before Him, would fill the mind with intolerable anguish': *Heaven*, pp. 9–10. Nelly Dean in *Wuthering Heights* (1847), declares that 'all sinners would be miserable in heaven' (9).

95 Maurice, *Lectures on Apocalypse*, pp. 63–4.

96 Thomas Carlyle, *Past and Present* (1843), book III, chapter 14.

97 Maurice, *Lectures on Apocalypse*, p. 65.

98 See, e.g., Adelaide Procter's 'The Lost Chord', with music by Arthur Sullivan (1877), in M. R. Turner, p. 239.

99 Although Victorian hymnody often described a static, theocentric heaven, the popular hymns of late-nineteenth-century revivalists such as Moody and Sankey were more anthropocentric in their emphasis on the heavenly home: see McDannell and Lang, pp. 288–9.

100 See Lincoln, note 9 above.

101 *Hymns Ancient and Modern*, p. 378.

102 See *The English Hymnal* (Oxford and London, 1906), p. 81.

103   I need Thy Presence every passing hour;
                      What but Thy grace can foil the tempter's power?
                      Who like Thyself my guide and stay can be?
                      Through cloud and sunshine, Lord, abide with me.
     See also note 61 above.

104 *Hymns Ancient and Modern*, p. 249.

105 Ibid., p. 323.

106 *Historical Companion to 'Hymns Ancient & Modern'*, edited by Maurice
     Frost, new edition (1962), p. 284.

107 Lincoln, p. 61.

108 *Hymns Ancient and Modern*, p. 257.

109 *Historical Companion*, p. 276.

110 *Hymns Ancient and Modern*, p. 793.

111 *Historical Companion*, p. 282.

112 *Hymns Ancient and Modern*, p. 839.

113 Ibid., p. 369.

114 Ibid., p. 257.

115 Ibid., p. 255.

116 Ibid., p. 495.

117 Ibid., p. 334.

118 Ibid., p. 154. See also pp. 151, 152, 153, 159.

119 Ibid., p. 150.

120 Ibid., p. 155.

121 Ibid., p. 157.

122 See [Hallam Tennyson], *Alfred Lord Tennyson: A Memoir* (1899), p. 754.

123 *The New International Version Interlinear Greek-English New Testament*,
     The Nestle Greek Text with a Literal English Translation by Alfred Mar-
     shall (Grand Rapids, Mich., 1976), p. 969.

124 *Hymns Ancient and Modern*, p. 170.

125 Günther Bornkamm, *'presbys'*, in Kittel, ed., *Theological Dictionary of the
     New Testament*, VI, 668.

126 D. M. R. Bentley has called Hall Caine's often quoted reminiscence in
     question: '"The Blessed Damozel": A Young Man's Fantasy', *Victorian
     Poetry*, 20 (1982), 31–43 (p. 31).

127 *Collected Works of Edgar Allan Poe*, edited by Thomas Ollive Mabbott, 3
     vols. (Cambridge, Mass., 1969–78), I, 364–5. All further quotations from
     the poem are taken from this edition.

128 For discussion of parallels between this aspect of 'The Raven' and Ross-
     etti's poem see Paul Lauter, 'The Narrator of "The Blessed Damozel"',
     Modern Language Notes, 73 (1958), 344–8.

129 Item 19A in Virginia Surtees, *The Paintings and Drawings of Dante Gabriel Rossetti (1828–1882): A Catalogue Raisonné*, 2 vols. (Oxford, 1971), I, 4. Surtees's description of the sketch ('A man sitting by a table rises from a chair and gazes at the face of an angel; other angels, behind and in front') ignores the fact that the female figure who leans towards the man is not winged.

130 Bentley, p. 43.

131 Ibid., p. 42.

132 Ibid., p. 43. Cf. David G. Riede, *Dante Gabriel Rossetti and the Limits of Victorian Vision* (Ithaca and London, 1983), p. 21.

133 See Dante Gabriel Rossetti, *The Blessed Damozel: The Unpublished Manuscript, Texts and Collation*, edited by Paull Franklin Baum (Chapel Hill, 1937). All quotations from the poem are taken from Baum. Unless otherwise stated, the 1856 version (*Oxford and Cambridge Magazine*) is quoted (pp. 17–21). Bentley argues that these changes reflect Rossetti's 'urge to secularize his early poems', and that the poem 'assumed the burden of his wish-fulfillment fantasies': Bentley, p. 33. David G. Riede's disagreement with Bentley's view that Rossetti displayed genuine religious belief in the early version of the poem is based on comparisons he draws between it and a roughly contemporary elegy by Rossetti: 'A "Juvenile Affair": D. G. Rossetti's "Sacred to the Memory of Algernon R. G. Stanhope"', *Victorian Poetry*, 20 (1982), 187–98 (pp. 195–8). Cf. Reide, *Rossetti*, p. 53.

134 Bentley explains this as empathy on the part of the 'percipient': Bentley, p. 40. Schulz believes that in the poem 'Rossetti appears to be fusing the spiritual message of divine love related to the *hortus conclusus* with the guilty tale of carnal love enacted in Eden': Schulz, p. 251.

135 The two stanzas at this point in the 1850 version in *The Germ* are less ambiguous and less dramatic in effect. The earthly lover bemoans the isolation of the damozel in heaven, and wonders whether he himself could worship in heaven:

> (Alas! to *her* wise simple mind
>   These things were all but known
> Before: they trembled on her sense, –
>   Her voice had caught their tone.
> Alas for lonely Heaven! Alas
>   For life wrung out alone!
>
> Alas, and though the end were reached? . . .
>   Was *thy* part understood
> Or borne in trust? And for her sake
>   Shall this too be found good? –
> May the close lips that knew not prayer
>   Praise ever, though they would?)

136 See Surtees, I, 142.

137 Cited in Surtees, I, 58.

138 Ibid.

139 Cf. Peter and Linda Murray, *The Art of the Renaissance* (1963), p. 217.

140 See *Blessed Damozel*, ed. Baum, p. xiii.

141 See Joan Rees, *The Poetry of Dante Gabriel Rossetti: Modes of Self-Expression* (Cambridge, 1981), p. 169.

142 See Christina Rossetti, *The Face of the Deep: A Devotional Commentary on the Apocalypse*, sixth edition (1911), e.g. pp. 539–51.

143 See p. 135 above.

144 See Jerome J. McGann, 'Rossetti's Significant Details', *Victorian Poetry*, 7 (1969), 41–54 (pp. 48–52).

145 See J. C. Reid, *The Mind and Art of Coventry Patmore* (1957), p. 91.

146 'Homo' (XIX), in *The Rod, the Root and the Flower*, edited by Derek Patmore (1950), p. 124. The first edition of *The Rod* was published in 1896.

147 *The Rod*, p. 125.

148 See Reid, pp. 81, 90.

149 Ibid., p. 36.

150 Cf. Antony H. Harrison, *Christina Rossetti in Context* (1988).

151 See Rod Edmond, 'Death Sequences: Patmore, Hardy, and the New Domestic Elegy', *Victorian Poetry*, 19 (1981), 151–65. Patmore's first wife brought up their children to anticipate having a step-mother one day, and in her will left her wedding ring to the second wife, with her 'love and blessing': see Basil Champneys, *Memoirs and Correspondence of Coventry Patmore*, 2 vols. (1900), I, 133–4.

152 Cf. Reid, p. 167.

153 See 'Departure', *The Unknown Eros* (I.VIII), in Coventry Patmore, *Poems*, edited by Basil Champneys (1906), p. 284. All further quotations from Patmore's verse are taken from this edition.

154 See Champneys, *Memoirs and Correspondence*, I, 146.

155 Compare the following words and phrases from the poem with verses from Luke: 'body' (23.55), 'vows of faith' (22.32, 48, 60); 'as, Lord, Thou wilt' (22.42); 'agony' (22.44), 'crucify' (23.33), 'treason' (23.2), 'devotion' (23.55–6), 'grace . . . in a fair stranger' and 'thy delusive likeness' (24.13–31), 'chilly dawn' (24.1), 'I lived again' (24.1–53). Also see the use of the Johannine post-Resurrection experiences in 'Vesica Piscis' (I.XXIV).

156 See Reid, p. 161.

157 Ibid., p. 5.

158 Ibid., pp. 21, 29.

159 See Brigid M. Boardman, *Between Heaven and Charing Cross: The Life of Francis Thompson* (London and New Haven, 1988), p. 171.

160 'Paganism Old and New', in *The Works of Francis Thompson*, edited by Wilfrid Meynell, 3 vols. (1913), III, 38–51 (p. 48).

161 *Poems of Francis Thompson*, edited by Terence L. Connolly, revised edition (New York, 1941), p. 77. All further quotations from Thompson's verse are taken from this edition.

162 Cf. R. L. Mégroz, *Francis Thompson, The Poet of Earth in Heaven: A Study in Mysticism and the Evolution of Love-Poetry* (1927), pp. 153f.

163 For an alternative reading, which sees the ending as more open, see Boardman, p. 139.

164 Cited in Boardman, p. 140.

165 Ibid., p. 120.

166 Ibid., pp. 124, 308.

167 Ibid., p. 306.

168 See pp. 134–5 above.

4 Hell

1 [John Keble], *The Christian Year: Thoughts in Verse for the Sundays and Holydays throughout the Year*, second edition (Oxford, 1827), p. 88 (Second Sunday in Lent).

2 The standard work on hell in the period is Geoffrey Rowell's *Hell and the Victorians: A Study of the Nineteenth-Century Theological Controversies Concerning Eternal Punishment and the Future Life* (Oxford, 1974).

3 Robert Pollok, *The Course of Time: A Poem*, Illustrated Edition (1857), p. 15.

4 E. H. Bickersteth, 'Milton's "Paradise Lost"', in *Companions for the Devout Life: Seven Lectures Delivered in St. James's Church, Piccadilly, A.D. 1876*, St James's Lectures, second series (1876), pp. 89–110 (p. 104).

5 See W. E. Gladstone, *Studies Subsidiary to the Works of Bishop Butler* (Oxford, 1896), p. 206, and Rowell, p. 212; David Lodge, *How Far Can You Go?* (Harmondsworth, 1981), p. 113.

6 Robert Hughes, *Heaven and Hell in Western Art* (London, 1968), p. 281.

7 Mark Pattison, *Memoirs* (1885), p. 249.

8 See D. P. Walker, *The Decline of Hell: Seventeenth-Century Discussions of Eternal Torments* (1964), pp. 3–4.

9 St Chrysostom, *Homilies*, III, cited in Henry Nutcombe Oxenham, *Catholic Eschatology and Universalism: An Essay on the Doctrine of Future Retribution*, second edition (1878), pp. 80–1.

10 J[oseph] Furniss, *The Sight of Hell*, Books for Children and Young Persons, 10 (Dublin, 1861), p. 27.

11 A figure of over four million copies of Furniss's booklets is recorded in *The*

Catholic Encyclopedia, edited by Charles G. Herbermann, *et al.*, 15 vols. (1907–12; rpt. New York, 1913), VI, 324.

12 Coffin's translation of Liguori's *The Eternal Truths* was published in 1857. (See Rowell, pp. 154–7.) Liguori's 'considerations' on 'The Pains of Hell' and 'The Eternity of Hell' clearly influenced Furniss's tract entitled *The Sight of Hell*.

13 Furniss, pp. 13–14.

14 Ibid., pp. 18–21.

15 Pollok, p. 18.

16 On the *Spiritual Exercises* of St Ignatius, see pp. 344–5 above.

17 Furniss, *Sight of Hell*, p. 24.

18 Ibid., p. 18.

19 See S. G. F. Brandon, *The Judgment of the Dead: An Historical and Comparative Study of the Idea of a Post-Mortem Judgment in the Major Religions* (1967), p. 116.

20 E. B. Pusey, *What is of Faith as to Everlasting Punishment?: In Reply to Dr. Farrar's Challenge in his 'Eternal Hope,' 1879*, second edition (Oxford and London, 1880), p. 19.

21 See Harold Begbie, *Life of William Booth: The Founder of the Salvation Army*, abridged edition, 2 vols. (1926), I, 183–4.

22 See Chapter 2, note 74.

23 See Chapter 6, note 47.

24 *Poems and Ballads*, in *The Complete Works of Algernon Charles Swinburne*, edited by Edmund Gosse and Thomas James Wise, Bonchurch Edition, 20 vols. (1925; rpt. New York, 1968), I, 298.

25 E. H. Bickersteth, *The Second Death; or, the Certainty of Everlasting Punishment: A Paper Read before the London Clerical Conference, in the Vestry Room of St. Giles-in-the-Fields* (1869), pp. 6, 12. On Tennyson and Swinburne, see pp. 52–3 above.

26 Furniss, p. 9. Cf. Liguori, p. 252.

27 Austin Holyoake, *Heaven & Hell: Where Situated?: A Search after the Objects of Man's Fervent Hope & Abiding Terror* [1873], p. 8.

28 Frederic W. Farrar, *Eternal Hope: Five Sermons Preached in Westminster Abbey, November and December, 1877* (1904), p. 120.

29 See above, p. 10.

30 Matthew Arnold, *Culture and Anarchy, with Friendship's Garland and Some Literary Essays*, edited by R. H. Super, Complete Prose Works, 11 vols. (Ann Arbor, Mich., 1960–77), V, 186.

31 Oxenham, p. xxxvii.

32 Gladstone, pp. 199–206.

33 J. B. Mozley, 'Professor Maurice's Theological Essays' (January 1854), in *Essays Historical and Theological*, 2 vols., third edition (1892), II, 297.

34 See p. 76 above.

35 Cf. Robert Lee Wolff, *Gains and Losses: Novels of Faith and Doubt in Victorian England* (1977), p. 227.

36 See *Irish Ecclesiastical Record*, 8 (1872), 245, cited in Rowell, *Hell and the Victorians*, p. 173.

37 Cited in F. W. Farrar, *Mercy and Judgment: A Few Last Words on Christian Eschatology with Reference to Dr. Pusey's "What is of Faith?"* (1881), p. 31.

38 Gladstone, p. 205.

39 See Chapter 6, notes 45 and 76.

40 A. C. Charity, *Events and their Afterlife: The Dialectics of Christian Typology in the Bible and Dante* (Cambridge, 1966), p. 210.

41 Frederick Denison Maurice, *Theological Essays*, second edition (Cambridge, 1853), pp. 455, 473.

42 [Hallam Tennyson], *Alfred Lord Tennyson: A Memoir* (1899), pp. 719–20.

43 Hans Küng, *Eternal Life?*, translated by Edward Quinn (1984), p. 179; John Bowker, 'The Human Imagination of Hell', *Theology*, 85 (1982), 403–10 (pp. 407–8).

44 See Furniss, *Sight of Hell*, p. 3.

45 See Holyoake, *Heaven and Hell*, p. 4.

46 *Catholic Encyclopedia*, VII, 207.

47 Catherine Crowe, for example, argued that 'it is a vulgar notion to imagine that Heaven and Hell are *places*; they are states; and it is in ourselves we must look for both': *The Night Side of Nature; or, Ghosts and Ghost Seers*, 2 vols. (1848), I, 370.

48 Bickersteth, *The Second Death*, p. 4.

49 Ibid., p. 9.

50 Ibid., p. 10.

51 Ibid., p. 11.

52 Ibid., p. 13.

53 Ibid., pp. 13, 16.

54 Robert Hughes prefers to relate hell as the 'image of total injustice' to the totalitarian atrocities of the twentieth century: see Hughes, p. 42.

55 James Anthony Froude, *The Nemesis of Faith*, Victorian Fiction: Novels of Faith and Doubt (New York and London, 1975), p. 15.

56 Ibid., p. 19.

57 Ibid., p. 205.

58 Ibid., p. 216.

59 Ibid., p. 160.

60 Randall Thomas Davidson and William Benham, *Life of Archibald Campbell Tait, Archbishop of Canterbury*, 2 vols. (London and New York, 1891), II, 129.

61 Ibid., II, 126.

62 Anthony Trollope, *Clergymen of the Church of England,* introduction by Ruth apRoberts (Leicester, 1974), p. 126.

63 See Davidson and Benham, II, 133, 140.

64 Ibid., II, 142.

65 Ibid., II, 160–1.

66 Bickersteth, *The Second Death*, pp. 20–1.

67 Ibid., p. 29.

68 Wilfrid Ward, *The Life of John Henry Cardinal Newman: Based on his Private Journals and Correspondence*, 2 vols. (1912), II, 46.

69 Trollope, p. 124.

70 *The Brontës: Their Lives, Friendships and Correspondence*, edited by Thomas James Wise and John Alexander Symington, 4 vols., Shakespeare Head Brontë (Oxford, 1932), II, 166. Cited in Arthur Pollard, 'The Brontës and their Father's Faith', *Essays and Reviews*, NS 37 (1984), 46–61 (p. 61).

71 *The Traveller's Guide, from Death to Life*, edited by Mrs Stephen Menzies (n.d.), p. 53.

72 Gladstone, p. 207.

73 [Richard Whateley], *A View of the Scripture Revelations Concerning a Future State: Laid Before his Parishioners, by a Country Pastor* (1829), p. 53.

74 Farrar, *Eternal Hope*, pp. xxxviii–xli.

75 Bickersteth, *The Second Death*, pp. 16–17.

76 Ibid., pp. 19–20.

77 Farrar, *Eternal Hope*, pp. 78–9; also cf. pp. 197–202.

78 Maurice, p. 450.

79 Farrar, *Mercy and Judgment*, p. 1.

80 Stewart D. F. Salmond, *The Christian Doctrine of Immortality* (1895), p. 376.

81 G. Somers Bellamy, *Essays from Shakspeare* (1879), pp. 15–16.

82 *Notes on Poems and Reviews*, in *Works of Swinburne*, XVI, 365.

83 Francis D. Klingender, *Art and the Industrial Revolution* [1947], edited and revised by Arthur Elton (1972), p. 109.

84 Thomas Balston, *John Martin, 1789–1854: His Life and Works* (1947), p. 236.

85 [William] Booth, *In Darkest England and the Way Out* [1890], p. 13. For further examples see *Into Unknown England, 1866–1913: Selections from the Social Explorers*, edited by Peter Keating (Glasgow, 1976).

86 See Gustave Doré and Blanchard Jerrold, *London: A Pilgrimage* (1872), e.g. facing pp. 30, 138, 148.

87 Frederick Engels, *The Condition of the Working-Class in England, From Personal Observation and Authentic Sources* (German, 1845; English, 1892), introduction by Eric Hobsbawm (1969), p. 58.

88 Engels, p. 86.

89 Alexis de Tocqueville, *Journeys to England and Ireland*, translated by George Lawrence and K. P. Mayer, edited by J. P. Mayer (1958), p. 107.

90 Alexander Welsh, *The City of Dickens* (Oxford, 1971), p. 65; S. E. Finer, *The Life and Times of Sir Edwin Chadwick* (1952), p. 315.

91 Booth, pp. 13–14.

92 See, e.g., Alfred Hall, *The Beliefs of a Unitarian* (1932), p. 35; Rowell, pp. 32–61.

93 For more detailed discussion on biblical allusion in *Mary Barton* see Michael Wheeler, *The Art of Allusion in Victorian Fiction* (London and Basingstoke, 1979), pp. 50–7.

94 Theophilus Lindsey, *Sermons, with Appropriate Prayers Annexed*, 2 vols. (1810), I, 507.

95 See *Into Unknown England*, pp. 20–2.

96 *The Letters of George Meredith*, edited by C. L. Cline, 3 vols. (Oxford, 1970), I, 48.

97 *Meredith: The Critical Heritage*, edited by Ioan Williams, Critical Heritage series, general editor B. C. Southam (1971), p. 76; cf. also pp. 74–5.

98 *The Poems of George Meredith*, edited by Phyllis B. Bartlett, 2 vols. (New Haven and London, 1978), I, 116. (All further quotations from *Modern Love* are taken from this edition.) Cf. also: 'By stealth / Our eyes dart scrutinizing snakes' (XXXIV).

99 George Meredith, *Selected Poems*, edited by Keith Hanley (Manchester, 1983), p. 20.

100 Ibid., p. 105.

101 Ibid., p. 106; the three phases are those suggested by Norman Friedman.

102 Williams, pp. 97–9.

103 See Donald Thomas, *Swinburne: The Poet in his World* (1979), p. 114.

104 See Thomas, p. 130.

105 *Swinburne: The Critical Heritage*, edited by Clyde K. Hyder, Critical Heritage series, general editor B. C. Southam (1970), p. 26.

106 Ibid., pp. 33, 67.

107 Ibid., p. 36.

108 Ibid., pp. 42–3.

109 See *Works of Swinburne*, XVI, 354–5.

110 See Thomas, p. 15.

111 *Works of Swinburne*, XIII, 423.

112 See Hyder, p. 42.

113 F. W. J. Hemmings, *Baudelaire the Damned: A Biography* (1982), pp. vii–viii.

114 Ibid., p. x.

115 Charles Baudelaire, *Les Fleurs du Mal* (Montreal, 1950), p. 158.

116 Hughes, pp. 42, 155.

117 *Works of Swinburne*, I, 298. (All further quotations from Swinburne's verse are taken from this edition.)

118 Ibid., XVI, 354.

119 Ibid., XVI, 360.

120 Ibid., XVI, 365.

121 See, for example, Bickersteth, *Yesterday, To-Day, and For Ever: A Poem In Twelve Books*, eighth edition (1873), III, 573.

122 Barbara Charlesworth, *Dark Passages: The Decadent Consciousness in Victorian Literature* (Madison and Milwaukee, 1965), p. 119.

123 Arthur Symons, 'Aubrey Beardsley', *Fortnightly Review*, NS 58 (1898), 752–61 (p. 757).

124 See H[enry] S. Salt, *The Life of James Thomson ('B.V.'), with a Selection from his Letters and a Study of his Works* (1889), p. 295. The poet's mother, Sarah Kennedy, was a 'deeply religious woman of the Irvingite faith, whose nature, unlike that of her husband, seems to have been of a somewhat melancholy cast' (Salt, p. 1).

125 Ibid., pp. 182, 297.

126 Ibid., p. 184.

127 *The City of Dreadful Night*, Proem, line 8: *Poems and Some Letters of James Thomson*, edited by Anne Ridler (1963), p. 177. (All further quotations from *The City* are taken from this edition.)

128 See William Sharpe, 'Learning to Read *The City*', *Victorian Poetry*, 22 (1984), 65–84 (p. 81).

129 *Poems of Thomson*, ed. Ridler, p. 271.

130 Cf. Sharpe, p. 82.

131 See also *The City*, I.78; II.24; IV.15; VI.15; VII.21f.; IX.19; XI.7; XIV.35; XXI.48, 60.

132 See Salt, p. 287. For further Dante echoes and parallels see *The City*, II.2, 11–12, 45; IV.25–33; IX–XI.

133 The first of the three epigraphs finally chosen by Thomson was from the *Inferno*, in the Italian (III.1: 'Through me you pass into the city of woe').

134 See Sharpe, pp. 66, 75.

135 See Charles Dickens, *A Tale of Two Cities*, edited by Andrew Sanders, World's Classics (Oxford and New York, 1988), pp. 388, 518.

5 Tennyson, *In Memoriam*

1 [Hallam Tennyson], *Alfred Lord Tennyson: A Memoir* (1899), p. 89.

2 *Remains in Verse and Prose of Arthur Henry Hallam*, [edited by Henry Hallam] (1863), p. xlii.

3 'Besides the coffin, there was a square iron box deposited in the vault,

which may have contained "The darken'd heart that beat no more"':
Alfred Gatty, *A Key to Lord Tennyson's 'In Memoriam'*, third edition
(1885), p. 23.

4 See Robert Bernard Martin, *Tennyson: The Unquiet Heart* (Oxford,
1980), p. 187. Later in life Tennyson did not attend the burial of his
stillborn son.

5 See A. Dwight Culler, *The Poetry of Tennyson* (New Haven and London,
1977), p. 155.

6 See *The Poems of Tennyson*, edited by Christopher Ricks, Longman
Annotated English Poets, general editor F. W. Bateson (1969), and Tennyson, *In Memoriam*, edited by Susan Shatto and Marion Shaw (Oxford,
1982). (All *In Memoriam* quotations are from the latter edition; further
references below are given as Shatto and Shaw.)

7 See pp. 63–4 above.

8 When Tennyson later visited Clevedon he found that Hallam was buried in
a transept and not, as Hallam's father had recorded, in the chancel. He
therefore altered 'chancel' in lyric 67 to 'dark church'. See Shatto and
Shaw, pp. 87, 228.

9 Cf. T. S. Eliot, 'In Memoriam' (1936), in *Selected Essays*, third edition
(1951), pp. 333–4.

10 See H. Tennyson, *Memoir*, p. 269.

11 Eliot, p. 336.

12 Jerome Buckley, for example, argues that '*In Memoriam* is seldom specifically Christian': *Tennyson: The Growth of a Poet* (Cambridge, Mass.,
1960), p. 127.

13 Eliot, p. 374.

14 Cf. John Beer, *Wordsworth and the Human Heart* (1978), p. 11. Various
sources were available to Tennyson at Somersby, including encyclopedias
and medical dictionaries. In Perceval B. Lord's *Popular Physiology* (1834),
for example, which was given to Tennyson on Christmas Day 1838, chapter 8 is on the circulation. Of particular interest is Peter Mark Roget's
Bridgewater Treatise, entitled *Animal and Vegetable Physiology, Considered with Reference to Natural Theology*, 2 vols. (1834), in which both
the circulation of the blood and respiratory circulation are explained, with
diagrams, although the copy from Tennyson's library at Lincoln looks very
little used.

15 See *Remains*, p. xliii.

16 See Alan Sinfield, *The Language of Tennyson's 'In Memoriam'*, Language
and Style series, edited by Stephen Ullmann (Oxford, 1971), pp. 178–9.

17 Kingsley's comment of 1850 is quoted in Christopher Ricks, *Tennyson*,
Masters of World Literature series, edited by Louis Kronenberger (1972),
p. 228.

18 Lyric 19 provides a particularly striking example of this effect.

19 See Eric Smith, *By Mourning Tongues: Studies in English Elegy* (Ipswich and Totowa, N.J., 1977), pp. 56–7.

20 J. C. C. Mays, '*In Memoriam*: An Aspect of Form', *University of Toronto Quarterly*, 35 (1965), 22–46; rpt. in *Tennyson, 'In Memoriam': A Casebook*, edited by John Dixon Hunt, Casebook series, general editor A. E. Dyson (1970), pp. 259–89 (pp. 267–8).

21 See, however, Martin J. Svaglic, 'A Framework for Tennyson's *In Memoriam*', *Journal of English and Germanic Philology*, 61 (1962), 810–25; James Kilroy, 'The Chiastic Structure of *In Memoriam, A.H.H.*', *Philological Quarterly*, 56 (1977), 358–73. For the original suggestion, see James Knowles, 'Aspects of Tennyson II (A Personal Reminiscence)', *Nineteenth Century*, 33 (1893), 164–88 (p. 182).

22 *Pascal's Pensées*, translated by H. F. Stewart (1950), p. 345.

23 See Friedrich Schleiermacher, *The Christian Faith*, edited by H. R. Mackintosh and J. S. Stewart (Edinburgh, 1928), pp. 103, 6, 12.

24 See James C. Livingston, *Modern Christian Thought: From the Enlightenment to Vatican II* (New York and London, 1971), p. 145.

25 S. T. Coleridge, *Aids to Reflection in the Formation of a Manly Character on the Several Grounds of Prudence, Morality and Religion*, revised by Thomas Fenby, New Universal Library (London and New York, [1905]), p. 134.

26 John Tulloch, *Movements of Religious Thought in Britain during the Nineteenth Century* [1885], Victorian Library (Leicester and New York, 1971), p. 138.

27 Ibid., p. 139.

28 See Chapter 3, note 50.

29 Frederick Denison Maurice, *The Kingdom of Christ; or, Hints to a Quaker, Respecting the Principles, Constitution, and Ordinances of the Catholic Church*, edited by Alec R. Vidler, 2 vols. (1958), II, 231.

30 Benjamin Jowett, *The Interpretation of Scripture, and Other Essays*, London Library Edition (London and New York, [1906]), p. 98.

31 Baden Powell quotes the relevant passage from *Aids to Reflection* in 'On the Study of the Evidences of Christianity', in *Essays and Reviews*, seventh edition (1861), pp. 94–144 (p. 120).

32 In *The Analogy of Religion*, which was still a set text at Cambridge in Tennyson's day, Butler's argument for the existence of a 'future state' anticipates the poet's at several points. Butler reflects, for example, upon the word 'continuance', the fact that 'the bodies of all animals are in a constant flux', the experience of dreams, the social nature of our new state after death, and the observation that 'we are plainly made for improvement of all kinds': *The Works of Joseph Butler*, edited by W. E. Gladstone,

2 vols. (Oxford, 1896), I, 23; I, 31; I, 34–5; I, 45; I, 182. On Tennyson's negative views on natural theology, see Culler, pp. 187–8.

33 See Shatto and Shaw, pp. 137, 283.

34 See Marion Shaw, 'In Memoriam and Popular Religious Poetry', Victorian Poetry, 15 (1977), 1–8 (p. 5).

35 Frederick Denison Maurice, Theological Essays, second edition (Cambridge, 1853), p. vi.

36 See H. Tennyson, Memoir, p. 362. On Tennyson and love see Charles F. G. Masterman, Tennyson as a Religious Teacher (1900), p. 82; L. S. Peake, 'Tennyson and the Search for Immortality: III. Reason and Love', The Saturday Review, 12 March 1932, p. 266.

37 The Writings of Arthur Hallam, edited by T. H. Vail Motter (New York and London, 1943), p. 210.

38 See G. C. Joyce, 'Analogy', in Encyclopaedia of Religion and Ethics, edited by James Hastings and J. A. Selbie, 13 vols. (Edinburgh and New York, 1908–26), I, 419.

39 Michael Edwards, Towards a Christian Poetics (London and Basingstoke, 1984), p. 228.

40 I endorsed this view in 'Tennyson, Newman and the Question of Authority', in The Interpretation of Belief: Coleridge, Schleiermacher and Romanticism, edited by David Jasper (London and Basingstoke, 1986), pp. 185–201 (p. 196), but now consider it to be mistaken. The most extreme version of the argument is Alan Sinfield's in Alfred Tennyson, Rereading Literature series, general editor Terry Eagleton (Oxford, 1986), pp. 113, 119, 150.

41 See pp. 260–3 above.

42 See, however, Philip Flynn, 'Hallam and Tennyson: The "Theodicaea Novissima" and In Memoriam', Studies in English Literature, 1500–1900, 19 (1979), 705–20 (p. 719); Peter Allan Dale, '"Gracious Lies": The Meaning of Metaphor in In Memoriam', Victorian Poetry, 18 (1980), 147–67 (p. 167).

43 Writings of Hallam, ed. Motter, p. 202; cf. Flynn, 'Hallam and Tennyson', pp. 709–10, 719.

44 Cf. M. Shaw, 'In Memoriam and Popular Religious Poetry', pp. 6–7.

45 The Life of Frederick Denison Maurice, Chiefly Told in his Own Letters, edited by Frederick Maurice, 2 vols. (1884), II, 16–17.

46 Edward Moore, Studies in Dante, Second Series: Miscellaneous Essays (Oxford, 1899), p. 5. See also Carl Dawson, Victorian Noon: English Literature in 1850 (Baltimore and London, 1979), pp. 43–5.

47 Moore, pp. 43, 47.

48 Maurice, Theological Essays, pp. 454–5.

49 Ibid., pp. 442, 444.

50 Ibid., p. 476. Gladstone's marginalia in his copy of this second edition indicate that he followed Maurice's argument carefully. He put a strong vertical line next to the passage on the 'abyss of love', for example, and annotated the discussion of Dante in a way which suggests that he had reservations about specific points. (Gladstone's copy is in St Deiniol's Library, Hawarden, and is cited here by kind permission of the Warden/Librarian of the library on behalf of the Trustees.) Gladstone was a serious student of Dante. He discussed Dante with Tennyson at Hawarden in 1876 (H. Tennyson, *Memoir*, p. 598) and accepted Moore's dedication to him of the second series of *Studies in Dante* in the last year of his life. In his own edition of the *Commedia* he underlined the word *Amore* (adding 'NB' in the margin) in the passage from the inscription on the gates of hell which Tennyson himself often quoted: see Gladstone's *Commedia*, 3 vols. (Padova, 1822), in St Deiniol's Library, Hawarden.

51 H. Tennyson, *Memoir*, p. 37.

52 'Mr Tennyson's Poetry' (1871) in *Richard Simpson as Critic*, edited by David Carroll, Routledge Critics series, general editor B. C. Southam (1977), p. 307.

53 See Gordon D. Hirsch, 'Tennyson's *Commedia*', *Victorian Poetry*, 8 (1970), 93–106 (p. 96); Flynn, p. 710.

54 *Remains*, pp. xvii–xviii, xxxv.

55 H. Tennyson, *Memoir*, p. 255.

56 See Hirsch; also e.g. James R. Kincaid, *Tennyson's Major Poems: The Comic and Ironic Patterns* (New Haven and London, 1975), pp. 10, 82–3. For further discussion on Dante parallels see pp. 254–5 above.

57 Hirsch, p. 98.

58 Tennyson is reported to have lost a portmanteau 'full of Dantes and dressing gowns' in August 1833: see Peter Allen, *The Cambridge Apostles: The Early Years* (Cambridge, 1978), p. 153.

59 Dante, *The Divine Comedy*, [trans. Henry Francis Cary], edited by Edmund Gardner, Everyman's Library, 1308 (London and New York, 1967), p. 10. (All further quotations from the *Divine Comedy* are taken from this edition.)

60 See Dante, e.g. pp. 2, 10, 161 (*Inferno*, I.54, III.9; *Purgatorio*, IV.30).

61 Dante, p. 406. (*Paradiso*, XXV.67f.)

62 H. Tennyson, *Memoir*, p. 270.

63 Hallam Tennyson, *Materials for a Life of A.T.*, 4 vols. [1895], II, 17; quoted in *Poems*, ed. Ricks, p. 861.

64 W. E. Gladstone, *Studies Subsidiary to the Works of Bishop Butler* (Oxford, 1896), p. 212.

65 James Anthony Froude, *Thomas Carlyle: A History of his Life in London, 1834–1881*, new edition, 2 vols. (1897), I, 311–12.

66 Frederic Harrison, *Tennyson, Ruskin, Mill, and Other Literary Estimates* (London and New York, 1899), p. 11.

67 Malcolm Woodfield, *R. H. Hutton, Critic and Theologian: The Writings of R. H. Hutton on Newman, Arnold, Tennyson, Wordsworth, and George Eliot* (Oxford, 1986), p. 141.

68 The dedication begins:

My Dear Sir,

   I have maintained in these Essays that a Theology which does not correspond to the deepest thoughts and feelings of human beings cannot be a true Theology. Your writings have taught me to enter into many of those thoughts and feelings. Will you forgive me the presumption of offering you a book which at least acknowledges them and does them homage?

Maurice, *Theological Essays*, p. v.

69 See Allen, p. 56.

70 F. W. Farrar, *Mercy and Judgment: A Few Last Words on Christian Eschatology with Reference to Dr. Pusey's 'What is of Faith?'* (1881), p.v.

71 See the article on Farrar in the *Dictionary of National Biography*.

72 See *Tennyson and his Friends*, edited by Hallam Tennyson (1911), p. 270.

73 See, e.g., Stephen Prickett, *Romanticism and Religion: The Tradition of Coleridge and Wordsworth in the Victorian Church* (Cambridge, 1976), p. 126.

74 See p. 235 above.

75 See the article on Robertson in the *Dictionary of National Biography*; also Owen Chadwick, *The Victorian Church*, second edition, 2 vols., Ecclesiastical History of England, edited by J. D. Dickinson, vols. VII–VIII (1970), I, 545.

76 Frederick W. Robertson, *Lectures and Addresses on Literary and Social Topics* (1858), pp. 125–6; also cited in preface to his *Analysis of 'In Memoriam'* (1862).

77 See Shatto and Shaw, p. 206.

78 See Geoffrey Rowell, *Hell and the Victorians: A Study of the Nineteenth-Century Theological Controversies Concerning Eternal Punishment and the Future Life* (Oxford, 1974), pp. 76–89.

79 H. Tennyson, *Memoir*, p. 362.

80 Ibid., p. 270.

81 *William Allingham's Diary*, introduced by Geoffrey Grigson (Fontwell, Sussex, 1967), p. 328.

82 Shatto and Shaw, p. 214.

83 See pp. 95–6 above.

84 The nine groups are lyrics 1–8, 9–20, 21–7, 28–49, 50–8, 59–71, 72–98, 99–103, 104–31. This assumes that the printed 'xx. to xxvii.' in Knowles should read 'xxi. to xxvii.'. See also note 18 above.

85 James Kilroy argues that a 'chiastic pattern is found in the entire poem', and that the 'poem's greatest intensity occurs in the middle': 'The Chiastic Structure of *In Memoriam, A.H.H.*', pp. 358, 360.

86 See Sinfield, *Language of 'In Memoriam'*, pp. 116–17.

87 See pp. 74–5 above.

88 Frederic W. Farrar, *Eternal Hope: Five Sermons Preached in Westminster Abbey, November and December, 1877* (1904), p. xxiv. Farrar was accused of using universalist arguments while repudiating universalist conclusions in *Eternal Hope*, and he wrote *Mercy and Judgment* in order to clarify his position. There he again quoted lyric 54, describing Tennyson as 'the great poet who, more perhaps than any living man, has taught us, not at any rate to be afraid of the wish and hope' that this may be so, 'even if it can never amount to a tenet of faith': *Mercy and Judgment*, p. 134. See also pp. 76–7 above.

89 H. Tennyson, *Memoir*, pp. 142–3.

90 See note 10 above.

91 See Culler, pp. 167, 189; W. David Shaw, *The Lucid Veil: Poetic Truth in the Victorian Age* (1987), p. 27. John D. Boyd endorses the view that Tennyson confuses personal immortality and the 'immortality' of mankind, and argues that they are 'related not logically but by an emotive bond': 'The Principle of Analogy and the Immortality Question in Tennyson's *In Memoriam*', *University of Toronto Quarterly*, 45 (1975–6), 123–38 (pp. 127–9). I would argue that for Tennyson they are related by their common ground in divine love.

92 See 'On Sympathy', in *Remains*, pp. 97–111, and in *Writings of Hallam*, pp. 133–42.

93 H. Tennyson, *Memoir*, p. 255.

94 See John D. Rosenberg, 'The Two Kingdoms of "In Memoriam"', *Journal of English and Germanic Philology*, 58 (1959), 228–40; rpt. in *Tennyson, 'In Memoriam': A Casebook*, p. 204.

95 See, e.g., Culler, pp. 166, 176.

96 Boyd, pp. 123, 127.

97 For a summary of these arguments, see Ray S. Anderson, *Theology, Death and Dying* (Oxford and New York, 1986), pp. 57–8.

98 See Knowles, p. 169.

99 See p. 135 above.

100 [William Branks], *Heaven our Home* (Edinburgh, 1861). For further reference to Branks, see p. 128 above.

101 Cf. Dante, p. 274 (*Purgatorio*, xxx.24).

102 For discussion on the euphemistic description of the grave as a bed see pp. 55–8 above, and the excellent analysis of lyric 67 by Isobel Armstrong in *Language as Living Form in Nineteenth-Century Poetry* (Brighton and New Jersey, 1982), pp. 197–9.

103 W. D. Shaw treats the phrase as a paradigm for poetic language: see note 91 above.

104 See Mary Joan Ellmann, 'Tennyson: Revision of *In Memoriam*, Section 85', *Modern Language Notes*, 65 (1950), 22–30.

105 Shatto and Shaw, pp. 240–1.

106 See Dale, p. 155.

107 Dale argues (p. 158) that 'Tennyson's problem in the poem . . . is to overcome Nature's literalism and reaffirm the metaphorical and mystical content of the word "breath," to show that the word "breath" has a God-imparted significance that does not at first meet the eye.' This he achieves at the end of lyric 95.

108 Shatto and Shaw, p. 251.

109 See, e.g., Ashton Nichols, 'The Epiphanic Trance Poem: Why Tennyson is not a Mystic', *Victorian Poetry*, 24 (1986–7), 131–48.

110 Knowles, p. 186.

111 See, e.g., Alan Sinfield, 'Matter-moulded Forms of Speech: Tennyson's Use of Language in *In Memoriam*', in *The Major Victorian Poets: Reconsiderations*, edited by Isobel Armstrong (1969), pp. 51–67 (p. 63); Carlisle Moore, 'Faith, Doubt and Mystical Experience in *In Memoriam*', *Victorian Studies*, 7 (1963), 155–69, rpt. in *Tennyson, 'In Memoriam': A Casebook*, pp. 241–58 (p. 251).

112 Philip James Bailey, *Festus: A Poem*, ninth edition (1875), p. 555.

113 Dante, p. 410 (*Paradiso* XXVI.82).

114 Coleridge, *Aids*, p. 4.

115 E.g. lyric 122: 'Be quicken'd with a livelier breath.' See Dale, p. 161.

116 *The Confessions of Saint Augustine*, translated by E. B. Pusey, Everyman's Library, 200 (London and New York, 1907), pp. 138–9. The similarity between lyric 95 and this passage is briefly noted by Percy H. Ormond in *The Mystical Poets of the English Church* (1919), pp. 309–10; cited in Buckley, pp. 123, 276.

117 Shatto and Shaw, p. 255.

118 See, e.g., F. C. Happold, *Mysticism: A Study and an Anthology*, revised edition (Harmondsworth, 1970), pp. 228–9.

119 See pp. 102–9, 124–5, above.

120 H. Tennyson, *Memoir*, p. 268.

121 See Sinfield, *Language of 'In Memoriam'*, pp. 111–12.

122 See Dante, p. 292 (*Paradiso*, I.3–9).

123 Cf. Shatto and Shaw, p. 256.

124 John Hick, *Death and Eternal Life* (1976), pp. 49–53.

125 Ibid., p. 458.

126 See Shatto and Shaw, p. 262.

127 See p. 229 above.

128 See *Poems*, ed. Ricks, p. 961.

129 Cf. M. Shaw, '*In Memoriam* and Popular Religious Poetry', p. 2.

130 See Julian of Norwich, *The Revelations of Divine Love*, translated by James Walsh (1961), p. 98.

131 See pp. 79–81 above.

132 Rosenberg, pp. 209–10.

133 *Poems*, ed. Ricks, p. 976.

134 See Shatto and Shaw, p. 291.

135 Ibid.

136 Ibid., p. 142; cf. 1 Corinthians 13.12.

137 See p. 19 above.

138 Shatto and Shaw point out (p. 293) that the 'traditional idea that all the physical elements of the body are periodically renewed is explained in a book which Tennyson was given at Christmas, 1838, Perceval B. Lord, *Popular Physiology* (1834), 353'. But also cf. Bishop Butler, in the opening section of his very influential *Analogy of Religion*: see p. 60 above.

139 See pp. 50–1 above; cf. Shatto and Shaw, pp. 294–5.

140 See above pp. 150–69.

141 Boyd (p. 128) cites Eliot's statement that the 'hope of immortality is confused (typically of the period) with the hope of gradual and steady improvement of this world', and Paull F. Baum's comment on 'the illogical conclusion, the happy ending wherein the immortality of mankind through evolution is substituted for the immortality of the individual soul'.

142 *The Penguin Book of English Christian Verse*, edited by Peter Levi (Harmondsworth, 1984), pp. 19–20.

6 Dickens, *Our Mutual Friend*

1 Jenny Wren puts this question to Riah: 'Is it better to have had a good thing and lost it, or never to have had it?' (III.2); cf. *In Memoriam*, 27. This and all subsequent quotations from *Our Mutual Friend* are taken from the Penguin English Library edition, edited by Stephen Gill (Harmondsworth, 1971).

2 Alexander Welsh, *The City of Dickens* (Oxford, 1971), p. 228.

3 Ibid., p. 141.

4 Ibid., pp. 196–7.

5 Ibid., p. 197.

6 In Bert Hornback's view, for example, Dickens learns to 'deny himself Eden and Heaven' and to 'see the inadequacy of Noah and his Ark as a response to the chaos of the Deluge': *'Noah's Arkitecture': A Study of Dickens's Mythology* (Athens, Ohio, 1972), p. 158. Joseph Gold's Dickens is 'the radical visionary, the artist who refuses to shelter in theology': *Charles Dickens: Radical Moralist* (Minneapolis and London, 1972), p. 232.

7 Dennis Walder, *Dickens and Religion* (1981), p. 2.

8 Ibid., p. 3.

9 Ibid., pp. 113, 170.

10 Andrew Sanders, *Charles Dickens, Resurrectionist* (London and Basingstoke, 1982), p. xi.

11 Sanders, p. 176. Sanders here draws attention to the significance of Nicodemus Boffin's name, adding that 'although it would be mistaken to limit *Our Mutual Friend* to a meditation on Christian doctrine, it is surely possible to closely relate these references to baptism, and to regeneration through water and the spirit to the novel's themes and incidents'. He cites the Book of Common Prayer, but does not examine its implications for Dickens in the detailed way that Janet Larson does in *Dickens and the Broken Scripture* (Athens, Georgia, 1985), a study which tends to present too negative a view of Dickens's scriptural and liturgical allusion, but is often suggestive. I am indebted to both these studies.

12 Walder, p. 2. Cf. also George Levine, *Darwin and the Novelists: Patterns of Science in Victorian Fiction* (Cambridge, Mass. and London, 1988), chapter 5.

13 Henry Bristow Wilson, 'Séances Historiques de Genève: The National Church', in *Essays and Reviews*, seventh edition (1861), pp. 145–206 (pp. 205–6). Cf. p. 77 above.

14 Ibid., p. 206.

15 *The Letters of Charles Dickens*, edited by Walter Dexter, Nonesuch Edition, 3 vols. (1938), III, 352; part of the letter is cited in Walder, p. 175.

16 See Frederick Temple, 'The Education of the World', in *Essays and Reviews*, pp. 1–49 (pp. 3–6). Dickens had a copy of Temple's *Sermons Preached in Rugby School Chapel, in 1858, 1859, 1860* (1861): see *Catalogue of the Libraries of Charles Dickens and W. M. Thackeray*, edited by J. H. Stonehouse (1935), p. 109.

17 *Essays and Reviews*, p. 47.

18 Benjamin Jowett, 'On the Interpretation of Scripture', *Essays and Reviews*, pp. 330–433 (p. 387). Cf. p. 9 above. The following extracts from Jowett's essay are also of interest in relation to various kinds of 'reconciling' or 'harmonizing' to which I refer later:

   . . . any true doctrine of inspiration must conform to all well-

ascertained facts of history or of science . . . there is no need of elaborate reconcilements of revelation and science; they reconcile themselves
the moment any scientific truth is distinctly ascertained. As the idea of
nature enlarges, the idea of revelation also enlarges . . . And as the
knowledge of nature which is possessed by the few is communicated in
its leading features at least to the many, they will receive with it a higher
conception of the ways of God to man [*sic*].   (pp. 348–9)

The letter is in many cases really or apparently in harmony with existing
practices, or opinions, or institutions.   (p. 358)

The harmony between Scripture and the life of man, in all its stages, may
be far greater than appears at present.   (pp. 375–6)

The applications of Scripture should be harmonized and, as it were,
interpenetrated with the spirit of the Gospel, the whole of which should
be in every part . . .   (p. 410)

19 Ibid., p. 373.
20 Ibid., p. 411. Andrew Sanders believes (p. 197) that *Our Mutual Friend*
can persuade us 'of the reality of the hope that the resurrected few may
show the way to the many'.
21 See p. 230 above.
22 There was a copy of *Essays and Reviews*, eighth edition (1861) in Dickens's library: see Stonehouse, p. 43.
23 Owen Chadwick, *The Victorian Church*, second edition, 2 vols.,
Ecclesiastical History of England, edited by J. D. Dickinson, vols. VII–VIII
(1970), II, 33. F. W. Farrar's conception of the origins of man, for example,
underwent a dramatic change between 1860 and 1865: see Stephen Prickett, *Words and 'The Word': Language, Poetics and Biblical Interpretation*
(Cambridge, 1986), p. 57.
24 See Stonehouse, pp. 9, 68, 80. In his letter of thanks to Hugh Miller's
widow, Dickens assured her that her husband's book would 'fill no neglected place on [his] book-shelves', but would always be precious to him:
Dexter, II, 845.
25 Hugh Miller, *The Testimony of the Rocks: or, Geology in its Bearings on
the Two Theologies, Natural & Revealed* (Edinburgh, 1884), p. 190; lecture 5 is reprinted in *Science and Religion in the Nineteenth Century*, edited
by Tess Cosslett, Cambridge English Prose Texts (Cambridge, 1984), pp.
67–85 (p. 79).
26 *Essays and Reviews*, p. 210.
27 Ibid., p. 211.
28 Ibid., p. 215.
29 Cf. Larson, p. 10.
30 See, for example, [Edward Greswell], *A Harmony of the Four Gospels, in*

the English Authorized Version, Arranged According to Greswell's *'Harmonia Evangelica' in Greek* (1833).

31 See James Hastings, *Dictionary of the Bible*, second edition, revised by Frederick C. Grant and H. H. Rowley (Edinburgh, 1963), p. 518. A Victorian liberal like Jowett, however, could write in 1860, 'the comparison of St. John and the "synoptic" Gospels . . . will tend rather to confuse than to elucidate the meaning of either': *Essays and Reviews*, p. 383. See also note 18 above.

32 Frank Kermode, 'John', in *The Literary Guide to the Bible*, edited by Robert Alter and Frank Kermode (1987), pp. 440–66 (p. 448).

33 Ibid., pp. 449–50.

34 Ibid., pp. 463–4.

35 See Chadwick, I, 250–71.

36 See above, pp. 6–7.

37 See above, pp. 9–10. Cf. Dickens's treatment of Magwitch's trial in *Great Expectations*, where the true verdict is deferred to the 'great Judgement that knoweth all things and cannot err': see above pp. 111–12.

38 Cf. Michael Wheeler, *The Art of Allusion in Victorian Fiction* (London and Basingstoke, 1979), pp. 61–77.

39 Steven Marcus, *Dickens from Pickwick to Dombey* (1965), p. 51.

40 See Sanders, p. xi.

41 Charles Dickens, *The Life of Our Lord: Written Expressly for his Children* (1934), p. 127.

42 Dexter, II, 408.

43 Ibid., II, 679–80; cited in Sanders, p. 174.

44 See e.g. Walder, p. 198.

45 *Dickens' Working Notes for His Novels*, edited by Harry Stone (Chicago and London, 1987), pp. 329–31.

46 Cf. *Our Mutual Friend*, ed. Gill, p. 17; Annabel M. Patterson, '*Our Mutual Friend*: Dickens as the Compleat Angler', in *Dickens Studies Annual*, 1 (1970), pp. 252–64 (p. 259). Patterson reads the fishing for bodies in the London Thames as 'a demonic parody of the true occupation in the pastoral world upstream', which she relates to the Christian symbolism in Isaak Walton's *Compleat Angler* (1653), for her a major parallel text in the novel.

47 Cf. Larson, p. 303.

48 Cf. p. 53 above.

49 Northrop Frye, *The Great Code: The Bible and Literature* (1983), pp. 149, 172–3.

50 In Dickens's library there was a copy of the 1825 edition of the *Decline and Fall* in 8 volumes, with portrait and map, published by Baynes, *et al.*: see Stonehouse, p. 50.

51 Modern biblical scholarship has, however, contested the identification of John the apostle with the disciple whom Jesus loved: see Hastings, *Dictionary of the Bible*, pp. 507–8.

52 This episode provides crucial evidence for Garrett Stewart's argument in *Death Sentences: Styles of Dying in British Fiction* (Cambridge, Mass. and London, 1984), a study of the novel from Dickens to Nabokov. For Stewart, what he calls the 'polysemous ambiguities on which the vocabulary of the Victorian death scene thrives' become 'strategies' in 'postponing the void, deferring the effacements of the blank page' (p. 7). Betty Higden's death scene is thus Dickens's most subtle 'conjuring' with the connection between his own narrative prose in the proximity of death and the failing voice of the dying character. Garrett does not quote the sentence in which Betty mistakes Lizzie for an angel. He also ignores the crucial sentence in the previous paragraph, where Betty leans against the tree: 'It brought to her mind the foot of the Cross, and she committed herself to Him who died upon it.' These omissions make it easier for Stewart to empty the episode of specifically religious reference:

> The balanced, momentarily stabilized chiastic assonance of 'weather-stained grey head' passes through the aspirant iambic alliteration of 'her as high as Heaven' in a suggested transcendence that needs no religious validation.
>
> Subjective and objective rendering are thereby hinged about a slippery phrasing that seems half analogy, half hyperbole: so high it seemed like heaven; every bit as high as heaven. The euphemism or periphrasis we might expect at such a time – 'she raised her beyond reach of any poorhouse' – is transformed into an indirect voucher of redemption that still avoids the mention of death while speeding to its visionary destination . . . the 'as high as' transition is a differential that allows for the quantum leap of the last capitalized word. (pp. 13–14)

Stewart's analysis is more sensitive to narrative strategies than to a specifically nineteenth-century religious consciousness.

53 Stone, p. 359.

54 A famous example is Wordsworth's 'angels or commissioned spirits', *The Prelude* (1850), VII, 244. For a different approach to this subject see Jonathan Arac, *Commissioned Spirits: The Shaping of Social Motion in Dickens, Carlyle, Melville, and Hawthorne* (New Brunswick, N.J., 1979).

55 The Catechism in the Book of Common Prayer has the question 'Who gave you this Name?', to which the response is, 'My Godfathers and Godmothers in my Baptism; wherein I was made a member of Christ, and child of God, and an inheritor of the kingdom of heaven.'

56 See note 38 above.

57 See pp. 208–14 above.

58 In his notes Dickens jotted down Amos Headstone, Amos Deadstone and Bradley Deadstone before settling on Bradley Headstone: see Stone, p. 345.

59 Cf., e.g., Dickens's treatment of the Murdstones in the early chapters of *David Copperfield*.

60 See pp. 74–5 above.

61 Dickens, *Life of Our Lord*, pp. 27–8.

62 Stone, p. 345.

63 See Wheeler, *Art of Allusion*, pp. 75–6; Sanders, p. 183.

64 See Walder, p. 204; Michael Cotsell, *The Companion to 'Our Mutual Friend'*, Dickens Companions, edited by Susan Shatto and Michael Cotsell (1986), p. 141.

65 See, e.g., pp. 254–5 above.

66 Cf. Frye, p. 56.

67 For the Southey, see p. 85 above; see also Robert Pollok, *The Course of Time: A Poem*, Illustrated Edition (1857), p. 150.

68 See p. 72 above. The apocalyptic symbolism associated with Eugene Wrayburn's assault is more reminiscent of Browning's *Easter-Day* than of Carlyle's *Sartor Resartus, pace* Barry V. Qualls, *The Secular Pilgrims of Victorian Fiction: The Novel as Book of Life* (Cambridge, 1982), p. 131: see pp. 106–7 above.

7 Newman, *The Dream of Gerontius*

1 John Henry Newman, *An Essay on the Development of Christian Doctrine* (1920), p. 36.

2 Wilfrid Ward, *The Life of John Henry Cardinal Newman*, 2 vols. (1912), I, 246; cited in Geoffrey Rowell, *Hell and the Victorians: A Study of the Nineteenth-Century Theological Controversies Concerning Eternal Punishment and the Future Life* (Oxford, 1974), p. 163.

3 John Henry Newman, *Apologia Pro Vita Sua: Being a History of his Religious Opinions*, edited by Martin J. Svaglic (Oxford, 1967), p. 256.

4 Ibid., p. 261.

5 Ibid., p. 37.

6 Geoffrey Rowell, '"The Dream of Gerontius"', *Ampleforth Journal*, 73 (1968), 184–92 (p. 192).

7 See pp. 73–83 above.

8 See Jacques Le Goff, *The Birth of Purgatory*, translated by Arthur Goldhammer (1984).

9 Ibid., p. 293.

10 Ibid., pp. 306, 12.

11 See p. 78 above.

12 See Esther R. B. Pese, 'A Suggested Background for Newman's *Dream of Gerontius*', *Modern Philology*, 47 (1949–50), 108–16.

13 See Edward Moore, *Studies in Dante, Second Series: Miscellaneous Essays* (Oxford, 1899), pp. 56–7.

14 See E. Moore, p. 56.

15 See E. Moore, p. 45. This and other revisionary aspects of Dante, such as his refusal to 'infernalize' purgatory as the church had done, and his portrayal of purgatory as 'straining in the direction of Paradise', encourages Le Goff (p. 346) to claim that he was 'in a sense more orthodox than the Church, more faithful to Purgatory's underlying logic'.

16 E. Moore, p. 47.

17 See pp. 232–4 above.

18 E. Moore (p. 59) describes the *Dream* as a poem 'singularly devoid of traces of the influence of Dante'.

19 [John Henry Newman], *Remarks on Certain Passages in the Thirty-Nine Articles*, Tracts for the Times, 90 (1841), pp. 23, 25.

20 Newman, *Essay on Development*, pp. 388–9.

21 Ibid., p. 390.

22 See pp. 74–7 above.

23 Newman, *Essay on Development*, p. 388.

24 Rowell, '"The Dream of Gerontius"', p. 190.

25 Catherine of Genoa, *Purgation and Purgatory, The Spiritual Dialogue*, translated by Serge Hughes, Classics of Western Spirituality (1979), p. 86.

26 Henry James Coleridge, *The Prisoners of the King: Thoughts on the Catholic Doctrine of Purgatory* (1878).

27 [John Henry Newman], *Verses on Various Occasions*, second edition (1869), pp. 294–5.

28 Newman, *Verses*, p. 358. (Further references to the *Dream* in the text are by section numbers.) In section 6 the Angel of the Agony prays for 'these souls which are so dear to Thee, / Who in prison, calm and patient, wait for Thee'. Earlier, in a hymn of praise by the Angel (3), Newman originally wrote the line 'By whom the suppliant captive is set free', but in the fair copy manuscript substituted 'prisoner' for 'captive': John Henry Newman, *The Dream of Gerontius, with a Complete Facsimile of the Original Fair Copy and of Portions of the First Rough Draft* (1909), MS p. 10.

29 Newman, *Apologia*, pp. 100–1.

30 Newman, *Essay on Development*, p. 48.

31 John Henry Newman, *Parochial and Plain Sermons*, 8 vols. (1891), I, 10.

32 See Meriol Trevor, *Newman: The Pillar of the Cloud* (1962), p. 633.

33 Rowell, '"The Dream of Gerontius"', p. 192.

34 Newman, *Apologia*, p. 112.

35 Ward, II, 357.

36 Newman, *Apologia*, p. 137.

37 John Henry Newman, *Discourses to Mixed Congregations* (1881), pp. 38–9; cited in Rowell, *Hell and the Victorians*, p. 158.

38 *The Manual of Prayers, Authorized by the Hierarchy of England and Wales for Congregational Use* (1886; rpt. 1953), pp. 235–6.

39 See *Rituale Romanum, Pauli V. Pontificis Maximi* (Mechliniae, 1860), pp. 112ff.

40 Originally the speech may have ended with the words 'In Thine own agony', as the following line ('Mary, pray for me . . .') is inscribed with a finer nib than the bulk of the fair copy manuscript, perhaps indicating that it was a late addition: see *The Dream of Gerontius, with a Complete Facsimile*, MS p. 4.

41 Gerhard Kittel, '*angelos* in the NT', in *Theological Dictionary of the New Testament*, edited by Gerhard Kittel, translated and edited by Geoffrey W. Bromiley, 10 vols. (Grand Rapids, Mich., 1964–76), I, 83–7 (p. 85).

42 Newman made late changes to the fair copy manuscript which emphasize the idea of sleep in the Angel's last speech, including, in its last line, replacing the word 'fetch' with 'wake': see *Facsimile*, MS p. 29.

43 Interestingly, a deleted line in the fair copy manuscript includes the words, 'Nor are there synchronisms': see *Facsimile*, MS p. 12.

44 Farrar used this passage to illustrate the second sense of *aiōnios* as 'something "spiritual" – something above and beyond time, – as when the knowledge of God is said to be eternal life': Frederic W. Farrar, *Eternal Hope: Five Sermons Preached in Westminster Abbey, November and December, 1877* (1904), p. 79, and n. 1. In a modern discussion of a theme similar to the Angel's, John Hick addresses the problem of 'times and spaces' in relation to 'psycho-physical re-creation after death in another space': 'Why should there not be a single time sequence in which events can occur simultaneously in different spaces, even though within each space the measurement of time must be in relation to physical movements peculiar to that space?' *Death and Eternal Life* (1976), p. 290. Also see Ina Rae Hark, 'Newman's *Dream of Gerontius*: Beyond Time and Sense', *Renascence*, 28 (1975), 15–26, for a somewhat uneven discussion of the theme in the *Dream*.

45 See *The Little Flowers of Saint Francis of Assissi*, translated by H. E. Manning (1915), p. 178.

46 See, e.g., Newman, *Parochial and Plain Sermons*, II, 366.

47 See, e.g., William E. Addis and Thomas Arnold, *A Catholic Dictionary, Containing some Account of the Doctrine, Discipline, Rites, Ceremonies, Councils, and Religious Orders of the Catholic Church* (1884), p. 26, to which Newman gave his official approval as Cardinal.

48 Cf. Stephen Prickett, *Romanticism and Religion: The Tradition of Coleridge and Wordsworth in the Victorian Church* (Cambridge, 1976), p. 208.

49 See Edward Bellasis, *Cardinal Newman as a Musician* (1892), pp. 10, 13, 18–19.

50 John Henry Newman, *The Scope and Nature of University Education*, second edition (1859), p. 346.

51 Newman, *Discourses*, p. 349.

52 See Howard E. Smither, *A History of the Oratorio*, 2 vols. (Chapel Hill, N.C., 1977), I, 29–76.

53 See Jerrold Northrop Moore, *Edward Elgar: A Creative Life* (Oxford, 1984), p. 166, n. 74.

54 Ibid., p. 290.

55 Ibid., p. 319, 313.

56 Elgar visited Newman's literary executor, Father Neville, at the Birmingham Oratory in order to obtain permission to abridge the *Dream*. See J. N. Moore, p. 296.

57 See I, cue 30. Quotations are from the Novello full orchestral score, and references are by part and cue number, given hereafter in the text.

58 See A. J. Jaeger, *'The Dream of Gerontius', John Henry Newman & Edward Elgar: Analytical & Descriptive Notes* (1901; rpt. Sevenoaks, 1974), p. 4.

59 This B flat is higher than the A flat on 'death' (I, cue 43) and the A on 'God' (I, cue 52).

60 Cf. Jaeger, p. 25.

61 See J. N. Moore, p. 312.

62 Cf. Jaeger, p. 31.

63 Ibid., p. 32.

64 Ibid.

65 See J. N. Moore, pp. 217–21.

66 See Jaeger, p. 33.

67 Howard E. Smither, 'Oratorio', in *The New Grove Dictionary of Music and Musicians*, edited by Stanley Sadie, 20 vols. (1980), XIII, 655–78 (p. 675).

8 Hopkins, *The Wreck of the Deutschland*

1 Letter to his mother, 26 June 1876, in Gerard Manley Hopkins, *Selected Prose*, edited by Gerald Roberts (Oxford, 1980), p. 64.

2 See Alfred Thomas, SJ, *Hopkins the Jesuit: The Years of Training* (1969), p. 232.

3 John Henry Newman, *Discourses to Mixed Congregations*, third edition (1862), pp. 402–3.

4 *The Letters of Gerard Manley Hopkins to Robert Bridges*, edited by Claude Colleer Abbott (1935), p. xxvi.

5 John Robinson, *In Extremity: A Study of Gerard Manley Hopkins* (Cambridge, 1978), p. 119.

6 Tom Paulin, 'On the Rampage', *TLS*, 14 August 1987, p. 863.

7 See David A. Downes, *Gerard Manley Hopkins: A Study of his Ignatian Spirit* (1959; rpt. 1960); Donald Walhout, *Send My Roots Rain: A Study of Religious Experience in the Poetry of Gerard Manley Hopkins* (Athens, Ohio and London, 1981); Elisabeth W. Schneider, *The Dragon in the Gate: Studies in the Poetry of G. M. Hopkins* (Berkeley and Los Angeles, 1968); Jerome Bump, *Gerard Manley Hopkins*, Twayne's English Authors series, general editor Herbert Sussman, 332 (Boston, 1982). See also Walter J. Ong, SJ, *Hopkins, the Self, and God*, The Alexander Lectures (Toronto, 1986).

8 See J. Hillis Miller, *The Linguistic Moment: From Wordsworth to Stevens* (Princeton, N.J., 1985), pp. 254–5; James Finn Cotter, *Inscape: The Christology and Poetry of Gerard Manley Hopkins* (Pittsburgh, 1972), pp. 146–52.

9 Miller, *Linguistic Moment*, p. 254.

10 See note 4 above.

11 *The Poems of Gerard Manley Hopkins*, fourth edition, edited by W. H. Gardner and N. H. MacKenzie (Oxford and New York, 1967), p. 51. (All further quotations from Hopkins's poetry are taken from this edition.)

12 Letter to Dixon, 27 February/13 March 1879, in *The Correspondence of Gerard Manley Hopkins and Richard Watson Dixon*, edited by Claude Colleer Abbott (1935), p. 24.

13 Francis Quarles, *Emblems, Divine and Moral; The School of the Heart; and Hieroglyphics of the Life of Man* (1866), p. 360. Interestingly, Walter Ong (p. 71) finds parallels between the *Spiritual Exercises* and the emblem books that were popular in St Ignatius's time.

14 Hans Frei, *The Eclipse of Biblical Narrative: A Study in Eighteenth and Nineteenth Century Hermeneutics* (New Haven and London, 1974), p. 130.

15 R[obert] Aitken, *The Teaching of the Types*, Tracts for the Clergy and the Earnest Minded, 1 (Oxford, 1854), p. 4: cited in Bump, *Hopkins*, pp. 98–9.

16 *The Note-Books and Papers of Gerard Manley Hopkins*, edited by Humphry House (London and New York, 1937), pp. 309, 331. See also Ong, pp. 4–6, *et passim*.

17 *The Spiritual Exercises of Saint Ignatius*, translated by Thomas Corbishley, SJ (1963), pp. 30–2.

18 Ibid., p. 30.

19 Ibid., pp. 36, 47.

20 Ibid., p. 69.

21 Ibid., p. 98.

22 See A. Thomas, pp. 231–5.

23 *Note-Books*, p. 128.

24 Anne Catherine Emmerich, *The Dolorous Passion of Our Lord Jesus Christ*, twelfth edition (1889), p. 102.

25 Ibid., p. 116.

26 Ibid., p. 268.

27 Ibid., p. 40.

28 Anon., *The Life and Revelations of Saint Gertrude, Virgin and Abbess, of the Order of St. Benedict* (1865), p. 186.

29 *Life of Gertrude*, pp. 35–6.

30 Ibid., p. 80.

31 See *The Catholic Encyclopedia*, edited by Charles G. Herbermann, *et al.*, 15 vols. (1907–12; rpt. New York, 1913), xv, 714.

32 See Emmerich, p. 31.

33 Ibid., p. 33.

34 *The Acts of the Christian Martyrs*, translated by Herbert Musurillo, Oxford Early Christian Texts, general editor Henry Chadwick (Oxford, 1972), pp. 27, 127.

35 See A. Thomas, pp. 35, 222–3; [John R.] Shortland, *The Corean Martyrs: A Narrative* [1869]; Bertrand A. Wilberforce, *Dominican Missions and Martyrs in Japan*, new edition (1897).

36 *The Times*, 9 December 1875, p. 6.

37 Miller, *Linguistic Moment*, p. 64.

38 Ibid., p. 255; Cotter, p. 146; Downes, p. 55.

39 Cited in Cotter, p. 100.

40 *Note-Books*, p. 337. See also Alan Heuser, *The Shaping Vision of Gerard Manley Hopkins* (1958), p. 44.

41 Cf., e.g., Leo Martin van Noppen, *Gerard Manley Hopkins, 'The Wreck of the Deutschland'* (Groningen, 1980), p. 89.

42 See Ignatius, p. 36; cf. Robinson, p. 23.

43 Walter Ong (p. 42) describes Hopkins as being 'exquisitely responsive' to Christianity's 'teaching on the Trinity of three Persons in God and its related teaching on the Incarnation'.

44 See Schneider, pp. 23–4.

45 Emmerich, pp. 56–7.

46 Newman, *Discourses*, p. 395.

47 *Note-Books*, p. 344.

48 See Cotter, pp. 40–8.

49 See illustration 17 above, and note 13.

50 See *Note-Books*, p. 263.

51 *The Times*, 10 December 1875, p. 10.

52 *The Times*, 11 December 1875, p. 7; 13 December 1875, p. 10.

53 See Alison G. Sulloway, *Gerard Manley Hopkins and the Victorian Temper* (1972), pp. 158–95.

54 See p. 28 above.

55 See Cotter, pp. 42–4.

56 See Jerome Bump, '"The Wreck of the Deutschland" and the Dynamic Sublime', *ELH*, 41 (1974–5), 106–29 (p. 129).

57 See Quarles, p. 285.

58 See Colleen McDannell and Bernhard Lang, *Heaven: A History* (New Haven and London, 1988), p. 102.

59 *Life of Gertrude*, p. 52.

60 Ibid., pp. 78–9.

61 St Ignatius (pp. 45–6) encourages the exercitant to 'see' the 'Three Divine Persons . . . watching the great round of the earth's surface, with all its people in a great blindness, going to Hell when they die'.

62 J. Hillis Miller, '"Orion" in "The Wreck of the Deutschland"', *Modern Language Notes*, 76 (1961), 509–14 (pp. 512–14).

63 *Life of Gertrude*, p. 54. Cf. also Quarles, p. 327; Charles Collins's painting, *Convent Thoughts* (1850–1), in *The Pre-Raphaelites* (1984), pp. 87–8; and J. M. Neale's translation from St Ambrose in *Hymns Ancient and Modern, For Use in the Services of the Church; With Accompanying Tunes* [edited by Henry Williams Baker, *et al.*], Standard Edition (1916), p. 529.

64 Emmerich, p. 59.

65 W. Harry Rogers, *Spiritual Conceits, Extracted from the Writings of the Fathers, the Old English Poets, etc.* (1862), p. 130.

66 Robinson, p. 120.

67 Emmerich, p. 246.

68 See Sulloway, pp. 186–7.

69 Ibid., pp. 189–90.

70 Oscar Cullmann, *The Christology of the New Testament*, second edition (1963), pp. 208–15; cited in Cotter, p. 147.

71 See Schneider, p. 29, where she argues cogently for a 'supernatural event' rather than an ambiguous 'vision'.

72 In *The School of the Heart*, the heart is depicted with a single eye in 'The Watching of the Heart': Quarles, p. 333. It is in 'The Enlightenment of the Heart', however, that he more closely anticipates Hopkins's treatment of the drowning of the tall nun:

> Now I perceive
> Presumption doth bereave
> Men of all hope of help, and leave
> Them, as it finds them, drown'd in misery:
> Despairing of themselves, to cry

> For mercy is the only remedy
> That sin-sick souls can have; to pray
> Against this darkness, may
> Turn it to day.
> Then unto thee,
> Great Lord of light, let me
> Direct my prayer, that I may see.

Quarles, pp. 313–14.

73 Cotter, p. 148.

74 See Julian Treuherz, 'The Pre-Raphaelites and Medieval Illuminated Manuscripts', in *Pre-Raphaelite Papers*, edited by Leslie Parris (1984), pp. 153–69 (p. 157).

75 See Owen Chadwick, *The Victorian Church*, second edition, 2 vols., Ecclesiastical History of England, edited by J. D. Dickinson, vols. VII–VIII (1970), II, 419.

Appendix: The Old Testament as the book of hope

1 Rudolf Bultmann and Karl Heinrich Rengstorf, *Hope*, Bible Key Words, 12 (1963), p. 9.

2 Ibid., pp. 10–11.

3 Ibid., p. 13.

4 See George P. Landow, *Victorian Types, Victorian Shadows: Biblical Typology in Victorian Literature, Art, and Thought* (1980).

5 *Lux Mundi: A Series of Studies in the Religion of the Incarnation*, edited by Charles Gore, eighth edition (1890), pp. 328–9.

6 Ibid., p. 346.

7 Ibid., p. 362.

8 *Encyclopaedia of Religion and Ethics*, edited by James Hastings and J. A. Selbie, 13 vols. (Edinburgh and New York, 1908–26), VI, 779.

9 See John Hick, *Death and Eternal Life* (1976), p. 63.

10 Ibid., pp. 58–9.

11 See Hans Küng, *Eternal Life?* (1982), translated by Edward Quinn (1984), p. 109.

12 See Hick, pp. 70–1; also p. 77, n. 60, where he cites the view of George W. E. Nickelsburg, Jr, that Daniel 12.2 is 'our earliest dateable intertestimental reference to a resurrection from the dead'.

13 S. G. F. Brandon, *The Judgment of the Dead: An Historical and Comparative Study of the Idea of a Post-Mortem Judgment in the Major Religions* (1967), pp. 100ff.

Bibliography

Place of publication is London unless otherwise stated.

Primary works (including Victorian criticism)

Addis, William E. and Thomas Arnold. *A Catholic Dictionary, Containing some Account of the Doctrine, Discipline, Rites, Ceremonies, Councils, and Religious Orders of the Catholic Church* (1884).

Aitken, Robert. *The Teaching of the Types*, Tracts for the Clergy and the Earnest Minded, 1 (Oxford, 1854).

Alexander, Mrs Cecil Frances. *Hymns for Little Children* (1848).

Alger, William Rounseville. *The Destiny of the Soul: A Critical History of the Doctrine of a Future Life*, tenth edition (New York, 1878).

Allingham, William. *William Allingham's Diary*, intro. Geoffrey Grigson (Fontwell, Sussex, 1967).

Anon. *The Acts of the Christian Martyrs*, trans. Herbert Musurillo, Oxford Early Christian Texts, general ed. Henry Chadwick (Oxford, 1972).

Anon. *The English Hymnal* (Oxford and London, 1906).

Anon. ['A Dean']. *'The Gates Ajar' Critically Examined* (1871).

Anon. *The Life and Revelations of Saint Gertrude, Virgin and Abbess, of the Order of St. Benedict* (1865).

Anon. *The Manual of Prayers, Authorized by the Hierarchy of England and Wales for Congregational Use* (1886; rpt. 1953).

Anon. *Methodist Free Church School Hymns* (1888).

Anon. *Rituale Romanum, Pauli V. Pontificis Maximi* (Mechliniae, 1860).

Arnold, Matthew. *Complete Prose Works*, ed. R. H. Super, 11 vols. (Ann Arbor, Mich., 1960–77).

The Poems of Matthew Arnold, ed. Kenneth Allott, second edn, ed. Miriam Allott, Longman Annotated English Poets, gen. eds. F. W. Bateson and John Barnard (London and New York, 1979).

Augustine, St. *The City of God*, trans. Marcus Dods, Modern Library (New York, 1950).

425

The Confessions of Saint Augustine, trans. E. B. Pusey, Everyman's Library, 200 (London and New York, 1907).

Bailey, Philip James. *Festus: A Poem*, ninth edn (1875).

Baker, Henry Williams, *et al.*, eds. *Hymns Ancient and Modern, For Use in the Services of the Church; With Accompanying Tunes*, Standard Edition (1916).

Baudelaire, Charles. *Les Fleurs du Mal* (Montreal, 1950).

Baynes, Robert H., ed. *The Illustrated Book of Sacred Poems* (London and New York, 1867).

Beattie, James. *Elements of Moral Science*, 2 vols. (Edinburgh, 1790–3).

Bell, Mackenzie. *Christina Rossetti: A Biographical and Critical Study* (1898).

Bellamy, G. Somers. *Essays from Shakspeare* (1879).

Bellasis, Edward. *Cardinal Newman as a Musician* (1892).

Benham, William, ed. *Catharine and Crauford Tait, Wife and Son of Archibald Campbell, Archbishop of Canterbury: A Memorial* (1879).

Bickersteth, Edward Henry. *The Blessed Dead: What Does Scripture Reveal of their State before the Resurrection?*, second edn, rev. (1863).

Companions for the Devout Life: Seven Lectures Delivered in St. James's Church, Piccadilly, A.D. 1876, St. James's Lectures, second ser. (1876).

The Holy Bible, with a Devotional and Practical Commentary by R. Jamieson and E. H. Bickersteth, 3 vols. (London and New York, 1861–5).

The Master's Home-Call: A Memoir of Alice Frances Bickersteth (1872).

A Practical and Explanatory Commentary on the New Testament (1868).

The Risen Saints: What does Scripture Reveal of their Estate and Employments? (1865).

The Shadowed Home, and the Light Beyond (1875).

The Two Brothers, and Other Poems, second edn (1872).

Yesterday, To-Day, and For Ever: A Poem in Twelve Books, eighth edn (1873).

Bickersteth, Robert, *et al. The Recognition of Friends in Heaven* (1866).

Blair, Robert. *The Grave: A Poem*, preface F. W. Farrar (Edinburgh, 1858).

Booth, William. *In Darkest England and the Way Out* (1890).

Branks, William. *Heaven our Home* (Edinburgh, 1861).

Life in Heaven (Edinburgh, 1863).

Meet for Heaven (Edinburgh, 1862).

Bridges, Robert. *Poetical Works of Robert Bridges, Excluding the Eight Dramas*, Oxford Edition (1914).

Brontë, Anne, Charlotte, Emily. *The Novels of the Brontës*, Clarendon edn, gen. eds. Ian and Jane Jack (Oxford, 1969–88).

Browning, Robert. *The Complete Works of Robert Browning*, ed. Roma A. King, Jr, *et al.* (Athens, Ohio, 1969–   ).

Buchanan, James. *Analogy, Considered as a Guide to Truth, and Applied as an Aid to Faith* (Edinburgh and London, 1864).

Bunyan, John. *The Pilgrim's Progress, Grace Abounding and A Relation of his Imprisonment*, ed. Edmund Venables, second edn, rev. Mabel Peacock (Oxford, 1900).

Butler, Joseph. *The Works of Joseph Butler*, ed. W. E. Gladstone, 2 vols. (Oxford, 1896).

Butler, Samuel. *Erewhon; or, Over the Range*, new popular edition (1923).
  The Way of all Flesh, ed. James Cochrane, Penguin English Library (Harmondsworth, 1966).

Carlyle, Thomas. *The Collected Letters of Thomas and Jane Welsh Carlyle*, Duke-Edinburgh Edition, gen. ed. Charles Richard Sanders, 7 vols. (Durham, N.C., 1970–7).
  Past and Present, Everyman's Library (London and New York, n.d.).
  Sartor Resartus; On Heroes and Hero Worship, Everyman's Library, 278 (London and New York, 1908).

Catherine of Genoa. *Purgation and Purgatory, The Spiritual Dialogue*, trans. Serge Hughes, Classics of Western Spirituality (1979).

Champneys, Basil. *Memoirs and Correspondence of Coventry Patmore*, 2 vols. (1900).

Clemens, Samuel Langhorne. ('Mark Twain'.) *Extract from Captain Stormfield's Visit to Heaven* (New York and London, 1909).

Clough, Arthur Hugh. *The Poems of Arthur Hugh Clough*, ed. A. L. P. Norrington (1968).

Coleridge, Henry James. *Prisoners of the King: Thoughts on the Catholic Doctrine of Purgatory* (1878).

Coleridge, Samuel Taylor. *Aids to Reflection in the Formation of a Manly Character on the Several Grounds of Prudence, Morality and Religion*, ed. Thomas Fenby, New Universal Library (London and New York, 1905).
  Confessions of an Inquiring Spirit, ed. H. St J. Hart, Library of Modern Religious Thought (1956).

Craik, Dinah Maria, née Mulock. *John Halifax, Gentleman* (London and Newcastle-on-Tyne, 1903).

Crowe, Catherine. *The Night Side of Nature; or, Ghosts and Ghost Stories*, 2 vols. (1848).

Dante Alighieri. *The Divine Comedy*, trans. Henry Francis Cary, ed. Edmund Gardner, Everyman's Library, 1308 (London and New York, 1967).

Davidson, Randall Thomas and William Benham. *Life of Archibald Campbell Tait, Archbishop of Canterbury*, 2 vols. (London and New York, 1891).

Dickens, Charles. *Bleak House*, ed. Norman Page, Penguin English Library (Harmondsworth, 1971).

The Clarendon Dickens, gen. eds. John Butt, Kathleen Tillotson, and James Kinsley (Oxford, 1966–).

Dickens' Working Notes for His Novels, ed. Harry Stone (Chicago and London, 1987).

Hard Times, for These Times, ed. David Craig, Penguin English Library (Harmondsworth, 1969).

The Letters of Charles Dickens, ed. Walter Dexter, Nonesuch Edition, 3 vols. (1938).

The Life of Our Lord: Written Expressly for his Children (1934).

Our Mutual Friend, ed. Stephen Gill, Penguin English Library (Harmondsworth, 1971).

The Posthumous Papers of the Pickwick Club, ed. Robert L. Patten, Penguin English Library (Harmondsworth, 1972).

A Tale of Two Cities, ed. Andrew Sanders, World's Classics (Oxford and New York, 1988).

Doré, Gustave and Blanchard Jerrold. *London: A Pilgrimage* (1872).

East, Timothy. *Death Bed Scenes; or, The Christian's Companion; On Entering the Dark Valley* (1825).

Eliot, George. See Evans, Marian.

Emmerich, Anne Catherine. *The Dolorous Passion of Our Lord Jesus Christ*, twelfth edn (1889).

Engels, Frederick. *The Condition of the Working-Class in England, From Personal Observation and Authentic Sources*, intro. Eric Hobsbawm (1969).

Erskine, Thomas. *The Unconditional Freeness of the Gospel: In Two Essays*, fourth edn (Edinburgh, 1831).

Essays and Reviews, by Frederick Temple, *et al.*, seventh edn (1861).

Evans, Marian. ('George Eliot'.) *Essays of George Eliot*, ed. Thomas Pinney (New York and London, 1963).

The Novels of George Eliot, Clarendon Edition, gen. ed. Gordon Haight (Oxford, 1980–).

Scenes of Clerical Life, ed. David Lodge, Penguin English Library (Harmondsworth, 1973).

Farrar, Frederic William. *The Bible: Its Meaning and Supremacy*, second edn (1901).

Eric; or, Little by Little: A Tale of Roslyn School, Black's Boy's Library (1928).

Eternal Hope: Five Sermons Preached in Westminster Abbey, November and December, 1877 (1904).

Mercy and Judgment: A Few Last Words on Christian Eschatology with Reference to Dr. Pusey's 'What is of Faith?' (1881).

Farrer, Austin. *The Glass of Vision*, Bampton Lectures (1948).

Feuerbach, Ludwig. *The Essence of Christianity*, trans. Marian Evans, second edn, English and Foreign Philosophical Library, 15 (1881).

Fowles, John. *The French Lieutenant's Woman* (1969).

Francis, St. *The Little Flowers of Saint Francis of Assissi*, trans. H. E. Manning (1915).

Froude, James Anthony. *The Nemesis of Faith* (1849).

['Zeta'.] *Shadows of the Clouds* (1847).

Thomas Carlyle: A History of his Life in London, 1834–1881, new edn, 2 vols. (1897).

Furniss, Joseph. *The House of Death*, Books for Children and Young Persons, 7 (Dublin, 1860).

The Sight of Hell, Books for Children and Young Persons, 10 (Dublin, 1861).

Gaskell, Elizabeth Cleghorn. *Mary Barton: A Tale of Manchester Life*, ed. Stephen Gill, Penguin English Library (Harmondsworth, 1970).

North and South, ed. Angus Easson, Oxford English Novels, gen. ed. James Kinsley (London and New York, 1973).

Gatty, Alfred. *A Key to Lord Tennyson's 'In Memoriam'*, third edn (1885).

Gissing, George. *The Nether World*, intro. Walter Allen, Everyman's Library, 1,362 (London and New York, 1973).

Workers in the Dawn, Victorian Fiction: Novels of Faith and Doubt (New York and London, 1976).

Gladstone, William Ewart. *Studies Subsidiary to the Works of Bishop Butler* (Oxford, 1896).

Gore, Charles, ed. *Lux Mundi: A Series of Studies in the Religion of the Incarnation*, eighth edn (1890).

Gosse, Edmund. *Father and Son: A Study of Two Temperaments*, popular edition (1909).

Greenoak, Francesca. *God's Acre: The Flowers and Animals of the Parish Churchyard* (1985).

Greswell, Edward. *A Harmony of the Four Gospels, in the English Authorized Version, Arranged According to Greswell's 'Harmonia Evangelica' in Greek* (1833).

Gurney, Edward. *Tertium Quid* (1887).

Hall, Alfred. *The Beliefs of a Unitarian* (1932).

Hallam, Arthur. *Remains in Verse and Prose of Arthur Henry Hallam*, ed. Henry Hallam (1863).

The Writings of Arthur Hallam, ed. T. H. Vail Motter (New York and London, 1943).

Hardy, Thomas. *The Complete Poems of Thomas Hardy*, ed. James Gibson, New Wessex Edition (1976).

Jude the Obscure, ed. Patricia Ingham, World's Classics (Oxford and New York, 1985).

Tess of the d'Urbervilles, ed. Juliet Grindle and Simon Gatrell, Clarendon Edition (Oxford, 1983).

Hare, Augustus J. C. *Memorials of a Quiet Life*, 3 vols. (1872–6).

Hare, Julius and Augustus. *Guesses at Truth* (1867).

Harrison, Frederic. *Tennyson, Ruskin, Mill, and Other Literary Estimates* (London and New York, 1899).

Henry, Matthew. *The Life of the Rev. Philip Henry, A.M., with Funeral Sermons for Mr. and Mrs. Henry*, enlarged J. B. Williams (1825).

Holyoake, Austin. *A Burial Service*, Secular Ceremonies (1870).

Heaven & Hell: Where Situated?: A Search after the Objects of Man's Fervent Hope & Abiding Terror (1873).

Hood, Thomas. *The Complete Poetical Works of Thomas Hood*, ed. Walter Jerrold (1906).

Hopkins, Gerard Manley. *The Correspondence of Gerard Manley Hopkins and Richard Watson Dixon*, ed. Claude Colleer Abbott (1935).

The Letters of Gerard Manley Hopkins to Robert Bridges, ed. Claude Colleer Abbot (1935).

The Note-Books and Papers of Gerard Manley Hopkins, ed. Humphry House (London and New York, 1937).

The Poems of Gerard Manley Hopkins, ed. W. H. Gardner and N. H. MacKenzie, fourth edn (Oxford, 1967).

Selected Prose, ed. Gerald Roberts (Oxford, 1980).

Horne, Thomas Hartwell. *An Introduction to the Critical Study and Knowledge of the Holy Scriptures*, tenth edn (1856).

Hughes, Thomas. *Tom Brown's Schooldays* (1857).

Hutchison, John. *Our Lord's Signs in St. John's Gospel: Discussions Chiefly Exegetical and Doctrinal on the Eight Miracles in the Fourth Gospel* (Edinburgh, 1892).

Ignatius Loyola, St. *The Spiritual Exercises of St Ignatius*, trans. Thomas Corbishley, SJ (1963).

Jaeger, A. J. *'The Dream of Gerontius', John Henry Newman & Edward Elgar: Analytical & Descriptive Notes* (1901; rpt. Sevenoaks, 1974).

James, John Angell. *Heaven; or, The Church Triumphant in its State of Celestial Repose* (1859).

Jowett, Benjamin. *The Interpretation of Scripture, and Other Essays*, London Library Edition (London and New York, 1906).

Julian of Norwich. *The Revelations of Divine Love*, trans. James Walsh (1961).

Kant, Immanuel. *Lectures on Philosophical Theology*, trans. Allen W. Wood and Gertrude M. Clark (Ithaca and London, 1978).

Keble, John. *The Christian Year: Thoughts in Verse for the Sundays and Holydays Throughout the Year*, second edn (Oxford, 1827).

Ker, William. *'The Things which must Shortly come to Pass': A Series of*

Discourses on the Prophecies of 'The Last Days,' Delivered in the Parish Church of Tipton, Staffordshire (Dudley, 1868).

Kingsley, Charles. *Alton Locke: Tailor and Poet*, ed. Herbert van Thal, First Novel Library (1967).

Yeast: A Problem (1851).

Knowles, James. 'Aspects of Tennyson II (A Personal Reminiscence)', *Nineteenth Century*, 33 (1893), 164–88.

Levi, Peter, ed. *The Penguin Book of English Christian Verse* (Harmondsworth, 1984).

Liddon, Henry Parry. *Passiontide Sermons* (London and New York, 1891).

Liguori, Alphonsus, St. *The Eternal Truths*, trans. R. A. Coffin (1857).

Lindsey, Theophilus. *Sermons, with Appropriate Prayers Annexed*, 2 vols. (1810).

Lodge, David. *How Far Can You Go?* (Harmondsworth, 1981).

Lord, Perceval B. *Popular Physiology* (1834).

Luckock, Herbert Mortimer. *After Death: An Examination of the Testimony of Primitive Times Respecting the State of the Faithful Dead, and their Relationship to the Living*, second edn (1880).

Lytton, Edward G. E. L. Bulwer. *A Strange Story*, 2 vols. (1862).

Lytton, Edward R. B. ('Owen Meredith'.) 'Last Words', *Cornhill Magazine*, 2 (July–Dec. 1860), 513–17.

Macaulay, Thomas Babington. *Lord Macaulay's Essays, and Lays of Ancient Rome*, popular edition (1899).

The Miscellaneous Writings and Speeches of Lord Macaulay, popular edition (1891).

MacBeth, George, ed. *The Penguin Book of Victorian Verse* (Harmondsworth, 1969).

Mallock, William Hurrell. *The New Republic; or, Culture, Faith, and Philosophy in an English Country House*, Rosemary Library, ed. John Squire (1937).

Marvin, Frederic Rowland. *The Last Words (Real and Traditional) of Distinguished Men and Women, Collected from Various Sources* (Troy, N.Y. 1900).

Masterman, Charles F. G. *Tennyson as a Religious Teacher* (1900).

Maurice, Frederick Denison. *Christmas Day, and Other Sermons*, second edn (1892).

Death and Life: A Sermon Preached in Lincoln's Inn Chapel on the 25th March, 1855 (Cambridge and London, 1855).

The Gospel of St. John: A Series of Discourses (Cambridge, 1857).

The Kingdom of Christ; or, Hints to a Quaker Respecting the Principles, Constitution and Ordinances of the Catholic Church, ed. Alec R. Vidler, 2 vols. (1958).

Lectures on the Apocalypse; or, Book of Revelation of St. John the Divine, second edn (Cambridge and London, 1865).

Theological Essays, second edn (Cambridge, 1853).

Maurice, Frederick, ed. *The Life of Frederick Denison Maurice, Chiefly Told in his Own Letters*, 2 vols. (1884).

Maurice, Priscilla. *Prayers for the Sick and Dying* (1853).

ed. *Sacred Poems for Mourners*, intro. R. C. Trench (1846).

Menzies, Mrs Stephen, ed. *The Traveller's Guide, from Death to Life* (n.d.).

Meredith, George. *The Letters of George Meredith*, ed. C. L. Cline, 3 vols. (Oxford, 1970).

The Poems of George Meredith, ed. Phyllis B. Bartlett, 2 vols. (New Haven and London, 1978).

Selected Poems, ed. Keith Hanley (Manchester, 1983).

The Works of George Meredith, Mickleham Edition, 18 vols. (1922–4).

Meredith, Owen. See Lytton, Edward R. B.

Miller, Hugh. *The Testimony of the Rocks; or, Geology in its Bearings on the Two Theologies, Natural & Revealed* (Edinburgh, 1884).

Montgomery, Robert. *The Omnipresence of the Deity: A Poem*, fourth edn (1828).

Moore, Edward. *Studies in Dante, Second Series: Miscellaneous Essays* (Oxford, 1899).

Mozley, J. B. *Essays Historical and Theological*, third edn, 2 vols. (1892).

Newman, John Henry. *Apologia Pro Vita Sua: Being a History of his Religious Opinions*, ed. Martin J. Svaglic (Oxford, 1967).

Discourses to Mixed Congregations (1881).

The Dream of Gerontius, with a Complete Facsimile of the Original Fair Copy and of Portions of the First Rough Draft (1909).

An Essay on the Development of Christian Doctrine (1920).

Lectures on the Prophetical Office of the Church, Viewed Relatively to Romanism and Popular Protestantism (London and Oxford, 1837).

Parochial and Plain Sermons, new edn, 8 vols. (1868).

Remarks on Certain Passages in the Thirty-Nine Articles, Tracts for the Times, 90 (1841).

The Scope and Nature of University Education, second edn (1859).

Verses on Various Occasions, second edn (1869).

Nicoll, W. Robertson, ed. *The Expositor's Greek Testament*, 5 vols. (1897–1910).

Oxenham, Henry Nutcombe. *Catholic Eschatology and Universalism: An Essay on the Doctrine of Future Retribution*, second edn (1878).

Paley, William. *The Works of William Paley*, 4 vols. (Edinburgh, 1823).

Pascal, Blaise. *Pascal's Pensées*, trans. H. F. Stewart (1950).

Pater, Walter. *Marius the Epicurean: His Sensations and Ideas*, Victorian Fiction: Novels of Faith and Doubt (New York and London, 1975).

Patmore, Coventry. *Poems*, ed. Basil Champneys (1906).

The Rod, the Root and the Flower, ed. Derek Patmore (1950).

Pattison, Mark. *Memoirs* (1885).

Phelps, Elizabeth Stuart. *The Gates Ajar*, ed. Helen Sootin Smith, John Harvard Library, gen. ed. Bernard Bailyn (Cambridge, Mass., 1964).

Poe, Edgar Allan. *The Collected Works of Edgar Allan Poe*, ed. Thomas Ollive Mabbott, 3 vols. (Cambridge, Mass., 1969–78).

Pollok, Robert. *The Course of Time: A Poem*, Illustrated Edition (1857).

Pusey, Edward Bouverie. *What is of Faith as to Everlasting Punishment?: In Reply to Dr. Farrar's Challenge in his 'Eternal Hope,' 1879*, second edn (Oxford and London, 1880).

Quarles, Francis. *Emblems, Divine and Moral; The School of the Heart; and Hieroglyphics of the Life of Man* (1866).

Reade, Charles. *The Cloister and the Hearth: A Tale of the Middle Ages*, Everyman's Library (London and New York, 1906).

Richmond, Legh. *The Dairyman's Daughter* (1810).

Robertson, Frederick W. *Analysis of 'In Memoriam'* (1862).

Lectures and Addresses on Literary and Social Topics (1858).

Sermons, Preached at Trinity Chapel, Brighton, third ser. (1857).

Rogers, W. Harry. *Spiritual Conceits, Extracted from the Writings of the Fathers, the Old English Poets, etc.* (1862).

Roget, Peter Mark. *Animal and Vegetable Physiology, Considered with Reference to Natural Theology*, Bridgewater Treatise, 2 vols. (1834).

Rossetti, Christina. *The Complete Poems of Christina Rossetti*, Variorum Edition, ed. R. W. Crump, 2 vols. (Baton Rouge and London, 1979–86).

The Face of the Deep: A Devotional Commentary on the Apocalypse, sixth edn (1911).

Rossetti, Dante Gabriel. *The Blessed Damozel: The Unpublished Manuscript, Texts and Collation*, ed. Paull Franklin Baum (Chapel Hill, 1937).

Ruskin, John. *The Works of John Ruskin*, ed. E. T. Cook and Alexander Wedderburn, Library Edition, 39 vols. (1902–12).

Salmond, Stewart D. F. *The Christian Doctrine of Immortality* (Edinburgh, 1895).

Salt, Henry S. *The Life of James Thomson ('B.V.'), with a Selection from his Letters and a Study of his Works* (1889).

Schleiermacher, Friedrich. *The Christian Faith*, ed. H. R. Mackintosh and J. S. Stewart (Edinburgh, 1928).

Shortland, John R. *The Corean Martyrs: A Narrative* (1869).

Simpson, Richard. *Richard Simpson as Critic*, ed. David Carroll, Routledge Critics series, gen. ed. B. C. Southam (1977).

Southey, Robert. *The Poetical Works of Robert Southey*, 10 vols. (1837–8).

Stanley, Arthur Penrhyn. *The Epistles of St. Paul to the Corinthians*, fourth edn (1876).

Stone, Elizabeth. *God's Acre; or, Historical Notices Relating to Churchyards* (1858).

Strauss, David Friedrich. *The Life of Jesus, Critically Examined*, trans. Marian Evans, 3 vols. (1846).

Swinburne, Algernon Charles. *The Complete Works of Algernon Charles Swinburne*, ed. Edmund Gosse and Thomas James Wise, Bonchurch Edition, 20 vols. (1975; rpt. New York, 1968).

Symons, Arthur. 'Aubrey Beardsley', *Fortnightly Review*, NS 58 (1898), 752–61.

Taylor, Isaac. *Physical Theory of Another Life* (1836).

Temple, Frederick. *Sermons Preached in Rugby School Chapel, in 1858, 1859, 1860* (1861).

Tennyson, Alfred. *In Memoriam*, ed. Susan Shatto and Marion Shaw (Oxford, 1982).
  The Poems of Tennyson, ed. Christopher Ricks, Longman Annotated English Poets, gen. ed. F. W. Bateson (1969).

Tennyson, Hallam. *Alfred Lord Tennyson: A Memoir* (1899).
  Materials for a Life of A. T. (p.p., n.d.).

Thackeray, William Makepeace. *The Works of William Makepeace Thackeray*, 26 vols. (1894–8).

Thompson, Francis. *Poems of Francis Thompson*, ed. Terence L. Connolly, rev. edn (New York, 1941).
  The Works of Francis Thompson, ed. Wilfrid Meynell, 3 vols. (1913).

Thomson, James. *Poems and Some Letters of James Thomson*, ed. Anne Ridler (1963).

Tocqueville, Alexis de. *Journeys to England and Ireland*, trans. George Lawrence and K. P. Mayer, ed. J. P. Mayer (1958).

Todd, Robert B., ed. *The Cyclopaedia of Anatomy and Physiology*, 5 vols. (1835–9).

Trollope, Anthony. *Barchester Towers*, World's Classics, 268 (1925).
  Clergymen of the Church of England, intro. Ruth apRoberts (Leicester, 1974).
  The Last Chronicle of Barset, World's Classics, 398 (1946).
  The Warden, World's Classics, 217 (1918).

Tulloch, John. *Movements of Religious Thought in Britain during the Nineteenth Century* (1885).

Twain, Mark. See Clemens, Samuel Langhorne.

Tyrrell, George. *Letters from a 'Modernist'*, ed. M. J. Weaver (1981).

Vaughan, Charles John. *Revisions of the Liturgy: Five Discourses* (Cambridge and London, 1860).

W., A. M. H. *Glimpses of a Brighter Land* (1871).

Warren, Charles F. S. *The Dies Irae: On this Hymn and its English Versions*, Part I, The Hymn (1897).

Watts, Isaac. *Divine Songs, Attempted in Easy Language for the Use of Children* (1715).

Weaver, Robert. *Heaven: A Manual for the Heirs of Heaven; Designed for the Satisfaction of the Inquisitive, as well as for Assistance to the Devout. Also, on Angels and their Ministry* (1837).

Whateley, Richard. *A View of the Scripture Revelations Concerning a Future State: Laid Before his Parishioners, by a Country Pastor* (1829).

Wilberforce, Bertrand A. *Dominican Missions and Martyrs in Japan*, new edn (1897).

Wood, Ellen (Mrs Henry). *East Lynne*, 3 vols. (1861).

Wordsworth, Christopher. *On Burning of the Body; and on Burial: A Sermon Preached in Westminster Abbey on Sunday July 5th, 1874* (Lincoln, 1874).

Wordsworth, William. *The Poetical Works of William Wordsworth*, ed. Ernest de Selincourt and Helen Darbishire, 5 vols. (Oxford, 1940–9).

Yonge, Charlotte M. *The Heir of Redclyffe*, Victorian Fiction: Novels of Faith and Doubt (New York and London, 1976).

Young, Edward. *The Complaint; or, Night Thoughts, on Life, Death and Immortality* (1812).

Secondary works

Abrams, M. H. *Natural Supernaturalism: Tradition and Revelation in Romantic Literature* (New York and London, 1971).

Aglionby, Francis Keyes. *The Life of Edward Henry Bickersteth, D.D., Bishop and Poet* (1907).

Allen, Peter. *The Cambridge Apostles: The Early Years* (Cambridge, 1978).

Allott, Miriam, ed. *The Brontës: The Critical Heritage*, Critical Heritage series, gen. ed. B. C. Southam (London and Boston, 1974).

Alter, Robert and Frank Kermode, eds. *The Literary Guide to the Bible* (1987).

Anderson, Ray S. *Theology, Death and Dying* (Oxford and New York, 1986).

Anon. *The Pre-Raphaelites*, Tate Gallery exhibition catalogue (1984).

Arac, Jonathan. *Commissioned Spirits: The Shaping of Social Motion in Dickens, Carlyle, Melville, and Hawthorne* (New Brunswick, N.J., 1979).

Ariès, Philippe. *The Hour of our Death*, trans. Helen Weaver (1981).

  Western Attitudes Toward Death: From the Middle Ages to the Present, trans. Patricia M. Ranum (Baltimore and London, 1974).

Armstrong, Isobel. *Language as Living Form in Nineteenth-Century Poetry* (Brighton and New Jersey, 1982).

ed., *The Major Victorian Poets: Reconsiderations* (1969).

ed., *Robert Browning*, Writers and their Background series, gen. ed. R. L. Brett (1974).

Balston, Thomas. *John Martin, 1789–1854: His Life and Works* (1947).

Barnes, Malcolm. *Augustus Hare* (1984).

Barr, James. *Biblical Words for Time* (1962).

Barrett, C. K. *A Commentary on the Second Epistle to the Corinthians* (1973).

Bartsch, H. W., ed. *Kerygma and Myth* (New York, 1961).

Beer, John. *Wordsworth and the Human Heart* (1978).

Begbie, Harold. *Life of William Booth: The Founder of the Salvation Army*, abridged edn, 2 vols. (1926).

Bentley, D. M. R. '"The Blessed Damozel": A Young Man's Fantasy', *Victorian Poetry*, 20 (1982), 31–43.

Birley, Robert. *Sunk Without Trace: Some Forgotten Masterpieces Reconsidered*, The Clark Lectures, 1960–1 (New York, 1962).

Blackmur, R. P. *A Primer of Ignorance*, ed. Joseph Frank (New York, 1967).

Boardman, Brigid M. *Between Heaven and Charing Cross: The Life of Francis Thompson* (London and New Haven, 1988).

Bowker, John. 'The Human Imagination of Hell', *Theology*, 85 (1982), 403–10.

Boyd, John D. 'The Principle of Analogy and the Immortality Question in Tennyson's *In Memoriam*', *University of Toronto Quarterly*, 45 (1975–6), 123–38.

Brandon, S. G. F. *The Judgment of the Dead: An Historical and Comparative Study of the Idea of a Post-Mortem Judgment in the Major Religions* (1967).

Brooks, Chris. *Signs for the Times: Symbolic Realism in the Mid-Victorian World* (1984).

Brown, Colin, ed. *The New International Dictionary of New Testament Theology*, 3 vols. (Exeter, 1978).

Buckley, Jerome. *Tennyson: The Growth of a Poet* (Cambridge, Mass., 1960).

Bultmann, Rudolf. *The Gospel of John: A Commentary*, trans. G. R. Beasley-Murray (Oxford, 1971).

Life and Death, Bible Key Words series, 14 (1965).

Bultmann, Rudolf and Karl Heinrich Rengstorf. *Hope*, Bible Key Words series, 12 (1963).

Bump, Jerome. *Gerard Manley Hopkins*, Twayne's English Authors series, gen. ed. Herbert Sussman, 332 (Boston, 1982).

'"The Wreck of the Deutschland" and the Dynamic Sublime', *ELH*, 41 (1974–5), 106–29.

Chadwick, Owen. *The Victorian Church*, second edn, 2 vols., Ecclesiastical History of England, ed. J. D. Dickinson, vols. VII–VIII (1970).

Chamberlain, William B. *Heaven Wasn't his Destination: The Philosophy of Ludwig Feuerbach* (1941).

Charity, A. C. *Events and their Afterlife: The Dialectics of Christian Typology in the Bible and Dante* (Cambridge, 1966).

Charlesworth, Barbara. *Dark Passages: The Decadent Consciousness in Victorian Literature* (Madison and Milwaukee, 1965).

Clarke, W. K. Lowther, ed. *Liturgy and Worship: A Companion to the Prayer Books of the Anglican Communion* (London and New York, 1932).

Cockshut, A. O. J. *Truth to Life: The Art of Biography in the Nineteenth Century* (1974).

Cohn, Norman. *The Pursuit of the Millennium: Revolutionary Millenarians and Mystical Anarchists of the Middle Ages* (1970).

Cosslett, Tess, ed. *Science and Religion in the Nineteenth Century* (Cambridge, 1984).

Cotsell, Michael. *The Companion to 'Our Mutual Friend'*, Dickens Companions, ed. Susan Shatto and Michael Cotsell (1986).

Cotter, James Finn. *Inscape: The Christology and Poetry of Gerard Manley Hopkins* (Pittsburgh, 1972).

Coveney, Peter. *The Image of Childhood, the Individual and Society: A Study of the Theme in English Literature*, rev. edn (Harmondsworth, 1967).

Culler, A. Dwight. *The Poetry of Tennyson* (New Haven and London, 1977).

Cullmann, Oscar. *The Christology of the New Testament*, second edn (1963).

Curl, James Stevens. *The Victorian Celebration of Death* (Newton Abbot, 1972).

Dale, Peter Allan. '"Gracious Lies": The Meaning of Metaphor in *In Memoriam*', *Victorian Poetry*, 18 (1980), 147–67.

Dawson, Carl. *Victorian Noon: English Literature in 1850* (Baltimore and London, 1979).

DeVane, William Clyde. *A Browning Handbook*, second edn (New York, 1955).

Dillistone, F. W. *Christianity and Symbolism* (1955).

Downes, David A. *Gerard Manley Hopkins: A Study of his Ignatian Spirit* (1959; rpt. 1960).

Drew, Philip. *The Poetry of Browning: A Critical Introduction* (1970).

Edmond, Rod. 'Death Sequences: Patmore, Hardy, and the New Domestic Elegy', *Victorian Poetry*, 19 (1981), 151–65.

Edwards, Michael. *Poetry and Possibility* (London and Basingstoke, 1989).

Towards a Christian Poetics (London and Basingstoke, 1984).

Eliot, T. S. *Selected Essays*, third edn (1951).

Ellmann, Mary Joan. 'Tennyson: Revision of *In Memoriam*, Section 85', *Modern Language Notes*, 65 (1950), 22–30.

Feaver, William. *The Art of John Martin* (Oxford, 1975).

Finer, S. E. *The Life and Times of Sir Edwin Chadwick* (1952).

Flynn, Philip. 'Hallam and Tennyson: The "Theodicaea Novissima" and *In Memoriam*', *Studies in English Literature, 1500–1900*, 19 (1979), 705–20.

Frei, Hans. *The Eclipse of Biblical Narrative: A Study in Eighteenth and Nineteenth Century Hermeneutics* (New Haven and London, 1974).

Frost, Maurice, ed. *Historical Companion to 'Hymns Ancient & Modern'*, new edn (1962).

Frye, Northrop. *The Great Code: The Bible and Literature* (1983).

Gauld, Alan. *The Founders of Psychical Research* (1968).

Gaustad, Edwin S., ed. *The Rise of Adventism: Religion and Society in Mid-Nineteenth-Century America* (New York, 1974).

Gennep, Arnold van. *The Rites of Passages*, trans. Monika B. Vizedom and Gabrielle L. Caffee (Chicago, 1960).

Gold, Joseph. *Charles Dickens: Radical Moralist* (Minneapolis and London, 1972).

Guskin, Phyllis J. 'Ambiguities in the Structure and Meaning of Browning's *Christmas-Eve*', *Victorian Poetry*, 4 (1966), 21–8.

Happold, F. C. *Mysticism: A Study and an Anthology*, rev. edn (Harmondsworth, 1970).

Hark, Ina Rae. 'Newman's *Dream of Gerontius*: Beyond Time and Sense', *Renascence*, 28 (1975), 15–26.

Harrison, Antony H. *Christina Rossetti in Context* (1988).

Harrison, J. F. C. *The Second Coming: Popular Millenarianism, 1780–1850* (London and Henley, 1979).

Hastings, James. *Dictionary of the Bible*, second edn, rev. Frederick C. Grant and H. H. Rowley (Edinburgh, 1963).

  ed., *The Great Texts of the Bible: Revelation* (1915).

Hastings, James and J. A. Selbie, eds. *Encyclopaedia of Religion and Ethics*, 13 vols. (Edinburgh and New York, 1908–26).

Hemmings, F. W. J. *Baudelaire the Damned: A Biography* (1982).

Herbermann, Charles G., *et al.*, eds. *The Catholic Encyclopedia*, 15 vols. (1907–12; rpt. New York, 1913).

Heuser, Alan. *The Shaping Vision of Gerard Manley Hopkins* (1958).

Hick, John. *Death and Eternal Life* (1976).

Hirsch, Gordon D. 'Tennyson's *Commedia*', *Victorian Poetry*, 8 (1970), 93–106.

Hornback, Bert. '*Noah's Arkitecture*': A Study of Dickens's Mythology* (Athens, Ohio, 1972).

Hoskyns, Edwyn Clement. *The Fourth Gospel*, ed. Francis Noel Davey, second edn (1947).

Hughes, Robert. *Heaven and Hell in Western Art* (1968).

Hunt, John Dixon, ed. *Tennyson, 'In Memoriam': A Casebook*, Casebook series, gen. ed. A. E. Dyson (1970).

Hyder, Clyde K., ed. *Swinburne: The Critical Heritage*, Critical Heritage series, gen. ed. B. C. Southam (1970).

Irvine, William and Park Honan. *The Book, the Ring, and the Poet: A Biography of Robert Browning* (1975).

Jack, Ian. *Browning's Major Poetry* (Oxford, 1973).

Jasper, David, ed. *The Interpretation of Belief: Coleridge, Schleiermacher and Romanticism* (London and Basingstoke, 1986).

Jay, Elisabeth. *The Religion of the Heart: Anglican Evangelicalism and the Nineteenth-Century Novel* (Oxford, 1979).

Johnston, Kenneth R. *Wordsworth and 'The Recluse'* (New Haven and London, 1984).

Keating, Peter, ed. *Into Unknown England, 1866–1913: Selections from the Social Explorers* (Glasgow, 1976).

Kermode, Frank. *The Genesis of Secrecy: On the Interpretation of Narrative*, The Charles Eliot Norton Lectures, 1977–8 (Cambridge, Mass. and London, 1979).

The Sense of an Ending: Studies in the Theory of Fiction (1967).

Kilroy, James. 'The Chiastic Structure of *In Memoriam, A.H.H.*', *Philological Quarterly*, 56 (1977), 358–73.

Kincaid, James R. *Tennyson's Major Poems: The Comic and Ironic Patterns* (New Haven and London, 1975).

Kittel, Gerhard, ed. *Theological Dictionary of the New Testament*, trans. and ed. Geoffrey W. Bromiley, 10 vols. (Grand Rapids, Mich., 1964–76).

Klingender, Francis D. *Art and the Industrial Revolution* (1947).

Kübler-Ross, Elisabeth. *On Death and Dying* (1970).

Küng, Hans. *Eternal Life?*, trans. Edward Quinn (1984).

Landow, George P. *Victorian Types, Victorian Shadows: Biblical Typology in Victorian Literature, Art, and Thought* (1980).

Larson, Janet. *Dickens and the Broken Scripture* (Athens, Georgia, 1985).

Lauter, Paul. 'The Narrator of "The Blessed Damozel"', *Modern Language Notes*, 73 (1958), 344–8.

Leeuwen, Arend Th. van. *Critique of Heaven* (1972).

Le Goff, Jacques. *The Birth of Purgatory*, trans. Arthur Goldhammer (1984).

Levine, George. *Darwin and the Novelists: Patterns of Science in Victorian Fiction* (Cambridge, Mass. and London, 1988).

Lincoln, Andrew. *Paradise Now and Not Yet: Studies in the Role of the*

Heavenly Dimension in Paul's Thought with Special Reference to his Eschatology, Society for New Testament Studies Monograph series, ed. R. McL. Wilson and M. E. Thrall, 43 (Cambridge, 1981).

Litzinger, Boyd and Donald Smalley, eds. *Robert Browning: The Critical Heritage*, Critical Heritage series, gen. ed. B. C. Southam (1970).

Livingston, James C. *Modern Christian Thought: From the Enlightenment to Vatican II* (New York and London, 1971).

McDannell, Colleen and Bernhard Lang. *Heaven: A History* (New Haven and London, 1988).

McFague, Sallie. *Metaphorical Theology: Models of God in Religious Language* (1983).

McGann, Jerome J. 'Rossetti's Significant Details', *Victorian Poetry*, 7 (1969), 41–54.

MacQuarrie, John. *God-Talk: An Examination of the Language and Logic of Theology* (1967).

Marcus, Steven. *Dickens from Pickwick to Dombey* (1965).

Martin, Robert Bernard. *Tennyson: The Unquiet Heart* (Oxford, 1980).

Mégroz, R. L. *Francis Thompson, The Poet of Earth in Heaven: A Study in Mysticism and the Evolution of Love-Poetry* (1927).

Miller, J. Hillis. *The Linguistic Moment: From Wordsworth to Stevens* (Princeton, N.J., 1985).

'"Orion" in "The Wreck of the Deutschland"', *Modern Language Notes*, 76 (1961), 509–14.

Moore, Jerrold Northrop. *Edward Elgar: A Creative Life* (Oxford, 1984).

Moorman, Mary. *William Wordsworth, A Biography: The Later Years, 1803–1850* (1965).

Morley, John, Viscount. *The Life of William Ewart Gladstone*, 3 vols. (1904).

Morley, John. *Death, Heaven and the Victorians* (1971).

Murray, Peter and Linda. *The Art of the Renaissance* (1963).

Neill, Stephen. *The Interpretation of the New Testament, 1861–1961*, The Firth Lectures, 1962 (1966).

Nichols, Ashton. 'The Epiphanic Trance Poem: Why Tennyson is not a Mystic', *Victorian Poetry*, 24 (1986–7), 131–48.

The Poetics of Epiphany: Nineteenth-Century Origins of the Modern Literary Movement (Tuscaloosa and London, 1988).

Noppen, Leo Martin van. *Gerard Manley Hopkins, 'The Wreck of the Deutschland'* (Groningen, 1980).

Ong, Walter J., SJ. *Hopkins, the Self, and God*, The Alexander Lectures (Toronto, 1986).

Oppenheim, Janet. *The Other World: Spiritualism and Psychical Research in England, 1850–1914* (Cambridge, 1985).

Ormond, Percy H. *The Mystical Poets of the English Church* (1919).

Pagels, Elaine. *The Gnostic Gospels* (1980).

Paley, Morton D. *The Apocalyptic Sublime* (New Haven and London, 1986).

Parris, Leslie, ed. *Pre-Raphaelite Papers* (1984).

Patterson, Annabel M. '*Our Mutual Friend*: Dickens as the Compleat Angler', in *Dickens Studies Annual*, 1 (1970), 252–64.

Paulin, Tom. 'On the Rampage', *TLS*, 14 August 1987, p. 863.

Peake, L. S. 'Tennyson and the Search for Immortality: III. Reason and Love', *The Saturday Review*, 12 March 1932, p. 266.

Pese, Esther R. B. 'A Suggested Background for Newman's *Dream of Gerontius*', *Modern Philology*, 47 (1949–50), 108–16.

Pollard, Arthur. 'The Brontës and their Father's Faith', *Essays and Reviews*, NS 37 (1984), 46–61.

Prickett, Stephen. *Romanticism and Religion: The Tradition of Wordsworth and Coleridge in the Victorian Church* (Cambridge, 1976).

 Words and 'The Word': Language, Poetics and Biblical Interpretation (Cambridge, 1986).

Qualls, Barry V. *The Secular Pilgrims of Victorian Fiction: The Novel as Book of Life* (Cambridge, 1982).

Ramm, Bernard. *The Pattern of Religious Authority* (Grand Rapids, Mich., 1957).

Rees, Joan. *The Poetry of Dante Gabriel Rossetti: Modes of Self-Expression* (Cambridge, 1981).

Reeves, Marjorie and Warwick Gould. *Joachim of Fiore and the Myth of the Eternal Evangel in the Nineteenth Century* (Oxford, 1987).

Reid, J. C. *The Mind and Art of Coventry Patmore* (1957).

Richardson, Alan and John Bowden, eds. *A New Dictionary of Christian Theology* (1983).

Ricks, Christopher. *Tennyson*, Masters of World Literature series, ed. Louis Kronenberger (1972).

Riede, David G. *Dante Gabriel Rossetti and the Limits of Victorian Vision* (Ithaca and London, 1983).

Robinson, John. *In Extremity: A Study of Gerard Manley Hopkins* (Cambridge, 1978).

Rowell, Geoffrey. '"The Dream of Gerontius"', *Ampleforth Journal*, 73 (1968), 184–92.

 Hell and the Victorians: A Study of the Nineteenth-Century Theological Controversies Concerning Eternal Punishment and the Future Life (Oxford, 1974).

Rowland, Christopher. *The Open Heaven: A Study of Apocalyptic in Judaism and Early Christianity* (1982).

Sanders, Andrew. *Charles Dickens, Resurrectionist* (London and Basingstoke, 1982).

Schneider, Elisabeth W. *The Dragon in the Gate: Studies in the Poetry of G. M. Hopkins* (Berkeley and Los Angeles, 1968).

Schulz, Max F. *Paradise Preserved: Recreations of Eden in Eighteenth- and Nineteenth-Century England* (Cambridge, 1985).

Selwyn, Edward Gordon. *The First Epistle of St. Peter* (1946).

Sharpe, William. 'Learning to Read *The City*', *Victorian Poetry*, 22 (1984), 65–84.

Shaw, Marion. '*In Memoriam* and Popular Religious Poetry', *Victorian Poetry*, 15 (1977), 1–8.

Shaw, W. David. *The Lucid Veil: Poetic Truth in the Victorian Age* (1987).

Sherry, Patrick. *Spirits, Saints and Immortality*, Library of Philosophy and Religion, ed. John Hick (1984).

Simon, Ulrich. *Heaven in the Christian Tradition* (1958).

Sinfield, Alan. *Alfred Tennyson*, Rereading Literature series, gen. ed. Terry Eagleton (Oxford, 1986).

  The Language of Tennyson's 'In Memoriam', Language and Style series, ed. Stephen Ullmann (Oxford, 1971).

Smith, Eric. *By Mourning Tongues: Studies in English Elegy* (Ipswich and Totowa, N.J., 1977).

Smither, Howard E. *A History of the Oratorio*, 2 vols. (Chapel Hill, N.C., 1977).

Steiner, George. *After Babel: Aspects of Language and Translation* (Oxford, 1975).

Stewart, Garrett. *Death Sentences: Styles of Dying in British Fiction* (Cambridge, Mass. and London, 1984).

Stonehouse, J. H., ed. *Catalogue of the Libraries of Charles Dickens and W. M. Thackeray* (1935).

Sulloway, Alison G., *Gerard Manley Hopkins and the Victorian Temper* (1972).

Surtees, Virginia. *The Paintings and Drawings of Dante Gabriel Rossetti (1828–1882): A Catalogue Raisonné*, 2 vols. (Oxford, 1971).

Svaglic, Martin J. 'A Framework for Tennyson's *In Memoriam*', *Journal of English and Germanic Philology*, 61 (1962), 810–25.

Swinden, Patrick, ed. *George Eliot, 'Middlemarch': A Casebook*, Casebook series, gen. ed. A. E. Dyson (London and Basingstoke, 1972).

Thomas, Alfred, SJ. *Hopkins the Jesuit: The Years of Training* (1969).

Thomas, Donald. *Swinburne: The Poet in his World* (1979).

Thompson, E. P. *The Making of the English Working Class* (1963; rpt. Harmondsworth, 1968).

Travis, Stephen H. *Christian Hope and the Future of Man*, Issues in Contemporary Theology series, ed. I. H. Marshall (Leicester, 1980).

Trevor, Meriol. *Newman: The Pillar of the Cloud* (1962).

Tucker, Robert C. *Philosophy and Myth in Karl Marx* (Cambridge, 1961).

Turner, Michael R., ed. *The Parlour Song Book: A Casquet of Vocal Gems* (London and Sidney, 1972).

Turner, Victor W. *The Ritual Process: Structure and Anti-Structure* (1969).

Turner, Victor W. and Edith Turner, *Image and Pilgrimage in Christian Culture: Anthropological Perspectives* (New York, 1978).

Walder, Dennis. *Dickens and Religion* (1981).

Walhout, Donald. *Send My Roots Rain: A Study of Religious Experience in the Poetry of Gerard Manley Hopkins* (Athens, Ohio and London, 1981).

Walker, D. P. *The Decline of Hell: Seventeenth-Century Discussions of Eternal Torments* (1964).

Waller, John O. 'Christ's Second Coming: Christina Rossetti and the Premillennialist William Dodsworth', *Bulletin of the New York Public Library*, 73 (1969), 465–82.

'Tennyson and Philip James Bailey's *Festus*', *Bulletin of Research in the Humanities*, 82 (1979), 105–23.

Ward, Wilfrid. *The Life of John Henry Cardinal Newman: Based on his Private Journals and Correspondence*, 2 vols. (1912).

Watson, J. R. *The Victorian Hymn*. Inaugural Lecture, 1981 (Durham, 1981).

Welsh, Alexander. *The City of Dickens* (Oxford, 1971).

Wendel, François. *Calvin: The Origin and Development of his Religious Thought*, trans. Philip Mairet (London and New York, 1965).

Wheeler, Michael. *The Art of Allusion in Victorian Fiction* (London and Basingstoke, 1979).

'Austin Farrer's *Glass of Vision*: A Literary and Theological Debate', *National Conference on Literature and Religion Newsletter*, 6 (April 1985), 14–21.

Wiles, Maurice. *The Remaking of Christian Doctrine* (1974).

Williams, Ioan, ed. *Meredith: The Critical Heritage*, Critical Heritage series, gen. ed. B. C. Southam (1971).

Wood, Christopher. *Victorian Panorama: Paintings of Victorian Life* (1976).

Woodfield, Malcolm. *R. H. Hutton, Critic and Theologian: The Writings of R. H. Hutton on Newman, Arnold, Tennyson, Wordsworth, and George Eliot* (Oxford, 1986).

Woolf, Robert Lee. *Gains and Losses: Novels of Faith and Doubt in Victorian England* (1977).

Index

445